Mine Errand
from the Lord

Mine Errand from the Lord

*Selections
from the Sermons
and Writings of*

Boyd K. Packer

DESERET
BOOK

SALT LAKE CITY, UTAH

© 2008 Boyd K. Packer

Visit us at DeseretBook.com

Library of Congress Cataloging-in-Publication Data

Packer, Boyd K.
    Mine errand from the Lord : selections from the sermons and writings of Boyd K. Packer / compiled by Clyde J. Williams.
        p.   cm.
    Includes bibliographical references and index.
    ISBN 978-1-60641-023-3 (hardbound : alk. paper)
    1. Packer, Boyd K.—Quotations.   2. Church of Jesus Christ of Latter-day Saints—Doctrines.   3. Mormon Church—Doctrines.
I. Williams, Clyde J.   II. Title.
    BX8609.P33 2008
    289.3'32—dc22   2008024942

Printed in the United States of America
Malloy Lithographing Incorporated, Ann Arbor, MI

10   9   8   7   6   5   4   3   2   1

"Wherefore I, Jacob, gave unto them these words as I taught them in the temple, having first obtained mine errand from the Lord."

—JACOB 1:17

Contents

Integrity and Keeping Confidences 544
Joy and Happiness 547
Gospel Standards versus the World 550
Christmas 552

26 MUSIC AND THE ARTS 555

27 TO THE YOUTH OF THE CHURCH 565

28 I HAVE THAT WITNESS 576

    NOTES 581

    SOURCES 599

    INDEX 617

Illustrations

Photo section following page 296

Significant Dates in the Life of Boyd K. Packer

September 10, 1924	Born in Brigham City, Utah, the tenth child of Ira Wright Packer and Emma Jensen Packer
October 1, 1932	Baptized by Robert Francis Johnson; confirmed by Elder Anthony M. Hansen
1943–1946	Pilot in the U.S. Air Force; served in the Pacific Theater Occupational Forces
July 28, 1947	Marries Donna Edith Smith in the Logan Temple
June 1948	Receives associate of science degree from Weber State College
June 3, 1949	Receives bachelor of science degree from Utah State University

September 1949	Begins career in Religious Education as a seminary teacher in Brigham City, Utah
March 12, 1950	Ordained a seventy by Elder Ezra Taft Benson
December 11, 1950	Ordained a high priest by Elder Joseph F. Merrill
January 21, 1955	Receives Distinguished Service Award from the Brigham City Junior Chamber of Commerce
June 1955	Appointed supervisor of Church Seminaries and Institutes with A. Theodore Tuttle
August 1961	Appointed to the Administrative Council of Brigham Young University
September 30, 1961	Sustained as an Assistant to the Twelve
March 12, 1962	Appointed a member of the Governor's Commission on Children and Youth for State of Utah
May 25, 1962	Received doctorate of education from Brigham Young University
August 1965–June 1968	President of the New England Mission
October 27, 1968	Participates in the creation of the first serviceman's stake in Berchtesgaden, Germany, with Elder Thomas S. Monson
April 6, 1970	Called to the Quorum of the Twelve Apostles
April 9, 1970	Ordained an Apostle
November 7, 1970	Receives the Utah State University Alumni Association Distinguished Alumni Award
August 27–29, 1971	Speaks at the first area conference of the Church in Manchester, England

October 1972	Begins service on the Scripture Committee, along with Elders Thomas S. Monson and Bruce R. McConkie, charged with overseeing a project to publish a new edition of the Standard Works of the Church
October 26, 1972	Receives Distinguished Alumni Award from Weber State College
November 21, 1974	Participates in the dedication of the Washington D.C. Temple
June 13, 1976	Travels to Idaho with President Spencer W. Kimball for follow-up on Teton Dam disaster, which took place June 5, 1976
October 1977	Travels to Israel to meet with various government, education, and religious leaders
1979	New LDS version of the King James Bible is published
1981	New editions of the Book of Mormon, Doctrine and Covenants, and Pearl of Great Price are published
May 1981	Tours China with Brigham Young University's International Folk Dancers and with BYU President Jeffrey R. Holland
April 18–22, 1983	Organizes the Arabian Peninsula Stake
June 10, 1983	Receives honorary doctorate from Weber State College
October 15, 1983	Conducts first regional conference with Elder Neal A. Maxwell in London, England
April 19, 1985	Receives honorary doctorate of humanities from BYU
April 12, 1987	Rededicates the Brigham City Tabernacle

September 1991	Travels to Bulgaria, Ukraine, Romania, and Germany; dedicates Ukraine for the preaching of the gospel, accompanied by Elder Dallin H. Oaks
March 19, 1992	Receives the Silver Beaver Award from the Boy Scouts of America
June 5, 1994	Sustained as Acting President of the Quorum of the Twelve Apostles
June 8, 1996	Receives honorary doctorate of humanities from Utah State University
July 31–August 8, 1998	Travels to Canada on Church business with President Gordon B. Hinckley
November 14, 1999	Dedicates Regina Saskatchewan Temple
April 6, 2000	Participates in the Palmyra New York Temple dedication
November 5, 2000	Participates in the Nauvoo Illinois Temple cornerstone service
June 27–28, 2002	Participates in the Nauvoo Illinois Temple dedication
January 11, 2003	Participates in the first worldwide training broadcast for LDS Church leaders
2004	An exhibit of artwork by President Packer, entitled "Boyd K. Packer: The Lifework of an Amateur Artist," is displayed at the Museum of Church History and Art
February–March 2005	Travels to Indonesia to review tsunami relief efforts
February 3, 2008	Set apart as President of the Quorum of the Twelve

Preface

One summer evening on a little island of the Pacific, while he was serving as a pilot in the Air Force during World War II, young Boyd K. Packer made a decision that would permanently affect the course of his life. He said, "I was thinking about what I wanted to do with my life after the war, should I be fortunate enough to survive. What did I want to be? It was on that night that I decided I wanted to be a teacher." (From *TYD*, p. 340. For key to abbreviations and reference codes, see Sources on p. 599.) In 1949 he began his career as a seminary teacher in Brigham City and has continued as a teacher to the present day as President of the Quorum of the Twelve Apostles. Beginning with his call as an Assistant to the Twelve in 1961 and then as a member of the Quorum of the Twelve in 1970, he has served as a General Authority for forty-seven years. During this time of service he has traveled to some seventy countries, many of them multiple times, and he has spoken at more than 1,300 stake, regional, area, and general conferences. In the words of Elder Dallin H. Oaks, "Whenever this man speaks he teaches." His desire to teach well and to help others do the same led him to write his remarkable book, *Teach Ye Diligently.* It has blessed the lives of countless teachers. As a master teacher he has had a profound impact upon the Church. Indeed, it has been one of his lifelong goals to become more like *the* Master Teacher, Jesus Christ.

President Packer has spent a lifetime developing his keen spiritual sensitivity and prophetic capacity to discern the issues that lie ahead. He has consistently, carefully, and powerfully addressed the major doctrinal, social, and moral issues of our day. Regularly when he speaks, he delivers what many consider to be a classic address on the subject at hand. One of my great challenges in compiling this book has been deciding what to leave out. Because I deemed it important to preserve nuance, there are statements in the book that may appear to be duplicates. However, each statement adds some unique insight that warranted leaving it in the collection.

The book is a little larger than had been anticipated, but there was much that needed to be preserved. President Packer has often taken a classic story or parable and then built his message around the symbolism or message from that story. Because the initial story or parable is frequently needed to help clarify the meaning, it therefore becomes very difficult to excerpt a short statement. While space has not allowed us to preserve all such stories, we have endeavored to preserve many of the best. Headings referencing "spiritual crocodiles"; "the mind is like a stage"; "spiritually speaking, I have tasted salt"; "John, leave it alone"; "the inheritance"; and many more are found within these pages.

In the preparation of this volume his books, *The Holy Temple, Teach Ye Diligently,* and *Our Father's Plan,* as well as more than four hundred of his talks and articles (many which were also published in other books), have been carefully searched for principles and priceless gems. While doing this reading and selecting, an impression came to me for a title for this work. It was a phrase from the prophet Jacob, often cited by President Packer. Jacob felt the tremendous weight of being called to counsel and caution his people because of the weaknesses or sins they were involved with. He felt he could not extend this counsel without first obtaining his errand or direction from the Lord.[1] This is precisely how President Packer has approached each opportunity to speak. He has had no interest in advancing his personal views or ideas. Rather, like Lehi's son Jacob, he has desired to take matters before the Lord to "obtain mine errand from the Lord."

Because of his desire to express himself in a very clear and precise manner, President Packer has always been meticulous in the preparation of his talks and writings. He has painstakingly spent hours, sometimes over periods of weeks, months, and even years, in preparation for his addresses.

President Packer's lifetime of preparation, careful attention to the scriptures and the doctrine they teach, and yearning desire to be sensitive to the promptings of the Spirit have enabled him to leave a legacy of profound insights on many gospel themes. His insights about the plan of happiness leave us with a deepened understanding that what goes on in this world need not determine our happiness.[2] He gives compelling reasons to submit to the Lord by using our precious gift of agency to live a life of obedience. He explains the power of ordinances and covenants, which help us fix our position and set our course in life. Few other writers have given such clear instruction on learning to recognize the voice of the Spirit and follow its promptings. President Packer has repeatedly shared profound principles of effective gospel teaching. He explains the power and benefits that come from regular, persistent study of the scriptures. He has clearly taught the supreme importance of marriage and family, together with remarkable promises of hope for those with wayward children. He gives significant direction on resisting temptation and obtaining the power to control one's thoughts. He has put into perspective the temple and the work done therein, explaining the foundational doctrines with uncommon clarity.

These teachings, and so many more, are clear and precise and can lead one to a much deeper understanding of the gospel. While the teachings in this book are not given to represent the official position of the Church on any doctrinal matters, President Packer's careful, thoughtful, and spiritual preparation make them of inestimable worth.

In President Packer's biography we learn that "collectively his talks are his journal. In them are found experiences with members of his

family, whom he does not name, lessons learned from friends and men-
tors, his approach to challenges that have confronted him, his feelings of
compassion for the poor and suffering, his firm stand on moral issues,
his views on doctrinal and organizational matters within the ministry,
his observations of peoples within the worldwide Church, and his
powerful witness of Jesus Christ, of the Prophet Joseph Smith and his
successors, and of the Book of Mormon and the other standard works
of scripture. Collectively these create a base for assessing the man and
his ministry."[3]

President Packer would be the first to acknowledge that his wife has
been his inspiration and sounding board for much of what he has
taught. Furthermore, he has said: "Most of what I know about how our
Father in Heaven really feels about us, his children, I have learned from
the way I feel about my wife and my children, and their children."
(98–07, p. 24.) A loving home with his wife and ten children proved to
be a most fruitful laboratory of learning.

In the production of this book the compiler is particularly grateful
to Kari, Matthew, and Nathan Johnson, Joseph Nance, and Nancy
Prater, whose help and expertise have greatly assisted in the arranging,
editing, and organizing of this work. Their efforts have helped move
this volume to a much more timely publication. Many thanks are given
to President Packer's secretary, Luella Thompson, and others in his
office who, with an already full schedule, gave considerable help with
providing materials, making corrections, and coordinating all that
needed to be done to keep this project moving forward. Appreciation
is expressed to Cory Maxwell at Deseret Book for his encouragement,
enthusiasm, and efforts to see this book through to a timely publication.

Naturally, the greatest appreciation goes to President Packer himself, for his years of untiring preparation and dedication that made this
book a necessity and for his willingness to allow me the privilege of
helping to make these important teachings available to faithful Latter-
day Saints and others who will benefit greatly from them long after he
has gone. From my days as a young seminary student to the present,
my life has been blessed and influenced by his teachings. I have been

much enlightened, inspired, motivated, and instructed by the wise counsel of President Boyd K. Packer. My capacity to discern pure doctrine and my ability to teach and reach those I have taught in both professional and ecclesiastical roles have been significantly influenced because of his teachings. I would call his teachings supernal, and I reaffirm my witness from the Spirit that he truly has obtained his "errand from the Lord."

CLYDE J. WILLIAMS

CHAPTER 1

The Great Plan of Happiness

*"If you understand the great plan of happiness
and follow it, what goes on in the world will not determine
your happiness."[1] (94–01, p. 20)*

Our Father's Plan. We rightly call it the Great Plan of Happiness, for so it is. It should be known as well as Our Father's Plan. As we grow older and, we hope, wiser, particularly when we have children of our own, we come to realize that the whole plan of happiness was designed for us and for them by our Father. (93–07, pp. 59–60)

The Great Plan of Happiness. Let me tell you in brief headlines what the scriptures say about this drama of the ages, "The Great Plan of Happiness."

The spirits of men and women are eternal.[2] All are sons and daughters of God and lived in a premortal life as His spirit children.[3] The spirit of each individual is in the likeness of the person in mortality,[4] male and female.[5] All are in the image of heavenly parents.

In the council of the Gods[6] the plan of the Eternal Father[7] was sustained. It provided for the creation of an earth[8] whereupon His children would receive physical bodies[9] and would be tested according to His

1

commandments.[10] Each spirit in premortal life was provided opportunities for learning and obedience. Each was given agency.[11]

A grand council in heaven was convened.[12] The divine plan required one to be sent as a Savior and Redeemer to fulfill the plan of the Father. The firstborn of the Eternal Father, Jehovah, willingly volunteered and was chosen.[13]

Most sustained this choice. Others rebelled and there was a "war in heaven." Satan and those who followed him in rebellion against the Father's plan were cast out and denied mortality.[14]

Those who kept the first estate (you are among them) were to be added upon with a physical body and were permitted to live upon the earth in this planned second estate.[15] Each was appointed the "times . . . and the bounds of their habitation."[16] Some were foreordained to be prophets.[17]

An earth was then organized.[18] Adam and Eve, in a paradisiacal state, were the first man and first woman.[19] They were married eternally[20] and were given commandments. They were in a state of innocence and knew no sin.[21]

Eve, beguiled by Satan,[22] transgressed and was to be cast out of the Garden. Adam chose to obey the first commandment to multiply and replenish the earth. He, with Eve, was subject to the Fall, which introduced mortality to the earth.[23] Adam and Eve became the first parents of the family of all the earth.[24]

Angels were sent to reveal to Adam the eternal plan of redemption,[25] and an atonement was wrought by Jesus Christ. Through the Atonement the effects of the Fall, mortal death and spiritual death, could both be overcome.[26] Christ unconditionally provided a resurrection for all mankind and thereby overcame physical death.[27]

But to overcome spiritual death, which is separation from God, requires that we be obedient to the laws and ordinances of the gospel of Jesus Christ.[28]

These principles and ordinances were instituted before the foundation of the world. They are not to be altered or changed. All must be saved by the same requirements.[29] The priesthood administers the ordinances of salvation.[30] The keys of the priesthood control the use of the priesthood.[31]

When you die, you are introduced to the spirit world.[32] It is happiness, a paradise, for the righteous. It is misery for the wicked.[33] In either, we continue to learn and are accountable for our actions.[34]

After all have been dealt with equally,[35] a judgment will be rendered.[36] Each will be resurrected in his or her own order.[37] The glory one receives, however, will depend on obedience to the laws and ordinances of our Father's plan.[38]

Those who have become pure, through repentance, will obtain eternal life and return to the presence of God. They will be exalted as heirs of God and joint heirs with Christ.[39] (95–06, pp. 3–4)

The Great Plan of Happiness is like a three-act play. The course of our mortal life, from birth to death, conforms to eternal law and follows a plan described in the revelations as The Great Plan of Happiness. The one idea, the one truth I would inject into your minds is this: *There are three parts to the plan. You are in the second or the middle part, the one in which you will be tested by temptation, by trials, perhaps by tragedy.* Understand that, and you will be better able to make sense of life and to resist the disease of doubt and despair and depression.

The plan of redemption, with its three divisions, might be likened to a grand three-act play. Act I is entitled "Premortal Life." The scriptures describe it as our First Estate.[40] Act II, from birth to the time of resurrection, the "Second Estate." And Act III, "Life after Death or Immortality and Eternal Life."

In mortality, we are like one who enters a theater just as the curtain goes up on the second act. We have missed Act I. The production has many plots and sub-plots that interweave, making it difficult to figure out who relates to whom and what relates to what, who are the heroes and who are the villains. It is further complicated because you are not just a spectator; you are a member of the cast, on stage, in the middle of it all! (95–06, p. 2)

Within these three epochs of truth rest all we know of the plan of salvation. They encompass all that is taught in the scriptures, and in the temple endowment—indeed all that has been revealed to us. (84–05)

Is the plan really the great plan of happiness? We sometimes wonder: if the plan really is the great plan of happiness, why must we struggle to find the fulness of it in mortal life?

If you expect to find only ease and peace and bliss during Act II [mortality], you surely will be frustrated. You will understand little of what is going on and why things are permitted to be as they are.

Remember this! The line *"And they all lived happily ever after"* is *never written into the second act.* That line belongs in the third act when the mysteries are solved and everything is put right. (95–06, p. 3)

Knowledge of the plan protects us. Without a knowledge of the gospel plan, transgression seems natural, innocent, even justified. There is no greater protection from the adversary than for us to know the truth—to know the plan! (*OFP*, p. 27)

A knowledge of the plan puts the commandments in perspective. Most of the difficult questions we face in the world now cannot be answered without some knowledge of the plan as a background.

Alma said this, and this is one of my favorite scriptures: "God gave unto them *commandments, after* having made known unto them the *plan of redemption.*"[41] Let me say that again: "God gave unto them command-ments, *after* having made known unto them the plan of redemption." Now, let me say it again: "God gave unto them commandments, AFTER having made known unto them the plan of redemption."

As President Harold B. Lee often said: "Don't tell them so they'll understand; tell them so they can't possibly misunderstand."[42] If you are trying to give them a "why," follow that pattern: "God gave unto them commandments, *after* having made known unto them the plan of redemption." (93–05)

Knowing the Father's plan will keep us from being lost. If we have come to know our Father's plan, we are never completely lost. We know something of how it was before our mortal birth. We know much of what lies beyond the horizon on either side, and which path will be safe for us to follow. With a knowledge of the plan comes also the determination to live the principles leading to eternal life.

With that knowledge comes testimony. For we find along the way spiritual provisions of insight, courage, and direction. There are experiences that convince us that we are never alone.

We come to know through our feelings the presence of a divine providence watching over us as we move through mortality.

When we know the plan, we understand why mortality must be a test. We know why so very much must be taken on faith alone. We develop patience with the unanswered questions of life and face with greater resolution the trials and tribulations that are the lot of humankind.

When we know the plan, we know who we are, we know why we are, and we know where we are. We know that each is a son or daughter of God. One day, if we will, we may return to His presence. For this is the grand purpose of the Father and of the Son, who spoke to Moses, saying, "Behold, this is my work and my glory—to bring to pass the immortality and eternal life of man."[43] (*OFP*, pp. 61–62)

One need not fear the future if following the plan of happiness. Whatever your age, if you follow the right plan, you will be all right. Come what may, wherever you go, whatever happens to the world, whatever trials you face, you need not fear the future. "If ye are prepared ye shall not fear."[44] I assure you, you need not fear the future. You will be happy—if, that is, you follow "the great plan of happiness."[45] (93–07, p. 47)

We must not be diverted from the plan. The plan of redemption, as contained in the standard works, must be the foundation of all that we do as members of His church. All of the elements of the plan must be retained in pure form.

We must not be diverted from them. They must not be ignored or clouded or diluted or diminished or superseded by any interest that we may have. To do otherwise is to waste the days of our probation purchased for us at so great a price. (84–05)

Events from the creation to the final winding-up scene are based on choice not chance. How well I know that among learned men are those who look down at animals and stones to find the origin of man. They do not look inside themselves to find the spirit there. They train themselves to measure things by time, by thousands and by millions, and say these animals called men all came by chance. And this they are free to do, for agency is theirs.

But agency is ours as well. We look up, and in the universe we see the handiwork of God and measure things by epochs, by eons, by dispensations, by eternities. The many things we do not know we take on faith.

But this we know! It was all planned before the world was. Events from the Creation to the final, winding-up scene are not based on *chance;* they are based on *choice!* It was planned that way.

This we know! This simple truth! Had there been no Creation, no Fall, there should have been no need for any Atonement, neither a Redeemer to mediate for us. Then Christ need not have been. (88–03, pp. 71–72)

PREMORTAL EXISTENCE

The doctrine of premortal life helps put all things in perspective. There is no way to make sense out of life without a knowledge of the doctrine of premortal life.

The idea that mortal birth is the beginning is preposterous. There is no way to explain life if you believe that.

The notion that life ends with mortal death is ridiculous. There is no way to face life if you believe that. . . .

When we understand the doctrine of premortal life, then things fit together and make sense.

We are the children of God, created in His image.

Our child-parent relationship to God is clear.

The purpose for the creation of this earth is clear.

The testing that comes in mortality is clear.

The need for a redeemer is clear.

When we do understand that principle of the gospel, we see a Heavenly Father and a Son; we see an Atonement and a Redemption.

We understand why ordinances and covenants are necessary.

We understand the necessity for baptism by immersion for the remission of sins. We understand why we renew that covenant by partaking of the sacrament. (83–05, p. 18)

Our state in premortal life. No more profound truth has been conveyed to us in the Restoration than the knowledge of our premortal existence. No other church knows or teaches this truth. The doctrine is given only in outline form, but salient facts are repeated often enough in the revelations to assure us of certain fundamental truths.

The facts are these.

We lived in the presence of God our Eternal Father prior to our mortal birth.

We use such words as *omnipotent* and *omniscient* to describe Him and feel them inadequate. Should not the word *God* be enough? Does it not bespeak such glory that, without the presence of priesthood power of godliness, mortal man could not behold His face and live?[46]

He is Elohim our father. The familiar word *father* reverently spoken does not demean him but greatly lifts us up.

The scriptures teach us that we are His offspring, His children.

And they further teach that intelligence, or spirit, has existed from all eternity.[47] We know also that we were individuals. We are told more than once in the revelations that we were clothed in a spirit body.[48] We know no more than that the spirit body was created in the image of our Father.[49]

The most fundamental of all endowments given to us is agency.[50]

To repeat, the few crucial facts we know about our status in premortal life: "man was also in the beginning with God."[51] We lived in the presence of God our Eternal Father; we are His offspring. Intelligence, or spirit, was organized as spirit bodies before the world was.[52]

We were endowed with agency. Authority had been conferred and leaders chosen.[53]

From the scriptures:

"God saw these souls that they were good, and he stood in the midst of them, and he said: These I will make my rulers; for he stood among those that were spirits, and he saw that they were good."[54]

In the words of the Prophet Joseph Smith:

"God himself, finding he was in the midst of spirits and glory, because he was more intelligent, saw proper to institute laws whereby the rest could have a privilege to advance like himself."[55]

We know little more than this of what our condition was then. Nor does it serve useful purpose to speculate or wrest the scriptures seeking after mysteries. (84–05)

We know that our birth into mortal existence was not our beginning; that we lived in a premortal state; that this life is one chapter of experience in our eternal progression.

While our knowledge is limited on our premortal state, we do know

1. That we were individual;
2. That we were intelligent;
3. That we had spirit bodies;
4. That we had, and yet have, a child-parent relationship with God, the Father;
5. That Jesus Christ was chosen from before the world was;
6. That as He is a Son of God, that likewise we, all mankind, are sons and daughters of God;
7. We, therefore, at times, refer to Him as our Elder Brother.

He is apart from the rest of us. For when the meridian of time had come and He was to enter mortality, the preparation of His mortal body was such that He was the Son of God in the Flesh, as well as in the spirit. (79–08)

The doctrine of premortal life is an essential part of the equation of life. The doctrine is so logical, so reasonable, and explains so many things, that it is a wonder that the Christian world rejected it. It is so essential a part of the equation of life that, left out, life just cannot add up, it remains a mystery.

The doctrine is simply this: life did not begin with mortal birth. We lived in spirit form before we entered mortality. We are spiritually the children of God.

This doctrine of premortal life was known to ancient Christians. For nearly five hundred years the doctrine was taught, but it was then rejected as a heresy by a clergy that had slipped into the Dark Ages of apostasy.

Once they rejected this doctrine, the doctrine of premortal life, and the doctrine of redemption for the dead, they could never unravel the mystery of life. They became like a man trying to assemble a strand of pearls on a string that was too short. There is no way they can put them all together.

Why is it so strange a thought that we lived as spirits before entering mortality? Christian doctrine proclaims the resurrection, meaning that we will live after mortal death. If we live beyond death, why should it be strange that we lived before birth? (83–05, pp. 16–17)

A knowledge of our premortal life helps bring understanding to our mortal existence. Our premortal existence. I don't know of any idea that helps us make sense out of life as much as this fundamental truth: We lived as spirit children—individual, intelligent sons and daughters of God—before our mortal birth. So many things in life can be understood only if we know there was a premortal life, and so many things can never be understood without that knowledge.

Why is it that two children born of the same earthly parents, so alike in physical appearance, frequently are so different in personality, temperament, and disposition—which seem inborn with them? . . . I don't know how to answer such questions without the doctrine of a premortal life. (93–07, p. 48)

Our memory of premortal life is veiled. As part of the eternal plan, the memory of our premortal life, Act I, is covered with a veil. Since you enter mortality at the beginning of Act II with no recollection of Act I, it is little wonder that it is difficult to understand what is going on.

That loss of memory gives us a clean start. It is ideal for the test; it secures our individual agency, and leaves us free to make choices. Many of them must be made on faith alone. Even so, we carry with us some whispered knowledge of our premortal life and our status as offspring of immortal parents.

You were born in innocence, for "every spirit of man was innocent in the beginning."[56] And you have an inborn sense of right and wrong, for the scriptures tell us in the Book of Mormon, we "are instructed sufficiently that [we] know good from evil."[57] (95–06, p. 2)

The plan was presented in premortal life. This great plan of happiness was first presented in a grand council in our premortal life. Each of us was there, a son or a daughter of God. Each had a choice to accept or to reject it. There was a rebellion, and a war erupted over the plan. Our being here with a mortal body tells us we were on the right side.

The leader of the rebellion formulated a plan of his own. It is described in the revelations as the "cunning plan of the evil one" or the "very subtle plan . . . of the adversary"[58] or the "great plan of destruction."[59]

Each of us chose the great plan of happiness. We know this because otherwise we would not be here in mortality. So far, so good.

But in mortal life, with both good and evil present, we must decide again. We must undergo the test. We have been given our agency and cannot escape confirming or rejecting the decision we made in the first estate. It is "choose you *this* day whom ye will serve."[60] (93–07, pp. 48–49)

The scriptures and the teachings of the Apostles and prophets speak of us in premortal life as sons and daughters, spirit children of God.[61] Gender existed before, and did not begin at mortal birth.[62]

In the great council in heaven,[63] God's plan was presented:[64] the plan of salvation,[65] the plan of redemption,[66] the great plan of happiness.[67] The plan provides for a proving; all must choose between good and evil.[68] His plan provides for a Redeemer, an Atonement, the resurrection, and, if we obey, our return to the presence of God.

The adversary rebelled and adopted a plan of his own.[69] Those that followed him were denied the right to a mortal body.[70] Our presence here confirms that we sanctioned our Father's plan.[71] (93–06, p. 21)

The Council in Heaven. We know that God the Father had a plan. We know He called a council. We know something of what transpired, and what the outcome was.

We were present during that grand council. God the Father announced the plan. It provided that we, His spirit children, already endowed with agency, would have the opportunity to receive a body of flesh and bone and would be made free to choose between good and evil—we would be tested. Through the test we would retain, as given by the Apostle Paul, a "hope of eternal life, which God, that cannot lie, promised before the world began."[72]

Two spirits arose in that council. The first, a glorious spirit, offered to fulfill the purposes of the plan and asked no recompense.

The second, a "son of the morning"[73] who "was in authority in the presence of God"[74] would redeem all. He would do it by compulsion and deny the spirits agency. He demanded as recompense that the glory be given him.

The Father chose the first, and the other rebelled. When the war was over, Lucifer "was cast out into the earth, and his angels were cast out with him."[75]

He did not receive a temporal body. He was an unclean spirit. He became the tempter, the evil one. (84–05)

We waited anxiously for our time to enter mortality. It is my conviction that in the spirit world prior to mortal birth, we waited anxiously for our time to enter mortality. I also believe that we were willing to accept whatever conditions would prevail in life. Perhaps we knew that nature might impose limits on the mind or on the body or on life itself. I believe that we nevertheless anxiously awaited our turn. (88–07, p. 19)

Spirits were reserved to come forth at this time. I am firmly convinced that the pattern of the coming of spirits into this world is managed and arranged beyond the veil. When I was a boy, I thought I was born a hundred years too late. I didn't see why I couldn't have been born and come west with the pioneers and been able to hunt buffalo, and to see the country when it was natural. But there was never a more glorious time to be born and be a member of the Church, never a more challenging time. For that reason, I believe the pattern of reserving spirits to come forth at this time to be a true principle. (91–03)

LAYING THE FOUNDATIONS OF EARTH LIFE—CREATION

The Creation. Obedient to the plan, they, that is the gods, organized matter in the epoch known as the creation.[76] It is described in Genesis, in the Pearl of Great Price, and in the endowment.

The light was divided from the darkness. The waters were gathered together and dry land appeared.

The earth brought forth plants of every kind, each bearing seed within itself.

Living creatures of every kind were created and blessed to bring forth, each after its own kind.

A garden was planted eastward in Eden.

When all of this was done, God pronounced all of it to be good, very good.[77] Then, as required in the plan, came the crowning creation:

"And I, God, created man in mine own image, in the image of mine Only Begotten created I him; male and female created I them."[78] (84–05)

The sequence of the creation is crucial. All things were created spiritually before they were naturally upon the face of the earth.[79] And we are told, and this is crucial, the sequence of the creation. We know it from Genesis, from Moses, from Abraham, and from the endowment. We know it from the Book of Mormon.

The Spirit of God "moved upon the face of the waters."[80] The water was divided. Light was divided from darkness. In turn came grass and herbs, and trees yielding seed and fruit. Then came fishes and fowl, beasts and creeping things. All things which were created, each in its *separate* kind, were commanded to multiply each *after its own kind.*[81]

How long this took, I do not know. How it was done, I do not know. This I do know: After it was declared to be good, it was not yet complete, for man was not yet found upon the earth. Man was created separately and last. (88–08, pp. 12–13)

The earth was created or formed of imperishable substance. The scriptures use the words *organize* and *form* when discussing the Creation.[82] The earth was created or formed of imperishable substance, for the revelations tell us that "the elements are eternal."[83] Matter already existed, but it was "without form, and void."[84]

That word *beginning* applies only if *create* is defined as *form* or *organize.* There was no beginning and there shall be no end to matter. This is also said of intelligence, that spiritual part of man. "Intelligence, or the light of truth, was not created or made, neither indeed can be."[85]

. . . How the earth was made, I do not know! I do know that even that will be revealed.[86] (88–08, pp. 11–12)

Man's mortal creation was a separate creation. We are taught in Genesis, in Moses, in Abraham, in the Book of Mormon, and in the endowment that man's mortal body was made in the image of God in a separate creation. Had the Creation come in a different way, there would have been no Fall.

If men were merely animals, then logic favors freedom without accountability. (88–03, p. 71)

Laws do not change. Laws govern the physical universe with such constancy and precision that once man has discovered them, he can, by their effect, demonstrate their existence with unfailing accuracy. . . . Laws do not change. A law, like truth, "abideth and hath no end."[87] A theory is tentative, subject to change, and may or may not be true. A theory is a means to an end, not the end in itself. . . . There are moral and spiritual laws pertaining to values—good and evil, right and wrong—laws as constant, precise, and valid as those which govern the physical universe. . . . Laws governing spiritual things were irrevocably decreed in heaven before the foundation of the earth.[88] (93–05)

We came to this earth to grow through the power of correct choice. He knew you there. Because He loved you, He was anxious for your happiness and for your eternal growth. He wanted you to be able to choose freely and to grow through the power of correct choice, so that you may become much as He is. To achieve this, it was necessary for us to leave His presence. Something like going away to school. A plan was presented, and each agreed to leave the presence of our Heavenly Father to experience life in mortality. (72–01, p. 111)

There are yet questions unanswered. How old is the earth? I do not know! But I do know that matter is eternal. How long a time has man been upon the earth? I do not know! But I do know that man did not evolve from animals.

Both questions have to do with time. Time is a medium for measurement, perhaps no more than that. Occasionally I wonder if time exists at all. Quantum physicists are now beginning to say strange things like that. "Time" comes from the word *tempus;* so do temporal and temporary. The revelations say that the day will come when "there should be time no longer."[89] In any case, they say "time only is measured unto men."[90] (88–08, p. 24)

The Fall

The doctrine of the Fall. Temporal bodies were organized for Adam and Eve, and their spirits entered their bodies.

They were placed in the garden and commanded to multiply and replenish the earth, a commandment they could not keep while there.

"And I, the Lord God, planted the tree of life also in the midst of the garden, and also the tree of knowledge of good and evil."[91] . . . Although they were commanded not to partake [of the tree of knowledge of good and evil], they had their agency and were told: "nevertheless, thou mayest choose for thyself, for it is given unto thee; but, remember that I forbid it, for in the day thou eatest thereof thou shalt surely die."[92]

Satan beguiled Eve with half truths and she partook of the tree of knowledge of good and evil.[93]

Whatever else occurred, for whatever purpose, Adam was left to decide, his agency was protected. The entire plan depended upon choice, upon decision, upon volition. "Adam fell that men might be; and men are, that they might have joy."[94]

The law had been broken, the penalty was decreed, and quickly meted out.

"Wherefore, I, the Lord God, caused that he should be cast out from the Garden of Eden, from my presence, because of his transgression, wherein he became spiritually dead, which is the first death."[95]

With the Fall came the first spiritual penalty—spiritual death!

The separation of Adam and of his posterity from the presence of God constituted spiritual death, for it separated them from things spiritual.

There is another death: the temporal death which is the separation of the body from the spirit.

The penalty for transgression was that, with the Fall, Adam and his posterity became subject to both of them.

The law had been broken and justice was upheld. But mercy would appeal. Mercy won a stay of temporal death and a probation was granted to man.[96] But temporal death was only delayed, for justice cannot be robbed, even by mercy. "It was not expedient that man should be reclaimed from this temporal death, for that would destroy the great plan of happiness."[97]

Even mercy could not waive repentance or the ordinances essential to redemption. The part mercy won was that a redemption could occur at all.

A probationary time was granted "that they should not die as to the temporal death, until I, the Lord God, should send forth angels to declare unto them repentance and redemption, through faith on the name of mine Only Begotten Son."[98]

It was an essential part of the plan in the very beginning that we are to be taught the gospel of salvation. (84–05)

The Fall by choice was necessary to the plan. Whatever else happened in Eden, in his supreme moment of testing, Adam made a choice.

After the Lord commanded Adam and Eve to multiply and replenish the earth and commanded them not to partake of the tree of knowledge of good and evil, He said: "Nevertheless, thou mayest choose for thyself, for it is given unto thee; but, remember that I forbid it, for in the day thou eatest thereof thou shalt surely die."[99]

There was too much at issue to introduce man into mortality by force. That would contravene the very law essential to the plan. The plan provided that each spirit child of God would receive a mortal body and each would be tested. Adam saw that it must be so and made his choice. "Adam fell that men might be; and men are, that they might have joy."[100]

Adam and Eve ventured forth to multiply and replenish the earth as they had been commanded to do. The creation of their bodies in the image of God, as a separate creation, was crucial to the plan. Their subsequent fall was essential if the condition of mortality was to exist and the plan proceed. (88–03, p. 70)

The Fall brought change of location and condition. Mortal death came into the world at the Fall.

It is easier for me to understand that word *fall* in the scriptures if I think both in terms of *location* and of *condition*. The word *fall* means to descend to a lower place.

The Fall of man was a move from the presence of God to mortal life on earth. That move down to a lower place came as a consequence of a broken law.

Fall may also describe a change in *condition*. For instance, one can fall in reputation or from prominence. The word *fall* well describes what transpired when Adam and Eve were driven from the garden. A transformation took place in their bodies. The bodies of flesh and bone became temporal bodies. *Temporal* means temporary. The scriptures say, "the life of all flesh is the blood thereof."[101]

President Kimball explained, "Blood, the life-giving element in our bodies, replaced the finer substance which coursed through their bodies before. They and we became mortal, subject to illness, pains, and even the physical dissolution called death."[102]

After the transformation of the Fall, bodies of flesh and bone and *blood* (unlike our spirit bodies) could not endure. Somehow the ingredient of blood carried with it a limit to life. It was as though a clock were set and a time given. Thereafter, all living things moved inexorably toward mortal death. (88–07, p. 18)

The Fall came by transgression, not sin. The transfer from the first estate in heaven to the second estate in mortality is in effect the Fall of man. Even though we may not fully understand it now, we need to accept the Fall as truth or we will not understand the ministry of Christ as our Redeemer, the Atonement, the ordinances and covenants, or the purposes of life itself.

The Fall came by transgression of a law, but there was no sin connected with it. There is a difference between transgression and sin. Both always bring consequences. While it may not be a sin to step off a roof, in doing so one becomes subject to the law of gravity, and consequences will follow.

The Fall of man was made from the presence of God to this mortal life, where, now in the presence of both good and evil, we face the test. (93–07, p. 49)

OPPOSITION OF SATAN

The adversary has sworn to spoil the plan for everyone. There is, of course, a villain in all this, the adversary, the schemer, the destroyer. He got off track in Act I [premortality]. He has sworn to spoil the plan for everyone. And he has legions of angels, dark angels, to help him do it. He, too, has a plan called the cunning plan,[103] a very subtle plan,[104] a secret plan,[105] the plan of destruction.[106] (95–06, p. 5)

The single purpose of Lucifer is to oppose the plan. The single purpose of Lucifer is to oppose the great plan of happiness, to corrupt the purest, most beautiful and appealing experiences of life: romance, love, marriage, and parenthood.[107] The specters of heartbreak and guilt[108] follow him about. Only repentance can heal what he hurts. (93–06, p. 21)

Angels of the devil are working to influence members to do evil. When you become familiar with the scriptures, you will read that there is a "devil . . . [who] inviteth and enticeth [men] to sin, . . . for he persuadeth no man to do good, no, not one; neither do his angels; neither do they who subject themselves unto him."[109]

Angels of the devil are working to influence members to do evil. Now that is worth knowing! [You] should understand and know from reading the scriptures that the devil is real. And you should know he has angels, and that communications with angels of the devil can appear as coming through the same channels as revelations that come from angels of God. (05–06)

The adversary can attack on many fronts. Many are the fronts on which the adversary can attack: the enticements of sexual sin, worldliness in its many forms, exalting man's reasoning over God's revelation, criticizing the Church leaders, to mention only a few. "After they [have] partaken of the fruit of the tree they [do] cast their eyes about as if they [are] ashamed. . . . And after they [have] tasted of the fruit they [are] ashamed, because of those that [are] scoffing at them, and they [fall] away into forbidden paths and [are] lost."[110]

How can one be unfaltering? First, be alert enough to know that the challenge, when it comes, is individual. While the youth (or, for that matter, the more mature) of Zion will not falter, *you* might. . . .

There does not have to be the great battle of Gog and Magog in order for a Church member to falter and fall in mortal combat in defense of his faith. (66–02, p. 101)

If we are righteous we can prevail over evil. Look at the world and see all that is wrong with it. You ought to know that the Lord never did let any wickedness reign or have dominion in the world except that He put a more than equivalent power and authority of righteousness to prevail over it. Ultimately each of us, individually, can have dominion over any influence that is evil—provided we take care of the ordinary things. (79–02)

The devil has no power over us unless we permit him. The punishment of the adversary was that he did not receive a body. All beings who have bodies, as the Prophet said it, will have power over those who do not. "The devil has no power over us only as we permit him."[111] (03–04, p. 168)

Lucifer cannot destroy us without our consent. How supernally precious freedom is; how consummately valuable is agency.

Lucifer in clever ways manipulates our choices, deceiving us about sin and consequences. He, and his angels with him, tempt us to be unworthy, even wicked. But he cannot, in all eternity he cannot, with all his power he cannot completely destroy us—not without our own consent. Had agency come to man without the Atonement, it would have been a fatal gift. (88–03, p. 71)

If you can understand how the Spirit operates, you will be all right. There is not enough evil that it could destroy you, even if it was all brought together as some kind of a dark, ugly laser beam and focused on you, unless somehow you consented to it. (02–02)

Powers of darkness cannot endure light. While light and virtue and truth at times will not endure the presence of darkness and evil and will not, by choice, stay in their presence, ultimately the powers of darkness cannot endure the presence of light.

By analogy, this can be demonstrated to a degree with electricity.

We are able to run a wire into a room and through a system of connections and switches turn on a light. The instant that happens, the darkness is gone. Some little of it may hide as shadows under the furniture; but, wherever the light can penetrate, the darkness must vanish.

In other words, we have the capacity to introduce light into a room; and, as we do, darkness must dissipate. I do not know of anyone who can do the opposite—that is, introduce such darkness into a room that light will vanish.

The ultimate power rests with the Lord and with His priesthood, with His servants. That idea should be an encouragement to members of the Church when they are intruded upon by forces that are evil and dark. Ultimately the power of light can hold them in abeyance. (*THT,* p. 123)

The Lord has never abandoned this earth to the adversary. The Lord has never abandoned this earth. He has never left it alone so that Satan could have full charge or have charge over all of it or any of it. That is another thing to learn, because if we understand that, we know that we will not be overtaken by or controlled by the adversary unless we exercise our choice and allow it to be. Sometimes that is unwitting; sometimes he comes upon us so suddenly that we do not realize it. And yet, we know that we have the power within us to thwart his desires just by choosing the other course. (00–05)

The Lord has never abandoned the earth to the power of the adversary. Always there has been a superior compensating power of inspiration and righteousness. (93–07, p. 58)

The adversary is jealous of those who have power to beget life. The adversary is jealous toward all who have power to beget life. He cannot beget life. He and those who followed him were cast out of heaven and forfeited the right to a mortal body. He will, if he can, take possession of *your* body, direct how you use it. His angels even begged to inhabit the bodies of swine.[112] He knows the supernal value of our power of procreation and jealously desires to rule those who have it. And, the revelations tell us, "he seeketh that all men might be miserable like unto himself."[113] He will tempt you, if he can, to degrade, to corrupt, if possible to destroy this gift by which we may, if we are worthy, have eternal increase.[114] (92–02, p. 110)

The adversary always goes to an excess. The adversary cannot be moderate or temperate; he always goes to an excess. (08–02)

A warning: there is a dark side. A warning: there is a dark side to spiritual things. In a moment of curiosity or reckless bravado some teenagers have been tempted to toy with Satan worship. Don't you ever do that! Don't associate with those who do! You have no idea of the danger! Leave it alone! And there are other foolish games and activities that are on that dark side. Leave them alone! (89–01, p. 54)

MAN'S NATURE, ORIGIN, AND POTENTIAL

To understand the nature of man we must not ignore the revelations. Any position which ignores the revelations of the Lord pertaining to the nature of man must ultimately prove to be inadequate, if not downright false and destructive. (66–05, p. 251)

As sons and daughters of God we are inherently good. How glorious it is to have the revealed word of God, to know that we have a child-parent relationship with Him. If we are of His family, we have inherited the tendency to be good, not evil. We are sons and daughters of God. (*TYD*, p. 88)

It is the nature of humankind to be good. I believe that the tendency in the human family is to be good and to do the thing that is right. I believe it is the desire of men to want to possess the noblest virtues. Men, women, and children, given the opportunity, have within them the disposition to do that which they ought to do. Furthermore, it is natural with men to want to learn. (*TYD*, p. 90)

Men are created to be righteous. There is a doctrine taught through much of traditional Christianity that men are conceived in wickedness and that men by nature are depraved and wicked and evil. You can be misled, and you can arrange some scriptures, if you don't understand them, to sustain that idea. The doctrine that men are basically evil is false. It is wrong. It is a tremendous perversion of the truth. To teach that men are basically evil and corrupt and that somehow through some generous extension of grace that sometime they might be decent for a little while is a debilitating, debasing, discouraging doctrine when in truth we are the sons and daughters of the Almighty. We basically are good. Men have the tendency to be righteous.

The Book of Mormon tells us that all "men are instructed sufficiently that they know good from evil."[115]

When I see somebody that is depraved almost beyond belief, I do not become discouraged because I know down deep inside somewhere is an innate knowledge and the ability to tell good from evil. Now men can be led from a pattern of virtue into almost unspeakable depths of wickedness, but that is against their nature, because we are the sons and daughters of God. (79–04)

All have a spiritual endowment to know right from wrong. All "men are instructed sufficiently that they know good from evil."[116]

Parents and teachers need to know that a youngster can tell right from wrong. This knowledge may be distorted or perverted or covered up in unfortunate life experiences, but intuitively, as a part of the spiritual endowment of all humanity, there is a knowledge of right from wrong.

That gives me great hope, for then I understand that every child of God, however reprobate he may have become, however degenerate he may seem to be, has hidden within him the spark of divinity and a sensitivity to that which is wrong as compared to that which is right. (*TYD*, pp. 99–100)

We were not created with overpowering unnatural desires. Some think that God created them with overpowering, unnatural desires, that they are trapped and not responsible.[117] That is not true. It cannot be true. Even if they were to accept it as true, they must remember that He can cure and He can heal.[118] (00–06, p. 74)

The adversary wants to convince us we are merely animals. Can you not see how careful, how clever, the adversary is? He need not even challenge the *existence* of moral laws; simply convince us that, as animals, we are not accountable and therefore exempt from them. To regard myself as but an animal would cost my agency, my accountability; I would forfeit justice, mercy, love, faith, the *Atonement*—all that endures beyond mortality: values more dear than life itself. I will not do it! (88–08, p. 24)

The idea that men are animals is spiritually destructive. No greater ideal has been revealed than the supernal truth that we are the children of God, and we differ, by virtue of our creation, from all other living things.

No idea has been more *destructive* of happiness, no philosophy has produced more sorrow, more heartbreak and mischief, no idea has done more to destroy the family than the idea that we are not the offspring of God, only advanced animals, compelled to yield to every carnal urge.

Animals are not subject to moral law. Nevertheless, while by and large they are promiscuous in responding to their mating instincts, their mating rituals have set patterns and have rigid limitations. For instance, animals do not pair up with their own gender to satisfy their mating instincts. Nor are these instincts expressed in the molestation of their offspring. (92–03, p. 67)

Belief that man evolved from animals promotes moral irresponsibility. The comprehension of man as no more than a specialized animal cannot help but affect how one behaves. A conviction that man did evolve from animals fosters the mentality that man is not responsible for moral conduct. Animals are controlled to a very large extent by physical urges. Promiscuity is a common pattern in the reproduction of animals. In many subtle ways, the perception that man is an animal and likewise controlled by urges invites that kind of behavior so apparent in society today. A self-image in which we regard ourselves as children of God sponsors one kind of behavior. A conclusion which equates man to animals fosters another kind of behavior entirely. Consequences which spring from that single false premise account for much of what society now suffers. (88–08, pp. 6–7)

Mankind are not mere animals. Animals cannot be responsible for breaking moral laws. If man is but an animal, he cannot morally be made accountable for restraints governing reproduction, social relationships, power, wealth, life, and death. The laws of morality themselves tell us that. "Where there is no law given there is no punishment; and where there is no punishment," Nephi said, "there is no condemnation."[119] Alma, in his remarkable counsel to his son Corianton on the subject of repentance, said:

"Now, how could a man repent except he should sin? How could he sin if there was no law? How could there be a law save there was a punishment?

"Now, there was a punishment affixed, and a just law given, which brought remorse of conscience unto man."[120]

There is that word *conscience* again, that obvious part of human nature not found in animals.

Moral law regulates the behavior of human beings and sets man apart from, and above, the animal kingdom. If moral law is *not* an issue, then organic evolution is no problem. If moral law is an issue, then organic evolution as the explanation for the origin of man is *the* problem. (88–08, p. 6)

The sealing authority cannot admit to ancestry from beasts. The sealing authority with its binding of the generations into eternal families cannot admit to ancestral blood lines to beasts. Let me repeat: *An understanding of the sealing authority with its binding of the generations into eternal families cannot admit to ancestral blood lines to beasts.* (88–08, p. 22)

Convictions about the theory of evolution. It is my conviction that to the degree the theory of evolution asserts that man is the product of an evolutionary process, the offspring of animals—it is false!

What application the evolutionary theory has to animals gives me no concern. That is another question entirely, one to be pursued by science. But remember, the scriptures speak of the spirit in animals and other living things, and of each multiplying after its own kind.[121]

And I am sorry to say, the so-called theistic evolution, the theory that God used an evolutionary process to prepare a physical body for the spirit of man, is equally false. I say I am sorry because I know it is a view commonly held by good and thoughtful people who search for an acceptable resolution to an apparent conflict between the theory of evolution and the doctrines of the gospel. (88–08, p. 21)

Some things must remain unknown. Science is seeking; science is discovery. Man finds joy in discovery. If all things were known, man's creativity would be stifled. There could be no further discovery, no growth, nothing to decide—no agency. All things not only *are not* known but must not be so convincingly clear as to eliminate the need for faith. That would nullify agency and defeat the purpose of the plan of salvation. Tests of faith are growing experiences. We have unanswered questions. Seeking and questioning, periods of doubt, in an effort to find answers, are part of the process of discovery. The kind of doubt which is spiritually dangerous does not relate to *questions* so much as to *answers.* For that and other reasons, it is my conviction that a full knowledge of the origin of man must await further discovery, further revelation.

Latter-day Saints may safely follow an interest in science and pursue it with commitment, dedication, and with inspiration. Laws which govern *both* the temporal and the spiritual are ordained of God. After all of the tomorrows have passed and after all things have been revealed, we will know that those laws are not in conflict, but are in harmony. (88–08, p. 8)

The revelations testify of the separate creation of man in the image of God. The revelations testify of the separate creation of man in the image of God—this after the rest of creation was finished. When the revelations do not fully explain something (and there is purpose in their not doing so), there is safety in clinging to whatever they do reveal. The creation of man and his introduction into mortality by the Fall as revealed in the scriptures conform to eternal laws governing *both* body and spirit.

If the theory of evolution applies to man, there was no Fall and therefore no need for an Atonement, or a gospel of redemption, or a Redeemer. (88–08, pp. 21–22)

Our bodies were provided with the power of creation. Under the accepted plan, Adam and Eve were sent to the earth as our first parents. They could prepare physical bodies for the first spirits to be introduced into this life.

There was provided in our bodies, and this is sacred, a power of creation. A light, so to speak, that has power to kindle other lights. It is a sacred and significant power. This power is good. (64–01)

Your body becomes an instrument of your mind. Your body becomes an instrument of your mind and the foundation of your character. Through life in a mortal body you can learn to control matter, and that will be very important to you through all eternity. (73–04, p. 52)

The mortal body is the instrument of our mind and the foundation of our character. Through it we are tested. The sacred power of procreation gives us an essential part in the plan. There are laws, eternal laws, set to govern our use of it. It is to operate in very narrow limits. And there are penalties of eternal consequence if we disobey. (*OFP,* pp. 24–26.)

Man can become like God. Man is the child of God, formed in the divine image and endowed with divine attributes, and even as the infant son of an earthly father and mother is capable in due time of becoming a man, so the undeveloped offspring of celestial parentage is capable, by experience through ages and eons, of evolving into a God. (88–08, p. 26)

The Father is the one true God. The Father *is* the one true God. *This* thing is certain: no one will ever ascend above Him; no one will ever replace Him. Nor will anything ever change the relationship that

Boyd K. Packer with President David O. McKay, June 15, 1963

we, His literal offspring, have with Him. He is Elohim, the Father. He is God; of Him there *is* only one. We revere our Father and our God; we *worship* Him. (84–07, p. 69)

The fact that we are children of God should inspire us to live pure lives. What could inspire one to purity and worthiness more than to possess a spiritual confirmation that we are the children of God? What could inspire a more lofty regard for oneself, or engender more love for mankind?

This thought does not fill me with arrogance. It fills me with overwhelming humility. Nor does it sponsor any inclination to worship oneself or any man.

The doctrine we teach has no provision for lying or stealing, for pornography, for immoralities, for child abuse, for abortion, for murder. We are bound by the laws of the Lord's church, as *sons and daughters of God,* to avoid all of these and every other unholy or impure practice. (84–07, pp. 68–69)

The true heritage and potential of man. Since *every living thing* follows the pattern of its parentage, are we to suppose that God had some other strange pattern in mind for His offspring? Surely we, His children, are not, in the language of science, a different species than He is.

What is in error, then, when we use the term *Godhood* to describe the ultimate destiny of mankind? We may now be young in our progression—juvenile, even infantile, compared with God. Nevertheless, in the eternities to come, if we are worthy, we may be like unto Him, enter His presence, "see as [we] are seen, and know as [we] are known," and receive a "fulness."[122] (84–07, pp. 67–68)

As children of God we have inherited powerful resources. It is critically important that you understand that you already know right from wrong, that you're innately, inherently, and intuitively good. When you say, "I can't! I can't solve my problems!" I want to thunder out, "Don't you realize who you are? Haven't you learned yet that you are a son or a daughter of Almighty God? Do you not know that there are powerful resources inherited from Him that you can call upon to give you steadiness and courage and great power?" (75–01, p. 88)

Men and women are of equal value in the eyes of God. There is nothing in the revelations which suggests that to be a man rather than to be a woman is preferred in the sight of God, or that He places a higher value on sons than on daughters.

All virtues listed in the scriptures—love, joy, peace, faith, godliness, charity—are shared by both men and women,[123] and the highest priesthood ordinance in mortality is given only to man and woman together.[124] (93–06, p. 21)

Man is a dual being. To study mankind and his beginnings by analyzing his physical body and environment only is to study but half of him. Regardless of how much physical truth is discovered, it is but half the truth.

Man is a dual being: "For man is spirit. The elements are eternal, and spirit and element, inseparably connected, receive a fulness of joy."[125] (88–08, p. 3)

Spiritual diseases come when one ignores rules of spiritual health. There is another part of us, not so tangible, but quite as real as our physical body. This intangible part of us is described as mind, emotion, intellect, temperament, and many other things. Very seldom is it described as spiritual.

But there is a *spirit* in man; to ignore it is to ignore reality. There are spiritual disorders, too, and spiritual diseases that can cause intense suffering.

The body and the spirit of man are bound together. Often, very often, when there are disorders, it is very difficult to tell which is which.

There are basic rules of physical health that have to do with rest, nourishment, exercise, and with abstaining from those things which damage the body. Those who violate the rules one day pay for their foolishness.

There are also rules of spiritual health, simple rules that cannot be ignored, for if they are we will reap sorrow by and by. (77–10, p. 59)

One can explain the spirit of man. "The spirit and the body are the soul of man."[126] Man is a dual being, a spirit within a mortal body.

It is difficult to teach about the intangible, spiritual part. But there are ways to do it. For example, your students know about computers. A personal computer made of metal, plastic, glass, and a dozen other materials will hold an astonishing amount of information. All of the standard works can be stored there, and in addition, sets of encyclopedias, dictionaries, books on a whole library of subjects, even illustrations and mathematical formulas.

With the press of a few keys, one can select any part of what is stored and see it instantly on a screen. One may, by pressing a few more keys, rearrange, add to, or subtract from what is stored in the computer. Press another key or two and you can print a copy of whatever you desire, even in full color. You then can hold in your hand tangible, absolute proof of what is inside there and how it is arranged.

If, however, you should take the computer completely apart, you could not find one word of it, not one illustration, not one tangible evidence that there are volumes, verses, poems, and illustrations inside the computer.

You could dissolve the computer with acids or burn it and you would not find one tangible word of evidence. You could no more find words in the ashes of a computer than you can find the spirit in the ashes of a cremated human body.

No one doubts that this great base of information is actually stored in the computer. It should not be too difficult to teach each youngster that there is within the human body a spirit. Notwithstanding that it is invisible and intangible, it is the very essence of reality. You can, in context of the gospel plan, explain what that spirit is. Let me say that again. You can, in context of the gospel plan, explain what that spirit is, where it came from, and what the destiny of each of us is. (93–05)

MORTALITY—BIRTH

A chronic disease. I was exposed the day after I was born to a chronic disease. It's called aging. (08–02)

The plan and the purpose of mortality. The purpose for coming into mortality is twofold: spirits come to receive a body and each is tested against both good and evil preparatory to reentering the presence of our Father.

Over us always and continually hangs the specter of temporal death, the separation of the body and the spirit, which death is the grave.[127]

The temporal death, although mercifully delayed for a time of probation, will surely come. We will be separated from our mortal bodies.

If there were no more to the plan, should it have ended there, the purposes of God would be frustrated. Our bodies would be lost forever.

Jacob explained that "this flesh must have laid down to rot and to crumble to its mother earth, to rise no more. . . . [O]ur spirits must become subject to that angel who fell from before the presence of the Eternal God, . . . and our spirits must have become like unto him."[128]

If the plan had provided only for the resurrection of the temporal body, an unclean spirit would reunite with the body. We could not return to the presence of God. The result would be spiritual death. Seven times in explicit brevity the scriptures state that "no unclean thing can dwell with God."[129]

Consider our plight. Because of the testing each of us, to one degree or another, becomes unclean. Without a way to cleanse ourselves, we would remain forever spiritually dead and forever subject to the evil one.

But there is more to the plan, for it is the plan of redemption. The coming of a savior, a redeemer, is the central message of the scriptures and is stated as simply as this: "The Messiah cometh in the fulness of time, that he may redeem the children of men from the fall."[130] To quote Jacob again, "Oh how great the plan of our God!"[131] (84–05)

The mortal body, agency, and testing. The mortal body is the instrument of our mind and the foundation of our character. Through it we are tested. The sacred power of procreation gives us an essential part in the plan. There are laws, eternal laws, set to govern our use of it. It is to operate in very narrow limits. And there are penalties of eternal consequence if we disobey.

And there is the ever-present tempter: "Because he had fallen from heaven, and had become miserable forever, he sought also the misery of all mankind."[132] He, with his angels, tempts us to degrade or misuse this and every other sacred gift we have received. He is determined to have us serve him and conspires to replace every feeling of love with one that is corrupt.

Agency requires that we be free to use the power as we will. The laws of nature provide that every time the natural conditions are met, whether under the bonds of marriage or not, a body will be conceived and a spirit assigned.

But who, knowing of the plan of salvation, could think of misusing the power of procreation?

The teaching of the plan of salvation, the doctrine of the kingdom of God, became preeminent among all the commandments of God.

Angelic messengers were sent and prophets were commissioned to teach mankind of their beginnings with God. The plan of redemption was given them.

Without a knowledge of the gospel plan, transgression seems natural, innocent, even justified.

There is no greater protection from the adversary than for us to know the truth—to know the plan!

And, there is the Holy Spirit. The Spirit is our tie to that realm from which we came. It always works by persuasion, never by compulsion, never by force. (84–05)

Two great purposes of mortality. Two great things were in store for us as we came into the world. One, we would receive a mortal body, created in the image of God. Through it, by proper control, we might achieve eternal life and happiness. Two, we would be tried and tested in such a way that we could grow in strength and in spiritual power. (64–01)

Our body is the foundation of our character. I remember a blessing I received when I was serving in the military. It included counsel that's good for every young person: "You have been given a body of such physical proportions and fitness as to enable your spirit to function through it. . . . You should cherish this as a great heritage. Guard [it] and protect it. Take nothing into it that shall harm the organs thereof because it is sacred. It is the instrument of your mind and [the] foundation of your character." That counsel had great influence on me. (96–01, p. 18)

Mortality does not make sense without an eternal perspective. A lot of what goes on in the second act [mortality] does not make sense unless you know about the first act [premortal life] and about the third act [life after death]. The second act will seem often very, very unfair if all you know is what goes on in the second act.

Did you ever know a play that concluded "and they all lived happily ever after" at the end of the second act? The only thing that matters seems to get done at the end of the third act as they drive away into the sunset.

Because we are in the second act, we're not all that knowledgeable if we don't read the script of what's going on later.

Why does it matter that we know the third act? If we don't know the third act, then we don't know how exceptions are handled. . . . Life is full of exceptions. They will not be solved at the end of the second act. In the third act, blessings that would have been received or that have been earned or desires unfulfilled will be answered, will be solved in the eternal plan. (95–01)

Prepare for the "degrees" of life and the life hereafter. Preeminent among life's lessons is the training we receive in courtship and in marriage and in family life. . . . There is a sequence of courses in this field of study that leads to an advanced degree of happiness. First comes the elementary course—boy meets girl. Then come various opportunities for companionship. Soon you are over the awkward, stupid feeling characteristic of those first serious relationships. The boyish attributes give way to manhood and the girlish manners blossom into womanhood.

After a preliminary course called engagement, one may have conferred upon him the first of the truly major degrees of life—the degree of "Mr." for him, and "Mrs." for her.

Then you graduate, as it were, from the ranks of the single and commence into the field of higher learning. The study continues. As partners, you delve more deeply into the arts and sciences of life than ever before. So many things that had once been anticipated, now are fulfilled. So many things that had previously been theoretical now become real.

In the course of the normal pattern of life's experience comes another commencement. A new and an ultimate in degrees is conferred. "Father" for him, and "Mother" for her. A consummation in the education of the whole man and the whole woman, and yet at once it is, as always, a beginning.

There are other degrees ahead—"Grandfather" for him, and "Grandmother" for her.

Some of you may not be privileged to enroll in this important school of life. You will be tested and trained in other ways, and will receive a fulness in other spheres. For all of us, there are other degrees ahead, eternal ones.

There are achievements relating to the spiritual nature of man that do not come as the result of any crash course. For, as it is with school, so it is with life. It was never intended that we stay here forever. We came to accomplish two great purposes. The first of them, to receive a mortal body. The second has to do with learning and testing and receiving a spiritual education. Then the plan is that we graduate and move on to greater things.

Death is not as consummate as many believe; it is another graduation. When you come to your commencement from life, you will find a conclusion which is another beginning, this time to have no ending.

Each of us will move on, some having completed the course with high honors, and others perhaps who have failed.

But each will move forward for the conferring of a degree, a degree that is telestial, a degree that is terrestrial, or for some a degree that is celestial—this one a degree of glory. Each one of us here is still eligible to receive it, but as with all things that are eternal, it must be paid for in advance. (75–05)

Time is the basic commodity of life. Time, the basic commodity of life, is the medium from which all activities of life are created. Time is inexorable and relentless in its progress. "A few minutes ago" vanishes to join a column of yesterdays that follow last year into the country called the past. Time has never been successfully stockpiled. Elusive of all storage procedures, it must—absolutely must—be consumed in one fashion or another as it is produced.

So commonplace is time that it is frequently wasted. Around us we constantly see those who are throwing large amounts of time to waste with such abandon as to suggest that they have a great surplus, even unlimited wealth of the commodity. Almost never in this life does one see a balance sheet showing a total of just how much remains. Such a statement of account would surely compel us to use our time prudently.

Often we awaken to the realization that we have been duped— swindled of part of our priceless legacy by one of many agencies clamoring for the attention of mankind. No protective agency can redeem it. It cannot be insured; it will never be recovered and returned. (*TYD*, p. 256)

There is much to learn in the latter years of life. There are some things you need to learn in mortality that you don't really know and learn and understand until the later years, when you have a little time on your hands and you can be a little more sensible and contemplative, when you are not under quite so much pressure to provide food and clothing and shelter.

Make use of the years ahead, and stay awake and alert. Capitalize on the tremendous opportunity to learn, through meditation and some of the quieter processes, those powerful things the Lord reveals; things that transcend what you have known even though you have taught the gospel all these years. If you sit and ponder on these things and begin to reflect and to be prayerful, I think you will understand something you may not have known before. (77–07)

How to miss old age. I spoke at the funeral of an eighty-four-year-old man. He was a man of singular achievement. Other speakers outlined his life and listed the many things he had done in his life. It was said that he had not missed anything in life.

When it came my turn to speak, I pointed out there was one thing that he had missed. One thing that he had never experienced. And that was old age. He never experienced it at all.

He died at eighty-four. He had the physical frailties common to people of such age. A few years ago he had open heart surgery. And yet, somehow he missed old age. He never experienced it at all.

Why? Because he was possessed of a bit of higher learning. He always was interested in others, and there was so much to be done for the blessing and benefit of others that he always regarded the system as being beautiful and marvelous.

He was always looking ahead. On the last day, knowing what was to be, he was looking ahead in happy anticipation. (78–03)

Keep nostalgia in perspective. My counsel to you is this: On occasion it's marvelous to get together and renew acquaintances, but nostalgia should be limited just to a glance at the trail you've come up; then look ahead. . . . Always capitalize on the experience and the training you received, but don't keep looking back over your shoulder. (77–07)

Keep busily engaged as you move to retirement. It is important to keep a positive and forward-looking and active mind. And if you are wondering how to keep your body active and operating and moving about as much as you can for as long as you can, the answer is to be busily engaged. When we come to the milestone in life where we move to retirement, or from one activity to another, we need to fill our lives. (77–07)

In your golden years there is so much to do and so much to be.
In your golden years there is so much to *do* and so much to *be*. Do not withdraw into a retirement from life, into amusement. That, for some, would be useless, even selfish. You may have served a mission and been released and consider yourself as having completed your service in the Church, but you are never released from being active in the *gospel.* "If," the Lord said, "ye have desires to serve God ye are called to the work."[133]

You may at last, when old and feeble, learn that the greatest mission of all is to strengthen your own family and the families of others, to seal the generations.

Now, I am teaching a true principle. I am teaching doctrine. It is written that "the principle [agrees] precisely with the doctrine which is commanded you in the revelation."[134]

In the hymn "How Firm a Foundation," which was published in 1835 in the first Latter-day Saint hymnbook, we find these words:

> *E'en down to old age, all my people shall prove*
> *My sov'reign, eternal, unchangeable love;*
> *And then, when gray hair shall their temples adorn,*
> *Like lambs shall they still in my bosom be borne.*[135]

Keep the fire of your testimony of the restored gospel and your witness of our Redeemer burning so brightly that our children can warm their hands by the fire of your faith. That is what grandfathers and grandmothers are to do! (03–05, p. 84)

JESUS CHRIST AND THE ATONEMENT

Through the Atonement of Christ, all mankind may be saved.
Before the Crucifixion and afterward, many men have willingly given their lives in selfless acts of heroism. But none faced what the Christ endured. Upon Him was the burden of all human transgression, all human guilt.

And hanging in the balance was the Atonement. Through His willing act, mercy and justice could be reconciled, eternal law sustained, and that mediation achieved without which mortal man could not be redeemed.

He, by choice, accepted the penalty for all mankind for the sum total of all wickedness and depravity; for brutality, immorality, perversion, and corruption; for addiction; for the killings and torture and terror—for all of it that ever had been or all that ever would be enacted upon this earth.

In choosing, He faced the awesome power of the evil one, who was not confined to flesh nor subject to mortal pain. That was Gethsemane!

How the Atonement was wrought, we do not know. No mortal watched as evil turned away and hid in shame before the light of that pure being.

All wickedness could not quench that light. When what was done was done, the ransom had been paid. Both death and hell forsook their claim on all who would repent. Men at last were free. Then every soul who ever lived could choose to touch that light and be redeemed.

By this infinite sacrifice, through this Atonement of Christ, all mankind may be saved by obedience to the laws and ordinances of the gospel. (88–03, p. 69)

Meaning of the Atonement. *Atonement* is really three words: *At-one-ment,* meaning to set at one, one with God; to reconcile, to conciliate, to expiate. (88–03, p. 69)

The Atonement was absolutely essential. Jacob described what would happen to our bodies and our spirits except an atonement, an infinite atonement, were made. We should, he said, have become "like unto [the devil]."[136]

I seldom use the word *absolute.* It seldom fits. I use it now—twice. Because of the Fall, the Atonement was absolutely essential for resurrection to proceed and overcome mortal death.

The Atonement was absolutely essential for men to cleanse themselves from sin and overcome the second death, which is the spiritual death, which is separation from our Father in Heaven. For the scriptures tell us, seven times they tell us, that no unclean thing may enter the presence of God. (88–03, p. 70)

The crowning principle of the gospel is the Atonement. The crowning principle of the gospel is the Atonement of the Lord Jesus Christ. He is the Messiah, the Mediator, the Redeemer. As the "weak things of the world," we do the best we can. Through repentance, we can repair our mistakes. The doctrines of the Church teach us how to do that.

The Atonement of Christ provides for those things that we cannot ourselves make whole. Jesus Christ is the Son of God, the Only Begotten of the Father, our Savior, our Redeemer, and the Head of the Church which bears His name. (04–04)

The purpose of the Atonement. Christ went below all things that He might rise above all things. He was pure and without blemish. He had no part with the adversary. Therefore He could reenter the presence of God.

What happened in Gethsemane and at Golgotha satisfied the law. He atoned for the transgressions of mankind, a supernal expression of mercy.

Just how the Atonement was wrought, we do not know. But thereafter, the resurrection began and eventually all mankind will reclaim their bodies.

With the atoning sacrifice of Jesus Christ, the terrible specter of the eternal death of the body no longer hovers over us. We are redeemed from temporal death, which death is the grave. He offered resurrection without condition, without cost.

This restoration comes to all, the just and the unjust. Otherwise man would be punished for Adam's transgression, and an injustice would have prevailed.

But redemption from spiritual death, from hell, is another matter. For this, there are conditions set. There are requirements established which are as eternal and absolute as the laws of mercy and justice themselves. Nevertheless the way was opened for us to become clean once more and to be eligible to return to the presence of God if we will.

Our redemption from spiritual death can be worked out only under the conditions which God has established, beginning with faith in the Lord Jesus Christ and repentance. Covenants and ordinances are required. (84–05)

The Atonement can help us alleviate spiritual pain. The spiritual part of us is subject likewise to pain. In the case of our spiritual bodies, the worst pain, the most constant pain, is guilt. Suppose that guilt were cumulative, that whatever you did from the time you were little, whatever you did that was wrong, that it would be added upon by whatever else you do that is wrong. There would be a cumulative power of guilt.

Some of us do that on our own. We collect guilt, worrying endlessly about things that are past. We know that the remedy for guilt is repentance, and we know that one of the conditions of repentance first is to recognize our transgressions and feel sorrow for them. Then we are to repent of them, and then there is to be a restoration.

But there are many things that we do that we cannot restore. There are transgressions that we get into almost innocently, and we break something that we cannot fix. . . .

The law of justice is compensated by the law of mercy. When we cannot pay, when there are things that we cannot fix, what do we do? Except Christ had come, guilt and the penalty for transgression would be accumulative. Then we would be "of all men most miserable."[137] Then our lives would be hopeless. But He came! (00–07)

The Atonement is an ever-present power to be called upon in our daily lives. The Atonement offers redemption from spiritual death and from suffering caused by sin.

For some reason, we think the Atonement of Christ applies *only* at the end of mortal life to redemption from the Fall, from spiritual death. It is much more than that. It is an ever-present power to call upon in everyday life. When we are racked or harrowed up or tormented by guilt or burdened with grief, He can heal us. While we do not fully understand how the Atonement of Christ was made, we can experience "the peace of God, which passeth all understanding."[138] (01–03, p. 23)

You need not know everything before exercising the power of the Atonement. You need not know everything before the power of the Atonement will work for you. Have faith in Christ; it begins to work the day you ask! (97–02, p. 10)

Understanding the Atonement brings a liberating, exalting feeling. It was through reading the scriptures, and listening, that I could understand, at least in part, the power of the Atonement. Can you imagine how I felt when finally I could see that if I followed whatever conditions the Redeemer had set, I need never endure the agony of being spiritually unclean? Imagine the consoling, liberating, exalting feeling that will come to you when you see the reality of the Atonement and the practical everyday value of it to you individually. (97–02, p. 10)

There are requirements to fully effect the Atonement in our lives. I quote the third article of faith. It has two parts: "We believe that through the Atonement of Christ, all mankind may be saved, [then the conditions] by obedience to the laws and ordinances of the Gospel."

Justice requires that there be a punishment.[139] Guilt is not erased without pain. There are laws to obey and ordinances to receive, and there are penalties to pay.

Physical pain requires treatment and a change in lifestyle.

So it is with spiritual pain. There must be repentance and discipline, most of which is self-discipline. But to restore our innocence after serious transgressions, there must be confession to our bishop, who is the appointed judge.

The Lord promised, "A new heart . . . will I give you, and a new spirit will I put within you."[140] That spiritual heart surgery, like in the body, may cause you pain and require a change in habits and conduct. But in both cases, recovery brings renewed life and peace of mind. (01–03, p. 24)

The Atonement helps fix things that we alone cannot cure. We all make mistakes. Sometimes we harm ourselves and seriously injure others in ways that we alone cannot repair. We break things that we alone cannot fix. It is then in our nature to feel guilt and humiliation and suffering, which we alone cannot cure. That is when the healing power of the Atonement will help.

The Lord said, "Behold, I, God, have suffered these things for all, that they might not suffer if they would repent."[141]

If Christ had not made His Atonement, the penalties for mistakes would be added one on the other. Life would be hopeless. But He willingly sacrificed in order that we may be redeemed. (01–03, pp. 23–24)

Under the plan mistakes can be overcome through the Atonement. The plan presupposes mistakes. Under the plan, penalties connected with bad choices, our sins, may be cancelled on condition that we keep the commandments which activate the influence of the Atonement.

We are commanded to *do* some things, and we are commanded *not* to do others in order to merit the redeeming power of that sacrifice, the Atonement of Christ. The choice is ours. Alma said, "God gave unto them commandments, after having made known unto them the plan of redemption."[142] (93–07, p. 50)

It is justice that invokes the Atonement on our behalf. Justice can seem to be so very demanding. But we must learn that when we put everything as right as we can put it right, it is Justice who invokes the Atonement, orders the adversary off our property, and posts the notice that his agents will make no more collections from us. Our debt will have been paid in full by the only perfect, pure person who ever lived. (93–07, p. 59)

Jesus remained perfectly clean. Prophets and teachers were sent among men to tell them of the plan that someday a Savior would come upon the earth. He would be a son of God. He would remain perfectly clean. No matter how much the rebellious spirits tried to influence Him to do wrong, He would do that which is right. (67–08)

Christ used His agency and chose to die. Although He was innocent and clean every whit, He was rejected, betrayed, and condemned to mortal death.

But with Him, there is a difference. He is the Only Begotten Son of God. Man cannot of himself choose to live, for man has no power over death. But Christ possessed the power of life, and He need not choose to die. Volition, decision, and *agency:* these are central to the plan. His death, His sacrifice had to be by His own choice.

There is no more majestic moment in the history of the world than when Christ stood before Pilate and was told, "Knowest thou not that I have power to crucify thee, and have power to release thee?" His answer: "Thou couldest have no power at all against me, except it were given thee from above."[143]

Christ chose to die. He accepted the penalty for our transgressions to satisfy justice if we would but repent, for the law of justice cannot be broken; otherwise God would cease to be God. (*OFP,* pp. 35–37)

Mercy and redemption are made possible because of the Mediator. By eternal law, mercy cannot be extended save there be one who is both willing and able to assume our debt and pay the price and arrange the terms for our redemption.

Unless there is a mediator, unless we have a friend, the full weight of justice untempered, unsympathetic, must, positively must, fall on us. The full recompense for every transgression, however minor or however deep, will be exacted from us to the uttermost farthing.

But know this: Truth, glorious truth, proclaims there is such a Mediator.

"For there is one God, and one mediator between God and men, the man Christ Jesus."[144]

Through Him mercy can be fully extended to each of us without offending the eternal law of justice.

This truth is the very root of Christian doctrine. You may know much about the gospel as it branches out from there, but if you only know the branches and those branches do not touch that root, if they have been cut free from that truth, there will be no life nor substance nor redemption in them. (77–06, pp. 55–56)

The Mediator. Let me tell you a story—a parable.

There once was a man who wanted something very much. It seemed more important than anything else in his life. In order for him to have his desire, he incurred a great debt.

He had been warned about going into that much debt, and particularly about his creditor. But it seemed so important for him to do what he wanted to do and to have what he wanted right now. He was sure he could pay for it later.

So he signed a contract. He would pay it off some time along the way. He didn't worry too much about it, for the due date seemed such a long time away. He had what he wanted now, and that was what seemed important.

The creditor was always somewhere in the back of his mind, and he made token payments now and again, thinking somehow that the day of reckoning really would never come.

But as it always does, the day came, and the contract fell due. The debt had not been fully paid. His creditor appeared and demanded payment in full.

Only then did he realize that his creditor not only had the power to repossess all that he owned, but the power to cast him into prison as well.

"I cannot pay you, for I have not the power to do so," he confessed.

"Then," said the creditor, "we will exercise the contract, take your possessions, and you shall go to prison. You agreed to that. It was your choice. You signed the contract, and now it must be enforced."

"Can you not extend the time or forgive the debt?" the debtor begged. "Arrange some way for me to keep what I have and not go to prison. Surely you believe in mercy? Will you not show mercy?"

The creditor replied, "Mercy is always so one-sided. It would serve only you. If I show mercy to you, it will leave me unpaid. It is justice I demand. Do you believe in justice?"

"I believed in justice when I signed the contract," the debtor said.

"It was on my side then, for I thought it would protect me. I did not need mercy then, nor think I should need it ever. Justice, I thought, would serve both of us equally as well."

"It is justice that demands that you pay the contract or suffer the penalty," the creditor replied. "That is the law. You have agreed to it and that is the way it must be. Mercy cannot rob justice."

There they were: One meting out justice, the other pleading for mercy. Neither could prevail except at the expense of the other.

"If you do not forgive the debt there will be no mercy," the debtor pleaded.

"If I do, there will be no justice," was the reply.

Both laws, it seemed, could not be served. They are two eternal ideals that appear to contradict one another. Is there no way for justice to be fully served and mercy also?

There is a way! The law of justice *can* be fully satisfied and mercy *can* be fully extended—but it takes someone else. And so it happened this time.

The debtor had a friend. He came to help. He knew the debtor well. He knew him to be shortsighted. He thought him foolish to have gotten himself into such a predicament. Nevertheless, he wanted to help because he loved him. He stepped between them, faced the creditor, and made this offer.

"I will pay the debt if you will free the debtor from his contract so that he may keep his possessions and not go to prison."

As the creditor was pondering the offer, the mediator added, "You demanded justice. Though he cannot pay you, I will do so. You will have been justly dealt with and can ask no more. It would not be just."

And so the creditor agreed.

The mediator turned then to the debtor. "If I pay your debt, will you accept me as your creditor?"

"Oh yes, yes," cried the debtor. "You save me from prison and show mercy to me."

"Then," said the benefactor, "you will pay the debt to me and I will set the terms. It will not be easy, but it will be possible. I will provide a way. You need not go to prison."

And so it was that the creditor was paid in full. He had been justly dealt with. No contract had been broken.

The debtor, in turn, had been extended mercy. Both laws stood fulfilled. Because there was a mediator, justice had claimed its full share, and mercy was fully satisfied. (77–06, pp. 54–55)

There is a Redeemer, a Mediator. There is a Redeemer, a Mediator, who stands both willing and able to appease the demands of justice and extend mercy to those who are penitent, for, "He offereth himself a sacrifice for sin, to answer the ends of the law, unto all those who have a broken heart and a contrite spirit; and unto none else can the ends of the law be answered."[145]

Already He has accomplished the Redemption of all mankind from mortal death; resurrection is extended to all without condition.

He also makes possible redemption from the second death, which is the spiritual death, which is separation from the presence of our Heavenly Father.

This redemption can come only to those who are clean, for no unclean thing can dwell in the presence of God.

If justice decrees that we are not eligible because of our transgression, mercy provides a probation, a penitence, a preparation to enter in.

Without our Redeemer, our Mediator, justice untempered, unsympathetic would prevail. (79–08)

Christ gave the greatest of all gifts. He was more than a great man. He was more than just a great teacher. He was the Savior, the Messiah. He made atonement for our sins and opened the resurrection. For as in Adam all men die (or were sent out from the presence of God), so in Christ would all men be made alive (or be able to return to the presence of God) knowing good from evil and having a resurrected body. This was the greatest of all gifts. (67–08)

Physical Death

Mortal death is a mechanism of rescue. Mortal death, the penalty justice imposed upon Adam and his posterity, is in fact a mechanism of rescue. It is the process by which we may return to the presence of God. Man *must* be released from mortality lest he live forever in his sins. Without mortal death, the plan of happiness would not just be disturbed or delayed, it would be destroyed! Alma was right when he said, "Now behold, it was not expedient that man should be reclaimed from this temporal death, for that would destroy the great plan of happiness."[146] (88–08, p. 14)

Death is a sacred event. You couldn't call it an ordinance, but death is a very sacred event. It's out of our hands. We know the spirit world is right here upon us. (08–02)

Death is an essential part of life. Death is a part of life. It is an essential part. It can be a beautiful part. (80–11)

Death is not an ending. Mortal death is no more an ending than birth was a beginning. (*THT,* p. 17)

There is no distance in death. There is no distance in death. The spirit world we know is here around us, but the veil is there, and the curtain is there. On occasions we can see and on more occasions we can feel those who have gone beyond. . . .

I saw my mother once. It was in a vision or a dream, more real than just a dream. She had died in her seventies, died a very painful, long-suffering death. There are two words that I could use to describe my mother when I saw her: the one is beautiful, and the other is glorious. I wondered why it was that I was privileged to see her.

Then one day President Spencer W. Kimball in a meeting said that he had seen his father. He described an experience about like I have described it to you. He said, "I wondered for a long time why I was blessed with that experience. I finally came to know that it was his way of saying that he approved of me, that he approved of my life and what I was doing." (08–03)

We need not fear death. We know that we live beyond the grave. That is the testimony. That is the thing, perhaps, most worth knowing, for then fear is gone. The Lord said: "Fear not . . . unto death; for in this world [ye have not a fulness of] joy . . . , but in me [ye have a fulness of] joy."[147] So the plan is working; it's progressing just as it should. . . .

On one occasion when Brother Romney was very old, I brought him home one night when he was very weary. We said nothing to one another. I thought he was too tired to talk. Then he said, "Boyd, when I think that in a short time I will be beyond the veil and be with Ida, I'm filled with such great joy that I just cannot contain myself." And I thought, "Thus speaks the prophet and Apostle." (98–05)

Our body is like a glove. Pretend . . . that my hand represents your spirit. It is alive. It can move by itself.

A glove is like your body. It cannot move. But when your spirit entered into your body, then you could move and act and live. Now you are a person—a spirit with a body—living on the earth.

While you are alive, the spirit inside your body causes it to work and to act and to live. But it was not intended that we stay here on earth forever. Some day, because of old age or perhaps a disease or an accident, the spirit and the body will be separated. When this happens, we say that a person has died. Death is a separation—a separation of the body and the spirit.

When the glove, which is like your body, is taken away from your spirit, it cannot move anymore. It just falls down. It is dead. But the part of you that looks out through your eyes and allows you to think and to smile, to act and to know, and to be, that is your spirit and that is eternal. It cannot die.

When our Heavenly Father made it possible for us to come into this world, He also made it possible for us to return to Him, because He is our Father and He loves us. Do not think that because we are living on this earth away from Him and because we can't see Him that He has forgotten us.

Our Heavenly Father knew that we would need help. So in the plan He provided for someone to come into the world and help us so that we can some day return to Him.

This was Jesus Christ, the Son of God. He is a spirit child as all of us are, but Jesus was also Heavenly Father's Only Begotten Son on the earth. And it was Jesus who made it possible for us to overcome death. He made it possible for our spirits and bodies to be one again. Because of Him, we will be resurrected. That means our spirit and body will be put back together. That is a gift from Him. That is why He is called our Savior, our Redeemer. (73–04, pp. 51–53)

Death ultimately is not untimely. We sometimes speak of death as an "untimely" death. I suppose that would be true when young people die, when there are families that are pulled apart through accident and difficulties that might be called untimely. But death itself is not. Time is measured only to man, the Lord said. And He said that He can recompense and put things together. (99–02)

The faithful who die young will not be denied any eternal blessings. Now the question may linger in your mind—what about the things he missed in life. He hadn't been married in the temple. What about parenthood and the experience of raising children? Well, let your minds and hearts be at peace. You know how you would manage it if you were his father. You know that if he had worked for something and deserved something and then by some chance of accident it was taken from him—you know that as his father you would provide it, wouldn't you? You must know that [he] will be denied nothing. For as the ordinances of the eternities unfold, he will be found with all of the blessings. You will remember Joseph Smith saw his brother, Alvin, in the celestial kingdom and he asked why—how did Alvin get there, and the message came back to him that those who would have, but couldn't, would not be denied. So don't let your mind worry over that. He will have all of the things, all of the blessings, that he would have had had he lived.[148] (71–05)

The spirit of reverence should prevail at funerals. There is the need to reestablish the spirit of reverence at funerals, whether in a chapel, a mortuary, or at other locations.

We should always have a tender regard for the feelings of the bereaved.

We are close, very close, to the spirit world at the time of death. There are tender feelings, spiritual communications really, which may easily be lost if there is not a spirit of reverence.

At times of sorrow and parting one may experience that "peace . . . which passeth all understanding"[149] which the scriptures promise. That is a very private experience. . . .

Three elements combine in a funeral as in no other meeting: the doctrines of the gospel, the spirit of inspiration, and families gathered in tender regard for one another.

May we reintroduce the attitude of reverence each time we gather to memorialize one who has moved through the veil to that place where one day each of us will go.

No consolation in parting compares with that "peace . . . which passeth all understanding." That is fostered by reverence. Reverence, please, brothers and sisters, reverence. (88–07, pp. 20–21)

A funeral is one of the most solemn and sacred meetings of the Church. One of the most solemn and sacred meetings of the Church is the funeral for a departed member. It is a time of caring and support when families gather in a spirit of tender regard for one another. It is a time to soberly contemplate doctrines of the gospel and the purposes for the ministry of the Lord Jesus Christ. (88–07, p. 19)

I know of no meeting where the congregation is in a better state of readiness to receive revelation and inspiration from a speaker than they are at a funeral. (96–07)

Bishops should remember that when funerals are held under priesthood auspices the service should conform to the instructions given by the Church. We should regard the bishop rather than the family or the mortician as the presiding authority in these matters. (88–07, p. 20)

A comforting, spiritual funeral is of great importance. A comforting, spiritual funeral is of great importance. It helps console the bereaved and establishes a transition from mourning to the reality that we must move forward with life. Whether death is expected or a sudden shock, an inspirational funeral where the doctrines of resurrection, the mediation of Christ, and certainty of life after death are taught strengthens those who must now move on with life. (88–07, p. 19)

Funerals should be characterized by spirituality and reverence. Sometimes family members tell things that would be appropriate at a family reunion or at some other family gathering but not on an occasion that should be sacred and solemn. While quiet humor is not out of order in a funeral, it should be wisely introduced. It should be ever kept in mind that the funeral should be characterized by spirituality and reverence. (88–07, p. 20)

RESURRECTION, JUDGMENT, AND KINGDOMS OF GLORY

Because of Jesus Christ we will all be resurrected. [Jesus Christ] overcame the mortal death for us. Through the Atonement, He made it possible for our spirit and body to be one again. Because of Him we will be resurrected. . . . That is a gift from Him. And all men will receive it. That is why He is called our Savior, our Redeemer. (73–04, p. 53)

As the Savior, Jesus Christ set in action the resurrection. He would set in action a resurrection so that our spirits could reenter a perfected body, never to be separated again. And He would teach us how to make ourselves clean and worthy to enter back into the presence of our Father in Heaven. This is why He was a Savior. He saved us from death by starting the resurrection—that is, the reuniting of the spirit with a wonderful perfected body. (67–08)

Resurrection can be a dual redemption. Resurrection is our redemption from temporal death, from the grave. There is also a redemption from the spiritual death and an exaltation for those who are worthy to receive it. We shall receive celestial, terrestrial, or telestial bodies in the resurrection. Those who inherit the celestial glory shall inherit bodies like unto the Father, bodies which have a glory akin to the glory of the sun. Our memory of premortal life will be restored in perfect clarity. Those who have been endowed, sealed, and have kept their covenants will assemble with their families. (83–04)

In the resurrection your body will be glorious. You can look forward to the day when you are "unwrapped" and your spirit is separated from the body. Your spirit is young and vibrant and beautiful. Even if your body is old and diseased or crippled or disabled in any way, when the spirit and body are put together in the resurrection, then you will be glorious, then you will be glorified. (02–02)

Because of the resurrection we do ordinance work for the dead. You believe in the resurrection. You must know that baptism for someone who is dead is quite as essential as baptism for someone who is living. There is no difference in the importance of it. One by one it must happen. They must do it here while living or it must be done for them here after they die.

The whole New Testament centers on the resurrection of the Lord. The message is that *all* are to be resurrected. Every scripture and every motivation that apply to missionary work have their application to ordinance work for the dead. (*THT,* p. 234)

Life beyond the grave—the resurrection and the judgment. Our knowledge of life beyond the veil, like our knowledge of the premortal life, is given only in outline form. But salient facts are repeated in the scriptures, and we are given sufficient doctrine to know what we must do to prepare for it.

As with our knowledge of the premortal life, there is little to be gained by seeking after the mysteries, for there is hardly time in a lifetime to master the plain and precious things.

The facts we know are these:

When we die as to mortality, the spirit leaves the body and is taken to a place of rest. Just as Eden was a place between the premortal world and mortality, there is prepared a place between temporal death and our return to the presence of God.

Those who are righteous are taken to paradise.

Those who are wicked are consigned to a spirit prison.

Justice will be upheld to the very letter of the law and demands that no one of us can be redeemed without the ordinances. That same justice requires that those who were denied a knowledge of the plan of salvation upon the earth will have the gospel preached to them. The dead must have the opportunity to receive the ordinances. They can repent and make covenants if they will.

The essential ordinances of the gospel which they did not receive in mortality (baptism, ordination to the priesthood, the endowment, and the sealing ordinance) will be vicariously provided for them. Justice, so often feared by man, is in truth a friend, a protector.

Mercy is revealed in full tenderness and in the commandment that we, the living, do for them vicariously what they cannot do for themselves. Those who do this work on earth have a crucial part in the plan.

Beyond the veil we will await a judgment, the resurrection, and thereafter the final judgment. We will be called forth from paradise or from prison to inherit, after the final judgment, that degree of glory that we merit, that which we have earned.

There is yet another death, a second spiritual death, which will be pronounced only upon the sons of perdition who have "denied the Holy Spirit after having received it, and having denied the Only Begotten Son of the Father, having crucified him unto themselves and put him to an open shame." They are "the only ones on whom the second death shall have any power."[150] After the resurrection they shall be cast into outer darkness.

We may, if we have been worthy, come forth in the morning of the first resurrection. If we have been true and faithful in all things, we shall approach the veil and there will be extended the sublimest of all invitations: "Enter into the joy of thy Lord."

An exaltation awaits each of us who are worthy to receive it. We shall receive celestial, terrestrial, or telestial bodies in the resurrection.

Those who inherit the celestial glory shall possess bodies like unto the Father, bodies which have a glory akin to the glory of the sun. Our memory of premortal life will be restored in perfect clarity.

If we have been endowed, sealed, and kept our covenants, we will assemble with our families. And there is the promise of eternal increase.

The doctrine of the eternal nature of family ties is neither known nor taught elsewhere in Christianity. To be worthy of exaltation in the presence of God and enjoy association with our own family is to receive the consummation of all blessings that God has provided in His plan.

What happens thereafter, we do not know; more than this we have not been given. But in due time if we are righteous we shall know, for unto them the father will "reveal all mysteries," the "wonders of eternity."[151] If we are righteous all that the Father hath shall be given us,[152] for we shall be gods.

With each of us the resurrection is a certainty. For each of us our degree of exaltation awaits the test. (84–05)

The Lord only gives directions to the celestial kingdom. The principles and ordinances of the gospel all point to the celestial kingdom. The Lord has not given us direction as to the lower kingdoms, save to warn us that by falling short of the higher mark we will inherit a lesser reward. (*THT,* p. 19)

No shortage of room in the celestial kingdom. There is no shortage of room in the celestial kingdom. There is room for all. (75–03, p. 105)

CHAPTER 2

Obedience and Faith

"Obedience is a powerful spiritual medicine.
It comes close to being a cure-all." (77–10, p. 60)

OBEDIENCE

Latter-day Saints are obedient because they see. Latter-day Saints are not obedient because they are compelled to be obedient. They are obedient because they know certain spiritual truths and have decided, as an expression of their own individual agency, to obey the commandments of God.

We are the sons and daughters of God, willing followers, disciples of the Lord Jesus Christ, and "under this head . . . [we] are made free."[1]

Those who talk of blind obedience may appear to know many things, but they do not understand the doctrines of the gospel. There is an obedience that comes from a knowledge of the truth that transcends any external form of control. We are not obedient because we are blind; we are obedient because we can see. The best control, I repeat, is self-control. (83–01, p. 66)

We are free to be obedient. Some people are always suspicious that one is obedient only because he is compelled to be. They indict themselves with the very thought that one is obedient only because he is compelled to be. They feel that one would obey only through compulsion. They speak for themselves. I am *free* to be obedient, and I decided that—all by myself. I pondered on it; I reasoned it; I even experimented a little. I learned some sad lessons from disobedience. Then I tested it in the great laboratory of spiritual inquiry—the most sophisticated, accurate, and refined test that we can make of any principle. So I am not hesitant to say that I want to be obedient to the principles of the gospel. *I want to.* I have decided that. My volition, my agency, has been turned in that direction. The Lord knows that. (71–11, p. 255)

We should be obedient. We also should be obedient! The fact that we have received a commandment from God is reason enough in itself to go and do as we have been directed to do.

I have come to know that if we will do so, even though we may not understand at first, the Lord will tell us, as He told Adam, why we are so commanded.[2] (*THT,* p. 264)

Do the will of the Father. We should put ourselves in a position before our Father in Heaven and say, individually, "I do not want to do what I want to do. I want to do what Thou wouldst have me do." Suddenly, like any father, the Lord could say, "Well, there is one more of my children almost free from the need of constant supervision."

I know that I am free to do as I will. If the First Presidency or the president of the Twelve were to assign me to attend a conference north in the winter or south in the summer, I could have my own way concerning that. I could settle that with two words. I could just say, "I won't." In fact, I could say it in one word, "No." I could have my way every single time.

But I will it to be the other way. I want to do what they want me to do. Why? Because I have the witness, the conviction, that they are the servants of the Lord. They are placed as my leaders. (71–11, pp. 257–58)

Now is the time to make the choice. Most of us have been taught the gospel all our lives. We know the difference between good and evil, between right and wrong. Isn't it time then that we decide that we are going to do right? In so doing we are making a choice—not just *a* choice but *the* choice. Once we have decided that, with no fingers crossed, no counterfeiting, no reservations or hesitancy, the rest will fall into place. (*TYD,* pp. 242–43)

You can be whatever you desire. You can be whatever you desire. The prophet Alma said: "I know that he granteth unto men according to their desire, whether it be unto death or unto life; yea, I know that he allotteth unto men . . . according to their wills, whether they be unto salvation or unto destruction. Yea, and I know that good and evil have come before all men; he that knoweth not good from evil is blameless; but he that knoweth good and evil, to him it is given according to his desires, whether he desireth good or evil, life or death, joy or remorse of conscience."[3]

Do you have the simple childlike humility to desire to be good? Do you know how important it is to mankind that goodness exist? Do you realize that somewhere in the world happiness must exist, that there must be happy families? Do you see how important it is to all of humanity that somewhere there be spiritually successful, reverent people? . . . The Lord said, "Be ye therefore perfect."[4] Are you embarrassed, or hesitant, or too proud to commit yourself? Too arrogant and lifted up? Do you think you are above a simple, personal, reverent desire to be good? Can you now . . . commit yourself and say: "I want to be good. Without hesitation I say that. I desire, really desire, to be good, as an act of volition—a voluntary gesture. As an exercise of my agency, I consent and choose to be good." (68–06)

We can give our agency to God. I will not consent to any influence from the adversary. I have come to know what power he has. I know all about that. But I also have come to know the power of truth and of righteousness and of good, and I want to be good. I'm not ashamed to say that—I want to be good. And I've found in my life that it has been critically important that this was established between me and the Lord so that I knew that He knew which way I had committed my agency. I went before Him and in essence said, "I'm not neutral, and You can do with me what You want. If You need my vote, it's there. I don't care what You do with me, and You don't have to take anything from me because I give it to You—everything, all I own, all I am." And that makes the difference. (70–09, p. 272)

Give yourself totally to the Lord. We have to give ourselves totally and completely, with nothing reserved, and we have to let the Lord know that all we want is for His will to be done, and that kind of devotion and conviction and consecration means that we have to listen spiritually. (08–02)

Each of us must learn obedience. When President Joseph Fielding Smith was the President of the Quorum of the Twelve, I was close to him. He made the conference assignments. I learned a great lesson from him.

I was in the Missionary Department at that time. I went to President Smith's office one day. He was making out the assignments for conferences. He said, "Here, take your pick."

That was tempting, because in those days it was something of a plum, something of a reward to be able to travel. I cannot even imagine that now! There was a stake in Mexico and one in New Zealand. They were talking about a stake in England. International travel was something sought after.

He handed me the list and said, "You put your name down where you would like to go."

I said, "Will you assign me where I say?"

He said, "Yes."

I said, "Are you sure?"

He said, "Oh, yes. I will let you go anywhere you want."

I said, "I want to go where I'm sent!"

He said, "That is the right answer."

*Elders Harold B. Lee, Gordon B. Hinckley, and Boyd K. Packer
meeting about LDS servicemen, May 22, 1965*

That was a great awakening: "I want to go where I'm sent!" He looked at me differently thereafter.

I learned that to obey can become a prime attribute. Each of us must somehow learn obedience. It is not always easy because the scriptures say, "My people must needs be chastened until they learn obedience, if it must needs be, by the things which they suffer."[5] It is not always easy to obey, but it is always wise and right to obey. (07–07)

Obey, and you cannot go wrong. Obey is a four-letter word. It is the most protecting word, the most revealing word. You obey, and you cannot go wrong. You will be provided for. (05–02)

Obedience leads to happiness. I cannot overemphasize that one's independence and spiritual strength depend on obedience to the laws and ordinances of the gospel. As we do so willingly we will learn to trust those delicate, sensitive, spiritual promptings. We will learn that they invariably lead us to righteousness, to happiness. (93–07, p. 58)

It is through obedience that we gain freedom. Some of us are very jealous of our prerogatives and feel that obedience to priesthood authority is to forfeit one's agency. If we only knew, my brethren and sisters, that it is through obedience that we gain freedom. (65–01, p. 239)

Obedience is the key to freedom. Obedience to God can be the very highest expression of independence. Just think of giving to Him the one thing, the one gift that He would never take. Think of giving Him that one thing that He would never wrest from you. . . .

Obedience—that which God will never take by force—He will accept when freely given. And He will then return to you freedom that you can hardly dream of—the freedom to feel and to know, the freedom to do, and the freedom to *be,* at least a thousand fold more than we offer Him. Strangely enough, the key to freedom is obedience. (71–11, p. 256)

Nothing can free us spiritually more than obedience. Each of us has agency; each is free to choose. Nothing can free us spiritually more than obedience—obedience to the laws, to the Lord. Nothing is more liberating spiritually than the worthiness which is maintained, and at times perhaps must be reclaimed, through repentance. We need to keep the Word of Wisdom (that is the key to revelation, to treasures of knowledge, even hidden treasures); pay tithes and offerings; sustain our leaders; study the scriptures (therein is a testimony of the Restoration as it relates to the great plan of happiness.) We must live the gospel. The gospel is the great plan of happiness. By following its path, "Ye shall know the truth, and the truth shall make you free."[6] (93–07, pp. 57–58)

FAITH

Faith must go beyond evidence. Faith, to be faith, must center around something that is not known. Faith, to be faith, must go beyond that for which there is confirming evidence. Faith, to be faith, must go into the unknown. Faith, to be faith, must walk to the edge of the light, and then a few steps into the darkness. If everything has to be known, if everything has to be explained, if everything has to be certified, then there is no need for faith. Indeed, there is no room for it. (68–08, p. 62)

Some years ago I learned a lesson that I shall never forget.

I had been called as an Assistant to the Council of the Twelve, and we were to move to Salt Lake City and find an adequate and permanent home. President Henry D. Moyle assigned someone to help us.

A home was located that was ideally suited to our needs. Elder Harold B. Lee came and looked it over very carefully and then counseled, "By all means, you are to proceed."

But there was no way we could proceed. I had just completed the course work on a doctor's degree and was writing the dissertation. With the support of my wife and our eight children, all of the resources we could gather over the years had been spent on education.

By borrowing on our insurance, gathering every resource, we could barely get into the house, without sufficient left to even make the first monthly payment.

Brother Lee insisted, "Go ahead. I know it is right."

I was in deep turmoil because I had been counseled to do something I had never done before—to sign a contract without having the resources to meet the payments.

When Brother Lee sensed my feelings he sent me to President David O. McKay, who listened very carefully as I explained the circumstances.

He said, "You do this. It is the right thing." But he extended no resources to make the doing of it possible.

When I reported to Brother Lee he said, "That confirms what I have told you."

I was still not at peace, and then came the lesson. Elder Lee said, "Do you know what is wrong with you—you always want to see the end from the beginning."

I replied quietly that I wanted to see at least a few steps ahead. He answered by quoting from the sixth verse of the twelfth chapter of Ether: "Wherefore, dispute not because ye see not, for ye receive no witness until after the trial of your faith."

And then he added, "My boy, you must learn to walk to the edge of the light, and perhaps a few steps into the darkness, and you will find that the light will appear and move ahead of you."

And so it has—but only as we walked to the edge of the light. (*THT,* pp. 183–85)

Believing is seeing. In a world filled with skepticism and doubt, the expression "seeing is believing" promotes the attitude, "You show me, and I will believe." We want all of the proof and all of the evidence first. It seems hard to take things on faith.

When will we learn that in spiritual things it works the other way about—that believing is seeing? Spiritual belief precedes spiritual knowledge. When we believe in things that are not seen but are nevertheless true, then we have faith. (68–08, p. 63)

How to exercise faith. You exercise faith by causing, or by making, your mind accept or believe as truth that which *you* cannot, by reason alone, prove for certainty.

The first exercising of your faith should be your acceptance of Christ and His Atonement. (94–05, p. 60)

Faith can be likened to a fire. Faith can be likened to a fire. It can be kindled and fanned and fed. Like a fire, it can be smothered and put out. Faith can be doubted. (84–02)

Faith and humility go hand in hand. Faith and humility go hand in hand. The person who can acknowledge his dependence upon God and accept a child-parent relationship with Him has prepared a place for faith. (68–08, p. 62)

There must be tests of faith. The Book of Mormon warns of "the vainness, and the frailties, and the foolishness of men! When they are learned they think they are wise, and they hearken not unto the counsel of God, for they set it aside, supposing they know of themselves."[7]

All things are not and must not be so convincingly clear as to require no test of faith. That would nullify agency and defeat the purpose of the plan of salvation. . . .

Be humble. Endure the . . . tests of faith [that come] with intellectual mocking. . . . You will be safe. (85–15)

Fear is the antithesis of faith. Fear is the antithesis of faith. In this Church, we do not fear. I have been sitting in the councils of the Brethren now for many years. I have seen disappointment, shock, and concern. Never once, for one second, have I ever seen any fear. And you should not. (95–06, p. 9)

POWER OF FAITH—MIRACLES

There are two kinds of faith. There are two kinds of faith. One of them functions ordinarily in the life of every soul. It is the kind of faith born by experience; it gives us certainty that a new day will dawn, that spring will come, that growth will take place. It is the kind of faith that relates us with confidence to that which is scheduled to happen. . . .

There is another kind of faith, rare indeed. This is the kind of faith that *causes* things to happen. It is the kind of faith that is worthy and prepared and unyielding, and it calls forth things that otherwise would not be. It is the kind of faith that moves people. It is the kind of faith that sometimes moves things. Few men possess it. It comes by gradual growth. It is a marvelous, even a transcendent, power, a power as real and as invisible as electricity. Directed and channeled, it has great effect. (68–08, pp. 62–63)

Miracles are attendant in our day. Did you know that the Lord told His Twelve Apostles that it was not only their privilege but their responsibility to perform miracles. These miracles were signs. We don't seek after signs, but they are attendant to the authority, and they are attendant in our day. (00–01)

The greatest miracles are the miracles of spiritual growth and healing. This is His Church. We are His servants. We who hold the priesthood have His authority and power. We can perform miracles. We do not talk about them. Most of those miracles have to do with healing the body. The greater miracles are the miracles of spiritual growth and healing in the lives of every one of us. (03–04, p. 175)

Miracles are regarded with reverence. Miracles have always been a witness of His church on the earth, and they are known among us—I could even say they are common among us—but they are not often talked about. We regard them with humility and with unmeasured reverence. (73–03, p. 18)

Has the day of miracles ceased? I know by experience too sacred to touch upon that God lives, that Jesus is the Christ, that the gift of the Holy Ghost conferred upon us at our confirmation is a divine gift. The Book of Mormon is true! This is the Lord's Church! Jesus is the Christ! There presides over us a prophet of God! The day of miracles has not ceased, neither have angels ceased to appear and minister unto man! The spiritual gifts are with the Church. (82–04, p. 7)

CHAPTER 3

Repentance and Forgiveness

"Never make the same mistake once." *(08–02)*

SIN AND TEMPTATION

Indulgence is bondage. Indulgence is bondage. True freedom comes from righteousness. *(69–06)*

Evil can overcome us only when we are undisciplined. Evil is not powerful enough to destroy the Church or any individual of the Church who is living in righteousness. That much power does not exist. Where there is unity, all certainly will be saved. However, where there are the undisciplined who will not follow, there arises a question as to whether there is enough power to save them. Certainly they can't be saved in their undisciplined mischief. *(64–08)*

Acceptance of wickedness cannot turn it into happiness. There are some things that are false, that are wrong. For instance, we cannot be happy and at once be wicked. Never. Regardless of how generally accepted that course may be.

If [wickedness] were printed in every book, run on every news press, set forth in every magazine; if it were broadcast on every frequency, televised from every station, declared from every pulpit, taught in every classroom, advocated in every conversation, still it would be wrong.

Wickedness never was happiness, neither indeed can it be, neither indeed will it ever be. (73–05, p. 170)

Avoid spiritual crocodiles. I have always been interested in animals and birds. When I learned to read, I found books about birds and animals and came to know much about them. By the time I was in my teens, I could identify most of the African animals. I could tell a klipspringer from an impala, or a gemsbok from a wildebeest.

I always wanted to go to Africa and see the animals, and finally that opportunity came. Sister Packer and I were assigned to tour in South Africa. We had a very strenuous schedule and had dedicated eight chapels in seven days.

The mission president was vague about the schedule for September 10th. (That happens to be my birthday.) I thought we were planning to return to Johannesburg, South Africa. But he had other plans. "There is a game reserve some distance from here," he explained, "and I have rented a car, and tomorrow, your birthday, we are going to spend seeing the African animals."

Now I might explain that the game reserves in Africa are unusual. The people are put in cages, and the animals are left to run free. That is, there are compounds where the park visitors check in at night and are locked behind high fences until after daylight. They are allowed to drive about, but no one is allowed out of his car.

Because of a delay in getting our evening meal, it was long after dark when we left to go to our isolated cabin. We found the turnoff and had gone up the narrow road just a short distance when the engine stalled. We found a flashlight, and I stepped out to check under the hood. As the light flashed on the dusty road, the first thing I saw was lion tracks!

Back in the car, we determined to content ourselves with spending the night there! Fortunately, we were rescued by the driver of a gas truck who had left the compound late because of a problem.

In the morning we had no automobile and no way to get a replacement until late in the afternoon. Our one day in the park was ruined and, for me, the dream of a lifetime was gone.

I talked with a young ranger, and he was surprised that I knew many of the African birds. Then he volunteered to rescue us. "We are building a new lookout over a water hole about twenty miles from the compound," he said. "It is not quite finished, but it is safe. I will take you out there with a lunch. You may see as many animals, or even more, than if you were driving around."

On the way to the lookout he volunteered to show us some lions. He turned off through the brush and before long located a group of seventeen lions all sprawled out asleep and drove right up among them.

We stopped at a water hole to watch the animals come to drink. It was very dry that season and there was not much water, really just muddy spots. When the elephants stepped into the soft mud, the water would seep into the depression and the animals would drink from the elephant tracks.

The antelope, particularly, were very nervous. They would approach the mud hole, only to turn and run away in great fright. I could see there were no lions about and asked the guide why they didn't drink. His answer, and this is the lesson, was "Crocodiles."

I knew he must be joking and asked him seriously, "What is the problem?" The answer again: "Crocodiles."

"Nonsense," I said. "There are no crocodiles out there. Anyone can see that."

I thought he was having some fun at the expense of his foreign game expert, and finally I asked him to tell us the truth. Now I remind you that I was not uninformed. I had read many books. Besides, anyone would know that you can't hide a crocodile in an elephant track.

He could tell I did not believe him and determined, I suppose, to teach me a lesson. We drove to another location where the car was on an embankment above the muddy hole where we could look down. "There," he said. "See for yourself."

I couldn't see anything except the mud, a little water, and the nervous animals in the distance. Then all at once I saw it!—a large crocodile, settled in the mud, waiting for some unsuspecting animal to get thirsty enough to come for a drink.

Suddenly I became a believer! When he could see I was willing to listen, he continued with the lesson. "There are crocodiles all over the park," he said, "not just in the rivers. We don't have any water without a crocodile somewhere near it, and you'd better count on it."

The guide was kinder to me than I deserved. My "know-it-all" challenge to his first statement, "crocodiles," might have brought an invitation, "Well, go out and see for yourself!"

I could see for myself that there were no crocodiles. I was so sure of myself I think I might have walked out just to see what was there. Such an arrogant approach could have been fatal! But he was patient enough to teach me.

I hope you'll be wiser in talking to your guides than I was on that occasion. That smart-aleck idea that I knew everything really wasn't worthy of me, nor is it worthy of you. I'm not very proud of it, and I think I'd be ashamed to tell you about it except that telling you may help you.

Those ahead of you in life have probed about the water holes a bit and raise a voice of warning about crocodiles. Not just the big, gray lizards that can bite you to pieces, but *spiritual crocodiles,* infinitely more dangerous, and more deceptive and less visible, even, than those well-camouflaged reptiles of Africa.

These spiritual crocodiles can kill or mutilate your souls. They can destroy your peace of mind and the peace of mind of those who love you. Those are the ones to be warned against, and there is hardly a watering place in all of mortality now that is not infested with them.

On another trip to Africa I discussed this experience with a game ranger in another park. He assured me that you can *indeed* hide a crocodile in an elephant track—one big enough to bite a man in two.

He then showed me a place where a tragedy had occurred. A young man from England was working in the hotel for the season. In spite of constant and repeated warnings, he went through the compound fence to check something across a shallow splash of water that didn't cover his tennis shoes.

"He wasn't two steps in," the ranger said, "before a crocodile had him, and we could do nothing to save him."

It seems almost to be against our natures, particularly when we are young, to accept much guidance from others. But there are times when, regardless of how much we think we know or how much we think we want to do something, our very existence depends on paying attention to the guides.

Now, it is a gruesome thing to think about that young man who was eaten by the crocodile. But that is not, by any means, the worst thing that could happen. There are moral and spiritual things far worse even than the thought of being chewed to pieces by a monstrous lizard.

Fortunately there are guides enough in life to prevent these things from happening if we are willing to take counsel now and again. If you will listen to the counsel of your parents and your teachers and your leaders when you are young, you can learn how to follow the best guide of all—the whisperings of the Holy Spirit. That is individual revelation. There is a process through which we can be alerted to spiritual dangers. Just as surely as that guide warned me, you can receive signals alerting you to the spiritual crocodiles that lurk ahead.

Fortunately, there is spiritual first aid for those who have been bitten. The bishop of the ward is the guide in charge of this first aid. He can also treat those who have been badly morally mauled by these spiritual crocodiles—and see them completely healed.

That experience in Africa was another reminder for me to follow the Guide. I follow Him because I want to. I bear witness that He lives, that Jesus is the Christ. (76–03, pp. 8–11)

Repentance

The key to escaping the power of the adversary is repentance and forgiveness. In the universal battle for human souls, the adversary takes enormous numbers of prisoners. Many, knowing of no way to escape, are pressed into his service. Every soul confined in a concentration camp of sin and guilt has a key to the gate. The key is labeled Repentance. The adversary cannot hold them, if they know how to use it. The twin principles of repentance and forgiveness exceed in strength the awesome power of the tempter. (92–02, p. 114)

We should repent often. Repentance, like soap, should be used frequently. (97–02, p. 9)

The scriptures show the path to repentance. Most mistakes you can repair yourself, alone, through prayerful repentance. The more serious ones require help. Without help, you are like one who can't or doesn't wash or bathe or put on clean clothes. The path you need to follow is in the scriptures. Read them and your faith in Christ will grow. Listen to those who know the gospel.

You will learn about the Fall of man, about the purpose of life, about good and evil, about temptations and repentance, about how the Spirit works. Read what Alma said of his repentance: "I could remember my pains no more; yea, I was harrowed up by the memory of my sins no more."[1]

Hear the Lord say, "Behold, he who has repented of his sins, the same is forgiven, and I, the Lord, remember them no more."[2] Doctrine *can* change behavior quicker than talking about behavior will. (97–02, p. 10)

There could be no peace without repentance. I readily confess that I would find no peace, neither happiness nor safety, in a world without repentance. I do not know what I should do if there were no way for me to erase my mistakes. The agony would be more than I could bear. It may be otherwise with you, but not with me.

An atonement was made. Ever and always it offers amnesty from transgression and from death if we will but repent. Repentance is the escape clause in it all. Repentance is the key with which we can unlock the prison from inside. We hold that key within our hands, and agency is ours to use it. (88–03, p. 71)

Too many live as though the Redeemer had never been born. If Christ had not come, that guilt, that racking, that torment, that harrowing up, that lake of fire and brimstone, would follow us around. It follows many of us around now. How foolish many of us are to endlessly go over in our mind things that we have done, things that we have hoped for that have not been fulfilled, mistakes that we have made that we cannot repair! We go on through life as though the Redeemer had never been born.

What can He cure? "Though your sins be as scarlet, they shall be as white as snow; though they be red like crimson, they shall be as wool."[3] There is nothing that He cannot cure. There is one thing that He says He will not forgive, but that would not apply to any of us. Otherwise, no matter what mistakes we have made, no matter how we have hurt other people, how we have been offended by other people, it can all be made right. (00–07)

It is a satanic lie to believe we cannot repent and be forgiven. It is a wicked, wicked world in which we live and in which our children must find their way. Challenges of pornography, gender confusion, immorality, child abuse, drug addiction, and all the rest are everywhere. There is no way to escape from their influence.

Some are led by curiosity into temptation, then into experimentation, and some become trapped in addiction. They lose hope. The adversary harvests his crop and binds them down. Satan is the deceiver, the destroyer, but his is a temporary victory. The angels of the devil convince some that they are born to a life from which they cannot escape and are compelled to live in sin. The most wicked of lies is that they cannot change and repent and that they will not be forgiven. That cannot be true. They have forgotten the Atonement of Christ.

"For, behold, the Lord your Redeemer suffered death in the flesh; wherefore he suffered the pain of all men, that all men might repent and come unto him."[4]

Christ is the Creator, the Healer. What He made, He can fix. The gospel of Jesus Christ is the gospel of repentance and forgiveness.[5] "Remember the worth of souls is great in the sight of God."[6] (06–02, pp. 27–28)

Heavenly Father can help us make things right. Who made you? Who is your Creator? There is not anything about your life that gets bent or broken that He cannot fix and will fix. You have to decide. If some of you have made mistakes and you think you are broken and cannot be put together, you do not know the doctrine of the Church. You do not know what the Atonement was about and who the Lord is and what a power He is in your life. (03–04, p. 175)

It is never too late to repent. Those who make one serious mistake tend to add another by assuming that it is then too late for them. It is never too late! Never!

While your temptations are greater than were ours, that will be considered in the judgments of the Lord. He said that "his mercies [are suited] according to the conditions of . . . men."[7] That is only just. . . .

The discouraging idea that a mistake (or even a series of them) makes it everlastingly too late does not come from the Lord. He has said that *if* we will repent, not only will He forgive us our transgressions, but He will forget them and remember our sins no more.[8] Repentance is like soap; it can wash sin away. Ground-in dirt may take the strong detergent of discipline to get the stains out, but out they will come. (89–01, p. 59)

The formula for repentance requires that we confess. The formula for repentance requires that we confess. Our first confession is to the Lord in prayer. When our mistakes are not grievous ones, and if they are personal, that may be all that is required by way of confession.

If our transgression includes tampering with the procreative capacities of another of either gender, then there is a necessary confession beyond prayer. From His priesthood the Lord has designated the bishop to be the common judge. If your transgression is serious, and your conscience will tell you whether it is or not, seek out the bishop.

The bishop represents the Lord in extending forgiveness for the Church. At times he must administer bitter medicine. Alma told Corianton, "Now, repentance could not come unto men except there were a punishment."[9] I would not want to live in a world where there was no repentance, and if punishment is a condition of that, I will willingly accept that. (92–02, p. 115)

Serious mistakes need to be confessed. Sometimes a member of the Church will go for years carrying some burden of guilt and pain. If you want to get rid of that, you doctor it up the way you would physical pain. You go to the one that can help heal it. If you have been carrying some heavy burden of transgression and want to get rid of it, go confess it. The forgiveness comes, and the bright morning of forgiveness, like the brightness of the morning sun, will shine in your life. You will go forward happily with the joy of knowing that you can be clean and, in due course, return to the presence of our Heavenly Father. (08–08)

Get transgressions settled in the right way. I have mentioned the corrosive guilt of unsettled transgression. Be wise enough to learn not to talk about your problems with the wrong people. Unfortunately, many young people who have made mistakes, particularly if these are in the category of moral transgression, end up telling a roommate about it. If there is something weighing heavily on your mind, talk it over first with the Lord in prayer, and then with your parents. Learn what a bishop is for, and confide in him when faced with such problems. If you have been immorally involved you should *get it settled*—get that page torn out of your life so that you can go on. (66–05, p. 248)

Impenitence is widespread. There is much evil in the world today, and modern means of communication have allowed it to spread faster and further than ever before: it gets to more people. There is impenitence of all kinds in the world. We must look at ourselves. The Lord has set rules and standards and will hold us accountable unless we seek forgiveness. If we truly repent and ask for forgiveness, we will receive it. We all need to get our lives in order. I don't know of anyone who does not. (68–04, p. 78)

Repentance cannot come except there be a punishment. Alma bluntly told his wayward son that "repentance could not come unto men except there were a punishment."[10]

The punishment may, for the most part, consist of the torment we inflict upon ourselves. It may be the loss of privilege or progress. (Forgiveness will come eventually to all repentant souls who have not committed the unpardonable sin.[11] Forgiveness does not, however, necessarily assure exaltation, as is the case with [King] David.[12]) We are punished *by* our sins, if not *for* them. (95–12, p. 19)

We are punished as much by our sins as for them. Ultimately we are punished quite as much by our sins as we are for them. (73–05, p. 167)

In paying our debts to the Lord we can participate in an atonement. The Lord provides ways to pay our debts to Him. In one sense we ourselves may participate in an atonement. When we are willing to restore to others that which we have not taken, or heal wounds that we did not inflict, or pay a debt that we did not incur, we are emulating His part in the Atonement. (95–12, p. 20)

We must settle our account with the Lord. All mankind can be protected by the law of justice, and at once each of us individually may be extended the redeeming and healing blessing of mercy.

A knowledge of what I am talking about is of a very practical value. It is very useful and very helpful personally; it opens the way for each of us to keep his spiritual accounts paid up.

You, perhaps, are among those troubled people. When you come face to face with yourself in those moments of quiet contemplation—that many of us try to avoid—are there some unsettled things that bother you?

President of the New England Mission in his office in Cambridge, Massachusetts

Do you have something on your conscience? Are you still, to one degree or another, guilty of anything small or large?

We often try to solve guilt problems by telling one another that they don't matter. But somehow, deep inside, we don't believe one another. Nor do we believe ourselves if we say it. We know better. They do matter!

Our transgressions are all added to our account, and one day if it is not properly settled, each of us, like Belshazzar of Babylon, will be weighed in the balance and found wanting.

There is a Redeemer, a Mediator, who stands both willing and able to appease the demands of justice and extend mercy to those who are penitent, for "he offereth himself a sacrifice for sin, to answer the ends of the law, unto all those who have a broken heart and a contrite spirit; and unto none else can the ends of the law be answered."[13] (77–06, p. 56)

Often the most difficult part of repentance is to forgive yourself. That great morning of forgiveness may not come at once. Do not give up if at first you fail. Often the most difficult part of repentance is to forgive yourself. Discouragement is part of that test. Do not give up. (95–12, p. 20)

It is not wise to speak of past mistakes. There is an inflexible rule in the Church that leaders who receive confessions from members must keep those matters confidential. That rule is very well kept in the Church.

Sometimes, however, members themselves are not wise in the ways they talk about the mistakes in their past.

One might, for instance, refer to the years when he did not keep the Word of Wisdom. It is not a good thing for reactivated members to talk about their past problems.

Young people, particularly, take license from such things. An immature mind might reason that if the speaker could transgress, return to activity, and perhaps hold a high position, why should they not enjoy the same thing.

[We] counsel members to let the dead past bury its dead. A

member should come back into activity without being continually reminded of his or her past mistakes. (81–03)

True repentance means don't look back! Sometimes, even after confession and penalties, the most difficult part of repentance is to forgive oneself. President Joseph Fielding Smith told of a woman who had repented of immoral conduct and was struggling to find her way. She asked him what she should do now. In turn, he asked her to read to him from the Old Testament the account of Sodom and Gomorrah, of Lot, and of Lot's wife, who was turned to a pillar of salt.[14] Then he asked her what lesson those verses held for her.

She answered, "The Lord will destroy those who are wicked."

"Not so," President Smith told this repentant woman. "The lesson for *you* is '*Don't look back!*'" (92–02, p. 116)

CHURCH DISCIPLINE

Some transgressions require church discipline. There are some transgressions which require a discipline which will bring about the relief that comes with the morning of forgiveness. If your mistakes have been grievous ones, go to your bishop. . . . [B]ishops can guide you through the steps required to obtain forgiveness insofar as the Church is concerned. Each one of us must work out individually forgiveness from the Lord. (95–12, p. 19)

What should we confess? What should we confess? There are some things that require that we confess to our bishop. Most things we do not have to and should not confess. We should not bother the bishop with little things that do not matter, but if the transgressions are serious, then we confess them to the bishop. (00–07)

Often bishops will "remember [the sins] no more." Local leaders such as bishops are called upon to handle many serious problems. Someone will come in for an interview, perhaps for a mission, and will not be worthy. Whether he or she is a youth or a mature person, ugly transgressions may be involved. Yet it is not too uncommon an experience that, if he repents, on meeting him in other circumstances later the bishop won't remember the reason for that earlier meeting. Thus the divine generosity is given in some measure even to the Lord's earthly servants, and they "remember [the sins] no more." (68–04, p. 76)

Leaders should know the principles as well as procedures. It is our responsibility to discipline members when there has been a very serious transgression. The *organization* and the *procedures* for holding such a council are explained in detail in the Church handbook of instructions.

Unless a leader knows the *principles* that apply in such cases, however, he might hold a Church disciplinary council in technical compliance with the handbook, even follow proper procedures, and yet injure rather than heal the wayward member.

If a leader does not know the *principles*—by principles I mean the principles of the gospel, the doctrines, what's in the revelations—if he does not know what the revelations say about justice or mercy, or what they reveal on reproof or forgiveness, how can he make inspired decisions in those difficult cases that require his judgment? (84–03, pp. 64–65)

Discipline is a demonstration of love. We understand why some feel we reject them. That is not true. We *do not* reject you, only immoral behavior. We *cannot* reject you, for you are the sons and daughters of God. We *will not* reject you, because we love you.[15]

You may even feel that we do not love you. That also is not true. Parents know, and one day you will know, that there are times when parents and we who lead the Church must extend *tough* love when failing to teach and to warn and to discipline is to destroy.

We did not make the rules; they were revealed as commandments. We do not cause nor can we prevent the consequences if you disobey the moral laws.[16] In spite of criticism or opposition, we must teach and we must warn. (00–06, p. 74)

Spiritual discipline will help redeem souls. More lost sheep will respond quicker to high standards than they will to low ones. There is therapeutic value in spiritual discipline.

Discipline is a form of love, an expression of it. It is necessary and powerful in people's lives.

When a toddler is playing near the road, we steer carefully around him. Few will stop and see him to safety or, if necessary, discipline him. That is, unless it is our own child or grandchild. If we love them enough we will do it. To withhold discipline when it would contribute to spiritual growth is an evidence of lack of love and concern.

Spiritual discipline framed in love and confirmed with testimony will help redeem souls. (69–03, p. 19)

The love of Christ does not presuppose approval of all conduct. Some members wonder why their priesthood leaders will not accept them just as they are and simply comfort them in what they call pure Christian love.

Pure Christian love, the love of Christ, does not presuppose approval of all conduct. Surely the ordinary experiences of parenthood teach that one can be consumed with love for another and yet be unable to approve unworthy conduct.

We cannot, as a church, approve unworthy conduct or accept into full fellowship individuals who live or who teach standards that are grossly in violation of that which the Lord requires of Latter-day Saints.

If we, out of sympathy, should approve unworthy conduct, it might give present comfort to someone but would not ultimately contribute to that person's happiness.[17] (95–12, p. 20)

One ultimately excommunicates himself. I recall a conversation with President Henry D. Moyle. We were driving back from Arizona and were talking about a man who destroyed the faith of young people from the vantage point of a teaching position. Someone asked President Moyle why this man was still a member of the Church when he did things like that. "He is not a member of the Church," President Moyle answered firmly. Another replied that he had not heard of his excommunication. "He has excommunicated himself," President Moyle responded. "He has cut himself off from the Spirit of God. Whether or not we get around to holding a [disciplinary council] doesn't matter that much; he has cut himself off from the Spirit of the Lord." (81–07, pp. 109–10)

FORGIVENESS

We must be ever forgiving. To get the relief, the forgiveness, we want, we had better be ever forgiving. (00–07)

Forgiveness is powerful spiritual medicine. Forgiveness is powerful spiritual medicine. To extend forgiveness, that soothing balm, to those who have offended you is to heal. And, more difficult yet, when the need is there, forgive yourself! . . .

Purge and cleanse and soothe your soul and your heart and your mind and that of others.

A cloud will then be lifted, a beam cast from your eye. There will come that peace which surpasseth understanding. (87–07, p. 18)

Can I ever be forgiven? Letters come from those who have made tragic mistakes. They ask, "Can I *ever* be forgiven?"

The answer is *yes!*

The gospel teaches us that relief from torment and guilt can be earned through repentance. Save for those few who defect to perdition after having known a fulness, there is no habit, no addiction, no rebellion, no transgression, no offense exempted from the promise of complete forgiveness. (95–12, p. 19)

The Atonement makes complete forgiveness possible. I repeat, save for the exception of the very few who defect to perdition, there is no habit, no addiction, no rebellion, no transgression, no apostasy, no crime exempted from the promise of complete forgiveness. That is the promise of the Atonement of Christ.

How all can be repaired, we do not know. It may not all be

accomplished in this life. We know from visions and visitations that the servants of the Lord continue the work of redemption beyond the veil.[18]

This knowledge should be as comforting to the innocent as it is to the guilty. I am thinking of parents who suffer unbearably for the mistakes of their wayward children and are losing hope. (95–12, p. 20)

All transgressions against the moral law can be forgiven. I know of no sin connected with transgression of the moral law which cannot be forgiven, assuming, of course, full and complete repentance. I do not exempt abortion.

The formula is stated in forty words: "Behold, he who has repented of his sins, the same is forgiven, and I, the Lord, remember them no more. By this ye may know if a man repenteth of his sins—behold, he will confess them and forsake them."[19] I know of no more beautiful words in all of revelation than these. "The same is forgiven, and I, the Lord, remember them no more." (92–02, p. 115)

Moral transgressions can be forgiven. Now, what of you who have already made mistakes or have lost yourselves to an immoral lifestyle? What hope do you have? Are you cast off and lost forever?

These are not unforgivable sins. However unworthy or unnatural or immoral these transgressions may be, they are not unforgivable.[20] When completely forsaken and fully repented of, there can open the purifying gift of forgiveness, and the burden of guilt will be erased. There is a way back—long, perhaps; hard, certainly; possible, of course![21]

You need not, you cannot find your way alone. You have a Redeemer. The Lord will lift your burden if you choose to repent and turn from your sins and do them no more. That is what the Atonement of Christ was for.[22] (00–06, p. 74)

Our Father in Heaven will remember our sins no more. Each of us has a loving Father in Heaven. Through the Father's redeeming plan, those who may stumble and fall "are not cast off forever."[23] "And how great is his joy in the soul that repenteth!"[24] "The Lord cannot look upon sin with the least degree of allowance; nevertheless,"[25] the Lord said, "he who has repented of his sins, the same is forgiven, and I, the Lord, remember them no more."[26] Could there be any sweeter or more consoling words, more filled with hope, than those words from the scriptures? "I, the Lord, remember [their sins] no more."[27] (06–02, p. 28)

Forgiveness is earned through great personal effort. Forgiveness from the Lord is earned through great personal effort. It takes courage to face the reality of your transgression, accept whatever penalty is required, and allow sufficient time for the process to work. When that is done, you will be *innocent* again. The Lord said: "I, even I, am he that blotteth out thy transgressions for mine own sake, and will not remember thy sins."[28] (92–02, p. 116)

There is the idea abroad that one can send a postcard of prayer and receive in return full forgiveness and be ready at once for a mission or for marriage in the temple. Not so; there are payments to be made. If a bishop offers comfort only and, in misguided kindness, seeks to relieve you of the painful but healing process in connection with repentance, he will not serve you well. (92–02, pp. 115–16)

John, leave it alone. There are spiritual disorders and spiritual diseases that can cause intense suffering.

If you suffer from worry, from grief or shame or jealousy or disappointment or envy, from self-recrimination or self-justification, consider this lesson taught to me many years ago by a patriarch. He was as saintly a man as I have ever known. He was steady and serene, with a deep spiritual strength that many drew upon.

He knew just how to minister to others who were suffering. On a number of occasions I was present when he gave blessings to those who were sick or who were otherwise afflicted. His was a life of service, both to the Church and to his community.

He had presided over one of the missions of the Church and always looked forward to the missionary reunions. When he was older, he was not able to drive at night, and I offered to take him to the reunions. That modest gesture was repaid a thousandfold.

On one occasion, when the Spirit was right, he gave me a lesson for my life from an experience in his own. Although I thought I had known him, he told me things about his life I would not have supposed.

He grew up in a little community with a desire to make something of himself. He struggled to get an education.

He married his sweetheart, and presently everything was just right. He was well employed, with a bright future. They were deeply in love, and she was expecting their first child.

The night the baby was to be born, there were complications. The only doctor was somewhere in the countryside tending to the sick.

After many hours of labor, the condition of the mother-to-be became desperate.

Finally the doctor was located. In the emergency, he acted quickly and soon had things in order. The baby was born and the crisis, it appeared, was over.

Some days later, the young mother died from the very infection that the doctor had been treating at another home that night.

John's world was shattered. Everything was not right now; everything was all wrong. He had lost his wife. He had no way to tend both the baby and his work.

As the weeks wore on, his grief festered. "That doctor should not be allowed to practice," he would say. "He brought that infection to my wife. If he had been careful, she would be alive today."

He thought of little else, and in his bitterness, he became threatening. Today, no doubt, he would have been pressed by many others to file a malpractice suit. And there are lawyers who would see in his pitiable condition only one ingredient—money!

But that was another day, and one night a knock came at his door. A little girl said simply, "Daddy wants you to come over. He wants to talk to you."

"Daddy" was the stake president. A grieving, heartbroken young man went to see his spiritual leader.

This spiritual shepherd had been watching his flock and had something to say to him.

The counsel from that wise servant was simply, "John, leave it alone. Nothing you do about it will bring her back. Anything you do will make it worse. John, leave it alone."

My friend told me then that this had been his trial—his Gethsemane. How could he leave it alone? Right was right! A terrible wrong had been committed and somebody must pay for it. It was a clear case.

But he struggled in agony to get hold of himself. And finally, he determined that whatever else the issues were, he should be obedient.

Obedience is powerful spiritual medicine. It comes close to being a cure-all.

He determined to follow the counsel of that wise spiritual leader. He would leave it alone.

Then he told me, "I was an old man before I understood! It was not until I was an old man that I could finally see a poor country doctor—overworked, underpaid, run ragged from patient to patient, with little medicine, no hospital, few instruments, struggling to save lives, and succeeding for the most part.

"He had come in a moment of crisis, when two lives hung in the balance, and had acted without delay.

"I was an old man," he repeated, "before I finally understood! I would have ruined my life," he said, "and the lives of others."

Many times he had thanked the Lord on his knees for a wise spiritual leader who counseled simply, "John, leave it alone."

And that is the counsel I bring again to you. If you have a festering grudge, if you are involved in an acrimonious dispute, "Behold what the scripture says [and it says it fifty times and more]—man shall not smite, neither shall he judge; for judgment is mine, saith the Lord, and vengeance is mine also, and I will repay."[29]

I say therefore, "John, leave it alone. Mary, leave it alone." (87–07, pp. 17–18)

CHAPTER 4

Covenants, Baptism, and the Gift of the Holy Ghost

*"Keep your covenants and you will be safe.
Break them and you will not." (90–09, p. 84)*

COVENANTS AND ORDINANCES

Covenants and ordinances are essential. Good conduct without the ordinances of the gospel will neither redeem nor exalt mankind; covenants and the ordinances are essential. We are required to teach the doctrines, even the unpopular ones. (85–13, p. 82)

Nothing transcends in importance the covenants and ordinances. Nothing in the Church transcends in importance the covenants and ordinances. No calling or assignment, no program or procedure, no interest or activity is an end in itself. All are to prepare us and inspire us to enter into and to keep our covenants. Holding meetings, building chapels, changing boundaries, organizing wards and stakes and missions are means to this end. (87–02)

The covenants and ordinances help us set a true course in life.
The mariner gets his bearing from light coming from celestial bodies—
the sun by day, the stars by night. . . .

The spiritual sextant, which each of us has, also functions on the
principle of light from celestial sources. Set that sextant in your mind
to the word *covenant* or the word *ordinance*. The light will come
through. Then you can fix your position and set a true course in life.
(87–03, p. 24)

One should not take ordinances and covenants lightly. When
you receive an ordinance, whether it be baptism, the sacrament, an ordination or setting apart, an endowment, or a sealing, you receive an obligation. Thereafter, you are under covenant not to steal, nor to lie, nor to
profane, nor to take the name of the Lord in vain. You are obligated to
maintain the moral standard. This standard—by commandment of the
Lord—requires that the only authorized use of the sacred power of procreation is with one to whom one is legally and lawfully wed. You have
responsibility to support every principle of the gospel and the servants
the Lord has ordained to administer them.

President Joseph Fielding Smith said this: "Each ordinance and
requirement given to a man for the purpose of bringing to pass his salvation and exaltation is a covenant."[1]

Be careful not to take the ordinances and covenants of the gospel
lightly, nor to maintain them carelessly. It will take increased courage
to keep your covenants. The world has moved away from those high
standards. (80–03, pp. 192–93)

*Ordinances and covenants become our credentials for admis-
sion.* No matter what citizenship or race, whether male or female, no
matter what occupation, no matter your education, regardless of the
generation in which one lives, life is a homeward journey for all of us,
back to the presence of God in His celestial kingdom.

Ordinances and covenants become our credentials for admission
into His presence. To worthily receive them is the quest of a lifetime;
to keep them thereafter is the challenge of mortality.

Once we have received them for ourselves and for our families, we are obligated to provide these ordinances vicariously for our kindred dead, indeed for the whole human family. (87–03, p. 24)

A covenant is a sacred promise. A covenant is a sacred promise, as used in the scriptures, a solemn, enduring promise between God and man. The fulness of the gospel itself is defined as the new and everlasting covenant.[2] (87–03, p. 23)

Covenants are powerful and motivating. The First Presidency frequently report to the Quorum of the Twelve that when they have called a man and his wife in to counsel with them over whether or not they will accept a mission call the immediate answer is, "We've been to the temple!" Meaning: We are under covenant. That word *covenant* is a powerful, motivating word. It makes men and women and children rise above themselves, reach beyond themselves and come within grasp of celestial exaltation. (*THT,* p. 166)

It is important to keep your covenants. It is for each of us to be loyal and true, to keep our covenants. Keep your spiritual premiums paid up. Do not let your spiritual policy lapse. Do not cause it to be cancelled in some moment of rebellion. Extend your policy by adding endorsements as you qualify for the higher ordinances of the gospel. Make a list of them; keep them in mind; work to qualify for each of them. And pray earnestly for help to do so. (*THT,* p. 168)

Be a keeper of the covenants. Be faithful to the covenants and ordinances of the gospel. Qualify for those sacred ordinances step by step as you move through life. Honor the covenants connected with them. Do this and you will be happy.

Your lives will then be in order—all things lined up in proper sequence, in proper ranks, in proper rows. Your family will be linked in an order that can never be broken.

In the covenants and ordinances center the blessings that you may claim in the holy temple. Surely the Lord is pleased when we are worthy of the title: A keeper of the covenants. (*THT,* pp. 170–71)

Keeping one's covenants does not require a call. Several years ago I installed a stake president in England. In another calling, he is here in the audience today. He had an unusual sense of direction. He was like a mariner with a sextant who took his bearings from the stars. I met with him each time he came to conference and was impressed that he kept himself and his stake on course.

Fortunately for me, when it was time for his release, I was assigned to reorganize the stake. It was then that I discovered what that sextant was and how he adjusted it to check his position and get a bearing for himself and for his members.

He accepted his release, and said, "I was happy to accept the call to serve as stake president, and I am equally happy to accept my release. I did not serve just because I was under *call.* I served because I am under *covenant.* And I can keep my covenants quite as well as a home teacher as I can serving as stake president."

This president understood the word *covenant.*

While he was neither a scriptorian nor a gospel scholar, he somehow had learned that exaltation is achieved by keeping covenants, not by holding high position. (87–03, pp. 23–24)

Beware of covenant-breakers. Beware of covenant-breakers inside the Church and out. Beware of those who mock the prophets. When you have been to the temple you are under covenant to support the leaders of the Church, your local officers and the General Authorities. Keep your covenants. Keep your faith. Be loyal. (*THT,* pp. 167–68)

Qualify for each ordinance in proper sequence. It is important to fix in our mind so serious an interest in the ordinances of the gospel that we will seek to qualify for each ordinance in proper sequence, to make and keep the covenants that are connected with them, and to make sure that everything in this regard, for us, is in proper order. (80–03, p. 187)

The ordinances are designed to help us put things in order. The word *ordinance* means, "A religious or ceremonial observance," "an established rite."

The Oxford Dictionary gives as the first definition of the word ordinance, "Arrangement in ranks or rows," and as the second definition, "Arrangement in sequence or proper relative positions."

That may not strike you, at the moment, as having much religious significance, but indeed it has.

Among the ordinances we perform in the Church are these:

Baptism

Sacrament

Naming and blessing of infants

Administering to the sick

Setting apart to callings in the Church

Ordaining to offices

And there are higher ordinances, performed in the temples. These include the endowment and the sealing ordinance spoken of generally as temple marriage.

The word ordinance comes from the word *order,* which means "a rank, a row, a series."

The word *ordain,* a close relative to the other two words, has, as its first definition, "To put in order, arrange, make ready, prepare."

And also, "To appoint or admit to the ministry of the Christian church . . . by the laying on of hands or other symbolic action."

From all of this dictionary work there comes the impression that an ordinance, to be valid, must be done in proper order.

Order,

Ordain,

Ordinance!

Order—To put in ranks or rows, in proper sequence or relationship.

Ordain—The process of putting things in rows or proper relationship.

Ordinance—The ceremony by which things are put in proper order. (80–01)

Ordinances must be performed by one who is authorized. In the matter of the ordinances of the gospel, there are no discounts. There is no credit buying. Nothing is ever put on sale at special, reduced prices. There is never something for nothing. There is no such thing as a "bargain." You pay full value. Requirements and covenants are involved. And you will get, in due time, full value. But you must, positively must, deal with an authorized agent or your claims will not be honored [cites D&C 132:7–14]. (80–03, p. 188)

One cannot be happy or exalted without the ordinances. Now, what about the ordinances of the gospel? How important are they to us as members of the Church?

Can you be happy, can you be redeemed, can you be exalted without them? Answer: They are more than advisable or desirable, or even than necessary. More even than essential or vital. They are *crucial* to each of us. (*THT,* pp. 145–46)

BAPTISM

There is significant symbolism in baptism. Baptism must be by immersion, for it is symbolic of both the coming forth from temporal death, from the grave, and of the cleansing required for redemption from spiritual death.

To complete the remission of sins, baptism is followed by the laying on of hands for the gift of the Holy Ghost.[3]

Under the plan, baptism is not just for entrance into the Church of Jesus Christ. It begins a spiritual rebirth that may eventually lead back into the presence of God.

If we really understood what baptism signifies we could never consider it trivial, nor alter the form of this sacred ordinance. (84–05)

Baptism is essential to obtain eternal life. There is an essential ordinance—baptism—standing as a gate through which every soul must pass if he would obtain eternal life. . . . Since baptism is essential, there must be an urgent concern to carry the message of the gospel of Jesus Christ to every nation, kindred, tongue, and people. That came as a commandment from Him. (75–06, p. 97)

Only when children reach accountability is baptism essential. In the days of the prophet Mormon, some who did not understand that little children are "blameless before God"[4] and are "alive in Christ"[5] wanted to baptize little children. Mormon said they "[denied] the mercies of Christ, and [set] at naught the atonement of him and the power of his redemption."[6]

Mormon sternly rebuked them, saying: "He that supposeth that little children need baptism is in the gall of bitterness and in the bonds of iniquity; for he hath neither faith, hope, nor charity; wherefore, should he be cut off while in the thought, he must go down to hell. . . .

"Behold, I speak with boldness, having authority from God."[7]

Only when a child reaches that age of accountability, set by the Lord at eight years of age,[8] is their baptism essential. Before that age, they are innocent. (02–03, p. 8)

Keeping our baptismal covenants is essential. Generally we understand that, conditioned upon repentance, the ordinance of baptism washes our sins away. Some wonder if they were baptized too soon. If only they could be baptized now and have a clean start. But that is not necessary! Through the ordinance of the sacrament, you renew the covenants made at baptism. When you meet all of the conditions of repentance, however difficult, you may be forgiven and your transgressions will trouble your mind no more. (97–02, p. 10)

Baptism is a call to lifelong service to Christ. Our baptism is a call to lifelong service to Christ. Like those at the waters of Mormon, we are "baptized in the name of the Lord, as a witness before him that [we] have entered into a covenant with him, that [we] will serve him and keep his commandments, that he may pour out his Spirit more abundantly upon [us]."[9] (97–04, p. 6)

Baptism and confirmation must be tightly fixed together. Missionaries sometimes think they are only to do half the work; they are to teach and then baptize by water, and that concludes their work. In many cases the other half, the teaching about the baptism of fire, never really gets done. Put the two together so that you almost forbid yourself to say "baptism" without saying "confirmation"—that is baptism of the water and confirmation and the conferring of the gift of the Holy Ghost. Get that idea in your mind with those two fixed together so tightly that, as one, it becomes part of you. Then we will not have the first half done, as is often the case at present, and the other half left undone. . . .

Missionaries—and parents as well—are to teach both halves: "Baptism by immersion for the remission of sins [and the] laying on of hands for the gift of the Holy Ghost."[10] Make it one sentence. Fix it in the front of your minds so that when you say one, you say the other, and when you think one, you think the other. Then you will begin to *feel* and understand, and the promptings will come. (03–08, p. 50)

GIFT OF THE HOLY GHOST

The Holy Ghost is the spirit of revelation. After baptism the ordinance of confirmation confers upon us the gift of the Holy Ghost. It is the supernal gift. The Holy Ghost is the spirit of revelation.[11] (93–07, p. 55)

The supernal, consummate spiritual gift. [The Holy Ghost is] the supernal, consummate, spiritual gift! It is so simple and so present that we often ignore it. It is almost overwhelming when you come to understand that the Holy Ghost, when it is conferred, is a gift! Now, those outside of the Church can be influenced by the Holy Ghost, can be inspired by it. That must be true or else how could they receive the inspiration to convert. But after baptism, we have conferred upon us the gift of the Holy Ghost as a presence. . . . This is the supernal gift—the one that each one of us has access to, if we will. (87–01, pp. 108–9)

The gift of the Holy Ghost is to be a shield, comfort, protection, and guide. When you were baptized, in a separate ordinance, you were confirmed a member of The Church of Jesus Christ of Latter-day Saints and were told in that ordinance, "Receive the Holy Ghost," to be a shield and a comfort to you, to be a warning agent to you, to be a protection and a guide to you. Every member of the Church has that, even the eight-year-olds. Before that time they are innocent. That is a power that you can call on. (07–06)

There is a pattern for receiving the gift of the Holy Ghost. On the day of Pentecost, the Twelve were assembled in a house:

"Suddenly there came a sound . . . of a rushing mighty wind. . . .

"And there appeared unto them cloven tongues like as of fire, and it sat upon each of them.

"And they were all filled with the Holy Ghost."[12]

With that the Twelve were fully empowered.

When they spoke that day, the people marveled, for each heard it in their own language—eighteen different languages.[13]

The Apostles set out to baptize all who would believe on their words. But baptism unto repentance was not enough.[14]

Paul found twelve men who had already been baptized by John the Baptist and asked, "Have ye received the Holy Ghost . . . ? [They replied], We have not so much as heard whether there be any Holy Ghost."[15]

"They were [then] baptized in the name of the Lord Jesus,"[16] and "Paul . . . laid his hands upon them, [and] the Holy Ghost came on them."[17]

The pattern was set, as it had been from the beginning.[18] Entrance into the Church of Jesus Christ is through "baptism by immersion for the remission of sins."[19] Then, in a separate ordinance, the priceless gift of the Holy Ghost is conferred "by the laying on of hands by those who are in authority, to preach the Gospel and administer in the ordinances." (00–02, pp. 7–8)

We can learn to follow the promptings of the Holy Ghost. [The Holy Ghost] is awakened with prayer and cultivated "by obedience to the laws and ordinances of the Gospel."[20] It can be smothered through transgression and neglect. And soon we learn that the tempter—the adversary—uses those same channels of the mind and heart to inspire us to evil, to laziness, to contention, even to acts of darkness. He can take over our thoughts and lead us to mischief. But each of us has agency; ever and always light presides over darkness. (00–02, p. 9)

Learn to call upon and live by the Holy Ghost. Go forward without fear. Do not fear the future. Do not fear whatever is ahead of you. Take hold of that supernal gift of the Holy Ghost. Learn to be taught by it. Learn to call upon it. Learn to live by it. And the Spirit of the Lord will attend you, and you will be blessed as it was intended that we should all be blessed by this supernal gift of the Holy Ghost. It can be conferred only by the laying on of hands by one who has authority, and there is no other church on the face of the earth that has the authority to confer this supernal gift. (00–01)

We must learn to trust the voice of the Spirit. We can learn in our early youth to follow the Spirit. Then the Lord can use us to answer prayers. The Lord can use us to do His work. Many of you, perhaps most of you, could bear testimony that you have been prompted by the Spirit. These are sacred experiences to us. We don't talk much about them, but they are an important part of our lives, for we are Latter-day Saints. If we live as Saints should live, His Spirit can guide us.

Members of the Church, especially our young members, must learn to trust in that Spirit. It will never prompt you to do wrong. In order to have it, we must live for it. That voice of inspiration is a still and a quiet voice. We do not hear the words so much as we feel the words. That feeling could be explained away by those who doubt, but it is a clear signal to Latter-day Saints. (78–10)

Learn as children to be obedient to the Spirit. We need to learn when we are children to be obedient to the Spirit. . . . I have found over the years, as we have raised our family, that if we have a sensitivity to the Spirit that the Holy Ghost will watch over us. The Lord has said that it will be a shield and a protection. It will be a teacher to us. And it will bring to our remembrance things that we need to know. (07–02)

We must open our lives to the Holy Ghost. The Lord said, "Behold, I stand at the door, and knock: [he that heareth] my voice, and open the door, I will come in . . . , and will sup with him."[21]

You know there is that famous painting of Christ at the door holding a lantern. One little boy said, "There is no latch on the door." And the painter said, "The painting is accurate. That is the heart's door. It opens only from within."

You will not be forced! Change your lives and admit the inspiration of the Holy Ghost. Begin to get your feelings sensitive enough so that you can be guided. You will not be denied! (00–01)

To enjoy the guidance of the Spirit one must live worthily. Through the Holy Ghost we will always have a very clear signal to follow. If we are living worthily that signal will be a constant guide to us.

It is a quiet gift. It is unknown in the world. To Latter-day Saints it is a great blessing. It can guide us in all we do in life. All of us, particularly our young people, must learn to trust in that Spirit. We must learn to be spiritually minded.

The prophet said, "To be carnally-minded is death, and to be spiritually-minded is life eternal."[22] (78–08)

The Spirit won't rescue us unless we do our part. I have learned that the Spirit will not teach you something that you should have learned by yourself. . . . But I know that you will not be left comfortless in your life and that there will be "wisdom and great treasures of knowledge, even hidden treasures."[23] (01–01)

If we are not careful we will drive the Spirit away. If we begin to do things that kill the Spirit, if we break the Word of Wisdom and do other things that are improper, then the Spirit will back off. It will leave us alone to find our way. That is a very dangerous place to be in. (07–02)

Describing the promptings of the Holy Ghost is difficult. To one who thought that revelation would flow without effort, the Lord said:

You have not understood; you have supposed that I would give it unto you, when you took no thought save it was to ask me.

But, behold, I say unto you, that you must study it out in your *mind;* then you must ask me if it be right, and if it is right I will cause that your bosom shall burn within you; therefore, you shall *feel* that it is right.[24]

This burning in the bosom is not purely a physical sensation. It is more like a warm light shining within your being. Describing the promptings from the Holy Ghost to one who has not had them is very difficult. Such promptings are personal and strictly private![25] (94–05, pp. 59–60)

The Holy Ghost speaks with a voice that you feel more than you hear. The Holy Ghost speaks with a voice that you *feel* more than you *hear.* It is described as a "still small voice."[26] And while we speak of "listening" to the whisperings of the Spirit, most often one describes a spiritual prompting by saying, "I had a *feeling . . .". . .* Revelation comes as words we *feel* more than *hear.* Nephi told his wayward brothers, who were visited by an angel, "Ye were past *feeling,* that ye could not *feel* his words."[27]

The scriptures are full of such expressions as "The veil was taken from our minds, and the eyes of our understanding were opened"[28] or "I will tell you in your mind and in your heart"[29] or "I did enlighten thy mind"[30] or "Speak the thoughts that I shall put into your hearts."[31] There are hundreds of verses which teach of revelation. (94–05, p. 60)

The Holy Ghost can help keep us off forbidden paths. The Holy Ghost was conferred upon you following baptism. The Holy Ghost becomes your Teacher and your Comforter. Through the Holy Ghost, you receive inspired direction in your personal life, in your family, in your occupation, and in your callings in the Church. . . .

The Holy Ghost is like a sextant. For centuries sailors have found their way across the trackless oceans by looking to the heavens with a sextant. They set a small mirror to catch the light of the stars by night or the sun by day. From that light they got their bearings and set their course.

A small sextant was used by a fisherman who rowed his boat out into the Atlantic Ocean off the coast of France to fish. If he drifted beyond the horizon or was blown off course by a storm, he could look to the heavens and get his bearings and find his way home.

Light from heaven can keep the fisherman from drifting off course. The Spirit of the Holy Ghost will keep you from wandering into forbidden paths. (03–01)

The Spirit can warn you of dangers. Part of the responsibility of the Spirit is to warn you of dangers. If you ever have a feeling that you should not go somewhere, then even though you may be coaxed by others, you say, "No, I am not free to go that way. I feel like I shouldn't go." They may tease you or even mock you, but as soon as you learn to follow that Spirit, then your way through life will be easier. You will eventually know how to conduct your life. . . . In due time, you will be guided as to what you should do about a marriage partner, which young man or young woman should be a part of your life. That is the thing in The Church of Jesus Christ of Latter-day Saints that is unique, and it rests upon every member, and it is in every country. . . . They have learned about this gift of the Holy Ghost. It is a powerful and a precious thing. (07–02)

There will be whisperings of approval or warning when you have decisions to make. You had conferred upon you the gift of the Holy Ghost. There will be whisperings of approval or warning when you have decisions to make.[32] The Holy Ghost can guide you away from evil and bring you back if you have wandered and lost your path. Never forget that you are sons and daughters of God. Satan cannot forever imprison you. You always hold the key of repentance to unlock the prison door. (03–09, p. 26)

The Gift of the Holy Ghost carries certain rights. While the Holy Ghost may inspire all mankind, the gift carries the right to have it as a "constant companion."[33] It is "by the power of the Holy Ghost [that you] may know the truth of all things."[34]

We are told that "angels speak by the power of the Holy Ghost."[35] We are even told that when we speak by the power of the Holy Ghost, we "speak with the tongue [or in the same language] of angels."[36] (94–05, p. 59)

One can speak with the tongue of angels. Nephi explained that angels speak by the power of the Holy Ghost, and you can speak with the tongue of angels, which simply means that you can speak with the power of the Holy Ghost. It will be quiet. It will be invisible. There will not be a dove. There will not be cloven tongues of fire. But the power will be there. (03–08, pp. 49–50)

"And they knew it not." We have had the Holy Ghost conferred upon us. I quote now this sentence: "And they knew it not."

The Lord said to the Nephites, "Whoso[ever] cometh unto me with a broken heart and a contrite spirit [shall receive baptism] with fire and with the Holy Ghost, even as the Lamanites [had been] baptized with fire and with the Holy Ghost, and they knew it not."[37]

Can you imagine that? I think every one of us at times, and many of us all the time, have no appreciation or understanding of the gift. We have the power and authority that comes with that gift. As you read the revelations, you will find the Holy Ghost referred to as a comforter (think of that—a comforter) and as a teacher, and we are told that it will abide with us and be in us. . . .

We live in a day when the moral and spiritual values of the world are low. We can look forward with great yearning, and hope things get better. Well, they are not going to get better! The trend that is happening all around us—in society and government and education and all else—is a continuous trend.

And yet with all of that, I stand with great hope and great optimism. I have no fear. Fear is the antithesis of faith. With all that is happening and with all the impossible challenges that we face, we have that supernal gift of the Holy Ghost conferred upon us. And yet, for the most part, we know it not. It's interesting how in our lives we are operating, to an extent, as though we had not received it. . . .

It is for everyone who will. Whosoever will come with a contrite spirit and a broken heart will receive the baptism of fire and the Holy Ghost.[38] It is conferred equally on men and women. (00–01)

Many benefit unknowingly from the Holy Ghost. Too many of us are like those whom the Lord said came "with a broken heart and a contrite spirit . . . [and] at the time of their conversion, were baptized with fire and with the Holy Ghost, *and they knew it not.*"[39] Imagine that: "And they knew it not." It is not unusual for one to have received the gift and not really know it. I fear this supernal gift is being obscured by programs and activities and schedules and so many meetings. There are so many places to go, so many things to do in this noisy world. We can be too busy to pay attention to the promptings of the Spirit. The voice of the Spirit is a still, small voice—a voice that is *felt* rather than heard. It is a spiritual voice that comes into the mind as a thought put into your heart. All over the world ordinary men, women, and children, not completely aware that they have the gift, bless their families, teach, preach, and minister by the Spirit within them. In every language, the Spirit of God—the Holy Ghost—guides, or can guide, every member of the Church. Everyone is invited to come and repent and be baptized and receive of this sacred gift. (00–02, pp. 8–9)

CHAPTER 5

Spiritual Development

"Prayer is your personal key to heaven.
The lock is on your side of the veil." [1] *(94–05, p. 59)*

PRAYER AND ANSWERS TO PRAYER

A lesson on faith and prayer. Several years ago we had a cow ready to calve. I had not been home in daylight hours for several weeks. One day before catching a plane for a conference, I went out to see the cow. She was in trouble. I called the veterinarian, who came immediately and looked at her. He tested her and said, "She has swallowed a wire, and it has punctured her heart. She will be dead before the day is over."

The next day the calf was to come. The cow was important to our economy. I asked the veterinarian if he could do anything, and he said he could take some measures, "but it will likely be useless—money down the drain." After asking, "What will it cost me?" I told him to go ahead.

The next morning the calf was born, but the cow was lying down gasping. I called the vet again, thinking the calf might need some attention. He looked the cow over and said she would be dead within an hour or so. I went to the house, got the telephone directory, copied down the number of an animal by-products company, put it on the hook by the phone, and told my wife to call them to come and get the cow later in the day.

We had our family prayer before I left for the plane. Our little boy was praying, and in the middle of his prayer—after he said all that he usually said, such as, "Bless daddy that he won't get hurt in his travels, bless us at school," and so on—he started to pray with deep feeling. He said, "Heavenly Father, please bless Bossy so that she will get to be all right."

While I was in California I remembered that prayer, and when the subject of prayer came up in a meeting, I told of the incident, saying, "I am glad he prayed that way, because he will learn something. He will mature, and he will learn that you do not get everything you pray for just by asking. There is a lesson to be learned."

And truly there was—but it was I who learned it, not my son, because when I got home Sunday night Bossy had "got to be all right." And it was the father who had learned the lesson about faith and prayer as much as, if not more than, the son. (*TYD*, pp. 201–2)

Prayer is the avenue to spiritual power. Prayer is the avenue you have to spiritual power. (06–09)

The loss of revelation and answers to prayer would leave this church weak. If we lose the spirit and power of individual revelation, we have lost much in this church. . . . If we become so independent and insecure that prayer and the answer to prayer are such that we are hesitant to rely on them, then we are weak. (*TYD*, p. 247)

Prayer is powerful spiritual medicine. If you need a transfusion of spiritual strength, then just ask for it. We call that prayer. Prayer is powerful spiritual medicine. The instructions for its use are found in the scriptures. (87–07, p. 18)

It is important to use reverential terms in our prayers. We are drifting from the use of reverential words in our prayers. Familiar terms such as *you* and *yours* are replacing *thee* and *thine* in prayer. Teach the children and gently inform new members that we use reverential terms when addressing our Heavenly Father in prayer. (91–06, pp. 22–23)

It is important to say "Amen." One of the things I've noticed as this meeting has progressed is that there was a very quiet "amen" among you when the prayer was said. . . . Do you know, that worried President Harold B. Lee? On several occasions he talked to the Brethren and said, "Brethren, we're losing something with our youth. They don't say, 'amen.'"

Then he explained that that tradition, which was developed through inspiration, is the way we have in our meetings of giving consent and committing ourselves as approving what has been said. President Lee called it "spiritual applause." When someone pronounces a testimony with which we're in harmony, or gives a prayer in which we want to join, as they conclude, "in the name of Jesus Christ, amen"— it's not just our privilege, but there's something of a responsibility, for us to *audibly* do likewise. (75–04)

Pray for one another. Do you remember in the Book of Mormon, the account of Alma? Alma was president of the church. Alma the younger was his wayward son. When his father would go preach a sermon in the city, the son often would follow him and he would ridicule what his father had said. Can you hear him saying something like this: "I suppose my old father has been telling you that nonsense again. Don't believe it. I don't."

Then something happened. An angel appeared to him, and he was struck down as though he was dead. The angel said this; he made this point very clear: Not because of any worthiness of thyself, but in order that the prayers of thy father would be answered have I come to give you this experience.[2] Think of that. Now most of us have relatives who are not yet members of the Church. We'd better pray as fervently as that father did.

As the Book of Mormon unfolds, we see the son succeeding his father as president of the church, and using the lesson of his youth to redeem thousands and tens of thousands.[3] And so it can be with us if we heed the voice of warning. (76–10)

We should constantly appeal to the Lord for correction and guidance. As far as I know in my personal life, there must be a constant sensitivity and appeal for correction. . . . [I rarely] ever give a prayer that I do not ask the Lord to help me, to correct me, and to guide me. . . . We are His sons and daughters. Our appeals do not go unheard. (02–08)

Prayer is an essential part of revelation. You have your agency, and inspiration does not—perhaps cannot—flow unless you ask for it, or someone asks for you.

No message in scripture is repeated more often than the invitation, even the command, to pray—to ask.

Prayer is so essential a part of revelation that without it the veil may remain closed to you. Learn to pray. Pray often. Pray in your mind, in your heart. Pray on your knees. (94–05, p. 59)

Learn how to pray. Learn how to pray and how to receive answers to your prayers. When you pray over some things, you must patiently wait a long, long time before you will receive an answer. Some prayers, for your own safety, must be answered immediately, and some promptings will even come when you haven't prayed at all. (76–03, p. 31)

Answers can come in different ways. Put difficult questions in the back of your minds and go about your lives. Ponder and pray quietly and persistently about them.

The answer may not come as a lightning bolt. It may come as a little inspiration here and a little there, "line upon line, precept upon precept."[4]

Some answers will come from reading the scriptures, some from hearing speakers. And, occasionally, when it is important, some will come by very direct and powerful inspiration. The promptings will be clear and unmistakable. (79–10, p. 21)

Answers to prayers come in a quiet way. We succeed in the Church, by and large, in teaching our members to pray. Even our little ones are taught to fold their arms and bow their heads, and with whispered coaching from their parents and from brothers and sisters, they soon learn to pray.

There is one part of prayer—the answer part—that perhaps, by comparison, we neglect.

There are some things about answers to prayer that you can learn when you are very young, and they will be a great protection to you. . . .

One of our sons has always been interested in radio. When he was a little fellow, his Christmas present was a very elementary radio construction set.

As he grew, and as we could afford it, and as he could earn it, he received more sophisticated equipment.

There have been many times over the years, some very recently, when I have sat with him as he talked with someone in a distant part of the world.

I could hear static and interference and catch a word or two, or sometimes several voices at once.

Yet he can understand, for he has trained himself to tune out the interference.

It is difficult to separate from the confusion of life that quiet voice of inspiration. Unless you attune yourself, you will miss it.

Answers to prayers come in a quiet way. The scriptures describe that voice of inspiration as a still, small voice.

If you really try, you can learn to respond to that voice. (79–10, p. 19)

There is a spiritual beam with a constant signal. It has been many years, but I have not forgotten that as pilots in World War II we did not have the electronic equipment that we have today. Our hope in a storm was to follow a radio beam.

A steady signal and you were on course. If you moved to one side of the steady signal, it would break up to a "dit-da," the Morse code for the letter A.

If you strayed to the other side of the signal, the beam would break up into a "da-dit," the Morse code signal for N.

In stormy weather there was always static and interference. But the life of many a pilot has depended on his hearing, above the roar of the engines and through all the static and interference, that sometimes weak signal from a distant airfield.

There is a spiritual beam, with a constant signal. If you know how to pray and how to listen, spiritually listen, you may move through life, through clear weather, through storms, through wars, through peace, and be all right. (79–10, p. 21)

Make every major decision on the basis of prayer. I would suggest that you make every major decision on the basis of prayer, on the basis of having prayed and communicated with the Lord, and that then you follow the pattern of the gospel. (63–02)

We can solve most problems by taking them to our Father in Heaven. There is one authorized "end run" around the bishop, the stake president, the General Authority, and everyone else in our line of authority. That is to our Father in Heaven in prayer. If we do that, we will in most instances solve our own problems. (96–07)

Spiritual things cannot be forced. It is good to learn when you are young that spiritual things cannot be forced.

Sometimes you may struggle with a problem and not get an answer. What could be wrong?

It may be that you are not doing anything wrong. It may be that you have not done the right things long enough. Remember, you cannot force spiritual things.

Sometimes we are confused simply because we won't take no for an answer. (79–10, p. 21)

GIFTS OF THE SPIRIT

Spiritual gifts are a product of faith. Spiritual gifts . . . are a product of our faith and if we don't have them, something is less than it should be. (87–01, p. 104)

We are to seek to be worthy of spiritual gifts. Spiritual gifts belong to the Church, and their existence is one of the great and abiding testimonies of the truth of the gospel. They really are not optional with the Church. Mormon taught that if they were absent, then "awful is the state of man."[5]

We are to seek to be worthy to receive these gifts according to the way that the Lord has directed.

Now, I say that again—we are to seek for spiritual gifts in the Lord's way. (87–01, p. 99)

Spiritual gifts cannot be forced. I must emphasize that the word "gift" is of great significance, for a gift may not be demanded or it ceases to be a gift. It may only be accepted when proffered.

Inasmuch as spiritual gifts are gifts, the conditions under which we may receive them are established by Him who offers them to us. Spiritual gifts cannot be forced, for a gift is a gift. They cannot, I repeat, be forced, nor bought, nor earned in the sense that we make some gesture in payment and expect them to automatically be delivered on our own terms.

There are those who seek such gifts with such persistence that each act moves them further from them. And in that persistence and determination they place themselves in spiritual danger. Rather, we are to live to be worthy of the gifts and they will come according to the will of the Lord. (87–01, p. 98)

Seeking spiritual gifts versus signs. We have the assignment to seek after spiritual gifts.[6] Then we have the very clear notice that signs will follow those that believe.[7] The scriptural direction that we should seek after spiritual gifts and that these signs would follow those that believe has a very important counterbalance, for by warnings that are unmistakable, we are not to seek after the signs.

I would like to give something of a definition of my own of the two terms—*spiritual gifts* and *signs.*

A spiritual gift is an endowment of spiritual power. For example, the gift of faith or gift of discernment, neither of which may be visible.

Signs, on the other hand, are evidences of visible manifestations that a spiritual power is present: visible miracles, such as a healing or raising one from the dead.

The scriptures make it clear that we are not to seek after signs, and it explains in many references that spiritual gifts, and the signs which follow them, are a product of faith and that faith is not an outgrowth of the signs. Let me repeat that. Spiritual gifts and the signs that follow them are the product of faith and not the reverse—faith is not an outgrowth of the signs. If we misunderstand this, surely we will place ourselves in spiritual jeopardy. In four places in the Bible and various other places, there is this very clear statement:

"An evil and adulterous generation seeketh after a sign; and there shall no sign be given to it, but the sign of the prophet Jonas."[8] (87–01, pp. 101–2)

The gift to be guided. There is another gift, a little difficult to describe, but I think we could maybe say that it is the gift to be guided, or the gift of guidance—difficult to define but I think you will know what I mean. When certain events happen (often small events in our lives) that could not possibly be coincidental, we get the impression that there is a Power and a Source that knew we would be there and what we would be about. (87–01, p. 97)

The power of discernment is real. This power of discernment is a very real spiritual gift. It is often conferred as a blessing upon men ordained as bishops, stake presidents, and so forth. Many can bear witness to the fact that they do not have to hear or to see all that they know, that they can discern thoughts when the purpose of their office is served. (67–05, p. 34)

Discerning right in a wicked world. We live in a day when evil is everywhere. At times it almost seems that right is wrong and wrong is right. We would hardly know which way to go if we did not have somewhere to turn in making many of the decisions we must make in life.

As members of the Church we are not just cut loose and left to shift for ourselves in this world. That would be a terrible thing. We are not left adrift. That constant spiritual guidance that we have in the Church is a clear signal, if we live for it and if we follow it. (74–06, p. 234)

LIGHT OF CHRIST

What is the Light of Christ? The Light of Christ is defined in the scriptures as "the Spirit [which] giveth light to *every* man that cometh into the world";[9] "the light which is in all things, which giveth life to all things, which is the law by which all things are governed."[10]

And the Light of Christ is also described in the scriptures as "the Spirit of Jesus Christ,"[11] "the Spirit of the Lord,"[12] "the Spirit of truth,"[13] "the light of truth,"[14] "the Spirit of God,"[15] and "the Holy Spirit."[16] Some of these terms are also used to refer to the Holy Ghost.

The First Presidency has written:

> There is a universally diffused essence which is the light and the life of the world, "which lighteth every man that cometh into the world," which proceedeth forth from the presence of God throughout the immensity of space, the light and power of which God bestows in different degrees to "them that ask him," according to their faith and obedience.[17]

Regardless of whether this inner light, this knowledge of right and wrong, is called the Light of Christ, moral sense, or conscience, it can direct us to moderate our actions—unless, that is, we subdue it or silence it. (04–05, pp. 8–9)

The more we know about the Light of Christ, the more we will understand about life. The Holy Ghost and the Light of Christ are

*The Paul Revere Award is given to Boyd K. Packer by
Governor John A. Volpe of Massachusetts and C. Robert Yeager,
president of L. G. Balfour Company, June 29, 1968*

different from each other. While they are sometimes described in the scriptures with the same words, they are two different and distinct entities. It is important for you to know about both of them.

The more we know about the Light of Christ, the more we will understand about life and the more we will have a deep love for all mankind. We will be better teachers and missionaries and parents, and better men and women and children. We will have deeper regard for our brothers and sisters in the Church and for those who do not believe and have not yet had conferred upon them the gift of the Holy Ghost. (04–05, p. 8)

The Light of Christ binds the human family together. There is a light, a "true Light, which lighteth every man that cometh into the world."[18] This Light of Christ is the ingredient which binds the whole human family together and forms something of a universal conscience. There is nothing that is right that we cannot achieve if our individual and our national conscience is clear. (89–03, p. 67)

From before our birth we were all equally endowed with the Light of Christ. The Light of Christ existed in you before you were born,[19] and it will be with you every moment that you live and will not perish when the mortal part of you has turned to dust. It is ever there.

Every man, woman, and child of every nation, creed, or color— everyone, no matter where they live or what they believe or what they do—has within them the imperishable Light of Christ. In this respect, all men are created equally. The Light of Christ in everyone is a testimony that God is no respecter of persons.[20] He treats everyone equally in that endowment with the Light of Christ. (04–05, p. 10)

The Light of Christ is like sunlight. I do not know how to teach about the Spirit of Christ except to follow what the Lord did when He taught invisible, intangible truths to His disciples.

To describe the Light of Christ, I will compare or liken it to the light of the sun. Sunlight is familiar to everyone; it is everywhere present and can be seen and can be felt. Life itself depends upon sunlight.

The Light of Christ *is* like sunlight. It, too, is everywhere present and given to everyone equally.

Just as darkness must vanish when the light of the sun appears, so is evil sent fleeing by the Light of Christ.

There is no darkness in sunlight. Darkness is subject unto it. The sun can be hidden by clouds or by the rotation of the earth, but the clouds will disappear, and the earth will complete its turning.

According to the plan, we are told that "it must needs be, that there is an opposition in all things."[21]

Mormon warned that "the devil . . . persuadeth no man to do good, no, not one; neither do his angels; neither do they who subject themselves unto him.

"[Now] seeing that ye know the light by which ye may judge, which light is the light of Christ, see that ye do not judge wrongfully."[22]

This Light of Christ, which gives life, is within you. The evil one will attempt to obscure it. It can be so clouded with confusion so far as to convince you that it does not even exist.

Just as sunlight is a natural disinfectant, the Spirit of Christ can cleanse the spirit. (04–05, p. 13)

The Light of Christ is as universal as sunlight itself. The Light of Christ is as universal as sunlight itself. Wherever there is human life, there is the Spirit of Christ. Every living soul is possessed of it. It is the sponsor of everything that is good. It is the inspirer of everything that will bless and benefit mankind. It nourishes goodness itself.

Mormon taught: "Search diligently in the light of Christ that ye may know good from evil; and if ye will lay hold upon every good thing, and condemn it not, ye certainly will be a child of Christ."[23] (04–05, p. 13)

The Light of Christ fosters everything that is good. This Spirit of Christ fosters everything that is good, every virtue.[24] It stands in brilliant, indestructible opposition to anything that is coarse or ugly or profane or evil or wicked.[25]

Conscience affirms the reality of the Spirit of Christ in man. It affirms, as well, the reality of good and evil, of justice, mercy, honor, courage, faith, love, and virtue, as well as the necessary opposites—hatred, greed, brutality, jealousy.[26] Such values, though physically intangible, respond to laws with cause-and-effect relationships as certain as any resulting from physical laws.[27] The Spirit of Christ can be likened unto a "guardian angel" for every person.[28]

The Spirit of Christ can enlighten the inventor, the scientist, the painter, the sculptor, the composer, the performer, the architect, the author to produce great, even inspired things for the blessing and good of all mankind.

This Spirit can prompt the farmer in his field and the fisherman on his boat. It can inspire the teacher in the classroom, the missionary in presenting his discussion. It can inspire the student who listens. And of enormous importance, it can inspire husband and wife, and father and mother.

This inner Light can warn and guard and guide. But it can be repulsed by anything that is ugly or unworthy or wicked or immoral or selfish. (04–05, p. 10)

By fostering the Light of Christ one can be brought to receive the Holy Ghost. The Spirit of Christ is always there. It never leaves. It cannot leave.

Everyone everywhere already has the Spirit of Christ, and while the Spirit of the Holy Ghost can visit anyone, the *gift* of the Holy Ghost is obtained "by obedience to the laws and ordinances of the Gospel,"[29] by submitting to "baptism by immersion for the remission of sins; [and the] laying on of hands for the gift of the Holy Ghost."[30] It is not automatically present like the Spirit of Christ is present. This gift must be conferred by one holding authority.[31]

That is what we are commissioned to do, to foster the Light of Christ, which is within every soul we meet, and bring souls to the point where the Holy Ghost may visit them. And then, in due time, they can receive, through the ordinance, the gift of the Holy Ghost, which is conferred upon every member of the Church. Once a person has received that gift of the Holy Ghost and can cultivate it together with the Light of Christ, which they already have, then the fulness of the gospel is open to their understanding. (04–05, p. 13)

Understanding the reality of the Light of Christ will give us greater understanding. If we understand the reality of the Light of Christ in everyone we see and in every meeting we attend and within ourselves, and understand the great challenge that we have—the surroundings in which we live, the danger which sometimes besets us—we will have courage and inspiration beyond that which we have known heretofore. And it *must* be so! And it *will* be so! All of this is a dimension of gospel truth that too few understand. (04–05, p. 14)

TESTIMONY

Spiritually speaking I have tasted salt. I will tell you of an experience I had before I was a General Authority which affected me profoundly. I sat on a plane next to a professed atheist who pressed his disbelief in God so urgently that I bore my testimony to him. "You are wrong," I said. "There is a God. I *know* He lives!"

He protested, "You don't *know*. Nobody *knows* that! You can't *know* it!" When I would not yield, the atheist, who was an attorney, asked perhaps the ultimate question on the subject of testimony. "All right," he said in a sneering, condescending way, "you say you know. Tell me *how* you know."

When I attempted to answer, even though I held advanced academic degrees, I was helpless to communicate.

Sometimes our youth, you young missionaries, are embarrassed when the cynic, the skeptic, treats you with contempt because you do not have ready answers for everything. Before such ridicule, some turn away in shame. (Remember the iron rod, the spacious building, and the mocking?)[32]

When I used the words *Spirit* and *witness,* the atheist responded, "I don't know what you are talking about." The words *prayer, discernment,* and *faith* were equally meaningless to him. "You see," he said, "you don't really know. If you did, you would be able to tell me *how you know*."

I felt, perhaps, that I had borne my testimony to him unwisely and was at a loss as to what to do. Then came the experience! Something came into my mind. And I mention here a statement of the Prophet Joseph Smith: "A person may profit by noticing the first intimation of the spirit of revelation; for instance, when you feel pure intelligence flowing into you, it may give you sudden strokes of ideas . . . and thus by learning the Spirit of God and understanding it, you may grow into the principle of revelation, until you become perfect in Christ Jesus."[33]

Such an idea came into my mind and I said to the atheist, "Let me ask if you know what salt tastes like."

"Of course I do," was his reply.

"When did you taste salt last?"

"I just had dinner on the plane."

"You just think you know what salt tastes like," I said.

He insisted, "I know what salt tastes like as well as I know anything."

"If I gave you a cup of salt and a cup of sugar and let you taste them both, could you tell the salt from the sugar?"

"Now you are getting juvenile," was his reply. "Of course I could tell the difference. I know what salt tastes like. It is an everyday experience—I know it as well as I know anything."

"Then," I said, "assuming that I have never tasted salt, explain to me just what it tastes like."

After some thought, he ventured, "Well—I—uh, it is not sweet and it is not sour."

"You've told me what it isn't, not what it is."

After several attempts, of course, he could not do it. He could not convey, in words alone, so ordinary an experience as tasting salt. I bore testimony to him once again and said, "I know there is a God. You ridiculed that testimony and said that if I *did* know, I would be able to tell exactly *how* I know. My friend, spiritually speaking, I have tasted salt. I am no more able to convey to you in words how this knowledge has come than you are to tell me what salt tastes like. But I say to you again, there is a God! He does live! And just because you don't know, don't try to tell me that I don't know, for I do!"

As we parted, I heard him mutter, "I don't need your religion for a crutch! I don't need it."

From that experience forward, I have never been embarrassed or ashamed that I could not explain in words alone everything I know spiritually. The Apostle Paul said it this way:

"We speak, not in the words which man's wisdom teacheth, but which the Holy Ghost teacheth; comparing spiritual things with spiritual.

"But the natural man receiveth not the things of the Spirit of God: for they are foolishness unto him: neither can he know them, because they are spiritually discerned."[34] (82–04, pp. 51–52)

A testimony will not come to the skeptic. Because of the way the Spirit operates, the skeptic will never know the truth. He will never meet the requirements of faith and humility and obedience to qualify him for a visitation of the Spirit. Testimony is perfectly protected from the insincere, the purely intellectual, the experimenter, the arrogant, the faithless, and the proud. It will not come to them. (91–04)

A testimony does not come by compelling spiritual experiences. The most important lessons come from ordinary events in life.

Some wait for compelling spiritual experiences to confirm their testimony. It doesn't work that way. It is the quiet promptings and impressions of ordinary things that give us the assurance of our identity as children of God. We live far below our privileges when we seek after signs and look "beyond the mark"[35] for marvelous events. (99–06, p. 15)

One cannot force a spiritual witness. I have come to know that the witness does not come by seeking after signs. It will not yield itself to pressure or to force. It comes through fasting and prayer, through activity and testing, through obedience. It comes through sustaining the servants of the Lord and following them. (93–07, p. 57)

Testimony comes by the power of the Spirit. Testimony comes by the power of the Spirit. We do not learn such things as testimony in the same way, exactly, as we do other things which we know. A testimony does not come by "natural" means.

"But the natural man receiveth not the things of the Spirit of God: for they are foolishness unto him: neither can he know them, because they are spiritually discerned."[36]

Some people doubt they have testimonies because they have not acquired their testimonies in just the same way they have acquired other knowledge.

There are many people with firm testimonies in the gospel of Jesus Christ who are really not aware that they possess them.[37] (68–01)

As you test gospel principles by believing without knowing, the Spirit will begin to teach you. Gradually your faith will be replaced with knowledge. (94–05, p. 60)

More powerful than you know. A testimony is not thrust upon you. A testimony grows. We can become taller in testimony like we become taller in physical stature, and hardly know it happens because it comes by growth.

There are many with firm testimonies of the gospel of Jesus Christ who are not really aware that they possess them. The Lord, speaking very directly to the people at the time of His appearance to the Nephites, said:

"Whoso cometh unto me with a broken heart and a contrite spirit, him will I baptize with fire and with the Holy Ghost, even as the Lamanites, because of their faith in me at the time of their conversion, were baptized with fire and with the Holy Ghost, and they knew it not."[38]

You may have much more power in your testimony than you realize and it will not be known, even by you, until you start to use it, to share it, to bear it to others. Is not this a perfect demonstration of the spirit of true Christianity? You cannot find it, nor keep it, nor enlarge it unless and until you are willing to share it, to give it away. It is by giving it away freely that it becomes yours. (82–05)

Principles of testimony bearing. Let's talk just a minute about testimony. After hearing 206 missionaries stand up and make an expression, I finally came to the realization that we had heard 205 talks and only one testimony. The responses went something like this: "I'm grateful to be a missionary. I'm glad to be on a mission. I have a great companion. I love my companion. I've had good companions all the time. We had a great experience last week. We were tracting [and so on], . . . and so you see how grateful I am to be on a mission. I have a testimony of this gospel. In the name of Jesus Christ, amen."

These missionaries had talked *about* testimony, but they had talked *around* and *through* it, *underneath* it and *over* it, but never *to* it. It was marvelous what happened when we were able to show them how one bears testimony.

There are two ways to spell *bear. Bear* means to carry. All of the missionaries were bearing testimonies—carrying them all over New England. Everywhere they went, their testimony went with them. There's another spelling to that word (and I wonder if we don't use the wrong one.) *Bare* means to expose or reveal or make known. So we may carry a testimony but not reveal it! Teach our young people to bear their testimonies instead of saying they have testimonies and then not saying what they are. Teach them to bear direct witness.

While a witness may come from hearing a testimony borne by another, I am convinced that *the* witness comes when the Spirit of the Lord falls upon a man or woman when he or she is bearing testimony personally. . . . Teach our young people to bear testimony—to bear testimony that Jesus is the Christ, that Joseph Smith is a prophet of God, that the Book of Mormon is true, that we lived before we came here, that Christ died to redeem us, and that He is the Son of God. As they testify of those things the Holy Ghost will bear witness in their hearts, and it will be compounded a thousandfold more powerfully than if they just listen to a witness borne by others. (68–05, pp. 153–54)

Bearing testimony is something of an experiment. Bear testimony of the things that you hope are true, as an act of faith. It is something of an experiment, akin to the experiment that the prophet Alma proposed to his followers. We begin with faith—not with a perfect knowledge of things. That sermon in the thirty-second chapter of Alma is one of the greatest messages in holy writ for it is addressed to the beginner, to the novice, to the humble seeker. And it holds a key to a witness of the truth.

The Spirit and testimony of Christ will come to you for the most part *when,* and remain with you only *if,* you share it. In that process is the *very essence* of the gospel. (82–04, p. 55)

Bearing testimony is an act of faith. It is when you exercise faith and begin to bear witness that the confirmation of truth comes. In this way it is hidden from the cynic, from the unworthy, from the unrepentant, from the curious and the experimenter.

Bear testimony of the things that you hope are true. Do it as an act of faith even though you may not know for certain that they are true. You will find in the process of bearing your testimony the confirmation will come to you that they are true. And, you will know as you bear it that you speak the truth. Then will come to you the greatest experience of bearing witness under the power of the Spirit. You will testify of things that you have believed in and hoped for and only now, in the bearing of them, do you know for certain that they are true. Then you will feel the Spirit speaking through you. (68–01)

A testimony is found in the bearing of it. A testimony is to be found in the bearing of it! Somewhere in the quest for spiritual knowledge there is that leap of faith. As the philosophers call it, it is a moment when your missionary has gone to the edge of the light and then taken a step or two into the unknown, into the darkness to discover that the way is lighted ahead just a footstep or two. "The spirit of man is the candle of the Lord," the Proverbs told us.[39]

It is one thing to receive a witness from what you have read or what another has said; that's a necessary beginning. . . . It is quite another to

have the Spirit affirm to you in your bosom that what you have testified is true. Do you understand? . . . What you give by way of testimony
will come back with increase and replacement. (91–04)

Oh, if I could teach you this one principle. A testimony is to be
found in the *bearing* of it! (82–04, p. 54)

There are two dimensions to testimony. There are two dimensions
to testimony. The one, *a testimony we bear to them,* has power to lift and
bless them. The other, infinitely more important, *the testimony they bear
themselves,* has the power to redeem and exalt them. You might say they
can get *a* testimony from what we say. *The* testimony comes when they
themselves bear a witness of the truth and the Holy Ghost confirms it
to them. James said, "Be ye doers of the word, and not hearers only."[40]
And the Lord said, "If any man will do his will, he shall know of the
doctrine."[41] (69–03, p. 15)

There is strength in testimony bearing. The testimony of ward
and stake and general leaders of the Church strengthens everyone who
comes within their influence. Those who serve in the organizations are
strengthened, and in turn they strengthen those who attend. Priesthood
holders, who go out as home teachers, are strengthened, and they bear
testimony to strengthen the members. The home teachers themselves
have home teachers. Thus there is a cycle of strength and spiritual nourishment that can make each of us as an individual and the Church as
an organization like a magnet, drawing more of the lost sheep into the
fold. (69–03, pp. 20–21)

Can one really know for sure? Young people, do not apologize or
be ashamed because you cannot frame into words that which you know
in your heart to be true. Do not repudiate your testimony merely
because you have no marvelous manifestations to discuss. . . .

We sympathize with you and know how difficult it is to hold to the
truth, particularly when professors of worldly knowledge—some of
them counterfeit Christians—debunk and scoff. We know from personal experience that you may have some doubts. You may wonder at

times, "Can I ever really know for sure?" You may even wonder, "Does anyone really know for sure?" . . .

In answer to your question, "Can I ever really know for sure?" we answer, "Just as certainly as you fill the requirements, that testimony will come." The Lord has never said, nor was it ever pretended, that this testimony yields itself to scientific investigation, to mere curiosity, or to academic inquiry.

In answer to your question, "Does anybody really know?" yes, tens of thousands know. The Brethren know. . . .

. . . And I bear my solemn witness that Jesus is the Christ. I say that I know Jesus is the Christ, that the gospel of Jesus Christ was restored to Joseph Smith, a prophet of God. (64–12, p. 1097)

CHAPTER 6

Revelation and Spiritual Experiences

"No one of us can survive in the world of today, much less in what it soon will become, without personal inspiration." (91–06, p. 23)

PERSONAL REVELATION

The voice of revelation. We could come away from a study of Elijah[1] with no more important lesson than to recognize how the Lord communicates with His children here upon the earth: through the still, small voice that is so difficult to describe to one who has never experienced it and is almost unnecessary to describe to one who has. That sweet, quiet voice of inspiration that comes more as a feeling than it does as a sound. That process through which pure intelligence can be spoken into the mind and we can know and understand and have witness of spiritual things. The process is not reserved for the prophets alone, but every righteous, seeking soul who will qualify and make himself worthy can have that manner of communication, even as a gift. (*THT,* p. 107)

Revelation is a language of the Spirit. We are dual beings, a spirit son or daughter of God, alive and intelligent in the first estate, confined now to a body of flesh and bone. "The spirit and the body are the soul of man."[2] The spirit is eternal; the body will become so. There are languages we can speak and hear with the body. There are languages of the Spirit, one being revelation. (93–07, p. 54)

Revelation is the process of communication to our spiritual eyes and ears. Revelation is the process of communication to the spiritual eyes and to the spiritual ears that were ours before our mortal birth. The scriptures speak of "the eyes of our understanding,"[3] and of "blindness of mind"[4] and of heart.[5] They speak of "feeling" words, rather than hearing them,[6] and of the still, small voice.[7] (93–07, p. 55)

The voice of inspiration comes as a feeling. That voice of inspiration is so quiet and still that it can be explained away. It is easy to be disobedient to that voice. It often takes great courage to follow it. But to Latter-day Saints it is a clear signal.

There is a very important message on this subject in the Book of Mormon. On one occasion Nephi scolded his brothers Laman and Lemuel for their unbelief, telling them: "Ye are swift to do iniquity but slow to remember the Lord your God. Ye have seen an angel, and he spake unto you; yea, ye have heard his voice from time to time; and he hath spoken unto you in a still small voice, but ye were past *feeling*, that ye could not *feel* his words."[8]

Someone once criticized the Book of Mormon by saying that it did not use correct language, and pointed to the above verse as the example: "You were past *feeling*, that ye could not *feel* his words." You don't *feel* words, the person insisted, you *hear* them. If the book were true, the passage would read, "You were past *hearing*, that you did not *hear* his words."

That correction would only be made by someone who did not know about the Spirit. (74–06, pp. 232–33)

The voice of the Spirit is generally felt rather than heard. We do not have the words (even the scriptures do not have words) which perfectly describe the Spirit. The scriptures generally use the word voice, which does not exactly fit. These delicate, refined spiritual communications are not seen with our eyes, nor heard with our ears. And even though it is described as a voice, it is a voice that one feels, more than one hears.[9] (82–04, p. 52)

The depth of personal revelation comes as a feeling. If you listen with your mortal ears for the revelations of the Almighty, you will receive part of it because of the patterns of preaching. But that depth of personal revelation comes to you when you *feel.* You don't *hear* the words of an angel, you *feel* the words of an angel, because "angels speak by the power of the Holy Ghost; wherefore, they speak the words of Christ."[10] (94–04)

Inspiration comes as thoughts, feelings, and impressions. The Holy Ghost communicates with the spirit through the mind more than through the physical senses. This guidance comes as thoughts, as feelings, through impressions and promptings. It is not always easy to describe inspiration. The scriptures teach us that we may "feel" the words of spiritual communication more than hear them, and see with spiritual rather than with mortal eyes.[11]

The patterns of revelation are not dramatic. The voice of inspiration is a still voice, a small voice. There need be no trance, no sanctimonious declaration. It is quieter and simpler than that. (89–04, p. 14)

Spiritual communication comes into the mind. Spiritual communication comes into the *mind,* it comes more as a feeling, an impression, than simply as a thought. Unless you have experienced it, it is very difficult to describe that delicate process.

The witness is not communicated through the intellect alone, however bright the intellect may be. (91–06, p. 21)

Pure intelligence may be conveyed instantly. There is a sacred process by which pure intelligence may be conveyed into our minds and we can come to know instantly things that otherwise would take a long period of time to acquire. He can speak inspiration into our minds, especially when we are humble and seeking. (75–03, p. 105)

Learn to receive inspiration. The Lord has a way of pouring pure intelligence into our minds to prompt us, to guide us, to teach us, to warn us. You can know the things you need to know *instantly!* Learn to receive inspiration. (79–10, p. 20)

Revelation usually comes as an impression. I have learned that revelation, which showers down on all of us "as the dews from heaven,"[12] usually comes as a noun not as an adjective. The Lord does not describe what it is He is talking about. He just gives you the impression. I have learned to follow those impressions. (08–05)

We must train ourselves to hear the voice of inspiration. You can train yourself to hear what you want to hear, to see and feel what you desire, but it takes some conditioning.

There are so many of us who go through life and seldom, if ever, hear that voice of inspiration, because "the natural man receiveth not the things of the Spirit of God: for they are foolishness unto him: neither can he know them, because they are spiritually discerned."[13] (79–10, p. 20)

The greatest education. The greatest education you can get is to learn the voice of the Spirit. (01–01)

The whisperings of the Spirit come gently and quietly. The Spirit does not get our attention by shouting or shaking us with a heavy hand. Rather it whispers. It caresses so gently that if we are preoccupied we may not feel it at all. (No wonder that the Word of Wisdom was revealed to us, for how could the drunkard or the addict feel such a voice?)

Occasionally it will press just firmly enough for us to pay heed. But most of the time, if we do not heed the gentle feeling, the Spirit will withdraw and wait until we come seeking and listening and say in our manner and expression, like Samuel of ancient times, "Speak [Lord], for thy servant heareth."[14] (82–04, p. 53)

There is a power of spiritual communication. There is a power of communication as real and tangible as electricity. Man has devised the means to send images and sound through the air to be caught on an antenna and reproduced and heard and seen. This other communication may be likened to that, save it be a million times more powerful, and the witness it brings is always the truth.

There is a process by which pure intelligence can flow, by which we can come to know of a surety, nothing doubting. (71–04, p. 88)

Angels can communicate by the power of the Spirit. "Angels speak by the power of the Holy Ghost."[15] Should an angel converse with you, neither you nor he would be confined to corporeal sight or sound in order to communicate. For there is that spiritual process described by the Prophet Joseph by which pure intelligence can flow into our minds and by which we can know what we need to know without either the effort or study or the passage of time, because that is revelation. We talk about confining on little computer chips vast amounts of information; through the processes of revelation and through this language of the Spirit, tremendous amounts of inspiration and information can be given to us instantly. (91–04)

One of the most important things we can teach is how to receive revelation. During unsettled times . . . the most important thing we can teach to members of the Church worldwide is how to receive revealed instruction, prompting, guidance, direction, warning, and to learn to trust it. (08–02)

It should not be difficult to teach how revelation can come through light. It should not be difficult to teach how revelation can come through Light, even though we do not know exactly how inspiration works.

Man himself, with all his limitations, can convey messages through fiber-optic cables. A single tiny fiber of glass, smaller than a human hair, can carry 40,000 messages at the same time. These can then be decoded and turned into sight and sound and color, even motion. Man can do that.

A laser beam, where there is no wire or fiber at all, can carry 100 billion bits of information in a second.

If man can do that, why should we marvel at the promise that the Light of Christ is in all of us and that the Holy Ghost can visit any of us?

It should not be difficult, therefore, to understand how revelation from God to His children on earth can come to all mankind through both the Spirit of Christ and the Holy Ghost. (04–05, p. 14)

Learn to listen to the voice of the Spirit. Many years ago my parents lived on a little farm. It was a poor farm. One day my father was plowing and he broke the plow. He came to the house to tell mother he had to take the plow to town to be welded. Mother was washing, with water on the stove. She hurried and got the children ready. She didn't go to town very often, and was anxious to go. Father hitched the horse to the buggy and brought it to the door. She lifted the children into the buggy.

As she went to climb in, she hesitated. "I don't think I will go with you today," she said to my father. "What's the matter?" Father asked. "I don't know," she answered. "I just have the feeling that I shouldn't go."

When she said the word *feeling* that meant something to my father. He was wise enough not to talk her out of it. "Well, if you have that feeling, perhaps you had better stay home."

She lifted the children out of the buggy, and of course, you knew what they started to do. She stood and watched as the buggy went down the road, the children crying with disappointment. And then she said to herself, "Now wasn't that silly of me." She returned to the house to finish the washing.

She had only been in the house a few minutes when she smelled smoke. The house was afire up in the ceiling. The children formed a bucket brigade and soon they had the fire out. And so ends an ordinary incident; except when you ask a question, Why didn't she go to town that day?

My mother prayed earnestly that the Lord would bless them that they could feed and clothe their children. They were saving money to pay for the farm. The money was in the house. If the house had burned, they would have lost everything.

I repeat, she prayed often.

Young people, we should learn that often our prayers are not answered at the very moment we ask them. If we learn to respond to the Spirit, they may be answered at any time.

Again the question, Why did she not go to town that day? She didn't hear a voice saying, "Don't go to town today; I'm going to answer your prayers." She did not see a written message. She stayed home because of a feeling. A still, small voice had spoken to her. She had told my father: "I just have a feeling I shouldn't go." That was a great lesson my mother taught to us.

And this is my counsel to you. . . . Learn to live by the Spirit. (78–10)

GUIDELINES FOR RECEIVING REVELATION

Prerequisite for revelation. One of the prerequisites to receiving revelation is obedience. (81–01)

To enjoy the guidance of the Spirit we must keep our covenants. In order to have that Spirit guide us we must prepare ourselves for it. To do that, to be worthy of constant inspiration, we must keep the covenants we made at the time of baptism. (74–06, p. 233)

Through worthiness we have the right to spiritual guidance. We are to be in the world but not of the world. And in the world we have the right, if we would live for it, to be possessed of that quiet spiritual guidance—if we will not seek for the manifestations of it, if we will not seek after signs. If we will live to be worthy, there will attend us a guiding Spirit that will preclude our doing anything in mortality, if we are obedient, that would ultimately interfere with our exaltation and our right to return to the presence of Him who is our Father. (87–01, pp. 109–10)

The Lord expects us to use all our resources first. We are expected to use the light and knowledge we already possess to work out our lives. We should not need a revelation to instruct us to be up and about our duty, for we have been told to do that already in the scriptures; nor should we expect revelation to replace the spiritual or temporal intelligence which we have already received—only to extend it. We must go about our life in an ordinary, workaday way, following the routines and rules and regulations that govern life.

Rules and regulations and commandments are valuable protection. Should we stand in need of revealed instruction to alter our course, it will be waiting along the way as we arrive at the point of need. (82–04, pp. 53–54)

Be obedient to promptings. Be obedient to the promptings you receive. I learned a sobering lesson as a mission president. I was also a General Authority. I had been prompted several times to release one of my counselors. Besides praying about it, I had reasoned that it was the right thing to do. But I did not do it. I feared that it would injure a man who had given long service to the Church.

The Spirit withdrew from me. I could get no promptings on who should be called as a counselor should I release him. It lasted for several weeks. My prayers seemed to be contained within the room where I offered them. I tried a number of alternate ways to arrange the work, but to no avail. Finally, I did as I was bidden to do by the Spirit. Immediately, the gift returned! Oh, the exquisite sweetness to have that gift again. You know it, for you have it, the gift of the Holy Ghost. And the brother was not injured; indeed, he was greatly blessed and immediately thereafter the work prospered. (82–04, p. 55)

We must follow the promptings of the Spirit. We must be sensitive to the Spirit. We must be tuned in, and have the courage and faith to follow the promptings of the Spirit. If we do not listen to the voice of the Spirit, there is not much purpose in the Lord's communicating to us through that channel. (*TYD*, p. 358)

If one ignores promptings, the Spirit will leave. This voice of the Spirit speaks gently, prompting you what to do or what to say, or it may caution or warn you. Ignore or disobey these promptings, and the Spirit will leave you. It is your choice—your agency. (94–05, p. 60)

Follow the inspiration of the still, small voice. When we are confused and at a loss to know which way to go, we can turn first to the local leader of the Church—to our branch president or bishop. As appropriate, he in turn can counsel with the stake president, or the mission president, who if necessary can counsel with the General Authorities, who themselves are in constant counsel with the prophet himself.

As with the Israelites in the wilderness,[16] it is not necessary to have the President of the Church or the other General Authorities hear all of the problems of the people. It is not necessary for the stake president or the mission president to personally judge all of these matters.

Even the bishops or branch presidents do not need to hear all of these matters, although it is true that they will hear more of them than the leaders above them will. The point is that each of us should live in such a way as to be able to follow the inspiration of that still, small voice. We must have the courage to follow these feelings. Such inspiration will always lead us to do right, to be active in the Church. This inspiration will always teach Latter-day Saints to be Latter-day Saints indeed. (74–06, p. 237)

Spiritual vision is necessary when facing problems. When you have a problem, work it out in your own mind first. Ponder on it and analyze it and meditate on it. Read the scriptures. Pray about it. I've come to learn that major decisions can't be forced. You must look ahead and have vision. What was it the prophet said in the Old Testament? "Where there is no vision, the people perish."[17]

Ponder on things a little each day and don't always be in the crisis of making major decisions on the spur of the moment. If you're looking ahead in life, you can see major problems coming down the road toward you from some considerable distance. By the time you meet one another, you are able at the very beginning to take charge of the conversation. Once in a while a major decision will jump out at you from the side of the road and startle the wits out of you, but not very often. If you've already decided that you're going to do what is right and let all of the consequences follow, even those encounters won't hurt you. (75–01, p. 88)

You cannot force spiritual things. You cannot force spiritual things. Such words as compel, coerce, constrain, pressure, and demand do not describe our privileges with the Spirit. You can no more force the Spirit to respond than you can force a bean to sprout, or an egg to hatch before its time. You can create a climate to foster growth, nourish, and protect, but you cannot force or compel: you must await the growth.

Do not be impatient to gain great spiritual knowledge. Let it grow, help it grow, but do not force it or you will open the way to be misled. (82–04, p. 53)

It is hard to listen to the voice of the Spirit if we are doing wicked things. We are told in the Book of Mormon that "angels speak by the power of the Holy Ghost; wherefore, they speak the words of Christ. Wherefore . . . the words of Christ will tell you all things what ye should do."[18]

In order to follow this voice, we must stay worthy. It's hard to listen to this voice if we are in a wicked place. It is hard to listen to this voice if we are doing wicked things. It is hard to listen to this voice if we are listening to wild music, or if we are watching films that are not worthy, or if we are being prompted to do things that are not right. It is hard to listen to this voice if we are partaking of alcohol or using other things that would disturb our bodies.

I repeat, it is a very quiet voice, a still voice. One that we must feel. Young people, you can learn to feel that voice. It can be a companion to you. Then when you have a decision to make, you can receive help. This voice responds to those who are obedient. (78–10)

You cannot make a major mistake without having been warned. I will make a promise to you, and you can test it. I have no hesitancy in making this promise in your young life. As you move forward in life, you cannot make a major mistake, any mistake that will have any lasting consequence in your life, without having been warned and told not to do it. It cannot be done in this Church. It doesn't work that way. You try to do something that is wrong, and the Spirit will say no. Now you may plug your ears—you don't plug your ears, you plug your feelings, and you let your desires or some other thing get hold of you. But you cannot make a mistake that is going to have any consequence without knowing about it. (05–02)

You will be warned of danger. . . . You cannot make a major mistake in your life without being warned. (00–05)

How do I know when I have received revelation? The question I'm most often asked about revelation is, "How do I know when I have received it? I've prayed about it and fasted over this problem and prayed about it and prayed about it, and I still don't quite know what to do. How can I really tell whether I'm being inspired so I won't make a mistake?"

First, do you go to the Lord with a problem and ask Him to make your decision for you? Or do you work, read the revelations, and meditate and pray and then make a decision yourself? Measure the problem against what you know to be right and wrong, and then make the decision. Then ask Him if the decision is right or if it is wrong. Remember what He said to Oliver Cowdery about working it out in your mind.[19] (75–01, p. 89)

The best time to ponder and study is in the early morning hours. I have learned that the best time to wrestle with major problems is early in the morning. Our minds are then fresh and alert. The blackboards of our minds have been erased by a good night's sleep. The accumulated distractions of the day are not in our way. Our bodies have been rested also. That is the time to think something through carefully and to receive personal revelation. For me, it is the best time to prepare lessons for a class I am to teach.

I heard President Harold B. Lee begin many a statement about matters involving revelation with an expression something like this: "In the early hours of the morning, while I was pondering upon that subject . . ." He made it a practice to work in the fresh, alert hours of the early morning on the problems that required revelation.

The Lord knew something when He directed in the Doctrine and Covenants, "Cease to sleep longer than is needful; retire to thy bed early, that ye may not be weary; arise early, that your bodies and your minds may be invigorated."[20] . . . I counsel our children to do their critical studying in the early hours of the morning when they're fresh and alert, rather than to fight physical weariness and mental exhaustion at night. I've learned the power of the dictum, "Early to bed, early to rise." When I'm under pressure, you won't find me burning the midnight oil. I'd much rather be in bed early and getting up in the wee hours of the morning, when I can be close to Him who guides this work. (*TYD,* pp. 243–45)

Spiritually speaking—learn to be alone in a crowd. You have to learn to be alone in a crowd. You have to have such control. That is so important. We spend so much time in airports and in other noisy places. But I do not go there. I might be standing there physically, but I am not there spiritually, because I am thinking things and doing things in my mind. If you will learn to do that, then the Spirit will teach you.

The promise is that when you receive the Holy Ghost, "[It will] teach you all things, and bring all things to your remembrance, whatsoever I have said unto you."[21]

You will be doing some things automatically, almost unwittingly. Without thinking, you will find you have been prompted and guided by the Holy Spirit. (02–02)

Revelation is not confined to the prophet. Revelation is not confined to the prophet. It is shared by the General Authorities. . . . Fathers and mothers also may receive inspiration, revelation . . . to help guide their families. And of course each of us, if we will live for it, may be the recipient of spiritual communications for our own personal guidance. (74–03, p. 93)

Revelation comes in an orderly pattern. The Lord reveals His will through dreams and visions, visitations, through angels, through His own voice, and through the voice of His servants.[22] "Whether by mine own voice," He said, "or by the voice of my servants, it is the same."[23]

The Lord's house is a house of order. The Prophet Joseph Smith taught that "it is contrary to the economy of God for any member of the Church, or any one [else], to receive instruction for those in authority, higher than themselves."[24]

You may receive revelation individually, as a parent for your family, or for those for whom you are responsible as a leader or teacher, having been properly called and set apart. (94–05, p. 61)

We live below our privileges concerning inspiration. One thing I have said more times than a few is that we live far below our privileges. Members of the Church live far below their privileges as far as inspiration is concerned. (98–02)

SPIRITUAL EXPERIENCES

It is not wise to continually talk of unusual spiritual experiences. I have come to believe also that it is not wise to continually talk of unusual spiritual experiences. They are to be guarded with care and shared only when the Spirit itself prompts you to use them to the blessing of others. I am ever mindful of Alma's words:

"It is given unto many to know the mysteries of God; nevertheless they are laid under a strict command that they shall not impart only according to the portion of his word which he doth grant unto the children of men, according to the heed and diligence which they give unto him."[25]

I heard President Marion G. Romney once counsel mission presidents and their wives in Geneva, "I do not tell all I know; I have never told my wife all I know, for I found out that if I talked too lightly of sacred things, thereafter the Lord would not trust me." (82–04, p. 53)

Strong spiritual experiences do not come frequently. I have learned that strong, impressive spiritual experiences do not come to us very frequently. And when they do, they are generally for our own edification, instruction, or correction. Unless we are called by proper authority to do so, they do not position us to counsel or to correct others. (82–04, p. 53)

Personal spiritual experiences should be treated with care. Dreams and visions and visitations are not uncommon in the Church and are a part of all that the Lord has revealed in this dispensation. Thus a worthy Church member may be the recipient of a marvelous spiritual experience. I have come to know that these experiences are personal and are to be kept private. Recipients should ponder them in their heart and not talk lightly about them.[26]

Those personal spiritual experiences do not convey any authority to direct the lives of others unless the recipient is the father or the mother or one who has been properly called and set apart.[27] (93–07, pp. 56–57)

Spiritual experiences should be spoken of with care. We may be prompted on occasion to tell of our spiritual experiences, but generally we should regard them as sacred. It is not out of order, however, to present some experiences from those who have lived in years past.

The fact that sacred spiritual experiences are not discussed widely— for instance, by the General Authorities—should not be taken as an indication that the Saints do not receive them. Such spiritual gifts are with the Church today as they were in years past.

Experiences which involve dreams or visions or visitations might be recorded and put away in family records to serve as a testimony and an inspiration to our descendants in the generations ahead. (*THT,* p. 243)

Use caution when sharing spiritual experiences. I made a rule for myself a number of years ago with reference to this subject. When

Speaking at the October 1968 general conference

someone relates a spiritual experience to me, personally or in a small, intimate group, I make it a rigid rule not to talk about it thereafter. I assume that it was told to me in a moment of trust and confidence, and therefore I never talk about it. If, however, on some future occasion I hear that individual talk about it in public in a large gathering, or where a number of people are present, then I know that it has been stated publicly and I can feel free under the right circumstances to relate it. But I know many, many sacred and important things that have been related to me by others that I will not discuss unless I am privileged to do so under the rule stated above. (*TYD*, p. 326)

There are some questions too sacred to discuss. There are some questions that we could not in propriety ask.

One question of this type I am asked occasionally, usually by someone who is curious, is, "Have you seen Him?" That is a question that I have never asked of another. I have not asked that question of my Brethren in the Council of the Twelve, thinking that it would be so sacred and so personal that one would have to have some special inspiration—indeed, some authorization—even to ask it.

Though I have not asked that question of others, I have heard them answer it—but *not* when they were asked. I have heard one of my Brethren declare, "I know, from experiences too sacred to relate, that Jesus is the Christ." I have heard another testify, "I know that God lives, I know that the Lord lives, and more than that, I know the Lord." I repeat: they have answered this question not when they were asked, but under the prompting of the Spirit, on sacred occasions, when "the Spirit beareth record."[28]

There are some things just too sacred to discuss: not secret, but sacred; not to be discussed, but to be harbored and protected and regarded with the deepest of reverence. (*TYD*, pp. 86–87)

CONTINUING REVELATION

The Church moves forward with constant revelation. This Church couldn't move forward one day without a constancy of revelation, not just to the President of the Church or to the Twelve, but to the membership of the Church across the world. (97–01)

Changes in organization or procedures are a testimony that revelation is ongoing. While doctrines remain fixed, the methods or procedures do not. (89–04, p. 15)

Revelation continues in the Church. Revelation continues in the Church: the prophet receiving it for the Church; the president for his stake, his mission, or his quorum; the bishop for his ward; the father for his family; the individual for himself.

Many revelations have been received and are found in evidence in the on-rolling work of the Lord. Perhaps one day other revelations which have been received and recorded will be published; and we stand in expectation that "He will yet reveal many great and important things pertaining to the Kingdom of God."[29] (74–03, p. 95)

Revelation is a continuous principle in the Church. In one sense the Church is still being organized. As light and knowledge are given, as prophecies are fulfilled and more intelligence is received, another step forward can be taken. (_THT,_ p. 137)

Revelation has not ceased. The very beginning of this Church was initiated by the veil parting and visitations from beyond the veil. That has not ceased. That process, if anything, has been intensified in our generation, and I bear witness to that. (99–08)

We live in a period of intense revelation. When I was a young seminary teacher, I thought, "I missed the days of the great revelation in the Church when the Prophet Joseph Smith and those who followed him were receptive to constant revelation and instruction from the Almighty."

In due time (and it takes time), I came to realize that we now live in a more intense period of revelation than it was then. The Lord is close to us and is revealing Himself to us as the great work of the Restoration moves forward. (07–07)

Not all revelation is printed in the scriptures. There are revelations which are not printed in the scriptures, nor in the handbooks. They are found in the Church. You might call them our tradition, but they are more than that, they are revelation. You find them in sentences and paragraphs scattered here and there in books and sermons of the Brethren.

The best source for these truths is found when we will listen to some who were there, who participated and watched and became students of the past like Brother Lee, Brother Kimball, Brother Romney, who are gone. . . . Men whose minds and experiences stretch back to the past. (92–01)

Revelation in the Church comes through proper channels. The Lord has set up some precise channels in the Church, and He invariably extends inspiration through these channels. However, we are often guilty of an "end run" to someone in higher authority than those who are immediately available. While we do not always follow the proper channels of authority and while we sometimes preempt responsibility that belongs to the parent or to a bishop, the Lord invariably stays in channel. He will not yield revelation and inspiration to us when we are out of those channels. (*TYD,* pp. 229–30)

Revelation in the Church is vertical. Revelation in the Church is vertical. It generally confines itself to the administrative or geographic boundaries or limitations assigned to the one who is called. For instance, a bishop who is trying to solve a problem will not get revelation from a bishop in another ward or stake to whom he is related or with whom he might work at the office.

My experience has taught me that revelation comes from above, not from the side. However more experienced or older or however more spiritual someone to the side may appear to be, it is better to go up through proper channels. (96–07)

Revelation is the essence of priesthood government. An ordinary young elders quorum president knows what revelation is and how to receive it. An ordinary young man knows how to approach the Lord through the veil and get revealed instruction.

That is the essence, the very essence, of priesthood government. That is a principle of the gospel. It is a law of God that He will reveal His will to His servants. Not just to the prophets and Apostles, but to His servants across the world. It is a precious principle that must be guarded and nurtured, but when we are overprogrammed it sometimes gets smothered. (84–03, p. 68)

The language of the Spirit. Several years ago I was assigned to come to Germany to take care of some important Church business. As I looked forward to that assignment, I worried a great deal. I knew there would be some very important interviews and that I do not speak German. I knew that most of those with whom I would conduct the Church business did not speak English. I felt helpless. After taking care of some work in England for about two weeks, I was finally on the plane to Germany. As I sat there pondering and praying, the voice of the Lord came into my mind and gave me some instructions. You know the Lord does not speak in either English or German and that He can speak pure intelligence into our minds without passage of time. The message was something like this: "What are you worried about? There is another language, the language of the Spirit. Those brethren will know that language. You know that language. There will be no problem." I was greatly comforted, and I had a great experience on that occasion.

I witness that there is that universal language, the language of the Spirit; since then I have never been very anxious when I have had to go into other countries. Sometimes we will visit among people of seven or eight languages on one trip, but always there is that language of the Spirit. (76–09, p. 79)

PATRIARCHAL BLESSINGS

Patriarchal blessings are blessings from the Lord. A number of years ago, I ordained a patriarch in a distant stake. Three months later he came to my office and told this experience.

After he was ordained, he was overwhelmed. He brooded over the awesome responsibility of giving blessings which must include a declaration of lineage and prophetic insights personal to each individual. He was weighed down with a feeling of inadequacy and could not get himself to attempt to give his first patriarchal blessing.

The stake president would ask if he was ready to give the blessings. Each time he would say he did not feel up to the great responsibility. Finally he realized that he must prepare himself. He talked to a revered Church leader in the community and asked, "Could I write out two or three brief paragraphs that could be an appropriate introduction to any patriarchal blessing? I could memorize these paragraphs as a beginning with the expectation that the Spirit would then provide the inspiration that I needed."

It was agreed that it would be all right. So he prepared a short introduction. He wrote and rewrote the paragraphs until he was satisfied that it was worthy of an introduction to a patriarchal blessing. Then he informed the stake president he was ready.

Soon the first young person came with his recommend to receive a blessing. Confident that his memorized introduction would get him started, he placed his hands on the young person's head and did not use a word of it!

"That day," he said, "I found out whose blessings they are. They are not my blessings; they are the blessings of the Lord, and He will, through His Spirit, dictate what should be said." Thereafter he never lost confidence in either his own ability or that the Spirit would be there to give him words. (05–01)

A patriarchal blessing comes by revelation. President Harold B. Lee told of calling a patriarch. . . . After the morning session of conference, where the man had borne a remarkable testimony, they went to a basement office.

The stake president's wife was present and wrote to President Lee:

> As you walked over to put your hands on [his] head, I thought to myself, he is a man with whom we socialize. We have gone on trips with him, to dances. . . . Now part of his

responsibility is to declare the lineage from which each one has come in these blessings. He hasn't been a student of ancient languages—how is he going to know?

. . . You walked over and put your hands on his head, and a light came from behind you and went right through you and into him. And I thought to myself, Isn't that a strange coincidence that the sunlight has come in just at that moment. And then I realized that there was [no window,] no sunlight. I was witnessing the answer to my question. . . . That light came from somewhere beyond Brother Lee and went through Brother Lee into this patriarch. Then I knew where he was going to get that information—by the revelations of Almighty God.[30]

And so it must be. Whenever a patriarch is ordained or pronounces a blessing, that same light, though it may be unseen, is present. It empowers a patriarch to declare lineage and to give a prophetic blessing, notwithstanding that he himself may be a man of very ordinary capacity.

Do not let the office of stake patriarch be neglected or ignored. It is essential to the spiritual power of a stake. (02–09, p. 45)

Counsel on seeking patriarchal blessings. Patriarchs do not advertise for blessings. Members should seek blessings as they feel inspired to do so. There is no fixed age at which one may receive a patriarchal blessing. The bishop ensures that the member is of sufficient age and maturity to understand the meaning and significance of the blessing. (02–09, p. 43)

Patriarchal blessings should be kept personal. Except for members of the immediate family, we should not permit others to read our blessing nor should we ask others to interpret it. Neither the patriarch nor the bishop can or should interpret it. (02–09, p. 43)

Strength can come by re-reading our blessings. The patriarch, who had never seen me before, made a promise that applies to every one of us. He told me to "face toward the sunlight of truth so that the shadow of error, disbelief, doubt and discouragement shall be cast behind you."[31] Many times I have gained strength from reading that patriarchal blessing given by an inspired servant of the Lord. (02–09, p. 45)

Patriarchal blessings apply beyond the veil. Sometimes someone will worry because a promise made in a patriarchal blessing is not yet fulfilled. For instance, a blessing may indicate that a member will be married, and they do not find a companion. That does not mean that the blessing will go unfulfilled. It is well to know that things happen in the Lord's due time, not always in ours. Things of an eternal nature have no boundaries. From the premortal existence to our existence beyond the veils of death, our life is an eternal life. (02–09, p. 45)

The work of the patriarch. The work of the patriarch draws near to the very central purpose of the Lord's work. It is in performing his duties that a patriarch will learn the language of the Spirit. It is a humbling and marvelous privilege and a great responsibility to be ordained a patriarch.

There is a respect accorded to the patriarch. He knows the gospel, he knows the scriptures, and he lives in harmony with the Spirit. In all of his own personal affairs, he is above reproach. His duties are completely spiritual. He is called to give blessings. He has no administrative responsibilities. He is not responsible to counsel the people. He is to give blessings. (05–01)

The calling of a patriarch. The calling of a patriarch is the calling of revelation. The patriarch in a sense is a prophet to give blessings which really in effect are a prophecy for each individual. (95–11)

Counsel to patriarchs. Speaking to the patriarchs, you have been chosen as few other men are chosen. You must live in such a way that through spiritual inspiration, you can give prophetic and inspired blessings. Be an exemplary patriarch in your own family. Live to be worthy of the Spirit. And experience the joy of your calling. (02–09, p. 45)

There are three kinds of patriarchs. The scriptures speak of three kinds of patriarchs: fathers of families[32]; the prophet leaders of ancient times; and the stake patriarch, an ordained office in the Melchizedek Priesthood.[33]

The father is a patriarch to his family and can and should give father's blessings to his children. (02–09, p. 42)

DISCERNING FALSE REVELATION

There are two sources of revelation. There are two sources of revelation—the one consistent with the great plan of happiness, the other growing from the "cunning plan of the evil one."[34] So that we will not be deceived, there is order in the Church and there are established channels through which revelation is given to the Church and to us, its members, as individuals. (93–07, p. 54)

No message is repeated more times in scripture than the simple thought: "Ask, and ye shall receive."[35]

I often ask the Lord for direction from Him. I will not, however, willingly accept promptings from any unworthy source. I refuse them. I do not want them, and I say so. (79–10, p. 21)

Inspiration versus Sinspiration: the choice is yours. You are the focus of two conflicting patterns trying to influence you in your life, trying to have you go this way or that way.[36] You are the one who makes the decision.

As the old man a generation ago said, "The Lord's votin' for me, and the devil's votin' against me, but it's *my* vote that counts!" And that is good, solid doctrine.

You will have just what you want. On one hand, you have inspiration from the Holy Ghost, and, on the other hand, you have what President Ezra Taft Benson called "sinspiration" from the angels of the devil. They are with you all of the time. (03–04, p. 171)

Revelation comes in an orderly way in the Church. Revelation comes in an orderly way in the Church. We are entitled to personal revelation. However, unless we are set apart to some presiding office, we will not receive revelations concerning what others should do.

Revelation in the Church comes to those who have been properly called, sustained, ordained, or set apart. A bishop, for instance, will not receive any revelation concerning a neighboring ward, because that is out of his jurisdiction. (89–04, pp. 14–15)

You will not receive revelation for anyone else's jurisdiction. Now, if you start receiving revelations for anyone else's jurisdiction, you know immediately that you're out of order, that they come from the wrong source. You will not receive revelation to counsel your bishop or to correct the leaders of the Church. (75–01, p. 89)

An unusual spiritual experience is not a call to direct others. An unusual spiritual experience should not be regarded as a personal call to direct others. It is my conviction that experiences of a special, sacred nature are individual and should be kept to oneself.

Few things disturb the channels of revelation quite so effectively as those people who are misled and think themselves to be chosen to instruct others when they are not chosen. (89–04, p. 15)

There can be counterfeit revelation. All inspiration does not come from God.[37] The evil one has the power to tap into those channels of revelation and send conflicting signals which can mislead and confuse us. There are promptings from evil sources which are so carefully counterfeited as to deceive even the very elect.[38]

Nevertheless, we can learn to discern these spirits. Even with every member having the right to revelation, the Church can be maintained as a house of order. (89–04, p. 14)

Be ever on guard lest you be deceived by inspiration from an unworthy source. You can be given false spiritual messages. There are counterfeit spirits, just as there are counterfeit angels.[39] Be careful lest you be deceived, for the devil may come disguised as an angel of light.

The spiritual part of us and the emotional part of us are so closely linked that it is possible to mistake an emotional impulse for something spiritual. We occasionally find people who receive what they assume to be spiritual promptings from God, when those promptings are either centered in the emotions or are from the adversary. (82–04, pp. 55–56)

We can be given false spiritual messages. How are we protected? By obedience. By following the true servants of the Lord. By standing firm in His Church. (82–05)

Avoid counterfeit revelations. "There are many spirits which are false spirits."[40] There can be counterfeit revelations, promptings from the devil, temptations! As long as you live, in one way or another the adversary will try to lead you astray. "For after this manner doth the devil work, for he persuadeth no man to do good, no, not one; neither do his angels; neither do they who subject themselves unto him."[41] The Prophet Joseph Smith said that "nothing is a greater injury to the children of men than to be under the influence of a false spirit when they think they have the Spirit of God."[42] The seventh chapter of Moroni in the Book of Mormon tells you how to test spiritual promptings. Read it carefully—over and over. By trial, and some error, you will learn to heed these promptings. If ever you receive a prompting to do something that makes you *feel* uneasy, something you know in your *mind* to be wrong and contrary to the principles of righteousness, do not respond to it! (94–05, p. 61)

There are potentially destructive effects of false revelation. Occasionally we will find someone who claims to receive spiritual revelations. One of the evidences of false revelation that you had better be careful of is that individuals begin to include others as though they are receiving spiritual instruction for them. They seem to think somehow that the inspiration they receive supersedes that which the bishops or stake presidents might receive and comes from some higher source than these brethren are privileged to have.

Some are deceived, and endless mischief occurs and sorrow results. The destructive result of these who are misled is twofold. One of the problems is that thereafter many become afraid, themselves thinking that they might be misled or go too far. And then they hold back and submerge the spiritual part of their lives. Then, for fear of going too far, they avoid the very spiritual feelings that can lead them and make them worthy to receive these gifts. (87–01, p. 103)

Beware of false promptings that "quench" the Spirit. The spiritual communications from the Holy Ghost can be interrupted by the promptings and influence of the evil one. You will learn to recognize that.

To further our understanding of this principle, Nephi taught: "If ye would hearken unto the Spirit which teacheth a man to pray ye would know that ye must pray; for the evil spirit teacheth not a man to pray, but teacheth him that he must not pray. But behold, I say unto you that ye must pray."[43]

So when we speak of angels communicating by the power of the Holy Ghost and we are told by the prophets that we can speak with the tongue of angels, then we must know that there is an opposing influence. We must be able to detect it.

There is one word in the book of Jacob that should alert us: "Behold, will ye reject these words? Will ye reject the words of the prophets; and will ye reject all the words which have been spoken concerning Christ, after so many have spoken concerning him; and deny the good word of Christ, and the power of God, and the gift of the Holy Ghost, and *quench* the Holy Spirit, and make a mock of the great plan of redemption?"[44]

So the Spirit can be quenched! (03–08, p. 51)

One can learn to recognize counterfeit signals. You should know also that, in addition to static and interference which jam the circuits, there are counterfeit signals.

Some have received revelations and heard voices that are put there deliberately by wicked sources to lead astray. You can learn to recognize those and tune them out, if you will.

Now, how do you tell the difference? How can you know if a prompting is an inspiration or a temptation?

My answer to that must surely expose my great confidence in young people. I believe young people, when properly taught, are basically sensible.

In the Church we are not exempt from common sense. You can know to begin with that you won't be prompted from any righteous source to steal, to lie, to cheat, to join anyone in any kind of moral transgression.

You have a conscience even as a little boy and girl. It will prompt you to know the things that are wrong. Don't smother it. . . .

Read . . . Moroni, chapter 7. . . . It tells of a way to judge such things. If ever you are confused and feel that you are being misled, go for counsel to your parents, and to your leaders. (79–10, pp. 20–21)

Avoid chattering about evil spirits. Spiritual gifts carry great responsibility and we are not to talk about them lightly. I see no purpose, for instance, of chattering endlessly about evil spirits. Missionaries somehow are wont to do that. And returned missionaries are not exempt from that. There is no purpose in that. I would not do it. And I wouldn't stay where it is done. Do not sit around and talk about the so-called experiences of those who have confronted evil spirits. (87–01, p. 108)

CHAPTER 7

The Scriptures

"I love the revelations. I love the scriptures.
They are always new." (01–01)

The scriptures must be the things of our soul. Responsibility for the Book of Mormon, as well as for the Doctrine and Covenants, the Pearl of Great Price, and the other revelations, rests upon the prophets and Apostles today. They must be the things of *our* soul. We must convey them to the coming generation. In this we have no accountability but to Him who is our Master, whose church this is, and whose servants we are. (86–04, p. 285)

The scriptures contain the answers to the difficult questions. Teach [your students] from the revealed word—the Bible, the Book of Mormon, the Doctrine and Covenants, and the Pearl of Great Price. Teach them! If you can induce in them a love for the scriptures, therein they can find the answers to the difficult questions. . . . Teach them that when their faith wanes and they need more knowledge, they should seek in the revealed word of the Lord. (68–05, pp. 150–51)

The scriptures can provide us with positive optimism. The Apostle Paul prophesied that in our day, these last days, men would be "disobedient to parents, . . . without natural affection, . . . despisers of those that are good, . . . lovers of pleasures more than lovers of God."[1] And he warned: "Evil men and seducers shall wax worse and worse, deceiving, and being deceived."[2] He was right. Nevertheless, when I think of the future, I am overwhelmed with a feeling of positive optimism.

Paul told young Timothy to continue in the things he had learned from the Apostles and said he would be safe because "from a child thou hast known the holy scriptures, which are able to make thee wise unto salvation through faith which is in Christ Jesus."[3]

A knowledge of the scriptures is important. From them we learn about spiritual guidance. (05–08, p. 70)

The inspiration from the scriptures will keep us safe on Zion's hill. There is in the Church a central core of power deeper than programs or meetings or associations. It does not change. It cannot erode. It is constant and certain. It never recedes or fades. While the Church is housed in chapels, it lives in the heart and soul of every Latter-day Saint. Everywhere in the world, humble members draw inspiration from the scriptures to guide them through life, not fully understanding that they have found that "pearl of great price"[4] about which the Lord spoke to His disciples. When Emma Smith, wife of the Prophet Joseph, collected hymns for the first hymnbook, she included "Guide Us, O Thou Great Jehovah," which is, in fact, a prayer:

> *When the earth begins to tremble,*
> *Bid our fearful thoughts be still;*
> *When thy judgments spread destruction,*
> *Keep us safe on Zion's hill.*[5]

Every soul who willingly affiliates with The Church of Jesus Christ of Latter-day Saints and seeks to abide by its principles and ordinances is standing "on Zion's hill." (05–08, p. 73)

SCRIPTURE STUDY

The importance of the scriptures. I have the conviction that in the generations ahead the publication of the new editions of the standard works [1979–80], with all of the resource helps they now contain, will emerge as one of the most important events in the Church that we shall witness in our lifetime on the earth.

With the passing of years, the scriptures will produce successive generations of faithful Latter-day Saints who know the Lord Jesus Christ and are willing to obey His will.

Nothing compares with the scriptures—no book written by scholars, no course of study. Even books written by the leaders of the Church do not carry the same authority as do the scriptures. (85–05, p. 49)

Read the scriptures and inspiration will come. Read the scriptures. I know that the matter of reading the scriptures and doing it in a systematic way becomes very difficult in our busy lives, but if you will read them continually and get the feel for them, you will have the Spirit. Which scripture? It doesn't matter. Just find yourself in the scriptures—the revelations—reading. And begin asking for the Holy Ghost to inspire you and guide you. (00–01)

Most answers to questions will come through scripture study. Naturally, when studying the gospel, many questions arise. There isn't time for the General Authorities to answer all the gospel questions for every individual member of the Church. It is not advisable for us even to try to do so. The Lord said in the preface of the Doctrine and Covenants that it was His purpose to have "every man . . . speak in the name of God the Lord, even the Savior of the world."[6]

We are counseled to find the answers for ourselves. Most of our answers will come through reading the four standard works from beginning to end. You should do that—read each of the four books of scripture from beginning to end more than once. You could hardly use your time to more advantage. (88–01)

Deep spiritual impressions come as we read the scriptures. We spoke of the scriptures as a library. I hope you have been convinced that this library is open to you now. You can enter therein. Alone in that library, in quiet individual study and prayer, you may receive the kind of revelation that is available to you, so that you too can be an instrument in the hands of God in bringing about His mighty work.

Deep spiritual impressions come to us as we read the scriptures. Those impressions come long before we have read them all. The reading of the scriptures, whether from beginning to end, or following a subject from book to book, brings a tempering, soothing feeling to us, even in the midst of the turmoil of life.

There comes the realization that all of the scriptures teach the same message. They all testify of Christ, from the early pages of the Old Testament to the recent revelation added to the Doctrine and Covenants. (85–05, p. 53)

True spiritual nourishment comes from the scriptures. Buildings, budgets, reports, programs, and procedures are very important. But, by themselves, they do not carry that essential spiritual nourishment and will not accomplish what the Lord has given us to do. . . . The right things, those with true spiritual nourishment, are centered in the scriptures. (82–02)

The scriptures should be likened unto us personally. When I understood that the Holy Ghost could communicate through our feelings, I understood why the words of Christ, whether from the New Testament or the Book of Mormon or the other scriptures, carried such a good feeling. In time, I found that the scriptures had answers to things I needed to know.

I read, "Now these are the words, and ye may liken them unto you and unto *all* men."[7] I took that to mean that the scriptures are likened to me personally, and that is true of everyone else.

When a verse I had passed over several times took on personal meaning, I thought whoever wrote that verse had a deep and mature understanding of my life and how I felt. (05–03, p. 7)

I love the scriptures. I love the revelations. I love the scriptures. They are always new. You would think now that after all these years in the leadership of the Church being dependent upon the scriptures, there would come a time when one would grow weary of them. Oh, no! They are so fresh and so wonderful and so powerful. What a privilege it is to go back to them when challenges arise. Challenges will come to all of us, because that is what life is about. (01–01)

God is inspiring the creation of ways to further His work. Never before have Church members had such excellent tools for studying and understanding the scriptures. Family home evenings, talks in Church, seminary and Sunday lessons, and missionary work can provide exceptional benefit. The doctrines taught will be purer and surer. Gospel perspective will grow. Testimonies will increase. There will be greater devotion and dedication to the Lord.

We are blessed to be living in such an exciting gospel dispensation. God is inspiring the minds of great people who create inventions that further the work of the Lord in ways this world has never known. (88–01)

Our knowledge of the scriptures should be ever growing. The Lord Himself, when confronted by Perdition himself, protected Himself and deflected that temptation by simply quoting scripture.

We do not ask that everyone in the Church be a scriptorian, but all of us should have a constant and continuous knowledge of the scriptures and the revelations. It should be ever-growing. (00–01)

There is great purpose in the way the scriptures are arranged. Individual doctrines of the gospel are not fully explained in one place in the scriptures, nor presented in order or sequence. They must be assembled from pieces here and there. They are sometimes found in large segments, but mostly it is in small bits scattered through the chapters and verses.

You might think that if all the references on baptism, for instance, were assembled in one chapter of each standard work, and all references on revelation in another, it would make the learning of the gospel much simpler. I have come to be very, very grateful that scriptures are arranged as they are. Because the scriptures are arranged the way they are, there are endless combinations of truths which will fit the need of every individual in every circumstance. (93–05)

The scriptures provide the basis for correct doctrine. Do you understand that we emphasize the teaching of the scriptures because they are the constant? From them we learn the purposes of life, the gifts of the Spirit. From them we learn about personal revelation, how to discern good from evil, truth from error. The scriptures provide the pattern and the basis for correct doctrine. (94–01, p. 20)

Avoid making decisions based solely on obscure passages of scripture. Sometimes someone will bring in a scriptural phrase and will make a major decision on the basis of some idea they found in a sentence in the revelations. I have to temper them a little with this idea: if something is essential to us, if it's a part of our plan of salvation, the Lord isn't going to hide it in some obscure phrase or verse of the scripture. It will be repeated over and over again in the revelations. (91–03)

A precise formula for knowing the scriptures are true. As surely as a person may determine whether a purported diamond is genuine by subjecting it to well-known tests for diamonds, the scriptures may be subjected to well-known tests for scriptures.

There is a very precise formula. To apply it, one must of necessity move from criticism to spiritual inquiry. . . . It is when many years are quietly committed to the search with sincerity and humility that one can know for sure. Many elements of truth come only after a lifetime of preparation.

A testimony of them, however, can come very quickly. We should not belittle the possibility that many humble folk, both young and old, possess such a testimony. Many possess a testimony that transcends the knowledge to be gained in academic and scientific fields. (74–03, pp. 14–15)

The importance of underlining scriptures. There are a number of plans for underlining scriptures. They vary somewhat and should suit the individual. The important thing is to underline them and make marginal notes of some kind so you can find them again. (*TYD,* pp. 196–97)

BOOK OF MORMON AND LATTER-DAY SCRIPTURE

The central message of the Book of Mormon is that Jesus is the Christ. To present the Book of Mormon properly to others, members and missionaries must know that the message of the book is a testimony to the world that Jesus is the Christ. That message recurs through the pages like a golden thread. Indeed, the Book of Mormon is another testament of Jesus Christ. (86–04, pp. 277–78)

After the people of Lehi had arrived in the Western Hemisphere, Lehi had a vision of the tree of life. His son Nephi prayed to know its meaning. In answer, he was given a remarkable vision of Christ. . . . That vision is the central message of the Book of Mormon. The Book of Mormon is in truth another testament of Jesus Christ. (86–02, pp. 60–61)

Mormon was influenced by Nephi's prophecies of Christ. I have the conviction that Mormon's reading of the small plates of Nephi greatly influenced what he chose from the large plates to include in the rest of his abridgment; for while we have some history of the people, we have much "preaching which [is] sacred, [and] revelation which [is] great, [and] prophesying."[8]

Being able to choose but a hundredth part, Mormon chose the better part. He was, however, not able to resist putting in a generous amount of military science and tactics—for he was a general. This unusual human insight is also a testimony!

Mormon was drawn to the prophecies concerning the coming of Christ. The inspiration that came to him as he abridged the records resulted in his work being, indeed, another testament of Jesus Christ. (86–04, p. 276)

The Book of Mormon is an endless treasure of wisdom and inspiration. The Book of Mormon is an endless treasure of wisdom and inspiration, of counsel and correction, "adapted to the capacity of the weak and the weakest [among us]."[9] At once, it is rich in nourishment for the most learned, if they will humble themselves.[10]

From the Book of Mormon we learn about:

The plan of salvation or "the great plan of happiness."[11]
The doctrine of Christ and the Atonement.[12]
Why death is necessary.[13]
Life after death in the spirit world.[14]
The workings of the evil one.[15]
The order of the priesthood.[16]
Sacramental prayers.[17]
A sure way to judge between good and evil.[18]
How to retain a remission of your sins.[19]

Clear, prophetic warnings and many, many other things pertaining to the redemption of man and to our lives. All are parts of the fulness of the gospel.[20]

The Book of Mormon confirms the teachings of the Old Testament. It confirms the teachings of the New Testament. It restores "many plain and precious things"[21] lost or taken from them.[22] It is in truth another testament of Jesus Christ. (05–03, p. 9)

Anyone can read the Book of Mormon and receive inspirational insights. I read that the prophet Lehi partook of the fruit of the tree of life and said, "Wherefore, I began to be desirous that my family should partake of it also; for I knew that it was desirable above all other fruit."[23] I had read that more than once. It did not mean much to me.

The prophet Nephi also said that he had written "the things of my soul . . . for the learning and the profit of my children."[24] I had read that before, and it did not mean all that much to me, either. But later when we had children, I understood that both Lehi and Nephi felt just as deeply about their children as we feel about our children and grandchildren.

I found these scriptures to be plain and precious. I wondered how young Joseph Smith could have such insights. The fact is I do not believe he had such penetrating insights. He did not have to have them. He just translated what was written on the plates.

Such plain and precious insights are everywhere in the Book of Mormon. They reflect a depth of wisdom and experience that is certainly not characteristic of a twenty-three-year-old.

I learned that anyone, anywhere, could read in the Book of Mormon and receive inspiration. (05–03, p. 7)

Use the Book of Mormon to help you through life's difficulties. As you are in trouble, read the Book of Mormon. As you are facing great events in your life, read the Book of Mormon. As you are trying to find your way through the difficulties of life and make decisions, read the Book of Mormon, and you will find it to be a great power. (08–07)

A most usable lesson from the Book of Mormon. Perhaps the most usable, everyday lesson that came to me over the years from the Book of Mormon is the instruction on the Spirit, that the Spirit of Christ is born in us, that the gift of the Holy Ghost is conferred upon us at the time of our confirmation, and that the Spirit is there to guide us. (08–07)

The Book of Mormon can heal starving spirits. Amos prophesied of "a famine in the land, not a famine of bread, nor a thirst for water, but of hearing the words of the Lord."[25]

In a world ever more dangerous . . . , the Book of Mormon: Another Testament of Jesus Christ has the nourishing power to heal starving spirits of the world. (01–05, p. 64)

Use the Book of Mormon when you are feeling weak or discouraged. Life moves all too fast. When you feel weak, discouraged, depressed, or afraid, open the Book of Mormon and read. Do not let too much time pass before reading a verse, a thought, or a chapter. (05–03, p. 8)

The Book of Mormon is the most rewarding book one can read. Except for the Bible, the Book of Mormon is different from any book you have read. It is not a novel. It is not fiction. For the most part, it is not difficult to read. However, like all books of profound value, it is not casual reading. But if you persist, I assure you that it will be the most rewarding book you have ever read. (86–02, p. 59)

I love the Book of Mormon. I love the Book of Mormon. It is a part of my being. Over the years, as I have grown from a young man to what I call "upper middle age," I find in the Book of Mormon an ever new and refreshing fountain of information and blessings. If you were to ask me what parts of the Book of Mormon were my favorite or what parts impressed me most, I can answer that very quickly: All of it. (08–07)

How one can come to know the Book of Mormon is true. Near the end of the book, you will find a promise addressed to you and to everyone who will read the book with intent and sincerity. Let me read that promise to you, from the last chapter in the Book of Mormon:

"And when ye shall receive these things, I would exhort you that ye would ask God, the Eternal Father, in the name of Christ, if these things are not true; and if ye shall ask with a sincere heart, with real intent, having faith in Christ, he will manifest the truth of it unto you, by the power of the Holy Ghost.

"And by the power of the Holy Ghost ye may know the truth of all things."26

No missionary, no member can fulfill that promise—neither Apostle nor president can fulfill that promise. It is a promise of direct revelation to you on the conditions described in the book. After you have read the Book of Mormon, you become qualified to inquire of the Lord, in the way that He prescribes in the book, as to whether the book is true. You will be eligible, on the conditions He has established, to receive that personal revelation. (86–02, p. 61)

***The Book of Mormon will verify and help one understand the
Bible.*** The Book of Mormon is a book of scripture. It is another testament of Jesus Christ. It is written in biblical language, the language of
the prophets.

For the most part, it is in easy-flowing New Testament language,
with such words as *spake* for *spoke, unto* for *to,* with and *it came to pass,*
with *thus* and *thou* and *thine.*

You will not read many pages into it until you catch the cadence of
that language and the narrative will be easy to understand. As a matter
of fact, most teenagers readily understand the narrative of the Book of
Mormon.

Then, just as you settle in to move comfortably along, you will
meet a barrier. The style of the language changes to Old Testament
prophecy style. For interspersed in the narrative are chapters reciting the
prophecies of the Old Testament prophet Isaiah. They loom as a barrier, like a roadblock or a checkpoint beyond which the casual reader,
one with idle curiosity, generally will not go.

You, too, may be tempted to stop there, but do not do it! Do not
stop reading! Move forward through those difficult-to-understand chapters of Old Testament prophecy, even if you understand very little of it.
Move on, if all you do is skim and merely glean an impression here and
there. Move on, if all you do is look at the words.

Soon you will emerge from those difficult chapters to the easier
New Testament style which is characteristic of the rest of the Book of
Mormon.

Because you are forewarned about that barrier, you will be able to
surmount it and finish reading the book.

You will follow the prophecies of the coming of the Messiah
through the generations of Nephite people to that day when those
prophecies are fulfilled and the Lord appears to them.

You will be present, through eyewitness accounts, at the ministry
of the Lord among the "other sheep" of whom he spoke in the New
Testament.[27]

Thereafter, you will be able to understand the Bible as never before.
You will come to understand much in the Old Testament and to know

why we, as a people, hold it in such esteem. You will come to revere the New Testament, to know that it is true. The account of the birth and the life and the death of the man Jesus as recorded in the New Testament is true. He is the Christ, the Only Begotten Son of God, the Messiah, the Redeemer of mankind.

The Book of Mormon, another testament of Jesus Christ, will verify the Old and the New Testaments. (86–02, p. 61)

Joseph Smith, with divine inspiration, translated and published the Book of Mormon: Another Testament of Jesus Christ.

The Book of Mormon verifies the Old Testament as a rich source of information, prophecy, and writings on the priesthood by the ancient prophets.

The Book of Mormon confirms the New Testament account of the life and ministry of Jesus Christ and His Apostles. (03–01)

The scriptures present a powerful affirmation that we are Christians. Some of them say that we have lost our way, that we are not Christians. Should they turn to that one thing in which they show the least interest and in which they have the least knowledge, the scriptures and the revelations, they would find in the Topical Guide fifty-eight categories of information about Jesus Christ; eighteen pages of small print, single-spaced, list literally thousands of scriptural references on the subject.

These references from the four volumes of scripture constitute the most comprehensive compilation of scriptural information on the mission and teachings of the Lord Jesus Christ that has ever been assembled in the history of the world.

The work affirms an acceptance of, a reverence for, and a testimony of the Lord Jesus Christ. Follow those references and you will open the door to whose church this is, what it teaches and by whose authority— all anchored to the sacred name of Jesus Christ, the Son of God, the Messiah, the Redeemer, our Lord. (82–06, p. 53)

The scriptures came through Joseph Smith. The scriptures did not come so much from Joseph Smith as they did through him. He was a conduit through which the revelations were given. He was otherwise an ordinary man, as were the prophets in ancient times and as are the prophets in our day. (74–03, p. 13)

The prophetic impact of the LDS edition of the scriptures. The stick or record of Judah—the Old Testament and the New Testament—and the stick or record of Ephraim—the Book of Mormon, which is another testament of Jesus Christ—are now woven together in such a way that as you pore over one you are drawn to the other; as you learn from one you are enlightened by the other. They are indeed one in our hands. Ezekiel's prophecy now stands fulfilled.

With the passing of years, these scriptures will produce successive generations of faithful Christians who know the Lord Jesus Christ and are disposed to obey His will.

The older generation has been raised without them, but there is another generation growing up. The revelations will be opened to them as to no other in the history of the world. Into their hands now are placed the sticks of Joseph and of Judah. They will develop a gospel scholarship beyond that which their forebears could achieve. They will have the testimony that Jesus is the Christ and be competent to proclaim Him and to defend Him.

Without the inspired help of hundreds of dedicated workers it would have been impossible! Among them were scholars in Hebrew, Greek, Latin, Old and New Testament studies. More than this, they are worthy men and women in whose lives the gospel of Jesus Christ is the dominating influence. Their work, if they only knew it, may well be their greatest contribution in mortality.

As the generations roll on, this will be regarded, in the perspective of history, as one of the crowning achievements in the administration of President Spencer W. Kimball. (82–06, p. 53)

This work [the new edition of the scriptures] will one day emerge as a signal inspired event of our generation. Because of it, we shall raise up generations of Latter-day Saints who will know the gospel and know the Lord. (85–10, p. 262)

The plan of happiness is not apparent in the Bible. The plan of happiness is not apparent in the Bible. Only after one studies the Book of Mormon, particularly, the Doctrine and Covenants, and the Pearl of Great Price, and then revisits the Bible, does one see elements of the plan scattered through it from beginning to end. (93–07, p. 58)

Latter-day scripture reveals the plan of salvation. Such knowledge of the plan of salvation as remained in the Old Testament and the New Testament was not a fulness. There came, as a voice from the dust, the testimony of other ancient prophets—The Book of Mormon, Another Testament of Jesus Christ. It contains the fulness of the gospel. It is a supernal gift and is the cornerstone of our religion. From it we have a knowledge of the plan of salvation. He reopened the channels of revelation. The Doctrine and Covenants and the Pearl of Great Price were given. And he adds from time to time, by revelation, further light and knowledge. . . .

He has revealed all of the principles, laws, doctrines, covenants, and ordinances required for the salvation and exaltation of man. All of this was restored by revelation and bestowed in successive visitations from beyond the veil. (84–05)

CHAPTER 8

Righteousness and Perfection

*"No blessing will be denied the righteous who
are striving to do that which is good." (07–09)*

STRIVING FOR PERFECTION

We must strive for perfection. Now, the Lord is very generous. He
tells us to strive to be perfect, so that He may bless us even more richly
as we travel that path. It is very difficult to be perfect. I am not sure I
know anyone who is perfect. Someone asked Brigham Young, "Are you
perfect?" He said, "No, I am not. If I were perfect, I would be taken to
heaven so fast it would scare this whole congregation." But he was striving for perfection. He was trying to do everything he could to be perfect. He was keeping his covenants. If we will keep our covenants and
do as we promise to do, then the Lord is bound and we will receive the
blessing. (86–01, pp. 256–57)

A missionary in Denmark asked me a question: "I am striving for
perfection. Some of the other missionaries [have] said, 'You are foolish;
you can't really be perfect.' What do you believe?" I told him I believe

the scriptures when they say: "Be ye therefore perfect, even as your Father which is in heaven is perfect."[1] Then I humbly admitted that I was perfect in some things. I am perfect when it comes to never touching tobacco, never; alcohol, never; tea and coffee, never. I am perfect there. Now there are many things where I am not perfect yet, but I *am* perfect if it comes to not committing murder. I have never done that. I will never do that. We can be perfect, a little bit at a time. (76–09, p. 83)

Spiritual growth comes gradually. "Whoso cometh unto me with a broken heart and a contrite spirit, him will I baptize with fire and with the Holy Ghost, even as the Lamanites, because of their faith in me at the time of their conversion, were baptized with fire and with the Holy Ghost, *and they knew it not.*"[2]

Several years ago I met one of our sons in the mission field in a distant part of the world. He had been there for a year. His first question was this: "Dad, what can I do to grow spiritually? I have tried so hard to grow spiritually and I just haven't made any progress."

That was his perception: to me it was otherwise. I could hardly believe the maturity, the spiritual growth that he had gained in one year. He "knew it not," for it had come as growth, not as a startling spiritual experience. (82–04, p. 54)

On the way to perfection. Some of you are so convinced not only that you are not perfect, but that you are not much of anything. That foolishness gets in your way. There is a way for you to move toward perfection.

When I was just a young man, there were not very many Church books. There was one that was written by one of the Brethren titled *On the Way to Perfection*. That is where we are, "on the way to perfection." Will we arrive there? Not in mortality, but we can improve ourselves. (02–04)

It is not expected that we would be perfect in mortality. It was not expected that you would be perfect. Only One that has ever lived has been perfect, and that is the Lord. But the key of repentance and forgiveness He has brought in the process of His Atonement and Resurrection. (08–08)

It does not please the Lord when we worry that we never do enough. As the Lord told Oliver Granger, "When [they fall they] shall rise again, for [their] sacrifice shall be more sacred unto me than [their] increase."[3]

Some worry endlessly over missions that were missed, or marriages that did not turn out, or babies that did not arrive, or children that seem lost, or dreams unfulfilled, or because age limits what they can do. I do not think it pleases the Lord when we worry because we think we never do enough or that what we do is never good enough.

Some needlessly carry a heavy burden of guilt which could be removed through confession and repentance.

The Lord did not say of Oliver, "*If* he falls," but "*When* he falls he shall rise again."[4] (04–09, p. 87)

MAINTAINING OUR STANDARDS

We do not set the standards. We do not set the standards, but we are commanded to teach them and maintain them. The standard remains abstinence before marriage and total fidelity in marriage. However out of step we may seem, however much the standards are belittled, however much others yield, we will not yield, we cannot yield. Obedience to the moral standard and observance of the Word of Wisdom will remain as requirements for ordination to the priesthood, for a mission, and for a temple recommend. (03–09, p. 26)

Exceptions prove the rule. When I speak of the law and of rules, I always get a letter or two pointing out a variation or an exception. There is an old saying that the exception proves the rule. That's a true statement.

You be careful that you don't look for exceptions as an excuse to avoid keeping the rules and don't trust those who do. If something has to be labeled an exception, really it does prove the rule. (95–06, p. 8)

Diversity self-destructs if handled carelessly. Diversity is a very popular word which self-destructs if handled carelessly. Properly respected, diversity is the friend to the word *choice.* But, like freedom, diversity can devour itself and choice will disappear.

Beware of those who teach a diversity in which everybody, every philosophy, and all behavior must be accepted everywhere with standards adjusted to accommodate and to please everyone. They are really arguing for their own brand of conformity. . . .

The hidden trap connected with diversity is that a misunderstanding of it can cause you to accept what *is* and lose sight of what *ought to be.*

We must and will maintain high standards in the Church in the name of choice and diversity. We have the right to create environments in our Church schools, in our institutes of religion, and individually in our minds, in our homes, in the Church at large to create a Zion. (95–06, p. 6)

It is important to maintain gospel standards across cultures. Since the Church is all over the world and across many cultures, there are things that are accepted in some cultures that are not acceptable to the Lord. There are patterns in some countries where they uniformly and normally drink a lot of alcoholic beverages. In the Church, we do not. And they will say, "Well, everybody's doing it."

And we say, "Well, when you come into the Church, you stop that."

And they say, "Do we have to?"

And we say, "No, you don't have to, but if you don't, you won't get two things. You won't get the inspiration of the Holy Ghost. And the other thing you won't get is a temple recommend." So that is an adjustment that has to be made. (06–01)

PROFANITY

Irreverence and profanity are wrong. However common irreverence and profanity become, they are nonetheless wrong. We teach our children so. In The Church of Jesus Christ of Latter-day Saints we revere His name. We worship in His name; we love Him. (67–06, p. 97)

The reality of profanity is no argument for its acceptance. Many things that are *real* are not *right*. Disease germs are real, but must we therefore spread them? A pestilent infection may be real, but ought we to expose ourselves to it? Those who argue that so-called "real life" is license must remember that where there's an *is*, there's an *ought*. Frequently, what *is* and what *ought* to be are far apart. When *is* and *ought to be* come together, an ideal is formed. The reality of profanity does not argue for the toleration of it. (67–06, p. 96)

Profanity is mockery. Profanity is more than just untidy language, for when we profane we relate to low and vulgar words, the most sacred of all names. I wince when I hear the name of the Lord so used, called upon in anger, in frustration, in hatred.

This is more than just a name we deal with. This relates to spiritual authority and power and lies at the very center of Christian doctrine.

The Lord said: "Therefore, whatsoever ye shall do, ye shall do it in my name."[5]

In the Church that Jesus Christ established, all things are done in His name. Prayers are said, children are blessed, testimonies borne, sermons preached, ordinances performed, sacrament administered, the infirm anointed, graves dedicated.

What a mockery it then becomes when we use that sacred name profanely. (67–06, p. 97)

You can break the habit of profanity. Nobody needs to swear! . . . [M]any of us . . . may have fallen victim to the habit of profanity. If this has been your misfortune, I know a way that you can break the habit quickly. This is what I suggest you do: Make an agreement with someone not in your family but someone who works closest with you. Offer to pay him $1 or $2, even $5, each time he hears you swear. For less than $50 you can break the habit.

Smile if you will, but you will find it is a very practical and powerful device. (67–06, p. 97)

SERVICE AND UNSELFISHNESS

Serve-us versus Service. [I present] a brief lesson in spelling. The word is service. Careful, lest you misspell it. Often it is spelled:

SERVE-US.

This, according to Packer's Practical Dictionary, means to accumulate, to acquire, to receive—to get! That dictionary lists a synonym—selfishness!

Webster spells the word:

S-E-R-V-I-C-E

which means to share, to give—to give freely—unselfishly. (87–05)

In rendering service, we must be concerned about what we are, not just what we do. I firmly believe that to render the greatest service to this Church, we must show quite as much concern for what we *are* as for what we *do.*

What we are, the very quality of our actual selves, may be of greater service than some things we are required to do. To be competent, even to be highly skilled, and able to perform some difficult procedures may be of great service. But if we *are* less than we should be, we may actually be a disservice. (80–02)

I see two kinds of service. I see two kinds of service: one, the service we render when we are called to serve in the Church; the other, the service we willingly give to those around us because we are taught to care. (97–04, p. 6)

No other service transcends that given in the home. To attend, to tithe, and to learn is to serve, and we often speak of serving as a worthy example.

No service in the Church or in the community transcends that given in the home. Leaders should be very sure that a call to serve in the Church will not weaken the family. (97–04, p. 7)

Spirit of service is best taught at home. The spirit of service is best taught at home. We must teach our children by example and tell them that an unselfish spirit is essential to happiness. (97–04, p. 6)

SELF-MASTERY AND THOUGHTS

Our salvation depends on controlling our thoughts. Because you may be susceptible to the plague and knowing that healthy, clean thoughts are resistant, even immune to it, I venture to talk with you about your thoughts, and to point out the danger of the undisciplined mind. Each of us must learn self-control of his thoughts. We *must* learn to control our thoughts, or someone or something else *will* control them. Untrained, unemployed thoughts are soon enslaved. . . . Success in life depends upon the management of your thoughts. Your very salvation depends upon it. (67–05, p. 32)

Put your "No Trespassing" sign up. I have the idea that many go through life with their minds something like a corner lot at a city intersection, just a lot on which there is no house. . . . Here is a mind, a vacant playing field; and anyone who comes by can crisscross it. I don't have that anymore. On my lot I have some signs that say No Trespassing, and then I list to whom that refers. I will not consent to contamination of the slightest single spot from a perverse source. I will not consent to it. If a thought like that enters my mind, it comes as a trespasser, an unwanted intruder. I do consent openly—without reservation, with hope, with anxiety—pleadingly with all invitation—for inspiration from the Lord.

Now I just ask you, do you have your No Trespassing signs up? (70–09, p. 271)

Replace inappropriate thoughts with edifying ones. I've had to evict some thoughts a hundred times before they would stay out. I have never been successful until I have put something edifying in their place.

I do not want my mind to be a dumping place for shabby ideas or thoughts, for disappointments, bitterness, envy, shame, hatred, worry, grief, or jealousy.

If you are fretting over such things, it's time to clean the yard. Get rid of all that junk! Get rid of it!

Put up a "no trespassing" sign, a "no dumping" sign, and take control of yourself. Don't keep anything that will not edify you.

The first thing a doctor does with a wound is to clean it out. He gets rid of all foreign matter and drains off infection—however much it hurts.

Once you do that spiritually, you will have a different perspective. You will have much less to worry about. (77–10, p. 60)

Things we should know about our thoughts. We *are accountable* for what we think; we *are responsible* for what we think. We can tell good from evil *if we will*. Therefore, I repeat again those things that we should know about our thoughts:

—That they are the control center for all action;
—That they are powerful;
—That they are individual, meaning that we can think of only one thing at a time;
—That they are subject to influence—both from the physical and from the environmental world, and from the realm of the spiritual—both good and bad;
—That we are free to choose. (67–05, pp. 36–37)

One thought at a time. Did you know that you can think of only one thing at a time? Did you know that every time you think a good thought, there is no room for a bad one?

To know this is of significant worth. Our minds may switch from one thought to another very quickly; nevertheless, there is only a single circuit—only one thought is processed at a time. . . . It is important that we know this because then we can give priority to significant and important thoughts. (67–05, p. 35)

Evil cannot tolerate the presence of good thoughts. While virtue, by choice, *will not* endure the presence of filth, that which is debased and unclean *cannot* endure the light.

Virtue *will not* associate with filth, while evil *cannot* tolerate the presence of good. (67–05, p. 39)

Thoughts are talks we hold with ourselves. Thoughts are talks we hold with ourselves. Do you see why the scriptures tell us to "let virtue garnish [our] thoughts unceasingly" and promise us that if we do, our "confidence [shall] wax strong in the presence of God; and the doctrine of the priesthood shall distil upon [our] soul[s] as the dews from heaven" and then "the Holy Ghost shall be [our] constant companion."[6] (99–07, p. 24)

Inappropriate thoughts can be spiritually fatal. Just as the air you breathe may expose you to a deadly virus, the thoughts you think may introduce spiritual diseases which, if untreated, may be spiritually fatal. (95–06, p. 5)

Thoughts cannot be hidden. It is important that we learn that we cannot hide our thoughts. You can't hide them. Sooner or later, they will be known; they will express themselves in actions. "As [a man] thinketh in his heart, so is he."[7] As a man thinketh in his heart, so he does. (67–05, p. 35)

Our thoughts control our actions. There are, if we control them, things we ought to know about thoughts. First, that they sponsor all action. Our thoughts are the switchboard, the control panel governing our actions. While some acts may seem so impulsive, and our reactions to things so automatic that they seem to be done without thinking, nonetheless, thought controls action. (67–05, p. 33)

We must immunize our minds and spirits with truth. When you were children, you went through an immunization program. Antibodies were injected into your system to protect you should you be exposed to contagions, enemies so small as to be invisible. . . .

I do not know how many times I have been exposed to, yet spared from, serious illness by having submitted to the momentary discomfort of an inoculation. . . .

While we can protect our bodies from contagious diseases with the proper serums, we cannot immunize our minds and spirits that way. We immunize our minds and our spirits with ideas, with truth. (95–06, p. 1)

Thoughts can be influenced. Our thoughts are subject to spiritual influence. Inspiration can and does come from God. He is real, and it is real.

Temptation, another kind of inspiration, can assert itself from the adversary; it is equally real. (My secretary, in typing the foregoing sentence, misspelled a word and inadvertently invented a very usable one—"sinspiration.") So we are subject to inspiration and sinspiration. But, regardless of the influence and regardless of the source, the most important consideration is that *we may choose.* We are free to choose. The Lord said to Adam: "Nevertheless, thou mayest *choose* for thyself, for it is given unto thee."[8] (67–05, p. 36)

Control your thoughts and you will be safe. "The Comforter, which is the Holy Ghost, whom the Father will send in my name, he shall teach you all things, and bring all things to your remembrance, whatsoever I have said unto you."[9]

Young people, the voice of the Spirit is felt rather than heard. You can learn when you are very young how the Holy Ghost works.

The scriptures are full of help on how good can influence your mind and evil control you, if you let it. That struggle will never end. But remember this:

> *All the water in the world,*
> *However hard it tried,*
> *Could never sink the smallest ship*
> *Unless it [gets] inside.*
> *And all the evil in the world,*
> *The blackest kind of sin,*
> *Can never hurt you the least bit*
> *Unless you let it in.*[10]

When you learn to control your thoughts, you will be safe. (99–07, p. 24)

Thoughts, like water, must be controlled. When I was about ten years old we lived in a home surrounded by an orchard. There never seemed to be enough water for the trees. The ditches, always fresh plowed in the spring, would soon be filled with weeds. One day, in charge of the irrigating turn, I found myself in trouble.

As the water moved down the rows choked with weeds, it would flood in every direction. I raced through the puddles trying to build up the bank. As soon as I had one break patched up, there would be another.

A neighbor came through the orchard. He watched for a moment, and then with a few vigorous strokes of the shovel he cleared the ditch bottom and allowed the water to course through the channel he had made. "If you want the water to stay in its course, you'll have to make a place for it to go," he said.

I have come to know that thoughts, like water, will stay on course if we make a place for them to go. Otherwise our thoughts follow the course of least resistance, always seeking the lower levels. (*TYD*, p. 55)

How to control thoughts. I had been told a hundred times or more as I grew up that thoughts must be controlled. But no one told me how.

I want to tell you young people about one way you can learn to control your thoughts, and it has to do with music.

The mind is like a stage. Except when we are asleep the curtain is always up. There is always some act being performed on that stage. It may be a comedy, a tragedy, interesting or dull, good or bad; but always there is some act playing on the stage of the mind.

Have you noticed that without any real intent on your part, in the middle of almost any performance, a shady little thought may creep in from the wings and attract your attention? These delinquent thoughts will try to upstage everybody.

If you permit them to go on, all thoughts of any virtue will leave the stage. You will be left, because you consented to it, to the influence of unrighteous thoughts.

If you yield to them, they will enact for you on the stage of your mind anything to the limits of your toleration. They may enact a theme of bitterness, jealousy, or hatred. It may be vulgar, immoral, even depraved.

When they have the stage, if you let them, they will devise the most clever persuasions to hold your attention. They can make it interesting all right, even convince you that it is innocent—for they are but thoughts.

What do you do at a time like that, when the stage of your mind is commandeered by the imps of unclean thinking?—whether they be the gray ones that seem almost clean or the filthy ones which leave no room for doubt.

If you can control your thoughts, you can overcome habits, even degrading personal habits. If you can learn to master them you will have a happy life.

This is what I would teach you. Choose from among the sacred music of the Church a favorite hymn, one with words that are uplifting and music that is reverent, one that makes you feel something akin to inspiration. . . . Go over it in your mind carefully. Memorize it. Even though you have had no musical training, you can think through a hymn.

Now, use this hymn as the place for your thoughts to go. Make it your emergency channel. Whenever you find these shady actors have slipped from the sidelines of your thinking onto the stage of your mind, put on this record [or CD], as it were.

As the music begins and as the words form in your thoughts, the unworthy ones will slip shamefully away. It will change the whole mood on the stage of your mind. Because it is uplifting and clean, the baser thoughts will disappear. For while virtue, by choice, will not associate with filth, evil cannot tolerate the presence of light.

In due time you will find yourself, on occasion, humming the music inwardly. As you retrace your thoughts, you discover some influence from the world about you encouraged an unworthy thought to move on stage in your mind, and the music almost automatically began.

"Music," said Gladstone, "is one of the most forceful instruments for governing the mind and spirit of man."

I am so grateful for music that is worthy and uplifting and inspiring.

Once you learn to clear the stage of your mind from unworthy thoughts, keep it busy with learning worthwhile things. Change your environment so that you have things about you that will inspire good and uplifting thoughts. Keep busy with things that are righteous. (73–09, pp. 26–27)

You can learn to control your thoughts. If you can learn to control your thoughts, you will be able to hedge up the way of the adversary when a thought comes as a temptation.

I know two ways to do that. One is through the use of music. You can choose a favorite hymn and record it in your mind. Did you know that you can think a hymn, you can sing it silently?

I know that can be done. I learned that from my brother. We were both bomber pilots in the military. He had been on very dangerous missions. When fear came to him, as it always will, he learned to hum his favorite hymn.

Before I went in the military, he told me, "When things looked very bad, I would inwardly, silently hum the music and the words to that hymn. Soon the propellers were singing back to me." That was a steadying influence. It was a valuable lesson for a young man—and for you.

You will find that if you choose a hymn to use for your protection, one day unconsciously you will start humming it to yourself silently and then stop and wonder. You will think back and find out that there was something to which you needed to be alert. The song started first as a warning, as a guide.

There is another thing you can do. You know more about computers than your dad does. Your little brother knows more than you do. On every computer board, in any language, there is one key that says delete. Have a "delete key" in your mind. Develop your use of the delete key. If you have one of these unworthy thoughts trying to push itself into your mind, delete it!

Now, what will that delete key be? Some little gesture that no one else would notice. I do not know what yours should be. That has to be yours. It is private. It might be, for instance, if you wear glasses, just touching your glasses. A thought comes into your mind, and you touch your glasses to delete it. No one but you will know. Or it might be any little gesture that is private to you, such as rubbing your hand. Learn to use your delete key when these thoughts, these temptations come. You can learn to delete them.

You can learn to control your thoughts. When you do that, and as you follow the rule of obedience, you are going to be all right. You will be guided. (02–07)

Bad thoughts and habits must be replaced with something good. Do not try merely to *discard* a bad habit or a bad thought. *Replace* it. When you try to eliminate a bad habit, if the spot where it used to be is left open it will sneak back and crawl again into that empty space. It grew there; it will struggle to stay there. When you discard it, fill up the spot where it was. Replace it with something good. Replace it with unselfish thoughts, with unselfish acts. Then, if an evil habit or addiction tries to return, it will have to fight for attention. Sometimes it may win. Bad thoughts often have to be evicted a hundred times, or a thousand. But if they are to be evicted ten thousand times, never surrender to them. You are in charge of you. I repeat, it is very, very difficult to eliminate a bad habit just by trying to discard it. Replace it. (78–01, p. 196)

Replace improper thoughts with good music. I found that, while not easy, I could control my thoughts if I made a place for them to go. You can replace thoughts of temptation, anger, disappointment, or fear with better thoughts—with music.

I love the sacred music of the Church. The hymns of the Restoration carry an inspiration and a protection. (99–07, p. 24)

No worthy thought is ever lost. The statement in the Book of Mormon, "Our words will condemn us, yea, all our works will condemn us; we shall not be found spotless; and our thoughts will also condemn us"[11] has a reciprocal—your words will bless you, your works will redeem you, yea even your very thoughts will redeem you. I have the conviction that no worthy thought is ever wasted. No worthy thought is ever lost. That becomes important when you're trying to build into the lives of your own children or into the lives of the missionaries some spiritual substance. Then some incident happens and some transgression takes place and you feel as though all of your efforts are in vain and that all has been erased. Maybe for the moment it has that appearance. It is not so. What was built in stays there. (93–03)

No good thought is ever lost. No turn of the mind, however brief or transitory or illusive, if it is good, is ever wasted. No thought of sympathy, or of forgiveness, no reflection on generosity or of courage or of purity, no meditation on humility or gratitude or reverence is ever lost. The frequency with which they are experienced is the measure of you. The more constant they become, the more you are worth, or, in scriptural terms, the more you are worthy. Every clean thought *becomes* you. Every clean thought becomes *you*. (67–05, p. 39)

AGENCY

Agency is the foundation on which all other doctrines rest. If you put all of the doctrines of the Church in boxes and laid them on a large floor and asked me to assemble them in some order, I would sort through the boxes and find one. It would be a long box and a heavy one, and it would say "Agency, Freedom, Agency." I would put that down first, and everything else we believe would be stacked in proper order on top of that. We are so concerned that we be free, that we decide that we are sons and daughters of God, and that we do what is right because we desire to do it. (82–08)

The crucial test of life. Our lives are made up of thousands of everyday choices. Over the years these little choices will be bundled together and show clearly what we value.

The crucial test of life . . . does not center in the choice between

In South Africa, September 1969

fame and obscurity, nor between wealth and poverty. The greatest decision of life is between good and evil. (80–10, p. 21)

The time is now for us to make the choice. Most of you have been taught the gospel all your lives. All of you know the difference between good and evil, between right and wrong. Isn't it time, then, that you decide that you're going to do right? In so doing you're making a choice. Not just *a* choice, but you're making *the* choice. Once you've decided that, with no fingers crossed, no counterfeiting, no reservations or hesitancy, the rest will all fall into place. (75–01, p. 88)

Each one of us can commit our agency to God. I want to be good! It has been critically important that an understanding of this was established between me and the Lord. It is very important that I know that He knows which way I committed my agency.

Each of us may go before Him and tell Him that we are not neutral, that He can do with us as He will. If He needs our vote, it is there. For myself, I do not care what He does with me. He does not have to take anything from me because I give it to Him—everything, all I own, all I am I will consecrate unto Him and His work. (*ABE,* p. 307)

I would expose you this morning to some tender, innermost feelings on this matter of agency. Perhaps the greatest discovery of my life, without question the greatest commitment, came when finally I had the confidence in God that I would loan or yield my agency to Him— without compulsion or pressure, without any duress, as a single individual alone, by myself, no counterfeiting, nothing expected other than the privilege. In a sense, speaking figuratively, to take one's agency, that precious gift which the scriptures make plain is essential to life itself, and say, "I will do as thou directs," is afterward to learn that in so doing you possess it all the more. (71–11, pp. 256–57)

We were given agency in premortality. I want to make this point: In the premortal existence, we were given spirit bodies, and we were given agency. So we are free. Let me read verses from the 93rd section of the Doctrine and Covenants:

And no man receiveth a fulness unless he keepeth his commandments.

He that keepeth his commandments receiveth truth and light, until he is glorified in truth and knoweth all things.

Man was also in the beginning with God. Intelligence, or the light of truth, was not created or made, neither indeed can be.

All truth is independent in that sphere in which God has placed it, to act for itself.[12]

So there we are. We have agency. What happens in our lives and in our pattern of eternal progression is just what we decide it will be. (03–04, p. 169)

Our destiny is not based on chance. The events from the creation to the final winding-up scene are all governed by law. Our destiny is not based on *chance.* It is based on *choice!* It was planned that way before the world was. It all works according to the plan, the great plan of happiness. (93–05)

Agency is not "free." The agency the Lord has given us is not a "free" agency. The term "free" agency is not found in the revelations. It is a *moral* agency. The Lord has given us freedom of choice:

"That every man may act in *doctrine* and *principle* pertaining to futurity, according to the *moral agency* which I have given unto him, that every man may be *accountable* for his own sins in the day of judgment."[13] There is no agency without choice; there is no choice without freedom; there is no freedom without risk; nor true freedom without responsibility. (90–05)

Freedom has to be earned. If you feel pressed in and pressured and not free, it may be for one of two reasons. One, if you have lost freedom, possibly it has been through some irresponsible act of your own. Now you must regain it. You may be indentured—indentured to some habits of laziness or indolence; some even become slaves to addiction. The other reason is that maybe if you are not free you have not earned it. Freedom is not a self-preserving gift. It has to be earned, and it has to be protected.

For instance, I am not free to play the piano, for I do not know how. I cannot play the piano. I could quickly prove that, but I think it may be a mistake on your part if you ask me to. The ability to play the piano, the freedom to do that, has to be earned. It is a relatively expensive freedom. It takes an investment of time and of discipline. (71–11, p. 254)

Moral agency does not free us from the consequences of our choices. Life is meant to be a test to see if we will keep the commandments of God.[14] We are free to obey or to ignore both the spirit and the letter of the law. But the agency granted to man is a *moral* agency.[15] We are not free to break our covenants and escape the consequences. (90–09, p. 84)

Freedom and agency require accountability. A little twisting the word freedom can lead to the loss of it. Individual freedom without responsibility can destroy freedom. . . .

We often speak of agency as a divine right. . . . If you do not temper freedom with responsibility and agency with accountability, they both will self-destruct. (95–06, p. 6)

Moral law assumes accountability. Moral law assumes accountability; no accountability, no penalties! Moral law will self-destruct if enforced against those not accountable. It is *not moral* to do so.

One of the strongest statements in all scripture speaks to those who would make little children accountable:

"Behold I say unto you, that he that supposeth that little children need baptism is in the gall of bitterness and in the bonds of iniquity; for he hath neither faith, hope, nor charity; wherefore, should he be cut off while in the thought, he must go down to hell."[16]

Those who mentally remain children are likewise innocent.[17] (88–08, p. 6)

We must choose to receive the full benefits of the Atonement. Regardless of the choices we make in life, our mortal body will be resurrected.

What happens thereafter will depend on the choices we make. Having chosen good over evil, we may be exalted and return to the presence of our heavenly parents. There is a condition: no unclean thing can enter there.

Since growth and experience come in part from having made bad choices through ignorance or inexperience, sometimes willfully or through temptation of the adversary, every one of us will need the cleansing which comes from repentance and forgiveness in order to return to the presence of our Heavenly Father.

The great plan of happiness provides a redeemer who has atoned for our mistakes and can wash away through that atonement our transgressions. Because choice and agency are ours, that cleansing cannot take place unless we want it and unless we ask for it. (95–01)

There is no true freedom without responsibility. It may seem unusual at first to foster *self-control* by centering on *freedom of choice,* but it is a very sound doctrinal approach.

While either subject may be taught separately, and though they may appear at first to be opposites, they are in fact parts of the same subject.

Some who do not understand the doctrinal part do not readily see the relationship between obedience and agency. And they miss one vital connection and see obedience only as restraint. They then resist the very thing that will give them true freedom. There is no true freedom without responsibility, and there is no enduring freedom without a knowledge of the truth. The Lord said, "If ye continue in my word, then are ye my disciples indeed; and ye shall know the truth, and the truth shall make you free."[18] (83–01, p. 66)

There is no true freedom without respect for the agency of others. We have always held the rights of the individual to be sovereign. But we have never before placed the collective rights of the majority in subjugation to the individual rights of any single citizen.

Any virtue, pressed to an extreme, becomes a vice; thrift becomes stinginess, generosity becomes wastefulness, self-confidence becomes pride, humility becomes weakness, and on and on. Individual rights as an ideal cannot endure except there be respect for the agency of others.

There is no true freedom without responsibility. Freedom without restraint becomes tyranny of a new and fatal kind. (89–03, p. 64)

We are free to listen to whom we will. In a lesson on delegation that few have noted, the Father in seven words commissioned the Son to represent him. In seven words it was done: "This is my Beloved Son, hear Him." We are free not to do it. We are free to listen to one another. We are free to heed those of the world. We are free to listen to perverse or wicked spirits. But if we want to know what counsel would be given from Elohim Himself we must seek our direction always "in the name of the Lord Jesus Christ." (*THT*, p. 7)

Some cite freedom as a justification for vice. It is interesting how one virtue, when given exaggerated or fanatical emphasis, can be used to batter down another. How clever the deception when freedom—the virtue—is invoked to justify vice! (92–02, p. 112)

Freedom of choice is distorted. While we pass laws to reduce pollution of the earth, any proposal to protect the moral and spiritual environment is shouted down and marched against as infringing upon liberty, agency, freedom, the right to choose.

Interesting how one virtue, when given exaggerated or fanatical emphasis, can be used to batter down another, with freedom, a virtue, invoked to protect *vice*. Those determined to transgress see any regulation of their lifestyle as interfering with their agency and seek to have their actions condoned by making them legal.

People who are otherwise sensible say, "I do not intend to indulge, but I vote for freedom of choice for those who do."

Regardless of how lofty and moral the "pro-choice" argument sounds, it is badly flawed. With that same logic one could argue that all traffic signs and barriers which keep the careless from danger should be pulled down on the theory that each individual must be free to choose how close to the edge he will go.

The phrase "*free* agency" does not appear in scripture. The only agency spoken of there is *moral agency*, "which," the Lord said, "I have given unto him, that every man may be *accountable* for his own sins in the day of judgment."[19]

And the Lord warned members of His church, "Let not that which I have appointed be polluted by mine enemies, *by the consent of those who call themselves after my name:* For this is a very sore and grievous sin against me, and against my people."[20] (92–03, pp. 66–67)

REWARDS OF RIGHTEOUSNESS

Much is given to those who are faithful. For all that we are required to do in this Church, we get a few things in return. We have the privileges of the priesthood. We can have our families sealed together for all eternity. We have the assurance of being happy in this life. We know the certainty of the resurrection and that if we will live worthily we have the assurance that we can return to the presence of our Heavenly Father, and that is worth everything. (72–02)

Good things must be paid for in advance. If I were to tell you one of the most important laws of life that I have learned, I should say this: The good things—that which is desirable, that which tends to elevate, glorify, and exalt—must be paid for in advance. Good must be earned. (62–04, p. 107)

Eternal rewards must be paid for in advance. Things that are eternal must be paid for in advance. With a down payment and an extension of credit, we can gain possession of material things, but there is no credit buying in eternity.

Things of the Spirit, things that are eternal must, positively must, be paid for in advance. (75–05)

Every man will be granted according to the desires of his own heart. Every man will be granted according to the desires of his own heart. Those who desire virtue and beauty and truth and salvation shall have it, and those who fail in that desire, or who unfortunately direct their desires in the opposite direction, shall have their agency respected. (62–04, p. 100)

You cannot get even with the Lord. You cannot get even with the
Lord, because He is always blessing ahead of you. (06–01)

***For the righteous, true success need not include fame and for-
tune.*** It is the misapprehension of most people that if you are good,
really good, at what you do, you will eventually be both widely known
and well compensated. It is the understanding of almost everyone that
success, to be complete, must include a generous portion of both fame
and fortune as essential ingredients. The world seems to work on that
premise. The premise is false! It is not true! The Lord taught otherwise.

The truth about this is remarkably difficult to teach and difficult
to learn. If one who is not well known and not well compensated claims
that he has learned that neither fame nor fortune is essential to success,
we tend to become suspicious of his statement as being self-serving.
What else could he say and not count himself a failure? If someone who
has possession of fame and fortune asserts that neither matters to success
or happiness, we suspect that his expression is patronizing.

Therefore, we reject as reliable authorities both those who have
fame and fortune and those who have not. We question that either is
an objective witness. That leaves us only one course—to learn for ourselves, by experience, about prominence and wealth and their opposites.
We therefore struggle through life, perhaps missing both fame and
fortune, to finally learn that we can indeed succeed without possessing
either; or we may one day have both and learn that neither is basic to
the recipe for true success and complete happiness. That is a very slow
way to learn. It was Benjamin Franklin who said, "Experience keeps a
dear school, but fools will learn in no other."[21]

Will we ever learn that the choice is not between fame and
obscurity, nor is the choice between wealth and poverty. The choice is
between good and evil, and that is a very different issue indeed. When
we finally understand that, our happiness will not be determined by the
material things, either on one hand or on the other. Our God has
vouchsafed to us our agency. If we can be shown where the deciding
pivotal choices are, we can succeed. (80–08, p. 4)

AFFLICTIONS, SUFFERING, AND TRIALS

There is a need for eternal perspective to understand trials and suffering. Until you have a broad perspective of the eternal nature of this great drama, you won't make much sense out of the inequities in life. Some are born with so little and others with so much, some in poverty, with handicaps, with pain, with suffering, premature death even of innocent children. There are the brutal, unforgiving forces of nature and the brutality of man to man. . . .

Do not suppose that God willfully causes that, which for His own purposes, He permits. When you know the plan and purpose of it all, even these things will manifest a loving Father in Heaven. (95–06, p. 3)

Sorrow and pain are to temper us, not consume us. Disappointment, sorrow, pain—these are all flames for the Refiner's fire, but they are meant to temper us only, not to consume us. (66–05, p. 252)

There is purpose in our struggles in life. We are indoctrinated that somehow we should always be instantly emotionally comfortable. When that is not so, some become anxious—and all too frequently seek relief from counseling, from analysis, and even from medication.

It was meant to be that life would be a challenge. To suffer some anxiety, some depression, some disappointment, even some failure is normal.

Teach our members that if they have a good, miserable day once in a while, or several in a row, to stand steady and face them. Things will straighten out.

There is great purpose in our struggle in life. (78–02, p. 93)

There are doctrines which bring perspective on mortal trials. The Apostle Paul said: "If in this life only we have hope in Christ, we are of all men most miserable."[22]

If our view is limited to mortal life, some things become unbearable because they seem so unfair and so permanent. There are doctrines which, if understood, will bring a perspective toward and a composure regarding problems which otherwise have no satisfactory explanation.

Truth: We are spirit children of a Father God. We lived with Him in our premortal existence, of which it must be said that there was not, neither could there have been, a beginning. The revelations speak of things "from before the foundation of the world" and "before the world was."[23]

Truth: Mortal life is temporary and, measured against eternity, infinitesimally brief. If a microscopic droplet of water should represent the length of mortal life, by comparison all the oceans on earth put together would not even begin to represent everlasting life.

Truth: After mortal death we will rise in the resurrection to an existence to which there will not, neither could there, be an end. The words *everlasting, never ending, eternal, forever and forever* in the revelations describe both the gospel and life.

That day of healing will come. Bodies which are deformed and minds that are warped will be made perfect. (91–02, p. 9)

Trials and tests can have opposite effects on individuals. The same testing in troubled times can have quite opposite effects on individuals. Three verses from the Book of Mormon, which is another testament of Christ, teach us that. . . .

And thus ended the thirty and first year of the reign of the judges over the people of Nephi; and thus they had had wars, and bloodsheds, and famine, and affliction, for the space of many years.

And there had been murders, and contentions, and dissensions, and all manner of iniquity among the people of Nephi; nevertheless for the righteous' sake, yea, because of the prayers of the righteous, they were spared.

But behold, because of the exceedingly great length of the war between the Nephites and the Lamanites many had become *hardened,* because of the exceedingly great length of the war; and many were *softened* because of their afflictions, insomuch that they did humble themselves before God, even in the depth of humility.[24]

Surely you know some whose lives have been filled with adversity who have been mellowed and strengthened and refined by it, while others have come away from the same test bitter and blistered and unhappy. (83–05, p. 18)

Mortality was not intended to be an effortless journey. It was never intended that we float in an effortless environment at 72 degrees and bathe constantly in the sensation of physical, sensational, and spiritual pleasures. We are here to grow. (66–05, p. 252)

It is quite normal to have a discouraging day now and again. We know from the Book of Mormon that there must be opposition.

"For it must needs be, that there is an opposition in all things. If not so, my first-born in the wilderness, righteousness could not be brought to pass, neither wickedness, neither holiness nor misery, neither good nor bad."[25]

It helps a great deal if we realize that there is a certain healthy element in getting the blues occasionally. It is quite in order to schedule a good, discouraging, depressing day every now and again just for contrast. (*TYD*, p. 102)

The Lord helps us to grow by not granting our every whim. What need was fulfilled when our forebears were persecuted and driven? What need was fulfilled when they suffered deprivation and want, hunger and cold? Whatever the Lord has in mind for us, our heritage was not established on the granting of every whim, seeing to every comfort, and fulfilling every supposed need of every member. That level of expectation can debilitate, even destroy them and the Church. I quote from Joseph Smith, "There must be decision of character aside from sympathy."[26] (*ABE*, p. 109)

A caution on overuse of sedatives. I am not always sure that the measures that are taken are wise. For instance, I am not sure it is always wise to try to erase grief with sedatives. Perhaps when we know the true nature of man, we may be more discriminating in the administering of sedatives in an attempt to erase grief or bring peace to broken hearts, and we may be more careful in the buffering of individuals from life through the use of tranquilizers. (66–05, p. 250)

We must not expect the laws of nature to be exempted for us. The very purpose for which the world was created, and man introduced to live upon it, requires that the laws of nature operate in cold disregard for human feelings. We must work out our salvation without expecting the laws of nature to be exempted for us. Natural law is, on rare occasions, suspended in a miracle. But mostly our handicapped, like the lame man at the pool of Bethesda, wait endlessly for the moving of the water. (91–02, p. 8)

Trials of the righteous. A life of righteousness does not necessarily lift from any soul the trials and difficulties, suffering and concerns of life. But the righteous do have some protection and blessings, and there is power working in their behalf. (*THT,* p. 104)

There is more equality in life's tests than one might expect. We may foolishly bring unhappiness and trouble, even suffering upon ourselves. These are not always to be regarded as penalties imposed by a displeased Creator. They are part of the lessons of life, part of the test.

Some are tested by poor health, some by a body that is deformed or homely. Others are tested by handsome and healthy bodies; some by the passion of youth; others by the erosions of age.

Some suffer disappointment in marriage, family problems; others live in poverty and obscurity. Some (perhaps this is the hardest test) find ease and luxury.

All are part of the test, and there is more equality in this testing than sometimes we suspect. (80–10, p. 21)

A caution against thriving on sympathy. I have known some who seemed to enjoy poor health and have interrupted the lives of those who were caring for them unnecessarily, making life miserable for all. They thrive on sympathy, which is generally very low in nourishment. To know just how far to press the handicapped when physical and emotional pain are involved may be the most difficult part for those who serve them. Nevertheless, as the Prophet Joseph Smith said, "There must be decision of character, aside from sympathy."[27] (91–02, p. 9)

Our body is a precious gift from God. However limited your body may be, it is a precious gift.

One of you may be well-born and well-formed while another is not. In either case, there is a testing. That is what mortality is all about. The poorly born may lack self-esteem, or the well-born infected with pride. Pride is the most deadly spiritual virus. In the eternal scheme of things, who is to say which is the most favored. (89–01, p. 59)

No room for guilt in connection with disabilities. I must first, and with emphasis, clarify this point: It is natural for parents with handicapped children to ask themselves, "What did we do wrong?" The idea that *all* suffering is somehow the direct result of sin has been taught since ancient times. It is false doctrine. That notion was even accepted by some of the early disciples until the Lord corrected them.[28]

There is little room for feelings of guilt in connection with handicaps. Some handicaps may result from carelessness or abuse, and some through addiction of parents. But most of them do not. Afflictions come to the innocent. (91–02, pp. 7–8)

Those with physical impediments will eventually be restored to a perfect frame. *Physical* means "temporal"; *temporal* means "temporary." Spirits which are beautiful and innocent may be temporally restrained by physical impediments.

If healing does not come in mortal life, it will come thereafter. Just as the gorgeous monarch butterfly emerges from a chrysalis, so will spirits emerge.

"Their sleeping dust [will] be restored unto its perfect frame, bone to . . . bone, and the sinews and the flesh upon them, the spirit and the body to be united never again to be divided, that they might receive a fulness of joy."[29] (91–02, p. 9)

The works of God can be manifest through those who help the handicapped. In Mendoza, Argentina, we attended a seminary graduation. In the class was a young man who had great difficulty climbing ordinary steps. As the class marched in, two strong young classmates gracefully lifted him up the steps. We watched during and after the proceedings, and it became apparent that the whole class was afflicted with a marvelous kind of blindness. They could not see that he was different. They saw a classmate, a friend. In *them* the works of God *were being* manifest. While there was no physical transformation in the boy or in his classmates, they were serving like angels, soothing a spirit locked in a deformed body awaiting that time when it would be everlastingly made perfect. (91–02, p. 8)

Those devoted to help handicapped loved ones are also being perfected. You parents and you families whose lives must be reordered because of a handicapped one, whose resources and time must be devoted to them, are special heroes. You are manifesting the works of God with every thought, with every gesture of tenderness and care you extend to the handicapped loved one. Never mind the tears and the hours of regret and discouragement; never mind the times when you feel you cannot stand another day of what is required. You are living the principles of the gospel of Jesus Christ in exceptional purity. *And you perfect yourselves in the process.* (91–02, p. 9)

Never ridicule those with disabilities. I must say this to parents. It is not unusual for foolish children and some very thoughtless adults to make light of the handicapped. The mimicking or teasing or ridiculing of those with handicaps is cruel. Such an assault can inflict deeper pain than can physical punishment—more painful because it is undeserved. It is my conviction that such brutality will not, in the eternal scheme of things, go unanswered, and there will come a day of recompense. . . .

Parents, take time in the next home evening to caution your family never to amuse themselves at the expense of the handicapped or of any whose face or form or personality does not fit the supposed ideal or whose skin is too light or too dark to suit their fancy. Teach them that they, in their own way, should become like angels who "move the water," healing a spirit by erasing loneliness, embarrassment, or rejection. (91–02, p. 8)

CHAPTER 9

Measurable Principles

*"We're not as good as we ought to be,
and we're not as good as we're going to be, but we're
better than we were." (08–02)*

REVERENCE

Revelation and reverence are inextricably combined. Revelation
and reverence are inextricably combined. You will not in irreverence
receive much revelation. . . .

There is a depth of personal reverence that is an essential if you are
going to receive revelation. Reverence means submission; it means obedience. (94–04)

Benefits will come if we maintain a spirit of reverence. Parents,
stake presidencies, bishoprics, auxiliary leaders, teachers: maintain a
spirit of reverence in meetings, encourage participation in congregational singing and the use of reverential terms in prayers.

While we may not see an immediate, miraculous transformation,
as surely as the Lord lives, a quiet one will take place. The spiritual
power in the lives of each member and in the Church will increase. The

Lord will pour out His Spirit upon us more abundantly. We will be less troubled, less confused. We will find revealed answers to personal and family problems without all the counseling which we seem now to need. (91–06, p. 23)

Reverence in meetings. For Sunday meetings, the music, dress, and conduct should be appropriate for worship. Foyers are built into our chapels to allow for the greeting and chatter that are typical of people who love one another. However, when we step into the chapel, we *must!*—each of us *must*—watch ourselves lest we be guilty of intruding when someone is struggling to feel delicate spiritual communications.

Leaders sometimes wonder why so many active members get themselves into such predicaments in life. Could it be that they do not feel what they need to feel because our meetings are less than they might be spiritually? (91–06, p. 22)

Reverence in chapels. Irreverent conduct in our chapels is worthy of a reminder, if not reproof. Leaders should teach that reverence invites revelation. (91–06, p. 22)

Reverence does not equate with absolute silence. [Reverence] does not equate with absolute silence. We must be tolerant of little babies, even an occasional outburst from a toddler being ushered out. (91–06, p. 22)

Irreverence suits the purposes of the adversary. We have watched patterns of reverence and irreverence in the Church. While many are to be highly commended, we are drifting. We have reason to be deeply concerned.

The world grows increasingly noisy. Clothing and grooming and conduct are looser and sloppier and more disheveled. Raucous music, with obscene lyrics blasted through amplifiers while lights flash psychedelic colors, characterizes the drug culture. Variations of these things are gaining wide acceptance and influence over our youth.

Doctors even say that our physical sense of hearing can be permanently damaged by all of this noise. This trend to more noise, more excitement, more contention, less restraint, less dignity, less formality is not coincidental nor innocent nor harmless. The first order issued by a commander mounting a military invasion is the jamming of the channels of communication of those he intends to conquer. Irreverence suits the purposes of the adversary by obstructing the delicate channels of revelation in both mind and spirit. (91–06, p. 22)

A caution concerning loud laughter. President Harold B. Lee was a man of quiet response to things that were humorous. Yet he enjoyed a very alert sense of humor and always had a ready story with some humorous twist to it. On one occasion while I was traveling with him he said that Elder Charles A. Callis had told him many years ago that loud laughter was a symptom of a vacant mind. He said, "I took that seriously, and since then I've tried to respond more quietly when I have been amused, not with an outburst of laughter." (*THT,* p. 59)

SABBATH

The Lord doesn't balance His books in October. There were two farmers once who had adjoining fields. The one never worked in his field on Sunday, and his neighbor used to chide him about it. He said, "Your crops aren't doing as well as mine are. Why don't you work on Sunday?"

The other farmer said, "Well, I want to do what the Lord said. I want to gain the blessings of the Lord."

Then one October day they stood at a fence line. The one farmer said, "Just look at it. Look at my field. It is beautiful, the grain is tall, the heads are full of wheat, and your field shows little signs of neglect. You haven't tended yours as well as I've tended mine. Look at my harvest compared to yours. What do you say now about the blessings you thought you were earning?"

This farmer thought for a few minutes and said, "The Lord doesn't balance his books in October." (07–09)

The Sabbath is a day for us to seriously check our course directions. Because the Lord is concerned about us and because He knows of all the difficulties awaiting us, He has prepared a plan or a map to give us the necessary guidance for a safe and profitable journey. This map is the *gospel of Jesus Christ* and is set forth in the revelations from our Father in Heaven. We also have the guidance and instructions of parents and of leaders of the Church who have journeyed along the road and who have previously made careful use of this gospel map. They have seen in the lives of others, or perhaps from some personal experience, what happens if we lose the trail. The Lord has explained that "the sabbath was made for man, and not man for the sabbath: Therefore the Son of man is Lord also of the sabbath."[1] We can see why it is to our benefit to schedule our time so that periodically, as we journey along, we stop and carefully consult the map. We may then lay plans for the journey ahead. This is essentially what the Sabbath day requires of us; and, therefore, the restrictions surrounding the Sabbath day are most beneficial. They tend to direct our attention to the map and to the seriousness of our journey. It is thus possible for us to eliminate the hazard of traveling on the wrong road. It is obvious that we must stop to check the direction we are taking and what destination we expect to reach.

We are old enough to understand that some things which appear to be merely restrictions and restraints are given in order that we might ultimately obtain the destination so clearly marked on the map. Once we understand this, we can look upon the Lord's gift of the Sabbath day with gratitude. (61–01, pp. 269–70)

Evidently the Lord was very much concerned about our earthly journey, for when He gave us life, He reserved every seventh day as His own in order that on that day we might consult the "map" that points the way to exaltation. (61–01, p. 270)

The Sabbath was made for us. We could prepare a detailed, specific list of the things to do on the Sabbath day, or we could prepare such a list of the things that we should not do. It may be more important, however, to remember that the Sabbath was made for us. If we keep it, we will have sufficient guidance and strength for every day of the week.

Is it any wonder that parents and leaders of the Church are constantly urging us to "Remember the Sabbath day, to keep it holy?" (61–01, p. 270)

SACRAMENT

The sacrament points back to the sacrifice and Atonement of Jesus Christ. The law of sacrifice had been observed since the days of Adam. It was symbolic of the redemption that would come with the sacrifice and the Atonement of the Messiah. The Mosaic law of sacrifice was fulfilled with the crucifixion of Christ.

Anciently they looked forward to the Atonement of Christ through the ceremony of the sacrifice. We look back to that same event through the ordinance of the sacrament.

Both sacrifice before, and the sacrament afterward, are centered in Christ, the shedding of His blood, and the Atonement He made for our sins. Both then and now the authority to perform these ordinances belongs to the Aaronic Priesthood. (81–08, p. 31)

The sacrament reminds us of our baptismal covenants and the Savior's sacrifice. At Gethsemane and Golgotha the Savior's blood was shed. Centuries earlier the Passover had been introduced as a symbol and a type of things to come. It was an ordinance to be kept forever.[2]

When the plague of death was decreed upon Egypt, each Israelite family was commanded to take a lamb, firstborn, male, without blemish. This paschal lamb was slain without breaking any bones, its blood to mark the doorway of the home. The Lord promised that the angel of death would *pass over* the homes so marked and not slay those inside. They were saved by the blood of the lamb.

After the crucifixion of the Lord, the law of sacrifice required no more shedding of blood. For that was done, as Paul taught the Hebrews, "once for all . . . one sacrifice for sins for ever."[3] The sacrifice thenceforth was to be a broken heart and a contrite spirit—repentance.

And the Passover would be commemorated forever as the sacrament, in which we renew our covenant of baptism and partake in remembrance of the body of the Lamb of God and of His blood, which was shed for us. (88–03, p. 72)

Through the sacrament we renew our baptismal covenants. Conditioned on repentance, the ordinance of baptism washes our sins away. Some wonder if they were baptized too soon. If only they could be baptized now and have a clean start. But that is not necessary! Through the ordinance of the sacrament you renew the covenants made at baptism. (97–02, p. 10)

It is not an easy thing in this world to stay worthy, to stay clean and pure. Each day may bring little irritations and temptations and mistakes. Our Heavenly Father has provided a way that we can renew the covenants we made with him at the time of our baptism. Each week we can gather together to partake of the sacrament for that purpose.

It is not very likely that during the course of a week, between sacrament meetings, we will get so far off the path of righteousness that we will lose our way. There is always that still, small voice to guide us. (74–06, pp. 233–34)

The sacrament renews the process of forgiveness. Every Sunday when the sacrament is served, that is a ceremony to renew the process of forgiveness. Listen to the sacramental prayer, and you will not get too far away from righteousness, and living a good life. You cannot do too much bad in a week if you are going each Sunday. Every Sunday you cleanse yourself so that, in due time, when you die your spirit will be clean. (08–08)

TITHING AND FAST OFFERINGS

There are spiritual blessings that come from offerings. The scriptures speak of tithes and of *offerings;* they do not speak of assessments or fundraising. To be an offering, it must be given freely—offered. The way is open now for many more of us to participate in this spiritually refining experience. . . .

For those who can and are willing, there comes the opportunity to make generous offerings. In leaving decisions to the individual, the Church is allowing the fundamental doctrine of moral agency asserting itself. Do you not see the change from *assessment* to *offering* as something of the testing that is fundamental to our mortal probation? . . .

It is a course correction; it is an inspired move. It will have influence upon the Church across the world, not just in our generation but also in the generations to come. (90–03, p. 91)

What is a full tithe? I get a little impatient with people every week when I am at conference and they say, "Brother Packer, can you tell me what is an honest tithing?"

I say, "What do you mean? Read the scriptures."

"I know," they say, "but the scriptures are a little vague. It talks about increase. What is a full tithing?"

Then I ask, "What is the problem?"

And they reply, "Well, I have a contract, I make $5,000 a year, so I know I'm supposed to pay $500, but Uncle George died and left some furniture and we didn't need it so we sold it and we got $200. Now is that—"

You know the rest. Well, "they had to ask." And if in doubt, why not be on the Lord's side? Why not be on the safe side? Why not pay that and a little more? (70–03)

Tithing should be a privilege rather than an imposition. Seek for the gift to teach by the Spirit. Then tithing, for instance, becomes less a matter of money than it does of faith and unselfishness and of obedience. We then see it as preparation for receiving the ordinances. It becomes a privilege rather than an imposition. We will then teach tithing without hesitation to even the tiniest of children. (82–02)

This is not an easy church to join. Several years ago I presided over one of our missions. Two of our missionaries were teaching a fine family, who had expressed a desire to be baptized; and then they suddenly cooled off. The father had learned about tithing, and he cancelled all further meetings with the missionaries.

Two sad elders reported to the branch president, who himself was a recent convert, that he would not have this fine family in his branch.

A few days later the branch president persuaded the elders to join him in another visit to the family. "I understand," he told the father, "that you have decided not to join the Church."

"That is correct," the father answered.

"The elders tell me that you are disturbed about tithing."

"Yes," said the father. "They had not told us about it; and when I learned of it, I said, 'Now, that's too much to ask. Our church has never asked anything like that.' We think that's just too much, and we will not join."

"Did they tell you about fast offering?" the president asked.

"No," said the man. "What is that?"

"In the Church we fast for two meals each month and give the value of the meals for the help of the poor."

"They did not tell us that," the man said.

"Did they mention the building fund?"

"No, what is that?"

"In the Church we all contribute toward building chapels. If you joined the Church, you would want to participate both in labor and with money. Incidentally, we are building a new chapel here," he told him.

"Strange," he said, "that they didn't mention it."

"Did they explain the welfare program to you?"

"No," said the father. "What is that?"

"Well, we believe in helping one another. If someone is in need or ill or out of work or in trouble, we are organized to assist, and you would be expected to help.

"Did they also tell you that we have no professional clergy? All of us contribute our time, our talents, our means, and travel—all to help the work. And we're not paid for it in money."

"They didn't tell us any of that," said the father.

"Well," said the branch president, "if you are turned away by a little

With Sister Packer in South Africa, September 1969

thing like tithing, it is obvious you're not ready for this Church. Perhaps you have made the right decision and you should not join."

As they departed, almost as an afterthought he turned and said: "Have you ever wondered why people will do all of these things willingly? I have never received a bill for tithing. No one has ever called to collect it. But we pay it—and all of the rest—and count it as a great privilege.

"If you could discover *why,* you would be within reach of the pearl of great price, for which the Lord said the merchant man was willing to sell all that he had so that he might obtain it.

"But," the branch president added, "it is *your* decision. I only hope you will pray about it."

A few days later the man appeared at the branch president's home. No, he did not want to reschedule the missionaries. That would not be necessary. He wanted to schedule the baptism of his family. They had been praying, fervently praying.

This happens every day with individuals and entire families attracted by the high standards, not repelled by them. (74–08, p. 88)

Children should be taught the principle of tithing. In the Church children are taught the principle of tithing, but it is at home that the principle is applied. At home even young children can be shown how to figure a tithe and how it is paid.

One time President and Sister Harold B. Lee were in our home. Sister Lee put a handful of pennies on a table before our young son. She had him slide the shiny ones to one side and said, "These are your tithing; these belong to the Lord. The others are yours to keep." He thoughtfully looked from one pile to the other and then said, "Don't you have any more dirty ones?" That was when the real teaching moment began! (98–07, p. 24)

WORD OF WISDOM—DRUGS

The body is a sacred possession. Latter-day Saints are taught that our body is a sacred possession. It is the instrument of our mind and the foundation of our character. We should take nothing into our bodies that would harm the organs thereof, or that would tamper with the delicate processes of thinking and feeling. There needs to be a vigorous reemphasis of this among the youth of the Church. The physical body is a priceless treasure. It should not be degraded by subjecting it to the influence of tobacco, or alcohol in any form, or, more dangerous than either of these, the slavery which comes through drug addiction. (71–03)

Take care of your body. Take care of your body. It is the instrument of your mind and the foundation of your character. Within it are kindled the life-giving capacities suited to prepare mortal bodies for the coming generations.

"Know ye not that ye are the temple of God, and that the Spirit of God dwelleth in you? If any man defile the temple of God, him shall God destroy: for the temple of God is holy, which temple ye are."[4]

When will we learn to do the following simple things:

1. Eat nourishing, balanced meals, particularly a well-balanced, sustaining breakfast.

2. Make sure that your body has plenty of rest. "Cease to sleep longer than is needful; retire to thy bed early, that ye may not be weary; arise early, that your bodies and your minds may be invigorated."[5]

3. Get proper exercise through both labor and recreation. Keep your bodies clean. It is marvelous at the university to have the vigor of youth developed through competitive athletic activities. But I urge you to pay attention to those instructions concerning the well-being of your bodies, not only in the vigor of youth but also in the childbearing, the middle, and the later years. The inseparable relationship between mind and body demands this. (66–05, p. 246)

We are to take care of our bodies. We are to take care of our bodies. If we do not, we will pay the consequences. Those of us who are a little older are paying the consequences now of the things that we did or did not do when we were young. (00–07)

The Word of Wisdom does not promise perfect health. The Word of Wisdom does not promise you perfect health, but it teaches how to keep the body you were born with in the best condition and your mind alert to delicate spiritual promptings. (96–01, p. 18)

The Word of Wisdom places restrictions upon us. The Word of Wisdom put restrictions on members of the Church. To this day those regulations apply to every member and to everyone who seeks to join the Church. They are so compelling that no one is to be baptized into the Church without first agreeing to live by them. No one will be called to teach or to lead unless they accept them. When you want to go to the temple, you will be asked if you keep the Word of Wisdom. If you do not, you cannot go to the house of the Lord until you are fully worthy. (96–01, p. 17)

The Word of Wisdom has been declared a commandment. While the revelation came first as a "greeting; not by commandment or constraint,"[6] when members of the Church had had time to be taught the import of the revelation, succeeding Presidents of the Church declared it to be a commandment. And it was accepted by the Church as such. (96–01, p. 17)

The standards of the Word of Wisdom will not change. We have accepted as the Word of Wisdom in the Church standards that we will not change. You are not going to go on a mission unless you observe it. You are not going to go to the temple for the more sacred ordinances unless you observe it. That is, no tea or coffee or liquor or tobacco or whatever else is covered by it.

We get strange letters asking if this or that is a part of the Word of Wisdom. Marijuana is not listed in section 89! And neither is strychnine or arsenic listed! But, of course, they are not habit-forming.

The point is, if you want to move on spiritually and do as you ought to do in this life, the principle outlined in the Word of Wisdom shows you the requirements. You cannot just toy with it. (03–04, p. 171)

The Word of Wisdom is a principle with a promise. I found in the Word of Wisdom a principle with a promise. The principle: Care for your body; avoid habit-forming stimulants, tea, coffee, tobacco, liquor, and drugs.[7] Such addictive things do little more than relieve a craving which they caused in the first place.

The promise: Those who obey will receive better health[8] and "great treasures of knowledge, even hidden treasures."[9] (00–06, p. 72)

The Word of Wisdom teaches the principle and the blessings. The Word of Wisdom was "given for a principle with promise."[10] That word *principle* in the revelation is a very important one. A principle is an enduring truth, a law, a rule you can adopt to guide you in making decisions. Generally, principles are not spelled out in detail. That leaves you free to find your way with an enduring truth, a principle, as your anchor.

Members write in asking if this thing or that is against the Word of Wisdom. It's well known that tea, coffee, liquor, and tobacco are against it. It has not been spelled out in more detail. Rather, we teach the principle together with the promised blessings. There are many habit-forming, addictive things that one can drink or chew or inhale or inject which injure both body and spirit which are not mentioned in the revelation.

Everything harmful is not specifically listed; arsenic, for instance—certainly bad, but not habit-forming! He who must be commanded in all things, the Lord said, "is a slothful and not a wise servant."[11] (96–01, p. 17)

The Word of Wisdom is a shield and protection. However much the Word of Wisdom has protected us over the years from the degrading influences of drunkenness, alcoholism, and from the use of tobacco, it now stands as a protection against evil and designs which are a greater threat. Although there was no extensive scientific information to support the Word of Wisdom when it was given, that has come as the years have unfolded. And now we find that adherence to the counsel contained in the Word of Wisdom is a shield before our youth, protecting them from the frightening invasion of narcotics.

Young people who keep the Word of Wisdom are not ordinarily

likely to indulge—even experiment—with drugs. If there are strong family ties and a warm family home life, the likelihood of their addiction is more remote than ever. (71–03)

The Word of Wisdom may be more valuable spiritually than physically. Young people, stay in condition to respond to inspiration.

I have come to know also that a fundamental purpose of the Word of Wisdom has to do with revelation.

From the time you are very little we teach you to avoid tea, coffee, liquor, tobacco, narcotics, and anything else that disturbs your health.

And you know that we get very worried when we find one of you tampering with those things.

If someone "under the influence" can hardly listen to plain talk, how can they respond to spiritual promptings that touch their most delicate feelings?

As valuable as the Word of Wisdom is as a law of health, it may be much more valuable to you spiritually than it is physically.

Even if you keep the Word of Wisdom, there are some things that can happen to you physically, but those things don't generally damage you spiritually. (79–10, p. 20)

The Word of Wisdom is a key to receiving individual revelation. How significant [the Word of Wisdom] is, "given for a principle with promise, adapted to the capacity of the weak and the weakest of all saints, who are or can be called saints."[12]

This principle comes with a promise: "Run and not be weary, . . . walk and not faint."[13] That is desirable.

But there is a more important promise: "And shall find wisdom and great treasures of knowledge, even hidden treasures."[14]

Can you see the necessity of the Word of Wisdom? We press our people, almost beg our people, to behave themselves, to keep their spiritual person in tune so that they can have the reception of the Holy Ghost. Your body is the instrument of your mind and spirit. You must take proper care of it. (03–08, p. 52)

In that marvelous revelation, the Word of Wisdom, we are told how to keep our bodies free from impurities which might dull, even destroy, those delicate physical senses which have to do with spiritual communication.

The Word of Wisdom is a key to individual revelation. (89–04, p. 14)

Living the Word of Wisdom will affect what you learn spiritually. Your body is the instrument of your mind. In your emotions, the spirit and the body come closest to being one. What you learn spiritually depends, to a degree, on how you treat your body. That is why the Word of Wisdom[15] is so important.

The habit-forming substances prohibited by that revelation—tea, coffee, liquor, tobacco—interfere with the delicate feelings of spiritual communication, just as other addictive drugs will do.

Do not ignore the Word of Wisdom, for that may cost you the "great treasures of knowledge, even hidden treasures"[16] promised to those who keep it. And good health is an added blessing. (94–05, p. 61)

The Word of Wisdom was given to help keep our spiritual nature alert. Surely the Word of Wisdom was given so that you may keep the delicate, sensitive, spiritual part of your nature on proper alert. Learn to "listen" to your feelings. You will be guided and warned and taught and blessed. (96–01, p. 19)

The promise of the Word of Wisdom is personal revelation. The "Word of Wisdom [was] given for a principle with promise."[17] But what is the promise? The promise, of course, is personal revelation.

"[Those who remember to do these things will] *receive health in their navel and marrow to their bones;* . . .

"And shall run and not be weary, and shall walk and not faint. [And that means we will have some measure of health, which, I have learned, is of secondary importance.]

"And I, the Lord, give unto them a promise, that the destroying angel shall pass by them, as the children of Israel, and not slay them."[18]

And this: "[You shall receive] *great treasures of knowledge, even hidden treasures.*"[19]

Now, the Word of Wisdom is, I think, only incidentally to keep us healthy, if we will observe it. . . .

It is not that you are going to be a healthy athlete all of your life, and it is not that you are going to avoid old age. It is that you *will* have the key to revelation. When your body begins to deteriorate, the patterns of revelation will be augmented and magnified. (03–04, pp. 170–71)

Living the Word of Wisdom is essential to keep us open to spiritual communication. Living this way is essential to keep members of the Church open to spiritual communication. It is defined as "*a principle with promise,* adapted to the capacity of the weak and the weakest of all saints, who are or can be called saints."[20] Keeping the Word of Wisdom (and we must keep it) will protect us from the destructive addictions which shackle us and interrupt our communication with our Heavenly Father.

You see why obeying the Word of Wisdom is set as a condition for ordination to the priesthood or entrance to the temple. (04–04)

Substance abuse closes off spiritual communication. If we abuse our body with habit-forming substances, or misuse prescription drugs, we draw curtains which close off the light of spiritual communication.

Narcotic addiction serves the design of the prince of darkness, for it disrupts the channel to the Holy Spirit of Truth. At present the adversary has an unfair advantage. Addiction has the capacity to disconnect the human will and nullify moral agency. It can rob one of the power to decide. Agency is too fundamental a doctrine to be left in such jeopardy.

It is my conviction, and my constant prayer, that there will come through research, through inspiration to scientists if need be, the power to conquer narcotic addiction through the same means which cause it.

I plead with all of you to earnestly pray that somewhere, somehow, the way will be discovered to erase addiction in the human body. (89–04, p. 14)

There are multiple reasons for living the Word of Wisdom. The greatest loss in failing to observe the Word of Wisdom is not what may happen to your lungs or to your brain or to your coordination. There is another reason much more important. No doubt you have noticed some who have achieved so-called success have not kept the Word of Wisdom. You may know someone who has violated the principles and yet seems immune from any penalties. To those who keep the Word of Wisdom, there is a specific promise given of "wisdom and great treasures of knowledge, even hidden treasures." Our spiritual senses are more delicately balanced than any of our physical senses. Like a fine radio receiver with a sensitive tuning mechanism, they can easily be thrown off channel, or even jammed by corrosive influences introduced into our minds and bodies. We can be sensitive to inspiration and spiritual guidance. To do this we need the wisdom and treasures of knowledge; they constitute a spiritual confirmation, a testimony of the truth. To have this witness fulfills the promise of the Lord. To be denied it is the penalty.

There is yet another reason, perhaps the most important of all. . . .

In addition to the other promises offered to those who observe the Word of Wisdom, we find in the last verse of the revelation this additional promise: "I, the Lord, give unto them a promise, that the destroying angel shall pass by them, as the children of Israel, and not slay them." Can you see why we stress so strongly this principle? It is certainly not to drive anyone from activity in the Church, but that their blessings may be full. (68–02)

Avoid becoming fanatical. Learn to use moderation and common sense in matters of health and nutrition, and particularly in medication. Avoid being extreme or fanatical or becoming a faddist.

For example, the Word of Wisdom counsels us to eat meat sparingly.[21] Lest someone become extreme, we are told in another revelation that "whoso forbiddeth to [eat meat] is not ordained of God."[22] (96–01, p. 18)

CHAPTER 10

Chastity and Dating

"I have warned that the awesome powers of the adversary will be employed to entice all mankind to sinfully use the sacred power of procreation. Do not yield, for every debt of transgression must be paid." (92–02, p. 114)

LAW OF CHASTITY

The power of procreation is the key to the plan of happiness. The commandment to multiply and replenish the earth has never been rescinded. It is essential to the plan of redemption and is the source of human happiness. Through the righteous exercise of this power, as through nothing else, we may come close to our Father in Heaven and experience a fulness of joy, even godhood! The power of procreation is not an incidental part of the plan of happiness; it is the key—the very key. (92–02, pp. 105–6)

Much of the happiness that may come to you in this life will depend on how you use this sacred power of creation. The fact that you young men can become fathers and that you young women can become mothers is of utmost importance to you. (72–01, p. 111)

How we employ the power to create life will determine our course in life. As we learn about ourselves and learn about the great plan of redemption, we know that in the premortal existence intelligence existed forever. It was not created. It will exist forever. In due course, we were given a spirit body.[1] We became then the sons and daughters of God. We had gender then. We were male or female.[2] While in that existence, we were valiant and chose good, as Alma recorded.[3] . . .

Then, in the course of our having chosen good . . . we had a body prepared by mortal parents, and we were born into mortality. With that came the power to create life, to follow the plan of redemption, the plan of happiness. How we employ that power and understand the supernal value of it is one major factor that will determine where we go in life. (03–04, pp. 169–70)

The power to act in the creation of life is sacred. This power to act in the creation of life is sacred. You can some day have a family of your own. Through the exercise of this power, you can invite children to live with you—little boys and little girls who will be your very own—created, in a way, in your own image. You can establish a home, a dominion of power and influence and opportunity. This carries with it great responsibility. (72–01, p. 111)

The process by which life is conceived was meant to be sacred. The process by which life is conceived is proper only for a man and woman who are legally and lawfully married. It was meant from the beginning to be veiled in total privacy. It was never to be degraded in idle conversation or to be the subject of unworthy humor. It was never to be exposed to public view, detailed in novels, illustrated in books, or acted out upon the stage or in films. It was never to involve children. And it was never to be perverted, never to be sold, and never to be bought for money. (89–02, p. 171)

There is only one legitimate employment of the power of procreation. The only legitimate employment of the power of procreation is between husband and wife, man and woman, who have been legally and lawfully married. Anything else violates the commandments of God. (92–03, p. 68)

Our mortal and eternal happiness depends on how we respond to physical desires. The desire to mate in humankind is constant and very strong. Our happiness in mortal life, our joy and exaltation, are dependent upon how we respond to these persistent, compelling physical desires.

As the procreative power matures in early manhood and womanhood there occurs, in a natural way, very personal feelings unlike any other physical experience. It is not without meaning that the process through which life is conceived should be accompanied by feelings of such depth and attraction that they draw the individual to seek a repetition of them. (92–02, p. 106)

The power of procreation is the very key to happiness. Protect and guard your gift. Your actual happiness is at stake. Eternal family life, now only in your anticipations and dreams, can be achieved because our Heavenly Father has bestowed this choicest gift of all upon you— this power of creation. It is the very key to happiness. Hold this gift as sacred and pure. Use it only as the Lord has directed.

My young friends, there is much happiness and joy to be found in this life. I can testify of that.

I picture you with a companion whom you love and who loves you. I picture you at the marriage altar, entering into covenants that are sacred. I picture you in a home where love has its fulfillment. I picture you with little children about you and see your love growing with them.

I cannot frame this picture. I would not if I could, for it has no bounds. Your happiness will have no ends if you obey his laws. (72–01, p. 113)

The power of procreation is good. The power of procreation is good. It is the power to create life. Think of that! The power to generate life given to man! Through its employment, a couple can unselfishly bring children into the world. This power becomes a binding tie in marriage. Those who employ this power in complete worthiness have the promise of eternal increase. Those who do not, face the possibility that it will be withdrawn from them.

In marriage a couple can unselfishly express their love to one another. They reap, as a result, a fulfillment and a completeness and a knowledge of their identity as sons and daughters of God.

The power of procreation is good—divinely good—and productive. Pervert it, and it can be bad—devilishly bad—and destructive.

This power is very different from our physical or emotional nature. We cannot toy with it, or employ it prematurely or unwisely, without being on some very dangerous ground. (78–01, p. 190)

Under the accepted plan, Adam and Eve were sent to the earth as our first parents. They could prepare physical bodies for the first spirits to be introduced into this life.

There was provided in our bodies—and this is sacred—a power of creation, a light, so to speak, that has the power to kindle other lights. This gift was to be used only within the sacred bonds of marriage. Through the exercise of this power of creation, a mortal body may be conceived, a spirit enter into it, and a new soul born into this life.

This power is good. It can create and sustain family life, and it is in family life that we find the fountains of happiness. It is given to virtually every individual who is born into mortality. It is a sacred and significant power, and I repeat, my young friends, that this power is good. . . .

It is a gift from God our Father. In the righteous exercise of it as in nothing else, we may come close to Him. (72–01, pp. 111–12)

When properly controlled the power of procreation will bless and sanctify. The eternal laws of the gospel of Jesus Christ do not prohibit our responding to inborn, God-given mating instincts. Alma admonished his son Shiblon, "See that ye bridle all your passions, that ye may be filled with love."[4] A bridle is used to guide, to direct. Our passion is to be controlled—but not controlled by extermination, as with a plague of insects; not controlled by eradication, as with a disease. It is to be controlled as electricity is controlled, to generate power and life. When lawfully used, the power of procreation will bless and it will sanctify.[5] (92–02, pp. 108–9)

The power of procreation must be strong and constant. It was necessary that this power of creation have at least two dimensions: one, it must be strong; and two, it must be more or less constant.

This power must be strong, for most men by nature seek adventure. Except for the compelling persuasion of these feelings, men would be reluctant to accept the responsibility of sustaining a home and a family. This power must be constant, too, for it becomes a binding tie in family life.

You are old enough, I think, to look around you in the animal kingdom. You soon realize that where this power of creation is a fleeting thing, where it expresses itself only in season, there is no family life.

It is through this power that life continues. A world full of trials and fears and disappointments can be changed into a kingdom of hope and joy and happiness. Each time a child is born, the world somehow is renewed in innocence. (72–01, pp. 111–12)

True love can be sublime, or if misused, it will bring suffering. You who are young adults are at an age when there is a compelling urgency for you to be complete. You want to find the fulfillment in life that you know you cannot find alone. The powers awakened earlier in your life have been growing. You have been responding to them, probably very clumsily, but they now form themselves into a restlessness that cannot be ignored. You are old enough now to fall in love—not the puppy love of elementary years, not the confused love of the teens, but the full-blown love of eligible men and women, newly matured, ready for life. I mean romantic love, with all the full intense meaning of the word, with all of the power and turbulence and frustration, the yearning, the restraining, and all of the peace and beauty and sublimity of love. No experience can be more beautiful, no power more compelling, more exquisite. Or, if misused, no suffering is more excruciating than that connected with love. (63–06, pp. 6–7)

No greater protection from the adversary than knowing the plan of salvation. The sacred power of procreation gave man an essential part in the plan of salvation. There were eternal laws set to govern their use of it. It was to operate in very narrow limits, and there were penalties of eternal consequence if they disobeyed. And there is ever the tempter and his angels who would tempt man to degrade or misuse this and every other sacred gift they had received. He is still determined to have them serve him and conspires to replace every feeling of love with one that is corrupt.

Agency required that man be free to use the power of procreation as he will. And the laws of nature provided that every time the natural conditions were met, whether under the bonds of marriage or not, a body would be conceived and a spirit assigned. But who, knowing of the plan of salvation, could think of misusing it? Who would seriously contemplate abortion or adultery or perversion? Or who would question the counsel of the prophets not to tamper with this process?

There is no greater protection for man than to know the plan, the gospel plan, the plan of salvation. . . . Without a knowledge of the gospel plan, fornication, adultery, perversion, and abortion would all seem natural, innocent, even justified. Do you see the connection between moral problems and a knowledge of the gospel? There is no greater protection from the adversary than truth, to know the plan of salvation. (83–04)

The inheritance. Once a man received as his inheritance two keys. The first key, he was told, would open a vault which he must protect at all costs. The second key was to a safe within the vault which contained a priceless treasure. He was to open this safe and freely use the precious things which were stored therein. He was warned that many would seek to rob him of his inheritance. He was promised that if he used the treasure worthily, it would be replenished and never be diminished, not in all eternity. He would be tested. If he used it to benefit others, his own blessings and joy would increase.

The man went alone to the vault. His first key opened the door. He tried to unlock the treasure with the other key, but he could not, for there were two locks on the safe. His key alone would not open it. No matter how he tried, he could not open it. He was puzzled. He had been given the keys. He knew the treasure was rightfully his. He had obeyed instructions, but he could not open the safe.

In due time, there came a woman into the vault. She, too, held a key. It was noticeably different from the key he held. Her key fit the other lock. It humbled him to learn that he could not obtain his rightful inheritance without her.

They made a covenant that together they would open the treasure and, as instructed, he would watch over the vault and protect it; she would watch over the treasure. She was not concerned that, as guardian of the vault, he held two keys, for his full purpose was to see that she was safe as she watched over that which was most precious to them both. Together they opened the safe and partook of their inheritance. They rejoiced for, as promised, it replenished itself.

With great joy they found that they could pass the treasure on to their children; each could receive a full measure, undiminished to the last generation.

Perhaps some few of their posterity would not find a companion who possessed the complementary key, or one worthy and willing to keep the covenants relating to the treasure. Nevertheless, if they kept the commandments, they would not be denied even the smallest blessing.

Because some tempted them to misuse their treasure, they were careful to teach their children about keys and covenants.

There came, in due time, among their posterity some few who were deceived or jealous or selfish because one was given two keys and another only one. "Why," the selfish ones reasoned, "cannot the treasure be mine alone to use as I desire?"

Some tried to reshape the key they had been given to resemble the other key. Perhaps, they thought, it would then fit both locks. And so it was that the safe was closed to them. Their reshaped keys were useless, and their inheritance was lost.

Those who received the treasure with gratitude and obeyed the laws concerning it knew joy without bounds through time and all eternity.

I bear witness of our Father's plan for happiness, and bear testimony in the name of Him who wrought the Atonement, that it might be. (93–06, pp. 23–24)

TEACHING THE LAW OF CHASTITY

Teach children the sacredness of the body. Teach the children the plan of salvation, the sacredness of the body, and the supernal nature of the power to give life. Mothers, guide them and warn them against misusing those sacred powers in your gentle way. The future of the family depends on how those powers are protected. . . .

When the sacred power to give life is used immorally, unnaturally, or in perversion, one stands in jeopardy of failing the test of mortality. Even then, through true repentance, the mercy of the Holy One has power to reclaim and to heal. (06–03)

Maturity and readiness are important when teaching morality. One of the major difficulties, and one of the monumental dangers, of sex education courses in public schools is that they disregard this significant principle of teaching. They tell all before the youngster is ready, and in so doing, they often wreak havoc with the spiritual, emotional, and moral stability of the students. They open them to great jeopardy. Things should be done in the season thereof, and there is a time for all things. A wise teacher and a wise parent will be alert to that fact. . . . The matter of teaching morality may be necessary, but the framework in which it is set should recognize the degree of maturity and readiness. . . . Unfortunately, there is no series of charts or graphs or measures or tests available that will enable the parent or the teacher to gain an accurate profile of maturation of each student and thereby tailor his teachings accordingly. This means that we must be careful and must be quiet observers of each youngster in order to be able to understand when he is ready. (*TYD*, pp. 130–31)

Two major problems in teaching procreation. I am convinced that two of the major mistakes are to teach too much about the [process of procreation] and to teach it at the wrong time. . . .

The notion that our young people need to be taught in great detail all of the facts relating to the physical processes involved in reproduction at an early age is nonsense. The overteaching of it is not a protection. Such things as they should know about the subject should be taught in a framework of reverence and modesty. (*TYD*, p. 302)

The challenge in teaching chastity. Perhaps no moral value is more challenging to teach than chastity. It is so easy to teach it negatively or to over-teach it. There is more danger of "over-kill" in teaching this subject than in teaching any other. (*TYD*, p. 301)

Chastity must be taught carefully. [Youth] are being taught—perhaps a better word would be bombarded—on the subject of chastity constantly and continually. Most of such teaching is negative and destructive; much of it is visually taught.

It is our responsibility to teach the subject in such a way that the principles of truth will overcome the misconceptions and misleading falsehoods that are taught so widely. We must teach so powerfully and so permanently that the truth cannot be overcome by the temptation to immorality, no matter how enticing. (*TYD*, p. 301)

The responsibility to teach about procreation rests with parents. The responsibility and the right to teach these sacred [procreative] processes rest with the parents in the home. I do not believe that it is the responsibility of the public schools, nor is it the responsibility of the organizations of the Church. The contribution of the Church in this respect is to teach parents the standards of morality that the Lord has revealed and to assist them in their responsibility of teaching these sacred subjects to their children. (*TYD*, p. 302)

Great care must be given when discussing chastity. The one place in the Church where some frank discussions [about chastity] may be appropriate is during an interview for priesthood advancement, for a call to a position, for a temple recommend, or in an interview in which a member is confessing transgression in order to get it resolved.

Occasionally, deep inquiry may be necessary. This teaching process, and that's what interviewing can be, ought likewise to be shrouded in modesty and the subject ought to be treated with reverence, wisdom, and restraint. . . .

Those who teach, and I refer to leaders, to teachers, and to parents, should keep in mind this message. Picture a father and mother leaving home for a period of time. Just as they go out the door they say to their little children who are to be left untended during their absence, "Now children, be good. Whatever you do while we are gone, do not take the footstool into the pantry, and do not climb to the fourth shelf and move the cracker box and reach back and get the sack of beans and take a bean and put it up your nose, will you?"

Some of us are just that foolish. The humor of the illustration is wry humor when you think of the first thing that happens after the parents are gone. Surely we can be wiser than that. (*TYD*, p. 303)

The remedy for infidelity never changes. The remedy for an infection in the physical body has changed dramatically over the centuries; the remedy for infidelity, not at all. Morality is not so easily conveyed from one generation to the next. It is acquired more from example, ideally in the home. (88–08, p. 9)

MODESTY

Your body is the instrument of your mind. Your body really *is* the instrument of your mind and the foundation of your character.

President Harold B. Lee taught of the important symbolic and actual effect of how we dress and groom our bodies. If you are well groomed and modestly dressed, you invite the companionship of the Spirit of our Father in Heaven and exercise a wholesome influence upon those around you. To be unkempt in your appearance exposes you to influences that are degrading.[6]

Avoid immodest clothing. Dress and groom to show the Lord that you know how precious your body is.

President Hinckley has warned you not to decorate your body with pictures or symbols that will never wash off or to pierce your body with rings or jewelry after the manner of the world.[7]

You would not paint a temple with dark pictures or symbols or graffiti or even initials. Do not do so with your body.[8] (00–06, pp. 72–73)

Don't follow the worldly pattern. On one occasion when I went to the temple to perform a marriage, I found one of the witnesses to be a young man, bearded, and with odd, hippie-type glasses. I felt uneasy. I did also a few days later at another marriage, when the groom wore a beard.

Not that there is anything wrong with a beard—not in and of itself. Many of our leaders have worn them. Brigham Young wore a beard, and Lorenzo Snow, and Joseph F. Smith, and George Albert Smith, to name a few. The thing that made me uneasy was just that it is another indication in our day. Here was an indication that this was a young man who apparently wanted to be in the world and to look like the world.

It seems so strange to me that young men would come to the temple and in effect say, "We want to experience the most exalted and the highest ordinance in this life," and yet at once insist on saying, "However, I am part of the world, and I want to be like the world and look like it."

To follow after the pattern of the world is to consent to influences that will erode and weaken and may ultimately destroy a marriage. It is extremely difficult to fight the world in the marriage relationship.

So I worry, not about the beard but about what it means. It must mean something, you know. (70–07, pp. 225–26)

Youth can be modest and yet in style. The youth of the Church, by and large, have found a sensible and reasonable adjustment to the grooming and dress styles of our day. Our young men and women can dress with decency and modesty and yet not be unstylish or look all that different or odd. (73–09, p. 25)

PROPER DATING PATTERNS

Dating should not be premature. When you are old enough you ought to start dating. It is good for young men and women to learn to know and to appreciate one another. It is good for you to go to games and dances and picnics, to do all of the young things. We encourage our young people to date. We encourage you to set high standards of dating.

When are you old enough? Maturity may vary from individual to individual, but we are rather of the conviction that dating should not even begin until you are sixteen. And then, ideal dating is on a group basis. Stay in group activities; don't pair off. Avoid steady dating. Steady dating is courtship, and surely the beginning of courtship ought to be delayed until you have emerged from your teens. (65–03, p. 517)

Dating should not be premature. You should appreciate your parents if they see to that. Dating should not be without supervision, and you should appreciate parents who see to that. . . . Dating leads to marriage. Marriage is a sacred religious covenant, and in its most exalted expression it may be an eternal covenant. Whatever preparation relates to marriage, whether it be personal or social, concerns us as members of the Church. (65–03, p. 517)

Parents have a sacred obligation to concern themselves with your dating habits. I speak very plainly to you, my young friends. If you are old enough to date, you are old enough to know that your parents have not only the right but the sacred obligation to concern themselves with your dating habits, and in doing this they are under counsel from the leaders of the Church.

If you are mature enough to date, you're mature enough to accept without childish, juvenile argument their authority as parents to set rules of conduct for you.

No sensible father would loan your new convertible to anybody, to go anyplace, to do anything, to come back anytime. If you are old enough to date, you are old enough to see the foolishness of parents who would loan their *children* on any such an arrangement. Don't ask your parents to permit you, their most precious possession, to go out on such flimsy agreements.

Actually, the loan of the car would not be so serious as you suppose, for should it be destroyed, it could be replaced. However, there are some problems and some hazards with dating for which there is no such fortunate solution. (*TYD*, pp. 293–94)

Be open with your parents. Communicate with them. Discuss your problems with them. Have prayer with them before a dating event. Stay in group activities. Don't pair off. Avoid steady dating. The right time to begin a courtship is when you have emerged from your teens. Heed the counsels from your bishop, from your priesthood and auxiliary teachers, from your seminary teacher. (65–03, p. 518)

Focus on measuring up to the ideals of your intended mate. I recall an experience with a young man who came to me asking my advice. He was a student at Brigham Young University, courting a lovely young woman. He said, "Brother Packer, I've got to have you tell me what to do. We've had an on-again, off-again, courtship and romance. If you tell me I should marry her, I will. If you tell me I shouldn't, I won't." He said, "She's my ideal. Intellectually, as I register all of her qualities, it all adds up to more than 100 percent of what I'd desire. But there's just one thing wrong with it."

I said, "What's that ?"

And he said, "We don't seem to like one another. We're miserable when we're together and more miserable when we're apart." . . .

I asked him a question I often ask young people. I said, "Are you going to accept the counsel you receive?" . . .

He said, "Well, that's what I'm here for. I'll accept your counsel."

I said, "Fine, you go home this weekend. You go to your father and you get him alone and you tell him what you've told me and you do what he tells you to do."

He went to his father and told him all he had told me, and his father said something to this effect: "Son, do you know what's wrong with you? You've been courting that girl as you've courted other girls and registered in your mind a set of specifications, and you go about it just as though you were buying a horse. You list all of the qualifications, the appearance, the temperament, and all of the rest. All of the time you're standing in judgment as to whether she will quite fit all of your specifications."

He continued, "My boy, your trouble is selfishness. If you'd spend half of the time worrying about whether you fit her ideals as you do worrying whether she fits yours, you wouldn't have this problem."

A few months later, we were assembled in one of the sealing rooms of the temple with this young couple and I had the privilege of officiating and sealing them for time and for all eternity, because he had learned the lesson of his life and had at once become unselfish.

I would suggest to you sweet sisters, why don't you be registering in your own mind not so much what specifications you have set for that prince valiant you're looking for, but rather a concern as to whether or not you would meet all of his. I think if you'll look at them with real intent and if you're prayerful about it, you're going to be looking toward some things that are homely and maybe dull, maybe a bit uninteresting, some might be dreary, some of them habit patterns that are hard to form, and yet you'll be preparing yourself in such a way that when the right young man does come along he will automatically and immediately and instantly see in you all that he has dreamed about and hoped for. And providentially there's some father teaching him so that he likewise is preparing himself so that he can be a better husband and a better father. (73–02)

SERIOUSNESS OF IMMORALITY

The overemphasis on physical gratification is the greatest deception in our day. The greatest deception foisted upon the human race in our day is that overemphasis of physical gratification as it is related to romantic love. It is merely a repetition of the same delusion that has been impressed on every generation in ages past. When we learn that physical gratification is only incident to, and not the compelling force of love itself, we have made a supreme discovery. If only physical gratification should interest you, you need not be selective at all. This power is possessed by almost everyone. Alone, without attendant love, this relationship becomes nothing—indeed, less and worse than nothing.

The adversary would draw down and make cheap and common and vulgar the sacred, sublime experience of love in its total expression, and in nothing is his villainy more loathsome, so tragic, as the invitation to man to look upon love with eyes and hearts and minds which are filthy. (63–06, p. 15)

Satan seeks to get us to misuse the powers of procreation. In the beginning there was one among us who rebelled at the plan of our Heavenly Father. He vowed to destroy and to disrupt the plan.

He was prevented from having a mortal body and was cast out— limited forever from establishing a kingdom of his own. He became satanically jealous. He knows that this power of creation is not just an incident to the plan, but a key to it.

He knows that if he can entice you to use this power prematurely, to use it too soon, or to misuse it in any way, you may well lose your opportunities for eternal progression.

He is an actual being from the unseen world. He has great power. He will use it to persuade you to transgress those laws set up to protect the sacred powers of creation.

In former times he was too cunning to confront one with an open invitation to be immoral. But rather, sneakingly and quietly he would tempt young and old alike to think loosely of these sacred powers of creation, to bring down to a vulgar or to a common level that which is sacred and beautiful.

His tactics have changed now. He describes it as only an appetite to be satisfied. He teaches that there are no attendant responsibilities to the use of this power. Pleasure, he will tell you, is its sole purpose.

His devilish invitations appear on billboards. They are coined into

At solemn assembly, April 1970. Standing, left to right: Boyd K. Packer, Hugh B. Brown, Howard W. Hunter, Gordon B. Hinckley, Thomas S. Monson.

jokes and written into the lyrics of songs. They are acted out on television and at theaters. They will stare at you now from most magazines. There are magazines—you know the word, pornography— open, wicked persuasions to pervert and misuse this sacred power. (72–01, p. 112)

Satan seeks to lead men and women into immorality. Because the power to create a mortal body is essential to our happiness and exaltation, the Lord has decreed severe penalties against the immoral use of that power to beget life.[9] Satan knows that if he can corrupt the process of mating and cause men and women to degrade it in immoral acts, he will, to that degree, for them disrupt the plan of happiness.

Paul taught, "God . . . will not suffer you to be tempted above that ye are able; but will with the temptation also make a way to escape, that ye may be able to bear it."[10]

I do not wish to offend the delicate feelings of you wonderful young people, but in your world awash with iniquity, you must be on guard. There are words we would rather not say. They describe things that we would rather not think about. But you are inescapably exposed to temptations in connection with fornication, adultery, pornography, prostitution, perversion, lust, abuse, the unnatural, and all that grows from them. Only with great effort can you escape the degrading profanity and wicked, joking humor that accompanies them. It is all paraded before you in unworthy entertainment—music, print, drama, film, television, and, of course, the Internet.

Remember the First Vision when young Joseph knelt in the grove. Immediately, thick darkness gathered around him. He was seized by the power of the enemy, an actual being from the unseen world. He did what every one of you can do. He called upon God, and the evil power left him.[11] There is great power in prayer. As a son or a daughter of God, you can, as Joseph did, pray to God in the name of Jesus Christ for strength.[12]

Satan, with his angels, will try to capture your thoughts and control what you do. If he can, he will corrupt anything that is good.[13] To him the Internet is just that—a net to ensnare you into wicked addiction with pornography. Unhappiness will follow.[14] (03–09, p. 25)

Moral violations occur step by step. I do not want to counsel you—I want to warn you. . . . There is a single moral standard in this Church and kingdom. It applies equally to men and to women. It holds that we shall be totally devoid of any moral implication; either with the opposite sex or with our own sex; that we will totally avoid any circumstances that could draw us into relationships that would be spiritually fatal to us.

My experiences in interviewing young people have been that the effects of these physical relationships are cumulative. We never find a young man that comes to us for a missionary interview that found himself in complete moral violation in one step. It is a stairway. He inched up it gradually. First, he was just holding hands with the girl. Then, the process that you full well know, ultimately because of repeated occurrences, brought him to the point of no resistance. He finds himself involved in a circumstance that may well be spiritually fatal. Now I say, I do not counsel you—I warn you against the possibility. (62–05)

Never tamper with the sacred powers of procreation. You grow up in a society where before you is the constant invitation to tamper with these sacred powers.

I want to counsel you and I want you to remember these words.

Do not let anyone at all touch or handle your body, not anyone! Those who tell you otherwise proselyte you to share their guilt. We teach you to maintain your innocence.

Turn away from any who would persuade you to experiment with these life-giving powers.

That such indulgence is widely accepted in society today is not enough! For both parties to willingly consent to such indulgence is not enough!

To imagine that it is a normal expression of affection is not enough to make it right.

The only righteous use of this sacred power is within the covenant of marriage.

Never misuse these sacred powers.

And now, my young friends, I must tell you soberly and seriously that God has declared in unmistakable language that misery and sorrow will follow the violation of the laws of chastity. "Wickedness never was happiness."[15] (72–01, p. 112)

Touch not the functions and powers of life within your body. Touch not the functions and powers of life within your body, and do not tamper with or explore these powers with any living soul. To seek some satisfaction by yourself is but to experience guilt, morbidity, and degradation. This exploration was never meant to be. I know there are those who say that things like this are to be excused. Some even say they are necessary. This is a lie. Such indulgence is neither necessary nor desirable. (63–06, p. 16)

Do not experiment with immorality. Do not experiment; do not let anyone of either gender touch your body to awaken passions that can flame beyond control. It begins as an innocent curiosity, Satan influences your thoughts, and it becomes a pattern, a habit, which may imprison you in an addiction, to the sorrow and disappointment of those who love you.[16] (00–06, p. 73)

Guard the sacred powers of creation. Do not ever let anybody touch your body in order to stimulate in any way those sacred powers of creation. Nobody! Not of your same gender or any gender! That power is to be expressed only and solely with your husband or wife to whom you are legally and lawfully married.[17] Then all of the happiness possible is open to you. You must guard that sacred power with your life. (03–04, p. 173)

We must fight unworthy desires. When any unworthy desires press into your mind, fight them, resist them, control them.[18] The Apostle Paul taught, "There hath no temptation taken you but such as is common to man: but God is faithful, who will not suffer you to be tempted above that ye are able; but will with the temptation also make a way to escape, that ye may be able to bear it."[19]

That may be a struggle from which you will not be free in this life. If you do not act on temptations, you need feel no guilt. They may be extremely difficult to resist. But that is better than to yield and bring disappointment and unhappiness to you and those who love you. (00–06, p. 74)

All must learn to control their impulses according to moral law. All of us are subject to feelings and impulses. Some of these are worthy and some are not; some of them are natural and some of them are not. We are to control them, meaning we are to direct them according to the moral law. (90–09, p. 85)

Beware of moral temptations that lead to unnatural behavior. I must speak of another danger, almost unknown in our youth but now everywhere about you.

Normal desires and attractions emerge in the teenage years; there is the temptation to experiment, to tamper with the sacred power of procreation. These desires can be intensified, even perverted, by pornography, improper music, or the encouragement from unworthy associations. What would have only been a more or less normal passing phase in establishing gender identity can become implanted and leave you confused, even disturbed.

If you consent, the adversary can take control of your thoughts and lead you carefully toward a habit and to an addiction, convincing you that immoral, unnatural behavior is a fixed part of your nature.

With some few, there is the temptation which seems nearly overpowering for man to be attracted to man or woman to woman. The scriptures plainly condemn those who "dishonour their own bodies between themselves; . . . men with men working that which is unseemly"[20] or "women [who] change the natural use into that which is against nature."[21]

The gates of freedom, and the good or bad beyond, swing open or closed to the password *choice*. You are free to choose a path that may lead to despair, to disease, even to death.[22]

If you choose that course, the fountains of life may dry up. You will not experience the combination of love and struggle, the pain and pleasure, the disappointment and sacrifice, that love which, blended together in parenthood, exalts a man or a woman and leads to that fulness of joy spoken of in the scriptures.[23] (00–06, p. 73)

Neither the spiritual nor the letter of the moral law condones perversion. [There are those who] defend and promote gay or lesbian conduct. They wrest the scriptures, attempting to prove that these impulses are inborn, cannot be overcome, and should not be resisted, and that therefore such conduct has a morality of its own. They quote scriptures to justify perverted acts between consenting adults. That same logic would justify incest or the molesting of little children of either gender. Neither the letter nor the spirit of moral law condones any such conduct. . . . Some choose to reject the scriptures out of hand and forsake their covenants. But they cannot choose to avoid the consequences. (90–09, p. 85)

The course we choose will lead to happiness or disappointment and tragedy. The legitimate union of the sexes is a law of God. The sacred covenants made by husband and wife with God protect the worthy expression of those feelings and impulses which are vital to the continuation of the race and essential to a happy family life. Illicit or perverted conduct leads without exception to disappointment, to suffering, to tragedy. (90–09, p. 85)

Misery and sorrow will follow the violation of the law of chastity. I must tell you soberly and seriously that God has declared in unmistakable language that misery and sorrow will follow the violation of the laws of chastity. "Wickedness never was happiness."[24] These laws were set up to guide all of His children in the use of this gift.

He does not have to be spiteful or vengeful in order that punishment will come from the breaking of the moral code. . . .

Crowning glory awaits you if you live worthily. The loss of the crown may well be punishment enough. Very often, we are punished as much by our sins as we are for them. (64–01)

Three transgressions of enormous proportion. Whatever the laws of man may come to tolerate, the misuse of the power of procreation, the destroying of innocent life through abortion, and the abuse of little children are transgressions of enormous proportion. For cradled therein rests the destiny of innocent, helpless children. (86–05, p. 18)

For those who have fallen it is possible to become clean. I am sure that within the sound of my voice there is more than one young person who already has fallen into transgression. Some of you young people, I am sure, almost innocent of any intent, but persuaded by the entice-ments and the temptations, already have misused this power.

Know then, my young friends, that there is a great cleansing power. And know that you can be clean. . . .

There is a way, not entirely painless, but certainly possible. You can stand clean and spotless before Him. Guilt will be gone, and you can be at peace. Go to your bishop. He holds the key to this cleansing power.

Then one day you can know the full and righteous expression of these powers and the attendant happiness and joy in righteous family life. In due time, within the bonds of the marriage covenant, you can yield yourselves to those sacred expressions of love which have as their fulfillment the generation of life itself.

Someday you will hold a little boy or a little girl in your arms and know that two of you have acted in partnership with our Heavenly Father in the creation of life. Because the youngster belongs to you, you may then come to love someone more than you love yourself. (72–01, pp. 112–13)

Instructions to those who have erred. To those who may have unwittingly, or in a moment of supreme temptation, made themselves unworthy or less worthy to love, instructions are simple. See your bishop. He will tell you what to do. Now, do not delay. Get it settled now, because mischief grows. It is hard to keep locked up. But the bishop has the keys, and he can lock it up for good.

There is forgiveness—complete forgiveness. It is based on repentance—complete repentance. (63–06, pp. 17–18)

A warning to unmarried couples. There is a practice, now quite prevalent, for unmarried couples to live together, a counterfeit of marriage. They suppose that they shall have all that marriage can offer without the obligations connected with it. They are wrong!

However much they hope to find in a relationship of that kind, they will lose more. Living together without marriage destroys something inside all who participate. Virtue, self-esteem, and refinement of character wither away.

Claiming that it will not happen does not prevent the loss; and these virtues, once lost, are not easily reclaimed.

To suppose that one day they may nonchalantly change their habits and immediately claim all that might have been theirs had they not made a mockery of marriage is to suppose something that will not be.

One day, when they come to themselves, they will reap disappointment.

One cannot degrade marriage without tarnishing other words as well, such words as *boy, girl, manhood, womanhood, husband, wife, father, mother, baby, children, family, home.*

Such words as *unselfishness* and *sacrifice* will then be tossed aside. Then self-respect will fade and love itself will not want to stay.

If you have been tempted to enter such a relationship or if you now live with another without marriage, leave! Withdraw from it! Run away from it! Do not continue with it! Or, if you can, make a marriage out of it.

Even a rickety marriage will serve good purpose as long as two people struggle to keep it from falling down around them. (81–04, pp. 13–14)

MORAL ISSUES

We must plant moral and spiritual values. If we do not plant moral and spiritual values firmly in place, something creeps in to replace them.

Some declare, "I'll let my children grow up uninfluenced; and when they are mature they'll choose for themselves, and then they'll not only be moral but they'll also be strong and free."

That's an interesting idea. Try it on your garden! Plant the seeds and leave the weeds, and see what you get.

If the nation's farmers did that, one season would see food shortages, another would produce a famine.

Morality, I repeat, is a very unstable element. Moral character does not develop by accident. It must be produced to exist, and it must be sustained to endure. (77–08, pp. 159–60)

The Church must speak out on moral issues. When a moral issue does arise, it is the responsibility of the leaders of the Church to speak out. Gambling, for instance, certainly is a moral issue. Life is a moral issue. When morality is involved, we have both the *right* and the *obligation* to raise a warning voice. We do not as a church speak on political issues unless morality is involved. (92–03, p. 67)

The Church must prepare to emerge as the major moral force in the world. (08–02)

When it comes to moral laws, the scriptures do not detail all that is approved or forbidden. Some challenge us to show where the scriptures specifically forbid abortion or a gay/lesbian or drug-centered lifestyle. "If they are so wrong," they ask, "why don't the scriptures tell us so in '*letter* of the law' plainness?" In fact, these issues are not ignored in the revelations.[25]

But the scriptures are generally positive rather than negative in their themes; therefore, it is a mistake to assume that anything not specifically prohibited in the "letter of the law" is somehow approved of the Lord. Not all of what the Lord approves is in the scriptures; neither is all that is forbidden. The Word of Wisdom, for instance, makes no specific warning against taking arsenic. Surely we don't need a revelation to tell us that is a harmful substance. (90–09, p. 84)

A tragic decline in the moral environment. As we test the *moral* environment, we find the *pollution* index is spiraling upward.

The Book of Mormon depicts humanity struggling through a "mist of darkness" and defines the darkness as the "temptations of the devil."[26] So dense was that *moral pollution* that many followed "strange roads" and "fell away into forbidden paths and were lost."[27]

The deliberate pollution of the fountain of life now clouds our moral environment. The gift of mortal life and the capacity to kindle other lives is a supernal blessing. Its worth is *incalculable!*

The rapid, sweeping deterioration of values is characterized by a preoccupation—even an obsession—with the procreative act. Abstinence before marriage and fidelity within it are openly scoffed at—marriage and parenthood ridiculed as burdensome, unnecessary. Modesty, a virtue of a refined individual or society, is all but gone. (92–03, p. 66)

In the world, tolerance has been elevated above morality, decency, and honor. (08–02)

Society is obsessed with immorality. Morality is no longer a measure of character for prominent role models for our youth—the politicians, the athletes, the entertainers. With ever fewer exceptions, what we see and read and hear has the mating act as the central theme. Censorship of any kind is forced offstage as a violation of individual freedom. That which should be absolutely private is disrobed and acted out center stage. In the shadows backstage wait addiction, pornography, perversion, infidelity, abortion, and—the ugliest of them all—incest and molestation. And all of them are on the increase. In company with them now is the pestilent disease, which, like a biblical plague, threatens races of mankind. In fact, all of mankind.

The philosophies which now converge all have one thing in common: either by insinuation or by declaration they reject God as our creator, as our Father, as our lawgiver. (92–02, p. 111)

Four transgressions that inflict suffering on little children. There is a sorry side to this subject as well. I wish not to dwell on that beyond listing four transgressions which plague mankind, all of which inflict suffering upon little children.

First, that consummate physical union of man and woman belonging to the marriage covenant is now falsely proclaimed an acceptable indulgence for any two adults.

Second, the misuse of that procreative power in degraded acts of perversion is widely promoted as the right of consenting adults. This selfish behavior carries neither the responsibility nor the rewards of parenthood.

Third, the deliberate destruction of the innocent and helpless by abortion is now widely fostered—even publicly funded.

Fourth, the bodies and minds and morals of increasing numbers of little children are brutalized and abused by those who should protect them.

In it all, mankind has sown a bitter wind and reaps heartbreak, guilt, abandonment, divorce, addiction, disease, and death; and little children suffer.

If these sins remain unchecked, civilization will be led unfailingly to destruction. (86–05, pp. 16–17)

Stay away from inappropriate environments. Young men and women, keep yourselves worthy. Stay away from those environments, the music, the films, the videos, the clubs, and the associations that draw you into immoral conduct.[28] (00–06, p. 73)

Don't ever watch or look at pornography. The adversary is busy with all his angels focusing right to the bull's-eye of what would destroy us quickest.

There is the matter of pornography. It has become almost a pornographic world. Now, you leave it alone! If you have any, destroy it! And if you know somebody that has it, help them destroy it! And do not look at it, not ever! It is destructive, and it will take you on a path that is not consistent with who you are and what you can decide. Do not watch it, not ever! (03–04, pp. 172–73)

The world seeks to redefine morality and marriage. Some work through political, social, and legal channels to redefine morality and marriage into something unrestrained, unnatural, and forbidden. But they never can change the design which has governed human life and happiness from the beginning. The deceiver preys upon some passion or tendency or weakness. He convinces them that the condition cannot be changed and recruits them for activities for which they never would volunteer.

But sooner or later that spark of divinity in each of them will ignite. They can assert their agency as sons and daughters created in the image of God[29] and renounce the destroyer. That which they had been led to believe could not be changed, will be changed, and they will feel the power of the redemption of Christ.[30] Their burden will be lifted and the pain healed up.[31] That is what the Atonement of Christ is all about.

They can claim their inheritance as children of heavenly parents and, despite the tortured, agonizing test of mortal life, know that they are not lost.

In the Church, one is not condemned for tendencies or temptations. One is held accountable for transgression.[32] If you do not act on unworthy persuasions, you will neither be condemned nor be subject to Church discipline. (03–09, pp. 25–26)

Beware of moral counterfeits. You will have to be very wise and discerning to know the path you should follow, for no age of youth seeking to be decent and to be honest have been subjected to so many counterfeits. The substitute standards of morality seem to be so genuine. They are, however, in the final analysis, so worthless. . . .

On virtually every path you will take in life you will find those who will urge or entice you to commit yourself to things that ultimately will dishonor you—to accept substitute standards of integrity, of morality, of family life. You may even become counterfeit yourself. When you listen to those who pretend to provide moral leadership, you will have to be spiritually sensitive if you wish to identify those that ring true. (74–05)

Man is not just an animal. Little do we humans realize what we have brought upon ourselves when we have allowed our children to be taught that man is only an advanced animal. We have compounded the mistake by neglecting to teach moral and spiritual values. Moral laws do not apply to animals, for they have no agency. Where there is agency, where there is choice, moral laws must apply. We cannot, absolutely cannot, have it both ways.

When youth are taught that they are but animals, they feel free, even compelled, to respond to every urge and impulse. We should not be so puzzled at what is happening to society. We have sown the wind, and now we inherit the whirlwind. (90–09, p. 85)

Every exalting relationship is provided for in the gospel. The following of every worthy instinct, the responding to every righteous urge, the consummating of every exalting human relationship are provided for and approved in the doctrines of the gospel of Jesus Christ and protected by commandments revealed to His church. (93–06, p. 21)

Identities of men and women must remain separate. Many in the world now press for a melding of the identities of man and woman, claiming that the virtue of equality requires a homogenization of all relationships. Following an absolutely hopeless quest, some seek an enduring physical and spiritual relationship with one of the same gender. That wicked deception has unleashed a pestilence which now threatens the whole of humanity. There can be no fulfillment there. To find fulfillment, they must—and, praise be to God, they can—find it where it has been from the beginning. (89–02, p. 173)

The separate natures of man and woman were designed by God. The separate natures of man and woman were designed by the Father of us all to fulfill the purposes of the gospel plan. Never can two of the same gender fulfill the commandment to multiply and replenish the earth. No two men or any number added to them, no matter how much priesthood they may think they possess, can do it. (89–02, pp. 171–72)

There are distinct roles for manhood and womanhood. There is a role for manhood and there is a role for womanhood. There is ominous persuasion in our society for those roles to blend. The adversary would have them disappear.

These days some men want to dress like women; and some women, like men. I say to our sisters, stay beautifully feminine, female. Stay a woman. For the sake and for the inspiration of his manhood, do that. You be yourself and don't beat him in his fields of activity. Be and improve yourself in the lovely, feminine fields, and then, in a subtle but powerful way, you will make him your captive.

There is great peril to this Church and kingdom of God if our men stray from the role of manhood and our sisters from the role of womanhood. (70–07, p. 223)

The abandonment of natural masculine and feminine roles threatens society as a whole. Those things that tend to make a man masculine and protective, and to enhance the feelings and virtues that are the ideal in a worthy male, ultimately benefit the woman.

Those things that accentuate the feminine, the womanly attributes of the girl and of the wife and of the mother, tend to secure the happiness of a man.

It is strange that we cannot see that we are doing many things in society now and in a frighteningly literal way are perverting ourselves as a society. (76–04)

The laws of God are ordained to make us happy. My message is to you who are tempted either to promote, to enter, or to remain in a lifestyle which violates your covenants and will one day bring sorrow to you and to those who love you.

Growing numbers of people now campaign to make spiritually dangerous lifestyles legal and socially acceptable. Among these are abortion, the gay/lesbian movement, and drug addiction. They are debated in forums and seminars, in classes, in conversations, in conventions, and in courts all over the world. Their social and political aspects are in the press every day.

The point I make is simply this: there is a *moral* and *spiritual* side to these issues which is universally ignored. For Latter-day Saints, morality is one component which must not be missing when these issues are considered—otherwise sacred covenants are at risk! Keep your covenants and you will be safe. Break them and you will not. . . . The laws of God are ordained to make us happy. Happiness cannot coexist with immorality: the prophet Alma told us in profound simplicity that "wickedness never was happiness."[33] (90–09, p. 84)

Many things cannot be understood except in terms of the plan of redemption. There are many things that cannot be understood or taught or explained unless it is in terms of the plan of redemption. Unless you understand the basic plan—the premortal existence, the purpose of life, the Fall, the Atonement, the Resurrection—unless you understand that, the unmarried, the abused, the handicapped, the abandoned, the addicted, the disappointed, those with gender disorientation, or the intellectuals will find no enduring comfort. You will not think life is fair unless you know the plan of redemption. (03–04, p. 173)

The tragedy of abortion. Those sacred life processes through which spirits may enter mortality are being tampered with. That path of life over which new spirits must cross to enter a mortal body is often walled up through contraceptive practice; and should, through some accidental means, those natural conditions be met and a body be generated, abortive procedures are now all too common, and the spirits are thrust back whence they came. These practices are looked upon as advancements for mankind. Both are founded upon selfishness. (70–11, p. 176)

A warning about abortion. Nowhere is the right of choice defended with more vigor than in the matter of abortion. When one has chosen to act, and a conception has occurred, it cannot then be unchosen. But there are still choices, always a best one.

Sometimes the covenant of marriage has been broken; more often none was made. In or out of marriage, abortion is not an individual choice. At a minimum, three lives are involved.

The scriptures tell us: "Thou shalt not . . . kill, nor do *anything* like unto it."[34]

Except where the wicked crime of incest or rape was involved, or where competent medical authorities certify that the life of the mother is in jeopardy, or that a severely defective fetus cannot survive birth, abortion is clearly a "thou shalt not." Even in these very exceptional cases, much sober prayer is required to make the right choice. (90–09, p. 85)

We have no license to destroy life. Once a life is conceived, to destroy that life, even before birth, is a major transgression, save conception results from rape, the mother's life hangs in the balance, or the life of the unborn is certified to be hopeless. We do not know all about when a spirit enters the body, but we do know that life, in any form, is very precious. While we are given the power to generate life and commanded to do so, we have no license to destroy it. "For the Lord . . . in all things hath forbidden it, from the beginning of man."[35] And the commandment given at Sinai was renewed in this dispensation: "Thou shalt not kill"[36] "nor do anything like unto it."[37] (92–02, p. 108)

We must continually resist inappropriate tendencies. Some say they are born with some tendency. Whether you are born with them or you acquired them or you got them through overmedication, addiction, or any other way, what should you do? Resist them! You resist them and push them away. How long? As long as you live. There are some things that are a life-long battle. (03–04, p. 173)

Resisting an addictive lifestyle is a genuine act of unselfishness. The suffering you endure from resisting or from leaving a lifestyle of addiction or perversion is not a hundredth part of that suffered by your parents, your spouse, or your children if you give up. Theirs is an innocent suffering because they love you. To keep resisting or to withdraw from such a lifestyle is an act of genuine unselfishness, a sacrifice you place on the altar of obedience. It will bring enormous spiritual rewards.

Remember that agency, that freedom of choice that you demanded when you forsook your covenants? That same agency can now be drawn upon to exert a great spiritual power of redemption. (90–09, p. 86)

A message of hope to those caught in a lifestyle of addiction. Now, in a spirit of sympathy and love I speak to you who may be struggling against temptations for which there is no moral expression. Some have resisted temptation but never seem to be free from it. Do not yield! Cultivate the spiritual strength to resist—all of your life, if need be.

Some are tortured by thoughts of covenants already forsaken and sometimes think of suicide. Suicide is no solution at all. Do not even think of it. The very fact that you are so disturbed marks you as a spiritually sensitive soul for whom there is great hope.

You may wonder why God does not seem to hear your pleading prayers and erase these temptations. When you know the gospel plan, you will understand that the conditions of our mortal probation require that we be left to choose. That test is the purpose of life. While these addictions may for a time have devoured your sense of morality or quenched the Spirit within you, it is never too late.

You may not be able, simply by choice, to free yourself at once from unworthy feelings. You can choose to give up the immoral expression of them. (90–09, p. 86)

CHAPTER 11

Marriage

*"I believe in marriage. I believe it to be the
ideal pattern for human living. I know it to be
ordained of God." (81–04, p. 15)*

PURPOSE OF MARRIAGE

The great plan of happiness was designed by God. Our destiny is
so established that man can only find complete fulfillment and fill the
divine purpose for his creation with a woman to whom he is legally and
lawfully married. The union of man and woman begets babies that are
conceived and cross that frail footpath into mortality.

This divine pattern was planned and the gospel designed from
"before the world was."[1] The plan provides for us to come to the world
into a mortal body. It is "the great plan of happiness."[2] We did not
design it. If we follow the pattern, happiness and joy will follow. The
gospel and the moral standards are set to prevent us from straying into
unworthy or unnatural behavior that will result in disappointment and
unhappiness. (06–03)

Marriage is the ideal pattern for human living. I believe in marriage. I believe it to be the ideal pattern for human living. I know it to be ordained of God. The restraints relating to it were designed to protect our happiness.

I do not know of any better time in all of the history of the world for a young couple who are of age and prepared and who are in love to think of marriage. There is no better time because it is *your* time. (81–04, p. 15)

A warning on placing a low value on marriage. Marriage is the shelter where families are created. That society which puts low value on marriage sows the wind and, in time, will reap the whirlwind—and thereafter, unless they repent, bring upon themselves a holocaust! (81–04, p. 14)

Marriage offers fulfillment all the way through life. God has ordained that life should have its beginning within the protecting shelter of marriage, conceived in a consummate expression of love and nurtured and fostered with that deeper love which is accompanied always by sacrifice.

Marriage offers fulfillment all the way through life—in youth and young love, the wedding and on the honeymoon, with the coming of little children and the nurturing of them. Then come the golden years when young ones leave the nest to build one of their own. The cycle then repeats itself, as God has decreed it should. (81–04, p. 15)

In marriage all worthy yearnings can be fulfilled. Marriage is yet safe, with all its sweet fulfillment, with all its joy and love. In marriage all of the worthy yearnings of the human soul, all that is physical and emotional and spiritual, can be fulfilled. (81–04, p. 15)

The primary purpose of marriage is to raise children in righteousness. Young Latter-day Saints do not get married so that they can have cars or furniture or parties or silverware or vacations or houses. All of these things may be had without marriage. We are married in order that we may have children. "Lo, children are an heritage of the Lord."[3] (62–03)

Man and woman were intended to be together. While fathers and sons bear the burden of the priesthood, it was declared in the very beginning that it was not good for man to be alone. A companion, or "help meet," was given him. The word *meet* implies equal.

Man and woman, together, were not to be alone. Together they were to constitute a fountain of life. While neither can generate life without the other, the mystery of life unfolds when these two become one. (89–02, p. 170)

The plan of happiness requires the righteous union of male and female. The plan of happiness requires the righteous union of male and female, man and woman, husband and wife.[4] Doctrines teach us how to respond to the compelling natural impulses which too often dominate how we behave.

A body patterned after the image of God was created for Adam,[5] and he was introduced into the Garden.[6] At first, Adam was alone. He held the priesthood,[7] but alone, he could not fulfill the purposes of his creation.[8]

No other man would do. Neither alone nor with other men could Adam progress. Nor could Eve with another woman. It was so then. It is so today.

Eve, an help meet, was created. Marriage was instituted,[9] for Adam was commanded to cleave unto his *wife* [not just to a *woman*] and "to none else."[10] (93–06, p. 21)

No man or woman can attain their full potential without the other. No man receives the fulness of the priesthood without a woman at his side. For no man, the Prophet said, can obtain the fulness of the priesthood outside the temple of the Lord.[11] And she is there beside him in that sacred place. She shares in all that he receives. The man and the woman individually receive the ordinances encompassed in the endowment. But the man cannot ascend to the highest ordinances—the sealing ordinances—without her at his side. No man achieves the supernal exalting status of worthy fatherhood except as a gift from his wife. (98–03, p. 73)

The gift of children is a two-way gift. The compelling need that draws a husband back to his wife is always to be expressed in tenderness and love. It is through this process that a wife may give her husband, and a husband his wife, a gift which can be received in no other way—the gift of children. (89–02, p. 171)

Plan and prepare for parenthood. Often when young couples come, they ask the specific question, "How many children should we plan to have?" This I cannot answer, for it is not within my province to know. With some persons there are no restrictions of health, and perhaps a number of children will be born into the family. Some good parents who would have large families are blessed with but one or two children. And, occasionally, couples who make wonderful parents are not able to have natural offspring and enjoy the marvelous experience of fostering children born to others. Planned parenthood involves a good deal more than just the begetting of children. Nothing in our lives deserves more planning than our responsibilities in parenthood. (66–04, p. 1150)

Approach parenthood with reverence. Whether you will be blessed with many children or but a few, or perhaps experience parenthood through the raising of little ones left homeless, is a matter that will be made known as your life unfolds. But I urge you, I warn you to approach parenthood with reverence. When you covenant in marriage and are free to act in the creation of life, when you stand at the threshold of parenthood, know that you stand on holy ground. Recognize also that in those areas of greatest opportunity lie the snares of persistent temptation. (66–04, p. 1150)

PREPARATION FOR MARRIAGE

The pattern is that we should get married. We are concerned in the Church and we talk in our councils about the pattern that is upon us where the young men are delaying marriage. It seems that they have the idea in their mind that they have got to have everything set before they get married—education complete, certainly a mission, then settled in an occupation before they get serious about getting married. . . . The pattern is that we should get married. It is part of the great blessing and obligation. Elder Bruce R. McConkie said that we should get married to "the right person, in the right place, by the right authority."[12] (05–10)

You must choose your eternal companion, not wait for a soul mate. Righteous love comes so naturally and so beautifully that it is apparent that there is a special providence about it. "They were meant for each other," we say. While I am sure some young couples have some special guidance in getting together, I do not believe in predestined love. If you desire the inspiration of the Lord in this crucial decision, you must live the standards of the Church, and you must pray constantly for the wisdom to recognize those qualities upon which a successful union may be based. You must do the choosing, rather than to seek for some one-and-only so-called soul mate, chosen for you by someone else and waiting for you. You are to do the choosing. You must be wise beyond your years and humbly prayerful unless you choose amiss. (63–06, p. 11)

Young adult men should desire a life's companion. A boy ought to love a girl. He ought to desire with all desire a life's companion. He ought to love fully and completely and righteously. He ought to be preoccupied with finding a sweetheart and, having found her, to love her— permanently. This power, this yearning to love and to be loved, is something so magnetic, so powerful, and so compelling, and so important that it is not to be ignored. (63–06, p. 5)

What young men should consider in choosing a wife. You, young man, will do well to consider if she is useful. It is not whether she is pretty or witty, or whether she dances well; it is not vital that she wear her clothes in fashion-model style. Some of these things may add a little to the interest, but they are essentially unessential. The question is, do you want her as the mother of your children? How wise is the man who does not expect perfection, but looks for potential. How wise the youth who looks for a mother for his children, not for an ornament to be admired by his friends, but a girl who wants to be a woman—a domesticated, feminine, motherly woman. (63–06, pp. 11–12)

What young women should consider in choosing a husband. How wise is the girl who looks for a man who will honor his priesthood, and who will not only be willing to take her to the temple, but indeed *insists* upon it.

Many of the things about a youthful boy so appealing to a girl may fade soon after marriage. She would do well to look deeply at his qualities. (63–06, p. 12)

Missionary service can prepare one well for fatherhood. I speak with emphasis on the moral preparation attendant to one who serves in the mission field—one who undergoes the necessary interviews, who is reinforced morally, strengthened, trained, through this dedicated service, so that he comes to you, my young sister, morally prepared. He is a priesthood holder, trained in honor in the priesthood, trained in that unselfishness and dedication that will equip him to be an ideal father. (62–03)

BUILDING A STRONG MARRIAGE

Marriage is not without trials. Marriage is not without trials of many kinds. These tests forge virtue and strength. The tempering that comes in marriage and family life produces men and women who will someday be exalted. (81–04, p. 15)

Mature love enjoys a bliss not imagined by newlyweds. If you suppose that the full-blown rapture of young romantic love is the sum of the possibilities which spring from the fountains of life, you have not yet lived to see the devotion and the comfort of longtime married love. Married couples are tried by temptation, misunderstandings, separation, financial problems, family crises, illness; and all the while love grows stronger, the mature love enjoys a bliss not even imagined by newlyweds. (92–02, pp. 106–7)

A woman needs genuine love. Each of you has a great need to have one to love you. More than that, as a woman you have a great and compelling need for an expression of your love. And however much other kinds of love may satisfy, the platonic, or charitable, or compassionate kinds of love, and however much we may enjoy a measure of love from our brothers and sisters in our family, and from our fellow man—a little love from many—to be really happy, to find true joy, it's crucial that you have the complete, unshared, fully-expressed love of one of God's sons. (70–04)

The highest degree of the celestial kingdom is unattainable without romantic love. [Romantic love] is not only a part of life, but literally a dominating influence of it. It is deeply and significantly religious. There is no abundant life without it. Indeed, the highest degree of the celestial kingdom is unattainable in the absence of it. (63–06, pp. 4–5)

Romantic love is incomplete; it is a prelude. Romantic love is incomplete; it is a prelude. Love is nourished by the coming of children, who spring from that fountain of life entrusted to couples in marriage. (92–02, p. 107)

Love in a worthy marriage is unexcelled. Participation in the mating process offers an experience like nothing else in life. When entered into worthily, it combines the most exquisite and exalted physical, emotional, and spiritual feelings associated with the word *love.* Those feelings and the lifelong need for one another bind a husband and wife together in a marriage, wherein all of the attributes of adult masculinity are complemented by the priceless feminine virtues of womanhood.

That part of life has no equal, no counterpart, in all human experience. (92–02, p. 107)

Expressions of love are the foundation of the marriage partnership. The introducing of spirits into this life is an expression of love. To invite children into this world and to care for them and to give to them, not indulgently but wisely, is an expression of love.

To order one's life for the benefit of others unselfishly is an expression of love. Nowhere are these lessons taught more effectively, nowhere are they of more necessity than in the marriage covenant which must be based on love, and every living minute must one way or another bear an expression of love. The fulfillment of the highest expressions of love are the foundation of the marriage partnership. (XX–01)

Children should be born out of love. The power of love between man and woman is not completely defined, but like electricity it can be used and controlled and directed, even though we do not know exactly what it is. We know that love has the power to create. Think of that! Just think of that! Love has the power to create life. When a young husband and young wife live together in love, the product of the most exalted and most sacred expression of love is life itself. Children are born out of love. (63–06, p. 13)

IMPORTANCE OF ETERNAL MARRIAGE

Marriage is meant to be eternal. There is another dimension to marriage that we know of in the Church. It came by revelation. This glorious, supernal truth teaches us that marriage is meant to be eternal.

There are covenants we can make if we are willing, and bounds we can seal if we are worthy, that will keep marriage safe and intact beyond the veil of death. . . .

Eternal love, eternal marriage, eternal increase! This ideal, which is new to many, when thoughtfully considered, can keep a marriage strong and safe. No relationship has more potential to exalt a man and a woman than the marriage covenant. No obligation in society or in the Church supersedes it in importance.

I thank God for marriage. I thank God for temples. I thank God for the glorious sealing power, that power which transcends all that we have been given, through which our marriages may become eternal. (81–04, p. 15)

Eternal love has no bounds. I picture you coming to the temple to be sealed for time and for all eternity. I yearn to talk to you about the sacred sealing ordinance, but this we do not do outside those sacred walls. The transcendent nature of all that is conferred upon us at the marriage altar is so marvelous, it is worth all the waiting and all the resisting. I picture you, as I have seen you often. The young man, masculine, clear of vision, stalwart of frame, firm to accept the responsibilities as a husband and as a father, and the bride, unassuming, beautifully feminine, an inspiration to her sweetheart, and dependent upon him. . . .

This picture, then, I see, and were I an artist, had I the power, I would paint this picture over and over again—not with oil or canvas or brush—but with counsel and admonition and encouragement and blessing, with forgiveness and reassurance, with the truth. . . . I cannot frame this picture—I would not if I could—for it has no bounds. Love like this may have a beginning, but never through all eternity need it have an end. (63–06, pp. 20–22)

Eternal marriage allows men and women to fulfill the full measure of their creation. From the very beginning, expressing the power to beget life was unlawful except there was a marriage between the man and the woman. Marriage is a covenant of lifelong fidelity and devotion which, by ordinance, may last for eternity.

The whole physical universe is organized in order that man and woman might fulfill the full measure of their creation. It is a perfect system where delicate balances and counter-balances govern the physical, the emotional, and the spiritual in mankind.

The Lord revealed that the purpose of it all is "to bring to pass the immortality and eternal life of man."[13] Ordinances and covenants were ordained to protect this power to generate life. When God's laws are obeyed, happiness follows, for "men are, that they might have joy."[14] (89–02, pp. 170–71)

Why is marriage in the Church so important? This power [of procreation] within you is good. It is a gift from God our Father. In the righteous exercise of it as in nothing else, we may come close to Him.

We can have, in a small way, much that our Father in Heaven has as He governs us, His children. No greater school or testing place can be imagined.

Is it any wonder, then, that in the Church marriage is so sacred and so important? Can you understand why your marriage, which releases these powers of creation for your use, should be the most carefully planned, the most solemnly considered step in your life? Ought we to consider it unusual that the Lord directed that temples be constructed for the purpose of performing marriage ceremonies? (64–01)

Staying in love is the life and breath of marriage. Marriage is eternal; family life is sacred; the falling in love of a young man and a young woman is the prelude to love, and staying in love is the vitality, the very breath and life of marriage.

Everyone hopes to experience romantic love. Rightly, it is not only a part of life, but literally a dominating influence of it. It is deeply and significantly religious. There is no abundant life without it. Indeed, the highest degree of the celestial kingdom is unobtainable in the absence of it. Truly, "it is not good that man should be alone."[15] (63–06, pp. 4–5)

DEALING WITH MARITAL PROBLEMS

Do not lose faith in marriage. I know that these are very troubled times. Troubles like we have now are very hard on marriages.

Do not lose faith in marriage. Not even if you have been through the unhappiness of a divorce and are surrounded with pieces of a marriage that has fallen apart.

If you have honored your vows and your partner did not do so, remember God is watching over us. One day, after all of the tomorrows have passed, there will be recompense. Those who have been moral and faithful to their covenants will be happy and those who have not will be otherwise.

Some marriages have broken up in spite of all that one partner could do to hold the marriage together. While there may be faults on both sides, I do not condemn the innocent one who suffers in spite of all that was desired and done to save the marriage. (81–04, p. 15)

You can stumble out of love. You can stumble out of love. I say "stumble" because the process of falling in love is so beautiful and so desirable that we ought to use a different designation for its opposite. If there is trouble, you stay married—both of you. You repent—both of you. You be worthy—both of you. You be prayerful—both of you. You be forgiving—both of you. Love can grow again from the same root stalk and bloom again with blossoms sweeter still. (63–06, pp. 18–19)

Important problems should be solved as a couple. My young sister, you have had some very choice, intimate, cherished times with your mother, talking over things that are sacred and personal. Now all of these moments belong to your husband, and only rarely and on superficial things would you have to run back to Mother—maybe for an occasional recipe or a remedy, but on all of the sacred and deep and important problems you belong to one another and you solve them between the two of you. (63–03, p. 227)

Never speak cross words to your spouse. Shortly before I was married I was assigned with an older companion to serve as home teacher to an aged little lady who was a shut-in. . . .

We somehow learned that she was very partial to lemon ice cream. Frequently we would stop at the ice cream store before making our visit. Because we knew her favorite flavor, there were two reasons we were welcome to that home.

On one occasion the senior companion was not able to go, for reasons that I do not remember. I went alone and followed the ritual of getting a half-pint of lemon ice cream before making the call. . . .

After a prayer, thinking of my coming marriage, I suppose, she said, "Tonight I will teach you." She said she wanted to tell me something and that I was always to remember it. Then began the lesson I have never forgotten. She recounted something of her life.

A few years after her marriage to a fine young man in the temple, when they were concentrating on the activities of young married life and raising a family, one day a letter came from "Box B." (In those days a letter from "Box B" in Salt Lake City was invariably a mission call.)

To their surprise they were called as a family to go to one of the far continents of the world to help open the land for missionary work. They served faithfully and well, and after several years they returned to their home, to set about again the responsibilities of raising their family.

Then this little woman focused in on a Monday morning. . . . There had been some irritation and a disagreement. Then some biting words between husband and wife. Interestingly enough, she couldn't remember how it all started or what it was over. "But," she said, "nothing would do but that I follow him to the gate, and as he walked up the street on his way to work I just had to call that last biting, spiteful remark after him."

Then, as the tears began to flow, she told me of an accident that took place that day, and he never returned. "For fifty years," she sobbed, "I've lived in hell knowing that the last words he heard from my lips were that biting, spiteful remark."

This was the message to her young home teacher. She pressed it upon me with the responsibility never to forget it. I have profited greatly from it. I have come to know since that time that a couple can live together without one cross word ever passing between them.

I have often wondered about those visits to that home, about the time I spent and the few cents we spent on ice cream. That little sister is long since gone beyond the veil. This is true also of my senior companion. But the powerful experience of that home teaching, the home teacher being taught, is with me yet, and I have found occasion to leave her message with young couples at the marriage altar and in counseling people across the world. (72–05, pp. 89–90)

Never should a husband be unkind to his wife or children. I say to you, young man, that never would you ever be brutal or unkind in any way—verbally, or in any other way—with this lovely young girl who will be your wife and the mother of your children. It is inconsistent with the priesthood that has been conferred upon you, and to the degree that you are an unworthy husband and an unworthy father, you likewise are an unworthy holder of the priesthood. (63–03, p. 230)

Never speak a cross word. Never speak a cross word—not one. It is neither necessary nor desirable. There are many who teach that it is normal and expected for domestic difficulty and bickering and strife to be a part of that marriage relationship. That is false doctrine. It is neither necessary nor desirable. I know that it is possible to live together in love with never the first cross word ever passing between you. (70–07, p. 224)

A warning to one who destroys a marriage. Now a word of warning. One who destroys a marriage takes upon himself a very great responsibility indeed. Marriage is sacred!

To willfully destroy a marriage, either your own or that of another couple, is to offend our God. Such a thing will not be lightly considered in the judgments of the Almighty and in the eternal scheme of things will not easily be forgiven.

Do not threaten nor break up a marriage. Do not translate some disenchantment with your own marriage partner or an attraction for someone else into justification for any conduct that would destroy a marriage.

This monumental transgression frequently places heavy burdens upon little children. They do not understand the selfish yearnings of unhappy adults who are willing to buy their own satisfaction at the expense of the innocent.

God Himself decreed that the physical expression of love, that union of male and female which has power to generate life, is authorized only in marriage. (81–04, p. 14)

HUSBAND AND WIFE RESPONSIBILITIES

Be careful to maintain the differences in the masculine and feminine nature. In the home and in the Church, sisters should be esteemed for their very nature. Be careful lest you unknowingly foster influences and activities which tend to erase the masculine and feminine differences nature has established. A man, a father, can do much of what is usually assumed to be a woman's work. In turn, a wife and a mother can do much—and in time of need, most things—usually considered the responsibility of the man, without jeopardizing their distinct roles. Even so, leaders, and especially parents, should recognize that there is a distinct masculine nature and a distinct feminine nature essential to the foundation of the home and the family. Whatever disturbs or weakens or tends to erase that difference erodes the family and reduces the probability of happiness for all concerned. (98–03, p. 73)

Except Adam and Eve by nature be different from one another, they could not multiply and fill the earth.[16] The complementing differences are the very key to the plan of happiness. Some roles are best suited to the masculine nature and others to the feminine nature. (93–06, p. 21)

Men and women have an equal right to exaltation. A man who holds the priesthood does not have an advantage over a woman in qualifying for exaltation. The woman, by her very nature, is also co-creator with God and the primary nurturer of the children. Virtues and attributes upon which perfection and exaltation depend come naturally to a woman and are refined through marriage and motherhood.

The priesthood is conferred only upon worthy men in order to conform to our Father's plan of happiness. With the laws of nature and the revealed word of God working in harmony, it simply works best that way. . . . Natural and spiritual laws which govern life were instituted from before the foundation of the world.[17] They are eternal, as are the consequences for either obeying or disobeying them. They are not based on social or political considerations. They cannot be changed. No pressure, no protest, no legislation can alter them. (93–06, p. 22)

Men and women are separate but equal. "The hand that rocks the cradle [does rule] the world."

"The plan of redemption, which was prepared from the foundation of the world, through Christ,"[18] was unfolded in the Creation. In the very beginning, man was created, and because "it is not good that the man should be alone," the Lord created a wife, "an help meet for him."[19] In the scriptures, the word *meet* means *equal*. Man and woman are separate but equal, complementary to one another. Both the equal and the separate natures are essential to the onrolling of the great plan of happiness.

Do not envy a man his manhood or his priesthood. Foster and encourage, in every way you can, his role and the role of your sons in the destiny ordained for them. To women is given a most supernal part of the plan of redemption. "And Adam called his wife's name Eve, because she was the mother of all living; for thus have I, the Lord God, called the first of all women."[20] Foster in yourself and in your daughters the exalted role of the woman, the incomparable gift of creation that attends motherhood. The man was given to provide and protect; the woman was given to make it all worthwhile.

The ultimate end of activity in the Church is that a man and his wife and their children can be happy at home, sealed together so that the family can continue throughout eternity. (06–03)

The husband should lead out in righteousness. The husband, the holder of the household, is established this day in this marriage covenant as the head of the family and the breadwinner. It may be hard for you to recognize this role, young lady, but your happiness is conditioned upon it. I will say to you plainly, you show me a woman who is in charge of a home, who directs the management of all affairs, including those of her husband—you show me such a woman—and I will show you an unhappy woman. I would hope that you would make a solemn resolution with reference to this marriage covenant. It does not negate democracy in marriage. When the final decision is to be made, when particularly it has reference to prayer and the need of special guidance, then you, as the wife, defer to your husband who holds the priesthood and place the responsibility upon his shoulders, and then you follow where he leads. (63–03, p. 230)

The husband should care for the needs of his wife. It was not meant that the woman alone accommodate herself to the priesthood

At solemn assembly, April 1970

duties of her husband or her sons. She is of course to sustain and support and encourage them, but holders of the priesthood, in turn, must accommodate themselves to the needs and responsibilities of the wife and mother. Her physical and emotional and intellectual and cultural well-being and her spiritual development must stand first among her husband's priesthood duties. (89–02, p. 174)

Be careful that hobbies do not consume your life. Let me talk to you, too, as the husband, about hobbies. I bring this up and talk to you as the husband more specifically than the wife because it is more often the husband who is the offender here. You will surely have an interest in some hobby; you ought to. But why don't you use moderation? I get a little impatient when I see a man who collects something, or raises something, or is involved in something, and this is more consuming than anything about him, including his family. If it is golfing, flying, boating, horses, or any other hobby, my friend, I urge you to look upon it in moderation so that it does not become an avocation, for it is way down the list with reference to the important things in life. I see many men involved in hobbies, and they are important and useful. Life may well be quite dull without them. But not infrequently we see a man possessed by his hobby, and it is similar to a man who eats teaspoonfuls of salt, or pepper, or ginger, or cloves, or nutmeg, or chili powder, and then just tastes now and again of mashed potatoes and the basics. Let your hobby be the flavoring, the spice, the thing that makes life interesting; but do not be possessed by it. (63–03, pp. 233–34)

It is better to be an occasional Church widow. Sometimes the wives of our priesthood leaders are jealous of their service. They say, "You are gone so much, I feel like a widow." They say, "We preach in the Church about a family, but you are never here." To that woman I say, "Careful!" There are other kinds of widows. There are beer hall widows; there are widows of men who spend all of their time with their hobbies. Being a so-called Church widow is not so bad. There is not any man that will not become a worthy priesthood leader if he is encouraged in the right way by his wife. Even the most clumsy and unspiritual man will respond to the right treatment. . . . Sisters, you have such power—just a gesture, a touch of the hand, and a kindly word, that's what keeps the brethren of the priesthood active and faithful. (76–07)

The impact of a righteous woman is profound. It is interesting . . . to know how man is put together—how incomplete he is. His whole physical and emotional and, for that matter, spiritual nature, is formed in such a way that it depends upon a source of encouragement and power that is found in the woman.

When he has found his wife and companion, he has, in a sense, found the other half of himself. He will return to her again and again for that regeneration that exalts his manhood and strengthens him for the testing that life will give him. . . .

The transformation of a man, the common, garden-variety man, into an able and effective priesthood leader is the privilege of a lovely Latter-day Saint woman. (70–15)

The young husband's needs. One suggestion with reference to [that young man], that as a prospective wife you may want to think about, is that he needs to know that he is taking care of you. He needs to feel and know that he is the leader in the family. He needs a wife and a sweetheart with whom he can share his love, with whom he can have its full, complete expression. He needs to have a circle—a family circle with children. This makes all that he must face out in the world seem worthwhile. He needs to feel that he is presiding. He needs to be the protector.

When he feels this, he is a better man. He is a better husband. He is a better employee, a better employer. He is better adjusted and happier in life. He can do better work. He can even be more prosperous. But for the sake of all that is important, above all he can be a better father and a better holder of the priesthood. (70–07, p. 223)

We are under obligation to multiply and replenish the earth. As you understand the sealing ordinance, you will know that the Lord wills that you live together naturally, and that of this relationship children will be born. You are under the obligation—it is not just a privilege—of multiplying to replenish the earth, and in consequence of this the Lord has promised all of the basic essential joys. Let me quote from the prophet, the President of the Church, David O. McKay:

"Love realizes his sweetest happiness and his most divine consummation in the home where the coming of children is not restricted, where they are made most welcome, and where the duties of parenthood are accepted as a co-partnership with the eternal Creator."[21]

I am fully aware what the pattern is in the world, but we are not of the world; and here is the temptation, I suppose, above any other temptation that you will face in your married life—to follow the pattern of the world and to adjust the standards of the Church to fit your so-called "special needs." I say to you solemnly and boldly that to do so places you under the responsibility of doing that which the Lord does not approve. You must understand that you are under disapproval of the Lord to follow such worldly practices. Again from the prophet:

"Some young couples enter into marriage and procrastinate the bringing of children into their homes. They are running a great risk. Marriage is for the purpose of rearing a family, and youth is the time to do it."[22] (63–03, p. 229)

A caution to those who would avoid parenthood. Frequently I receive letters and not infrequently young couples come, particularly of college age, struggling to achieve advanced degrees, and they ask for counsel on the coming of children in their lives.

Never has a generation been so surrounded with those who speak irreverently of life. *Never* has there been such persuasion to avoid responsibilities of parenthood. *Never* has it been so convenient to block that frail footpath of life across which new spirits enter mortality. (66–04, p. 1150)

A caution against avoiding and delaying children. There is great temptation in the world today and the attention of our young people is inclined toward the practice of avoiding or delaying after marriage the welcoming of children into our families. Sometimes we have yielded to the world-taught doctrine that children are a burden, an interference, an expense. We like to think that we as parents are to instruct our children and that our obligation and opportunity concluded there, but how much more have we as parents learned from our children! (62–03)

Wherever possible, wives should avoid joining the breadwinning line. There will be the temptation for you, when the budget is pinched, when the budget is small, and the children are small in size but many in number, for you to want to join your husband on the breadwinning line. This is the poorest of all economies. If you will do what the Lord would have you do, you will resist the temptation to leave the home and the children, and you will manage on the budget that the father and husband is able to provide. (63–03, p. 230)

It is important for young women to be trained in the event that the husband and breadwinner is taken in death. Under such circumstances a wife and mother perhaps has no alternative but to leave the home and seek employment, but I urge you, strongly urge you, to resist the temptation to join your husband in the breadwinning line. (63–03, p. 232)

Counsel to sisters whose husbands are less-active or not members. I address my remarks to the Relief Society sisters whose husbands are not at present active in the Church. . . . You'll notice I didn't say anything about nonmembers. I just said, to those of you whose husbands are not yet members.

Each weekend we meet one or two stake leaders who joined the Church after many years, through the encouragement of a patient, not infrequently a long-suffering, wife.

I have often said that a man cannot resist that step if his wife *really* wants him to, and if she knows how to give him encouragement.

Frequently we give up on this matter. Now, you can't ever give up. You can't ever give up, not in this life or in the next. You can never give up.

Some have joined the Church after finding it at a very late hour in their life, or after lingering (you almost could use the word *malingering*) for many years before taking that step. Then comes the regret over

the wasted years, and the question, "Why couldn't I have realized earlier? [Quotes Matthew 20:6–15.] . . . The gates of the celestial kingdom
will open to those who come early or late. Sisters, you must never give
up. If you have faith enough and desire enough, you will yet have at the
head of your home a father and a husband who is active and faithful in
the Church. (78–05, pp. 70–71)

Now one word to you sisters who are married to a man who is not
active or not yet a member.

Never say, "My husband is not a member. Instead say, "My husband
is not *yet* a member." Not *yet* a member. I've always maintained that the
man is helpless before a woman who would see him active and faithful
in the priesthood if she first, really wants to, and second, knows how. I
wonder if I could coach you just a little bit.

First I would urge you to act as though he is an active member.
Now if he isn't a member or if he isn't faithful, he isn't subject to the
inspiration that he could have otherwise. Be tolerant and faithful and
patient with him. I'd urge you to treat him just as though he were active
and faithful and honoring his priesthood and live in expectation.

There's no credit buying on eternal things, none at all. Anything
that is worthwhile has to be paid for in advance. No school in all of
England issues the diploma on the day of registration and then urges
the students to stay around and work it out. No, you work it out first,
and then the diploma comes. Nothing worth having, no eternal virtue,
can be achieved on credit terms. It must be paid for in advance.

Suppose you go to work and start making payments in faith, reverence, prayer, pleading with the Lord. (71–08, pp. 128–29)

***A nonmember husband needs to know how much you care about
the gospel.*** I was told of a home teacher trying to encourage the father
to pray in the home. The father resisted and sat down on the couch.
Finally he kneeled but wouldn't pray. His wife was then invited to pray
and through her tears she poured out her heart to the Lord, pleading
with Him for what she wanted most.

When the prayer was over, this husband, a startled man, and I think in many ways an innocent man, said, "I didn't know that. I didn't know that was what you wanted. You're going to see some changes in me."

You've heard the lyrics of that song of yesterday: "I've told every little star. . . . Why haven't I told you?" Why don't you tell him, sisters?

He needs to know; he needs to be told that you care about the gospel as deeply as you do and that you care about him infinitely more because of the gospel and what it means to you.

Let him know that your goodness as a wife and as a mother, as a sweetheart and as a companion in love, grows from your testimony of the gospel. (71–09, p. 73)

Help inactive and nonmember husbands feel at home with the Church. It is difficult to get a man to go to church when he doesn't feel at home. It may be new and different to him, or perhaps there are habits he has not yet overcome and he may feel self-conscious and just not feel at home at church. There is another solution, you know, that of making him feel like church while at home.

We often don't properly credit what he does at home. It's that going to the chapel that gets fixed in our minds as the symbol of church activity. In many ways it can be the things that he does at home that are more important as a beginning.

And so the suggestion, why don't you begin where you are, right at home, and I repeat, if your husband doesn't feel at home going to church, then do everything you can to make him feel at church while he's at home. . . . In a study which involved families with inactive or nonmember fathers, these fathers agreed, after some persuasion, to institute the family home evening program in their homes. Gradually the fathers were drawn into participation. It had an appeal because it was in their own comfortable environment and they could do it about as they wished. The family home evening program is just that adaptable.

There was an interesting result. When they felt comfortable with the Church at home then they began to go with their families to church.

To bring some of the things of heaven into the home is to insure that family members will graduate to Church participation. Family home evening is, of course, ready-made for this. It is a meeting at home that can be organized to fit every need; and it's just as much a church meeting, or can be, as those held at the chapel. (78–05, p. 73–74)

MAINTAINING MORAL FIDELITY

The only legitimate employment of the powers of procreation is between a husband and wife. The only legitimate employment of the powers of procreation is between husband and wife who have been legally and lawfully married. Anything other than this violates the commandments of God Himself. And as Alma said, "I say unto you, if ye speak against it, it matters not, for the word of God must be fulfilled."[23] (92–02, p. 113)

True love requires mutual respect and complete fidelity. True love requires a mutual respect and that the couple reserve until after the marriage the sharing of that affection which unlocks those sacred powers in that fountain of life. It means avoiding premarriage situations in which physical desire might take control. Courtship is a time to measure integrity, moral strength, and worthiness. The invitation, "If you love me, you will let me," exposes a major flaw in character. It deserves the reply: "If you really loved me, you would never ask me to transgress. If you understood the gospel, you couldn't!"

Pure love presupposes that only after a pledge of eternal fidelity, a legal and a lawful ceremony, and ideally after the sealing ordinance in the temple are those procreative powers released for the full expression of love. They are to be shared only and solely with that one who is our companion in marriage. (92–02, p. 107)

Breaking of marriage covenants offends the Lord. When we catch a vision of what the family is, what those binding ties are, and what the marriage covenant is, then we must know that surely few things in our day offend the Lord more than the silly and whimsical way in which many people enter into and release themselves from the marriage covenant. Indeed, we have reached a point in history when the marriage covenant, considered through all generations of history as sacred and vital, is now declared by many to be useless. (70–11, p. 176)

Never give your companion cause to question your fidelity. Young man, you have got to be worthy of faith. If your bride is to have faith in gospel things, it must start basically with you; and it does not matter where you are, how long you have been gone, or with whom you may be associating. Never once, at any time, is it your privilege to give this lovely little bride any reason to lack faith in you. She must know implicitly that under no circumstance ever would you be guilty of any infidelity. The same with you, my young sister, you must realize that no matter how far away he is or how lonely it is for you, or what the difficulties are, never must there be one word, one inflection, one joke, one comment, one suspicion that would permit him to lack faith in you. (63–03, pp. 228–29)

Never make light of the powers of creation. This day, as you become husband and wife, those powers of creation are released for your use. Herein lie the most cherished, sacred, and beautiful experiences in this life, that you might act in the creation of bodies for little spirits to inhabit. Now on this there is never any joking. It might have been appropriate as you were courting to tease one another a little bit, to joke about the third party, or to try to introduce into the relationship the strange powers of jealousy. But now as you accept this sealing ordinance, if it ever was appropriate (and this I question), after marriage it certainly has no place. There should never be any joking or jesting or teasing about these most personal and sacred of all human relationships. (63–03, p. 228)

It is not appropriate to discuss intimate things with friends. You belong to one another, and it would not be appropriate to talk about such intimate things with your friends. If on occasion there may develop a problem, you might then return and talk to your mother or to your father, or perhaps to your bishop or your family doctor, if the question was of that nature, but never would you discuss these most sacred of all things with just anyone—with someone at work, or with the neighbor woman. These are sacred and, of all things, most personal. (63–03, p. 228)

A caution to married couples. Accept this caution. A married couple may be tempted to introduce things into their relationship that are unworthy. Do not, as the scriptures warn, "change the natural use into that which is against nature."[24] If you do, the tempter will drive a wedge between you. If something unworthy has become part of your relationship, be wise and don't ever do it again. (92–02, p. 113)

ADVICE TO THE UNMARRIED

Counsel to those who are single. I refer to those of you who have not had the privilege of marriage or who have lost your husbands through the tragedy of divorce or perhaps through the inevitable call of death.

Some of you are struggling alone to raise little families, often on meager budgets and often with hours of loneliness. I know there is a great power of compensation. I know that there is a spirit that can give you power to be both father and mother if necessary.

There stands in our small circle of General Authorities more than one man who was raised in the home of an attentive, lovely widowed mother. I heard one of them bear testimony in conference that in his boyhood days they had all the things that money couldn't buy.

There is a priesthood shelter, sisters, under which you come. There is the bishop who stands as the father of the ward. Let him help, and the others he may delegate. Let your home teachers assist, particularly when you need the influence of manhood in the raising of boys.

Remember, you are not alone. There is a Lord who loves you and He watches over you, and there is the power of the Spirit that can compensate.

And so, to you also I say, you must never give up, never, neither in this world nor in the next. For there comes a time when the judgments are rendered and as the Lord said in that parable, "Whatsoever is right, that shall ye receive."[25] (78–05, pp. 77–78)

What about the exceptions? When we speak of marriage, family life, there inevitably comes to mind, "What about the exceptions? There are always exceptions!" Some are born with limitations and cannot beget children. Some innocent ones have their marriage wrecked because of the infidelity of their spouses. Others do not marry and live lives of single worthiness, while at once the wayward and the wicked seem to enjoy it all.

For now, I offer this comfort: God is our Father! All the love and generosity manifest in the ideal earthly father is magnified, beyond the capacity of mortal mind to comprehend, in Him who is our Father and our God. His judgments are just, His mercy without limit, His power to compensate beyond any earthly comparison.

Remember that mortal life is a brief moment, for we will live eternally. There will be ample—I almost used the word *time,* but time does not apply here—there will be ample opportunity for all injustices, all inequities to be made right, all loneliness and deprivation compensated, and all worthiness rewarded when we keep the faith. (92–02, pp. 113–14)

Righteous yearnings unfulfilled in mortality will one day be fulfilled. It suits the purpose of the Almighty to let it be that some will not have a marriage or find it broken through death or mischief. Some have great difficulty having any children, and some will not have children of their own—that is, it will not happen in mortal life. But in the eternal scheme of things, it will happen as surely as the commandments are kept. Those yearnings unfulfilled in mortality will be filled to overflowing in the life beyond where there is eternal love and eternal increase. (06–03)

No one will be denied blessings because of circumstances beyond their control. Any soul who by nature or circumstance is not afforded the blessing of marriage and parenthood, or who innocently must act alone in rearing children, working to support them, will not be denied in the eternities any blessing—provided they keep the commandments.[26]

As President Lorenzo Snow promised: "That is sure and positive."[27] (93–06, p. 23)

Blessings of eternal marriage and family will not be denied the faithful. For some all is not complete in mortal life, for marriage and a family of their own have passed them by. But the great plan of happiness and the laws which govern it continue after death. Watched over by a kind and loving Heavenly Father, they will not, in the eternal pattern of things, be denied blessings necessary for their exaltation, including marriage and family. And it will be sweeter still because of the waiting and the longing. (03–09, p. 25)

A message of hope. Hope is a great virtue. And I want to give an expression of comfort and love to you sisters who hope for things which you think will never be. I want to tell you of the goodness of the Heavenly Father who knows an eternity of things we shall see. "If in this life only we have hope in Christ, we are of all men most miserable."[28] I bless you lovely sisters who work through your lives with the hope that you can have every fulfillment as the eternities unfold. I have seen something of how it is beyond the veil; know that your greatest hopes will be fulfilled and more. (76–07)

Those limited in this life have a greater joy beyond the veil. Those who are limited in this life have a greater joy beyond the veil to find that all will be added upon you in that existence. (06–03)

A promise of hope to the unmarried. To the dear sister who moves past the usual age of marriage and yet has not found her companion and who is *temporarily*—I underline the word *temporarily*—without a companion: Your temporary plight, dear sister, may last through mortality. I say again, it is *temporary.*

We talk a lot about families. Sometimes in bitterness you are wont to say, "All of this talk about families, but I don't have a family and . . ." Stop there! Don't add that extra phrase: "I wish they'd stop talking so much about families." You pray that we do keep talking about families, about fathers and mothers and children, and family home evening, and temple marriage, and companionship, and all of the rest; because all of that will be yours. If we stop talking about it, then you, among all the others, will be the losers. (73–06)

Advice to those who are unmarried. Now a word to those who want to love and to be loved who are slipping past the usual age for marriage. I am thinking of many of these lovely, worthy sisters who feel that life is passing them by. Unfortunately, you sometimes feel that way when you are nineteen. These suggestions: Do not give up. Hold to your standards. It may well come to you as a September song and be twice more precious for the waiting. Stay attractive—and I do not mean the cover-girl appeal—but attractive in disposition and in attitude and in service. Stay available. Do not be so content with what you do that you cease to care. To some it may not come, but surely there is a compensation that the Lord has in store for the righteous who have held to His standards, but who remain unmarried through no choice of their own. (63–06, p. 17)

Heavenly Father cares about His daughters. I have never had the feelings I felt when my daughter was to be married. I know more about that word *Father* now. I know how fervently He wants His lovely daughters to be faithfully married to a holder of the priesthood, how with His almighty power He can and will cause that to be, if not now—then. It is worth every hope. Ultimately, all those things will be fulfilled. (76–07)

Counsel to those who are not privileged to marry. Some of you may not experience the blessings of marriage. Protect nonetheless these sacred powers of creation, for there is a great power of compensation that may well apply to you. (72–01, p. 113)

Encouragement for those who are not married or who are not parents. There are those who do not have children because they are not presented with a worthy opportunity for marriage, or because of limitations in one or both of the marriage partners they are not able to become parents.

Their test rests heavily on intent and motivation, and lies somehow in whether they would if they could. The unmarried must maintain the natural regard and attachment for children and find opportunities to teach and influence them for good. This must occur in place of the increasing numbers who express themselves of being glad to be rid of that obligation. (76–04)

Wise counsel to the divorcee. To the young divorcee, with perhaps three little children whose husband has gone away, a reprobate, I say: Careful, careful.

You may have been used and abused; all the criticism and evil that you might say about your husband might well be true. At least you might feel it is true. But I say to you, don't ever say those things to your little ones.

When that poignant moment comes when they say, "Mamma, why doesn't Daddy come home anymore? Doesn't Daddy love us anymore?" bite your tongue, dear sister. Don't say, "Your daddy is a liar" (or a cheat, or an adulterer, or an evil man). Just say, "Sweetheart, we don't understand everything and maybe one day we'll learn. There are lots of things in life that we must wait to know." Just pass it off. Careful, dear girl, lest you unwittingly teach your children that they are the offspring of a reprobate. That gets fixed into their minds and when the teenage challenges come, they let down the bars and say, "I can't help myself, it was born into me." Be the perfect Christian. (73–06)

CHAPTER 12

Family Relationships

"The ultimate purpose of every teaching, every activity in the Church, is that parents and their children are happy at home, sealed in an eternal marriage, and linked to their generations." (94–01, p. 19)

CHURCH PROGRAMS AND THE FAMILY

The family is an eternal organization. Today we have other organizations in the Church that are working on family ties. We have stakes and missions, wards, branches, and districts. Each is presided over by a priesthood officer. These organizations are temporarily essential; they are not eternal organizations. They can be organized or they can be dissolved. . . . But the family, on the other hand, can be an eternal organization. Though the family may move from one ward or stake to another, the family organization remains intact. It may even be transferred from mortality into the eternities in the spirit world. The family established under the priesthood in the temple is founded in what is perhaps the most profound of all ordinances. When a couple enters into the new and everlasting covenant, they have the possibility of entering full expression of their life powers, both spiritual and physical.

This is a responsibility not to be regarded lightly. Those sacred life-giving physical powers which have been reserved and protected through the entire life of the individual are at last released for a sacred and pure and holy purpose, the begetting of a family.

These positions in the family, the positions of parenthood, should not be temporary; they should be permanent. Presiding officers in the Church are changed from time to time, but not so with the father and mother. (70–11, pp. 175–76)

Nothing is more important to the Church and to civilization than the family. The great plan of happiness enables family relationships to last beyond the grave. Sacred ordinances and covenants, available only in the temple, make it possible for individuals to return to the presence of God and for families to be united eternally. Marriage, the family, and the home are the foundation of the Church.[1] Nothing is more important to the Church and to civilization itself than the family! (03–09, p. 25)

The ultimate purpose of the adversary is to disrupt and destroy the family. The ultimate purpose of every teaching, every activity in the Church, is that parents and their children are happy at home, sealed in an eternal marriage, and linked to their generations.

The ultimate purpose of the adversary, who has "great wrath, because he knoweth that he hath but a short time,"[2] is to disrupt, disturb, and destroy the home and the family. Like a ship without a rudder, without a compass, we drift from the family values which have anchored us in the past. Now we are caught in a current so strong that unless we correct our course, civilization as we know it will surely be wrecked to pieces. (94–01, p. 19)

The great plan of happiness is the plan for a happy family. The great plan of happiness[3] revealed to prophets is the plan for a happy family. It is the love story between husband and wife, parents and children, that renews itself through the ages. (95–05, p. 9)

Strong families build strong nations. We teach that families are sacred. We teach Latter-day Saint men to be totally faithful to their wives. We teach wives to be faithful to their husbands, to love and honor their children, to turn their hearts to their children, and to turn the hearts of the children to their parents. Then we have happy families. Then we have happy people. Then we have strong communities. Then we have strong nations. (79–11)

Worthy Latter-day Saint families are standards to the world. We know that activity in the Church centers in the family. Wherever members are in the world, they should establish a family where children are welcome and treasured as "an heritage of the Lord."[4] A worthy Latter-day Saint family is a standard to the world. (06–07, p. 87)

The relationship between Church and family. Faithful attendance at church, together with careful attention to the needs of the family, is a near-perfect combination. In church we are taught the great plan of happiness.[5] At home we apply what we have learned. Every call, every service in the Church brings experience and valuable insights which carry over into family life. (98–07, p. 23)

In the Church we care about the family. In the Church we show intense and constant concern for the home and for the family. I think it can be truly said that the ultimate end of activity in the Church is to see a father and a mother and their children happy at home, to see them happy as a family—eternally.

If the efforts of our Church officers and organizations and the influence of our Church building programs and curriculums are not ultimately to affect the happiness of the individual and the strength and stability of the family, there is grave question as to whether they are any good at all.

We care about the family. We study the family. We pray over the family. We work for the stability of the family. We work to preserve and protect the institution of the family.

We analyze the effect of every influence that comes along, as it may ultimately change by way of strengthening, or threaten by way of weakening, the family. (77–03, p. 8)

The purpose of all priesthood and auxiliaries is to protect and exalt the family. The offices and the quorums and the auxiliaries which support them are cradled in the stakes and wards and missions and branches and continue the kingdom of God on the earth.[6] All of the offices and all of the ordinances have as their foremost purpose the protection and exaltation of the family.

It was never intended that priesthood authority be limited to one man in a congregation but that every man as the head of his household become worthy to bless his family. The purpose of it all: the home and the family.

Brethren, you must be faithful to your wife and a protection to your children. You know the moral standard. You must keep it. Never neglect your wife or your children. Never abandon them. They are precious beyond any measure.

Ordinances were revealed and commandments were given to build temples, "for therein are the keys of the holy priesthood ordained"[7] that families can be sealed for time and for all eternity. (04–04)

The Church is built out of family units. We do not build the Church out of wards and branches and stakes and districts; we build the Church out of families and individuals. (08–02)

The home is the basic institution of the Church. The home is the basic institution of the Church. When our fight against sin is won, it will be won on home ground; consequently, our obligation as Church leaders is to strengthen the home. (64–04)

The Church and its leaders exist to strengthen the family. The purpose [of the Church organization] is to shelter families and individuals. They are grouped together in a ward or branch.

It is the responsibility of the bishop to see that each family is bound together in enduring covenants and each individual is safe and happy. The system works best when the bishop recognizes the preeminent responsibility of parents.

While the bishop is sometimes referred to as the "father of the ward," we should remember he is not called to rear the children of the ward.

Our handbook states:

"Parents have primary responsibility for the welfare of their children.[8] The bishopric and other ward leaders support but do not replace them in this responsibility."[9] (99–01, p. 63)

Parents have preeminent responsibility to lead their family. The home is the basic unit of the Church. When we succeed, and the home is presided over by the priesthood, it is established for time and all eternity.

Parents have preeminent responsibility to lead their families. Church organizations are *to sustain*, not *replace* them. Church organizations are not to usurp the responsibility from the parents because some *do not* and some *cannot* fulfill their responsibilities. (87–06)

The shield of faith is handcrafted and fitted in the home. Lest parents and children be "tossed to and fro," and misled by "cunning craftiness" of men who "lie in wait to deceive,"[10] our Father's plan requires that, like the generation of life itself, the shield of faith is to be made and fitted in the family. No two can be exactly alike. Each must be handcrafted to individual specifications.

The plan designed by the Father contemplates that man and woman, husband and wife, working together, fit each child individually with a shield of faith made to buckle on so firmly that it can neither be pulled off nor penetrated by those fiery darts.

It takes the steady strength of a father to hammer out the metal of it and the tender hands of a mother to polish and fit it on. Sometimes one parent is left to do it alone. It is difficult, but it can be done.

In the Church we can teach about the materials from which a shield of faith is made: reverence, courage, chastity, repentance, forgiveness, compassion. In church we can learn how to assemble and fit them together. But the actual making of and fitting on of the shield of faith belongs in the family circle. Otherwise it may loosen and come off in a crisis. (95–05, p. 8)

We began thirty years ago under the campaign called *correlation* to teach members of the Church that that which is most worth doing must be done at home. Some still do not see that too many out-of-home activities, however well-intended, can leave too little time to make and fit on the shield of faith at home. This shield of faith has never been successfully produced in a factory; it is a cottage industry. (95–04)

This shield of faith is handmade in a cottage industry. What is most worth doing ideally is done at home. It can be polished in the classroom, but it is fabricated and fitted in the home, handcrafted to each individual.

Many do not have support in the family. When that shield is not provided at home, we must, and we can, build it. (04–01, p. 4)

Weigh carefully the needs of dysfunctional and functional families. To serve the needs of an increasing number of dysfunctional families, the Church provides influences and activities to compensate for what is missing in those homes.

Priesthood and auxiliary leaders, and especially parents, must use wisdom born of inspiration to make very certain that those activities, for both leaders and members, are not over-demanding of time and money. If they are, it leaves too little of both and makes it difficult for attentive parents to influence their own children. Be very careful to sustain and support rather than supplant the home. (98–03, p. 74)

A caution about overscheduling activities. I must touch upon what must surely be the most difficult problem to solve. Some youngsters receive very little teaching and support at home. There is no question but that we must provide for them. But if we provide a constant schedule of out-of-home activities sufficient to compensate for the loss in those homes, it may make it difficult for attentive parents to have time to be with and teach their own children. Only prayer and inspiration can lead us to find this difficult balance. (98–07, p. 24)

Be careful not to overschedule families. Every time you schedule a youngster, you schedule a family—particularly the mother.

Consider the mother who, in addition to her own Church calling and that of her husband, must get her children ready and run from one activity to another. Some mothers become discouraged—even depressed. I receive letters using the word *guilt* because they cannot do it all.

Attending church is, or should be, a respite from the pressures of everyday life. It should bring peace and contentment. If it brings pressure and discouragement, then something is out of balance. (98–07, p. 23)

Care must be taken to not let Church programs overburden the family. In providing out-of-home activities for the family, we must use care; otherwise, we could be like a father determined to provide everything for his family. He devotes every energy to that end and succeeds; only then does he discover that what they needed most, to be together as a family, has been neglected. And he reaps sorrow in place of contentment.

How easy it is, in our desire to provide schedules of programs and activities, to overlook the responsibilities of the parent and the essential need for families to have time together.

We must be careful lest programs and activities of the Church become too heavy for some families to carry. The principles of the gospel, where understood and applied, strengthen and protect both individuals and families. (98–07, pp. 22–23)

The Brethren warned in advance of the disintegration of the family. [In 1964] the Brethren warned us of the disintegration of the family and told us to prepare. It was announced by the First Presidency and the Quorum of the Twelve Apostles that the Church would be restructured.

The weekly family home evening was introduced by the First Presidency, who said that "the home [is] the basis of a righteous life and . . . no other instrumentality can take its place nor fulfill its essential functions."[11]

Parents are provided with excellent materials for teaching their children, with a promise that the faithful will be blessed.[12]

While the doctrines and revealed organization remain unchanged, all agencies of the Church have been reshaped in their relationship to one another and to the home. . . . We can only imagine where we would be if we were just now reacting to this terrible redefinition of the family. But that is not the case. We are not casting frantically about trying to decide what to do. We know what to do and what to teach.

The family is very much alive and well in the Church. Hundreds of thousands of happy families face life with an unwavering faith in the future. (94–01, p. 20)

The family is safe within the Church. The family is safe within the Church. We are not in doubt as to the course we must follow. It was given in the beginning, and guidance from on high is renewed as need may be. (94–01, p. 21)

There is only one place where the family can be fully protected. When you young people who now look forward to marriage and a family life look around and see the dangers, there is only one place on this earth where the family can be fully protected, and that's within the ordinances and the doctrines of the gospel of Jesus Christ. Live the gospel and you're going to be all right.

The world isn't a very pleasant place to live in, and there are challenges and disorders and patterns of life and death and all of the problems that come to us, and yet the answers are found in understanding that the family is the fundamental unit of the Church. All of the activities of the Church are calculated to strengthen the family. (08–01)

Prophetic guidance for the family. How could the Brethren possibly have known that within half a lifetime social and cultural standards would drift so low and so rapidly and then slip into a free fall? How could they have possibly known that across the world leaders in business, industry, government, education, law enforcement, and courts would awaken to a sense that the future of civilization depends on stable families and that those leaders would cast about for answers, not able to recognize them when they were able to find them?

But the Brethren did know. I watched and, in a small way, participated as the whole curriculum of the Church was restructured and correlated with the family as the anchor. (98–06)

We have watched the standards of morality sink ever lower until now they are in a free fall. At the same time we have seen an outpouring of inspired guidance for parents and for families.

The whole of the curriculum and all of the activities of the Church have been restructured and correlated with the home:

- Ward teaching became home teaching.
- Family home evening was reestablished.
- Genealogy was renamed family history and set to collect records of all the families.
- And then the historic proclamation on the family was issued by the First Presidency and the Council of the Twelve Apostles.
- The family became, and remains, a prevailing theme in meetings, conferences, and councils.
- All as a prelude to an unprecedented era of building temples wherein the authority to seal families together forever is exercised.

Can you see the spirit of inspiration resting upon the servants of the Lord and upon parents? Can we understand the challenge and the assault now leveled at the family? (98–07, p. 22)

The establishment of family home evening is a warning to prepare ourselves. The establishment of family home evening as part of the organized pattern of activity in the Church is, in a sense, the sounding of an alarm to all parents and all young people. The warning is to prepare themselves and strengthen themselves against the challenges which now face us. . . . Strong home ties and warm family relationships produce a balance of character. They produce a satisfaction and offer such fulfillment that young people will feel no need to go beyond them to experiment with the things of the world. (71–03)

The promise of family home evening. This program is designed for a family meeting to be held once a week. In the Church, Monday night has been designated and set aside, Church-wide, for families to be at home together. . . . With this program comes the promise from the prophets, the living prophets, that if parents will gather their children about them once a week and teach the gospel, those children in such families will not go astray. (70–16, p. 108)

Family home evening is a powerful way to protect and draw children closer. [Family home evening is] a very practical and a very powerful place to begin, both to protect your children and, in the case of one you are losing, to redeem him. . . . There is much . . . to all of these special lessons—subtle, powerful magnets that help to draw your child closer to the family circle. (70–16, p. 108)

"The Family: A Proclamation to the World" is akin to scripture. "The Family: A Proclamation to the World"[13] was written by inspiration by members of the First Presidency and Quorum of the Twelve Apostles. There have been only five proclamations given in the history of the Church, and this one has come in our day. It is akin to scripture. You read it; it has that stature. (07–07)

The "Proclamation" explains why we are the way we are. When you wonder why we are the way we are and why we do the things we do and why we will not do some of the things that we will not do, you can find the authority for that in this proclamation on the family. There are times when we are accused of being intolerant because we won't accept and do the things that are supposed to be the norm in society. Well, the things we won't do, we won't do. And the things we won't do, we can't do, because the standard we follow is given of Him. (08–01)

PARENTS' OBLIGATION TOWARD CHILDREN

Deep and abiding happiness can be found in parenthood. The source of deep and abiding human happiness and joy is to be found in the responsibilities and the sacrifices which attend parenthood. (64–11)

Do not be afraid to bring children into the world. Do not be afraid to bring children into the world. We are under covenant to provide physical bodies so that spirits may enter mortality.[14] Children are the future of the restored Church. (04–03, p. 79)

Children are the past, the present, and the future all blended into one. Children are the past, the present, and the future all blended into one. They are consummately precious. Every time a child is born, the world is renewed in innocence.

I constantly think about and pray for the children and youth and their parents. (02–03, p. 8)

Parenthood carries with it an obligation to God. If you have wondered what security you could provide for the little persons who are your children or for those whom you love equally as much who are your children's children, two things are significant. First, parenthood carries with it sacred obligations that exceed the obligation of husband to wife and wife to husband, or parents to children or children to parents. Parenthood carries with it an obligation to God, our eternal parent. With parenthood should come a deep sensitive reverence for life and an uncommon respect for the miracle of life. (64–11)

Blessed are couples who desire children. Some years ago a president of a student stake asked if I would counsel with a young couple. The stalwart young man and his lovely wife had recently been told, with some finality, that they would never have children of their own. They were heartbroken as they sobbed out their disappointment. What they wanted most in life, what they had been taught and knew was an obligation and a privilege beyond price (part of the plan), they now were to be denied. Why? Why? Why?

I consoled them as best I could and offered comfort that really was insufficient to quiet the pain they felt. As they were leaving the office, I called them back and said, "You are a very fortunate and very blessed young couple."

They were startled and the young man asked why I would say such a thing as that. Did I not understand what they had told me? Why would I say they were fortunate and blessed, when they were to be denied the thing they wanted most, children of their own?

I answered, "Because you want them. In the eternal scheme of things, that will be of inestimable and eternal value." The Lord has said that He "will judge all men according to their works, according to the desire of their hearts."[15] Many people now do not want children or want few of them or consider them a burden rather than a blessing. They were a very blessed young couple.

When you understand the plan, you can cope with challenges in life which otherwise would be unbearable. (95–06, p. 8)

Parents are responsible to provide for their children. Children should not be ignored or neglected. They absolutely must not be abused or molested. Children must not be abandoned or estranged by divorce. Parents are responsible to provide for their children.

The Lord said, "All children have claim upon their parents for their maintenance until they are of age."[16]

We are to look after their physical, their spiritual, and their emotional needs. The Book of Mormon teaches, "Ye will not suffer your children that they go hungry, or naked; neither will ye suffer that they transgress the laws of God, and fight and quarrel one with another, and serve the devil, who is the master of sin, or who is the evil spirit which hath been spoken of by our fathers, he being an enemy to all righteousness."[17] (02–03, p. 8)

Children are blessed by righteous parents. Nothing compares with a father who is responsible and in turn teaches his children responsibility. Nothing compares with a mother who is present with them to comfort them and give them assurance. Love, protection, and tenderness are all of consummate worth.

The Lord said, "I have commanded you to bring up your children in light and truth."[18]

All too often, a parent is left alone to raise children. The Lord has a way of strengthening that parent to meet alone what should be the responsibility of two parents. For either parent to deliberately abandon their children is a very grievous mistake. (02–03, pp. 8–9)

Be prayerful in raising your children. As we move forward into a world that is very difficult, spiritually very dangerous with all that is going on, especially in the raising of children, fathers and mothers, as you are on your knees praying, the answers can come. (08–04)

Little children need to be loved. Little children need greatly to be loved, and their security is based on whether they can obtain it or not; and it cannot be false—it must be real and true and deep. They cannot learn to love without a pattern, and most will often respond in their adult lives as they have been taught to respond in their youth.

The great miracle of all existence, the mystery of life as it were, is that one obtains love by and large only by giving it. Great principles of life are demonstrated in the fact that the bestowal of love or attention or appreciation or interest or concern or companionship brings unto him who gives an abundance of the things that he gives. (XX–01)

The cycle of abuse can be broken. To you adults who repeat the pattern of neglect and abuse you endured as little children, believing that you are entrapped in a cycle of behavior from which there is no escape, I say:

It is contrary to the order of heaven for any soul to be locked into compulsive, immoral behavior with no way out!

It *is* consistent with the workings of the adversary to deceive you into believing that you *are*.

I gratefully acknowledge that transgressions, even those which affect little children, yield to sincere repentance. I testify with all my soul that the doctrine of repentance is true and has a miraculous, liberating effect upon behavior. (86–05, p. 18)

Nothing in the scriptures gives license to neglect or abuse children. There is nothing in the scriptures, there is nothing in what we publish, there is nothing in what we believe or teach that gives license to parents or anyone else to neglect or abuse or molest our own or anyone else's children.

There is in the scriptures, there is in what we publish, there is in what we believe, there is in what we teach, counsel, commandments, even warnings that we are to protect, to love, to care for, and to "teach [children] to walk in the ways of truth."[19] To betray them is utterly unthinkable.

Among the strongest warnings and the severest penalties in the revelations are those relating to little children. Jesus said, "But whoso shall offend one of these little ones which believe in me, it were better for him that a millstone were hanged about his neck, and that he were drowned in the depth of the sea."[20] (02–03, p. 8)

Misconduct can ultimately be traced to a deficiency of love. Strangely enough, almost every example of erratic behavior and misconduct can ultimately be traced to the deficiency of love and affection or an attempt to achieve love and affection on the part of the violator. (XX–01)

We must teach parents to be responsible. We often hear, "We must provide frequent and exciting activities lest our youth will go to less wholesome places." Some of them will. But I have the conviction that if we teach parents to be responsible and allow them sufficient time, over the long course their children will be at home.

There, at home, they can learn what cannot be effectively taught in either church or school. At home they can learn to work and to take responsibility. They learn what to do when they have children of their own. (98–07, p. 24)

Let the home environment dominate. You cannot always choose where you live, but often you can, and when you can, keep in mind that it is a wise thing to live so that children can be dominated by the home environment rather than by the neighborhood environment. That is, have a place where your children can play by themselves. If others venture into their playground area they come as guests and must meet the standards that have been set and the limitations that are established by the ideals that are yours. (70–07, p. 226)

Create an atmosphere of peace and reverence in your home. You can do a great deal to create in your home an atmosphere of peace and hominess and reverence and tranquility and security. You can do this without much to live on. By contrast, you can create something angular and cold and psychedelic and artificial. In a thousand different ways your youngsters will be influenced by the choice you make. You can set the tone. It can be quiet and peaceful, where quiet and powerful strength can grow, or it can be bold and loud and can turn the main-spring of tension a bit tighter in the little children as they are growing up, until at last that mainspring breaks. (70–07, p. 227)

Children must have full-time parents. Children must have full-time parents. A courageous, manly father who will not seek to escape his family responsibilities through intemperance, a masculine man who heads his household and whose family is primary, not secondary, a man who asserts himself in the moral development of his children, a man who makes no apology to his friends or co-workers for seeking a spiritual atmosphere in the home. A motherly, womanly mother who, with her husband, has held a little child in her arms and felt "here is someone we love more than we love ourselves, here is someone for whom we will do things we never would do for ourselves, and more important than this, here is someone for whom we will give up and cease to do things that we would not otherwise give up and cease to do for ourselves." (64–11)

It is vitally important to have a mother in the home. How wise and courageous are parents who realize that the little persons who are their children cannot be reared by a babysitter, or by one another. In this day when the family, as an institution, is in great jeopardy, when enemies circle about seeking to destroy the family, parents would do well to recognize that in the sacred institution of family life the organization is such that both the father and the mother have a post to guard, the father as breadwinner and head of the family and the mother as homemaker and heart of the family. How foolish we are if we pull the mother away from her post at home and set her with the father on the breadwinning line leaving one door, the home itself, and the children themselves, vulnerable to an enemy. (64–11)

Principles of good teaching are particularly important to parents. While everybody in the Church is a teacher, was a teacher, or will be a teacher, if you have children or grandchildren you are continuously a teacher. The principles of good teaching are particularly important to you, perhaps more important in your teaching responsibilities as a parent than in any other teaching assignment you may have.[21] (*TYD*, p. 6)

Parents must know when the time for the lesson is now. Parents must know when the time for the lesson is *now,* right now, for their children are ready for it.

My wife and I have made it a practice as parents never to put off a question from one of our youngsters. Regardless of how unimportant the question seems or how busily we are involved, we have always been willing to interrupt anything to respond to the question of a youngster. That is because the question is an indication that he is ready; he wants to know—now. (*TYD*, p. 135)

Let children help. I think one of the major mistakes in teaching children is the tendency for parents to be bothered when children want to participate and to learn something. If we let them help, it is amazing how quickly they become accomplished. How eagerly they learn, for they are ready.

We do a little woodwork around our home, and our boys have all wanted to get involved. We have let them and encouraged them. When I have been working on a project and a youngster wants to do the same thing, I let him try—always. (*TYD*, p. 136)

Prepare children with good home skills. Each Christmas, at least one of the presents for the boys has been a hand tool. When they were old enough, a good metal toolbox was included. When each has left home, he has had his own set of tools and some knowledge of how to use them. He can tune up a car, or drive a nail, or turn a screw, or replace a plug or a faucet washer.

The girls, in turn, have learned to cook and to sew, and each has left home with a sewing machine. This training is doubly important—

first, in frugal living at home, and then in their value as an employee. They would, we hoped, be not only good, but good for something.

Now, I have an idea that some soul will be very upset with us for not providing our boys with a sewing machine and our girls a box of tools as well.

So I hasten to explain that our boys can cook enough to survive a mission and they can sew on a button. The girls in turn can change a faucet washer and drive a nail, and both of them can type and even change a tire on a car. (82–03, p. 86)

Help your daughters retain their feminine nature. Somehow I have never been interested, as a father, in having our daughters reduce themselves to equality with men. It is against their natures. That would be to yield some heights that God intended that they should reach.

There are some things women, by nature, can do so much better than men. There are some spiritual virtues that women must protect for men—or great, very, very great will be the cost.

There seems to be, in the world now, more violence, more brutality, more vulgarity and coarseness. It's a signal that some essential ingredient is being lost. Whatever it is, that ingredient is vital to the future of society.

There is, at once, less tenderness, less reverence, less modesty. Things are more forward and less reserved. The delicate, tender, quiet, reverent, soft things in life that are more a part of the feminine nature somehow are becoming short in supply. . . .

You will not lose by raising daughters who are lovely, refined, feminine women. (79–06)

Parents have a responsibility to teach the doctrine. Responsibility for teaching the doctrines rests upon parents.

"The glory of God is intelligence, or, in other words, light and truth. Light and truth forsake [the] evil one. . . . *I have commanded you to bring up your children in light and truth.*"[22]

If all your children know about the gospel is what you have taught them at home, how safe will they be? Will they reject evil because they choose to reject it? (83–01, p. 66)

We must spiritually immunize our children against evil. We do not fear the future for ourselves or for our children. We live in dangerously troubled times. The values that steadied mankind in earlier times are being tossed away. We must not ignore Moroni's words when he saw our day and said, "Ye [must] awake to a sense of your awful situation."[23] We cannot take lightly this warning from the Book of Mormon:

> The Lord in his great infinite goodness doth bless and prosper those who put their trust in him . . . doing all things for the welfare and happiness of his people; yea, then is the time that they do harden their hearts, and do forget the Lord their God, and do trample under their feet the Holy One— yea, and this because of their ease, and their exceedingly great prosperity.
>
> And thus we see that except the Lord doth chasten his people with many afflictions, yea, except he doth visit them with *death* and with *terror,* and with *famine* and with all manner of *pestilence,* they will not remember him.[24]

Have you noticed that word *terror* in that prophetic Book of Mormon warning? The moral values upon which civilization itself must depend spiral downward at an ever-increasing pace. Nevertheless, I do not fear the future. . . . Parents now are concerned about the moral and spiritual diseases. These can have terrible complications when standards and values are abandoned. We must all take protective measures. With the proper serum, the physical body is protected against disease. We can also protect our children from moral and spiritual diseases.

The word *inoculate* has two parts: *in*—"to be within"—and *oculate* means "eye to see." When children are baptized and confirmed,[25] we place an *eye within them*—"the unspeakable gift of the Holy Ghost."[26] With the Restoration of the gospel came authority to confer this gift.

The Book of Mormon gives us the key: "Angels speak by the power of the Holy Ghost; wherefore, they speak the words of Christ. . . . Feast upon the words of Christ; for behold, the words of Christ will tell you [and your children as well] all things what ye should do."[27]

If you will accept it in your mind and cradle it in your feelings, a knowledge of the restored gospel and a testimony of Jesus Christ can spiritually immunize your children. One thing is very clear: the safest place and the best protection against moral and spiritual diseases is a stable home and family. This has always been true; it will be true forever. We must keep that foremost in our minds. . . .

Encourage our young people. They need not live in fear.[28] Fear is the opposite of faith. While we cannot erase wickedness, we can produce young Latter-day Saints who, spiritually nourished, are immunized against evil influences. (04–03, pp. 77–79)

Priceless lessons can be learned from our own children. When it comes to understanding our relationship with our Heavenly Father, the things my wife and I have learned as parents and grandparents that are most worth knowing, we have learned from our children.

This blessing has come to me as a gift from my wife. The Lord said of such women, "[A wife is given to a man] to multiply and replenish the earth, according to my commandment, and to fulfill the promise which was given by my Father before the foundation of the world, and for their exaltation in the eternal worlds, that they may bear the souls of men; for herein is the work of my Father continued, that he may be glorified."[29] (02–03, p. 10)

Teaching children brings its own reward. Teaching children brings its own reward. Have you not yet learned that when you teach, you learn more from teaching than do your children from learning? (99–06, p. 15)

Parenthood is the greatest of educational experiences. Some years ago two of our little boys were wrestling on the rug before the fireplace. They had reached the pitch—you know the one—where laughter turns to tears and play becomes a struggle. I worked a foot gently between them and lifted the older boy (then just four years of age) to a sitting position on the rug, saying, "Hey there, you monkey, you had better settle down." He folded his little arms and looked at me with surprising seriousness. His little boy feelings had been hurt, and he protested, "I not a monkey, Daddy—I a person."

I thought how deeply I loved him, how much I wanted him to be "a person"—one of eternal worth. For "children are an heritage of the Lord."[30]

That lesson has lingered with me. Among the many things we have learned from our children, this, perhaps, has been the most tempering.

Much of what I know—of what it matters that one knows—I have learned from my children.

Parenthood is the greatest of educational experiences. (66–04, pp. 1149–50)

Never correct a serious problem by reacting to the incident. I have a rule that I made for myself and have always tried to follow. It is this: Never correct a serious problem by reacting to the incident that brings it to my attention. . . . When you want to control the behavior of others and administer correction, you ought to have some reason for doing something about it as compared to doing nothing about it. There ought to be a very good reason for doing something right now as compared with doing something later when the atmosphere is less tense. (*TYD*, pp. 160–61)

You must never give up. Now, parents, I desire to inspire you with hope. You who have heartache, you must never give up. No matter how dark it gets or no matter how far away or how far down your son or daughter has fallen, you must never give up. Never, never, never.

I desire to inspire you with hope.

God bless you heartbroken parents. There is no pain so piercing as that caused by the loss of a child, nor joy so exquisite as the joy at his redemption. (70–16, p. 109)

The measure of a successful parent. It is a great challenge to raise a family in the darkening mists of our moral environment.

We emphasize that the greatest work you will do will be within the

At solemn assembly, April 1970

walls of your home,[31] and that "no other success can compensate for failure in the home."[32]

The measure of our success as parents, however, will not rest solely on how our children turn out. That judgment would be just only if we could raise our families in a perfectly moral environment, and that now is not possible.

It is not uncommon for responsible parents to lose one of their children, for a time, to influences over which they have no control. They agonize over rebellious sons or daughters. They are puzzled over why they are so helpless when they have tried so hard to do what they should.

It is my conviction that those wicked influences one day will be overruled.

> The Prophet Joseph Smith declared—and he never taught a more comforting doctrine—that the eternal sealings of faithful parents and the divine promises made to them for valiant service in the Cause of Truth, would save not only themselves, but likewise their posterity. Though some of the sheep may wander, the eye of the Shepherd is upon them, and sooner or later they will feel the tentacles of Divine Providence reaching out after them and drawing them back to the fold. Either in this life or the life to come, they will return. They will have to pay their debt to justice; they will suffer for their sins; and may tread a thorny path; but if it leads them at last, like the penitent Prodigal, to a loving and forgiving father's heart and home, the painful experience will not have been in vain. Pray for your careless and disobedient children; hold on to them with your faith. Hope on, trust on, till you see the salvation of God.[33] (92–03, p. 68)

Parents, keep your covenants. We cannot overemphasize the value of temple marriage, the binding ties of the sealing ordinance, and the standards of worthiness required of them. When parents keep the covenants they have made at the altar of the temple, their children will be forever bound to them. (92–03, p. 68)

Raising families is not easy. Sometimes there are wayward children, and parents mourn and wonder. . . .

The matter of raising families is not easy, and it does not all get done in this lifetime. The Lord does not harvest everything in October. It is not all accounted for here in this life. So you who have things that are worrying you or disappointing you or that are breaking your heart, just have faith, and do not fear. (07–09)

Avoid over-supervising your children's mate selection. I have noticed that a considerable amount of difficulty among our young people is occasioned from the over-supervision of parents in the selection of a mate for their children. They need to be very wise and very delicate in this matter. (63–03, p. 227)

A caution to parents of newlyweds. I would urge parents to use considerable restraint in reference to the two of you as they learn to regard you as a separate family. I hope they will see you splashing around in the water—not drowning, but splashing—and have the courage and restraint so as not to encumber you with help, but to just let you find your own way. If you are drowning, that is a different matter. I should hope that they would throw you a lifeline and tie it to the shore somewhere and then not forever stand around to try to direct your activities. (63–03, p. 227)

Our children fulfill our dreams when they live the gospel. I do not like to receive honors. Compliments always bother me, because the great work of moving the gospel forward has in the past, does now, and will in the future depend upon ordinary members.

My wife and I do not expect reward for ourselves greater than will come to our own children or to our parents. We do not press, nor do we really want our children to set great prominence and visibility in the world or even in the Church as their goal in life. That has so very little to do with the worth of the soul. They will fulfill our dreams if they live the gospel and raise their children in faith. Like John, "[We] have no greater joy than to hear that [our] children walk in truth."[34] (04–09, pp. 87–88)

Motherhood and Womanhood

God loves mothers. The gift of life and the mother-love that attends it surely are among the supreme gifts of God. I know that the Lord loves mothers. He has said that not even the fall of a sparrow would escape His notice. How readily, then, will He bless those mothers who seek Him.

Their mother gave my children to me, and my mother gave me life. With reverence I say, as well we all might say, God bless, please bless, mothers. (77–01)

Motherhood is a supernal role. As a Latter-day Saint young woman, be a princess. As you grow, be a queen. Glorify that role. The role of womanhood. The role of motherhood. That supernal role. To you are given the blessings and the joy of motherhood. (70–04)

Preserve the ideals of motherhood. There is so much to be lost if the ideals of womanhood and of motherhood are tampered with or tarnished.

When I speak of mothers, I speak not only of those women who have borne children, but also of those who have fostered children born to others, and of the many women who, without children of their own, have mothered the children of others.

The bearing of children is but the beginning—a few months and it is finished. Fostering and molding a child's character is never done. It takes a lifetime and more. (77–01)

The limitation of priesthood to men is a tribute to the incomparable place of women in the plan. The obligations of motherhood are never-ending. The addition of such duties as those which attend ordination to the priesthood would constitute an intrusion into, an interruption to, perhaps the avoidance of, that crucial contribution which only a mother can provide.

The limitation of priesthood responsibilities to men is a tribute to the incomparable place of women in the plan of salvation. (89–02, p. 172)

A woman's lot is not less than a man's. Those who tell you that in the kingdom of God a woman's lot is less than that of the man know nothing of the love, akin to worship, that the worthy man has for his wife. He cannot have his priesthood, not the fulness of it, without her. "For no man," the Prophet said, "can get the fulness of the priesthood outside the temple of the Lord."[35] And she is there beside him in that sacred place. She is there and shares in all that he receives. Each, individually, receives the washings and anointings, each may be endowed. But he cannot ascend to the highest ordinances—the sealing ordinances—without her at his side. (80–09, p. 111)

Men and women have complementary, not competing roles. Men and women have complementary, not competing, responsibilities. There is difference but not inequity. Intelligence and talent favor both of them. But on the woman's part, she is not equal to man; she is superior! She can do that which he can never do; not in all eternity can he do it. There are complementing rewards which are hers and hers alone. (89–02, p. 172)

Only a woman can bestow upon man that supernal title of father. Only a woman can bestow upon man that supernal title of father. She in turn becomes a mother. Can anyone dispute that her part is different from and more demanding than his? The mother must endure limitations while nature performs the miracle of creation. Through her sacrifice, once again another spirit clothed in a mortal body crosses that frail footpath of life to experience mortality and the testing required in the plan of salvation. (89–02, p. 172)

Only a woman can become a mother. Only a woman can become a mother. Never has it been otherwise. Never will it be otherwise. There are some realities that are certain, this is one of them, and to tamper with it is to pull some things apart that are very difficult to put back together.

Only a woman can become a mother. Because physically and emotionally she is structured to permit that to be, feelings will be in balance and she will be happy if she has reverent regard for that as a possibility.

There are things she feels because of it. There are things she needs because of it. There are things she must not do because of it. (76–04)

Motherhood refines spiritual sensitivity. Women, by virtue of their femininity, are more susceptible and responsible to pay attention to the whisperings of the Spirit. (01–01)

Looking back from upper middle-age, I think that women have the advantage. Women are more spiritually sensitive. I am thinking of my mother and of my wife and the things that a woman will feel because of the sensitivity of the feeling. (00–01)

Men may miss many things that are spiritual. Women somehow instinctively make time for these things. It is that sensitivity that is refined by motherhood. Should that be tampered with, or put aside, or smothered? Oh, how great the loss! Never were we more in need of those tender virtues than today.

Women are deeply sensitive spiritually. How tragic it would be to pull them into a man's world. Oh, what a loss! How tragic if a woman by decision avoids motherhood, resents it, becomes a part-time mother, or, sadder yet, forsakes it. (77–01)

Motherhood carries a special influence. While the responsibility to guide little children belongs to both parents, motherhood carries with it a special sacred influence. The program of The Church of Jesus Christ of Latter-day Saints will not preempt your privileges, Mother. It is structured to strengthen you as a mother. None of it is calculated to diminish your influence in the home. . . . There is a "home partnership" spirit in all that is done. How important it is that every mother be enthroned as a queen in her home, teaching the principles of life and salvation to her little ones. (64–05, p. 492)

Women, focus on the family and you will be blessed. You sisters may be surprised to learn that the needs of men are seldom, if ever, discussed in priesthood quorums. Certainly they are not preoccupied with them. They discuss the gospel and the *priesthood* and the family!

If you follow that pattern, you will not be preoccupied with the perceived needs of women. As you give first priority to your family and serve your organization, every need shall be fulfilled, every neglect will be erased, every abuse will be corrected, now or in the eternities. (98–03, pp. 72–73)

No teaching is equal to teaching children. No teaching is equal, more spiritually rewarding, or more exalting than that of a mother teaching her children. A mother may feel inadequate in scripture scholarship because she is occupied in teaching her family. She will not receive a lesser reward.

A man will be hard pressed to equal that measure of spiritual refinement that accrues naturally to his wife as she teaches their children. And if he understands the gospel at all, he knows that he cannot be exalted without her.[36] His best hope is to lead out as an attentive, responsible partner in teaching their children. (99–06, p. 16)

Blessings promised to mothers of children with disabilities. I speak a word to mothers who have little children who are handicapped, children whose little bodies were born incompletely formed or whose little minds are limited. No one knows the depth of agony that you have suffered. By way of consolation, I read from the Doctrine and Covenants:

> Ye cannot behold with your natural eyes, for the present time, the design of your God concerning those things which shall come hereafter, and the glory which shall follow after much tribulation.
>
> For after much tribulation come the blessings. Wherefore the day cometh that ye shall be crowned with much glory; the hour is not yet, but is nigh at hand.[37]

. . . Blessings will be extended to mothers such as you who have given tender and affectionate love to handicapped children. Trials such as these bring a reverence for life, a new depth of compassion and motherhood. (64–05, p. 492)

It is a dangerous trend to draw mothers out of the home. There is another dangerous trend as mothers, sometimes beyond their control, are being drawn out of the home. What could a mother possibly bring into the home that can equal her being at home with the children while they grow and mature? We may learn from events of the future that "the hand that rocks the cradle is the hand that rules the world." (06–03)

The sacred calling of a mother. The First Presidency counseled that

> the mother who entrusts her child to the care of others, that she may do non-motherly work, whether for gold, for fame, or for civic service, should remember that "a child left to himself bringeth his mother to shame."[38] In our day the Lord has said that unless parents teach their children the doctrines of the Church "the sin be upon the heads of the parents."[39]
>
> Motherhood is near to divinity. It is the highest, holiest service to be assumed by mankind. It places her who honors its holy calling and service next to the angels.[40]

That message and warning from the First Presidency is needed more, not less, today than when it was given [in 1942]. And no voice from any organization of the Church on any level of administration equals that of the First Presidency. (93–06, p. 23)

A mother's influence in the home is needed more than additional money. A [working] mother brings home a paycheck. That is an immediate, tangible, and valuable contribution to the home. The change that occurs in the children while she is gone is so subtle, so quiet, so unnoticeable that often the values are mistaken. The immediate,

Boyd K. Packer

Boyd K. Packer and family, April 1970

Boyd K. Packer and Donna Smith Packer at April 2007 general conference

Greeting President Gordon B. Hinckley, October 2003 general conference

The Quorum of the Twelve, October 1994

Donna Smith Packer and Boyd K. Packer

tangible, quickly noticed result of her labor is seldom compared with the subtle disintegration that takes place. . . .

If my experience in counseling is typical, and if experience is worth anything, if I could talk to a mother without hesitation, I would say only in a critical emergency, perhaps as serious as losing the breadwinner in the home, would I ever counsel a mother to leave her children and go outside the home to work. Now a babysitter doesn't love your children. A baby tender can't tend your children. Grandma can't. Grandma has filled her hitch. It is her privilege now to love them and spoil them and then send them home, but not to raise them. Now mothers, if you want to raise fine, stalwart children, then you take the domestic, feminine role. (63–07)

When I grew up there were eleven children. I was number ten, and I used to think we were poor. We weren't; we just didn't have any money. We did have a choice luxury, and that was a mother at home, and that was a hard-working mother, and when we would come home from school we would knock the screen door off the hinges, and the first word out of our mouths would be *Mom,* and she would answer from scrubbing, bottling fruit, or patching Levis, or some domestic role. She would say, "What?" We didn't know what. The conversation was over as soon as she would answer. Well now, I am grateful, humbly grateful, for that influence in the home, where in spite of economic pressure and in the face of the possibility of her going outside of the home to work, she stayed there. (63–07)

Mothers will never regret sacrifices made for their children. There is a trend in the world today—and unfortunately in the Church—for women to want to be emancipated. And we wonder at times—emancipated from what? From domesticity? From motherhood? From happiness? And to what are you in slavery? Your children? It is neither necessary nor desirable for the mother of little children to become a drudge or to be relegated to a position of servitude. It is not, however, uncommon to see women—interestingly enough many in the financially well-to-do category—over-surfeiting themselves with activities outside of the home at the expense of their little children.

I have never known a mother to regret in the closing years of her life a sacrifice made for her children or to begrudge the cost of guiding them to fine Christian citizenship.

On the other hand, we find almost universal remorse for neglect of family in the growing years or for over-indulging children, which is symptomatic of the most serious type of neglect.

Mothers, do not abandon your responsibilities! Be reverently grateful for your little children. (64–05, p. 492)

We need women with character. We need women who will applaud decency and quality in everything from the fashion of clothing to crucial social issues.

We need women who are organized and women who can organize. We need women with executive ability who can plan and direct and administer, women who can teach, women who can speak out.

There is a great need for women who can receive inspiration to guide them personally in their teaching and in their leadership responsibilities.

We need women with the gift of discernment who can view the trends in the world and detect those that, however popular, are shallow or dangerous.

We need women who can discern those positions that may not be popular at all, but are right. (78–06, p. 8)

Young women, stay wholly a woman. I would urge you to stay wholly a woman, a beautiful, lovely, feminine woman. I hope that you'll be modest in your dress and in your manner. I hope you'll be modest in your language. I hope you'll be the princess that will make the young prince invite you to be his queen and open up an eternity of joy and happiness. . . .

I have said on many occasions, and I say here again, there is no persuasion for a man to be good quite so powerful as the ideal of a lovely, virtuous woman. When we talk about priesthood and responsibility that rests upon this church and the critical necessity of brethren who hold the priesthood and who honor it, then we find the generating power for this coming through a lovely, virtuous woman. (73–02)

Faithful young women are set apart from the world. My sweet young sisters, . . . remember that in this Church and kingdom you will be set apart from the world. I pray that you will be wholly woman, that you'll think beautiful, lovely, feminine thoughts, that you'll dress in beautiful, lovely, feminine clothing, that you'll groom yourselves that way. Much depends on that, for from that strength and that obedience and that courage come the power by which the priesthood can function. (73–02)

FATHERHOOD

The meaning of the word "father." Through loving one more than you love yourself, you become truly Christian. Then you know, as few others know, what the word "father" means when it is spoken of in the scriptures. You may then feel something of the love and concern that He has for us.

It should have great meaning that of all the titles of respect and honor and admiration that could be given Him, that God Himself, He who is the highest of all, chose to be addressed simply as Father. (64–01)

How can one come to love someone more than himself? This experience of loving someone more than you love yourself can come, insofar as I know, only through the exercise of the power of creation. Through it you become really Christian, and you know, as few others know, what the word *Father* means when it is spoken of in the scriptures; and you feel some of the love and concern that He has for us; and you may experience some of the remorse and sorrow that must be His if we fail to accept all that is beautiful and praiseworthy and of good report in this world. (59–01, p. 60)

We learn most about what it means to be a father in the home. I
have studied much in the scriptures and have taught from them. I have
read much from what the prophets and apostles have spoken. They have
had a profound influence upon me as a man and as a father.

But most of what I know about how our Father in Heaven really
feels about us, His children, I have learned from the way I feel about
my wife and my children and their children. This I have learned at
home. I have learned it from my parents and from my wife's parents,
from my beloved wife and from my children, and can therefore testify
of a loving Heavenly Father and of a redeeming Lord. (98–07, p. 24)

The highest calling for a man is that of husband and father.
Now some highly important counsel . . . to you, young men. When you
go to the temple to be married, there will be organized a unit of the
Church, the eternal unit. You may be a bishop of a ward some day or
the president of a stake, but from such callings you will be released. The
highest calling that can come to you in mortality is to preside over a
home as a husband and a father. (70–07, p. 227)

Bishops, let fathers preside. Bishops, keep constantly in mind that
fathers are responsible to preside over their families. Sometimes, with
all good intentions, we require so much of both the children and the
father that he is not able to do so. If my boy needs counseling, Bishop,
it should be my responsibility first, and yours second. If my boy needs
recreation, Bishop, I should provide it first, and you second. If my boy
needs correction, that should be my responsibility first, and yours
second. If I am failing as a father, help me first, and my children second. Do not be too quick to take over from me the job of raising my
children. Do not be too quick to counsel them and solve all of the problems. Get me involved. It is my ministry. (78–02, p. 93)

A father's responsibility transcends any other interest in life.
Your responsibility as a father and a husband transcends any other
interest in life. It is unthinkable that a Latter-day Saint man would
cheat on his wife or abandon the children he has fathered, or neglect or
abuse them.

The Lord has "commanded you to bring up your children in light and truth."[41]

You are responsible, unless disabled, to provide temporal support for your wife and children.[42] You are to devote, even sacrifice yourself to the bringing up of your children in light and truth.[43]

That requires perfect moral fidelity to your wife, with no reason ever for her to doubt your faithfulness.

Never should there be a domineering or unworthy behavior in the tender, intimate relationship between husband and wife.[44]

Your wife is your partner in the leadership of the family and should have full knowledge of and full participation in all decisions relating to your home.

Lead your family to the Church, to the covenants and ordinances. (94–01, pp. 20–21)

No father or husband should exercise unrighteous dominion. Should a man "exercise control or dominion or compulsion . . . in any degree of unrighteousness,"[45] he violates "the oath and covenant which belongeth to the priesthood."[46] Then "the heavens withdraw themselves; the Spirit of the Lord is grieved."[47] Unless he repents he will lose his blessings. (93–06, p. 22)

No father should be rude or unkind to his wife or children. Any father who would strike his wife or his children dilutes to that degree the priesthood he holds. It is not worthy of him. There are other ways to do it. I cannot think of a man who holds the priesthood, particularly if he has been sealed in the temple, that would ever be rude or unkind or even impolite to his wife, the mother of his children. (06–01)

Husbands carry an equal obligation to help with the care and nurturing of children. There is no task, however "menial," connected with the care of babies, the nurturing of children, or the maintenance of the home that is not his equal obligation. The tasks that come with parenthood, which many consider to be below other tasks, are simply above them. (89–02, p. 174)

Fathers can help sons set worthy goals. As a father and son discuss goals, there develops the type of communication which strengthens and builds.

There are in the Church many fathers that long for this kind of contact with their sons. The fathers who could, if given the opportunity and encouragement to do so, carry on purposeful interviews with their sons and help them set goals.

When a boy who has had such a talk with his father goes in to his interview with the bishop, there would be little need for the bishop to spend a great deal of his busy time with such a boy. In such cases the bishop could serve as a second witness to what the father and the boy had already established. . . . There is little we could do in the Church which would bring fathers and sons closer together and which would more fully place the father in his true position as spiritual leader of his family than to have this interview take place between the father and his son. (71–06)

Fathers, don't get overly involved in hobbies. Now, Dad, don't get so involved in hobbies that it becomes your life. . . . Hobbies are essential and vital and necessary but not to be totally consuming at the expense of the family and the husband-wife relationship. (63–07)

Your most important objective should be your family and not your work. Your occupation must become a contributing factor toward the more important objective of building your home and family and not the major objective around which all else must revolve. We readily admit that there are occasions when you must be transferred by your employment and that many of the important things of family life must be geared in a measure to your occupation as the breadwinner, but it ought not to be the all-consuming, the single sole hub around which all that is important to you revolves. (63–03, p. 233)

HOME AND FAMILY

The eternal family is the ultimate blessing from God. The doctrine of exaltation and the eternal nature of family ties is neither known nor taught elsewhere in Christianity. To be worthy of exaltation in the presence of God and enjoy association with one's own family is to receive the ultimate of all blessings that God has provided in His plan. (83–04)

An eternal family begins a kingdom. Surely the most sacred relationships on this earth are those relationships that are established when young couples are sealed for time and all eternity in the temple of the Lord. As little children are born to them, they create a kingdom. (64–04)

Family relationships are ordained of God. To you who have stood, or do stand, or will stand at the head of a home as a parent, how deeply consoling and how eminently important is the knowledge that the family institution and these family relationships are ordained of God. (64–11)

The center core of the Church is the family. The center core of the Church is not the stake house; it is not the chapel; that is not the center of Mormonism. And, strangely enough, the most sacred place on earth may not be the temple, necessarily. The chapel, the stake house, and the temple are sacred as they contribute to the building of the most sacred institution in the Church—the home—and to the blessing of the most sacred relationships in the Church, the family. (63–03, pp. 234–35)

Strength comes from a religious influence in the home. There is security, strength, assurance, and stability that come to children who live in homes where there is a religious influence, where there is faith, prayer, and activity for the standards of morality and modesty, and where family relationships are geared by admittance that there is a spirit and influence that exceeds anything social or anything civic, or anything academic or intellectual, and preserves and makes family relationships beautiful and eternal. (63–07)

Happiness at home depends on spirituality. The ultimate end of all ambition is to be happy at home. Regardless of your achievements or accomplishments in fields of endeavor, unless you are happy at home you are not fully happy. . . .

Now happiness at home depends upon spirituality. If you miss spiritual development, if you avoid coming to a knowledge of God and developing a relationship with Him, you not only miss much, but possibly everything. (65–05)

The celestial kingdom is an extension of a happy home into the eternities. President David O. McKay was speaking quite literally when he said that the celestial kingdom is an extension of a happy home into the eternities.

Make sure, young man, that you treat your wife with reverence and with respect. Treat her as your sweetheart, your loving companion, the mother of your children. In this marriage relationship comes the greatest of exaltation and the greatest experiences of life. You will come to know that most of what you know that is worth knowing you learn from your children. Then you will come to know that success comes from following a simple pattern. All you have to do is live the gospel. All you have to do is go to church and pay your tithing and try to live the gospel and respond to calls and try to do a responsive and dedicated work in the callings that come to you. (70–07, pp. 227–28)

When troubles come remember they help us become like God. You are going to have some troubles in your life. You know, if I had all the power that the Almighty has, and it was within my province to make your way so straight that there would be never a bend and to make it so smooth that there would never be a rut and to make it so clear that there would be never an obstacle, for your sakes I would not do it; for from your troubles there will come growth. You will find moments of disappointment, even despair. You will not be free from illness or even death, and even stark tragedy may visit you in this great adventure of family living. From these things, however, your love will deepen, your testimony will increase, your faith will grow and your knowledge of the Lord will become more firm. In no other way can man or woman win the approval of the Lord; and in no other way can man or woman become as God is quite so quickly as in family living. (63–03, p. 234)

Put your homes in order. Put your homes in order. If mother is working outside of the home, see if there are ways to change that, even a little. It may be very difficult to change at the present time. But analyze carefully and be prayerful.[48] Then expect to have inspiration, which is revelation.[49] Expect intervention from power from beyond the veil to help you move, in due time, to what is best for your family. (04–03, p. 79)

I would go back to the home that has a mother there. I ask you, what good is the big picture window and the lavish appointments and the priceless decor in a home if there is no mother there? The mother as a mother, not a breadwinner, is an essential figure in this battle against immorality and wickedness. I would also go back to the family where children were accountable and where father was the head of the family. Would you think me naive if I were to propose that this battle ultimately will be won on such simple grounds as the children coming in after school to homemade bread and jam with Mama there? or on such grounds as Daddy and Mama taking their youngsters to sacrament meeting? or that tender hug as they are put to bed and Daddy or Mama saying, "We need you in this family. You are part of us, and no matter what your troubles are, you can come home"? Would you think me naive to believe that ultimately, on the home ground, this battle will be won? (58–02)

The standard pattern of the home must be preserved. There is a crucial need to preserve the standard pattern of the home. (08–02)

The priesthood functions differently in the home than in the Church. There is a difference in the way the priesthood functions in the home as compared to the way it functions in the Church. In the Church our service is by call. In the home our service is by choice. A calling in the Church generally is temporary for there comes a release. However, our place in the home and family, which is based on choice, is forever and beyond.

In the Church there is a distinct line of authority. We serve where called by those who preside over us.

In the home it is a partnership with husband and wife equally yoked together, sharing in decisions, always working together. While the husband, the father, has responsibility to provide worthy and inspired leadership, his wife is neither behind him nor ahead of him but at his side. (98–03, p. 73)

We should care for family members. The word *temple* to the Latter-day Saint suggests a reverence for life. It embraces a concern for the young and the very old in the family. The world now fosters another view of these family connections. There is a growing tendency to establish centers for the care of the very young and of the very old. This responsibility is being shifted outside the home and family. There may be times when institutional help is needed for the care of the infirm. But we are becoming too free nowadays to shift from the family the privilege (I call it a privilege rather than a burden) of caring for family members. It is wrong. We should not disconnect the generations in this way. We should not unlink ourselves from our generations. (*THT,* pp. 260–61)

CHAPTER 13

Teaching and Church Doctrine

*"Remember, teaching doctrine will improve behavior
more quickly and more permanently than teaching about behavior
will improve behavior." (00–04)*

CHURCH DOCTRINE

True doctrine, understood, changes behavior. True doctrine,
understood, changes attitudes and behavior. The study of the doctrines
of the gospel will improve behavior quicker than a study of behavior
will improve behavior. Preoccupation with unworthy behavior can lead
to unworthy behavior. That is why we stress so forcefully the study of
the doctrines of the gospel. (86–05, p. 17)

True doctrine answers the questions of life. I assure you there is,
underlying the programs and activities of this church, a depth and
breadth and height of doctrine that answers the questions of life.

When one knows the gospel of Jesus Christ, there is cause to
rejoice. The words *joy* and *rejoice* appear through the scriptures repeti-
tively. Latter-day Saints are happy people. When one knows the doctrine, parenthood becomes a sacred obligation, the begetting of life a

sacred privilege. Abortion would be unthinkable. No one would think of suicide. And all the frailties and problems of men would fade away. (83–05, p. 18)

Principles essential to our redemption are not hidden in obscure verses. I've lived to learn that anything that is essential for the redemption of mankind or for our citizenship in the Church is not hidden away in some obscure verse. It is repeated over and over again. Sometimes we don't recognize it. (93–03)

Understanding the doctrine gives cause to rejoice. Latter-day Saints are happy people. That is because when one knows the doctrines, the frailties of men tend to fade away.

When we understand the doctrines, then things fit together and make sense.

We are the children of God, created in His image.

Our child-parent relationship to God is clear.

The purpose for the creation of this earth is clear.

The testing that comes in mortality is clear.

The need for a redeemer is clear.

When we understand the principles of the gospel, we see a Heavenly Father and a Son; we see an atonement and a redemption.

We understand why ordinances and covenants are necessary.

We understand the necessity for baptism by immersion for the remission of sins. We understand why we renew that covenant by partaking of the sacrament. There is no better way to make sense out of life than a knowledge of the doctrines. When we understand those doctrines, we have cause to rejoice and we do rejoice, even celebrate. (88–01)

Convictions concerning understanding doctrine. I desire to share a few thoughts about a basic doctrine of the Church.

What I say is based on these convictions:

First: Instruction vital to our salvation is not hidden in an obscure verse or phrase in the scriptures. To the contrary, essential truths are repeated over and over again.

Second: Every verse, whether oft-quoted or obscure, must be measured against other verses. There are complementary and tempering teachings in the scriptures which bring a balanced knowledge of truth.

Third: There is a consistency in what the Lord says and what He does. That is evident in all creation. Nature can teach valuable lessons about spiritual and doctrinal matters. The Lord drew lessons from flowers and foxes, from seeds and salt, and from sparrows and sunsets.

Fourth: Not all that God has said is in the Bible. Other scriptures—the Book of Mormon, the Doctrine and Covenants, and the Pearl of Great Price—have equal validity, and the four sustain one another.

Fifth: While much must be taken on faith alone, there is individual revelation through which we may know the truth. "There is a spirit in man: and the inspiration of the Almighty giveth them understanding."[1] What may be obscure in the scriptures can be made plain through the gift of the Holy Ghost. We can have as full an understanding of spiritual things as we are willing to earn.

And I add one more conviction: There is an adversary who has his own channels of spiritual communication. He confuses the careless and prompts those who serve him to devise deceptive, counterfeit doctrine, carefully contrived to appear genuine. (84–07, p. 66)

The doctrine comes through prophets, not scholars. The doctrines of the gospel are revealed through the Spirit to prophets, not through the intellect to scholars. (93–02)

Be careful of the sources from which you learn doctrine. There is safety in learning doctrine in gatherings which are sponsored by proper authority. Some members, even some who have made covenants in the temple, are associating with groups of one kind or another which have an element of secrecy about them and which pretend to have some higher source of inspiration concerning the fulfillment of prophecies than do ward or stake leaders or the General Authorities of the Church. Know this: There are counterfeit revelations which, we are warned, "if possible . . . shall deceive the very elect, who are the elect according to the covenant."[2] (91–06, p. 21)

Beware of measuring the doctrine by the intellect alone. If doctrines and behavior are measured by the intellect alone, the essential spiritual ingredient is missing, and we will be misled. (91–06, p. 21)

When doctrine is overlooked, we are in great danger. The principles are overlooked—the gospel is overlooked; the doctrine is overlooked. When that happens we are in great danger! We see evidence of it in the Church today.

I wish to raise a voice of solemn and sober warning! We live in a day of great opposition, not just in the United States but worldwide. It grows by day and by night all across the world. Enemies from without, reinforced by apostates from within, challenge the faith of the rank and file members of the Church. It is not the programs of the Church they challenge. They are, in fact, quite complimentary of them. It is the doctrines they focus on. It is the doctrines they attack, and we notice that many Church leaders seem to be at a loss as to how to answer doctrinal questions. If our members are ignorant of the doctrines, we are in danger, notwithstanding efficient programs and buildings. (84–03, p. 67)

Principles and doctrine never change. Procedures, programs, the administrative policies, even some patterns of organization are subject to change. The First Presidency are quite free, indeed quite obliged, to alter them from time to time. But the *principles,* the *doctrines, never* change. If we overemphasize programs and procedures that can change, and will change, and must change, and do not understand the fundamental principles of the gospel, which *never* change, we can be misled. (84–03, p. 65)

The gospel includes every true element of any philosophy. I declare the gospel to be both true and inclusive of every true element of any philosophy; indeed, the gospel is a fulness of the truth in all of them. (88–08, p. 2)

A principle is an enduring truth, a law, a rule. A principle is an enduring truth, a law, a rule you can adopt to help you in making decisions. Generally, principles are not spelled out in detail. That leaves you free to adapt and to find your way with an enduring truth, a principle, as an anchor. (96–07)

What is needed is a revival of the basic gospel principles. Because the Church is growing so fast, there is a temptation to try to solve problems by changing boundaries, altering programs, reorganizing the leadership, or providing more comfortable buildings. What we really need is a retrenchment such as we have read about in Church history. What we really need is a revival of the basic gospel principles in the lives of all the Latter-day Saints. The true essence of priesthood administration is not in procedure—it is in principle, in doctrine! (84–03, p. 66)

We must see that each successive generation learns the gospel. We must see that the generations that follow us learn the gospel. It is our duty to deliver intact to them, the generations that follow us, the principles and the ordinances of the gospel and the authority of the priesthood.

We must foster those programs which are designed to teach the gospel. Primary, Sunday School, the priesthood lessons, Relief Society lessons, the Aaronic Priesthood and Young Women programs, and sacrament meetings can be powerful, if we will use them to preach the gospel. Sacrament meetings should be gospel oriented. And I do not see how a bishop or stake president could rest until seminary was operating for his young people and the teacher development program that makes these programs of the finest quality receives some attention. All of these deserve watchcare and endorsement. (84–03, p. 69)

From doctrine we learn principles of conduct. The scriptures provide the pattern and the basis for correct doctrine.

From doctrine, we learn principles of conduct, how to respond to problems of everyday living, even to failures, for they, too, are provided for in the doctrines. (94–01, p. 20)

Avoid seeking after mysteries. [It] does [not] serve any useful purpose to speculate or wrest the scriptures, seeking after mysteries. There is scarcely time to master the plain and precious truths revealed to guide us through mortality. (*OFP*, p. 16)

Belief in a false notion is not the problem. A member, at any given time, may not understand one point of doctrine or another, may have a misconception, or even believe something is true that in fact is false.

There is not much danger in that. That is an inevitable part of learning the gospel. No member of the Church should be embarrassed at the need to repent of a false notion he might have believed. Such ideas are corrected as one grows in light and knowledge.

It is not the *belief* in a false notion that is the problem; it is the *teaching* of it to others. In the Church we have the agency to believe whatever we want to believe about whatever we want to believe. But we are not authorized to teach it to others as truth. (85–08, p. 35)

You don't have to know all the answers. Do you have to know all the answers? Well, if you do . . . you don't need any faith. . . .

I have come to know one thing that is increasingly important, particularly with our college-age students, who at the moment are under more stress from some of the directions that are apparent in society. I have come to know that more important than giving them all the answers is giving them something of a posture or a position in confronting the difficult and challenging questions that come to them. I believe this. Our youth will be content without knowing everything. They are content to take many things on faith. They don't want to know everything right now. They want to know what to do when they don't know everything—or even much of anything—on the questions they meet every day from their associates. (68–05, p. 149)

TEACHING YOUTH

The plan is worthy of repetition over and over again. You will not be with your students or your own children at the time of their temptations. At those dangerous moments they must depend on their own resources. If they can locate themselves within the framework of the gospel plan, they will be immensely strengthened.

The plan is worthy of repetition over and over again. Then the purpose of life, the reality of the Redeemer, and the reason for the commandments will stay with them.

Their gospel study, their life experiences, will add to an ever-growing witness of the Christ, of the Atonement, of the restoration of the gospel. (93–05)

Help students push back the curtain and see into the eternities. Teach your students to see with the eyes they possessed before they had a mortal body; teach them to hear with ears they possessed before they were born; teach them to push back the curtains of mortality and see into the eternities. (93–05)

The Lord wants the youth to be taught the truth. I know that the inclination of our youth is to be good. Their basic, innate desire is to seek the truth rather than to shy from it. I know that the Lord wants them to be taught the truth, and that if we will submit ourselves, and purify ourselves and qualify ourselves, through the power of the Holy Ghost we can accomplish those things which the Lord has commanded us to do.

May the Lord bless you, all of you, who teach. . . . May His Spirit be with you as you go before the students, however unschooled you may think you are, however unqualified, that you will be able to teach in order that they can warm their hands by the fire of your faith and be preserved against those temptations which they will meet in the world. (66–03)

We must inoculate youth from spiritual diseases. Spiritual diseases of epidemic proportion sweep over the world. We are not able to curb them. But we can prevent our youth from being infected by them.

Knowledge and a testimony of the restored gospel of Jesus Christ are like a vaccine. We can inoculate them.

Inoculate: In means "to be within" and *oculate* means "eye to see."

We place an eye within them—"the unspeakable gift of the Holy Ghost."[3] (04–01, p. 5)

It is a great responsibility to build character. It is the responsibility of the teacher and the parent to mold and build the character and the attitude into something beautiful and enduring. That is a great responsibility. The Lord will not consider lightly how we use the opportunity. (*TYD*, p. 346)

It is important to feed the students. The easiest way to have control over those whom you teach is to teach them something—to feed them. Be well prepared and have an abundance of subject matter organized and ready to serve. There is no substitute for this preparation. As long as you are feeding the students well, few discipline problems will occur. (*TYD*, p. 182)

It is essential that those you teach be fed, that they be taught something. Each time they come, there should be at least one thought, one idea, one inspiration that is theirs for having been in the class. It can be a little thought, an ordinary one—in fact, the more fundamental it is, the more you have accomplished. (*TYD*, p. 183)

You are on the Lord's side. While you are staying at your post and while you are standing steady, make sure that you are committed, that you are non-neutral, that you are biased, that you are one sided, that you are on the Lord's side. We do not consent in any way to have the voice of the adversary or the other side speak in your classes. (70–09, p. 266)

These are days of great spiritual danger for our youth. The world is spiraling downward at an ever-quickening pace. I am sorry to tell you that it will not get better.

It is my purpose to *charge* each of you as *teachers* with the responsibility—to put you on alert. These are days of great spiritual danger for our youth.

I know of nothing in the history of the Church or in the history of the world to compare with our present circumstances. Nothing happened in Sodom and Gomorrah which exceeds in wickedness and depravity that which surrounds us now.

Words of profanity, vulgarity, and blasphemy are heard everywhere. Unspeakable wickedness and perversion were once hidden in dark places; now they are in the open, even accorded legal protection.

At Sodom and Gomorrah these things were localized. Now they are spread across the world, and they are among us.

I need not—I will not—identify each evil that threatens our youth. It is difficult for man to get away from it. (04–01, p. 4)

Peer group pressure is a powerful tool. Peer group pressure *is* a powerful tool. It can be used destructively or constructively. The wise teacher will be alert for opportunities to use it in a positive way in his classroom and in helping change for the better the lives of his students. (*TYD*, p. 181)

Effective leaders maintain dignity in their appearance. On occasions I have observed leaders of young people trying so hard to be like them. They have not realized that such actions demonstrate visually that they want to join them, not lead them. . . . When I have seen a stake presidency, a high council, or a bishopric dressed and groomed like teenagers, all of my teaching experience seems to confirm the probability that they are not as strong an influence among the youth as they would be if they were to maintain the dignity and image of their leadership callings.

There are times, on picnics and other informal occasions, when they can mingle with and dress like the young people, but that would be an exception.

I repeat, when young people want help—when they *really* want help—they reach up, not over. (*TYD*, p. 285)

Teachers, be careful about drawing students to you. The adulation of the young can easily be misunderstood and misused. If you are a talented teacher, you may have the tendency to be as foolish as the missionary who draws a convert, not to the gospel and the Church, but to himself. I caution you vigorously about that. (74–04, p. 53)

Teachers have the responsibility to be an anchor. You have a great responsibility; and, of course, there comes with that a great opportunity. You have the responsibility to be the anchor; you have the responsibility to stand steady. Somewhere on earth in our day our youth must, positively must, be able to tie to someone who is not confused and who is secure in his faith. (70–09, p. 268)

Students want to reach up to a teacher. Students want to reach *up* to a teacher, not *over* to him. When they have real problems, they want to go beyond what they can get from a buddy. They want to reach up. And there are some little elements of formality in dress and in grooming that help immeasurably in teaching classes. (*TYD*, p. 283)

Teachers should maintain their dignity. A teacher does better if the students refer to him in terms of respect. In the Church they call him "Brother" and not "Mister." He is aware that students do not need a friend—they have plenty of those. They need a teacher, a counselor, an adviser. They need to reach upward, not outward. This teaching distance that exists between the teacher and his students is always there, although it is crossed frequently from him to them. This teaching distance, this dignity, secures him—his office and his character and his kindness—from trespass by his students. (*TYD*, p. 173)

A sense of humor is powerfully important. A sense of humor is a powerfully important attribute of a good teacher. The gospel is a happy and a pleasant gospel. There are times when we may be solemn almost to tears, but a good teacher will develop a sense of humor. (*TYD*, p. 250)

A caution to teachers on counseling. If you are a classroom teacher, it is good advice to keep the deep personal problems of students in the proper channels. Remember, if you are a teacher, it does not make you the parent of the student, or his bishop. Just because counseling needs to be done—and it may very desperately need to be done—it does not mean you are the one who should give the counsel. (*TYD*, p. 229)

A wise teacher avoids improper relationships with students. I have known a student to hang around a teacher like a starved puppy waiting for any morsel of attention or affection that may be thrown to him. At times it takes restraint to keep the relationship formal enough that it does not injure the youngster. A wise teacher will use that devotion and hand out love in such a way that he leads the student to the proper channels and proper relationship so that the dependence does not become damaging. (*TYD*, p. 230)

Wise teachers direct students to proper channels to resolve serious problems. The desire to help someone is not justification for a teacher to want to follow every counseling opportunity to its conclusion. A teacher in the Church is a very wise teacher if he will have clearly in mind the kinds of problems that ought to be solved in channels other than the teacher-student relationship. Even at the risk of feeling inattentive or unsympathetic, he should make it a rigid rule to see that the problems are diverted to where revelation can be delivered. (*TYD*, p. 232)

Counsel to Teachers

Every member is a teacher. Every member of the Church teaches for virtually his whole lifetime. We are teaching when we preach or speak or respond in meetings, for preachers are teachers—at least they generally are, and certainly they always should be. The similarity of the words *preach, teach,* and *speech* is not accidental. When we are speaking and preaching, we are teaching. (*TYD*, p. 3)

Everybody is a teacher—the leader is a teacher, the follower is a teacher, the counselor is a teacher, and the parents are teachers. So we have a responsibility to learn the principles of teaching. The Lord set up His Church so that we all do everything in the Church. There's a statement in the Doctrine and Covenants that "every man might speak in the name of God the Lord, . . . the Savior of the world."[4] How blessed we are that we have a lay priesthood, as it is called, so that all of the brethren can hold the priesthood. All of the sisters are eligible for callings in the Church, and all of us will be parents. Therefore, teaching is the center of all that we do. (07–03)

Teachers must measure up to their calling. I do not use the word *absolute* very often, but I use it now. It is absolutely crucial that you as teachers in the Church measure up and do as you are called and ordained and appointed to do, and simply teach. Teach the gospel of Jesus Christ in its simplicity. (08–05)

There is a desperate need for stable families and teachers who know how to teach values. Now, in an absolutely remarkable consensus, leaders in politics, government, law enforcement, medicine, social agencies, and the courts recognize that the breakdown of the family is the most dangerous and frightening development of our time, perhaps in all human history. They are casting around for answers.

There is a desperate need for stable families and teachers who know how to teach values. (95–10, p. 51)

The gift to teach must be earned. The gift to teach must be earned, and once it is earned, it must be nourished if it is to be kept. If it sleeps too long, it may die. As it works, it grows. (*TYD*, p. 345)

The Church is sustained by teaching. The Church moves forward sustained by the power of the teaching that is accomplished. The work of the kingdom is impeded if teaching is not efficiently done. The growth of the Church depends upon teaching, for missionaries are, above all, teachers. They are constantly teaching the gospel of Jesus Christ. Their testimonies are borne in order that others may be taught, and perhaps the most important verb synonymous with teaching in the Church is the verb *testify.* (TYD, p. 4)

Becoming an effective teacher requires willingness to learn. We acclaim a teacher who is successful with group dynamics and is able to establish a spirit in a classroom in which everybody participates and everybody learns. Sometimes we credit that to his being a "born teacher" or someone who has a "real knack" or "a talent to teach," when in fact it may be that he uses basic principles anyone can apply if he is willing to learn about them and then to apply them. (*TYD*, pp. 125–26)

We learn best by teaching. There are some things you cannot have possession of until you give them away. That is why teaching is such a great blessing in the Church. That is why we want everyone to be teachers. In teaching you learn more than any of the students in your class. The teacher always gains more than the students gain. If you are humble enough to accept a call and go to work, even though you do not know much, you will grow. (00–05)

In teaching, knowing our objectives is important. In teaching we have a specific "somewhere" to get to, and there must be a plan. We must give careful attention to objectives. Fortunately much is done in preparing lesson materials in the Church. The objectives are carefully considered, and the plans are carefully organized so that with reasonable attention to the lesson manual, one can formulate objectives. (*TYD*, p. 141)

Teachers should remember the student is most important. It is easy for a teacher to develop an arrogant attitude that he is the most important person in the class. Always we must remember that the student is the most important. "He that is greatest among you shall be your servant"[5] is what the Lord said. The purpose of all that relates to teaching is to benefit the student. Sometimes teachers and administrators lose track of that. (*TYD*, p. 195)

The superb teacher studies his students. The superb teacher also studies the students; he studies them seriously and intently.

Two things may well occur. First, if you look at your students and wonder why they think and act and feel as they do, you may learn many, many things, and you will be more keenly equipped to help them. Second, as you study carefully their features and expressions, there may well up in your heart a warmth of Christian compassion that comes all too infrequently, even to a dedicated teacher. The feeling is akin to inspiration, a feeling of love. This love will compel you to find the way to do well the work of the Lord: feeding His sheep. (*TYD*, p. 104)

Teaching must be so effective that it cannot be erased. The teaching we do must be so indelible, effective, and impressive that it cannot be erased. Then if it is covered over temporarily by falsehoods or wickedness, a good scrubbing will still leave our work intact and perhaps even a little brighter. We must teach and teach well, and teach permanently. As parents, as teachers, as officers in the Church, that is our obligation and our opportunity. (*TYD*, p. 11)

As teachers we can have a perfect desire to do right. Is there any reason why every one of us, without exception, every single solitary soul, cannot be perfect in his desire to do that which is right?

Then it can be said one day when you're standing to be judged— either judged for your activities as a teacher of youth or judged for your ministry in life—that your desire was right. (70–09, p. 271)

No attempt to teach the gospel is ever futile. Don't be too anxious to call yourself a failure or to judge others as failures. When all accounts are settled, you will find that no effort to teach righteousness is ever completely lost. Nothing you do in the way of trying to convey the gospel of Jesus Christ is ever futile. (*TYD*, p. 339)

The real test of teaching comes after class. A teacher would do well to know that the test of her effectiveness does not come during class periods. A youngster is not going to steal a notebook from his companion during Sunday School class, nor is he apt to say that profane word while in class. Teaching must be so impressing and so reinforcing that after children leave, when they are not in the environment and atmosphere of class circumstances, they will be affected by our teaching. (64–04)

Teachers should avoid becoming puffed up. Some teachers have a tendency to become "puffed up" in their learning. They should exercise care not to do this, because students can quickly detect any signs of sham or hypocrisy. Wise men have written in the scriptures concerning this matter. (*TYD,* p. 217)

A teacher should take criticism. A teacher should be willing to take constructive criticism. If you can find someone who has the courage to give it to you wisely, it will be among the most valuable contributions to your life. (*TYD,* p. 346)

Don't let research and writing divert you from teaching. I caution you [about] . . . the tendency to be diverted from your teachings to do research and writing. Now, that may sound strange to you, but it seems to me that writing and research are, in true perspective, subsidiary to teaching. Both can make teaching more effective. Each has a proper place. I do not say ignore them; I say do not be diverted by them. (74–04, p. 53)

Avoid pedagogical hobbies. I speak of pedagogical hobbies. A teacher may see something to which others may not be paying adequate attention. He may appoint himself to see that it is not neglected, and then overdo it. Almost anything can be overemphasized, as well as neglected. (74–04, p. 54)

The commission of religious education teachers. We are now encircled. Our youth are in desperate jeopardy. These are the last days, foreseen by prophets in ancient times.

I will read one clear, descriptive, accurate prophecy, so old as to be ancient but so timely that evidence of every statement can be seen in today's news releases.

This know also, that in the last days perilous times shall come.

For men shall be lovers of their own selves, covetous, boasters, proud, blasphemers, disobedient to parents [Can you imagine that being prophesied?], unthankful, unholy,

Without natural affection [we see a tidal wave of sexual perversion now sweeping in around us, to say nothing of the hideous specter of child abuse that now is becoming common even among our people], truce-breakers, false accusers, incontinent, fierce, despisers of those that are good,

Traitors, heady, high-minded, lovers of pleasures more than lovers of God;

Having a form of godliness, but denying the power thereof: from such turn away.

When you think of what is happening in society today, the next verse has tremendous meaning.

For of this sort are they which creep into houses, and lead captive silly women laden with sins, led away with divers lusts,

Ever learning, and never able to come to the knowledge of the truth.[6]

That prophetic description of our day is accurate. The evil circumstances it describes encircle *every* student you teach.

While studying one day, I read to that point and sat pondering about all the evidence that now confirms every element in that prophecy. There was a mood of very deep gloom and foreboding, a very ominous feeling of frustration, almost futility. I glanced down the page, and one word stood out, not accidentally, I think. I read it eagerly and then discovered that the Apostle who had prophesied all of that trouble had included in the same discourse the immunization against all of it. Skipping a few verses, I will continue from the same chapter.

But evil men and seducers shall wax worse and worse, deceiving, and being deceived.

But continue thou in the things which thou hast learned

With President Harold B. Lee, 1970

and hast been assured of, knowing of whom thou hast learned them;

And that from a child thou hast known the holy scriptures, which are able to make thee wise unto salvation through faith which is in Christ Jesus.

All scripture is given by inspiration of God, and is profitable for doctrine, for reproof, for correction, for instruction in righteousness:

That the man of God may be perfect, thoroughly furnished unto all good works.[7]

And there you have it—your commission, your charter, your objective in religious education. You are to teach the scriptures. That is the word that stood out on the page—*scriptures.* If your students are acquainted with the revelations, there is no question—personal or social or political or occupational—that need go unanswered. Therein is contained the fulness of the everlasting gospel. Therein we find principles of truth that will resolve every confusion and every problem and every dilemma that will face the human family or any individual in it. (77–11, pp. 4–5)

TEACHING BY THE SPIRIT

One needs the Spirit to teach moral and spiritual values. We have been instructed in the revelations that "if ye receive not the Spirit ye shall not teach."[8] If there is one essential ingredient for the teaching of moral and spiritual values, for the teaching of the gospel, it is to have the Spirit of the Lord with us as we teach. Happily, the promise is given to us that this can be true. (*TYD,* p. 320)

We should constantly teach under inspiration. We should constantly teach under inspiration. We have the right to teach under inspiration in the home and in the Church. And should we have teaching to do in our other pursuits of life, it is not untoward to call upon the Lord for inspiration in that teaching also. (*TYD,* p. 357)

Having first obtained our errand from the Lord. I have always felt that we stand in holy places when we are given entrance to the hearts of those we teach. There are ways in which we may be sustained spiritually and made equal to the opportunity. One of the most important is found in these lines:

"Wherefore I, Jacob, gave unto them these words as I taught them in the temple, *having first obtained mine errand from the Lord.*"[9] . . . I emphasize the expression "having first obtained mine errand from the Lord."

There is a great power operative over the Church and kingdom of God. There are sources of intelligence available to all who teach in the Church—if they teach diligently. There is that sacred process by which pure intelligence may be conveyed to the mind in an instant, so that a teacher can know what he needs to know in his moment of need. (*TYD,* pp. 356–57)

This matter of obtaining one's errand from the Lord is basic preparation for one who teaches. Who would want to go before a class to teach righteousness without first having importuned the Lord for His Spirit to attend the occasion? . . . When [the Spirit] is present, permanent teaching can take place. (*TYD,* p. 322)

Promised blessings to faithful teachers. "Teach ye diligently and my grace shall attend *you* [the teacher], that you [the teacher, the mother, the father] may be instructed more perfectly in theory, in principle, in doctrine, in the law of the gospel, in all things that pertain unto the kingdom of God, that are expedient for you [the mother, the father] to understand."[10]

Notice the promise is to the teacher rather than to the student.

Teach ye diligently and my grace shall attend you [who teach your children or Primary, Sunday School, Young Women and Young Men, priesthood, seminary, Relief Society], that you may come to know:

Of things both in heaven and in the earth, and under the earth; things which have been, things which are, things which must shortly come to pass; things which are at home, things which are abroad; the wars and the perplexities of the nations, and the judgments which are on the land; and a knowledge also of countries and of kingdoms—

That ye [who teach] may be prepared in all things when I shall send you again to magnify the calling whereunto I have called you, and the mission with which I have commissioned you.[11] (99–06, p. 16)

A teacher never has to be alone. Teaching is a sacred calling, a holy calling. The thing I think I would tell teachers is that they never teach alone. They never have to be alone. The Lord has promised that in the scriptures. Alma said the Lord granteth unto all nations, in every tongue, teachers,[12] and the Lord said, "Teach ye diligently and my grace [will] attend you."[13]

I don't know how to teach the gospel without a constancy of prayer. (07–03)

Power comes to the teacher when he is prepared. Power comes when a teacher has done all that he can to prepare, not just the individual lesson, but in keeping his life in tune with the Spirit. If he will learn to rely on the Spirit for inspiration, he can go before his class—or, in the case of the parent, he can meet with his children—secure in the knowledge that he can teach with inspiration. (*TYD*, pp. 358–59)

Teachers should treasure up in their minds the words of life. While doing manual work, while traveling, during those all too often wasted moments of waiting, the resourceful teacher is preparing not only tomorrow's lesson but also making general preparations for many future lessons through observation of nature and of life and through prayer. . . .

The scriptural injunction to "treasure up in your minds continually the words of life, and it shall be given you in the very hour that portion that shall be meted unto every man"[14] has much significance for teachers of the gospel of Jesus Christ. Let your mind find constant employment in observation, in meditation, in prayer; then let your hand always be near a pencil and paper to record the essentials of such preparation before they vanish as quickly and completely as time itself. (*TYD,* pp. 260–61)

Learn the gospel in order to share it. If we learn in order to serve, to give to others, and to "feed" others, we will find the acquisition of subject matter much easier. We then are trying not to glorify ourselves, but to teach our own children or others in the Church. Then there will come to us the full meaning of this scripture: "He that findeth his life shall lose it: and he that loseth his life for my sake shall find it."[15]

We will also come to know the meaning of the scripture, "Treasure up in your minds continually the words of life, and it shall be given you in the very hour that portion that shall be meted unto every man."[16]

Our obligation is to share the gospel in everyday life, as parents, as missionaries, as teachers in the Church organizations. If you keep this constantly in mind, you will learn in order to give. It will then be so much easier to learn how to feed His sheep. (*TYD,* p. 191)

It is important to ask the Lord to help us teach. There is something important about our deciding that we want to be a good teacher—a good parent. There is something equally important about making that desire known to the Lord. Many of us have the desire, but we keep it to ourselves. An important key is turned when we go through the formality of stating our desires to Him who can grant them.

There is no theme in holy scripture more oft-repeated than the simple injunction, "Ask, and ye shall receive." (*TYD,* p. 14)

There is power in teaching with the Spirit. On a number of occasions I heard William E. Berrett, one of the greatest teachers I have known, pay tribute to a teacher he had as a boy when he lived in the south end of the Salt Lake Valley in a rural ward. He told of an experience in which an older gentleman was appointed to teach a class of boys. The new teacher was a convert from Europe who spoke with a heavy accent and had to struggle with the language. President Berrett would say, "He was an unlettered man, deprived of a formal education, who had a hard time speaking English. But I will ever be grateful to him. What he lacked in expression he made up in spirit. We could have warmed our hands by the fire of his faith." I know of no greater tribute to a teacher in the Church than that.

The gift to teach with the Spirit is a gift worth praying for. A teacher can be inept, inadequate, perhaps even clumsy, but if the Spirit is powerful, messages of eternal importance can be taught. (*TYD,* pp. 324–25)

Effective Teaching

A brief overview of the plan is of immense value to students. Whatever course you teach, a brief overview, even in outline form, can form a framework upon which our youth can place the truths you will present, many of which come at random.

There is one framework that fits every course you teach. Elements of it are everywhere in the scriptures. . . .

A brief overview of the "plan of happiness" (which is my choice, my favorite title, in talking of the plan), if given at the very beginning and revisited occasionally, will be of immense value to your students. (93–05)

Teachers can draw lessons from everyday life. I found that we can, as the Savior did, draw lessons from everyday occurrences. We can note the behavior of people in all their individuality and sameness. I developed the desire, as a teacher, to share the things I had observed. I found that by diligent, consistent observation, note taking, and filing, one can store up a vast reservoir of knowledge, examples, lessons, feelings, experiences, and stories. One can come to know the verity of the scripture [to] "treasure up in your minds continually the words of life, and it shall be given you in the very hour that portion that shall be meted unto every man."[17] That supply is there whenever one needs to draw from it for teaching or speaking assignments. Whatever else we are in life, we are teachers—as parents, in Church service, in all else that we do. (*ABE,* p. 6)

There is teaching that lives after the students are gone. If you use parables and stories and illustrations, it lives after the students are out of the class. (07–03)

There is power in using parables to teach. In the four Gospels in the New Testament are recorded thirty-six parables that the Lord used. With a little resourcefulness, all of us as teachers can use this technique. It is simply the process of developing, creating, or inventing an imaginary situation that represents a real-life situation. For some reason, it is used very little. This is unfortunate, because it is an easy way to drive home an otherwise difficult lesson. When I say an easy way, that is only comparatively speaking. It takes work and imagination and resourcefulness to create a parable, but great profit comes from the time expended when the results are considered. (*TYD,* p. 204)

Teachers who use the parables and imagery their students can understand find greater meaning is imparted. Gospel principles can come alive if they are related to the everyday experiences of the hearers. (*TYD,* p. 207)

Scrupulous care should be given when telling stories. Stories can be used effectively to interest a class and teach them. I suppose there are stories that might occasionally be used merely to entertain them. That would be true perhaps only of little children. Everyone has so many experiences that might be useful in teaching if they were alert to them and recorded them.

As useful as stories are, I have always been scrupulously careful in telling stories not to give the impression that a fictitious story is true or that I participated in an incident when I did not. I know there are those who will want to make the stories appear to be part of their own experience. Personally, I feel that is dishonest. I would not do it, nor would I recommend it to anyone else. If I ever tell a story in my teaching and indicate that it is from my own experience, it did happen to me or I would never identify it that way. Nor should you feel it necessary to embellish or extend or decorate a story. If it won't stand on its own to illustrate the point, then don't use it. . . .

There are enough simple true experiences in everyday life and there are many ways to construct lifelike stories such as in the parables of Jesus that a person doesn't need to fabricate an experience. (*TYD,* pp. 286–87)

Use care in relating inspirational stories. When we teach spirituality, there are many faith-promoting incidents in the lives of others and in our own lives that might be recalled by way of illustration or testimony. There are accounts of miraculous events in the lives of members of the Church past and present.

The seventh Article of Faith states: "We believe in the gift of tongues, prophecy, revelations, visions, healings, interpretation of tongues, and so forth." There are many inspiring and inspired accounts of these gifts among the Latter-day Saints.

The teacher must, however, be very judicious in the use of experiences of this type. First of all, he must *know* that they are true. There are many things that are passed about that are not true. From time to time there seems to be a rash of accounts of visitations, of experiences that are fallacious. (*TYD,* p. 325)

A teacher must capitalize on the readiness of his student. If teaching is to be effective, it must capitalize on the readiness of the students to learn. A number of years ago when I was teaching seminary, a student was killed in an automobile accident on the way to school. There was a pall of gloom and shock over the whole school that day. The students came to class more serious and ready to learn than I had ever seen them before. I was teaching Church history, and we were bringing the pioneers west. But that was not the time for a lesson on pioneering. That day they were ready for a lesson on the Atonement of Christ, the resurrection, life after death.

A good teacher will be alert and will seize upon the opportunity to teach when the youngster is ready. Many lessons that we have been anxious to teach our own children have had to wait until they were ready. (*TYD,* pp. 129–30)

Never apologize for repetition. Repetition is an important procedure in all teaching. Don't overlook the significance of the fact that
Moroni visited Joseph Smith three times during the night and a fourth
time the next day, with the same—precisely the same—message. Many
teachers and most speakers try to cover too much. They race from one
subject to another when they might better be repeating one simple idea.
It is good advice to tell your listeners what you are going to tell them,
tell them, and then tell them what you have told them. That is a useful
technique.

Never apologize for repetition. (*TYD,* pp. 354–55)

Audio and visual aids should be used sparingly. Teachers would
do well not to be extremists on anything and to be cautious and wise
in adopting new techniques or procedures.

Audio and visual aids in a class can be a blessing or a curse, depend-
ing upon how they are used. They might be compared to spices and fla-
vorings that go with a meal. They should be used sparingly to accent or
make a lesson interesting, but the basic instruction, when all is said and
done, will for the most part be lecture, question and answer, and recita-
tion. (*TYD,* p. 265)

How to help students with difficult questions. Anyone can ask a
difficult question. Anyone can tune in from the outside and want to
know all about statistical analysis, for example, before he has learned to
add and subtract. To attempt to satisfy him on that level is to confuse
him.

The most important thing we as teachers can do with our students
is to assure them that we are at peace; to understand difficult, even controversial, issues, we must realize there are some things that we can't
answer. I don't have the slightest embarrassment or hesitancy to say that
I do not know why the Lord has done some of the things He has done.

But there are some things I do know. I do know that we will never
be without some of these difficult questions. I do not feel that they have
ever hurt the Church and kingdom of God. I do not think we have
lost an honest convert because of the position of the Church on

controversial matters. I do know that the more arrogant and academic and self-centered a person is, the less likely he is to be satisfied with an answer that has spiritual implications. (*TYD*, pp. 84–85)

Answering difficult questions requires certain prerequisites. Most educational programs require the completion of basic or prerequisite courses before one can register for advanced courses. . . . If we apply this principle of prerequisites to a very difficult question, we will approach it in an entirely different way. There just isn't much use in trying to answer a difficult question for someone who has not undergone the prerequisite study of faith, repentance, baptism by immersion for the remission of sins, and the laying on of hands for the gift of the Holy Ghost. Unless he knows something about revelation and about authority, whatever answer we give will not be satisfying to him. (*TYD*, pp. 81–82)

Be careful lest you answer the question. When a student asks a question, be careful lest you answer it! Or more emphatically, be careful lest the teacher answer it. How easy it is for a teacher to respond quickly to simple questions, to close a conversation that might have ignited a sparkling and lively class discussion.

The wise teacher deftly and pleasantly responds, "That's an interesting question. What does the class think of this?"

Or, "Can anyone in the class help with this interesting problem?"

A simple two-way conversation, and you've involved the whole class and their minds come alive and are open to teaching. (*TYD*, p. 68)

There is only one stupid question. It is important for a teacher to make sure that the students understand there is only one stupid question, and that is the one that is never asked. It is worth a few minutes in class to explain that no one is all-knowledgeable. No one knows everything; everyone is uninformed in one area or another that is known to most people. It is not out of place for members of a class or for parents and children to ask questions. (*TYD*, pp. 73–74)

Don't be afraid to say "I don't know." A teacher must expect to be confronted frequently with difficult questions. Often these are questions to which there is no satisfying or comforting answer. A teacher cannot know everything. The Lord has not yet revealed everything. And yet, to a teacher the questions will come, asking about everything. He should have the humility to say, "I don't know." Often that will be the only true answer. If it is something that he should know, it is well to add, "I should know the answer to that, and I can find out the answer. When I have been able to do so, I will give it to you."

When we are teachers in the Church, we will often find ourselves saying, "I do not know the answer, and I do not know anyone who does know the answer to that." We needn't be afraid or ashamed to say that. It won't hurt the students to know that we're not all-knowing. (*TYD*, p. 80)

Leave the mysteries alone. There is good reason for the Brethren over the years to have counseled the people to leave the mysteries alone. There are those who dig deeply to find things that in some cases may be true but are not essential to the salvation of any mortal individual. How much better that we teach generously all who need to know the basic principles of the gospel. (*TYD*, pp. 197–98)

PRINCIPLES OF CLASSROOM MANAGEMENT

Teachers should be generous in their praise. Teachers should be generous in their praise and encouragement. They can do more to govern behavior through that channel than in any other way. (*TYD*, p. 109)

A key part of discipline is to remember that all are children of God. Remember that a fundamental part of discipline is to know and to understand and to believe that all men are basically good; that we are children with heavenly parentage; that all men are instructed sufficiently that they know good from evil; that there is hope for everyone. (*TYD*, pp. 91–92)

A teacher must acknowledge individual differences in students to succeed. No principle of education has received so much attention from professional educators as the principle of individual differences. No teacher will succeed without knowing something about this principle. One cannot get a group together without noting that each person is individually different. That is true of a family. It is true of any class or congregation. (*TYD*, p. 115)

One of the great miracles of life is that no two individuals are exactly alike. We know that fact from various measurements that can be taken of the physical body—fingerprints, for example, where no two are ever the same—and also from measurements of intelligence and from emotional reactions. It is helpful for a teacher to understand that many of those whom he teaches, his own children or those in the Church, just do not see things the same way he sees them. (*TYD*, p. 117)

The eyes have it. When it comes to controlling a child or a class, the eyes have more power than a club has. Expressive, friendly, demanding, appealing, forgiving, commanding—the eyes have it. The direct, unwavering, piercing look has called many a student back to the classroom, leaving broken conversations to be gathered after class and put together in surroundings more appropriate for chatter. The alert and sensitive teacher can discipline a student more effectively with his eyes than the clumsy teacher can ever do with accusations or ultimatums or pressure of any kind.

The eyes of the alert teacher move constantly back and forth across the class, taking in each movement, recording each expression, responding quickly to disinterest or confusion. They read immediately a puzzled expression or sense at once when learning has taken place. Just as the conductor of a symphony orchestra controls a complicated and magnificent organization and yet himself is silent, so the master teacher directs the workings of the class by gesture, inflection, expression, and, most of all, the use of his eyes. (*TYD*, pp. 164–65)

The cure for a deflated ego. We know how grateful we are when someone pumps our ego up a bit. A deflated ego, after all, need not really be a serious disorder, and a parent or a teacher can ordinarily correct the disorder in a moment or two. If it has been deflated several times, it may be a little more difficult, but a treatment of genuine compliments and kind words and encouragement extended over a period of time does the trick. (*TYD,* p. 108)

A good teacher never gives up. A teacher may labor with all the resources at hand and then have a bad day or find that one of his pupils has not responded. One thing that he must never do is give up.

It is comforting to realize that Jesus Himself was not successful in redeeming all with whom He came in contact, that even all those who heard Him speak and teach did not respond—those who were there, who were in the multitudes and listened, who perhaps touched Him. The important thing is that He *wanted* to redeem them all. (*TYD,* p. 334)

Easier to prevent than to rescue. The wise teacher does not kill a fly with a sledgehammer or try to adjust a watch with a crowbar. He takes control of the class at the beginning and then keeps that control. It is so much easier to maintain control than it is to try to rescue the situation once it has gotten out of hand. (*TYD,* p. 157)

What if it were your boy? As a young seminary teacher, a group of us were in a room with Antoine R. Ivins of the First Quorum of the Seventy, then a very venerable older man. He had been born in a dugout down in southern Utah. We were asking him questions. It is a wonderful thing to ask questions of a General Authority.

I asked him the question that was most on my mind as a young seminary teacher about a rascal of a boy in the class. The substance of my question was, "How long do I have to put up with that?"

He didn't answer for a long time. He sat on a table at the front of the room, swinging his feet a little, looking at the floor. Then he said six words, "What if it were your boy?" I had learned something that I have never forgotten. (00–04)

Jesus: The Master Teacher

Jesus was first and foremost a teacher. There is a clearer reason for describing Jesus as a teacher than for describing Him as a social reformer, philosopher, or any of the other names He has been called. He *was* a teacher. That is how He accomplished the things He was sent to do. He taught.

The fact that His followers were referred to as disciples is of great significance, for *disciple* literally means "pupil" or "scholar," and the disciples were literally His students. (*TYD*, p. 21)

The Savior is the master teacher. The teaching of Jesus Christ constitutes a treatise on teaching technique surpassed by none. Jesus has been described as a philosopher, an economist, a social reformer, and many other things. But more than these, the Savior was a teacher. If you were to ask, "What did Jesus have as an occupation?" There is only one answer: He was a teacher. It is He who should be our ideal. It is He who is the master teacher. (96–04)

How can one develop the gift of teaching? Many years ago I read this scripture [Moroni 10:7–10, 17] and pondered it. I thought that among the gifts one might have in order to make himself useful to the Lord, the gift to teach by the Spirit would be supreme. The gift to teach the word of Wisdom and to teach the word of knowledge by the Spirit is much to be desired. Why should such a gift not come to us if we desire it? If we desire to succeed as a teacher and we're willing to earn that ability, why should it not come to us? If we're willing to ask for it and pray for it, and we believe with sufficient faith that we can possess it, why should it be withheld from us?

Where would we turn to develop such a gift? Where do we go for an example? That, of course, brings us to Him who is the Master Teacher, Jesus Christ, the Son of God, the Only Begotten of the Father. In the scriptures He is addressed constantly as "Master," which by interpretation means "teacher." He is the Master Teacher, and from Him and His example we also may learn to be master teachers. (*TYD*, p. 20)

It is not unwise to aspire to teach as Jesus did. Although Jesus did not discuss the subject of teaching procedures, we can learn a great deal about how to teach moral and spiritual ideals by studying the accounts of His ministry in the Gospels. It is not untoward for any of us to aspire to teach as He taught. It is not untoward for any of us to aspire to be like Him. He was not just a teacher; He was *the* teacher. Through the centuries and through translation from language to language, His teachings have remained simple and compelling and direct, because they were designed to do just that. (*TYD,* p. 24)

Even as I am. I believe that to the degree you perform according to the challenge and charge which you have, the image of Christ does become engraven upon your countenances, and for all practical purposes, in that classroom at that time and in that expression and with that inspiration, you are He, and He is you.

We teach what we are. Our conduct may determine whether those we teach accept or reject our words. Again, "What manner of men [and we might say women] ought ye to be? . . . Even as I am."[18] President Spencer W. Kimball taught, "You will do all you teach your students to do: to fast, to bear testimony, to pay tithing, to attend your meetings, to attend temple sessions, to keep the Sabbath day holy, to give Church service ungrudgingly, to have home evenings and family prayers, and to keep solvent, and to be honest and full of integrity."

In the course of my efforts to teach His gospel, I have come to know Him, Jesus Christ, the Son of God, the Only Begotten of the Father. I stand in reverence before Him with deep regard for what He taught, and with deep regard for how He taught. It is not untoward for any of us to aspire to teach as He taught. It is not untoward for any of us to aspire to be like Him. He was not just a teacher; He was the master teacher. (96–03)

Jesus used comparisons to illustrate gospel principles. Keep in mind that Jesus was not merely talking to the people of His day about their experiences and the things in their environment. He was not teaching them about hens and chickens. He was using the hen and the chickens to teach them about something else. He related and interrelated these experiences in the visible world to the unseen world within. He made the application, the comparison, so that the lesson was obvious.

If we were to subtract from the discourses of Jesus the applications He made, we would end up with something of a disjointed commentary on peasant life in ancient Palestine. It is the teaching of the gospel that makes the illustrations come alive. The illustrations, in turn, make the meaning of the lessons clear to people of all ages. (*TYD*, p. 48)

The four Gospels are a treatise on teaching. There is no information in print on how to teach moral and spiritual values more important nor, if properly approached, more helpful than is found in the Gospels. They constitute a treatise on teaching technique surpassed by none. (*TYD*, pp. 22–23)

CHAPTER 14

Learning and Scholarship

"If all you know is what you see with your natural eyes and hear with your natural ears, then you will not know very much." (08–02)

KNOWLEDGE, WISDOM, AND EDUCATION

Gaining knowledge and wisdom is eternally worthwhile. In the midst of all that is transitory in our age, we may yet discover something permanent, something that will outshine and outlast the violence and struggle and brutality that is in the daily fare—not dominion over other lives and lands, but ourselves through learning. I believe that the art or process of acquiring knowledge, comprehension, understanding, skills, all of which may, with time and effort mature into wisdom, is eternally worthwhile. But quoting Spinoza, "All things excellent are as difficult as they are rare." (*ABE*, p. 3)

Knowledge versus education. A number of years ago there was a student at Columbia University who was known as the "perennial student." He had been left an inheritance which stipulated that it should continue as long as he was engaged in collegiate study. Thereafter, the income was to go to a charity.

This man remained a student until he died. It was said that he had been granted every degree offered by Columbia University and had taken practically every course. No field of knowledge was foreign to him. He was probably more widely read than the best of his professors. He was described as the "epitome of erudition." But he could not possibly be described as educated. He fit the description of those spoken of in the scripture who are "ever learning, and never able to come to the knowledge of the truth."[1] He was inherently selfish. What a pity! What a waste! (83–03, p. 26)

A balanced education is extremely important. It is important that we provide a balanced education. So many people attend institutions of higher learning and fail to learn the most important things of life.

Some graduates move through their careers with the precision and grace of a superbly trained athlete. They respond to every challenge and win every contest.

But at once, sadly enough, in their private lives they show no more coordination than a drunk. They trip over problems that any truly thoughtful person could avoid.

They stagger through life puzzled by broken marriages, by thankless children, and by the unhappiness they both experience themselves and cause for others.

How unworthy for an institution of higher learning to certify students for graduation, yet so ill-prepared for life itself, having denied them the things most worth knowing or, most unfortunate, having taught in their place philosophies that ultimately hold no lasting happiness. (81–02)

There can be great power in education. I confess I have a feeling of awe when I contemplate the power of education. I become encouraged when I see the great force for good when education accomplishes a righteous purpose. I am restless over the possibility, ever present, that education may be perversely used. We have many examples in the world where the misuse of this power has degraded men rather than exalted them. (81–02)

A dream worth pursuing. We encourage our youth in every country to get an education, even if at times it seems hopeless. With determination and faith in the Lord, you will be blessed with success. It is a dream well worth pursuing. (92–05, p. 73)

The difference between being well-schooled and well-educated. The difference between being well-schooled and well-educated rests somehow in what you do with the knowledge you have gained. (83–03, p. 25)

Ultimately we must learn the gospel for ourselves. It is important to know the gospel, for instance, according to the leaders of the Church. But an even better starting place is to know the gospel according to one's own self, that is, to take a subject such as the Word of Wisdom and really search our own minds as to how we feel about it. We should read what we can find in the scriptures about the subject and then write down our feelings. Then we may compare those feelings against what leaders of the Church have written or said.

If we are sincere, we will find our conclusions being sustained by their conclusions. If we are searching inside ourselves in the right way, and we have included prayer as part of that search, we are tapping the same source of intelligence that the leaders of the Church are tuned-in upon.

Then we may become independent witnesses of that principle from our own inquiry. Then our obedience is not blind obedience. Then our agency is protected, and we are on the right course. Then we will do things because we know they are right and are the truth. We will know this from our own inquiry, not simply because someone else knows it. (*TYD*, p. 119)

If you want to learn, the Lord will teach you. Elder Harold B. Lee and Elder Marion G. Romney were always teaching, and they would, in a sense, go out of their way to tell me something or teach me something. I think the reason they did it—I'm not sure they ever saw me in this position or calling—is that I had one virtue: I wanted to learn, and I didn't resent it. And if you don't resent it, and if you want to learn, the Lord will keep teaching you, sometimes things you really didn't think you wanted to know. (07–03)

We should cultivate a desire to be taught and corrected. A desire to learn is one thing. An expressed willingness to be taught and to be corrected is quite another. . . .

While there is great value in seeking a personal interview to receive counsel, what I am talking about is something else. It is an unstructured process, with counsel and suggestions offered in bits and pieces and you responding with thanks. That process survives only where there is a genuine desire to learn and an invitation to those who can teach and correct you.

That invitation is not always in words but more in attitude. Could that be the reason that the scriptures counsel, "Ask and ye shall receive" more than any other statement? I believe the priceless gift of the Holy Ghost, which can be a constant companion, operates on those terms. (90–04, p. 24)

Physical knowledge is cumulative, where moral knowledge is not. Contributions to scientific and practical knowledge are gathered from one generation to the next. As greater light and knowledge are discovered, tentative theories of the past are replaced.

Unlike knowledge of the physical universe, the moral knowledge of each generation begins where the previous generation began rather than where they *left off.* For example, the remedy for an infection in the physical body has changed dramatically over the centuries; the remedy for infidelity, not at all. Morality is not so easily conveyed from one generation to the next. It is acquired more from example, ideally in the home.

This apparent imbalance in accumulating knowledge can easily contribute to a spirit of arrogance in students of the physical world, especially in so-called intellectuals. They may feel they have inherited the larger and more valuable legacy of knowledge.

The Book of Mormon warns of "the vainness, and the frailties, and the foolishness of men! When they are learned they think they are wise, and they hearken not unto the counsel of God, for they set it aside, supposing they know of themselves, wherefore, their wisdom is foolishness and it profiteth them not. And they shall perish.

"But to be learned is good *if they hearken unto the counsels of God.*"[2] (88–08, pp. 8–9)

Gospel learning and understanding are lifetime pursuits. Not long before President McKay died, he spoke to the General Authorities in the temple meeting just prior to a general conference. He talked of the temple ordinances and quoted at length from the ceremonies. He explained them to us. (That was not inappropriate, considering that we were in the temple.) After he had spoken for some time, he paused and stood gazing up to the ceiling in deep thought.

I remember that his big hands were in front of him with his fingers interlocked. He stood gazing as people sometimes do when pondering a deep question. Then he spoke: "Brethren, I think I am finally beginning to understand."

Here he was, the prophet—an Apostle for over half a century and even then he was learning, he was growing. His expression "I think I am finally beginning to understand" was greatly comforting to me. Perhaps if he was learning still, I might not be quite so much condemned for my state of relatively little understanding on many spiritual matters, provided that I'm still striving and learning. (*THT,* p. 263)

SECULAR VERSUS RELIGIOUS

Both reason and revelation are required. Each of us must accommodate the mixture of reason and revelation in our lives. The gospel not only permits but *requires* it. An individual who concentrates on either side solely and alone will lose both balance and perspective. (91–07)

The combining of reason and revelation is the test of mortal life.
[There is a] catalytic process where two seemingly antagonistic influences can merge and each give strength to the other. The essential catalyst for the fusion of reason and revelation in both student and faculty is the Spirit of Christ. He is "the true light that lighteth every man that cometh into the world."[3] The blending medium is the Holy Ghost, which is conferred upon every member of the Church as a gift.

The blending of opposites is everywhere present in life. A base metal, fused with a precious one, can produce an alloy stronger and more resilient than either component alone.

Such a blending is seen in the priesthood of God, ordained to be conferred upon the ordinary man who must live in the base, workaday world where reason and the muscles of his body are the substance of his livelihood. The blending in of revelation will make him anything but ordinary. While such a man must remain in the world, he is not of the world. . . .

The fusion of reason and revelation will produce men and women of imperishable worth.

On the one hand is reason: the thinking, the figuring things out, the research, the pure joy of discovery, and the academic degrees man bestows to honor that process. On the other is revelation, with the very private and very personal, the very individual, confirmation of truth. The combining of them is the test of mortal life! (91–01, p. 90)

A balance of the intellectual and spiritual is required for real success. If only your intellect has been broadened in college, you will not be happy. It is the training of the spirit that strengthens the moral fiber of man. If you are immoral, you will create an immoral world, you may even live in such a world already in your mind. If you are not honest, you will make a dishonest world. If you are not decent, you will not be happy. That will be true in spite of how much you own or how prominent you become. Without a balance between the intellectual and the spiritual we move through life without achieving real success.

Yet it is the understanding of almost everyone that success, to be complete, must include as essential ingredients a generous portion of both fame and fortune. The world seems to work on that premise. But the premise is false. The Lord taught otherwise. (83–03, p. 28)

There is danger in leaving the things of the Spirit out of our professional study. If we are not careful, very careful, and if we are not wise, very wise, we first leave out of our professional study the things of the Spirit. The next step soon follows: we leave the spiritual things out of our lives. . . .

If we do not keep this constantly in mind—that the Lord directs this Church—we may lose our way in the world of intellectual and scholarly research. (81–07, p. 104)

Respect the truths of moral and spiritual law. You should not be hesitant to pursue knowledge; indeed, you should excel in fields of scientific inquiry. I repeat, if you respect the truths of moral and spiritual law, you are in little danger for your soul in any field of study. . . . Study to your heart's content any worthy field of inquiry; just remember that all knowledge is not equal in value. (88–08, p. 10)

We need not choose between developing our intellectual or spiritual capacity. The crucial test of life, I repeat, does not center in the choice between fame and obscurity, nor between wealth and poverty. The greatest decision of life is between good and evil. Nor need we choose between developing our intellectual capacities and our spiritual capacities. The sensors which assist us to make correct choices are only incidentally academic or intellectual. They are primarily spiritual. With balanced attention to each you may have the best of both, and then you will be educated. (83–03, p. 30)

There is a difference between acquiring temporal and spiritual knowledge. There is a difference between acquiring temporal knowledge and acquiring spiritual knowledge. Students learn that on test day. It is awfully hard to remember something you didn't learn in the first place.

That is true of temporal knowledge, but spiritually we can draw on a memory that goes back beyond birth. We may develop a sensitivity to things that were not understood when we were younger. (99–06, p. 15)

Seek learning by study and faith. "Seek learning, even by study and also by *faith!*"[4] Cultivate faith, that one ingredient essential to spiritual discovery. Then you will understand the *meaning* of what you see through microscopes or telescopes or any other scopes. Your knowledge will expand, even to a knowledge of "things which must shortly come to pass."[5] That is the spirit of prophecy. Do not mortgage your testimony for an unproved theory on how man was created. Have faith *in* the revelations; *leave man in the place the revelations have put him!* (88–08, p. 10)

There is a great need to learn by study and by faith. [In about 1926], the institutes of religion were established; and soon there was encouragement, both for the men in the institute program and for the teachers of religion at Brigham Young University, to go away and get advanced degrees. "Go study under the great religious scholars of the world," was the encouragement, "for we will set an academic standard in theology."

And a number of them went. Some who went never returned. And some of them who returned never came back. They had followed, they supposed, the scriptural injunction: "Seek learning, even by study and also by faith."[6] But somehow the mix had been wrong, for they had sought learning out of the best books, even by study, but with too little faith. They found themselves in conflict with the simple things of the gospel. One by one, they found their way outside the field of teaching religion, outside Church activity, and a few of them outside the Church itself. And with each went a following of his students—a terrible price to pay. I could name a number of these men, as could many of you. Somehow the mix had been wrong: too much "by study," too little "by faith."

Happily, though, some of those who went away to study returned magnified by their experience and armed with advanced degrees. They returned firm in their knowledge that a man can be in the world but not of the world. (74–04, pp. 43–44)

Do not yield your faith in payment for an advanced degree. Do not yield your faith in payment for an advanced degree or for the recognition and acclaim of the world. Do not turn away from the Lord nor from His Church nor from His servants. You are needed—oh, how you are needed!

It may be that you will lay your scholarly reputation and the acclaim of your colleagues in the world as a sacrifice upon the altar of service. They may never understand the things of the Spirit as you have a right to do. They may not regard you as an authority or as a scholar. Just remember, when the test came to Abraham, he didn't really have to sacrifice Isaac. He just had to be willing to. (81–07, p. 120)

Judge the professions of men against the revealed word of the Lord. It is an easy thing for a man with extensive academic training to measure the Church using the principles he has been taught in his professional training as his standard. In my mind it ought to be the other way around. A member of the Church ought always, particularly if he is pursuing extensive academic studies, to judge the professions of man against the revealed word of the Lord.

Many disciplines are subject to this danger. Over the years I have seen many members of the Church lose their testimonies and yield their faith as the price for academic achievement. (81–07, pp. 101–2)

There is ultimate truth. Pragmatism as a philosophy says there is no ultimate truth. We are not neutral. We are belligerent on one side. (08–02)

Do not "buy into" philosophies that contradict the Father's plan. We may safely study and learn about the theories and philosophies of men, but if they contradict the plan of redemption, the great plan of happiness, do not "buy into" them as truth. If you do, you may be putting a mortgage on your testimony, on your knowledge of premortal life, on the creation of man, on the Fall and the Atonement, on your

Redeemer, the resurrection, and exaltation; for "every plant, which my heavenly Father hath not planted, shall be rooted up."[7]

If you "buy into" the philosophies of men, you may have your testimony repossessed. Your respect for moral law may go with it, and you will end up with nothing. (93–07, pp. 51–52)

Civilization is in jeopardy when spiritual development is ignored. How sad it is to walk among men whose spiritual development has been retarded or arrested. How pathetic to see individuals who have missed the fundamentals of spiritual strength and security. When the prerequisites of spiritual strength are ignored, then moral fibers are weakened. Civilization is then in jeopardy.

It is not difficult today to find individuals who academically are giants, but spiritually and morally are the smallest size of pygmy. This imbalance, an impediment to happiness, places man and all around him, particularly his family, in jeopardy. (70–13)

A warning to teachers who introduce students to degradation. There is the temptation for college teachers, in the Church and outside of it, to exercise their authority to give assignments and thereby introduce their students to degradation under the argument that it is part of our culture. Teachers in the field of literature are particularly vulnerable.

I use the word *warning.* Such will not go unnoticed in the eternal scheme of things. Those who convey a degraded heritage to the next generation will reap disappointment by and by.

Teachers would do well to learn the difference between studying some things, as compared to studying *about* them. There is a great difference. (76–01, p. 284)

Beware of irreverent professors. The large body of university professors in the world today represent the finest standard of our civilization. However, some few professors delight in relieving the student of his basic spiritual values. Throughout the world more and more faculty members look forward to the coming of a new crop of green freshmen with a compulsive desire to "educate" them.

Each year, many fall victim in the colleges and universities. There, as captive audiences, their faith, their patriotism, and their morality are lined up against a wall and riddled by words shot from the mouths of irreverent professors. (73–05, pp. 164–65)

We ought to demand more protection from faithless philosophies. We are very particular to forbid anyone from preaching Catholicism, or Protestantism, or Mormonism, or Judaism in a public school classroom, but for some reason we are very patient with those who teach the negative expression of religion.

Where separation of church and state is proclaimed, we ought to demand more protection from the agnostic, from the atheist, from the communist, from the skeptic, from the humanist and the pragmatist, than we have yet been given. (*TYD,* p. 226)

Destruction of faith will destroy the moral fiber of society. I claim that the atheist has no more right to teach the fundamentals of his sect in the public school than does the theist. Any system in the schools or in society that protects the destruction of faith, and forbids, in turn, the defense of it, must ultimately destroy the moral fiber of society. (*TYD,* p. 226)

Atheism versus theism. The United States Supreme Court several years ago handed down a decision relating to prayer in the public schools. That decision was a partial decision. It was one-sided. Regardless of what the intent was—and I know what the intent was—the effect has been to offer great encouragement to those who would erase from our society every trace of reference to the Almighty. And an extension of that has been, as an effect, the abandonment of any concern for moral and spiritual values in the public schools.

The decision was partial because the plaintiff wanted to protect her son from any contact with religion in the public schools. Now her son is protected from my type of religion, and my son is exposed to hers.

There is a crying need for educators to understand and identify atheism for what it is—and that is, a religion. Though a negative one, nevertheless it is a religious expression.

We put sunshine and rain together under the heading of weather.

It would be a little ridiculous to talk about clear skies and cloudy ones and claim that the two are not related and could not be considered under the single heading—weather. It is equally ridiculous to separate theism from atheism and claim that they are two separate matters. This is particularly so when we condone in the classroom, and in some instances encourage, the atheist's preaching of his doctrine and the standards of conduct and morality that accompany his beliefs, and then at once, with great vigor, eliminate any positive reference to theism and the standards that accompany that belief. (77–08, p. 171)

The religion of atheism. There is a crying need for the identification of atheism for what it is, and that is, a religion albeit a negative one. Atheism is a religious expression; it is one extreme end of religious philosophy.

Those who are spiritually sensitive recognize God, a living being who rules in the affairs of man. The so-called atheist declares that God is not. Not just that He isn't the cause of things, but that He indeed is not. . . . Atheism, like theism, is divided into many sects: communism, agnosticism, skepticism, humanism, pragmatism, and others.

The atheist proclaims his own dishonesty in accepting pay to teach psychology, sociology, history, or English, while he is indeed preaching his atheistic religious philosophy to his students.

If the atheist wants to teach his doctrine at a public school, let him purchase property off campus and build himself a building and offer classes. Let him label the classes for what they are. (*TYD,* pp. 224–25)

We must spiritually prepare our minds to find answers to life's questions. I made up my mind a long time ago that I was going to put a fence around my mind and there would be some "no trespassing" signs on it. I'm not going to leave it vacant, and I'm going to be a little selective about who can put what there. And it isn't everybody that can cross my mind. Some are not welcome. Some are resisted. Some are forcibly excluded. My mind is not going to be a refuse pile of junk and litter that just anybody can add to any time they want. There's a fence around it.

The Quorum of the Twelve Apostles, 1971. Front row, left to right:
Spencer W. Kimball, Ezra Taft Benson, Mark E. Petersen, Delbert L. Stapley,
Marion G. Romney. Back row, left to right: LeGrand Richards, Hugh B. Brown,
Howard W. Hunter, Gordon B. Hinckley, Thomas S. Monson,
Boyd K. Packer, Marvin J. Ashton.

Because there are some questions that are so deep and so difficult and so searching, anybody with just a junk pile to search through to find a satisfactory answer has a long search, and certainly the brief span of a lifetime isn't enough for anyone to find an answer there.

Now, when you come to these basic questions of why people are born where they are, when you come to the basic questions relating to man's inhumanity to man, when you come to the basic imponderables that relate to why a natural calamity would be permitted on this earth, or the question of why there should be disease upon the earth, or why there should be frailties of flesh, why temptation should exist, or why pain and misery should be here—you're not going to find answers to questions like these in a littered junk yard. You're not going to find anything satisfactory by digging through the trash heaps that have accumulated on the vacant lot of a mind where anybody has trespassed back and forth and thrown there anything they didn't want.

No one could find any semblance to the word "justice." No one could find much meaning to the word "mercy" and surely no one could find any warrant even to the term of "god" unless you somehow came to know that this life is not all there is and that the life to come is just a continuation of a life that went on before we came into mortality. When we talk about that, we talk about . . . our premortal existence. When you start talking in those terms, you begin talking doctrine. You begin talking about revelation.

It's no wonder, no wonder that the members and clergy of the churches of the world find that once the major problems that have confronted mankind are before them, they stand aside in puzzled bewilderment. (71–02)

BYU and Religious Education

True education requires both an academic and spiritual foundation. True education includes more than thinking, more than training the natural man. Brigham Young University has as its purpose the training of every student to cultivate the spiritual part of their natures, to feel as well as to think.

That is the one subject which does not lead to a specific degree. When Brigham Young sent Karl G. Maeser to found this school, he admonished him not to even teach the times tables without the Spirit of the Lord. Spiritual refinement is to permeate every class in every subject leading to every degree, from the associate and technical degrees, to the lofty doctorates.

If you only got the academic part, only the thinking part, you may yet be unqualified to face the real challenges of life and you may be little safer spiritually than you would be physically if someone should take out your appendix, having as their only qualification an honorary Doctor of Medicine degree.

I pray that we have not failed to build into your lives a deep spiritual foundation. If you do not have both the thinking part and the feeling part, you may go forth and gain the whole world and yet lose your own soul.

We are counseled in the revelations to "study and learn, and become acquainted with all good books."[8]

And we have been urged by our leaders from the day the Church was founded to: "Seek ye diligently and teach one another words of wisdom; yea, seek ye out of the best books words of wisdom; seek learning, even by study and also by faith."[9] (85–09)

In the university environment, both reason and revelation must be nurtured. History confirms that the university environment always favors reason, with the workings of the Spirit made to feel uncomfortable. I know of no examples to the contrary. Spirituality, while consummately strong, reacts to very delicate changes in its environment. To have it present at all and to keep it in some degree of purity requires a commitment and a watch-care which can admit to no embarrassment when compared with what the scholarly world is about.

The moral and spiritual capacity of the faculty and what they shall give, and the spiritual atmosphere in which students are to learn and what they receive, will not emerge spontaneously! They happen only if they are *caused* to happen and thereafter maintained with unwavering determination. (91–01, p. 89)

In scholarship, be careful you are not giving equal time to the adversary. In an effort to be objective, impartial, and scholarly, a writer or a teacher may unwittingly be giving equal time to the adversary. (81–07, p. 110)

Keep a careful balance in academics and spirituality. Testimony and spirituality are the key elements of teaching religion. You can have both excellence and values, but you must nurture them carefully. Otherwise, in the purely academic environment which generates secular achievement, spirituality will wilt and die. (84–08)

Brigham Young University must maintain a style of its own. Tuition and fees do not make up one-fourth of the per-student cost of running this university. More than seventy percent comes from the tithes of the Church; from the widow's mite. There is too much toil and faith and self-denial represented in those funds to expend them on one who is unappreciative of the opportunities afforded to progress both spiritually and academically.

How can we justify expending those sacred funds on a student who will dishonor the agreement he signed at the time of admission or on the salary of a faculty member who has his own agenda, which is at variance with the central mission of the Church, particularly when there is a lineup, ever growing, of both students and teachers waiting and anxious to come to learn or to teach and advance the mission of the university and the central mission of the Church?

As to the student body—the lot of you—what a miracle! Where on earth, now or in any past generation, could you assemble such a student body? Individually you are impressive; together you are powerful, compelling. We admire you! You are unbelievable to the stranger who comes among you. You are a witness of the Restoration, you are a joy to your parents, to all of us. You are the object of approval before Him who is the Father of our spirits and His Son who is our Redeemer.

Granted, there may be a few among you who feel uncomfortable with the conservative philosophy at Church schools. Each has his choice. If it is a different lifestyle you choose, you are not chained here. There are plenty of places to find whatever lifestyle you desire.

But together with you, we will maintain this university with a style of its own. We who love this university will not allow some few to alter the lifestyle here.

And, with your help, we will maintain to the best of our ability an environment that is totally free from the use of narcotics, the abuse of prescription drugs, from steroids and stimulants, from gambling or any other destructive addiction; where chastity and decency and integrity are fostered; where their opposites are subject to correction or expulsion.

Always there are those who chafe under standards and guidelines and restraints and want them lowered or loosened or lifted. Always they play on the word *freedom* and ask, "Is not *free agency* a basic doctrine of the gospel?"

Those who think standards contradict their agency may wish to read the 78th verse of Section 101 in the Doctrine and Covenants. They will find that the agency vouchsafed to us from God is a *moral* agency and that every one is accountable. There can be no *freedom* without *choice*. We are determined to maintain standards, and guidelines, and restraints so those who want to live under them may have that choice. (90–04, pp. 40–41)

It is not the standards that are on trial, but the students. The standards of the school are not on trial to be tested, but as you enter here as a freshman, you are. (62–05)

The importance of continuing endorsement at Church colleges. Why would anyone feel unsettled at a review of your worthiness to remain at a Church college? It is no different than the test to measure your academic progress, no different than the requirement that you maintain a certain grade point average.

The continuing endorsement is no different than renewing a temple recommend. When President Harold B. Lee would hear that someone became indignant over a temple recommend or other worthiness interview, he would say, "The hit bird flutters!" (90–04, p. 40)

Those who teach at Church schools are to uphold the standards set by the Lord. Do not be intimidated by one who advocates philosophies or behavior that are in opposition to the standards set by the Lord and entrusted to His servants, those who have established, who finance, and who are responsible to administer our schools, our Institutes of Religion.

Students in our schools have both the right and the responsibility to challenge such teachings. That may be part of your test. A student or a teacher who feels uncomfortable in our environment is free to choose another, but they are not free to substitute their own ideals or standards of behavior for those expected in an institution supported by the tithes and offerings of the Saints. (95–06, p. 7)

Much is required. Several years ago while conducting a BYU graduation, because of time restraints, I set aside some prepared remarks and just spoke briefly of service. Paraphrasing a scripture, I said: "Where much is given, much is expected."

I received a letter from a woman pointing out that I had misquoted the scripture and distorted its meaning. The scripture, found both in the New Testament and in the Doctrine and Covenants, reads, "For of him unto whom much is given much is required."[10]

She pointed out that there is a big difference in expected and required. And so it is. From you who have been blessed, much will be expected and much more required of you. (96–02)

Look through your luggage. As you leave the campus satisfied at the things you have gained, go through your pockets, look through your luggage, see if something may have been lost—spiritual things—essential if there is to be happiness in your future.

Take with you your faith, your patriotism, your virtue. If they are battered a bit, they can be repaired. Even virtue, if tarnished, can be polished again. Carry them away with you. They can be renewed. You will come to know in the years ahead that life has precious little to offer without them. . . .

I know that many of the treasures that you may have set aside will prove to be that which was of most worth to you. (73–05, pp. 170–71)

Students must have their ladder leaning against the right tree. If students are going to partake of the fruit that is "desirable to make one happy," yea, "desirable above all other fruit,"[11] which Lehi saw in his vision, they had better have their ladder leaning against the right tree. And they had better hold onto the iron rod while they are working their way toward it. (95–10, p. 51)

In the Church we are not neutral. In the Church we are not neutral. We are one-sided. There is a war going on, and we are engaged in it. It is the war between good and evil, and we are belligerents defending the good. We are therefore obliged to give preference to and protect all that is represented in the gospel of Jesus Christ, and we have made covenants to do it. . . . And I want to say in all seriousness that there is a limit to the patience of the Lord with respect to those who are under covenant to bless and protect His Church and kingdom upon the earth but do not do it.

Particularly are we in danger if we are out to make a name for ourselves, if our "hearts are set so much upon the things of this world, and aspire to the honors of men."[12] (*HBT,* pp. 110–11)

Church schools must not be neutral. Brigham Young University is unique among universities. It is a private school established for a special spiritual purpose.

One time I heard the president of a great eastern university describe his school in these words, "We can best serve as a neutral territory—a kind of arbiter where people can come to reason."

This could not be said of this school. This school is not neutral; it is committed; it is one-sided; it is prejudiced, if you will, in favor of good, of decency, of integrity, of virtue, and of reverence; in a word, in favor of the gospel of Jesus Christ.

This school is not a playing field where good and evil are invited to joust with one another to see which one may win. Evil will find no invitation to contest here. This is a training ground for a single team.

Here the students are coached and given signals preparatory for the game of life. The scouts and the coaches of the opposing team are not welcome here. (81–02)

There should be no reticence in relating secular truths to revealed truths. As with the students, there are perhaps a few faculty and staff who are restless over the conservative philosophy of education in the Church.

There should be no reticence in relating secular truths to revealed truths. Indeed, that is what President McKay gave as the sole purpose of this university. Nor should there be a problem with teaching about any topic or philosophy or subject for we should seek all truth. However, to advocate an unworthy philosophy, rather than to teach about it, to appoint one's self as an alternate voice, is out of harmony with the purpose of Church schools and with the central mission of the Church. (90–04, p. 41)

Church schools are a forum for faith. There are philosophies and ideologies which are not taught at Church schools.

These schools are maintained as forums for faith. Insofar as higher education is concerned, they are some of the last citadels.

Faith in the world is fading. Its voice grows feeble. In almost every institution of higher learning, faith is closed out by court edict.

Do not allow our platforms of faith to be shared with the atheist, the skeptic, the destroyer of faith. If these are the voices the students want to hear, they are free to go where those voices speak. (81–02)

Seminaries and institutes are a godsend. The seminaries were an outgrowth of the old religion classes, and the institutes of religion were an outgrowth of the seminaries and originally were called college seminaries. In the history of the Church there is no better illustration of the prophetic preparation of this people than the beginnings of the seminary institute program. These programs were started when they were nice but were not critically needed. They were granted a season to flourish and to grow into a bulwark for the Church. They now become a godsend for the salvation of modern Israel in a most challenging hour. (77–11, p. 4)

Attendance in seminary increases positive outcomes with our youth. Do you know that seminary more than doubles the gospel teaching time for a young member of the Church? If you tabulate all of the instruction time he gets in all the organizations of the Church and total it up, the seminary will give him that much again and much more. There is a continuity of instruction, a formality of teaching, and a quality of instruction and materials that make this one of our most successful programs.

Did you know that the incidence of temple marriage when the bride and groom have graduated from seminary and/or institute is more than double the Church average? You could say, "Well, that's because the good kids go to seminary." But it can't be fully explained that way or we'd have higher temple marriage among the good kids where we have many members but don't have these programs. Every study we have made over the past generation has sustained that accomplishment. We have reason to believe that it has similar influence in the preparation for missions. (75–02)

Temple marriages are higher among seminary and institute graduates. The percentage of temple marriages among graduates of seminaries and institutes is more than double the Church average. Do you need any better endorsement than that? (90–06, p. 38)

Seminaries and institutes deserve our full support. All of these courses in seminary, institute, and Church schools are taught by dedicated teachers. These teachers deserve our respect, our deep gratitude, and our full support. Every parent, every Church leader, should act as an enrollment agent for seminaries and institutes. Parents and priesthood leaders should check on their college students and see that they attend the institute. (90–06, p. 38)

The importance of seminary and institute in helping youth learn the doctrine. If you want your son to play the piano, it is good to expose him to music. This may give him a feel for it and help greatly in his learning. But this is not enough. There is the practice and the memorization and the practice and the practice and the practice before he can play it well.

If you want your daughter to learn a language, expose her to those who speak it. She may get a feel for the language, even pick up many words. But this is not enough. She must memorize grammar and vocabulary. She must practice pronunciation. There is rote learning without which she will never speak or write the language fluently.

So it is with the gospel. One may have a feel for it. But some time one must learn the doctrine. Here, too, rote learning, practice, memorization, reading, listening, discussion, all become essential. There is no royal road to learning.

The Church can help parents because this kind of learning is effectively given in a classroom setting. So we have seminaries, institutes, religion classes; there are priesthood, Sunday School, and auxiliary classes. The curriculum for all of them centers in the scriptures and the history of the Church. Spiritual development is tied very closely to a knowledge of the scriptures, where the doctrines are found.

A school library may hold a world of knowledge. But unless a student knows the system of cataloging, a search for that knowledge will be discouraging; it will be an ordeal. Those systems are really not too difficult to learn. Then all of the knowledge in all of the books is opened to him. Searching becomes very simple indeed. But one must find it and read it. One must *earn* it.

It is so with the scriptures. They contain the fulness of the everlasting gospel, an eternity of knowledge. But one must learn to use them or the search will be discouraging. Again, there is a system. Learn about the concordance, the footnotes, the Topical Guide; memorize the books of the Bible and the Book of Mormon. And the scriptures will then yield their treasure. All of this is taught in the seminary and institute classes. The teachers are both worthy and well trained. But they cannot help if your students are not enrolled. (83–01, p. 67)

A caution about becoming too narrow as a religion teacher.
Please know that however specialized you become in one thing, you
must remain expert in several others. For instance, if you are a specialist
in the archaeology of the Old Testament, there is not the slightest excuse
for you to be deficient as a teacher of the Book of Mormon or of the
Doctrine and Covenants or of the New Testament. If you are assigned
to teach these areas to undergraduates and feel that you are being misused because you are a specialist, you need to repent. If you have a tendency to set aside these things, you are drifting from what it is all about.
(74–04, p. 53)

The Church must concentrate on moral and spiritual education.
The Church must concentrate on moral and spiritual education; we
may encourage secular education but not necessarily provide it. (92–05,
p. 71)

CHAPTER 15

Economics and Welfare Principles

"This couplet of truth has been something of a model:
'Eat it up, wear it out, make it do, or do without.'" (75–01, p. 85)

WELFARE PRINCIPLES

Welfare principles also apply in our spiritual lives. The basic principles underlying the Church welfare program have application in our emotional and spiritual lives: specifically that independence, industry, thrift, self-reliance, and self-respect should be developed; that work should be enthroned as a ruling principle in our lives; that the evils of an emotional or spiritual dole should be avoided; and that the aim of the Church is to help the members help themselves. (*TYD*, pp. 241–42)

The Church welfare program is a self-help system. [The Church welfare program] is a self-help system, not a quick handout system. It requires a careful inventory of all personal and family resources, all of which must be committed before anything is added from the outside.

It is not an unkind or an unfeeling bishop who requires a member to work to the fullest extent he can for what he receives from Church welfare.

There should not be the slightest embarrassment for any member to be assisted by the Church. *Provided,* that is that he has contributed all that he can. (78–02, p. 91)

There is no shame in any honorable work. There is one thought that must come at the very beginning of a discussion on occupations and careers in order to establish it as preeminent, and it is this:

Do not ever belittle anyone, including yourself, nor count them, or you, a failure, if your livelihood has been modest. Do not ever look down on those who labor in occupations of lower income. There is great dignity and worth in any honest occupation. Do not use the word *menial* for any labor that improves the world or the people who live in it.

There is no shame in any honorable work, and the principle of faith, which the Lord connected with learning, is precious above the technologies of man. (82–03, p. 84)

The gospel of Jesus Christ is the formula for success. There is a formula. The Lord said, "Verily I say unto you, that every man who is obliged to provide for his *own* family, let him provide, and he shall in nowise lose his crown; *and let him labor in the church.*"[1]

The gospel of Jesus Christ is the formula for success. Every principle of the gospel, when lived, has a positive influence over your choice of an occupation and on what you will achieve. The counsel to labor in the Church has great value. Living the gospel will give you a perspective and an inspiration that will see you successful, however ordinary your work may be or however ordinary your life may seem to others. (82–03, p. 87)

It is important to work honestly for what we get. There are so few nowadays who are really willing to work. We must train our children and ourselves to give, in work, the equivalent of the pay we receive and perhaps just a little extra.

There are so few who will come a bit early to get organized for the day, or stay a minute after to tidy up the work bench or the desk for tomorrow's work.

The attitude that demands compensation and benefits in excess of the value of labor has come near destroying the economy of the world. Now, however, many workers quite willingly accept reductions in pay just to keep their jobs. That spirit of doing a little extra would have prevented the crisis had it been evident earlier. (82–03, pp. 86–87)

There is a contribution the Church can make to our careers. While we cannot build schools for everyone, there is a most important contribution the Church *can* make to our careers, one that *is* central to the mission of the Church. And that is to teach moral and spiritual values.

There are ordinary virtues which influence our careers even more than technical training; among them are these:

Integrity.
Dependability.
Courtesy.
Respect for others.
Respect for property. (82–03, p. 86)

Men and women should choose careers that fit their nature. While many, many occupations suit a man or a woman equally well, I, for one, have grave concern over the growing trend for both men and women to choose careers which in some respects are against their very natures.

We have tried to prepare our boys for manly work and our girls for work that would suit the opportunities that womanhood will bring them. In defense of our doing that, I can only observe that in this Church we are not exempt from using common sense. (82–03, p. 86)

The idler shall not eat the bread of the laborer. When people are *able* but are *unwilling* to take care of themselves, we are responsible to employ the dictum of the Lord, that the idler shall not eat the bread of the laborer. The simple rule has been, to the fullest extent possible, to take care of one's self. This couplet of truth has been something of a model:

"Eat it up, wear it out, make it do, or do without." (75–01, p. 85)

Never fail to give to those in need. Many years ago, my parents lived in a very modest home in the northern end of the state of Utah. One morning, my mother answered a knock at the door and was confronted there by a large frightening-looking man, who asked her for money. She said, "We have no money." There were in that home many children, but very little money. He pressed his demands, insisting that she give him some money, finally saying "I am hungry; I would like to get something to eat."

"Well," she said, "if that is the case then I can help you." So she hurried to the kitchen and fixed him a lunch. And I am sure it was the most modest of provisions. She could tell as she gave him the lunch at the door that he was not pleased, but with little resistance he took the lunch and left. She watched him as he went down the lane through the gate and started up the road. He looked back, but he did not see her standing inside the door, and as he passed the property line, he took the lunch and threw it over the fence into the brush.

Now, my mother is a little Danish woman, and she was angered; she was angered at the ingratitude. In that house there was nothing to waste, and she was angered that he was so ungrateful.

The incident was forgotten until a week or two later; she answered another knock at the door. There stood a tall raw-boned teenage boy, who asked about the same question in essentially the same words, "We need help; we are hungry. Could you give us some money; could you give us some food?" But somehow the image of the first man appeared in her mind and she said "No," excusing herself, "I am sorry. I am busy; I cannot help you today. I just cannot help you." What she meant was, "I won't. I won't. I won't be taken in again." Well, the young man turned without protest and walked out the gate, and she stood looking after him. It wasn't until he passed through the gate that she noticed the wagon, the father and mother and the other youngsters, and as the boy swung his long legs into the wagon, he looked back rather poignantly;

the father shook the reins and the wagon went on down the road. She hesitated just long enough so that she could not call them back.

From that experience she drew a moral by which she has lived and which she has imparted to her children, and though that was, I suppose, nearly fifty years ago, there has always been just a tiny hint of pain as she recalled the incident with this moral: "Never fail to give that which you have to someone who is in need." I repeat, "Never fail to give that which you have to someone who is in need." (62–02, pp. 460–61)

SELF-SUFFICIENCY—COUNSELING

Sometimes divine restraint is needed to help others grow. In our lives, profound compassion must be paradoxically set against divine restraint and guide us in all areas of our jurisdiction. This restraint makes possible wise and effective succoring and comforting of those in need. Whether as parent to child, teacher to student, or Church leader to member or nonmember, we may deeply, acutely long to help. But we must recognize the necessity of sometimes withholding (out of love) immediate relief or supply so that child, student, member, or other may have unfettered opportunity to grow by helping themselves. (*ABE*, p. 111)

Live in such a way so as to enjoy the inspiration of the Spirit. When we are confused and at a loss to know which way to go, we can turn to the leader of the Church—to our branch president or our bishop.

They, in turn, can counsel with the stake president, or the mission president, who in turn can counsel with the General Authorities, who themselves are in constant counsel with the prophet, seer, and revelator.

It is not necessary to have the President of the Church hear all of the problems of the people; neither the other General Authorities of the Church. It is not necessary for the stake president, or the mission president, to personally judge all of these matters.

Nor is it necessary for the bishops or branch presidents to hear all of these matters, although it is true that they will hear more of them than do the mission presidents, or the General Authorities, or the President of the Church.

Live in such a way that you can follow the inspiration of that still, small voice. Have the courage to follow those feelings. Such inspiration will always lead one to do right, to be active in the Church. This inspiration will always teach Latter-day Saints indeed to be Latter-day Saints. (78–08)

Counsel in the Lord's way. Bishop, those who come to you are children of God. Counsel them in the Lord's own way. Teach them to ponder it in their minds, then to pray over their problems.

Remember that soothing, calming effect of reading the scriptures. Next time you are where they are read, notice how things settle down. Sense the feeling of peace and security that comes. (78–02, p. 93)

Following the right leads to increased spiritual self-reliance. The Lord is very generous with the freedom He gives us. The more we learn to follow the right, the more we are spiritually self-reliant, the more our freedom and our independence are affirmed. (75–01, p. 89)

An emotional dole system can be dangerous. I think an emotional dole system can be as dangerous as a material dole system, and we can become so dependent that we stand around waiting for the Church to do everything for us. (75–01, p. 86)

There is danger in the loss of emotional and spiritual self-reliance. I have been concerned that we may be on the verge of doing to ourselves emotionally (and therefore spiritually) what we have been working so hard for generations to avoid materially. If we lose our emotional and spiritual self-reliance, we can be weakened quite as much, perhaps even more, than when we become dependent materially. (*TYD,* p. 234)

It is normal and healthy to be depressed occasionally. Did you know that it is normal and healthy to be depressed occasionally? As General Authorities, we face a long line of people who call upon us because they are unhappy—they are depressed. They are worried about this and that and really not certain what they are worried about. They are a little like the man who insisted: "You can't tell me that worry doesn't help. The things I worry about never happen!"

When we search the revealed word for some evidence of the nature of man, we find statements such as this:

"For it must needs be, that there is an opposition in all things. If not so, . . . righteousness could not be brought to pass, neither wickedness, neither holiness nor misery, neither good nor bad."[2]

If you happen to hit a good sorry mood once in a while, relax and enjoy it—it is a good sign that you are normal. (66–05, p. 247)

An overabundance of counseling can lead to spiritual and emotional dependency. If we provide an overabundance of counsel without at once emphasizing the principle of self-reliance as it is understood in the welfare program, we can cause people to be so totally dependent emotionally and spiritually upon others that they subsist on some kind of emotional welfare. They can become unwilling to sustain themselves and become so dependent that they endlessly need to be shored up, lifted up, encouraged, and taught to contribute little of their own. (*TYD*, p. 234)

An epidemic of "counselitis." We seem to be developing an epidemic of "counselitis" which drains spiritual strength from the Church much like the common cold drains more strength out of humanity than any other disease.

That, some may assume, is not serious. It is very serious! . . .

We have become very anxious over the amount of counseling that we seem to need in the Church. Our members are becoming dependent.

We must not set up a network of counseling services without at the same time emphasizing the principle of emotional self-reliance and individual independence.

If we lose our emotional and spiritual independence, our

self-reliance, we can be weakened quite as much, perhaps even more, than when we become dependent materially.

If we are not careful, we can lose the power of individual revelation. What the Lord said to Oliver Cowdery has meaning for all of us.

> Behold, you have not understood; you have supposed that I would give it unto you, when you took no thought save it was to ask me.
>
> But, behold, I say unto you, that you must study it out in your mind; then you must ask me if it be right, and if it is right I will cause that your bosom shall burn within you; therefore, you shall feel that it is right.
>
> But if it be not right you shall have no such feelings, but you shall have a stupor of thought that shall cause you to forget the thing which is wrong.[3]

Spiritual independence and self-reliance is a sustaining power in the Church. If we rob the members of that, how can they get revelation for themselves? How will they know there is a prophet of God? How can they get answers to prayers? How can they know for *sure* for themselves? (78–02, pp. 91–92)

Some counseling may not be emotionally or spiritually healthy. There are those counselors who want to delve deeper into the lives of subjects than is emotionally or spiritually healthy. I think I should explain here that when I use the word *counselor* I'm not just talking about professional counselors. I'm talking about *all* of us who are responsible for counseling. There are those who want to draw out and analyze and take apart and dissect. While a certain amount of catharsis is healthy and essential, overmuch of it can be degenerating. It is seldom as easy to put something back together as it is to take it apart. (75–01, p. 87)

A caution on counseling. I remember seeing a little sign years ago in a photographer's shop on the island of Kauai that said, "If there is beauty, we will take it. If there is none, we will make it." I fear that some of us, in our counseling in the Church, seem to be saying, "If there are problems, we'll abate them. If there are none, we'll create them." (*TYD*, p. 240)

There is often need for strong direction in counseling. I think that if nondirective counseling is all one does, often that's precisely what we get from the counseling—no direction. When a counselor schedules an interminably long session to say as little as possible and allows the student to struggle with whether or not something is right or wrong, which the counselor already knows, that is a waste of time. So is fussing around trying to determine whether it is right for the student under the circumstances, or wrong for him under the circumstances. When anyone with any moral sense knows that a course is wrong, then it is wrong for *anybody* and it is wrong for *everybody*. (*TYD*, pp. 238–39)

Do not dole out counsel indiscriminately. We dole out counsel and advice without the slightest thought that the member should solve the problem himself or turn to his family, and that only when those resources are inadequate should he turn to the Church.

We ought to be very careful, therefore, not to dole out counsel indiscriminately, or try to totally sustain our members in every emotional need. If we are not careful, we can lose the power of individual revelation.[4] (*TYD*, pp. 234–35)

Avoid dependency on psychiatrists. I look with concern on the increased dependency upon psychologists and psychiatrists. Now, explicitly, I did *not* say I look with concern upon the use of them. I said I look with concern upon our growing *dependency* upon them. I have misgivings about the growing tendency to diagnose every aberration of behavior as the beginnings of "psycho-something-or-other." . . .

May I say that I recognize the need for professional help from psychiatrists. I have at times referred individuals to them, but I say again that I look with concern upon our growing dependency upon them. I would suppose that when there is that measure of difficulty or disorder which requires professional attention, that attention ought to be given on the referral from the bishop and from the medical doctor. But we are at the point now where at the slightest aberration in behavior we are sent for professional clinical inspection. (66–05, pp. 249–50)

WEALTH AND MATERIALISM—PRIDE

In finding happiness, the real choice is between good and evil. Position and wealth . . . are no more essential to true happiness in mortality than their absence can prevent you from achieving it. Mortal life is a school, and most of the tests we undergo are multiple-choice tests.

If your growth in college has been solely intellectual, you may not have learned in the course of earning your diploma that the choice in life is not between fame and obscurity, nor is it between wealth and poverty. The choice is between good and evil, and that is a very different matter indeed. When we finally understand this lesson, thereafter our happiness will not be determined by material things. We may be happy without them or successful in spite of them. (83–03, p. 29)

The challenge of material and spiritual success. The crucial decision of life does not center in the choice between fame and obscurity, nor between wealth and poverty. *The* decision of life is between good and evil. It is possible to be both rich and famous and at once succeed in the eternal spiritual sense, but the Lord warned of the difficulty of it when He talked about camels and needles. (80–08, p. 6)

True happiness is not dependent on wealth or fame. It is the misapprehension of most people that if you are good, really good, at what you do, you will eventually be both widely known and well compensated. It is the understanding of almost everyone that success, to be complete, must include a generous portion of both fame and fortune as essential ingredients. The world seems to work on that premise. The premise is false. It is not true. The Lord taught otherwise. . . . You need not be either rich or hold high position to be completely successful and truly happy. In fact, if these things come to you, and they may, true success must be achieved in spite of them, not because of them. (80–10, p. 21)

The gospel—not wealth—provides the anchor we need. I had a
bishop come to me once. He said, "I don't know what's wrong. We have
twenty-two couples in our ward that are, in one degree or another, expe-
riencing domestic difficulties, and," he said, "I think all twenty-two
couples are headed for divorce." He said, "Tell me, what am I not
doing? What's wrong?"

I happened to know the area where he was bishop, and I said,
"Bishop, I think there is nothing wrong with you. I know your area.
You just happen to have the misfortune of presiding over a ward where
everyone is financially very well-to-do. You live in a ward where there
are all very big homes (sometimes very small incomes), very big mort-
gages, and they've lost themselves. It is your responsibility to teach them
the gospel of Jesus Christ, and to give them the anchor that they need."
(95–07)

Pride is a deadly spiritual virus. Pride is the most deadly spiritual
virus. (89–01, p. 59)

CHAPTER 16

Government, Laws, War, and Freedom

"There is no freedom without law.
There is no freedom without responsibility." (68–11)

MORAL DECAY

Everything sacred is being trampled. There isn't anything that's sacred that isn't being stomped on now. (08–02)

It is important that the rights of women, men, and children be preserved. I am for protecting the rights of a woman to be a woman, a feminine, female woman; a wife and a mother.

I am for protecting the rights of a man to be a man, a masculine, male man; a husband and a father.

I am for protecting the rights of children to be babies, and children and youth to be nurtured in a home and in a family.

I am for recognizing the inherent God-given differences between men and women.

I am for accommodating them so that we can have physically and emotionally and spiritually stable, happy individuals and families and communities. (77–03, p. 9)

No civilization has survived the dismantling of the family. Everyone, in or out of the Church, now seems to agree that what is wrong with the world centers on the failing of the family structure.

While world leaders and court judges agree that the family must endure if we are to survive, many of them use the words *freedom* and *choice* as tools to pry apart the safeguards of the past and loosen up the laws on morality, marriage, abortion, and gender.

If enough people protest limits on conduct, the limits are moved farther out and behavior that was once prohibited is reclassified as normal, moral, legal, and socially acceptable. The bonds of marriage and kinship are seen as bondage rather than as sacred ties. In spite of the worthy intention to strengthen families and protect children, the United Nations, in recent declarations on the International Year of the Family, defined the family as most any collection of people who are living together.

And its view of children offers, in the U.N.'s own language, a "new concept of separate rights for children with the government accepting the responsibility of protecting the child from the power of parents."

No civilization has survived the dismantling of the family. (95–04)

If morality exists in a nation, it exists in individual hearts. There needs to be enough of us who have faith enough and who are moral enough to desire that which is right. Virtues, like love and liberty and patriotism, do not exist in general, they exist in particular. If morality exists at all, it exists in the individual heart and mind of the ordinary citizen. Such virtues cannot be isolated in any other place— not in the rocks or in the water, not in trees or air, not in animals or birds. If it exists at all, it exists in the human heart. Morality flourishes when the rank and file are free. It flourishes where a conscience is clear, where men have faith in God and are obedient to the restraints He has set upon human conduct. (89–03, p. 67)

The Lord will manifest the way to expose the world's problems.
The many problems facing us are complex. There are no simple
answers. The more I meditate upon them, the more they show themselves in their various forms and become almost too formidable to me
to even approach. Except for those eight words, . . . "having first
obtained mine errand from the Lord," except for that qualification, I
would quickly recommend retreat and capitulation. But with that, I
have no doubts . . . that within the foreseeable future we will give the
lie to much that is taught in the world today. (*ABE,* p. 151)

*The sins of Sodom and Gomorrah are now spread across the
world.* The sins of Sodom and Gomorrah were localized. They are now
spread across the world, wherever the Church is. The first line of
defense—the home—is crumbling. Surely you can see what the adversary is about. We are now exactly where the prophets warned we would
be. (04–02, p. 9)

Tolerance can be a dangerous trap. The virtue of "tolerance" has
been distorted and elevated to a position of such prominence as to be
thought equal to and even valued more than morality. It is one thing to
be tolerant, even forgiving of individual conduct. It is quite another to
collectively legislate and legalize to protect immoral conduct that can
weaken, even destroy the family.

There is a dangerous trap when tolerance is exaggerated to protect
the rights of those whose conduct endangers the family and injures the
rights of the more part of the people. We are getting dangerously close
to the condition described by the prophet Mosiah, who warned:

> Now it is not common that the voice of the people
> desireth anything contrary to that which is right; but it is
> common for the lesser part of the people to desire that which
> is not right; therefore this shall ye observe and make it your
> law—to do your business by the voice of the people.
>
> And if the time comes that the voice of the people doth
> choose iniquity, then is the time that the judgments of God
> will come upon you; yea, then is the time he will visit you

with great destruction even as he has hitherto visited this land.[1]

Tolerance can be a dangerous trap. (06–03)

The moral fiber of society is weakening. Something has happened to our collective conscience. Countries have a conscience, just as people do. Something in our national conscience became unsettled. In the end, a clouded conscience cannot conquer. In the end, a clear conscience cannot be defeated.

Something is weakening the moral fiber of the American people. We have always had couples live together without marriage, but we have not honored it as an acceptable lifestyle. We have always had children born out of wedlock, but we have never made it to be respectable. And we have never before regarded babies, whether conceived in or out of wedlock, to be an inconvenience and destroyed them by the thousands through abortion—and this while barren couples yearn for a child to raise.

We have always had some who followed a life of perversion, but we have never before pushed through legislation to protect that way of life lest we offend the rights of an individual. We have never been this "liberated" before.

We have always had those who were guilty of criminal acts, but we have not put the rights of the accused above the rights of the victim.

If one single soul does not wish to listen for a moment to a public prayer—one which does not offend, which even pleases the majority—we are told we must now eliminate prayer completely from all public life.

We have always had addictive drugs, but not in the varieties we have now and not widely sold near public schools, even elementary schools. When perversion and addiction are justified as the expression of individual rights and call up a pestilence which threatens even the innocent, must the right of privacy preclude even individual testing to help find out where it is moving? What kind of personal freedom is this, anyway? (89–03, pp. 63–64)

Justice is misrepresented. Nowadays justice is so misrepresented that the victim of a crime often receives much less of it than the criminal. And legislation which is supposed to vouchsafe freedom of speech is cleverly twisted to protect the pornographer and penalize the victim. (77–08, p. 159)

WAR AND THE GOSPEL—MILITARY

This nation has fought to protect her own and others' independence. Few generations have passed in this land without a call to arms. Threats to our independence have recurred with persistent regularity. Only twenty-one years passed between the armistice in 1918, which ended World War I, and September 1939, when World War II began! Who was it that said, "We learn from history that we learn nothing from history"? With little hesitation, this nation has responded to threats to freedom with military action. We have fought not only to protect our own independence but also to secure or protect it for other nations. Sustained by a courage that comes only from a moral people, we have fought for our homes and our families, our lands, our country, our rights, and our religion. "Chains," President David O. McKay said, "are worse than bayonets."[2] (89–03, pp. 61–62)

One can serve in the military and yet be a righteous example. To you who have answered that call [to military service], we say: Serve honorably and well. Keep your faith, your character, your virtue.

While war permits stomping out of a man's heart the reverent and tender virtues that exemplify true manhood, military service does not require it. You can serve and yet be exemplars of righteousness. (68–03, p. 60)

Those called into the military can enjoy the blessings of God. You brethren, as holders of the priesthood, now are called to answer this call to the military. We want you to know that you can deserve, and will deserve, as you serve, the blessings of Almighty God. You will come to know that you will find a closeness in a challenge that otherwise would be impossible. . . . We know you're physically prepared because you have been accepted on that basis. You are mentally alert and able, you have been able to qualify to the degree necessary. . . . And now if you have a balance with your spiritual maturity, then this is the beginning of a great and important thing in your lives and the Lord will bless you. (68–11)

We do not encourage our members to avoid military service. We do not take the position as a Church to aid, nor abet, nor to encourage our members to avoid their military service. We ought, as citizens, to have open to us any of the options that are offered as citizens, and yet finally, when our responsibilities are before us, and we find the necessity of answering the call to military service, then we answer that call honorably and fulfill our citizenship responsibilities. (68–09)

Often the innocent are victims of war. In armed conflicts there are casualties. Sometimes clean, worthy men, innocent of any desire to kill, devoid of any aggressive will to own that which belongs to someone else, fall victims of the confused, wicked ugliness of war.

"For," the prophet Moroni said, "the Lord suffereth the righteous to be slain that his justice and judgment may come upon the wicked; therefore ye need not suppose that the righteous are lost because they are slain; but behold, they do enter into the rest of . . . their God."[3] There are homes among us now where this heartbreak is known.

I read somewhere some simple lines of verse about a mother—and a telegram. Deep within lies a seed of strength and consolation—understood, perhaps, only by those who have faith. I can read but a few lines.

> *"Killed in action . . . in the line of duty."*
> *Blind went her eyes with pain. . . .*
> *A moan of mortal agony,*
> *Then all became still again.*
> *"Oh God! . . . my God! . . . where were you*
> *When my son was being slain?"*
> *And the scalding tears of bitterness*
> *Drenched her cheeks like the summer rain.*

Speaking at the April 1972 general conference

But a soft voice seemed to whisper
In the twilight's afterglow,
"I had a son . . . at Calvary . . .
Two thousand years ago." (68–03, pp. 60–61)

Our greatest national threat comes from moral decay within.
Following World War II, Winston Churchill wrote, "The human
tragedy reaches its climax in the fact that after all the exertions and sacrifice of hundreds of millions of people, and of all the victories of the
righteous cause, we have still not found peace or security, and that we lie
in the grip of even worse perils than those we have surmounted."

We find ourselves against a frightening prophetic certainty that it
is happening to us again—with an ominous terrible suspicion that this
time the decay is within.

It is one thing to be bound together, armed and united on a moral
course, fearless of the attack from godless or amoral or immoral adver-
saries. It is quite another to realize that we ourselves are becoming
amoral—even immoral—perhaps godless.

That is what we are to guard our nation against! (74–10)

The balance of decency has shifted. Strength that comes from
decency, from morality, is the one, the essential ingredient required for
the preservation of freedom, indeed for the preservation of humankind.
And there is reason to believe that we are losing it.

Something changed. Perhaps for the first time since Concord
Bridge that balance of decency and morality is shifting past the center.
The balance, which measures the morality of all of us put together, is
slowly tipping in the wrong, fatal direction. These lines written to
describe another time and place seem to fit our circumstance now.

That which they would never yield
To military might,
They threw away unwittingly
When evil came by night
And scattered tares among the grain.
They did not rouse to see

Their fundamental moral strength
In mortal jeopardy.[4] (89–03, p. 62)

WORKING FOR GOOD GOVERNMENT

How may the Constitution be saved? It has been prophesied that the Constitution of the United States will hang by a thread and that the elders of Israel will step forth to save it.[5] In my mind that does not require a few heroes in public office steering some saving legislation through the halls of Congress, neither some brilliant military leaders rallying our defense against an invading army. In my mind, it could well be brought about by the rank and file of men and women of faith who revere the Constitution and believe that the strength of democracy rests in the ordinary family and in each member of it.

That saving strength rests in ordinary fathers and mothers who do not neglect the spiritual development of their children. It rests in fathers and mothers who will send their sons and daughters to the four corners of the earth to teach that if we will follow in His word, "then [we will be his] disciples indeed; and [we] shall know the truth, and the truth shall make [us] free."[6] (89–03, p. 68)

This Church and its faithful members will defend the Constitution. There occurs from time to time reference to the Constitution hanging by a thread. President Brigham Young said:

> The general Constitution of our country is good, and a wholesome government could be framed upon it; for it was dictated by the invisible operations of the Almighty. . . .
>
> Will the Constitution be destroyed? No. It will be held inviolate by this people; and as Joseph Smith said, "the time will come when the destiny of this nation will hang upon a single thread, and at this critical juncture, this people will step forth and save it from the threatened destruction." It will be so.[7]

I do not know when that day will come or how it will come to pass. I feel sure that when it does come to pass, among those who will step forward from among this people will be men who hold the holy priesthood and who carry as credentials a bachelor or doctor of law degree, and women, also, of honor. And there will be judges as well.

Others from the world outside the Church will come, as Colonel Thomas Kane did, and bring with them their knowledge of the law to protect this people.

We may one day stand alone, but we will not change or lower our standards or change our course. (04–02, pp. 10–11)

This land will be a land of liberty unless our purposes run counter to God's. The Book of Mormon . . . in repeated references designates this land as "choice above all other lands,"[8] and "a land of liberty" unto those who possess it.[9] This book of prophecy also established a great responsibility upon the citizens of this land and declares that when the purposes of the people become destructive to the purposes of God, they are in danger of losing liberty, the most precious of all gifts. (55–01)

How to stand worthy of public trust. Occasionally we find an individual who holds, or is seeking to hold, high public office.

Such a man may claim to be worthy of public trust. He may insist that he would not cheat the public, or misrepresent them, or mislead them, or break faith with them.

We may ask ourselves, what does that individual do with a private trust? A good measure of him is to determine how he keeps covenants relating to his family. . . .

A man who is not faithful to his marriage partner and to his family is hardly worthy of confidence and trust.

If he would cheat on his marriage vows . . . surely he must stand unworthy of any great public trust.

He cannot claim this to be a private matter with no bearing on his integrity before the public. (80–01)

FREEDOM

It is God's will that men be free people. One of the most significant principles in the Church, even from the beginning, was the principle of liberty. The Lord declared in His revelations that it was not commensurate with His will that men should be in bondage one to another, that religiously and politically there was to be no aristocracy with dictatorial rights. And He declared that "for this purpose have I established the Constitution of this land, by the hands of wise men whom I raised up unto this very purpose, and redeemed the land by the shedding of blood."[10] (55–01)

Following the gospel plan will keep us free. In our search for happiness, let us set as our goal eternal life, and eternal joy. If mankind would but avail himself of the great gospel plan which includes all that is calculated to bring happiness and joy, there could be no fear of losing the priceless gift of freedom. We would then be on the Lord's side of the line. Perhaps then we could more fully realize the significance of the promise given by the greatest of all: "Ye shall know the truth, and the truth shall make you free."[11] (55–01)

Freedom must be built on righteous principles. Along with the great knowledge that this is the chosen land of God, we have been warned and forewarned that the foundation of freedom must be built on the observance of righteous principles. (55–01)

Freedom cannot survive when the rights of the individual are fanatically promoted. Neither can freedom long survive in a society where the rights of the individual are fanatically promoted regardless of what happens to society itself. The rights of the individual—the ideal, the virtue—when pressed to the extreme, like other virtues will presently become a vice. Unless they ensure some balance, activists, lawyers, legislators, judges, and courts who think they are protecting individual freedom are in fact fabricating a new and subtle and sinister kind of dictatorship. (89–03, p. 65)

CHAPTER 17

Church History and the Restoration

*"There is no such thing as an accurate, objective history
of the Church without consideration of the spiritual powers
that attend this work." (81–07, p. 104)*

CHURCH HISTORY

*Students should see the hand of the Lord in the history of the
Church.* You seminary teachers and some of you institute and BYU
men will be teaching the history of the Church this school year. This is
an unparalleled opportunity in the lives of your students to increase
their faith and testimony of the divinity of this work. Your objective
should be that they will see the hand of the Lord in every hour and
every moment of the Church from its beginning till now. (81–07,
p. 104)

*An accurate history of the Church must consider the influence of
spiritual powers.* There is no such thing as an accurate, objective history of the Church without consideration of the spiritual powers that
attend this work. . . . If we who research, write, and teach the history
of the Church ignore the spiritual on the pretext that the world may

not understand it, our work will not be objective. And if, for the same reason, we keep it quite secular, we will produce a history that is not accurate and not scholarly—this in spite of the extent of research or the nature of the individual statements or the incidents which are included as part of it, and notwithstanding the training or scholarly reputation of the one who writes or teaches it. We would end up with a history that left out the one most essential ingredient. (81–07, pp. 104–6)

Angels attend the rank and file of the Church. This rank and file of the Church—150 years of them—have brought the truth to this generation. It is planted where it is most likely to bear an abundant harvest—in the hearts of the ordinary people. . . .

Who would dare to say that angels do not now attend the rank and file of the Church who—

answer the calls to the mission fields,
teach the classes,
pay their tithes and offerings,
seek for the records of their forebears,
work in the temples,
raise their children in faith,
and have brought this work through 150 years?

There comes a witness, also, from some who have stumbled and fallen but have struggled back and have found the sweet, forgiving, cleansing influence of repentance. They now stand approved of the Lord, clean before Him; His Spirit has returned to them and they are guided by it. Without reviewing the hard lessons of the past they guide others to that Spirit. . . .

Who would dare to say that the day of miracles has ceased? Those things have not changed in 150 years, not changed at all. For the power and inspiration of the Almighty rests upon this people today as surely as it did in those days of beginning: "It is by faith that miracles are wrought; and it is by faith that angels appear and minister unto men; wherefore, if these things have ceased wo be unto the children of men, for it is because of unbelief."[1] (80–04, pp. 63–64)

A caution about belittling the Church and its past leaders. [I] caution [against] the idea that so long as something is already in print, so long as it is available from another source, there is nothing out of order in using it in writing or speaking or teaching.

Surely you can see the fallacy in that.

I have on occasion been disappointed when I have read in writings of those who are supposed to be worthy members of the Church statements that tend to belittle or degrade the Church or past leaders of the Church. When I have commented on my disappointment at seeing such things in print, the answer has been, "It was printed before, and it's available, and therefore I saw no reason not to publish it again."

You do not do well to see that such writing is disseminated. It may be read by those not mature enough for "advanced history," and a testimony in seedling stage may be crushed. (*HBT,* p. 114)

A caution to historians. One who chooses to follow the tenets of his profession, regardless of how they may injure the Church or destroy the faith of those not ready for "advanced history," is himself in spiritual jeopardy. If that one is a member of the Church, he has broken his covenants and will be accountable. After all of the tomorrows of mortality have been finished, he will not stand where he might have stood. (81–07, p. 109)

A caution to those who destroy faith. That historian or scholar who delights in pointing out the weakness and frailties of present or past leaders destroys faith. A destroyer of faith—particularly one within the Church, and more particularly one who is employed specifically to build faith—places himself in great spiritual jeopardy. He is serving the wrong master, and unless he repents, he will not be among the faithful in the eternities. (81–07, p. 109)

There is a limit to the patience of the Lord. I want to say in all seriousness that there is a limit to the patience of the Lord with respect to those who are under covenant to bless and protect His Church and kingdom upon the earth but do not do it.

Particularly are we in danger if we are out to make a name for ourselves, if our "hearts are set so much upon the things of this world, and aspire to the honors of men." (81–07, p. 111)

JOSEPH SMITH

Testimony of Joseph Smith. I'm unable, I confess, to stand apart and look at Joseph Smith with complete scholastic detachment; so any contemplations or appraisals that I make of him are tempered with this fact: I accept the Prophet Joseph Smith as a servant of God. I believe that he was divinely inspired to restore the gospel of Jesus Christ to the earth, that he was in every whit a prophet, seer, and revelator. And where I may apologize for the lack of objectivity, I might add that while objectivity has a head, subjectivity has a heart; and often the heart will know things that the head never will discover. So I bear conviction and testimony that Joseph Smith was a prophet of God. (59–03, p. 37)

Joseph Smith—a prophet teacher. Was he a teacher? Did his adherents learn? Are his teachings alive today? The answer, of course, is obvious. The kingdom of God is going forth; his name is yet being proclaimed throughout all the world; and he is known for good or for evil.[2] Joseph Smith was an ordinary man; he was possessed of few if any immunities; he was called of God; he was chosen; he suffered; he endured. And his work is with us; it can be tested. Throughout sacred writ is the constant invitation to "ask and ye shall receive," to "seek and ye shall find," to "knock, and it shall be opened unto you." We can know whether Joseph Smith was a prophet and a teacher.

With countless thousands of others, I know that Joseph Smith was a mighty prophet, seer, and revelator. With the exception of Jesus Christ, he is the greatest being who ever walked the face of this earth. I am deeply grateful for the influence his life has had upon me and will yet have in the eternities to come. (59–03, pp. 43–44)

We do not have to defend the Prophet Joseph Smith. There always were, are now, and ever will be those who stir into 200-year-old dust, hoping to find something Joseph is alleged to have said or done in order to demean him. The revelations tell us of "those that shall lift up the heel against mine anointed, saith the Lord, and cry they have sinned when they have not sinned before me, saith the Lord, but have done that which was meet in mine eyes, and which I commanded them."[3] They face very stern penalties, indeed.

We do not have to defend the Prophet Joseph Smith. The Book of Mormon: Another Testament of Jesus Christ will defend him for us. Those who reject Joseph Smith as a prophet and revelator are left to find some other explanation for the Book of Mormon. And for the second powerful defense: the Doctrine and Covenants, and a third: the Pearl of Great Price. Published in combination, these scriptures form an unshakable testament that Jesus is the Christ and a witness that Joseph Smith is a prophet. (05–03, p. 9)

APOSTASY AND RESTORATION

As a result of apostasy, the keys of authority were lost. Following the crucifixion of Christ, an apostasy occurred. Leaders began to "teach for doctrines the commandments of men."[4] They lost the keys of authority and closed themselves off from the channels of revelation. That lost authority could not just be repossessed. It had to be restored by those who held the keys of authority anciently.[5] (03–09, p. 24)

[The Twelve] taught, testified, and established the Church. And they died for their beliefs, and with their deaths came centuries of apostasy.

The most precious thing lost in the Apostasy was the authority held by the Twelve—the priesthood keys. For the Church to be *His* Church, there must be a Quorum of the Twelve who hold the keys and confer them on others. (08–09, p. 84)

When the Great Apostasy occurred, the Light of Christ was still present. The shadow of apostasy settled over the earth. The line of priesthood authority was broken. But mankind was not left in total darkness or completely without revelation or inspiration. The idea that with the crucifixion of Christ the heavens were closed and that they opened in the First Vision is not true. The Light of Christ would be everywhere present to attend the children of God; the Holy Ghost would visit seeking souls. The prayers of the righteous would not go unanswered.

The conferring of the *gift* of the Holy Ghost must await the restoration of the priesthood and the dispensation of the fulness of times, when all things would be revealed. Temple work—ordinance work—would then be revealed. Then those who lived during the many generations when essential ordinances were unavailable, when baptism was not available, would be redeemed. God never abandons His children. He never has abandoned this earth. (04–05, p. 11)

Joseph Smith became the instrument of the Restoration. Despite opposition, the Twelve established the Church of Jesus Christ; and despite persecution, it flourished. But as the centuries passed, the flame flickered and dimmed. Ordinances were changed or abandoned. The line was broken, and the authority to confer the Holy Ghost as a gift was gone. The Dark Ages of apostasy settled over the world. But always, as it had from the beginning, the Spirit of God inspired worthy souls.[6]

We owe an immense debt to the protestors and the reformers who preserved the scriptures and translated them. They knew something had been lost. They kept the flame alive as best they could. Many of them were martyrs. But protesting was not enough, nor could reformers restore that which was gone.

In time, a great diversity of churches arose. When all was prepared, the Father and the Son appeared to the boy Joseph in the Grove, and those words spoken at the river Jordan were heard once again: "This is My Beloved Son. Hear Him!"[7] Joseph Smith became the instrument of the Restoration. (00–02, p. 8)

The Apostles were martyred, and in time, an apostasy took place. The doctrines of the Church were corrupted and the ordinances changed. The keys of priesthood authority were lost. This universal

Apostasy required a restoration of authority—of the priesthood keys, of doctrines, and of ordinances.

Joseph Smith was visited in person by God the Eternal Father and His Son Jesus Christ. They told him they had a special work for him to do. Through him the keys would be restored, and the Church, as had been established by Jesus Christ when He was on the earth, would be restored.

Joseph Smith and Oliver Cowdery were ordained to the Aaronic Priesthood by John the Baptist.[8] They were ordained to the Melchizedek Priesthood by the ancient apostles, Peter, James, and John.[9] These ordinations restored the authority and the keys for the kingdom of God, never again to be taken from the earth.

In April of 1830, the Prophet Joseph Smith organized The Church of Jesus Christ of Latter-day Saints. The true Church of Jesus Christ was once again among men, with authority "to preach the Gospel and administer in the ordinances thereof."[10]

Other priesthood keys were conferred upon Joseph and Oliver by Moses, Elijah, Elias, and other ancient prophets.[11] (03–01)

The Restoration did not come all at once. John the Baptist returned through the veil to confer the Aaronic Priesthood, "which holds the keys of the ministering of angels, and of the gospel of repentance, and of baptism by immersion for the remission of sins."[12] A companion ordinance, confirmation and the conferral of the gift of the Holy Ghost, required a greater authority.[13]

Soon thereafter, Peter, James, and John, Apostle companions of the Lord, restored the higher or Melchizedek Priesthood[14]—"the Holy Priesthood, after the Order of the Son of God."[15] The Restoration did not come all at once. In a series of visitations, other prophets came to restore the keys of the priesthood.[16] With the authority restored, the organization was revealed. Apostles were ordained, and the Quorum of the Twelve Apostles and First Presidency were organized as they had been anciently.[17] The ordinances were revealed and authority given to perform them. (03–09, p. 24)

Joseph's vision of the Father and the Son opened this dispensation. Then came the restoration of the fulness of the gospel of Jesus Christ with the same organization that existed in the primitive Church, built upon the foundation of apostles and prophets.[18]

Some suppose that the organization was handed to the Prophet Joseph Smith like a set of plans and specifications for a building, with all of the details known at the beginning. But it did not come that way. Rather, it came a piece at a time as the Brethren were ready and as they inquired of God. (96–05, p. 6)

The Church of Jesus Christ of Latter-day Saints is not a correction. The Church of Jesus Christ of Latter-day Saints is not just an adjustment or a correction of what had become Christianity following the great Apostasy. It is a replacement, a restoration of organization and authority to what Christianity had been when Christ established it. (04–04)

Gospel dispensations culminate in the fulness of times. The administration of the gospel plan among men has been divided into dispensations of the gospel. Each of the dispensations is a gospel epic, a period in which portions of the plan would be revealed. These dispensations, one following another, move toward the final one—the dispensation of the fulness of times—when all things, the fulness of the gospel, would be revealed. The great plan, insofar as mortality was concerned, could then be consummated. (83–04)

PIONEER HERITAGE

The pioneers came because they "had to." A visitor to the Salt Lake Valley apologized to President George A. Smith for them having been driven from the pleasant scenes of Europe and the East into the western wilderness to the Utah desert.

President Smith replied, "No, No! You don't understand. We came here willingly—because we had to!"[19]

The "had to" part was not because of persecutions or mobbings or even the 2,000 soldiers sent after them. The "had to" was because of what was inside of them. They knew why they came.

They knew that there had been a restoration of the fulness of the gospel of Jesus Christ. They knew from the revelations to expect such treatment. They had firm, unshakable, individual testimonies of the life and death and Resurrection of Jesus Christ. They knew that the authority of the priesthood had been restored to earth by angelic messengers. Nothing could deter them. They had then, as we have now, individual testimonies, witness of the truth of the gospel of Jesus Christ.

Now the fulness of the gospel has spread across the earth. Today tens of thousands of messengers—missionaries—carry the message of the gospel. They represent millions of members with authority to baptize, ordain, and seal. That is why they came!

In ways, our journey today is harder than theirs and infinitely more dangerous. There are dark, ominous clouds ahead. Each one of us needs, and each can have, the same courage, the same assurance from the same source, the same testimony of the Risen Lord. We know why we are here and where we are going. God bless them for what they earned for us. (06–05)

The resolute pioneer spirit is preserved. We will teach people self-reliance, teach them to take care of themselves, and then feed the poor, clothe the naked, administer to the sick. We will do it ourselves. There is a tremendous network of projects and storehouses to witness this determination.

We will be temperate and hold to the one standard of chastity. We will speak for good and against evil, regardless of the criticism or the persecution that may follow.

In the aggregate, as a people, the resolute pioneer spirit is preserved. And the harder test now lies ahead, to protect this people from a different invasion—an immoral one. (79–05)

CHAPTER 18

Preparing in the Last Days

"Be composed; the Lord is watching over what
is happening on this earth." (08–02)

AVOIDING INDIVIDUAL APOSTASY

The gospel is like a piano keyboard. The gospel might be likened
to the keyboard of a piano—a full keyboard with a selection of keys on
which one who is trained can play a variety without limits: a ballad to
express love, a march to rally, a sweet melody to soothe, and a hymn to
inspire; an endless variety to suit every mood and satisfy every need.

How shortsighted it is, then, to choose a single key and endlessly
tap out the monotony of a single note, or even two or three notes, when
the full keyboard of limitless melody and harmony can be played!

How disappointing it is that when the fulness of the gospel, the
whole keyboard, is here upon the earth, many churches tap on a single
key! The note they stress may be essential to a complete harmony of
religious experience, but nonetheless it is not all there is. It isn't the
fulness.

For instance, one taps on the key of faith healing to the neglect of many principles that would bring greater strength than faith healing itself. Another taps on an obscure key relating to the observance of the Sabbath—a key that would sound different indeed if played in harmony with the other essential notes. A key used like that can get completely out of tune. Another repeats endlessly the key that relates to the mode of baptism and now and then taps one or two other keys as though there were not a full keyboard. And again, the very key used, essential as it is, just doesn't sound complete when played alone to the neglect of the others. (71–10, p. 41)

Avoid gospel hobbies. Some members of the Church who should know better pick out a hobby key or two and tap them incessantly, to the irritation of those around them. By doing this they can dull their own spiritual sensitivities. They can thus lose track of the inspired knowledge that there is a fulness of the gospel and can become, individually, as many churches have become: they may reject the fulness in preference to a favorite note. As this preference becomes exaggerated and distorted, they are led away into apostasy. (71–10, p. 42)

There is tragedy in personal apostasy. We hold steadfastly to standards the world now rejects. And we face more than an indifferent or hostile world. The spirit of opposition that brooded over Kirtland visited Missouri and Nauvoo and follows the Church in every generation. Today there are those in the Church who communicate through networks and publications. They hold symposia in which they turn over stones looking for things to criticize. Surely they will find plenty to occupy their time. How could it be otherwise? The Lord has chosen "the weak things of the world, those who are unlearned"[1] to bear his work along and none of us are exempt from temptation or human frailty.

The Brethren issued a caution to members saying, "We are especially saddened at the participation of our own members [in symposia], especially those who hold Church or other positions that give them stature among Latter-day Saints and who have allowed their stature to be used to promote . . . presentations that result in ridiculing sacred things or injuring The Church of Jesus Christ, detracting from its mission, or jeopardizing the well-being of its members."

We feel deep sorrow over the course such dissidents have chosen. But they must choose for themselves. The choice is theirs, for it is given to them.

The tragedy of their choice is personal with them and their posterity. For the Lord has said, "They shall be severed from the ordinances of mine house. Their basket shall not be full, their houses and their barns shall perish, and they themselves shall be despised by those that flattered them. They shall not have right to the priesthood, nor their posterity after them from generation to generation."[2]

While we sorrow after them, their efforts have negligible effect upon the Church. Should they lead hundreds to follow after them, they will be replaced by thousands, even tens of thousands as it was in Kirtland, and in the valleys of the West. For "the keys of the kingdom of God are committed unto man on the earth" and will, like the "stone which is cut out of the mountain without hands . . . roll forth, until it has filled the whole earth."[3] (95–04)

Beware of the fruits of criticism and expressing doubts. In the Church we have certain members who smart under the restrictions of rigid discipline. Their approach to the gospel is largely intellectual. They have not learned to tap into the great sources of intelligence available through spiritual inquiry.

A typical individual in this category is active in the Church. He responds to calls, accepts the doctrines "for the most part," but is disturbed by one or two things. . . . When called to teaching positions, he has a great deal of difficulty hiding his doubts. While basically he accepts the doctrines and tries to keep the standards, he frequently objects to "the way the Church is being run."

. . . None of us lives for himself alone. Others are following in our footsteps, watching carefully, and taking license from the things we say and the things we do. When we have doubts, it is wise to keep them to ourselves and to ponder on them and study and pray and inquire. One by one they are resolved. When we have questions that are unresolved, it is wise to take them on faith. Otherwise it may be that we will enjoy the fruits of the gospel and never stray "too" far, and yet those who come after us who depend upon us most may be robbed of their spiritual inheritance. They may forsake the standards and become ineligible for those redeeming ordinances that make life eternally happy. (*TYD*, pp. 213–15)

Those who seek to destroy faith will fade into spiritual oblivion. It is invariably true that those who set their hand to disturb or thwart the work of the Lord, or destroy faith—those who challenge or ridicule or criticize His chosen servants, whether in the wards, the stakes, or the Church—fade into spiritual oblivion and lose what might have been theirs. (*TYD*, p. 216)

Deception can be overcome. There have been those I have known who have been deceived or led astray but who, when corrected, have hung tenaciously to the principle of obedience and have become tractable and repentant. They move forward and upward much the stronger and the wiser for their experience. (*TYD*, p. 216)

Individuals can break the chain of apostasy. Years ago when I was teaching seminary, I remember a girl who stayed after class and wept over the fact that her father, her grandfather, and her great-grandfather were apostates. Her great-grandfather had been a great missionary in the Church and opened one of the continents of the world, a missionary that had become disaffected because of arrogance. The spirit of apostasy had set in, and his son and his grandson had fallen in that bitterness.

Here was an only child in the family, with a tender mother trying to raise her up in righteousness, who had encouraged her to be active in the Church. She was in a seminary class, and every day she had heard things that put her in opposition with her father.

One day she stayed after school and sobbed out her grief and said, "How can I change my father? What can I do to change my dad?"

Well, she couldn't erase those generations before her, but I pointed out that there was one thing she could do that she had not thought of.

In that chain of apostasy, while she could not go back and make the change herself, she could *be* the change.

And I have lived to know now that from her generation henceforth, they will all be under the covenant because she made the change. I told her to love her father, a good man in most ways, and to be reverent and obedient and respectful to him. She herself was to be the change. (70–12)

FALSE PROPHETS AND DECEIVERS

Claims of special authority or revelation are false. There are those who claim authority from some secret ordinations of the past. Even now some claim special revealed authority to lead or to teach the people. Occasionally they use the names of members of the First Presidency or of the Twelve or of the Seventy and imply some special approval of what they teach.

There have been too many names presented, too many sustaining votes taken, too many ordinations and settings apart performed before too many witnesses, too many certificates prepared, and too many pictures published in too many places for any Church member to be deceived as to who holds proper authority. Claims of special revelation or secret authority from the Lord or from the Brethren are false on the face of them and really are utter nonsense!

The Lord has never operated in that way. These things were not done in a corner[4]; there is light on every official call and every authorized ordination, and it has always been that way. (85–08, p. 34)

Beware of deceivers. There are some among us now who have *not* been regularly ordained by the heads of the Church and who tell of impending political and economic chaos, the end of the world— something of the "sky is falling, Chicken Little" of the fables. They are misleading members to gather to colonies or cults.

Those deceivers say that the Brethren do not know what is going on in the world or that the Brethren approve of their teaching but do not wish to speak of it over the pulpit. Neither is true. The Brethren, by virtue of traveling constantly everywhere on earth, certainly know what is going on, and by virtue of prophetic insight are able to read the signs of the times.

Do not be deceived by them—those deceivers. If there is to be any gathering, it will be announced by those who have been regularly ordained and who are known to the Church to have authority.

Come away from any others. Follow your leaders who have been duly ordained and have been publicly sustained, and you will not be led astray. (92–05, p. 73)

Beware of those who claim special authority. In the forty-second section of the Doctrine and Covenants it says "that it shall not be given to any one to . . . preach [the] gospel [or by implication to administer in the Church] except he be ordained by some one who has authority" and that he has received that authority by ordination from the leaders of the Church.[5] That is one principle.

The other principle is that "it is known to the Church that he has authority." So nothing goes on, as Paul said, "for this thing was not done in a corner."[6] If ever you see groups that are a little bit secretive, who claim to know something new, some supposed special knowledge that isn't in the regular routine patterns in the wards and stakes, leave it alone. If they lay claim to some special authority or some special ability to interpret the scriptures, you know on the surface that it isn't right and you can feel that it isn't right, even though sometimes they come with a powerful, attractive feeling that you might mistake for the Spirit of the Lord. That's when your head ought to operate, as well as your heart, and remember that the Lord works through channels. And that is why we do all the voting in the Church. . . . Unless they have been ordained by someone who has authority and has been ordained by the heads of the Church and it's known to the Church that they have authority, they are not to be followed. (91–07)

The Church is protected from imposters. We always know who is called to lead or to teach and have the opportunity to sustain or to oppose the action. It did not come as an invention of man but was set out in the revelations: "It shall not be given to any one to go forth to preach my gospel, or to build up my church, except he be ordained by some one who has authority, and *it is known to the church* that he has authority and has been regularly ordained by the heads of the church."[7] In this way, the Church is protected from any imposter who would take over a quorum, a ward, a stake, or the Church. (07–08, p. 6)

Avoid those who claim some special calling or revelation. If someone approaches you individually or invites you to very private meetings, claiming to have some special calling, whatever you do, follow Paul's counsel—"from such turn away."

They may claim special revelations and callings. They may claim visions and visitations. But where, pray tell me, can they claim the sustaining vote of the membership? In the revelation on organization and Church government given in 1830, the Lord said: "No person is to be ordained to any office in this church, where there is a regularly organized branch of the same, without the vote of that church."[8] (85–08, p. 35)

Avoid like a plague those who claim that some great spiritual experience authorizes them to challenge the constituted priesthood authority in the Church. Do not be unsettled if you cannot explain every insinuation of the apostate or every challenge from the enemies who attack the Lord's church. And we now face a tidal wave of that. In due time you will be able to confound the wicked and inspire the honest in heart. (82–04, p. 56)

PREPARING FOR THE SAVIOR'S COMING

We need not live in fear. We live in troubled times—very troubled times. We hope, we pray, for better days. But that is not to be. The prophecies tell us that. We will not as a people, as families, or as individuals be exempt from the trials to come. No one will be spared the trials common to home and family, work, disappointment, grief, health, aging, ultimately death.

400 MINE ERRAND FROM THE LORD

What then shall we do? That question was asked of the Twelve on the day of Pentecost. Peter answered, "Repent, and be baptized every one of you in the name of Jesus Christ for the remission of sins, and ye shall receive the gift of the Holy Ghost."[9] . . . We need not live in fear of the future. We have every reason to rejoice and little reason to fear. If we follow the promptings of the Spirit, we will be safe, whatever the future holds. We will be shown what to do. (00–02, p. 8)

Promote faith, not fear. Fear and faith are antagonistic to one another, and it is our obligation to promote faith, not fear; so stand steady. (70–09, p. 264)

No one knows the day nor the hour. Teenagers also sometimes think, "What's the use? The world will soon be blown all apart and come to an end." That feeling comes from fear, not from faith. No one knows the hour or the day,[10] but the end cannot come until all of the purposes of the Lord are fulfilled. Everything that I have learned from the revelations and from life convinces me that there is time and to spare for you to carefully prepare for a long life. (89–01, p. 59)

Plan and prepare for the future. There is a lot of difficulty in the world. What's the world coming to? Will it survive?

We had a family meeting a year or two ago. There was worry and foreboding: "Will the world hold together?" When they asked me to speak, I said, "I want you to buy two spruce trees, Colorado blue spruce, just little seedlings. The reason I choose those is because they are the slowest growing tree I know of. Plant them about thirty feet apart. Then buy a hammock and wait for the trees to grow. When they grow, you can swing in the hammock between the trees. Will the world still be there? Oh, yes. You will be able to marry and give in marriage, you'll be able to have a family, see your children and your grandchildren as we have done, and now, as we are doing, welcome great-grandchildren. The world will still be here and you will be somebody. You'll be in the right place!" (95–07)

We know we are tested. To you little children and to you parents I say: Don't be afraid; be happy; life is good. You can find a full and a righteous life ahead for children and grandchildren and great-grandchildren, because the work is not done. Parents, assure your children, particularly your little children, that they need not fear if they will be prayerful. (07–09)

Past struggles have helped prepare us for the coming of the Lord. All the struggles and exertions of past generations have brought to us in our day the fulness of the gospel of Jesus Christ, the authority to administer, and the wherewithal to accomplish the ministry. It all comes together in this dispensation of the fulness of times, in the which the consummation of all things will be completed and the earth prepared for the coming of the Lord. (06–07, pp. 87–88)

The Lord is sending those spirits reserved for the final days. I am very convinced that because of what is going on out in the world, the Lord is sending in His reserves, those spirits held in abeyance until the final days of the dispensation of the fulness of times, when wickedness would so overcome the world that there would be little hope. He sends them into the homes of the Latter-day Saints—young men and young women. They are better prepared and more powerful spiritually than we ever were to meet what is ahead for this Church. It is all part of what is going on. (05–06)

This is a day of hastening. There is a day of hastening. The Lord said, "I will hasten my work in its time."[11] That hastening we feel. Look at the world around us. There has been a decline. The world has been slipping for as long as we know. Since World War II, the plane dipped and it gets ever steeper. The world is slipping into mischief and wickedness and depravity at a rate faster than we have known or that we can find in the annals of history.

That means that in the Lord's work, likewise, there is a day of hastening. The work must be done, and we are always given the tools to do it. (02–08)

We are floating along on a quiet stream and all is calm. But if you listen closely, you can hear the sound of rapids ahead. (08–02)

All of the prophecies are coming to fruition. All of the things prophesied are coming to fruition. There are wars and rumors of wars and plagues and pestilence and earthquakes in diverse places. The Lord is fulfilling the things he prophesied and announced in the beginning of this dispensation. (03–03)

WHERE TO FIND SAFETY

The ensign to which we are to rally is Jesus Christ. We speak of the Church as our refuge, our defense. There is safety and protection in the Church. It centers in the gospel of Jesus Christ. Latter-day Saints learn to look within themselves to see the redeeming power of the Savior of all mankind. The principles of the gospel taught in the Church and learned from the scriptures become a guide for each of us individually and for our families.

We know that the homes we establish, and those of our descendants, will be the refuge spoken of in the revelations—the "light," the "standard," the "ensign" for all nations, and the "refuge" against the gathering storms.[12]

The ensign to which all of us are to rally is Jesus Christ, the Son of God, the Only Begotten of the Father, whose Church this is and whose name we bear and whose authority we carry. (06–07, p. 88)

There is no such thing as geographical security. There are dangers all around. Some of you may say, "If things get really tough, we will move here, or we will move back there, and then we will be safe; everything will be all right there." If you do not fix it so that you are safe and in good company when you are alone, or when you are with your own husband or your own wife and your own children, you will not be safe or find happiness anywhere. There is no such thing as geographical security. (*ABE,* p. 201)

Elder and Sister Packer at a servicemen's conference in Berchtesgaden, Germany, 1972

Where can one find refuge? We face the challenge of raising families in the world in darkening clouds of wickedness. Some of our members are unsettled, and sometimes they wonder: Is there any place one can go to escape from it all? Is there another town or a state or a country where it is safe, where one can find refuge? The answer generally is no. The defense and the refuge is where our members now live.

The Book of Mormon prophesies, "Yea, and then shall the work commence, with the Father among all nations in preparing the way whereby his people may be gathered home to the land of their inheritance."[13]

Those who come out of the world into the Church, keep the commandments, honor the priesthood, and enter into activity have found the refuge. (06–07, p. 87)

Steady as she goes. I do not doubt that we sail into troubled waters. There are storms to ride out, there are reefs and shoals to negotiate ere we reach port. But we have been through them before and found safe passage. "The heavens shall be darkened, and a veil of darkness shall cover the earth; and the heavens shall shake, and also the earth; and great tribulations shall be among the children of men, but my people will I preserve."[14] "Steady as she goes." Our craft has weathered storms before. It is seaworthy.

What a glorious time to be alive! What a marvelous age to live! Thank the Lord for the privilege of living in an adventuresome day of challenge. There is celestial radar—revelation from God—guiding us. There is an inspired captain, a prophet of God, leading us. (69–02, p. 100)

Do not fear the future. Why don't you . . . declare an independence and look forward with an optimism and a hope and a faith. Faith is characteristic of Latter-day Saints. Fear is not.

Do not fear the future—yours or generally. Keep your covenants. Participate in the ordinances. And there is a great guiding, protecting power that will be yours. (80–01)

Look forward with faith not fear. This is a great time to live. When times are unsettled, when the dangers persist, the Lord pours out His blessings upon His church and kingdom. I have been associated now in the councils of the Church for upwards of [forty-seven] years. During that time I have seen, from the sidelines at least, many a crisis. Among the leaders I have at times seen great disappointment, some concern, maybe some anxiety. One thing I have never seen is fear. Fear is the antithesis of faith. In this Church and in this kingdom there is faith.

So let us look forward with an attitude of faith and hope. (80–03, p. 195)

Each stake is a defense and a refuge and a standard. Some live with an unspoken fear of what awaits us and the Church in the world. It grows ever darker in morality and spirituality. If we will gather into the Church, live the simple principles of the gospel, live moral lives, keep the Word of Wisdom, tend to our priesthood and other duties, then we need not live in fear. The Word of Wisdom is a key to both physical health and revelation. Avoid tea, coffee, liquor, tobacco, and narcotics.

We can live where we wish, doing the best we can to make a living, whether modest or generous. We are free to do as we wish with our lives, assured of the approval and even the intervention of the Almighty, confident of constant spiritual guidance.

Each stake is a defense and a refuge and a standard. A stake is self-contained with all that is needed for the salvation and exaltation of those who would come within its influence, and temples are ever closer. (06–07, pp. 86–87)

The distance between the world and the Church will steadily grow. The distance between the Church and a world set on a course which we cannot follow will steadily increase.

Some will fall away into apostasy, break their covenants, and replace the plan of redemption with their own rules.

Across the world, those who now come by the tens of thousands will inevitably come as a flood to where the family is safe. Here they will worship the Father in the name of Christ, by the gift of the Holy Ghost, and know that the gospel is the great plan of happiness, of redemption. (94–01, p. 21)

We live in dangerous times. Like a ship without a compass, society drifts from the family values which anchored us in the past. We are caught in a current of moral pollution so strong that unless we correct our course, civilization as we know it will surely be wrecked to pieces.

The perilous times Paul prophesied would come "in the last days," have come.

> For men [are] lovers of their own selves, covetous, boast-
> ers, proud, blasphemers, disobedient to parents, unthankful,
> unholy, without natural affection, trucebreakers, false accus-
> ers, incontinent, fierce, despisers of those that are good, trai-
> tors, heady, high-minded, lovers of pleasures more than
> lovers of God; having a form of godliness, but denying the
> power thereof. . . . This sort are they which creep into
> houses, and lead captive silly women laden with sins, led
> away with divers lusts, ever learning, and never able to come
> to the knowledge of the truth.[15] (95–04)

Safety will come in living like a Latter-day Saint. Largely because of television, instead of looking over into that spacious build-ing, we are, in effect, living inside of it. That is your fate in this genera-tion. You are living in that great and spacious building. . . .

You will be safe if you look like and groom like and act like an ordi-nary Latter-day Saint: dress modestly, attend your meetings, pay tithes, take the sacrament, honor the priesthood, honor your parents, follow your leaders, read the scriptures, study the Book of Mormon, and pray, always pray. An unseen power will hold your hand as you hold to the iron rod.

Will this solve all your problems? Of course not! That would be contrary to the purpose of your coming into mortality. It will, however, give you a solid foundation on which to build your life.[16]

The mist of darkness will cover you at times so much that you will not be able to see your way even a short distance ahead. You will not be able to see clearly. But you can *feel* your way. With the gift of the Holy Ghost, you can *feel* your way ahead through life. Grasp the iron rod, and do not let go. Through the power of the Holy Ghost, you can *feel* your way through life.[17] (07–01, pp. 260–61)

The safety of the human family depends upon this Church maintaining its standards. (08–02)

CRITICS AND OPPOSITION

To oppose this work is to advertise it. We do not quarrel with people of other religions. They quarrel with us a lot, and they are free to do that. It gets quite interesting sometimes. They are always trying to find some ways to stop our work. Ordinarily, the harder they try, the quicker we prosper. They have not learned that yet, that to oppose us is to advertise us. (06–09)

Many who leave the Church can't leave it alone. There is something very interesting about a person who is anxious to forsake the standards of his church, particularly if he leaves them and encourages others to do likewise.

Have you ever wondered what it means when a person can leave the Church but he cannot leave it alone? Normal behavior would have him cancel his affiliation in the Church and let that be that. Not so with this individual. He can leave it, but he cannot leave it alone. He becomes consumed and obsessed with it. That says something about him. (*TYD*, p. 222)

We must not feel obligated to answer every criticism. We face ahead some narrow places, both as individuals and as a church. We are "shot at" with criticism and opposition from many directions.

If you feel that you must answer every criticism and challenge that comes your way, a single critic or one heckler can occupy your full time.

I have learned that there is one place to search for approval and that is up—to be approved of our Lord and of our Heavenly Father.

When I have received a prompting that something needed to be said, I have tried to say it as diplomatically and as wisely as possible. But I have tried to have the courage to say things that are difficult to say even though they may make some uncomfortable. (*ABE*, p. 249)

Never apologize for the sacred doctrines of the gospel. It is not an easy thing for us to defend the position that bothers so many others. But, brethren and sisters, never be ashamed of the gospel of Jesus Christ. Never apologize for the sacred doctrines of the gospel. Never feel inadequate and unsettled because you cannot explain them to the satisfaction of all who might enquire of you. Do not be ill at ease or uncomfortable because you can give little more than your conviction.

Be assured that, if you will explain what you know and testify of what you feel, you may plant a seed that will grow and blossom into a testimony of the gospel of Jesus Christ. (98–01, p. 67)

One can't please the Lord without offending the devil. We face in this generation, and the generations [ahead of] us, challenges beyond anything that have been experienced in previous generations in the Church.

There is no way that you can have the approval of the Lord without offending the devil, said President Romney. It is futile to suppose that you can be immune from the opposition or anger of the devil and at once please the Lord. Now "choose ye this day whom ye will serve."[18] If you choose the Lord you choose discomfort, opposition, criticism, and a lot of other things.

The compensation is the sustaining influence of the Spirit and the presence of the Spirit and the ministering of angels. (94–04)

No dispensation has had the gospel without opposition. No other dispensation has had the gospel without any challenge, without any opposition or resistance, without persecution from the world, and to expect that we shall be without such conditions is to expect that which will never be. We do not hold membership in the Church and its blessings without paying a price for it. (66–02, pp. 103–4)

The Church will always have critics. Do not expect to see the day when this Church, or those in it, will be free from resistance, criticism, even persecution. That will never be.

Just remember: "Blessed are ye, when men shall revile you, and persecute you, and shall say all manner of evil against you falsely, for my sake. Rejoice, and be exceeding glad: for great is your reward in heaven: for so persecuted they the prophets which were before you."[19] (79–03, p. 81)

There has been no end to opposition. There has been no end to opposition. There are misinterpretations and misrepresentations of us and of our history, some of it mean-spirited and certainly contrary to the teachings of Jesus Christ and His gospel. Sometimes clergy, even ministerial organizations, oppose us. They do what we would never do. We do not attack or criticize or oppose others as they do us. . . .

Strangest of all, otherwise intelligent people claim we are not Christian. This shows that they know little or nothing about us. It is a true principle that you cannot lift yourself by putting others down. (06–07, p. 87)

The Lord will fight our battles. We are in the middle of the opposition of the Church. That has gone on forever. We see so much published in the newspapers and particularly on the Internet, those who are criticizing the Church or criticizing the leaders, the priesthood or auxiliary leaders.

Sometimes I have been asked, "What do the Brethren think of this?"

And I can say, "Not much. We don't have time!"

We are trying to operate the Church across the world. We don't talk about those things, and in one way are not interested in them. When we see the enormous growth of the Church, the marvel that is there and the spread of the gospel of Jesus Christ, we are not turned away by that opposition. It has always been there.

In fact, it is not our problem. It is theirs. We do not oppose them, and we do not go out preaching against them or trying to disturb them. They can go their way. So it becomes their problem.

We can say, however, that they cannot escape the consequences.[20] . . .

The Lord has said that He will fight our battles. We do not wince much at opposition and challenges. We take care of our families and do the best we can. (07–09)

Do not confront those who teach we are not Christians. While we take the gospel of Christ to all people, we do not oppose other churches. If you meet someone who challenges our right to the title Christian, do not confront them. Teach them peaceably. We have but to remain humble and peaceable followers of Christ, for He has promised, "I will fight your battles."[21] (98–01, p. 66)

Be more concerned that people understand than agree with us. As I grow older in age and experience, I grow ever *less* concerned over whether others agree with us. I grow ever *more* concerned that they understand us. If they do understand, they have their agency and can accept or reject the gospel as they please. (98–01, p. 67)

Do not be discouraged by those who seek to destroy faith. Before us there are signs of great trials, and of *great* achievements. The enemy encircles about us, angered by our progress. Be ever watchful! For more ominous than this, they are aided by those within who destroy faith and feed that which has no lasting substance.

Brethren, do not be discouraged when disappointments come, as surely they will, for every soul has his agency. And some will not follow you, nor will they follow us. That is part of the testing. (82–02)

To argue over sacred things usually generates much more heat than light. There are doctrinal beliefs that will continue to be misunderstood and disturb our critics. . . . One need not have answers to all those questions to receive the witness of the Spirit, join the Church, and remain faithful therein. There is a knowledge that transcends rational explanations, sacred knowledge that leads to conversion.

While we can provide answers, they will not be satisfactory, however, to those who do not accept continuing revelation. To argue or debate over sacred things usually generates much more heat than light. (98–01, p. 65)

Beware of the testimony of one who seeks to tear down. Many an academic giant is at once a spiritual pygmy and, if so, is usually a moral weakling as well. Such a person may easily become a self-appointed member of a wrecking crew determined to destroy the works of God.

Beware of the testimony of one who is intemperate, or irreverent, or immoral, who tears down and has nothing to put in place of what he destroys. (74–03, p. 15)

Be careful of those who promote controversy. Be careful of those who promote controversy and contention, "For verily, verily I say unto you, he that hath the spirit of contention is not of me," saith the Lord.[22]

This next question concerns those who are shaking your faith.

Are they really being fair? Could it be that they point to alleged misconduct, insinuating that the Church is responsible, to excuse themselves from living the high standards of the Church or to cover some failure to do so? You think about that—carefully. (79–03, p. 80)

There are those who present a distorted view of some of our teachings. Recently someone quoted a sentence from an otherwise obscure source in which an early Church leader talked about the submission of wives to their husbands. It was presented as representative of the views of the Church and ridiculed. What he did not do is quote as well from many statements from that same leader to husbands of their responsibility to their wives and families. It therefore was a distorted picture that did not fairly or honestly represent the views of that early leader. That is not scholarship. That is not unbiased. It is a disservice to people past and present. (XX–02)

Beware of those who would persuade us to change direction. On one occasion I attended a meeting at Ricks College with a group of seminary teachers when President Joseph Fielding Smith, then the President of the Council of the Twelve, met with us. One of the teachers asked about a letter being circulated throughout the Church at that time from a dissident member who claimed that many of the ordinances were not valid because of some supposed mistake in the procedure in conferring the priesthood. When President Smith was asked what he thought about the man's claim, he said, "Before we consider the claim, let me tell you about that man." He then told us of several things about him and about the covenants he had not kept. He concluded with this statement: "And so you see, that man is a liar, pure and simple—well, perhaps not so pure."

There are those both outside the Church and in it who will try to persuade or compel us to change our direction. (80–03, pp. 193–94)

Beware of those who publish criticisms about our doctrine. There is another area where caution means safety. There are some who, motivated by one influence or another, seek through writing and publishing criticisms and interpretations of doctrine to make the gospel more acceptable to the so-called thinking people of the world.

They would do well to read very thoughtfully the parable of the tree of life in the eighth chapter of 1 Nephi, and to ponder very soberly verse twenty-eight:

"And *after*" [meaning after they were members of the Church] *after* "they had tasted of the fruit they were ashamed, because of those that were scoffing at them; and they fell away into forbidden paths and were lost."[23] (85–08, p. 35)

How should we react to the ridicule of temple ordinances? The sacred ordinances of the temple are now held up to open ridicule by enemies of the Church. Some foolish members take license from this and in an effort to defend the Church have been led to say more than is wise. . . .

How *should* we react when the sacred ordinances of the priesthood, of the temple, are held up to open public ridicule? What *should* we do in the face of the opposition that now confronts us? There is an answer in the Old Testament.

When the Israelites returned from captivity, they found Jerusalem destroyed. The prophet Nehemiah rallied the people to rebuild the wall about the city. Their enemies were amused. Sanballat mocked them and said, "Will they revive the stones out of the heaps of . . . rubbish?" Tobiah the Ammonite said, "Even that which they build, if a fox go up, he shall even break down their stone wall."[24]

But the wall went up, for "the people had a mind to work."[25]

When the enemies saw that the wall was nearly up and that it was strong, they became worried. Sanballat and Geshem invited Nehemiah to meet with them in one of the villages in the plain of Ono. But Nehemiah said, "They thought to do me mischief. And I sent messengers unto them, saying, I am doing a great work, so that I cannot come down: why should the work cease, whilst I leave it, and come down to you?"[26] Their defense was simple and effective: "We made our prayer unto our God, and set a watch against them"[27] and then went about the work.

And that is what we should do—go about our work, strengthen the wards and the stakes, the quorums and the families and the individual members. We have a work to do. Why should it cease while we do battle with our enemies? Brethren, set a watch and make a prayer and go about the work of the Lord. Do not be drawn away to respond to enemies. In a word, *ignore* them. (83–02, pp. 54–55)

CHAPTER 19

Meetings and Auxiliaries

*"Our meetings should be conducted in such a way that
members may be refreshed spiritually and remain attuned to the
Spirit as they meet the challenges of life." (96–07)*

SACRAMENT MEETING

Sacrament meetings should be spiritual, doctrinal meetings.
Sacrament meeting is the only meeting where there is provision for
members, on a regular and permanent basis, to participate in an ordinance of the gospel.

From the time that a little youngster sips from the sacrament cup
that is steadied by his mother or father, until he takes the sacrament
with the equally unsteady hand that comes with great age, that ordinance is repeated over and over and over and over again.

It is, in fact, the renewing of the covenants of the ordinance of
baptism.

Sacrament meetings should be spiritual, doctrinal, dignified meetings. Anything that is inconsistent with the sacred ordinance of the
gospel, that lacks dignity and formality and reverence, is not in order
in sacrament meeting. (81–03)

Bishops should not give our meetings away. Our bishops should not give our meetings away. That is true of our missionary farewells. We're deeply worried that they now have become kind of reunions in front of ward members. The depth of spiritual training and teaching which could go on is being lost. We have failed to remember that it is a sacrament meeting and that the bishop presides. (96–07)

All should sing the hymns in our meetings. Many times when we attend stake conferences and sacrament meetings we find that the young people are not singing. I hope you, as youth, and as adults, will learn the hymns of Zion and sing them. Sing them with joy and sing them with vigor. Many of the missionaries here have served in those parts of the world—Samoa and Germany, for instance—where the hymns are sung with great gusto and with great enthusiasm, so you know how hymns can be sung, and with all of that they are sung with great inspiration. (75–04)

Wearing our Sunday best is important. There are many things I could say about such matters as wearing Sunday best. Do you know what "Sunday best" means? It used to be the case. Now we see ever more informal, even slouchy, clothing in our meetings, even in sacrament meeting, that leads to informal and slouchy conduct. (96–07)

GENERAL CONFERENCE

Follow the counsel given at general conference. I say again, *follow the Brethren. . . .* In a few days there opens another general conference of the Church. The servants of the Lord will counsel us. You may listen with anxious ears and hearts, or you may turn that counsel aside. What you shall gain will depend not so much upon their preparation *of* the messages as upon your preparation *for* them. (65–01, p. 244)

Why should we follow the counsel given at general conference? We don't have to listen to [the Brethren] or pay heed to them—we have our agency. But there is a lesson in scripture to consider.

The children of Israel entered the land of Edom. It was infested with serpents and snakes, the bite of which was so painful and so dangerous that they called them fiery, flying serpents. They cried for deliverance.

> And Moses prayed for the people.
>
> And the Lord said unto Moses, Make thee a fiery serpent, and set it upon a pole: and it shall come to pass, that every one that is bitten, when he looketh upon it, shall live.
>
> And Moses made a serpent of brass, and put it upon a pole, and it came to pass, that if a serpent had bitten any man, when he beheld the serpent of brass, he lived.[1]

"How silly," some must have said. "How can such a thing cure me? I'll not show my stupidity by paying any attention," and some would not look. In First Nephi we read that "after they were bitten he prepared a way that they might be healed; and the labor which they had to perform was to look; and because of the simpleness of the way, or the easiness of it, there were many who perished."[2]

And today many say, "How silly! How could accepting Christ save me?" They will not turn their heads to look or incline their ears to hear. They ignore the great witness that comes from these [general] conferences. We ought to, indeed we must, heed the counsel of these men, for the Lord said, "What I the Lord have spoken, I have spoken, and I excuse not myself; and though the heavens and the earth pass away, my word shall not pass away, but shall all be fulfilled, whether by mine own voice or by the voice of my servants, it is the same."[3] (68–07, p. 80)

It is not so much what is heard in the sermons but what is felt. It is not so much what is heard in the sermons but what is felt. The Holy Ghost can confirm to all who come within that influence that the messages are true, that this is The Church of Jesus Christ of Latter-day Saints. (07–04, p. 28)

Auxiliaries

No organization in the Church should stand alone. There has been much attention given to the correlating of all the agencies of the Church. It is now established in the Church that no organization needs to stand alone, nor indeed can it fulfill its purpose if it were to do so. The strength of all organizations can sustain and help each organization. Then the power of the whole Church, indeed, the power of the priesthood, can be marshaled in defense of our children against the enticing of the evil one. (70–05)

What is an auxiliary organization? The dictionary defines auxiliary as conferring help or aid, assisting, supporting, subsidiary. Now we may ask, auxiliary to what? The answer I suggest is, auxiliary to the priesthood, and to the home and family.

Webster adds a second definition, and included therein we find a caution. "Auxiliary means also," it says, "serving to supplement," and this we can accept and endorse, but it goes on to say, "or to take the place of," and on this we would caution. An auxiliary is organized to confer help and aid, to assist and support, even to supplement the priesthood and the home, but it is not intended that it should replace them. (62–03)

Auxiliary teachers are to assist the home. Each [Primary or] Sunday School teacher should determine that she will never preempt the home. She will always have in her mind the fact that these are borrowed children, and they come to her under a sacred trust. They belong to the family at home. If teachers have that attitude in mind, they will find ways of assisting and blessing children. (64–04)

We must keep the "feel" of those who are in need. In our programming we must keep the "feel" of those who are in need. The mind will communicate with the mind, the heart with the heart, and the spirit with the spirit. What we feel they will feel. Somehow feeling must be kept in our work, or we will not redeem the lost sheep.

Somehow as priesthood and auxiliary leaders we must remember how it is to be spiritually hungry and poor. Somehow we must remember—or imagine—what it is like to be unrepentant, rebellious, and unforgiving. We must pray fervently for a feeling for it, and pray for the gift to teach by the Spirit. (69–03, p. 21)

The Relief Society organization has been blessed. I endorse the Relief Society without hesitation, for I know it to have been organized by inspiration from Almighty God. It has been blessed since its organization. I know that it is a rising and not a setting sun. I know that the light and the power that emanates from it will increase, not decrease.

I know that the Relief Society today is led by wise and inspired and strong women. Through them the frustrations of the poorly trained, the lonely, the single will give way to security and happiness. The bewilderment of the uninspired and the misled will be replaced with assurance and direction.

After months of prayerful concern over this matter, having inquired of Him whose organization it is, without reservation, without hesitancy, I endorse and applaud the Relief Society of The Church of Jesus Christ of Latter-day Saints and pray God to bless these, our sisters, to strengthen them, for this is His church and we are led by a prophet. (78–06, p. 9)

An endorsement of Relief Society. It is my purpose to give unqualified endorsement to the Relief Society—to encourage all women to join in and attend, and priesthood leaders, at every level of administration, to act so that the Relief Society will flourish.

The Relief Society was organized and named by prophets and apostles who acted under divine inspiration. It has an illustrious history. Always, it has dispensed encouragement and sustenance to those in need. . . . Relief Society inspires women and teaches them how to adorn their lives with those things which women need—things that are "lovely, or of good report or praiseworthy."[4] The First Presidency has urged women to attend "because in the work of the Relief Society are intellectual, cultural, and spiritual values found in no other organization and sufficient for all general needs of its members."[5] (98–03, p. 72)

The Relief Society is the greatest women's organization on this earth. The Relief Society is the greatest women's organization on this earth. And the Young Women's organization is preparatory for it. It is worth fostering.

If you devote yourself to Relief Society you will be guided with inspiration and no issue concerning women will need to be neglected. (79–06)

Sisters, build Relief Society! Sisters, you have a great work to do. Build Relief Society! Strengthen its organization! . . . Do not allow yourselves to be organized under another banner. Do not run to and fro seeking some cause to fulfill your needs. Your cause stands under the authority of the priesthood of Almighty God; that is the consummate, the ultimate power extant upon this earth! (80–09, p. 111)

A strong Relief Society is crucial to the future. Rally to the cause of Relief Society! Strengthen it! Attend it! Devote yourselves to it! Enlist the inactive in it and bring nonmember sisters under the influence of it. It is time now to unite in this worldwide circle of sisters. A strong, well-organized Relief Society is crucial to the future, to the safety of this Church.

We now move cautiously into the darkening mists of the future. We hear the ominous rumbling of the gathering storm. The narrow places of the past have been a preliminary and a preparatory testing. The issue of this dispensation now is revealed before us. It touches the life of every sister. We do not tremble in fear—for you hold in your gentle hands the light of righteousness. It blesses the brethren and nourishes our children. (80–09, p. 111)

The greatest challenge facing the Relief Society. The greatest challenge facing Relief Society in our day is to assist these lovely wives of these hundreds of thousands of men to encourage their husbands, to make a heaven in their homes. Sisters, make the gospel seem worthwhile to him and then let him know that that is your purpose. (78–05, p. 76)

Relief Society blesses men as well as women. Relief Society guides mothers in nurturing their daughters and in cultivating in husbands and sons and brothers courtesy and courage, and, indeed, all virtues essential to worthy manhood. It is quite as much in the interest of the men and boys that Relief Society prosper as in the interest of women and girls. (98–03, p. 72)

The safety of the family is greatly reinforced by Relief Society. However much priesthood power and authority the men may possess—however much wisdom and experience they may accumulate—the safety of the family, the integrity of the doctrine, the ordinances, the covenants, indeed the future of the Church, rests equally upon the women. The defenses of the home and family are greatly reinforced when the wife and mother and daughters belong to Relief Society. (98–03, p. 73)

Eternal blessings will come to the sisters by following the pattern of the priesthood. Relief Society is a great strength to the priesthood. Through it you will share in the privileges and blessings that belong to the priesthood. Indeed, the holders of the priesthood cannot have a fulness without you.

If you sisters follow after that pattern, you will not be preoccupied with the needs of women. You will serve your organization, your cause—the Relief Society—this great circle of sisters. Your every need shall be fulfilled, now, and in the eternities; every neglect will be erased; every abuse will be corrected. All of this can come to you, and come quickly, when you devote yourself to Relief Society. (80–09, p. 110)

Service in Relief Society sanctifies each sister. Service in the Relief Society magnifies and sanctifies each individual sister. Your membership in Relief Society should be ever with you. When you devote yourself to the Relief Society and organize it and operate it and participate in it, you sustain the cause that will bless every woman who comes within its influence. You are organized, I remind you again, after the pattern of and under the authority of the priesthood. (80–09, p. 110)

Relief Society provides "someone to do for." Shortly after the funeral held for the first wife of President Harold B. Lee, I was in a group which included his daughter Helen. Someone expressed sympathy to her for the passing of her mother and said: "She took such good care of your father. I'm sure he must be lonely and must miss all of the things she did for him."

Helen responded with an insight of remarkable wisdom. "You do not understand," she said. "It is not so much that he misses all of the things that Mother did for him. He misses her most because he needs *somebody to do for*."

We all need *someone to do for*. When that is unfulfilled as a need, we become lonely. In the Lord's own way, Relief Society provides for that need. (78–06, pp. 7–8)

Strong Relief Societies carry a powerful influence. Strong Relief Societies carry a powerful immunizing and healing influence for the mothers and the daughters, for the single parent, for the single sisters, for the aging, for the infirm. (98–03, p. 74)

Relief Society is like a refuge. The Relief Society might be likened to a refuge—the place of safety and protection—the sanctuary of ancient times. You will be safe within it. It encircles each sister like a protecting wall. (80–09, p. 110)

Attendance at Relief Society is important. Now to the sisters in the Church I say that attendance at Relief Society, in an important way, is not really optional.

It is as obligatory upon a woman to draw into her life the virtues that are fostered by the Relief Society as it is an obligation for the men to build into their lives the patterns of character fostered by the priesthood. (78–06, p. 8)

Sisters, to me there is something pathetic about those of our sisters who sit at home waiting to be *enticed* to Relief Society. That is not right!

When faithful sisters pray and work and make a worthy presentation, they deserve your support. Just to have you attend is a great help.

Sisters, it is your duty to attend Relief Society, just as it is the duty of the brethren to attend their priesthood meetings. . . . If you are absenting yourself from Relief Society because "you don't get anything out of it," tell me, dear sister, what is it that you are putting into it? (78–06, pp. 8–9)

Relief Society must increase sisterhood. During the study that concluded with the consolidated schedule, my main anxiety, and I expressed it in every discussion, was for the Relief Society. We had the concern that Relief Society might be regarded thereafter as little more than a Sunday class. That fear was not without some foundation, and I want to remind you—particularly you who are officers and teachers— that the Relief Society has very broad responsibilities.

Attendance at the Sunday meeting is but a small part of your duty. Some of you have not understood this and have set aside much of what Relief Society has meant over the years—the sisterhood, the charitable and practical parts of it.

You must gather them in again. You who lead this work must now find ways to bring back and to increase the sisterhood, the fraternal spirit of the Society. You must find ways to strengthen the charitable and the practical dimensions as well. Nothing must distract you from this. (80–09, p. 110)

Women need to feel they belong to Relief Society. The Brethren know they *belong* to a quorum of the priesthood. Too many sisters, however, think that Relief Society is merely a class to attend. The same sense of *belonging* to the Relief Society rather than just attending a class must be fostered in the heart of every woman. Sisters, you must graduate from *thinking* that you only *attend* Relief Society to *feeling* that you *belong* to it! (98–03, p. 73)

Young Women: join with the sisters in Relief Society. The First Presidency recently instructed young women approaching womanhood to join the mothers and grandmothers in Relief Society.[6] Some young women draw away. They would rather be with those their own age. Young women: Do not be so very foolish as to miss this association with the older sisters. They will bring more worth into your life than much of the activity you enjoy so much. (03–05, pp. 82–83)

The Young Women's organization is a preparatory organization. The Aaronic Priesthood is called the preparatory priesthood because the activities of it prepare young men for the day when they will hold the Melchizedek Priesthood, when they will move into their responsibilities as husbands, as fathers, and as leaders in the Church.

In a similar way, the Young Women's organization is a preparatory organization so that girls, as they move through young womanhood, will be prepared for membership in the Relief Society, prepared to be wives and mothers, and to be leaders and teachers in the organizations of the Church. (79–06)

CHAPTER 20

Priesthood and Its Exercise

"The priesthood . . . is not ours to change or modify; . . .
it is ours to honor [and] magnify." (89–02, p. 170)

PRIESTHOOD IN THE CHURCH

What is the priesthood? Priesthood is the authority and the power which God has granted to men on earth to act for Him.[1] When we exercise priesthood authority properly, we do what He would do if He were present. (92–04, p. 148)

What it means to hold the priesthood. We who hold the priesthood of God are joined together by a sacred bond. We often speak of "holding" the priesthood. The word *hold* is most often used in connection with things that we can pick up and set down and then pick up again. We may, if we are not properly taught, come to think of the priesthood in that way. The priesthood is not like that. It is an authority and a power that is a part of us.

We did not possess it when we came into mortality. But, if we honor it, we will keep it when we leave. We can hold it and at once share it with our wives. We can use the power of it to bless and nourish and protect our children. It is our duty to bless all of mankind. (83–02, pp. 53–54)

The oath and covenant of the priesthood. There is an oath and covenant of the priesthood. The covenant rests with man, the oath with God. The Melchizedek Priesthood is received by covenant. A man's covenant with God is to be faithful and magnify his callings in the priesthood, to give heed to the words of eternal life, and to live by every word that proceedeth forth from the mouth of God.[2]

God, for His part, declares with an everlasting oath that all who receive the priesthood and obey the covenants that pertain to that priesthood shall receive "all that [the] Father hath. And this is according to the oath and covenant which belongeth to the priesthood. Therefore, all those who receive the priesthood, receive this oath and covenant of my Father, which he cannot break, neither can it be moved."[3] (92–04, p. 153)

Priesthood holders act for the Lord. When we officiate in the priesthood, we always do it in the name of the Lord.[4] When we act according to the proper order of things, we act for the Lord, and it is as though He were there insofar as the validity of the ordinance is concerned. The Lord said to one man who was being set apart to preach the gospel: "I will lay my hand upon you *by the hand of my servant Sidney Rigdon,* and you shall receive my Spirit, the Holy Ghost, even the Comforter, which shall teach you the peaceable things of the kingdom."[5] (92–04, p. 159)

The priesthood is not ours to modify but to magnify. The priesthood, once defined as the authority given to man to act in the name of God, is not ours to remodel or change or modify or abridge. It is ours to honor as we magnify our callings. (89–02, p. 170)

Priesthood is conferred only on males. From the beginning the priesthood has been conferred only upon males. It is always described in the scriptures as coming through the lineage of the fathers.[6] (89–02, p. 170)

Priesthood is the cause for men and boys in the Church. When the priesthood is organized and functions as it should, the worthy aspirations of all who have part in it are satisfied. Through the priesthood men can be trained in the proper relationship with all sisters—their wives and daughters and mothers. Priesthood is the cause for men and boys in the Church. (80–09, p. 110)

We truly are "a kingdom of priests." Can you possibly imagine what it would be like to manage the Church today if we had to look for and hire ministers or pastors and then train them professionally and then provide them with a salary, regardless of how devout they might be? Can you see how difficult that would be in this very unsettled world?

In approximately 170 countries and 180 languages there is no need for that because the gospel was restored and the authority given, and we truly are "a kingdom of priests." Can anyone doubt that the Church was restored and that it is guided today by revelation both to leaders and to all of the members?

Do you men and boys understand how important you are to the work of the Lord? We are, all of us, just ordinary men. But having been given power by the priesthood, we have the commission to carry this work to every nation, kindred, tongue, and people.[7]

This sacred authority is placed in our keeping. It is conferred upon us by ordination, and offices are received by setting apart. It continues from our Prophet-President to you and to me. And because of the design that has been revealed, it can bless the lives of every individual who, when brought to a knowledge of it, can conform his life to the requirements of worthiness. (04–04)

One who holds the priesthood should conduct himself as such. When we hold the priesthood, we ought to act like it—not just in priesthood meeting, but all day every day and all night every night, not just the stake president and the high priest, but every holder of the priesthood—the deacon, the teacher, and the priest, the elder, the high priest, the bishop, the patriarch, indeed the apostles, all of us. (76–05)

Priesthood holders should be dependable. If we hold the priesthood, we ought to be dependable. That is just another way of being obedient. Now I'm sure sometimes we think, "Well, if I was given some great, marvelous thing to do, then I'd be obedient." But it all begins with the little things—doing our priesthood home teaching, attending our meetings, holding our family home evenings, paying our tithing, keeping the records. Whatever it is we are called to do, we must be dependable and we must do it. Our young men should learn in their youth to be dependable. Remember the assignment comes from the Lord; it is delivered through His servants. If we hold the priesthood (and we do) we ought to act like it. (76–05)

Priesthood holders treat their wives with respect. Surely there isn't a man here who holds the priesthood who would be brutal or unkind in any way to his wife, who would be oppressive in any way to the mother of his children, who would show anything but love and respect and affection. Surely every pattern of their relationship would be worthy and moral. You know it is possible to be immoral in our marriage relationships, but surely no holder of the priesthood would be guilty of that. (76–05)

The priesthood is not divisible. The priesthood is greater than any of its offices. When someone first receives the Aaronic or the Melchizedek Priesthood, it is conferred upon him by the laying on of hands. After the priesthood has been conferred upon him, he is ordained to an office in the priesthood. All offices derive their authority from the priesthood.

The priesthood is not divisible. An elder holds as much priesthood as an Apostle.[8] When a man receives the priesthood, he receives all of it. However, there are offices within the priesthood—divisions of authority and responsibility. A man may exercise his priesthood according to the rights of the office to which he is ordained or set apart. (92–04, p. 150)

There are limits to priesthood authority. Ordinarily the privileges connected with an ordination to the priesthood may be exercised anywhere in the Church. Priesthood holders need no prior authorization to perform ordinances or blessings that are not recorded on the records of the Church, such as consecrating oil, administering to the sick, and giving fathers' blessings.

The priesthood is always regulated by those who have the keys, and an ordinance must be authorized by the presiding authority who holds the proper keys and priesthood if the ordinance is to be recorded on the records of the Church.

Authority connected to an office to which one is set apart has limits, including geographic ones. The authority of a man set apart as president of a stake is limited to the boundaries of that stake. He is not a stake president to members in a neighboring stake, nor is a bishop the bishop over members outside his ward. When a man is ordained a bishop, he is also set apart to preside in a specific ward and has no authority outside its boundaries. When he is released as bishop of that ward he may still hold the ordained office of bishop, but he cannot function as such unless he is set apart again to preside over a ward. When a patriarch is ordained, he is set apart to give blessings to members of his own stake or to those who come into the boundaries of his stake with a recommend from proper authority from a stake where there is no patriarch. These principles of priesthood government are established by revelations. (92–04, p. 154)

The practice of delegating authority, and at once limiting it, is so commonly demonstrated in business and education, in government, in cultural organizations, that we should not have difficulty in understanding that principle in the Church.

A missionary is given authority to teach and to baptize. Given certain approval, he can ordain someone to a priesthood office. If he is an elder, however, he cannot ordain someone to be a high priest, for his authority is limited. . . . Those who hold the Melchizedek Priesthood can perform the ordinances relating to the higher priesthood.

But unless they are given special authorization they cannot endow, nor seal, nor perform those ordinances that pertain to the temple. There are limits. (*THT,* pp. 150–51)

The priesthood is always conferred by ordination. Do not miss that one simple, obvious absolute: The priesthood ever and always is conferred by ordination by one who holds proper authority, and it is known to the Church that he has it. And even when the priesthood has been conferred, an individual has no authority beyond that which belongs to the specific office to which one has been ordained. Those limits apply as well to an office to which one is set apart. Unauthorized ordinations or settings apart convey nothing, neither power nor authority of the priesthood. (93–01, p. 20)

There is order in ordinations and settings apart. To participate in an ordination, one must have equal or higher priesthood authority than is to be given in the ordinance. For instance, an elder should not stand in the circle where a high priest is ordained or a man is set apart to an office requiring him to be a high priest. Only presiding authorities can set apart presidents with keys. (03–07, p. 3)

Ordinations and settings apart must be under the direction of presiding authorities. All ordinations and settings apart must be by or under the direction of the presiding authorities. The priesthood can only be conferred by one who has priesthood authority and is authorized by one who holds the appropriate keys.

An ordination to an office in the priesthood is permanent and follows one ordained wherever he goes. Except for transgression, he is never released.

One set apart will eventually be released by the same authority by which he was called. (03–07, p. 2)

POWER IN THE PRIESTHOOD

The unseen power of the priesthood can be felt. I want to tell you about the unseen power of the Aaronic Priesthood. A boy of twelve is old enough to learn about it. As you mature you should become very familiar with this guiding, protecting power.

Some think that unless a power is visible it cannot be real. I think I can convince you otherwise. Do you remember when you foolishly put your finger in that light socket? While you did not see exactly what happened, surely you felt it!

No one has ever seen electricity, not even a scientist with the finest instruments. However, like you they have felt it. And we can see the results of it. We can measure it, control it, and produce light, and heat, and power. No one questions that it is real simply because he cannot see it.

Although you cannot see the power of the priesthood, you can *feel* it, and you can see the results of it. The priesthood can be a guiding and protecting power in your life. (81–08, p. 30)

Priesthood power comes only through obedience and worthiness. I have told you how the *authority* is given to you. The *power* you receive will depend on what you do with this sacred, unseen gift.

Your authority comes through your ordination; your power comes through obedience and worthiness. . . .

Power in the priesthood comes from doing your duty in ordinary things: attending meetings, accepting assignments, reading the scriptures, keeping the Word of Wisdom. (81–08, p. 32)

Worthiness is essential to have power in the priesthood. How crucial it is that we be worthy. Each must be absolutely faithful to his wife. Any attraction outside of marriage, however innocent, may be influenced by the adversary and lead straight to the bull's-eye of disaster.

Carefully observe the Word of Wisdom, that your body and your mind may be the instrument for revelation that is required in these ordinances.

If there is anything that is unworthy about you, if you have pictures or films or printed materials at home or at work that are unworthy, destroy them so that there will be no evil influence surrounding you.

If you have made a misstep so serious that it should have been confessed, and it was not, seek for the healing balm of confession and repentance and forgiveness.

It is in this manner that ordinary men exercise the authority and the power of the "priesthood . . . after the holiest order of God."[9] (03–07, pp. 3–4)

The measure of our authority depends on God. In The Church of Jesus Christ of Latter-day Saints there is no paid ministry, no professional clergy, as is common in other churches. More significant even than this is that there is no laity, no lay membership as such; men are eligible to hold the priesthood and to carry on the ministry of the Church, and both men and women serve in many auxiliary capacities. This responsibility comes to men in all walks of life, and with this responsibility also comes the authority. There are many who would deny, and others who would disregard it; nevertheless, the measure of that authority does not depend on whether men sustain that authority, but rather depends on whether God will recognize and honor that authority. (65–01, p. 237)

AARONIC AND MELCHIZEDEK PRIESTHOOD

The importance of quorums. In the dispensation of the fulness of times the Lord has instructed that priesthood bearers should be organized into quorums, meaning selected assemblies of brethren given authority so that His business might be transacted and His work proceed.

A quorum is a brotherhood. Except for the offices of bishop and patriarch, those ordained to offices in the priesthood are organized into quorums.

Though one may be called to and released from ecclesiastical assignments for which one is set apart, membership in a quorum is a steady, sustaining citizenship. It becomes a right of one ordained to an office in the priesthood. And the holding of the priesthood, including the attendant membership in the quorum, is to be regarded as a sacred privilege. (92–04, p. 152)

Priesthood quorum membership. Quorum membership is not optional. You may not be ordained to an office in the priesthood and yet choose not to belong to a quorum. You maintain your membership in that quorum until you are ordained to another office in the priesthood. Automatically you then become a member of another quorum. . . .

You may be called to and released from assignments. Your membership in your quorum is a steady, sustaining citizenship that becomes your right as a holder of the priesthood. The holding of the priesthood, including the attendant membership in the quorum, ought to be regarded as a sacred privilege. . . .

You ought to energetically determine to maintain your standards in order to be worthy of such membership. You should regard the priesthood you hold, from which all other offices and authorities must draw their power, as having preference and priority in your feelings and your attentions.

A man who becomes inactive does not lose his membership in the quorum. He may lose interest in the quorum, but the quorum must never lose interest in him. The quorum is responsible always and continually for each of its members. We are not to ignore an inactive member, or withdraw interest in and contact with him. . . .

You are a member of a priesthood quorum. By your actions you either sustain or degrade it. When his priesthood quorum functions properly, a man sustained by the brethren of his quorum almost could not fail in any phase of life's responsibility. (78–07)

What is the Aaronic Priesthood? Let me teach you some very basic things about the Aaronic Priesthood.

It "is called the Priesthood of Aaron, because it was conferred upon Aaron and his seed, throughout all their generations."[10]

The Aaronic Priesthood goes by other names as well. Let me list them and tell you what they mean.

First, the Aaronic Priesthood is sometimes called the lesser priesthood.

"Why it is called the lesser priesthood is because it is an appendage to the greater, or the Melchizedek Priesthood, and has power in administering outward ordinances."[11]

This means that the higher priesthood, the Melchizedek Priesthood, always presides over the Aaronic, or the lesser, Priesthood. . . .

The fact that it is called the lesser priesthood does not diminish at all the importance of the Aaronic Priesthood. . . .

The Aaronic Priesthood is also called the Levitical Priesthood. The word *Levitical* comes from the name Levi, one of the twelve sons of Israel. Moses and Aaron, who were brothers, were Levites.

When the Aaronic Priesthood was given to Israel, Aaron and his sons received the *presiding* and administrative responsibility. The male members of all other Levite families were put in charge of the ceremonies of the tabernacle, including the Mosaic law of sacrifice. . . .

Finally, the Aaronic Priesthood is referred to as the preparatory priesthood. This, too, is a proper title because the Aaronic Priesthood prepares young men to hold the higher priesthood, for missions, and for temple marriage. . . .

You would do well to watch your fathers and your leaders, to study how the Melchizedek Priesthood works. You are preparing to join the elders, high priests, and patriarchs and to serve as missionaries, quorum leaders, bishoprics, stake leaders, and as fathers of families.

A few of you who now sit there as deacons, teachers, and priests will one day sit here as Apostles and prophets and will preside over the Church. *You must be prepared.*

It is indeed correct to call the Aaronic Priesthood the preparatory priesthood. (81–08, pp. 30–31)

The Aaronic Priesthood is the preparatory priesthood. The Aaronic Priesthood . . . is the preparatory priesthood. It is the lesser priesthood. Preparatory for what? It is to prepare young men to hold the Melchizedek Priesthood. It is to prepare young men for life. It is to train them to be leaders. It is to train them in obedience. It is to train them to get control of things that are bigger than they are. It is to show them how to use more than their muscles. (78–11, pp. 42–43)

The Aaronic Priesthood is a sacred authority. You young men who hold the Aaronic Priesthood, you who are deacons, teachers, and priests, do not discount the authority that you have as . . . a holder of the Aaronic Priesthood. It is a sacred authority. (07–05)

Higher priesthood offices retain the authority of the lower offices. You always hold one of these [Aaronic Priesthood] offices. When you receive the next higher office, you still retain the authority of the first. For instance, when you become a priest, you still have authority to do all that you did as a deacon and teacher. Even when you receive the higher priesthood, you keep all of the authority of, and, with proper authorization, can act in the offices of, the lesser priesthood. (81–08, p. 31)

The Melchizedek or higher priesthood. There are in the Church two priesthoods, namely the Melchizedek and Aaronic, including the Levitical Priesthood. The first is called the Melchizedek Priesthood because Melchizedek was such a great high priest. "Before his day it was called *the Holy Priesthood, after the Order of the Son of God.*"[12]

The Melchizedek Priesthood is also spoken of in the scriptures as the "greater priesthood" or the priesthood "which is after the holiest order of God"[13] and the priesthood "after the order of mine Only Begotten Son."[14]

"Out of respect or reverence to the name of the Supreme Being, to avoid the too frequent repetition of his name, they, the church, in ancient days, called that priesthood after Melchizedek, or the Melchizedek Priesthood."[15] We can understand why that should be. The name of the priesthood is frequently mentioned in meetings and lessons and is printed in handbooks and manuals. It would be irreverent to use informally the sacred title which includes the name of Deity. (92–04, p. 148)

The patriarchal order is part of the Melchizedek Priesthood. There are references to a patriarchal priesthood. The patriarchal order is not a third, separate priesthood.[16] Whatever relates to the patriarchal order is embraced in the Melchizedek Priesthood. "All other authorities

At the General Relief Society Conference, October 3, 1973.
Seated to Elder Packer's right are the Relief Society General Presidency:
Belle S. Spafford, Marianne C. Sharp, and Louise W. Madsen.

or offices in the church are appendages to [the Melchizedek] priest-hood."[17] The patriarchal order is a part of the Melchizedek Priesthood that enables endowed and worthy men to preside over their posterity in time and eternity. (92–04, p. 149)

HOME TEACHING AND REACTIVATION

Home teaching is very important. The leaders of the Church expend great effort to see that priesthood home teaching works. Though it is much taken for granted, it is always provided for and always will be. The principles of it have never changed, not with chang-ing society or the various additions to programming in the Church. Without it the Church could very quickly cease to be the Church. And I say again, though some activities may be more inviting, none is more important. (72–05, p. 89)

Home teaching provides a watch-care. Home teaching, strangely enough, is taken so much for granted that most members pay little attention to it, participating routinely, sometimes almost with annoy-ance. Through it, nevertheless, there come to members of the Church a protection and a watch-care not known elsewhere. (72–05, p. 89)

Effective home teaching is twice a blessing. To you who are home teachers—you who perform the routine visit, not infrequently consid-ered a drudgery—do not take the assignment lightly or pass it off as being routine. Every hour you spend in it and every step you take in it and every door you knock upon, every home you greet, every encour-agement you give, is twice a blessing.

It is an interesting truth that the home teachers are often taught in the course of their visits to the family. In fact, it is often a question, even in a moment of sacrifice and service by a priesthood home teacher, who benefits the most—the family he serves or the home teacher. (72–05, p. 89)

Only a home teacher. There is a spiritual genius in priesthood home teaching. Every priesthood holder who goes forth under this assignment can come away repaid a thousand fold.

I have heard men say in response to a question about their Church assignment, "I am only a home teacher."

Only a home teacher. Only the guardian of a flock. Only the one appointed where the ministry matters most. Only a servant of the Lord!

It is because of you, the priesthood home teacher, that a verse of the hymn stands true:

> *Beneath his watchful eye,*
> *His saints securely dwell;*
> *That hand which bears all nature up*
> *Shall guard his children well.*[18] (72–05, p. 90)

Testimony is the moving power. Testimony, then, is the moving power. Testimony is the redeeming force.

Programs will redeem only to the degree that they produce testimony. Elaborate programming will not hurt us if the Spirit is there, nor help us if it is not. To send priesthood home teachers to the lost sheep as a program is not enough. They must go in the spirit of testimony. (69–03, p. 15)

Home teaching strengthens the youth. I say to our bishops, you might as well try to raise up an athlete on a diet of chocolate bars and soda pop as to attempt to sustain your youth with activity programs only. They may be drawn to them, but they will not be much nourished by them. No effort to redeem your youth can be more productive than the time and attention given to priesthood home teaching. For the object of priesthood home teaching is to strengthen the home, and as the teenager would say, and he usually knows, "That is where it is all at." (72–05, p. 89)

Through home teaching comes a sustaining power. There can pour through this channel of priesthood home teaching a sustaining power to the limits of the resources of the Church on this earth. This is not all. There can flow through this channel a redeeming spiritual power to the limits of heaven itself.

Through home teaching, tragedies have been averted. Sinking souls have been lifted. Material need has been provided. Grief has been assuaged. The infirm have been healed through administration. While the work goes on without being heralded, it is inspired of Almighty God and is basic to the spiritual nourishment of this people. (72–05, p. 89)

A blessing of having home and visiting teachers. In February [1973] I was in England. They were in the throes of a great nationwide strike and all the fuel had been turned off. It was winter and cold, and the radio announcements concluded generally with an appeal. They were appealing to the postmen, the letter-carriers, and the delivery boys to look in on the aged or the infirm. The government was concerned about many of the people there because they would be alone and without heat, perhaps in great need, with no one to look after them.

I thought how fortunate it is, how marvelous it is, that members in the Church have the priesthood home teachers, and they have the visiting teachers who can go about "according to their natures" and they can render the help that is necessary and desirable. (73–08)

The challenge in helping the spiritually malnourished. The *Deseret News* of 10 July 1956 printed a bulletin from the LDS Hospital on the condition of an eighteen-year-old girl who had been brought to the hospital six days earlier having survived nine days pinned under a car in Parley's Canyon, near Salt Lake City. The bulletin was, for a change, optimistic: "Attending physicians at the LDS Hospital said the girl's blood condition is so improved she likely will need no more transfusions. . . . Doctors said her diet has been increased to include potatoes, eggs, and puddings. She no longer requires intravenous feedings."

The injuries she had sustained in the accident were not of themselves the important factor. It was the lack of food and moisture that reduced her body to that poor condition. It was several days before the doctors gave much hope for her recovery.

It isn't easy to minister to one so starved. It was not a matter of just putting food before her. The food had to be carefully administered, for delicate balances could be upset, and her life was at stake. Doctors were extremely careful, for their very treatment might prove fatal. When she recovered, that was regarded as something of a miracle.

So it is with those around us who are spiritually undernourished, or starved. We refer to them as the lost sheep. We are called to minister to them. They are of all descriptions. Some have deficiencies of one kind or another that merely rob them of spiritual vigor. Others have so seriously starved themselves of spiritual things that we scarce can hope to save them.

Responsibility for redemption of the lost sheep rests with the priesthood. The doing of it rests upon the home teacher. He is the priesthood representative charged with the responsibility to see that every member of the Church is properly nourished spiritually and does not suffer physical want. He it is who must see that the parents in the home are aware of the need to provide adequate spiritual sustenance for their children. And he is the one who can relate all Church agencies to the home, calling for just the right blend of spiritual nourishment to sustain those who are well and heal those who are undernourished.

We wonder why home teaching is not more successful than it is. Members who have been instructed often enough, and ought to *know,* still are listed among the lost sheep. If we are to redeem them we must know what kind of nourishment to administer, and when, and in what amounts. It is not a matter of just putting it before them. (69–03, pp. 12–13)

A promise to the less active who will return. If you will return to the environment where spiritual truths are spoken, there will flood back into your minds the things that you thought were lost. Things smothered under many years of disuse and inactivity will emerge. Your ability to understand them will be quickened.

That word *quickened* is much used in the scriptures, you know.

If you will make your pilgrimage back among the Saints, soon you will be understanding once again the language of inspiration. And more quickly than you know, it will seem that you have never been away. Oh, how important it is for you to realize that if you will return, it can be made as though you have never been away. (75–03, p. 105)

PRIESTHOOD KEYS

The keys of the priesthood. There are keys of the priesthood. While the word *key* has other meanings, like keys of wisdom or keys of knowledge, the keys of the priesthood are the right to preside and direct the affairs of the Church within a jurisdiction. All priesthood keys are within The Church of Jesus Christ of Latter-day Saints, and none exist outside the Church on earth. (92–04, p. 149)

Who holds the keys of the kingdom? The keys of the kingdom are held by the Prophet, Seer, and Revelator. Only one man at any given time can exercise all of the keys. The keys are conferred upon every man that is ordained an Apostle and set apart as a member of the Quorum of the Twelve Apostles. Now there have been men ordained Apostles who were not in the Quorum of the Twelve a number of times during the history of the Church. Unless you are sustained in the Quorum of the Twelve, you are not given the keys of the kingdom. The Seventies have an apostolic authority, but they do not hold the keys. When the President of the Church passes away, then the presidency is dissolved and the counselors take their place in the quorum to which they belong. . . .

Someone asked President [Marion G.] Romney once, "Does the senior Apostle, the president of the Twelve, always become the President of the Church, or could someone else be sustained as President of the Church?"

Brother Romney said, "The answer is yes to both questions!" He said, "If the Lord wants someone else, he sees that he is the senior Apostle at the proper time." (91–08)

The prophet holds the keys of the priesthood. In 1976 following a conference in Copenhagen, Denmark, President Spencer W. Kimball invited us to a small church to see the statues of Christ and the Twelve Apostles by Bertel Thorvaldsen. The "Christus" stands in an alcove beyond the altar. Standing in order along the sides of the chapel are the statues of the Twelve, with Paul replacing Judas Iscariot.

President Kimball told the elderly caretaker that at the very time Thorvaldsen was creating those beautiful statues in Denmark, a restoration of the gospel of Jesus Christ was taking place in America with apostles and prophets receiving authority from those who held it anciently.

Gathering those present closer to him, he said to the caretaker, "We are living Apostles of the Lord Jesus Christ," and pointing to Elder Pinegar he said, "Here is a Seventy like those spoken of in the New Testament."

We were standing near the statue of Peter, whom the sculptor depicted holding keys in his hand, symbolic of the keys of the kingdom. President Kimball said, "We hold the real keys, as Peter did, and we use them every day."

Then came an experience I will never forget. President Kimball, this gentle prophet, turned to President Johan H. Benthin, of the Copenhagen Stake, and in a commanding voice said, "I want you to tell every prelate in Denmark that they do NOT hold the keys! I HOLD THE KEYS!"

There came to me that witness known to Latter-day Saints but difficult to describe to one who has not experienced it—a light, a power coursing through one's very soul—and I knew that, in very fact, here stood the living prophet who held the keys. (95–05, p. 8)

All essential priesthood keys rest with the First Presidency. All the priesthood keys essential to salvation and exaltation were conferred by heavenly authority upon the Prophet Joseph Smith. That authority is now reposed in the current First Presidency of the Church. And authority is delegated to priesthood leaders across the world. (03–01)

I heard President Kimball say on one occasion, as other Presidents of the Church have said, that, while he holds all of the keys that are held upon the earth, there are keys that he does not hold. There are keys that have not been given to him as President of the Church, because they are reserved to higher power and authority. For instance, he said that he does not hold the keys of the resurrection. The Lord holds them, but He has not delegated them—neither anciently, nor to modern prophets. (*THT,* p. 151)

The Twelve hold all the keys individually and collectively. Individually and collectively the Twelve hold the keys and have confirmed the authority to exercise all of the keys upon the senior Apostle, the one man who is to preside over the Church.

The Lord has provided a system in which there is no aspiring, no maneuvering for position or power, not even a hint of soliciting for votes or cultivating influence. The system does not allow it, neither would the Lord permit it. It does not work the way man usually works, and so it should be. The Lord reminded the prophet Isaiah, "My ways [are] higher than your ways, and my thoughts than your thoughts."[19] (95–05, p. 7)

Apostles receive all the keys. All men who are ordained Apostles and sustained as members of the Quorum of the Twelve Apostles have all the revealed priesthood keys conferred upon them.[20]

The President of the Church is the only person on earth who has the right to exercise all the keys in their fulness.[21] He receives that authority by being set apart by the Twelve Apostles. (92–04, p. 150)

What are the keys of the sealing power? The word *key* is symbolic. The word *sealing* is symbolic. Both represent, I repeat, the consummate authority on this earth for man to act in the name of God.

I have found that many members of the Church have a very limited view of what the sealing power is. Since it is used most frequently in connection with temple marriages, the *word* seal has come to mean, in the minds of many Church members, simply that—sealing two people in the eternal marriage bond. It is also used to designate the ordinance by which children who have not been born in the covenant are "sealed" to their parents. Other members of the Church have the idea that the sealing authority that Elijah brought had to do solely with baptism for the dead.

The authority is much more inclusive than that. The keys of the sealing power are synonymous with the keys of the everlasting priesthood. (*THT*, p. 84)

Nothing is regarded more sacred than the keys of the sealing power. The keys of the sealing power are synonymous with the keys of the everlasting priesthood [reads Matthew 16:13–19]. Peter was to hold the keys. Peter was to hold the sealing power, that authority which carried the power to bind or seal on earth or to loose on earth and it would be so in the heavens. Those keys belong to the President of the Church—to the prophet, seer, and revelator. That sacred sealing power is with the Church now. Nothing is regarded with more sacred contemplation by those who know the significance of this authority. Nothing is more closely held. There are relatively few men who have been delegated this sealing power upon the earth at any given time—in each temple are brethren who have been given the sealing power. (95–02, pp. 148–49)

No authorization transcends the sealing power. Thirteen years after Moroni appeared, a temple had been built adequate for the purpose, and the Lord again appeared and Elijah came with Him and bestowed the keys of the sealing power. Thereafter ordinances were not tentative but permanent. The sealing power was with us. No authorization transcends it in value. That power gives substance and eternal permanence to all ordinances performed with proper authority for both the living and the dead. (80–03, p. 192)

The sealing power is the consummate gift from God. In the Church we hold sufficient authority to perform all of the ordinances necessary to redeem and to exalt the whole human family. And, because we have the keys to the sealing power, what we bind in proper order here will be bound in heaven. Those keys—the keys to seal and bind on earth, and have it bound in heaven—represent the consummate gift from our God. With that authority we can baptize and bless, we can endow and seal, and the Lord will honor our commitments. (95–02, p. 150)

Priesthood authority comes only through authorized channels. You can receive the priesthood only from one who has the authority and "it is known to the church that he has authority."[22]

The priesthood cannot be conferred like a diploma. It cannot be handed to you as a certificate. It cannot be delivered to you as a message or sent to you in a letter. It comes only by proper ordination. An authorized holder of the priesthood has to be there. He must place his hands upon your head and ordain you.

That is one reason why the General Authorities travel so much—to convey the keys of priesthood authority. Every stake president everywhere in the world has received his authority under the hands of one of the presiding brethren of the Church. There has never been one exception.

Remember these things. The priesthood is very, very precious to the Lord. He is very careful about how it is conferred, and by whom. It is never done in secret. (81–08, p. 32)

We now have means by which we can teach and testify to leaders and members all over the world electronically. But in order to confer the keys of authority in that unbroken line upon the priesthood leaders, "by the laying on of hands," wherever they are in the world, one of us must be there every time. (08–09, p. 86)

The Church is a marvelous system. There is one thing that you cannot do for yourselves, and that is you cannot give yourselves the keys. We hold the keys, and we delegate the giving of those keys to the members of the quorums of Seventy, and they can come out and organize a stake, acting under the authority of our keys and the keys the President of the Church holds. They can call a new stake president, and if he needs to be a high priest, they can ordain him. He probably was ordained a high priest earlier by one of the leaders of the stake. Then the Seventy can set him apart as a stake president and can confer upon him the keys of the presidency.

This is a marvelous, marvelous system, because the Church cannot be destroyed now. There are too many places in well over 100 countries where we have congregations. We have not just tens of thousands but millions of men who hold the priesthood. Man could not have invented the Church. It is beyond the thought of mankind to have invented anything so marvelous, so supernal with the patterns of administration and the gospel of Jesus Christ. (06–01)

CHAPTER 21

Leadership and Following
the Brethren

*"Follow the Brethren. Three words. There is nothing in your life that will
destroy you if you will follow the Brethren." (68–04, pp. 79–80)*

EFFECTIVE LEADERSHIP

Qualities of a successful priesthood leader. There are qualities
which determine how successful a priesthood leader is going to be. I'd
like to list twelve of them, just briefly. You will succeed if these things
are in order:

1. What you feel—the strength of your testimony.
2. What you know—your knowledge of the gospel and
   the scriptures.
3. What you are—your personal qualities and your values.
4. What you do—your conduct and example.
5. How you inspire—your spirituality.
6. How you teach—your natural or your acquired skills.
7. What you foster—the use of manuals, proper Church
   music.

8. How you lead—your organizational structure.

9. How you train and manage the programs.

10. How you conform to policies and guidelines, to handbooks and procedures.

11. How you manage your budgeting and expenses.

12. How you provide materials, buildings, facilities, etc. (85–06)

The important things cannot be measured on reports. Unfortunately, we tend to center our efforts on things that can be written on reports. We do not, and should not, and will not require the most important things to be put on reports.

We cannot count faith, nor repentance, nor should we try to compute prayer, nor tabulate love. These are spiritual things that do not lend themselves to numbers and percentages.

But even these things can be measured. They lend themselves to spiritual assessment, in interviews, through meditation and prayer. They may be appraised by employing the powers of discernment, a precious spiritual gift which accompanies our callings.

Do not become so preoccupied with reports and procedures and programs and buildings that you neglect this part of your ministry. (82–02)

Focus on the things you cannot measure. If you can't focus on the things you can't count, you won't affect the things you can count. (08–02)

Good decisions lead toward making and keeping covenants. A good and useful and true test of every major decision made by a leader in the Church is whether a given course leads toward or away from the making and keeping of covenants. Centering your mind on ordinances and covenants gives purpose to all the many things we do in preaching the gospel and perfecting the Saints. (87–04)

Don't neglect the spiritual things. Do not forget discernment, inspiration, admonition, correction, and forgiveness.

Brethren, do not neglect the priesthood, the covenants, the ordinances, the scriptures.

Put them on your agendas, discuss them. (82–02)

You learn how to govern His Church from the scriptures. Now, these are very troubled times. In order that you will not drift, you must know the source of your authority and your power. You must measure everything you learn about your ordination and calling against fundamental truths. It is from the scriptures that you learn how to govern His Church. (03–01)

Every leader must understand the gospel. It is so important that every member, particularly every leader, understands and knows the gospel.

It is not easy to find time to study the gospel. It is harder for the stake president to do it and infinitely harder for the bishop to do it, but it is necessary and it is possible. Brethren must attend the classes as often as they can; bishops and stake presidents should find some way to attend at least a good share of the Gospel Doctrine classes and the appropriate priesthood quorum lessons. (84–03, pp. 68–69)

Priesthood leaders must give necessary correction. When a man in a leadership position resists giving counsel or necessary correction, he is thinking of himself. (08–02)

Church leaders are teachers first and foremost. The General Authorities are teachers. Stake presidents and mission presidents are teachers; high councilors and quorum presidents are teachers; bishops are teachers; and so through all of the organizations of the Church.

The Church moves forward sustained by the power of the teaching that is accomplished. (*TYD*, pp. 3–4)

Leaders have a responsibility to teach. Leaders have a responsibility to teach, whether they are in councils or interviews or worship services. They also have a responsibility to ensure that teacher development and effective gospel learning are ongoing in the lives of members. (07–03)

FOLLOWING CHURCH LEADERS

Follow the Brethren and be safe. On one occasion Karl G. Maeser was going with a group of young missionaries across the Alps. They were crossing a high mountain pass on foot. There were long sticks stuck into the snow of the glacier to mark the path so that travelers could find their way safely across the glacier and down the mountain on the other side.

When they reached the summit, Brother Maeser wanted to teach the young elders a lesson. He stopped at the pinnacle of the mountain and pointed to those sticks that they had followed. And he said, "Brethren, behold the priesthood of God. They are just common old sticks, but it's the position that counts. Follow them and you will surely be safe. Stray from them and you will surely be lost." And so it is in the Church. We are called to leadership positions and given the power of the priesthood. And we are just common old sticks, but the position we are given counts. (76–08, p. 51)

There is safety in following the counsel of leaders. Protection is embodied in that very unpopular word (particularly when we are young): *obedience!* We need to understand the order of the priesthood and the safety in following the counsel of priesthood leaders. (87–01, p. 104)

Why do we listen to the Brethren? When the council meetings [of the First Presidency and the Twelve] come in the middle of the week, we find the Brethren here again. They sit in council to prayerfully deliberate over the affairs of the Church and kingdom of God here upon the earth.

Traveling as they do across the earth (literally, the full extent of it), it is hardly conceivable that they could miss or would ignore any significant development—social, political, religious, national, or racial—

anywhere on the earth. Also, they have lifelong training and achievement in fields of activity so important to mankind.

However, it is not because of travel or professional success that we ought to pay heed to them. Nor is it because they are nimble of mind or wise in years. These things are incidental only.

We listen to them because they have been "called of God, by prophecy, and by the laying on of hands, by those who are in authority to preach the gospel and administer in the ordinances thereof."[1]

They are given divine authority. Not one of them aspired to the office he holds, nor did he call himself, for "in The Church of Jesus Christ of Latter-day Saints, one takes the place to which one is duly called," said President J. Reuben Clark, "which place one neither seeks or declines."[2] (68–07, p. 80)

It is the position that counts. In our home, we don't talk about the bishop. We talk about the *bishop*. We don't just have a bishop. We have a *bishop*. And we have *home teachers*. And we have a *stake president*. And in this Church we have a *prophet*. And it's the position that counts. And the power and the authority go together.

God grant that we who hold the priesthood will be obedient and sustain all those who are called to preside over us. (76–08, p. 52)

The mantle of priesthood authority. While the men who preside over you in the wards and stakes of the Church may seem like very ordinary men, there is something extraordinary about them. It is the mantle of priesthood authority and the inspiration of the call which they have answered. (65–01, p. 240)

We must learn to instantly heed warnings from those who guide us. When the Teton Dam collapsed and unleashed seventeen miles of backed-up water and accumulated debris upon the towns and farms beneath it, only eleven of nearly thirty-five thousand people in the path of the flood died. Why? Because they were warned; and more importantly, because they heeded the warning *instantly.* The result—a miracle of tremendous proportions made up of a myriad of small miracles.

What is happening in the world is much like a flood. A great wave of evil and wickedness has been loosed. It seeps around us and gets deeper and deeper. Our lives are in danger. Our property is in danger. Our freedoms are in danger.

We, too, have been warned. It seems almost against our natures to accept warning or guidance from others. There are, however, times when, regardless of how much we know, our very existence depends upon paying attention to those who guide us. (*ABE,* p. 203)

The Lord is with us when we sustain our leaders. When Moses led the children of Israel in Egypt, they sojourned out in the desert. . . . Word came that the Amalekite robbers were gathering their forces to conquer the Israelites. They were a terrible people and would sell the Israelites into slavery—those they didn't kill. The Israelites were poorly trained and virtually without arms.

Moses went before the Lord to plead for help. . . . The Lord gave a strange instruction. He said, "Tomorrow the Amalekites would come against you in the valley." Moses was to go up on the hillside overlooking the valley, and he was told to raise his hands to the heavens, as long as he did so the Israelites would win. And so it happened; the battle commenced and the Amalekites began to win. And Moses raised his arms, and the Israelites began to win. Moses was a very old man by our standards, and you can imagine how difficult it would be to stand for hours with your arms up. And as soon as his arms began to come down, the Israelites began to lose the battle.

Then two men, Aaron and a man by the name of Hur, went up to assist Moses. They moved a rock on the hillside where it would overlook the battle and had Moses seated on the rock. Then, standing on both sides of him, they held his arms in their arms. And the Old Testament closes that incident with these words: "And Joshua discomfited Amalek and his people with the edge of the sword"—meaning that he whipped them.[3]

Now you may say, "What a strange thing that the Lord would make the fate of his covenant people dependent upon whether an old man could hold his arms up in the air." But a great lesson was taught that day in Israel. The image of the presidency emerges: the president sustained by his counselors. Then all Israel was taught, and the lesson is good for us today, that as long as we sustain and uphold our leaders, we will prosper against all odds, against all the modern Amalekite robbers. And how are we asked to signify that we sustain our leaders? By raising our arms. So this day we've had the privilege of voting to sustain those who are called to preside over us—in this case, the General Authorities; in other meetings, your stake and ward authorities; and when anyone is called to office, we are called to sustain them with a vote—a great opportunity and a tremendous responsibility. (76–10)

A promise to those who follow the Brethren. Often overlooked . . . is a marvelous promise: "If my people will hearken unto my voice, and unto the voice of my servants whom I have appointed to lead my people, behold, verily I say unto you, they shall not be moved out of their place."[4]

Remember this promise; hold on to it. It should be a great comfort to those struggling to keep a family together in a society increasingly indifferent to, and even hostile toward, those standards which are essential to a happy family.

The promise is a restatement of what the Lord told the multitude: "Blessed are ye if ye shall give heed unto the words of these twelve whom I have chosen from among you to minister unto you, and to be your servants."[5] . . .

But the promise was followed with this caution: "But if they will not hearken to my voice, nor unto the voice of these men whom I have appointed, they shall not be blest."[6] (96–05, p. 8)

Important counsel to youth. Young brethren and sisters, . . . in three words the most important counsel I could give you, particularly at your age, in this generation, with the tremendous forces of evil now arrayed against the kingdom of God—that counsel, simple, yet I say the most important I can give: Follow the Brethren. (65–04)

If we follow our leaders we will be saved. I bear witness, brethren and sisters, that the leaders of the Church were called of God by proper authority, and it is known to the Church that they have that authority and have been properly ordained by the regularly ordained heads of the Church. If we follow them we will be saved. If we stray from them we will surely be lost. That is true of the file leaders down through the ranks of the Church, the heads of quorums and wards, of stakes and missions, and of the prophet, who stands at the head of the Church. (85–08, p. 35)

Follow the Brethren to avoid forfeiting blessings. Unless you arrive at the point where you can follow the brethren and sustain the authorities of the Church, you'll find yourself on a path that will lead down the sure road to apostasy and you'll forfeit all of the blessings that might have been yours. (65–04)

Follow the counsel of your bishop. Bishops are inspired! Each of us has agency to accept or reject counsel from our leaders, but never disregard the counsel of your bishop, whether given over the pulpit or individually, and never turn down a call from your bishop. (99–01, p. 58)

Counsel from leaders is inspired. I don't know anything more frustrating than to have someone come in for counsel, and you're praying about it as you listen carefully, and you do get an inspiration. You get an impression and inspiration. You know the statement in the Book of Mormon, "the voice of the Lord came into my mind." I know what that means. You have some counsel for them and you see them listen half-attentively, and then hardly listen, because you're counseling them to do something they don't want to do, and then they turn aside from that counsel in favor of a choice of their own that will surely lead them to destruction. (65–04)

It is important to be a willing learner. The other day I received a letter of apology, as I have on many occasions. It came from someone I do not know. This letter told how resentful and angry that member had been for a long period of time toward me because of a talk I had given. It was a request for forgiveness.

I am quick to forgive. I am only an agent both in giving the talk and in extending forgiveness.

The scriptures contain many references revealing how "hard"[7] to bear the teachings of the prophets and apostles were for the Israelites and for the Nephites. It is so easy to resist the teaching and resent the teacher. That has been the lot of the prophets and apostles from the beginning.

One of the Beatitudes teaches that:

"Blessed are ye, when men shall revile you, and persecute you, and shall say all manner of evil against you falsely, for my sake. Rejoice, and be exceeding glad: for great is your reward in heaven: for so persecuted they the prophets which were before you."[8]

Typically those letters of apology say, "I could not understand why you felt the need to make me feel so uncomfortable and so guilty." Then, out of their struggle, there emerges an insight, an inspiration, an understanding of causes and effects. Finally they come to see and understand why the gospel is as it is.

I mention one among several subjects. A sister may finally come to see why we stress the importance of mothers staying at home with their children. She understands that no service equals the exalting refinement which comes through unselfish motherhood. Nor does she need to forgo intellectual or cultural or social refinement. Those things are fitted in—in proper time—for they attend the everlasting virtue which comes from teaching children. (99–06, pp. 15–16)

We must be loyal in small things as well as large. Some of us suppose that if we were called to a high office in the Church immediately, we would be loyal and would show the dedication necessary. We would step forward and valiantly commit ourselves to this service.

But (you can put it down in your little black book) if you will not be loyal in the small things, you will not be loyal in the large things. If you will not respond to the so-called insignificant or menial tasks which need to be performed in the Church and kingdom, there will be no opportunity for service in the so-called greater challenges.

A man who says he will sustain the President of the Church or the

General Authorities, but cannot sustain his own bishop, is deceiving himself. The man who will not sustain the bishop of his ward and the president of his stake will not sustain the President of the Church. (65–01, pp. 238–39)

Which way do you face? [As a young supervisor of the seminaries] I was uneasy about some counsel I had received from my predecessor. A few days later I came from Brigham City for an appointment with Elder Harold B. Lee. It was the first time I was ever in his office. He congratulated me on my appointment and asked what he could do for me. I told him I had come to listen, and listen I did.

Let me tell you the most important thing he said. "You must decide, to begin with," he said, "where you stand and which way you face. You must decide whether you are a delegate representing the seminary and institute men before the Brethren, or whether you will, as I think you should, represent the Brethren to the seminary and institute teachers." He expanded on that theme, making sure that I knew I had a choice on which way I would face.

That interview changed my life. Without that counsel, I should not have been qualified later to be ordained as a member of the Quorum of the Twelve Apostles. (79–09)

Follow the Brethren. Some among us would rather criticize the Lord and His church than concentrate on the problems. That is a symptom of impenitence.

As a "spiritual doctor" I counsel you to follow the Brethren. If you don't understand a problem or a position the Church has taken, restrain your tongue. Check the mote in your own eye before you criticize.

Follow the Brethren. Three words. There is nothing in your life that will destroy you if you will follow the Brethren. Even if it were all brought together and focused on you, there is not enough evil in the world to destroy you unless you consent to it. (68–04, pp. 79–80)

A solemn warning to those who turn against the Lord's anointed. Some few within the Church openly, or perhaps far worse, in the darkness of anonymity, reproach their leaders in the wards and stakes and in the Church, seeking to make them "an offender for a word,"[9] as Isaiah said. To them the Lord said:

> Cursed are all those that shall lift up the heel against mine anointed, saith the Lord, and cry they have sinned when they have not sinned . . . but have done that which was meet in mine eyes, and which I commanded them. . . .
>
> . . . [B]ecause they have offended my little ones they shall be severed from the ordinances of mine house.
>
> Their basket shall not be full, their houses and their barns shall perish, and they themselves shall be despised by those that flattered them.
>
> They shall not have right to the priesthood, nor their posterity after them from generation to generation.[10]

That terrible penalty will not apply to those who try as best they can to live the gospel and sustain their leaders. Nor need it apply to those who in the past have been guilty of indifference or even opposition, if they will repent, confess their transgressions, and forsake them.[11] (96–05, p. 7)

The question is whether it is true. I remember once Elder Harold B. Lee gave a talk at BYU and he told me that he felt some unusual inspiration in that talk and gave emphasis to a point that he had not intended to discuss. A few days later one of the professors from BYU called at his office and interviewed him and said, "Brother Lee, I was very interested in your talk. I was very interested in one point particularly." Brother Lee said, "Yes, I was quite interested too." The professor said, "Would you mind citing the reference and the authority for that?"

Brother Lee thought for a few minutes and said, "Yes, the reference for that is Elder Harold B. Lee of the Council of the Twelve Apostles speaking at a devotional assembly at BYU," and then he gave the date of his sermon.

The point I make simply is this: It isn't a question of who said it or when, the question is whether it is true. (77–04, pp. 22–23)

The authority in the Church is not on trial. The test of authority in the Church isn't whether you sustain it or not, it's whether God sustains it. The authority that's held isn't on trial. (65–04)

A broad knowledge of the doctrines does not give one authority to counsel others. If it should be that a member has a broader knowledge of the doctrines than does his priesthood leaders, there is one thing that he does not have, and that is the office and authority to qualify him to counsel others under inspiration. (XX–02)

ROLE OF THE PROPHET AND GENERAL AUTHORITIES

The role of prophets. The prophets, as they walk and live among men, are common, ordinary men. Men called to apostolic positions are given a people to redeem. Theirs is the responsibility to lead those people in such a way that they win the battles of life and conquer the ordinary temptations and passions and challenges. And then, speaking figuratively, it is as though these prophets are tapped on the shoulder and reminded: "While you carry such responsibility to help others with their battles, you are not excused from your own challenges of life. You too will be subject to passions, temptations, challenges. Win those battles as best you can." (*THT,* p. 102)

The Lord will speak through His prophet. The Son, in organizing His church, organized all the apostles, prophets, and He said, in effect, "This is my prophet, hear him." We don't have to. We can listen to [others] . . . we don't have to use that channel. But the Lord invariably will use that channel and when He speaks to this earth, it will be through His prophet. (68–11)

What a prophet need not be. Now, there are some things a prophet does not of necessity have to be, and it's perhaps surprising to discover some of these. He need not be a classic example of physical perfection, nor need he be the most intelligent individual who has ever been born. It is not necessary, in order to be a prophet, to be the best educated among all the people of the world; and it isn't necessary, in the final part, to have a personality molded in any special iron-clad mold. (59–03, p. 36)

Prophets are to see and to warn. Perhaps young men do speak of the future because they have no past, and old men of the past because they have no future. However, there are fifteen old men whose very lives are focused on the future. They are called, sustained, and ordained as prophets, seers, and revelators. It is their right to see as seers see; it is their obligation to counsel and to warn. (95–10, p. 50)

The ultimate authority in religion rests with prophets, seers, and revelators. It is not to a university, however, that the world must turn for ultimate authority in the field of religion. . . . By direction of Him whose Church this is, that authority is held by a group of ordinary men called from many walks of life . . . who are ordained as Apostles, sustained as prophets, seers, and revelators, and presided over by one authorized to exercise all the keys of spiritual authority existing upon the earth. (74–04, pp. 48–49)

The gift of discernment is an awesome burden to carry. There is a power of discernment granted "unto such as God shall appoint . . . to watch over [His] church."[12] To discern means "to see."

President Harold B. Lee told me once of a conversation he had with Elder Charles A. Callis of the Quorum of the Twelve. Brother Callis had remarked that the gift of discernment was an awesome burden to carry. To see clearly what is ahead and yet find members slow to respond or resistant to counsel or even rejecting the witness of the apostles and prophets brings deep sorrow.

Nevertheless, "the responsibility of leading this church" must rest upon us until "you shall appoint others to succeed you."[13]

The Lord warned us of those few in the Church "who have professed to know my name and have not known me, and have blasphemed against me in the midst of my house."[14] (96–05, p. 7)

Apostles are to bear special witness. We lay no claim to being Apostles of the world—but of the Lord Jesus Christ. The test is not

With President Spencer W. Kimball and Sister Camilla Kimball in Uruguay at the South America area conferences, November 1978

whether men will believe, but whether the Lord has called us—and of that there is no doubt! We do not talk of those sacred interviews that qualify the servants of the Lord to bear a special witness of Him, for we have been commanded not to do so. But we are free, indeed, we are obliged, to bear that special witness. (80–04, p. 65)

Revelation continues with us. We who have been called to lead the Church are ordinary men and women with ordinary capacities struggling to administer a church which grows at such a pace as to astound even those who watch it closely. Some are disposed to find fault with us; surely that is easy for them to do. But they do not examine us more searchingly than we examine ourselves. A call to lead is not an exemption from the challenges of life. We seek for inspiration in the same way that you do, and we must obey the same laws which apply to every member of the Church.

We are sorry for our inadequacies, sorry we are not better than we are. We can feel, as you can see, the effect of the aging process as it imposes limitations upon His leaders before your very eyes.

But this we know. There are councils and counselors and quorums to counterbalance the foibles and frailties of man. The Lord organized His church to provide for mortal men to work as mortal men, and yet He assured that the spirit of revelation would guide in all that we do in His name.

And in the end, what is given comes because the Lord has spoken it, "whether by [His] own voice or by the voice of [His] servants, it is the same."[15] We know His voice when He speaks.

Revelation continues with us today. The promptings of the Spirit, the dreams, and the visions and the visitations, and the ministering of angels all are with us now. And the still, small voice of the Holy Ghost "is a lamp unto [our] feet, and a light unto [our] path."[16] Of that I bear witness. (89–04, p. 16)

What is the process by which decisions are made by the Brethren? When a matter comes before the First Presidency and the Quorum of the Twelve Apostles in a temple meeting, one thing that is determined very quickly is whether it is of serious consequence or not. One or another of us will see in an apparently innocent proposal issues of great and lasting consequence.

It is clear from the revelations that the decisions of the presiding quorums "must be by the unanimous voice of the same; . . . unless this is the case, their decisions are not entitled to the same blessings."[17] In order to ensure that to be the case, matters of consequence are seldom decided in the meeting where they are proposed. And, if the proposal is a part of a larger issue, sufficient time is taken to "bring us all along" so that it is clear that each of us has either a clear *understanding* of the issue or, as is often the case, has a very clear *feeling* about it. . . .

It would be unthinkable to deliberately present an issue in such a way that approval depended upon how it was maneuvered through channels, who was presenting it, or who was present or absent when it was presented.

Often one or more of us is away during regular meetings. We all know that the work must proceed and will accept the judgment of our Brethren. However, if a matter has been studied by one of the Quorum in more detail than the others or he is more familiar with it either by assignment, experience, or personal interest, the matter is very often delayed until he can be in on the discussion.

And always, if one of us cannot understand an issue or feels unsettled about it, it is held over for future discussion. . . .

There is a rule we follow: A matter is not settled until there is a *minute entry* to evidence that all of the Brethren in council assembled (not just one of us, not just a committee) have come to a unity of feeling. Approval of a matter in principle is not considered authority to act until a minute entry records the action taken—usually when the minutes are approved in the next meeting. . . .

That is how we function—in council assembled. That provides safety for the Church and a high comfort level for each of us who is personally accountable. Under the plan, men of very ordinary capacity may be guided through counsel and inspiration to accomplish extraordinary things. (91–01, pp. 83–84)

Succession in the Presidency. When the President of the Church dies, then the First Presidency is dissolved. . . . In the case of the Presidency and the Twelve, when the president passes away, the counselors take their place in the quorum to which they belong, which is the Quorum of the Twelve Apostles. Sometimes we have fourteen Twelve Apostles. Now that bothers the mathematicians, but it works all right. It's a temporary situation. Then the senior Apostle always becomes, actually is, the President of the Church. (97–01)

The death of a prophet is never accidental. The death of a prophet is never accidental. A prophet cannot be taken, save his ministry is complete. . . . This is His work and He will do as He will do. (74–01, pp. 123–24)

The Lord values wisdom and experience. Have you ever wondered why the Lord organized the First Presidency and the Quorum of the Twelve Apostles so that the senior leadership of the Church will always be older men? This pattern of seniority values wisdom and experience over youth and physical vigor. (03–05, p. 84)

The Lord's system of Church leadership permits no aspiring. There are those who wonder at the system where the senior Apostle, invariably now an older man, becomes the President of the Church.

Those who do not understand write to us or publish articles saying, "Isn't it time now to do the sensible thing and install a vigorous young leader to face the challenge of a growing international Church?"

They fail to see the divine inspiration in the system established by the Lord. Granted, it does not work as the wisdom of men would dictate. The Lord reminded Isaiah: "My thoughts are not your thoughts, neither are your ways my ways. . . . For as the heavens are higher than the earth, so are my ways higher than your ways, and my thoughts than your thoughts."[18]

See what the Lord has provided. Nowhere on this earth is there a body of men of the leadership and authority as completely devoid of aspiring. The very system that seems so strange to many just does not allow it; neither would the Lord permit it. There is no jockeying for position or power, no soliciting for votes, no hint of cultivating influence in any self-serving way.

There is a brotherhood that accommodates differing views and personalities, but we are one. The authority in the administration of the Church is independent of any individual and is held in trust by fifteen men who have been ordained as Apostles. (95–03)

CALLS TO CHURCH POSITIONS

A lesson in extending calls in the Church. Leaders must learn how to issue calls. When I was a young man, I heard Elder Spencer W. Kimball speak in a stake conference. He said that as a new stake president in Arizona, he left his office in the bank to call a man to be stake leader of the young men.

He said, "Jack, how would you like to be leader of the young men in the stake?"

Jack responded, "Aw, Spencer, you don't mean me. I couldn't do anything like that."

He tried to persuade him, but Jack refused the call.

Brother Kimball went back to his office to brood over his failure. He knew the stake presidency had been inspired to make the call. Finally it came to him: he had made a terrible mistake! Of course, *Jack* would not respond.

Perhaps he recalled what the prophet Jacob had said when he "taught them in the temple, *having first obtained mine errand from the Lord.*"[19]

President Kimball now did as Jacob had done in ancient times. He "obtained [his] errand from the Lord."

He returned to ask Jack to forgive him for not doing it right and started over: "Last Sunday the stake presidency prayerfully considered who should lead the young men in the stake. There were several names; yours was among them. We all felt that you were the man. We knelt in prayer. The Lord confirmed to the three of us, by revelation, that you were to be called to that position."

Then he said, "As a servant of the Lord, I am here to deliver that call."

Then Jack said, "Well, Spencer, if you are going to put it that way. . . ."

President Kimball replied, "I *am* putting it that way!"

Of course, *Jack* would not respond to a casual invitation from *Spencer,* but he could not refuse a call from the Lord through Stake President Kimball. He served faithfully and with inspiration. (97–04, pp. 7–8)

Responding to calls in the Church. We do not call ourselves to offices in the Church. Rather, we respond to the call of those who preside over us. It is the responsibility of those who preside to prayerfully consult the Lord as to His will concerning a position in the Church. Then the principle of revelation is at work. The call is then delivered by the presiding officer, who is acting for the Lord.

We do not, under ordinary circumstances, refuse a call. Neither do we ask for a release beyond calling to the attention of the presiding officer circumstances which may make a release advisable. (92–04, pp. 155–56)

It is important to accept opportunities to serve in the Church. Never say *no* to an opportunity to serve in the Church. If you are called to an assignment by one who has authority, there is but one answer. It is, of course, expected that you set forth clearly what your circumstances are, but any assignment that comes under call from your bishop or your stake president is a call that comes from the Lord. An article of our faith defines it so, and I bear witness that it is so.

Once called to such positions, do not presume to set your own date of release. A release is, in effect, another call. Men do not call themselves to offices in the Church. Why must we presume that we have the authority to release ourselves? A release should come by the same authority from whence came the call. (65–01, p. 243)

You have a right to inspiration for your callings. You have the right to *know* concerning calls that come to you. Be humble and reverent and prayerful concerning responsibilities that are placed upon your shoulders. Keep those standards of worthiness so that the Lord can communicate with you concerning the responsibilities that are yours in the call that you have answered. (65–01, p. 243)

A willingness to serve comes from individual testimonies. The willingness of Latter-day Saints to respond to calls to serve is a representation of their desire to do the will of the Lord. That arises from the individual witness that the gospel of Jesus Christ, restored through the Prophet Joseph Smith and contained in the Book of Mormon, is true. (97–04, p. 6)

Response to a call depends upon the testimony of the one being called. We live to know, in this church, that the response to a call does not depend on the testimony and witness of the one who delivers the call. It depends, rather, on the testimony and witness of the one who receives it. (73–03, p. 22)

We serve where we are called. It is not in the proper spirit for us to decide where we will serve or where we will not. We serve where we are called. It does not matter what the calling may be.

I was present at a solemn assembly when David O. McKay was sustained as President of the Church. President J. Reuben Clark Jr., who had served as first counselor to two presidents, was then sustained as second counselor to President McKay. Sensitive to the possibility that some might think that he had been demoted, President Clark said: "In the service of the Lord, it is not where you serve but how. In The Church of Jesus Christ of Latter-day Saints, one takes the place to which one is duly called, which place one neither seeks nor declines."[20] (97–04, p. 7)

One does not aspire to callings in the Church. One does not aspire to a call nor request or resent a release. Both a call and a release are directed by inspiration of our leaders. (03–07, p. 3)

One calling in the Church should not be esteemed over another. There is the natural tendency to look at those who are sustained to presiding positions, to consider them to be higher and of more value in the Church or to their families than an ordinary member. Somehow we feel they are worth more to the Lord than are we. It just does not work that way!

It would be very disappointing to my wife and to me if we supposed any one of our children would think that we think we are of more worth to the family or to the Church than they are, or to think that one calling in the Church was esteemed over another or that any calling would be thought to be less important. . . .

As General Authorities of the Church, we are just the same as you are, and you are just the same as we are. You have the same access to the powers of revelation for your families and for your work and for your callings as we do. . . .

No member of the Church is esteemed by the Lord as more or less than any other. It just does not work that way! Remember, He is a father—our Father. The Lord is "no respecter of persons." (07–08, pp. 8–9)

The pattern for being released. While we do not ask to be released from a calling, if our circumstances change it is quite in order for us to counsel with those who have issued the call and then let the decision rest with them. Nor should we feel rejected when we are released by the same authority and with the same inspiration by which we were called. (97–04, p. 8)

No calling is more important than parenthood. No calling is more important, no service more enduring, than parenthood. Generally callings in the Church help parents to be better parents. Nevertheless, leaders should use both judgment and inspiration to make certain that a call does not make it measurably difficult for parents to serve as parents.

One who has authority to issue a call must rely on inspiration to avoid overburdening those who are always willing. (97–04, p. 7)

The world doesn't understand that one must be called by prophecy. "We believe that a man must"—not could be, or might be, or sometimes is. "We believe that a man must be called of God, by prophecy, and by the laying on of hands by those who are in authority, to preach the Gospel and administer in the ordinances thereof."[21]

Now, the world doesn't see that. Some members of the Church don't see that. The man who said we're called by desperation or something else is a man who is not possessed of the right spirit. For "the natural man receiveth not the things of the Spirit of God: for they are foolishness unto him: neither can he know them, because they are spiritually discerned."[22] And I have come to know that whenever you find criticism, and cynicism, and ridicule over something as sacred as this, invariably also you find disobedience. (73–03, pp. 25–26)

The established order for callings in the Church. Man must be called by those who have the proper authority; sustained, or voted on, in an appropriate meeting; and ordained or set apart by one who has the authority. This is called "common consent," or the voice of the people.[23] This follows the instructions given in revelation: "Again I say unto you, that it shall not be given to any one to go forth to preach my gospel, or to build up my church, except he be ordained by some one who has authority, and it is known to the church that he has authority and has been regularly ordained by the heads of the church."[24]

Notice that there are two requirements: First, we must receive authority from someone who has it and has been ordained by the heads of the Church. Second, it must be known in the Church that he has the authority.

The sustaining in the priesthood and the setting apart to office is done openly where it can be known to the Church who has authority, as the scriptures require.

There is great safety to the Church in having the names of those called to offices in the Church presented in the proper meeting.[25] Anyone who is a pretender or a deceiver will be recognized. If someone claims to have been secretly ordained to a special calling or higher order of the priesthood, we may know immediately that the claim is false. (92–04, pp. 156–57)

The Church will always be led by those who have been called by the regularly ordained heads of the Church.

Now, this does not prevent any member from sharing the gospel in a missionary attitude; that is their duty. There are duties, such as home teaching, and ordinances, such as blessing the sick, which go with the priesthood, and no special setting apart is required for their performance. But for any and every office there is care to see that anyone given authority receives it from one who has authority and it is *known to the Church* that he has authority. (85–08, p. 33)

Sustaining, ordaining, and blessing. So that it will be known to the Church who is called to serve, names are presented in an appropriate meeting for a sustaining vote.[26] That vote is not just to approve; it is a commitment to support.

Following the sustaining, there is an ordination or setting apart. The pattern was set in the early Church when the Lord promised, "I will lay my hand upon you by the hand of my servant." He further promised, "You shall receive my Spirit, the Holy Ghost, even the Comforter, which shall teach you the peaceable things of the kingdom."[27]

When leaders set someone apart, they do more than authorize service. They pronounce a blessing. It is a marvelous thing to receive a blessing from the Lord Jesus Christ through the hands of His servants. That blessing can cause changes in the life of the one called or in the family. (97–04, p. 7)

How to choose one to be ordained or set apart. Let me explain how to choose one to be ordained to an office in the priesthood or set apart to lead or to teach. As a presidency or a bishopric, you counsel and pray, individually and together, about who should be called. The answer comes by revelation. The scriptures teach, "You must study it out in your mind; then you must ask me if it be right, and if it is right I will cause that your bosom shall burn within you; therefore, you shall feel that it is right."[28]

The priesthood must not be conferred upon a man or a boy who is unrepentant or unwilling to live by the covenants connected with it.

For both ordinations and settings apart, you interview to determine:

Are they worthy of the call?

Will they accept the call?

If they are married, will their spouse support them?

Are there family, work, or health problems which might interfere with their service? (03–07, p. 1)

Ordination and setting apart. There are two ways by which authority is conferred in the Church: by *ordination* and by *setting apart.* Offices in the priesthood—deacon, teacher, priest, elder, high priest, patriarch, seventy, and Apostle—always come by ordination. The keys of presidency and the authority to act in callings in the priesthood are received by setting apart.

For instance, the office of elder in the Melchizedek Priesthood is an ordained office, but the office of president of an elders quorum is an office to which a person is set apart rather than ordained. In either case, he is given a blessing to accompany his service in an office to which he is ordained or set apart.

There are many "set apart" offices in the Church in both the priesthood and the auxiliary organizations. Some duties are inherent in the priesthood, and one need not be set apart to do them. Visiting the homes of members as assigned (home teaching) is an example.

Because women are not ordained to the priesthood, when sisters are set apart to offices, including the office of president in an auxiliary, they receive authority, responsibility, and blessings connected with the office, but they do not receive keys. (92–04, pp. 153–54)

Ordination or setting apart is an opportunity to pronounce a blessing. An ordination or a setting apart is an opportunity to pronounce a blessing. A blessing is not to give counsel or instruction. That is done afterward when one is taught his duties.

There is no precise wording required. One of the great blessings of the Church is the way the priesthood is organized, with very few ordinances that must be word perfect and precise. We need not, indeed should not, memorize the blessing. As the Spirit directs, we might bless one in his home and his family and his work. He can be blessed with discernment and wisdom and understanding, with health. The words that we say will come by inspiration. Each blessing then is unique and personal to the individual member. (03–07, p. 3)

The responsibilities of a bishop. The bishop is responsible for the young men of the Aaronic Priesthood and for the young women as well. He receives and accounts for tithes and offerings. He is responsible for the temporal affairs of the Church, to seek out the poor, and he has many other duties.

The bishop is "to judge his people by the testimony of the just, and *by the assistance of his counselors,* according to the laws of the kingdom which are given by the prophets of God."[29] He is to judge them as to their worthiness to receive the ordinances and serve in offices.

He is to counsel and correct and to preach the gospel to his flock, individually and collectively. In all of this, he is to teach the gospel of Jesus Christ, the Crucifixion, the Atonement, the Resurrection, the Restoration. (99–01, p. 57)

There is nothing quite like the office of bishop. In all the world there is nothing quite like the office of bishop in The Church of Jesus Christ of Latter-day Saints. Except for parents, the bishop has the best opportunity to teach and to cause to be taught the things that matter most. And a bishop has the remarkable opportunity to teach parents about their responsibility; then he must allow them time to teach their children. (99–01, p. 57)

The bishop has the right to revelation. Inherent in the ordination to be bishop is both the right and the obligation to be directed by inspiration. The bishop has the power to discern by the Spirit what he is to do.

Revelation is the one credential that all bishops have in common. Bishops come from many cultures, many occupations. They vary in experience, personality, and age, but they do not differ in their right to be guided spiritually. (99–01, p. 58)

One does not aspire to be a bishop. One does not exactly volunteer or aspire to be bishop. He is *called* to be bishop, "called of God, by prophecy." Then he is both ordained and set apart "by the laying on of hands by those who are in authority, to preach the Gospel and administer in the ordinances thereof."[30]

A man is *ordained* a bishop, an office in the priesthood; then he is *set apart* and given the keys to preside over a ward. He with his two counselors form a bishopric—a type of presidency.

Once ordained, he is a bishop for the rest of his life. When he is released from presiding over a ward, his ordination becomes dormant. If called again to preside over a ward, his previous ordination is reactivated. When he is released, it becomes dormant again. (99–01, pp. 57–58)

The miracle of calling stake presidents. Think of going somewhere in the world and arriving on a Saturday afternoon. Sometimes, when planes are delayed, we come late and the meetings have to be rearranged. Yet the following morning there must be new leadership called, people we've never seen; and sometimes there's a language barrier. If we were doing it in man's way, there would be a personnel file; there would be interviews and more interviews; there would be times of study, the interviewing of many who know the individual, and so on. But it doesn't work that way; it can't, for there isn't time. The world is too large, and there are too many stakes and too many places to be. It's a marvelous thing to be able to go before the Lord, to present a simple question, and to get a direct, positive, unmistakable answer. I'm ever humbled by that. This is a miracle, this process of the call and release of members in the filling of Church positions. (73–03, p. 20)

Three things that come with calls to Church offices. Now, with each call in the Church there come, it seems to me, three things: First, something by way of preparation, not infrequently a spiritual prompting. On these weekends when we call a new stake president, it's an interesting thing to ask, "President, when did you first learn of this call?" knowing full well that the annunciation of that to him didn't come from me. He then will tell those sacred experiences, which we'll not repeat here, about how he knew, so that he could prepare for this call.

Usually the next thing that is related to a call is a trial. It's like a test, perhaps like a test one receives at school—and incidentally, like the tests at school, a person can fail if he will. . . .

The third thing, with reference to this quiet miracle, is that with the setting apart comes an endowment of power and inspiration, a sustaining power that will secure the success of anyone called to office in this church. (73–03, pp. 22–25)

All can get a confirmation about leaders who are called. Any seeking soul—any member—has the right to know by the gift of the Spirit about the call of our leaders.

On one occasion I was organizing a new stake on Upolu Island in Samoa. As is customary, we were conducting interviews with local priesthood leaders, asking each to suggest a few names of brethren of stature to be considered for a call.

One dignified branch president had walked from the other side of the island. He stood before us in a white shirt and tie, with a lava-lava, or skirt, tied about his waist. He wore no shoes; he had never owned shoes.

I asked for names. He gave but one: "Bishop Iono will be our stake president." He was right, for that had already been revealed to me. But I did not feel he should make the announcement.

So I asked for other names, for we had counselors and others to call as well. He replied, holding up his finger, "Just one name." "But," I said, "suppose he could not serve, would you not like to name others?" This humble priesthood president then asked me a question, "Brother Packer, are you asking me to go against the witness of the Spirit?"

How marvelous! This wonderful man had reminded me that each member of the Church, in prayer, can receive confirmation that the fifth article of faith has been honored. (85–08, p. 35)

ITEMS OF COUNSEL

We should call the Church by its name. Rather than using "Mormon Church," we should call the Church by its name—The Church of Jesus Christ of Latter-day Saints; "for thus," the Lord told us in a revelation, "shall my church be called in the last days."[31] (92–04, p. 159)

The name of the Church is important. This is The Church of Jesus Christ of Latter-day Saints. It isn't the Mormon Church. Never say "Mormon" when you can say The Church of Jesus Christ of Latter-day Saints. It is the Church.

Now that's a long name, and sometimes we kind of stumble over it in conversations. We say, "The Church of Jesus Christ of Latter-day Saints," and someone will say, "the church of what?" And so we miss an opportunity when we rely on the word Mormon. You can learn to say it. The—Church—of—Jesus Christ—of Latter-day—Saints! Every time you say that you bear a testimony. Remember which church you are in. The Church of Jesus Christ of Latter-day Saints! (68–11)

What it means to dedicate a building. I would like to explain something about a dedication. . . . By doing so, we each relinquish our ownership of the building. . . . In dedicating a building, we present it officially as our gift to the Lord. This means that tomorrow morning when anyone enters this building, they come here as guests of the Lord. It then belongs to Him. . . . [We] are under serious responsibility to maintain the building as beautiful and appealing as it can be made. [We] are under responsibility to have a spirit here in the building that is completely worthy of the ownership of the building. (70–01)

There is an order to follow when seeking counsel or blessings. There is an order of things as to where we go for counsel or blessings. It is simple—we go to our parents. When they are no longer available, if it is a blessing, then we may go to our home teacher. For counsel, you go to your bishop. He may choose to send you to his file leader—the stake president. But we do not go to the General Authorities. We do not

write to them for counsel or suppose that someone in a more prominent position will give a more inspired blessing. If we could get this one
thing taught in the Church, great power would rest upon us. (96–07)

We must speak of the rule first and then consider the exceptions.
Whenever we speak of home and family and motherhood, we fear we
might wound the tender hearts of those who may never marry or those
whose marriages have failed. There are those who are greatly disappointed with their children. There are heartbreaking gender problems,
untimely deaths, abortion, abuse, pornography, and, in addition, an
endless list of things which almost dissuade us from speaking with the
plainness that the scripture commands us to do.

I return, as I have on countless occasions, to the inspired words of a
Relief Society president. I will ever be grateful to Sister Alberta Baker. A
convert of the Church, she was mission Relief Society president when I
was mission president in New England. She was a very small woman
and walked with a very pronounced limp from childhood polio.

We had sixty Relief Societies scattered across the mission. Some of
them were off-course and some of them were little more than sewing
circles and a few had lost their way entirely. Sister Belle Spafford, president of the general Relief Society, provided some simple guidelines that
could be followed.

We called the Relief Society leaders together in the chapel at the
Joseph Smith Birthplace Memorial in Vermont. I asked Sister Baker to
explain the changes we were asking them to make. She gently invited
the sisters to conform more closely to the patterns set for the Relief
Society.

One sister stood and said defiantly, "That doesn't fit us. We're an
exception!" She repeated with more emphasis, "We are an exception!"

It was a very tense moment, something of a crisis. Sister Baker
turned to me for help. I was not interested in facing a fierce woman, so
I motioned for her to proceed. Then came the revelation!

With gentle firmness, she said: "Dear sister, we'd like not to take
care of the exception first. We will take care of the rule first, and then

we will see to the exception." She continued to explain what a Relief Society should be.

Later I told her I would be quoting her all over the world. And so I have. In many challenging moments, some very tense, I have quoted the revelation that came to that sweet, little Relief Society president. (06–03)

If you declare the standard (law, doctrine, principle) and in the same breath provide for exceptions—they will grasp the exception first. (08–02)

The rules of happiness must be taught first. When we speak plainly of divorce, abuse, gender identity, contraception, abortion, parental neglect, we are thought by some to be way out of touch or to be uncaring. Some ask if we know how many we hurt when we speak plainly. Do we know of marriages in trouble, of the many who remain single, of single-parent families, of couples unable to have children, of parents with wayward children, or of those confused about gender? Do we know? Do we care?

Those who ask have no idea how much we care; you know little of the sleepless nights, of the endless hours of work, of prayer, of study, of travel—all for the happiness and redemption of mankind.

Because we *do* know and because we *do* care, we must teach the rules of happiness without dilution, apology, or avoidance. That is our calling. (94–01, p. 20)

Bishops keep confidences. Often actions of bishops and stake presidents and others are misread by people who are not in a position to know the full truth.

Neither the bishop nor the member he is judging is obliged to confide in us. The bishop must keep confidences.

When all is said and done, in most cases, it is clearly none of our business anyway.

Often someone will not go to his bishop with a problem. He wants to see a General Authority instead. He says the bishop will talk—for what about the time when someone in the ward went to him and soon everyone knew about the problem?

Follow these cases through, as I have done, and you will probably find that, first, the member confided in her neighbor who didn't know what to counsel her. Then she talked it over with her best friend, and then her sister, and received conflicting advice. Finally, her husband was told by the man he rides with that they'd better see the bishop.

Indeed, it was noised about, but not by the bishop. Bishops keep confidences. (79–03, p. 81)

An unworthy leader flies against everything the Church stands for. If a leader does conduct himself unworthily, his actions fly against everything the Church stands for, and he is subject to release.

It has even been our sad responsibility, on some few occasions, to excommunicate leaders from the Church who have been guilty of very serious illegal or immoral conduct.

That should increase, not shake, your faith in the Church. (79–03, p. 80)

Do not speak of past transgressions. Not long ago I was in a stake and the stake president was talking about his earlier days. He said, "You know, when I was young I was inactive and did this and this and this."

Afterwards I quietly said, "President, don't ever do that again."

He said, "What do you mean?"

I said, "Don't ever talk about your days of inactivity, and let me tell you why. The older people will be all right and might be lifted up by it, but sitting out there will be a teenager, and they will look up at you and say, 'There is the stake president. If he can get out of the way and get in that much trouble and still be brought back, why should I worry about being out of the way and in that much trouble?' And some of them will get away and never come back. Your days of inactivity mean nothing. Those pages have been torn out of your book and thrown away. You never refer to them again, except as there may be an inquiry from someone presiding over you. But you never voluntarily talk about it." (80–07)

CHAPTER 22

The Kingdom Rolls Forth

*"The Church of Jesus Christ of Latter-day Saints will go
forth 'until it has filled the whole earth'¹ and the great Jehovah announces
that His work is done.² The Church is a safe harbor. We will be
protected by justice and comforted by mercy.³ No unhallowed hand
can stay the progress of this work."⁴ (04–03, p. 80)*

The Church has a three-fold mission. There is a three-fold mission of the Church.

First, we are to preach the gospel to every nation, kindred, tongue, and people. We are to persuade them to repent and convert them from the ways of the world and from apostate doctrines. When they repent, we are authorized to administer the ordinance of baptism and confer upon them the gift of the Holy Ghost. This is the work of preaching.

Second, we are thereafter to teach them obedience to all of the laws and ordinances of the new and everlasting covenant, which is the gospel. We are to worthily enter into the covenant of marriage and provide temporal bodies for spirits to enter mortality. We are to prepare the posterity of Adam in all things to enter the presence of God. This is the labor of perfecting the Saints.

Third, we are to receive the baptism of water and of the Spirit for and in behalf of those who died without the knowledge of the truth,⁵ and be ordained, endowed and sealed for them vicariously. This is our bond, our tie to life beyond the veil. When we know the plan of redemption, we understand why there must be a linking of all of the generations of man. This is our part in the redemption of the dead.

Through the work of preaching to the world, perfecting the Saints, and redeeming the dead, we become saviors of mankind. (84–05)

How to implement the mission of the Church. You may wonder how to proceed to implement the mission of the Church in the lives of your members. Where should you focus your attention and energy? You may not have noticed that the statement of the mission tells us how to do it.

We are to proclaim the gospel of the Lord Jesus Christ to every nation, kindred, tongue, and people, to prepare them to receive the ordinances of baptism and confirmation as members of the Church.

We are to perfect the Saints by preparing them to receive the ordinances of the gospel and by instruction and discipline to gain exaltation.

We are to redeem the dead by performing vicarious ordinances of the gospel for those who have lived on the earth.

We are to bring to pass the immortality and eternal life of man by concentrating on ordinances and on the covenants associated with them. That is written there in the mission statement of the Church.

A good and useful and true test of every major decision made by a leader in the Church is whether a given course leads toward or away from the making and keeping of covenants. Centering your mind on ordinances and covenants gives purpose to all the many things we do in preaching the gospel and perfecting the Saints. (87–04)

I know how to proclaim the gospel; it is by perfecting the Saints and redeeming the dead. I know how to perfect the Saints; it is by redeeming the dead and proclaiming the gospel. I know how to redeem the dead; it is by proclaiming the gospel and perfecting the Saints. (08–02)

There are some things the Church must do. There are some things that the Church *must* do, for we are commanded to do them. We must preach the gospel. We must build temples. We must perfect the Saints.

These things others cannot do. The many other good things (which are not central to the mission of the Church) must take second place. For we do not have the resources to do all that *is* worth doing, however worthy it may be. (82–03, p. 86)

The plan of redemption must be the foundation of all we do in the Church. The plan of redemption, as contained in the standard works, must be the foundation of all that we do as leaders of this Church. All of the elements of the plan must be retained in pure form. We must not be diverted from them. They must not be ignored, clouded, deluded, diminished, or superseded by any interest that we may have. To do otherwise is to waste the days of our probation purchased for us at so great a price. (83–04)

The Lord provides the means to help the work go forward. When the servants of the Lord determine to do as He commands, we move ahead. As we proceed, we are joined at the crossroads by those who have been prepared to help us. They come with skills and abilities precisely suited to our needs. And, we find provisions—information, inventions, help of various kinds—set along the way waiting for us to take them up. It is as though someone knew we would be traveling that way. We see the invisible hand of the Almighty providing for us.

For instance, inventions in the fields of travel and communication have come along just as we were ready for them. Surely we, His priesthood, have the true perspective on how this works. The airplane did not come as an accidental discovery to wicked men who were groveling to conquer one another. *Revelation* was involved. It came precisely when we could use it to move across the world to restore the gospel. It was given to *us!*

When we are ready, the Lord will reveal whatever we need—we will find it waiting at the crossroads. . . .

Elder LeGrand Richards some time ago said: "Brethren, the Lord has inspired men to invent these great tools. Now if we don't use them to teach His gospel, Satan will use them to lead the people astray."

We must get the vision of this, for where there is no vision the people perish. (77–05)

Learn the difference between the Church and the gospel. Learn the difference between the Church—which is a container, a vessel, a domicile for the gospel—and the gospel itself. Concentrate on learning the gospel and how the Spirit operates, then you will be wise indeed. (02–02)

The language of the Church is the language of the Spirit. Although we differ in language and custom and culture and in many ways, when we meet together we strengthen one another, and we become one. The language of the Church is the language of the Spirit. (03–01)

In one way faithful members are the same. One of the things I have learned in traveling about the Church for well over forty years and visiting members in perhaps one hundred countries, is that the Church is alike everywhere. The nationalities are different and there are sometimes differences in the buildings, but the people, the members of the Church, are always the same. There is something about Latter-day Saints when they are living the gospel. There is an aura around them. And when they are listening to the Spirit, the Spirit guides them through their lives. (07–02)

The righteous will continue to be gathered in all nations. The Church has grown now to cover the whole world. This gathering shall continue until the righteous are assembled in the congregations of the Saints in all nations of the world.

Joseph Smith said, "He who scattered Israel has promised to gather them; therefore inasmuch as you are to be instrumental in this great work"—listen carefully—"He will endow you with power, wisdom, might, and intelligence, and every qualification necessary . . . until you can circumscribe the earth."[6] (06–06)

This Church will prevail. This Church will prosper. It will prevail. Of this I am absolutely certain. (06–07, p. 88)

The spirit of gathering. There was, in the earlier days, a spirit of gathering. Kirtland, Ohio, was the first gathering place. A spirit of apostasy brooded over Kirtland, and at the very time the Prophet Joseph Smith needed protection and support, in an incredible act, he sent the Twelve Apostles abroad. When the winnowing was over, those who left the Church were replaced by thousands of converts coming from Europe.

The Church then gathered in Missouri. The mobs drove them to Nauvoo, Illinois. When driven out again, they went as pioneers into the western wilderness to gather again in the Rocky Mountains. Converts by the tens of thousands came from Europe.

That kind of gathering has now ended. Our members have been counseled to find their Zion in their homelands: the Belgians in Belgium; the Japanese in Japan; the Nigerians in Nigeria; and so on across the world. It can be Zion for them. For the scriptures tell us that "Zion is the pure in heart."[7] We build temples to which they can gather. (95–04)

Prophetic counsel to gather in one's native land. President Spencer W. Kimball taught, "The 'gathering of Israel' occurs when people in faraway countries accept the gospel and remain in their native lands."[8] . . . The counsel for us to gather in our own lands was counsel from the prophets. Now there's great importance in your young lives in following that counsel. Sometimes when we go out to seek our fortunes, we think we are an exception, and that there are so many more opportunities available in other lands. . . . I have a lingering, sensitive, prophetic idea that as you obediently follow the prophet you will live to know a stability and a fulness and a plenty in your own lands, that by comparison now seem deprived economically. You will have far more of what matters most than you would have if you should go elsewhere seeking your fortune. When you come to find that which matters most, you will find always in the long-run that to be the rule, and not the exception, is to see the fulness of life. Should there be exceptions, the Lord will designate those in an unmistakable way. (77–04, pp. 21–22)

This church will never be the biggest. Bigger is not necessarily better. Biggest is not best. Were that true, the Church itself would be in trouble even though it grows rapidly. The Book of Mormon strongly suggests that the Church will never be the biggest. You have read that passage, haven't you—that though it will be scattered among all nations, yet its dominions would be small.[9] We are not trying to be the biggest. (88–05)

In one sense the Church will always be no bigger than a ward. Whatever happens in the world, whatever heights of civility or depths of depravity emerge in society, the plan remains unaltered. The Church will grow until it fills the whole earth. At once it will remain no bigger than the ward.

The Church provides activities and associations and ordinances and ordinations and covenants and contracts and corrections which prepare each of us for exaltation. It follows a pattern made in the heavens, for no mortal mind could have designed it. (99–01, p. 63)

CHAPTER 23

Temple Work

"Temples are the single most tangible, impressive evidence
of our knowledge and our faith in the resurrection, and of our certain
knowledge that there is life beyond death." (81–09, p. 179)

Come to the temple. To all of you I say, "Come to the temple." If
not now, come then. Pray fervently, set your lives in order, save whatever you can in hopes that that day may come. Start now that very difficult and sometimes discouraging journey of repentance. . . . I urge you
all to keep your faith and your hope and determine that you will
come—that you will be worthy and that you will come to the temple.

It has been my observation that the temple transforms the individual and makes abundantly worthwhile any efforts made to get there.
(*THT,* p. 21)

Whether you need to put your personal life in order to obtain a
temple recommend or whether you are just careless about this work and
have allowed worldly matters to take precedence—whatever the reason,
be moved to make the change. Firmly resolve now that you will do
everything you can do to aid temple work and the genealogical work
that supports it and to assist every living soul and every soul beyond the

veil in every way you can with every resource at your disposal. Come to the temple! (*THT,* p. 23)

The temple is the house of the Lord. There are many reasons one should want to come to the temple. Even its external appearance seems to hint of its deeply spiritual purposes. This is much more evident within its walls. Over the door to the temple appears the tribute 'Holiness to the Lord.' When you enter any dedicated temple, you are in the house of the Lord. (95–02, p. 32)

The house of the Lord is sacred. Say the word *temple.* Say it quietly and reverently. Say it over and over again. *Temple. Temple. Temple.* Add the word *holy. Holy Temple.* Say it as though it were capitalized, no matter where it appears in the sentence.

Temple. One other word is equal in importance to a Latter-day Saint. *Home.* Put the words *holy temple* and *home* together, and you have described the house of the Lord! (93–01, pp. 20–21)

The purpose of temple dedications. While members of the Church may have contributed the money to build the temple and may themselves have labored to construct it, it is not theirs once it is dedicated. The dedication of a temple, in a real way, gives the building and all of the landscaping and structures related to the temple site to the Lord. The temple itself becomes literally the house of the Lord. The word *temple* comes from the word *templum,* which is defined as the abode of Deity or simply the house of the Lord. . . .

After a temple is dedicated we do not feel we own it. It is the Lord's house. He directs the conditions under which it may be used. He has revealed the ordinances that should be performed therein and has established the standards and conditions under which we may participate in them. (*THT,* pp. 34–35)

All our efforts should lead to the temple. We would do well to see that in administering the organizations of the Church, all roads lead to the temple. For it is there that we are prepared in all things to qualify us to enter the presence of the Lord. God grant that we can see, as He saw, that all we do to convert and baptize and activate and perfect them has its fulfillment through the consummate, supernal work of the house of the Lord. (87–04)

Temples are a tangible evidence of our faith in the resurrection. I have a deep regard for the work that is accomplished in our temples. Temples are the single most tangible, impressive evidence of our knowledge and our faith in the resurrection, and of our certain knowledge that there is life beyond death. (81–09, p. 179)

Testimony of temple work. I feel deeply—very, very deeply—this inspiration in the work of the temples. I have a profound regard for it.

I know as surely as I know that I live that the work relating to the temples is true. I know that it was revealed from beyond the veil. I know that that revelation continues.

I know also that revelation may come to each member of the Church individually concerning temple work.

Come to the temple—come and claim your blessings. It is a sacred work. Of this I give my witness. (*THT,* pp. 267–68)

Blessings come from temple service. I have the conviction that the Lord will bless us as we attend to the sacred ordinance work of the temples. Blessings there will not be limited to our temple service. We will be blessed in all of our affairs. We will be eligible to have the Lord take an interest in our affairs both spiritual and temporal. (*THT,* p. 182)

The temple—a place to take our cares. When members of the Church are troubled or when crucial decisions weigh heavily upon their minds, it is a common thing for them to go to the temple. It is a good place to take our cares. In the temple we can receive spiritual perspective. There, during the time of the temple service, we are "out of the world." . . . There is something cleansing and clarifying about the spiritual atmosphere of the temple.

Sometimes our minds are so beset with problems, and there are so many things clamoring for attention at once, that we just cannot think clearly and see clearly. At the temple the dust of distraction seems to settle out, the fog and the haze seem to lift, and we can "see" things that we were not able to see before and find a way through our troubles that we had not previously known. (*THT,* pp. 180–81)

Prerequisites for temple worship. Most educational programs require the completion of basic or prerequisite courses before one can register for advanced courses. At a university you cannot register for a graduate course in chemistry, or even an advanced course, until completing the basic or elementary courses. This principle of prerequisites is well understood in everyday life. . . . It should not seem unusual, then, that the Lord has decreed in His church that admission to the temple comes only after certain prerequisites have been filled. It should not seem unusual that certain preparation and worthiness should be established before these privileges are given. (*THT,* pp. 26–28)

Entrance to the temple requires personal worthiness. You must possess a current recommend to be admitted to the temple. This recommend must be signed by the proper officers of the Church. Only those who are worthy should go to the temple. Your local bishop or branch president has the responsibility of making inquiries into your personal worthiness. This interview is of great importance, for it is an occasion to explore with an ordained servant of the Lord the pattern of your life. If anything is amiss in your life, the bishop will be able to help you resolve it. Through this procedure, as you counsel with the common judge in Israel, you can declare or can be helped to establish your worthiness to enter the temple with the Lord's approval.

The interview for a temple recommend is conducted privately between the bishop and the Church member concerned. Here the member is asked searching questions about his personal conduct and worthiness and about his loyalty to the Church and its officers. The person must certify that he is morally clean and is keeping the Word of Wisdom, paying a full tithe, living in harmony with the teachings of the Church, and not maintaining any affiliation or sympathy with apostate groups. The bishop is instructed that confidentiality in handling these matters with each interviewee is of the utmost importance. (95–02, p. 32)

Come to the temple worthily. If you are eligible by the standards that are set, by all means you should come [to the temple] to receive your own blessings; and thereafter you should return again and again and again to make those same blessings available to others who have died without the opportunity to receive them in mortality. You should *not* come to the temple until you are eligible, until you meet the requirements that the Lord has set, but you should come; if not now, as soon as you can qualify. (*THT,* p. 11)

The importance of the temple recommend interview. I have come to know, in interviewing people who have made mistakes in their lives, that a very convincing evidence of repentance is that they are willing to do whatever is required of them. Occasionally, when a bishop is hesitant to issue a temple recommend, a member will resist the bishop and perhaps argue with him. That very attitude is a signal that the bishop may well need to consider very, very carefully whether or not someone with that spirit should be given the privilege of entering the house of the Lord. It indicates that member may not be quite ready.

Surely, when you appear to be interviewed for a temple recommend you would accept the judgment of him who is designated as the judge in Israel, who is responsible to represent the Lord in determining whether or not it is proper for you to enter this sacred place. (*THT,* pp. 54–55)

Dress and grooming in the temple. On occasion, when I have performed a marriage in the temple, there has been one there to witness it who obviously has paid little attention to the counsel that the Brethren have given about dress and grooming, about taking care not to emulate the world in the extremes of style in clothing, in hair length and arrangement, and so forth. I have wondered why it is that if such a person was mature enough to be admitted to the temple he would not at once be sensible enough to know that the Lord could not be pleased with those who show obvious preference to follow after the ways of the world.

How could a recommended member attend the temple in clothing that is immodest or worldly? How could one groom himself in such a way that the style of hair is not in keeping with refinement and dignity? . . . When you have the opportunity to go to the temple to participate in the temple ceremonies or to witness a sealing, remember where you are. You are a guest in the house of the Lord. You should groom yourself and clothe yourself in such a way that you would feel comfortable should your Host appear. (*THT,* p. 74)

There is another temple within the temple. However more imposing the temple at Salt Lake City may be, that invisible temple that lives in the building itself is the same in all temples. The ordinances are the same, the covenants equally binding, the blessings equally in force, the Holy Spirit of Promise equally present.

And the center of it all is another temple.

"Know ye not that ye are the temple of God, and that the Spirit of God dwelleth in you?

"If any man defile the temple of God, him shall God destroy; for the temple of God is holy, which temple ye are."[1] (93–04, p. 178)

THE TEMPLE—A HOUSE OF LEARNING

The temple is a great school. The temple is a great school. It is a house of learning. In the temples the atmosphere is maintained so that it is ideal for instruction on matters that are deeply spiritual. (95–02, p. 145)

The key to learning in the temple. What we gain *from* the temple will depend to a large degree on what we take *to* the temple in the way of humility and reverence and a desire to learn. If we are teachable we will be taught by the Spirit, in the temple. (*THT,* p. 42)

The purpose of temple learning. The instruction given in the endowment provides a firm perspective, a point of reference by which a person may gauge all his learning and wisdom, both spiritual and temporal; by which he may gather things together, determine their true meaning and significance, and fit them into their proper places.

It is at the temple that we may begin to see into the eternities. (*THT,* p. 45)

In the temple our vision of eternity expands. As we grow and mature and learn from all of the experiences in life, the truths demonstrated in the temple in symbolic fashion take on a renewed meaning. The veil is drawn back a little bit more. Our knowledge and vision of the eternities expands. It is always refreshing. (*THT,* p. 39)

The temple is symbolic. The temple itself becomes a symbol. If you have seen one of the temples at night, fully lighted, you know what an impressive sight that can be. The house of the Lord, bathed in light, standing out in the darkness, becomes symbolic of the power and the inspiration of the gospel of Jesus Christ standing as a beacon in a world that sinks ever further into spiritual darkness. (95–02, p. 146)

There is power in the symbolic teachings of the temple. If you will go to the temple and remember that the teaching is symbolic you will never go in the proper spirit without coming away with your vision extended, feeling a little more exalted, with your knowledge increased as to things that are spiritual. The teaching plan is superb. It is inspired. The Lord Himself, the Master Teacher, in His own teaching to His disciples taught constantly in parables, a verbal way to represent symbolically things that might otherwise be difficult to understand. He talked of the common experiences drawn from the lives of His disciples, and He told of hens and chickens, birds, flowers, foxes, trees, burglars, highwaymen, sunsets, the rich and the poor, the physician, patching clothes, pulling weeds, sweeping the house, feeding pigs, threshing grain, storing into barns, building houses, hiring help, and dozens of other things. He talked of the mustard seed, of the pearl. He wanted to teach His hearers, so He talked of simple things in a symbolic sense.

None of these things is mysterious or obscure, and all of them are symbolic. (*THT,* p. 41)

Look toward the temple. The temple ceremony will not be understood at first experience. It will be partly understood. Return again and again and again. Return to learn. Things that have troubled you or things that have been puzzling or things that have been mysterious will become known to you. Many of them will be the quiet, personal things that you really cannot explain to anyone else. But to you they are things known. . . .

So look toward the temple. Point your children toward the temple. From the days of their infancy, direct their attention to it, and begin their preparation for the day when they may enter the holy temple. (*THT,* pp. 41–42, 47)

The key to understanding temple ceremonies. Without the spiritual atmosphere of the temple itself, and without the worthiness and preparation required of those who go there, the temple ceremonies would not be quickly understood and might be quite misunderstood. Therefore I am content with the restrictions the Lord has placed on them. (*THT,* p. 36)

Importance of the Temple and Temple Ordinances

Temple work is centered in families. Temple work is centered in families. The ultimate end of all we do in the Church is to see that parents and children are happy at home and sealed together in the temple. (06–06)

The need for temple ordinances justified the Restoration. Surely it could be said today that very few of those who have experienced the endowment fully appreciate or fully know the supernal worth of the temple ordinances and the family history work which sustains them. This work is crucial to the redemption of both the living and the dead.

It is this doctrine more than any other we teach which sets The Church of Jesus Christ of Latter-day Saints apart from all of Christianity and must justify the Restoration. (93–04, p. 179)

Temple ordinances enrich us in three ways. To endow is to enrich, to give to another something long lasting and of much worth. The temple endowment ordinances enrich in three ways: (a) The one receiving the ordinance is given power from God. "Recipients are endowed with power from on high." (b) A recipient is also endowed with information and knowledge. "They receive an education relative to the Lord's purposes and plans."[2] (c) When sealed at the altar a person is the recipient of glorious blessings, powers, and honors as part of his endowment. (*THT,* p. 153)

Temple ordinances: sacred versus secret. Questions about the temple ceremony usually meet with the response, "We are not free to discuss the temple ordinances and ceremonies." Those who have not been to the temple sometimes ask, "Why is it so secret?"

If "secret" means that others are permanently prevented from knowing of them, then *secret* is the wrong word. These things are *sacred.*

It was never intended that knowledge of these temple ceremonies would be limited to a select few who would be obliged to ensure that others never learn of them. It is quite the opposite, in fact. Those who have been to the temple have been taught an ideal. Someday every living soul and every soul who has ever lived shall have the opportunity to hear the gospel and to accept or reject what the temple offers. If this opportunity is rejected, the rejection must be on the part of the individual himself. (*THT,* pp. 28–29)

Temple ordinances are to be kept sacred. A careful reading of the scriptures reveals that the Lord did not tell all things to all people. There were some qualifications set that were prerequisite to receiving sacred information. Temple ceremonies fall within this category.

We do not discuss the temple ordinances outside the temples. . . .

The ordinances and ceremonies of the temple are simple. They are beautiful. They are sacred. They are kept confidential lest they be given to those who are unprepared. Curiosity is not a preparation. Deep interest itself is not a preparation. Preparation for the ordinances includes preliminary steps: faith, repentance, baptism, confirmation, worthiness, a maturity and dignity worthy of one who comes invited as a guest into the house of the Lord.

All who are worthy and qualify in every way may enter the temple, there to be introduced to the sacred rites and ordinances. (95–02, pp. 143–44)

A major goal of the Church is to make the ordinances available. A major goal of the Church is as far as possible to make the fulness of the ordinances available to a growing membership worldwide. Now, what ordinances? Fundamental is the ordination to the priesthoods. When we get to the higher ordinances there are the washings and the anointings, the endowment, then the sealing, in which we organize the only permanent unit of the Church. This total process progressively moves the soul toward the perfection we all seek. (79–13, pp. 216–17)

Who may officiate and participate in temple ordinances. Those who are called as sealers in the temple are set apart only by direct authority held by the President of the Church. This should illustrate the deep regard in which these ordinances are held and the limitations that the Lord has set upon who may perform them. It should not be surprising that there should be limitations as to those who may receive them and those who may witness them. It should not, therefore, seem strange that the temples are held sacred, for all who will prepare themselves by repentance, by baptism, by preparation in worthiness to meet the qualifications, may enter therein to participate in the ordinances offered in the house of the Lord. When we go there we go as His servants. (*THT*, p. 35)

The endowment is required for exaltation. The blessing of the endowment is required for full exaltation. Every Latter-day Saint should seek to be worthy of this blessing and to obtain it. (*THT*, p. 154)

It is not safe to neglect the redemptive temple work. The work that goes on within the temples is a great redemptive, protective work of the Church. We are familiar with it in the sense of its being part of the three-fold mission of the Church: the preaching of the gospel (missionary work); the perfecting of the Saints (that work that goes on within the wards and the branches of the Church); and the redemption of our dead.

We have at home a little three-legged stool. One of the legs is set up so it can be removed. On occasions, to demonstrate some principle I will take that one leg from the stool and ask someone to cause the stool to stand. Most of the legs are there, but with one missing the stool cannot be made to stand on its own.

It is not safe for us collectively, nor is it safe for us individually, to neglect in our lives this sacred, redemptive work which constitutes one-third of the responsibility that rests upon this Church. (81–09, p. 181)

Making and keeping temple covenants brings us closer to our Heavenly Father. The work that goes on within our temples is a sacred work. The genealogical work which precedes it is an inspired work. By receiving the ordinances and making our covenants in the temple, by honoring those covenants, and wherever possible by regular temple attendance in service to those who have departed this life without having received these blessings, we can draw ever closer to our Father. (81–09, p. 184)

Temple covenants provide protection. It is in the ordinances of the temple that we are placed under covenant to Him—it is there we become the covenant people.

If we will accept the revelation concerning temple ordinance work, if we will enter into our covenants without reservation or apology, the Lord will protect us. We will receive inspiration sufficient for the challenges of life. (*THT,* p. 265)

Our labors in the temple cover us with a shield and a protection. No work is more of a protection to this church than temple work and the genealogical research that supports it. No work is more spiritually refining. No work we do gives us more power. No work requires a higher standard of righteousness.

Our labors in the temple cover us with a shield and a protection, both individually and as a people.

So come to the temple—come and claim your blessings. It is a sacred work. (95–02, p. 151)

The purpose of the temple garment. The garment represents sacred covenants. It fosters modesty and becomes a shield and protection to the wearer.

The wearing of such a garment does not prevent members from dressing in the fashionable clothing generally worn in the nations of the world. Only clothing that is immodest or extreme in style would be incompatible with wearing the garment. Any member of the Church, whether he or she has been to the temple or not, would in proper spirit want to avoid extreme or revealing fashions. (*THT*, p. 75)

Why we wear the temple garment. On one occasion I was invited to speak to the faculty and staff of the Navy Chaplains Training School in Newport, Rhode Island. The audience included a number of high-ranking naval chaplains from the Catholic, Protestant, and Jewish faiths. A class of chaplains then being trained were also invited to the meeting. My invitation asked me to explain the tenets of the Church and to respond to questions the chaplains might have. The idea was for them to learn more about what they might do for Latter-day Saint servicemen in their chaplaincy service, particularly in remote areas where such men were out of contact with the Church. At the time there was a need for them to be informed, because the Vietnam War was then in full fury.

In the question-and-answer period one of the chaplains asked, "Can you tell us something about the special underwear that some Mormon servicemen wear?" The implication was, "Why do you do that? Isn't it strange? Doesn't that present a problem?"

I knew of course that the matter of the garment was a concern to Latter-day Saint servicemen who had been to the temple. Since they generally were living in open barracks, on occasions their under-clothing was visible to the other men. Naturally they sometimes were questioned about it, and on some occasions uncharitable fellows ridiculed them. . . .

There are several circumstances in which nonmembers may have a legitimate reason to take an interest in the garment or special under-clothing that is worn by members of the Church who have been endowed. Those who have received their endowment know what the garment symbolizes and the sacred nature of the covenants connected with it. But it is important to satisfy the inquiry of those who are legit-imately interested, to the point at least of having them understand that this is a matter of very deep significance to us in the Church.

To the chaplain who made the inquiry I responded with a question: "Which church do you represent?" In response he named one of the Protestant churches.

I said, "In civilian life and also when conducting the meetings in the military service you wear clerical clothing, do you not?" He said that he did.

I continued: "I would suppose that that has some importance to you, that in a sense it sets you apart from the rest of your congregation. It is your uniform, as it were, of the ministry. Also, I suppose it may have a much more important place. It reminds you of who you are and what your obligations and covenants are. It is a continual reminder that you are a member of the clergy, that you regard yourself as a servant of the Lord, and that you are responsible to live in such a way as to be worthy of your ordination."

The chaplains all seemed to consent to this appraisal of the value of their own clerical clothing.

I then told them: "You should be able to understand at least one of our reasons why Latter-day Saints have a deep spiritual commitment concerning the garment. A major difference between your churches and ours is that we do not have a professional clergy, as you do. The con-gregations are all presided over by local leaders. They are men called from all walks of life. Yet they are ordained to the priesthood. They hold offices in the priesthood. They are set apart to presiding positions as presidents, counselors, and leaders in various categories. The women, too, share in that responsibility and in those obligations. The man who heads our congregation on Sunday as the bishop may go to work on Monday as a postal clerk, as an office worker, a farmer, a doctor; or he may be an air force pilot or a naval officer. By our standard he is as much an ordained minister as you are by your standard. He is recognized as such by most governments. We draw something of the same benefits from this special clothing as you would draw from your clerical vestments. The difference is that we wear ours under our clothing instead of outside, for we are employed in various occupations in addition to our service in the Church. These sacred things we do not wish to parade before the world."

I then explained that there are some deeper spiritual meanings as well, connecting the practice of wearing this garment with covenants that are made in the temple. We wouldn't find it necessary to discuss these—not that they are secret, I repeated, but because they are sacred.

I told them that if they would accept baptism into The Church of Jesus Christ of Latter-day Saints and live in harmony with its teachings, they too could share in all of the blessings connected with the holy temple.

They found that answer completely satisfying. They made a comment or two about it along the lines of understanding now why the Latter-day Saint men in the military service were so careful about this matter. They could then see that to ridicule that practice was, in a sense, to ridicule Christian clergy in general. I have found from making this explanation to military chaplains and to Christian ministers generally, individually and on occasions in large gatherings where the question has come up, that it is a dimension they had not previously considered. Having received this explanation, they tend to become more protective of the members of the Church who are wearing the garment. (*THT,* pp. 75–78)

The essence of the meaning of temples. When we say *temple* I would list what in essence are Latter-day Saint synonyms for the word:

marriage, family, children, happiness, joy, eternal life, resurrection, redemption, exaltation, inspiration, revelation. (*THT,* p. 260)

There will be opposition to temple work. Temple work brings so much resistance because it is the source of so much spiritual power to the Latter-day Saints and to the entire Church. (95–02, p. 150)

The adversary will try to interfere with temple work. Temples are the very center of the spiritual strength of the Church. We should expect that the adversary will try to interfere with us as a Church and with us individually as we seek to participate in this sacred and inspired work. The interference can vary from the terrible persecutions of the earlier days to apathy toward the work. The latter is perhaps the most dangerous and debilitating form of resistance to temple work. (*THT,* p. 177)

Do not let opposition deter you from temple work. If we face difficulties and frustrations and opposition, even persecution—both individually and as a church—it is of little moment in the eternal scheme of things. Do not let opposition deter you from your genealogical or temple work.

To those who sense the size of this challenge to provide temple ordinance work for all, both living and dead, and are overwhelmed by it, I say, "Have faith. We will win the day, and the Lord will provide." To those who are hesitant to move, I say, "Wake up and see the vision of it. We can accomplish the things we have been commanded, if we will but get started." (*THT,* p. 183)

Those who seek to prevent temple work will come away with nothing. We built a temple in Nauvoo. It was destroyed. It happened in Kirtland, in Independence, in Far West, and in Nauvoo. The Saints set about to build temples. In each case, either they were prevented from building the temple or it was taken away from them; and in Nauvoo the temple was defiled and destroyed.

Those who joined the unholy power to prevent temple work seemed to win. Time after time they had their way. They ended up, for a time at least, with the sites—leaving to the persecuted Saints nothing. Nothing? No! We have the keys, the ordinances. We have everything. *They* have nothing. They cannot baptize nor ordain. They cannot wash nor anoint nor endow nor seal. We came away with everything, and they have nothing. Our forebears were compelled, because of those deprivations in the early years, to focus on the things that mattered most. (*THT,* pp. 174–75)

TEMPLE ORDINANCES FOR THE DEAD

There is no other work so immersed in the Spirit. There is no work that I know of that is so immersed in the Spirit as this sacred work of preparing names for the temple and the subsequent ordinances that are performed there. (99–08)

The doctrine of redemption for the dead sets us apart from all other Christian churches. Except for the doctrine of the redemption of the dead, the gospel would be so nearly deficient that we would come close to being little better in our offering than any of the Christian churches. The problem is this, most of the people who live on the earth at any given time are not baptized by immersion for remission of sins. The Lord made very clear that except ye be baptized in the water and the Spirit ye will nowise enter the kingdom of heaven. Well, they are trapped. What kind of a God would make an absolute decree that baptism is the entrance into the kingdom of heaven, then let it be on earth that most of the population never came under the ordinance?

Well that is a question that can be answered only in The Church of Jesus Christ of Latter-day Saints. It is answered on the doctrine of baptism for the dead. (95–13)

Importance of vicarious work for the dead. Every Latter-day Saint is responsible for this work. Without this work, the saving ordinances of the gospel would apply to so few who have ever lived that the gospel could not be claimed to be true.

Probably no point of doctrine sets this Church apart from the other

With children in Guatemala, June 1979

claimants as this one does. Save for it, we would, with all of the other churches, have to accept the clarity with which the New Testament declares baptism to be essential and then admit that most of the human family could never have it. (*THT,* p. 20)

Baptisms for the dead are essential. We have been authorized to perform baptisms vicariously so that when those who have passed on hear the gospel preached and desire to accept it, that essential ordinance will have been performed. They need not ask for any exemption from that essential ordinance. Indeed, the Lord Himself was not exempted from it. . . .

"Strange," one may say. It *is* passing strange. It is transcendent and supernal. The very nature of the work testifies that Jesus Christ is our Lord, that baptism is essential, that He taught the truth. (75–06, p. 99)

The necessity of baptisms for the dead. There is a very provoking and a very disturbing question about those who died without baptism. What about them? If there is none other name given under heaven whereby man must be saved (and that is true), and they have lived and died without even hearing that name, and if baptism is essential (and it is), and they died without even the invitation to accept it, where are they now? . . . There are several non-Christian religions larger than most of the Christian denominations, and together those religions are larger than all of the Christian denominations combined. Their adherents for centuries have lived and died and never heard the word *baptism.* What is the answer for them?

That is a most disturbing question. What power would establish one Lord and one baptism and then allow it to happen that most of the human family never comes within the influence of its doctrines? With that question unanswered, the vast majority of the human family must be admitted to be lost, including the little boy who drowned—and against any reasonable application of the law of justice, or of mercy, either. In those circumstances, how could Christianity itself be sustained?

If a church has no answer to this dilemma, how can it lay claim to be the Lord's church? Surely He is not willing to write off the majority of the human family because they were never baptized while on earth. . . . The answer to the puzzling challenge could not be invented by men. It had to be, and was, revealed. . . . With proper authority a mortal person could be baptized for and in behalf of someone who had not had that opportunity before passing on. That individual would then accept or reject the baptism in the spirit world, according to his own desire. (*THT,* pp. 14–17)

Without the work for the dead the plan would be unfair. Provision is made in the plan for those who live in mortality without knowing of the plan. "Where there is no law given there is no punishment; and where there is no punishment there is no condemnation; . . . because of the Atonement; . . . they are delivered."[3] Without that sacred work of the redemption of the dead, the plan would be incomplete and would really be unfair. (95–06, p. 4)

Vicarious ordinances are Christlike. There are those who scoff at the idea of vicarious ordinances performed for the salvation of souls. They think it all to be very strange.

No thinking Christian should be surprised at such a doctrine. Was not the sacrifice of Christ a vicarious offering for and in behalf of all mankind? The very Atonement was wrought vicariously.

The Lord did for us what we could not do for ourselves. Is it not Christlike for us to perform in the temples ordinances for and in behalf of those who cannot do them for themselves? (87–03, p. 24)

The Lord will reveal means to accomplish missions and temple work. We do not now see how we can preach the gospel to every living soul. Nor do we yet know how we can find the names of those who did not have the opportunity to hear the gospel in mortality. But we can do what we can do now. And when we stand in need of further light and knowledge or more developed means of doing the work, the need will be supplied. Direction may be given on how we can hasten both the acquisition of names and the performing of the necessary vicarious ordinance work. (*THT,* p. 221)

We are under covenant to work to redeem all. All of the long-range goals will be tremendously expensive in both time and means. But we are under covenant to commit all that we have of both, to the building up of the Church and the kingdom of God and the establishment of Zion, both here and beyond the veil.

To those who sense the size of this challenge to redeem all who have ever lived, and are overwhelmed by it, I say, have faith. We will win the day, and the Lord will provide.

To those who are hesitant to move, I say, wake up and see the vision of it. (77–05)

No person ever born will be overlooked. The ordinance of vicarious baptism makes it possible for everyone who has been born or will yet be born, who missed baptism during their life on earth, to come under its redeeming influence.[4]

No person ever born to this earth, no matter where or when or what race or persuasion, will be overlooked or passed by or neglected. All are provided for, either in this life or in the next, that "all mankind may be saved, by obedience to the laws and ordinances of the Gospel."[5] (04–04)

We must love the deceased and desire to redeem them. One day while pondering prayerfully on this matter I came to a realization that there is something that any one of us can do for all who have died.

I came to see that any one of us, by himself, can care about them, all of them, and love them. That came as a great inspiration, for then I knew there was a starting point.

Whatever the number, we can love them, and desire to redeem them. Any one of us has within us the power to expand our concern to include them all. If a billion more are added, we can care for them also.

If the numbers seem staggering, we will move ahead. If the process is tedious, we will move ahead anyway. If the records have been lost, if the obstacles and opposition are overwhelming, we will move ahead anyway.

But now we must adopt a different *attitude,* different procedures, and technology. We must redeem the dead, all of them, for we are commanded to do it. (77–05)

Keys and authority are necessary for all ordinances. In the Church we hold sufficient authority to perform all of the ordinances necessary to redeem and to exalt the whole human family. And, because we have the keys to the sealing power, what we bind in proper order here will be bound in heaven. Those keys—the keys to seal and bind on earth, and have it bound in heaven—represent the consummate gift from our God. With that authority we can baptize and bless, we can endow and seal, and the Lord will honor our commitments. (*THT,* p. 151)

Those beyond the veil minister here that temple work might be completed. Veils can become thin, even parted. We are not left to do this work alone.

They who have preceded us in this work and our forebears there, on occasion, are very close to us. I have a testimony of this work; it is a supernal work in the Church. I am a witness that those who go beyond the veil yet live and minister here, to the end that this work might be completed. (87–03, p. 25)

The gospel must be available to all. We in the Church must not retreat before the overwhelming assignment of extending the gospel to all men, both living and dead. Not all those living to whom we preach the gospel may accept it. But we are obliged to extend it to them. If we go out to do it, that part which is consistent with the will of the Lord will be accomplished and we will stand approved of Him. (*THT,* p. 211)

FAMILY HISTORY WORK

Essential components of family history and temple work. There are several basic component parts to genealogical and temple work. Over the years, they may be rearranged somewhat in emphasis, or the approach in programming Church participation may change somewhat. But the responsibilities stay about the same.

1. Each of us is to compile his own life history.
2. Each of us is to keep a book of remembrance.
3. As individuals and families we are each to seek out our kindred dead, beginning first with the four most recent generations on each line, and then going back as far as we can.
4. We are each to participate in other programs such as name extraction when asked to do so.
5. We are to organize our families and hold meetings and reunions.
6. If we have access to a temple, each of us should go to the temple as often as possible to do ordinance work—first for ourselves, then for our progenitors, then for all the names that have been gathered by means other than our own. (*THT,* pp. 229–30)

Family history work is more than processing names. Family history is getting names processed to go to the temple. But it is also family relationships, and it is family reunions, and it is family connections, and it is keeping the accounts of the things that are handed down from parents to children and passed through families that connect and make the spiritual connection through this power of the Holy Ghost, the Spirit by which we operate. (02–08)

Parents should teach the importance of the temple and family history. Parents can teach the children about their grandparents and instill in them a love for their family name. They can teach them of the resurrection and the fact that their forebears actually live beyond the veil, and someday there will be a reunion.

Father and mother can speak of ordinances and covenants. By the inflection of their voices, they can italicize the word *temple* every time they say it. "Temple" can be made a companion to the word "worthiness." The words "tithes" and "offering" can be grouped together with "service" and "sacrifice," "missionary" and "calling," "prayer" and "sacrament" and "faith," "covenant" and "ordinance." These are the words that should live together with a family. (88–02)

There will always be a need to know the basics in family history research. There will never be an end to our need to know the basics. Speaking figuratively, we must know the routine, the dull, ordinary, maybe tiresome routine of recording names. What I know about family history work is not simply the administration of it, because I have been to the record office and with my wife sat and gone through the dusty books that I know haven't been opened since they were closed hundreds of years ago, making sure that we knew the footnotes were correct and understanding the proper family relationships and places and names and all of this. The laser does great work and the Internet does great work, but it doesn't do that. (99–08)

You do not need to be an expert to do temple and family history work. You can fulfill your obligation to your kindred dead and to the Lord without forsaking your other Church callings. You can do it without abandoning your family responsibilities. You can do this work. You can do it without becoming a so-called "expert" in it. (*THT*, p. 230)

Revelation has and will come. We have collected hundreds of millions of names, and the work goes forward in the temples and will go on in other temples that will be built. We do not suggest that the size of the effort should be impressive, for we are not doing nearly as well as we should be.

Those who thoughtfully consider the work inquire about those names that cannot be collected. "What about those for whom no record was ever kept? Surely you will fail there. There is no way you can search out those names."

To this I simply observe, "You have forgotten revelation." Already we have been directed to many records through that process. Revelation comes to individual members as they are led to discover their family records in ways that are miraculous indeed. And there is a feeling of inspiration attending this work that can be found in no other. When we have done all that we can do, we shall be given the rest. The way will be opened up. (75–06, p. 99)

Temple work is lineage-linked. All that I have learned from the revelations and from reading the statements of the prophets has fixed two things in my mind. First, we are individually responsible to seek after our kindred dead and see that the temple ordinances are performed for them. Second, once those names have been found, we are to establish family relationships. Genealogical and temple work is lineage-linked. We are linking the generations together. (*THT,* p. 225)

Temple and family history work—one eternal round. I have wondered over the years about the meaning of the scripture recorded three times in the Book of Mormon, that "the course of the Lord is one eternal round."[6]

I can see one meaning as it relates to our work for the dead. Genealogical work, the essential preparation for temple work, puts us to seeking through the records for those who have lived in the past. We look back to the past to find them. We perform temple ordinance work for them and then we look forward to the future to meet them. Something sacred is consummated when we have safely recorded, in the list of ordinances completed, the names of those who *lived* in our past and who yet *live* in our future. This ordinance work is crucial to us and to the Church. (*THT,* pp. 249–50)

Temple and family history work are pleasing to the Lord. Temple and genealogical work constitutes a living testimony of the ministry of the Lord Jesus Christ. He wrought the Atonement; He set in operation the resurrection.

If men were really "dead" when they die, why concern ourselves? Why the vast resources of time and money and effort directed at this work? If there were no resurrection, why would we do it?

But there is life beyond the veil. Every thought or word or act we direct at this sacred work is pleasing to the Lord. Every hour spent on genealogical research, however unproductive it appears, is worthwhile. It is pleasing to the Lord. It is our testimony to Him that we accept the doctrine of the resurrection and the plan of salvation. It draws us close to those who have gone before. It welds eternal links in family associations and draws us closer to Him who is our Lord and stands in the presence of Him who is our Eternal Father. (*THT,* p. 255)

Temple and genealogy work are visible testimonies of our belief in the Resurrection and Atonement. The more I have to do with genealogical work, the more difficulty I have with that word *dead.* I know of no adequate substitute. I suppose *departed* would suit me as well as any. I have had too many sacred experiences, of the kind of which we never speak lightly, to feel that the word *dead* describes those who have gone beyond the veil.

Temple and genealogy work are visible testimonies of our belief in the Resurrection and Atonement of the Lord Jesus Christ. Should we doubt that we live again beyond the veil, what reason would we have to do the things we are doing?

This work is our witness of the redemptive power of the sacrifice of the Lord Jesus Christ. (87–03, p. 25)

Family history work is spiritually refining. Genealogical work has the power to do something *for* the dead. It has an equal power to do something *to* the living. Genealogical work of Church members has a refining, spiritualizing, tempering influence on those who are engaged in it. They understand that they are tying their family together, their living family here with those who have gone before. (*THT,* p. 239)

Doing temple and family history work blesses you with perspective, patience, and spirituality. Members of the Church cannot touch this work without becoming affected spiritually. The spirit of Elijah permeates it. Many of the little intrusions into our lives, the little difficulties and the petty problems that beset us, are put into proper perspective when we view the linking of the generations for the eternities. We become much more patient then. So if you want the influence of dignity and wisdom and inspiration and spirituality to envelop your life, involve yourself in temple and genealogical work. (*THT,* pp. 224–25)

Temple and family history work lead to spiritual refinement. I know of no work in the Church more conducive to spiritual refinement and communication than temple and genealogical work. In this work our hearts and our minds are turned to those beyond the veil. Such a work helps us to sharpen our spiritual sensitivities. (*THT,* p. 241)

Family history and temple work are individual responsibilities. There are other things we can do collectively as a church. We microfilm records worldwide. We establish libraries for use of members and non-members. We build vaults to store records. As a Church we develop forms and procedures to help in research. We prepare research manuals. We program conferences, meetings, and seminars to motivate, instruct, and inspire.

Nevertheless genealogical and temple work are basically *individual* responsibilities. . . . We are all responsible, individually, to link our families in proper order. (*THT,* pp. 227–28)

Our responsibility for family history work. We should search the records for the names of our kindred dead. We are to run that chain of lineage sealings back as far as we can obtain the information. We are to do the ordinance work for our progenitors. (*THT,* p. 206)

Searching out our kindred dead is a duty of consummate importance. Genealogies, or family histories, as I prefer to call them, are an indispensable part of temple work. Temples are nourished with names. Without genealogies, ordinances could be performed only for the living. Searching out the names of our kindred dead is a duty of consummate importance. There is a spirit which accompanies this work very similar to that which attends us in the temple itself. (87–03, p. 24)

Do not belittle those who do family history research. There is the tendency on the part of some to regard genealogy work as a tedious, onerous burden. And they are quite content to leave it to the aged or to others "who have an interest in such things."

Be careful! It may well be that those who have that interest in such things have chosen the better part. And I would say to you, if you are called to other service, or do not have an interest in genealogy, do not belittle or stand in the way of those who do. Give them every encouragement; contribute what you can. (87–03, pp. 24–25)

Family history work justifies itself. Genealogical work in one sense would justify itself, even if one were not successful in clearing names for temple work. The process of searching, the means of going after those names, would be worth all the effort you could invest. The reason: You cannot find names without knowing that they represent people. You begin to find out things about people. When we research our own lines we become interested in more than just names or the number of names going through the temple. Our interest turns our hearts to our fathers—we seek to find them and to know them and to serve them.

In doing so we store up treasures in heaven. (*THT,* pp. 239–40)

The spirit of Elijah. There is a special spirit that attends the work that we do in gathering the names and recording the lineage of families preparatory to ordinances being performed in the holy temple. Those who discern that spirit know it to be the spirit of Elijah as it has been described over the years.

This spirit was present long before Elijah was upon the earth, for the revelations tell us that this work was ordained from before the foundation of the world. And the scriptures tell us that for thereunto were the keys of the holy priesthood ordained . . . that spirit is present when the Latter-day Saints kneel at the altars of the temple and perform the sealings and when the washings and the anointings and the endowments and the ordinances are performed so that the work of this dispensation might roll forward.

I have felt that spirit, know that spirit, know this to be a supernal work. The mind of man could not have invented this work. The mind of mortal man could not have contemplated it. And I'm grateful that that motivating spirit belongs not just to the presiding authorities of the Church or not just on some rare and marvelous occasion, but it follows all Latter-day Saints across the world and motivates those who are not members of the Church as they record these names to the end that the promises and the prophecies might be fulfilled. (88–10)

As the years have passed since Elijah restored the keys of the sealing power, the determination of the Latter-day Saints to turn their hearts to their fathers has become increasingly evident. This is not just a philosophical idea to be debated. It is a work to be performed. We receive further light and knowledge as the work requires. We can each receive inspiration—the spirit of Elijah—as we involve ourselves in this sacred labor of love. (*THT,* p. 208)

The spirit of Elijah is powerful and compelling. The spirit of Elijah spoken of by the Prophet here and on other occasions is something very real. When a member of the Church comes under its influence, it is a powerful, compelling force which motivates him with a desire to be attending to genealogical and temple work. It leaves him anxious over the well-being of his forebears. When that spirit comes, somehow we desire to know more about those forebears—we desire to *know* them. (*THT,* p. 210)

We will meet our forebears. The time will come when each one of us will be invited to pass through that separating veil. If we have done our duty in this great work for those who have passed on, well might we look forward with great anticipation to that time, for a great reward awaits us there. With all assurance, it awaits. I will meet my forebears and you will meet yours. (*THT,* p. 267)

The gradual revelation of the sealing to families. In the early days of the Church the Saints didn't know how to use this power in behalf of the dead. Overjoyed when given the knowledge that they could baptize for the dead, they went to the river and began doing so. Elder Wilford Woodruff recalled those days as follows: "[Joseph Smith] never stopped till he got the fulness of the word of God to him concerning baptism for the dead. But before doing so he went into the Mississippi River, and so did I, as well as others, and we each baptized a hundred for the dead, without a man to record a single act that we performed."

It seems they just ran out to the river and began baptizing for their ancestors.

And then this: "Why did we do it? Because of the feeling of joy that we had, to think that we in the flesh could stand and redeem our dead. We did not wait to know what the result of this would be, or what the whole of it should be."[7]

Similarly it took time for the Saints to understand the matter of sealings. They knew that there was a sealing, yet they didn't know quite what it was, so they began by getting themselves sealed to living prophets. . . .

In April 1894, this changed. In general conference President Wilford Woodruff explained a little about what the Saints had been doing, and from the pulpit he talked to the temple presidents. . . . He told them: "You have acted up to all the light and knowledge that you have had; but you have now something more to do. We have not fully carried out those principles in fulfillment of the revelations of God to us, in sealing the hearts of the fathers to the children and the children to the fathers."

For some time he had not felt satisfied with the way this important matter was being handled.

"When I went before the Lord to know who I should be adopted to (we were then being adopted to prophets and apostles), the Spirit of God said to me, 'Have you not a father who begot you?'

"'Yes, I have.'

"'Then why not honor him? Why not be adopted to him.'

"'Yes,' said I, 'that is right.'

"I was adopted to my father and should have had my father sealed to his father, and so on back. And the duty that I want every man who presides over a temple to see performed from this day henceforth and forever, unless the Lord God Almighty commands otherwise, is, let every man be adopted to his father. That is the will of God to this people."

And that's when we got the lineage straightened out and we knew what this sealing of families was all about. (79–13, pp. 214–16)

A simple process by which to begin your life history. There are two very simple instructions for those who are waiting for a place to begin. Here's what you might do:

Get a cardboard box. Any kind of a box will do. Put it some place where it is in the way, perhaps on the couch or on the counter in the kitchen—anywhere where it cannot go unnoticed. Then, over a period of a few weeks, collect and put into the box every record of your life, such as,

> your birth certificate,
> your certificate of blessing,
> your certificate of baptism,
> your certificate of ordination,
> your certificate of graduation.

Collect diplomas, all of the photographs, honors or awards, a diary if you have kept one, everything that you can find pertaining to *your* life; anything that is written, or registered, or recorded that testifies that you are alive and what you have done.

Don't try to do this in a day. Take some time on it. Most of us have these things scattered around here and there. Some of them are in a box in the garage under that stack of newspapers; others are stored away in drawers, or in the attic, or one place or another. Perhaps some have been tucked in the leaves of the Bible or elsewhere.

Gather all these papers together and put them in the box. Keep it there until you have collected everything you think you have. Then make some space on a table, or even on the floor, and sort out all that you have collected. Divide your life into three periods. The Church does it that way. All of our programming in the Church is divided into three general categories—children, youth, and adult.

Start with the childhood section and begin with your birth certificate. Put together every record in chronological order: the pictures, the record of your baptism, etc., up to the time you were twelve years of age.

Next assemble all that which pertains to your youth, from twelve to eighteen, or up until the time you were married. Put all of that together in chronological order. Line up the records—the certificates, the photographs, and so on—and put them in another box or envelope. Do the same with the records on the rest of your life.

Once you have done this, you have what is necessary to complete your life story. Simply take your birth certificate and begin writing: "I was born September 10, 1924, the son of Ira W. Packer and Emma Jensen Packer, at Brigham City, Utah. I was the tenth child and the fifth son in the family." Etc., etc., etc.

It really won't take you long to write, or dictate into a tape recorder, the account of your life, and it will have an accuracy because you have collected those records. (*THT*, pp. 232–33)

CHAPTER 24

Spreading the Gospel

*"We accept the responsibility to preach the gospel to every
person on earth. And if the question is asked, 'You mean you are out
to convert the entire world?' the answer is, 'Yes. We will try to
reach every living soul.'" (THT, p. 13)*

PREPARING AND CALLING MISSIONARIES

***Every Latter-day Saint young man should answer the call to
serve a mission.*** We, as members of the Church, have the fulness of the
gospel. Every conceivable manner of spiritual nourishment is ours.
Every part of the spiritual menu is included. It provides an unending
supply of spiritual strength. Like the widow's cruse of oil, it is replenished as we use it and shall never fail.[1]

And yet, there are people across the world and about us—our
neighbors, our friends, some in our own families—who, spiritually
speaking, are undernourished. Some of them are starving to death!

If we keep all this to ourselves, it is not unlike feasting before those
who are hungry.

We are to go out to them, and to invite them to join us. We are to
be missionaries.

It does not matter if it interrupts your schooling or delays your career or your marriage—or basketball. Unless you have a serious health problem, every Latter-day Saint young man should answer the call to serve a mission.

Even mistakes and transgressions must not stand in the way. You should make yourself *worthy* to receive a call. (84–04, p. 42)

Worthy young men should answer the call to be a missionary. Each young man who is physically able to serve has a sacred priesthood duty to remain worthy, to be willing to answer the call to be a missionary. And it is a call; it is not just an option or an invitation. The stake president and the bishop must teach them that, so that they never turn down a call from the Lord. (85–07, p. 132)

It is the Lord's mission, not ours. If you are going on *your* mission, you have a lot of problems ahead of you. You have no end of disappointment. If you are going on the *Lord's* mission and you get that fixed in your mind, you won't care where you go or what the circumstances are. (97–01)

Three keys for mission preparation. Missionary service is the work of the Lord. We who hold the priesthood are the only ones on earth with authority to perform the ordinances connected with it. It is the duty of the young men holding the priesthood to serve in the mission field. In preparation for that service you need to do three things.

First, you should decide now, in spite of temptation or opposition, that you will serve a mission. It is your duty! . . . Having made the decision, the second thing you must do is to remain worthy. In our society that will not be easy. But then why should it be easy? The physical strength of youth needs to be surpassed by the moral strength of your young manhood. . . . Finally, you need to prepare financially. Every one of you should have a savings account specifically reserved for your mission. I speak to that young man who doesn't have any idea how he can finance a mission. I do not know either. But I do know this: if you will go, there will be a way. Opportunities will come to you as manna from heaven. Do not let that deter you from your duty. Young brethren, a mission is a duty—it is your duty. And you have the help of your teachers and leaders in the Church—and most of all your parents. First, you should decide now, in spite of temptation or opposition, that you will serve a mission. It is *your* duty! (83–02, pp. 56–58)

Mission preparation is a moral protection. The obligation to prepare for a mission is a moral protection for our youth. They must come worthily. We must have each one of them arrive at the age of a mission call in worthiness. The call and the worthiness are inseparable. (85–07, pp. 134–35)

Young women should encourage young men to serve missions. Some young men are—now I must choose the right word—forced? persuaded? encouraged? compelled? to serve a mission by a sweet girl. She flashes her pretty eyelashes and says with some determination that she will one day marry one who has served an honorable mission.

It is interesting indeed what inspires spiritual patriotism. How quickly a young hero will line up to enlist with that kind of encouragement. God bless the sisters who have such power to recruit missionaries. (83–02, p. 59)

Missionary work is the responsibility of the priesthood. Missionary work is the responsibility of the priesthood. Sisters may serve on missions. It's a little different with the sisters than the brethren. If the sisters desire to serve on missions, then they may be called but there isn't the same pressure or emphasis for all of the sisters to serve on missions. There are some practical reasons for that and there are some ecclesiastical reasons, as well. One of the practical reasons is that in many missions, there are places where it isn't safe for sisters to serve. We are happy to have in the mission field a certain number of sisters but all of the sisters in the Church of missionary age are not really pressed to serve on missions. As your lives unfold, you will find that there are greater missions yet for the sisters. (97–01)

Missionary service is the best way to learn the gospel. If there is any best way for a young member of the Church to gain an in-depth knowledge of the gospel, it is to serve a mission. A mission is a near-perfect combination of study and application of principles as one learns them. Nothing can compare with it.

The calling of a missionary requires him to be able to teach the basic principles of the gospel all day every day. He teaches the plan of salvation over and over and over again.

The Lord is our example. It would be hard to describe the Lord as an executive. He was a teacher! That is the ideal, the pattern.

Missionaries are teachers. No student learns quite as much from hearing a lesson as a teacher does from preparing it.

Just imagine having a two-hour study period every day with a companion. The missionary studies the scriptures as he never has before and as he never will be able to do again, particularly if he is called to a leadership position. He is given a foundation in the very essence of the gospel. (84–03, p. 69)

Priesthood leaders must approach the call of missionaries prayerfully. Perhaps the most precious thing that we carefully maintain is the letter of call to a specific mission from the President of the Church. This is much to be treasured by every missionary. But the Church is so large now that the President of the Church cannot pray about each soul by name, individually. No ward is so large, however, nor any stake so extended, as to prevent both bishop and stake president from praying on their knees over the name of each young man, separate and apart from any other name—asking the Lord through the veil how to keep them worthy, when each should be called, and how to inspire each one with the sacred nature of the call. The stake presidents and bishops must be careful not to draw back from this sacred work in the calling of missionaries. (85–07, pp. 131–32)

The safety of the Church rests on successfully calling missionaries. The safety of the Church in generations ahead rests on our success in calling missionaries. If leaders and parents have concern for the future of this work, we will not rest until every able-bodied young man in the Church is made worthy and desires to receive a call to a mission. (84–03, p. 70)

A key to spiritual strength is the calling of missionaries. There is a cause-and-effect relationship between the calling of missionaries to go abroad and the growth of the Church at home.

There are countries which have received missionaries from the center stakes of Zion for a hundred years or more, where they have not yet developed the tradition that their young men serve on missions. As a result, in some missions the number of converts is fewer in a whole year than it is in many missions in a single month.

In other countries, where the gospel has been preached for only a generation or two, they enjoy very rapid growth, with more converts in a month than some missions produce in a year. In those countries their youth are called to missions in generous numbers, notwithstanding they are the developing countries where our members are poor, very poor.

The stakes that accept missionaries from the center stakes of Zion and do not send missionaries are not spiritually safe. They will not grow either in numbers or in spiritual strength. The key is the calling of missionaries. (85–07, p. 137)

We must not be casual about preparing and calling missionaries to serve. We need parents and teachers and leaders who will pray with and about our young people.

The youth will be casual about serving if we are casual about preparing and calling them. They need a "cause." Give them the cause, the greatest on earth. They will serve on missions if they are *called to serve on missions.* If they are invited or recommended or interviewed only, and asked to consider only, they may turn down a call from the Lord. (85–07, p. 137)

MISSIONARY WORK

We are commanded to preach the gospel. We are *commanded* to preach the gospel. We are commanded to preach, whether or not there are any extra benefits and blessings from it. Why? Because *it is our duty!* That is a principle, a *commanding principle!* (84–03, p. 70)

We have a duty to feed the sheep. Young brethren, I can hear the voice of the Lord saying to each of us just as He said to Peter, "Feed my lambs. . . . Feed my sheep. . . . Feed my sheep."[2]

I have unbounded confidence and faith in you, our young brethren. You are the warriors of the Restoration. And in this spiritual battle, you are to relieve the spiritual hunger and feed the sheep. It is your duty! (84–04, p. 43)

We accept the responsibility to preach the gospel to all. The powerful missionary spirit and the vigorous missionary activity in The Church of Jesus Christ of Latter-day Saints becomes a very significant witness that the true gospel and the authority are possessed in this church. We accept the responsibility to preach the gospel to every person on earth. And if the question is asked, "You mean you are out to convert the entire world?" the answer is, "Yes. We will try to reach every living soul."

Some who measure that challenge say quickly, "Why, that's impossible! It cannot be done!"

To that we simply say, "Perhaps, but we shall do it anyway."

Against the insinuation that it cannot be done, we are willing to commit to this work every resource that can be righteously accumulated. And while our effort may seem modest when measured against the challenge, it is hard to ignore when measured against what is being accomplished, or even what is being attempted, elsewhere. (*THT,* pp. 13–14)

You are called to serve. May the Lord bless you and bless those who sent you and who sustain you. Go in the Spirit, and go patiently. Go under call. You are under call. You have been called to serve. It is His Church, not yours. You are to do His bidding, not your own. As you do that, you will be greatly magnified. You will rise far and above yourselves to become humble servants and humble handmaidens of the Lord. (90–08)

A mission call is a sacred thing. Years ago when I was a new General Authority, I learned many lessons. I was assigned first to the

Missionary Department. President Henry D. Moyle of the First Presidency was responsible for missionary work and the calls, the recommendations would come in, and quite often he would call me to come up to his home so that he would be away from the office. We'd go into the little office he had in his home, and I would read the forms and he would make the designation and I would write on the form which mission the elder or sister was assigned to. So they were assigned to a mission.

One day I read a form and it was a young man. I had read his qualifications and told President Moyle where he was from and what his education was, his age, and then I said, "Six years of A-grade German."

President Moyle thought a minute and said, "Andes Mission." Spanish speaking in South America.

I said, "President, that was German not Spanish."

He thought for a minute, pondered, and said, "Andes Mission."

And I never did that again. I learned a great lesson.

I learned that the call of missionaries is a very sacred thing and that generally speaking a missionary knows why he is assigned to the mission he is. Sometimes it's well into his mission—he wonders why he wasn't assigned here because he was so qualified and yearned to go there. It's a very wise thing to accept the call. (97–01)

A strange formula that works. What a glorious opportunity to go into the mission field. Some of you are going into countries where there are struggles and difficulties, sometimes danger. All of that goes with the territory. Generally speaking, you are going to be patterned in a set of rules and regulations and disciplines typical of what you have had here. But when you get out there, you will be alone by yourselves.

You know, it is a strange formula. You take two teenagers, take them away from everything they are interested in, fix it so they have got something to live on and a place to live, sometimes an automobile, and say that we'll be back in a month or two to see you. And then say, "Now, go out and preach the gospel." This is something that just is not built in or born into a teenager. It is really a strange thing. The only defense of it is that it works. It works, not because of you and me, but it works because the gospel of Jesus Christ is true. (90–08)

It is the Lord's mission. The first great experience is to learn that it is not your mission at all—it is the Lord's mission. I know that we say, "I am going on my mission," but it is not my mission, it is His mission. You have the responsibility to bear witness of the Restoration of the gospel of Jesus Christ. You are to teach of the Atonement and of the resurrection. You are to teach of the establishment of The Church of Jesus Christ of Latter-day Saints. You will find through prayer, through challenge, through work, through study, and through the difficulties and disappointments you face that it is the Lord's mission. You will come to know that. That is your reward. (02–07)

Be susceptible to the inspiration of the Lord. The greatest commodity; . . . the greatest resource; . . . the greatest preparation, the greatest attribute that you can have as you go into the mission field is to be susceptible to the inspiration of the Lord. (81–01)

You will have to quell a warning in order to make a mistake. Go out and do your missionary work, and have your hearts open, and learn to receive revelation and inspiration, and keep your thoughts clean and pure. Keep an open mind, and go about the work with the intelligence and training and experience that you have, and you will be all right. But you try and make a mistake, and you will have it hedged up so that you will have to overrule your feelings. You will have to quell a warning in order to make a mistake, because the Lord isn't going to let you. He will warn you first. (81–01)

It is the Spirit, not the numbers that we need. We must labor incessantly and diligently by the Spirit. If we will not be preoccupied with records and recordings and procedures and numbers of baptisms, we will have baptisms aplenty. We will have converts aplenty. (00–04)

Follow the Spirit and everything else will be all right. The ingredient that will glue everything else together is the Spirit. If you will learn about the Spirit, then everything else will be all right. You will be warned of dangers. You will be lifted up and blessed. You can be healed. You can suffer disappointment and depression and challenge and illness and everything else and weather through it. (90–08)

Do your best, and the Spirit will make up the rest. It does not matter if you are a little tongue-tied or if your brain is a little tied. If you are hesitant and you look upon yourself as being something less than perfect, at least you are being honest. If you are struggling the best you can to do what you ought to do, then the Spirit of the Lord will make up the rest. (90–08)

Conversion takes place through the power of the Spirit. Remember, when conversion takes place, it is through the power of the Spirit. We need to bring a greater power to bear in the missions of the Church, in the lives of missionaries, in the lives of all who investigate the gospel.

"He that receiveth the word by the Spirit of truth receiveth it as it is preached by the Spirit of truth."[3] (85–06)

The Holy Ghost can work through the Light of Christ. It is important for a teacher or a missionary or a parent to know that the Holy Ghost can work through the Light of Christ. A teacher of gospel truths is not planting something foreign or even new into an adult or a child. Rather, the missionary or teacher is making contact with the Spirit of Christ already there. The gospel will have a familiar "ring" to them. Then the teaching will come "to the convincing of [those who will listen] that Jesus is the Christ, the Eternal God, manifesting himself unto all nations."[4] (04–05, p. 10)

Bear testimony. You are to learn the doctrines of the Church. You can learn them in many ways. You can learn them by listening to the sermons that you hear. Then there is another great principle: you can learn the doctrines from what you teach, as you teach.

The mission president may tell you to just go bear testimony. You may say to him, "But, I don't have a testimony." If you are a little better

schooled than some missionaries and consider yourself to be intellectually above those around you, you may say to your mission president,
"How can I bear a testimony that I don't have?"

The mission president may again say, "Just go bear testimony."

You may say to him, "Well, that will be a lie, because I don't have a
testimony."

And the mission president may say, "Go bear testimony."

Perhaps the words *obedience* and *duty* will come into your mind,
and you will go with great hesitation. You will begin to bear testimony.
The promptings of the Spirit will testify to you in your heart and in
your mind that what you say is true. You will then learn something
from what you have said. It will be the beginning and the germ of a
testimony that will come into your heart. You will be getting acquainted
with that other great companion that you have. (02–07)

Do not overlook the strength of your testimony. There are times
when some confirmation of your testimony, some evidence that you are
accepted of the Lord can remove discouragement and cause you to
rejoice and redouble your efforts. There is one evidence of the strength
of your testimony that many missionaries overlook. That is the effect
of your testimony and your teaching in the lives of others. When you
influence others to change their lives, even influence them to want to
change their lives—that is a signal to you that they "see" or "feel" something in you. (82–05)

You come to own some things by giving them away. There are
some things that you gain ownership of by giving them away. Generally that is true of things that endure. But you don't own them until you
give them away. We go out on missions to preach the gospel and we
don't know very much when we go out there, but in the process of giving it away, we claim it. (88–04)

The Spirit, like love, is not divisible. The Spirit, like love, is not
divisible. Each missionary may possess the full measure of it. Meaning
that the portion you may enjoy does not deprive another, indeed it may
assist another, to share in it. And, if you know Christian doctrine, as

you should know it, the Spirit and the testimony of Christ will come to you for the most part when, and remain with you, if you share it. In that process is the very essence of the gospel. (82–05)

A missionary learns more than those he teaches. "Thou therefore which teachest another, teachest thou not thyself? thou that preachest a man should not steal, dost thou steal?"[5]

Great truth! One of the great patterns and rewards of missionary service is that they learn what they teach. They, of course, learn more than anyone they teach. They learn more from their investigators and from their teaching than the investigators do from them. (99–05)

Testimony is the converting power of the gospel. The converting power of the gospel lies in the testimony borne by the missionary to the investigator. The missionaries who are baptizing regularly, are those who bear direct, firm witness. (68–01)

The measure of the Church is not in size. Frequently we find missionaries are moved by superficial motives.

I remind you missionaries that the measure of the Church is not in size. Some seem to feel that if it isn't the biggest, it isn't the truest. Brethren, the Church was just as true when there were six members as it is now with . . . million[s].

We are not merely seeking after baptisms, we want to help people. We are not obligated to selfishly get more members for the Church, we are obligated to generously share the truth. It is not that we need the membership, it is that they need the repentance.

And also it is an imperative duty that we owe to all the rising generation, and to all the pure in heart:

"For there are many yet on the earth among all sects, parties, and denominations, who are blinded by the subtle craftiness of men, whereby they lie in wait to deceive, and who are only kept from the truth because they know not where to find it."[6] (65–02)

The only true and living church. It is our firm conviction that The Church of Jesus Christ of Latter-day Saints is, as the revelations state, "the only true and living church upon the face of the whole earth."[7]

This doctrine often generates resistance and repels the casual investigator.

Some have said, "We want nothing to do with anyone who makes so presumptuous a claim as that."

The early Latter-day Saints were bitterly persecuted for holding to this doctrine. They were the butt of many clever stories. We, of course, are not free from that today.

Should we not then make one accommodation and set this doctrine aside? Would it not be better to have more accept what would be left of the gospel than the relatively few who are converted now? . . .

Could we not use the words *better* or *best?* The word *only* really isn't the most appealing way to begin a discussion of the gospel.

If we thought only in terms of diplomacy or popularity, surely we should change our course.

But we must hold tightly to it even though some turn away. (85–13, pp. 80–81)

We did not invent the doctrine of the only true Church. We did not invent the doctrine of the only true church. It came from the Lord. Whatever perception others have of us, however presumptuous we appear to be, whatever criticism is directed to us, we must teach it to all who will listen. (85–13, p. 82)

The Book of Mormon is our message. The Book of Mormon: Another Testament of Jesus Christ is the "keystone" of our message. Without gimmicks, without any huckstering, we must see that the Book of Mormon is moved out into the world. Every copy that can be placed anywhere must be placed there. That is the message: The Book of Mormon: Another Testament of Jesus Christ. (85–07, p. 136)

Do not be drawn from your work by critics. Do not be drawn from your work by critics.

Nehemiah, the prophet, set about to build a wall around Jerusalem. In spite of all of the opposition, he was steadfast in his purposes. Finally the enemy, Sanballat and Geshem, sought to draw him aside from his work. But Nehemiah said: "They thought to do me mischief" and answered: "I am doing a great work, so that I cannot come down: why should the work cease, whilst I leave it, and come down to you?"[8]

Some time ago a stake mission leader talked to me concerning an activity in his community. The representatives of one of the churches had hired the high school auditorium and announced a series of lectures, an exposé on Mormonism. He was greatly concerned and asked what they should do to counteract them.

I answered, "It is too bad you can't put them on your payroll. They will do you more good than ever they will do you harm. Ignore them. Go back to work. Teach the gospel."

Their misrepresentations became so extravagant that the honest in heart became curious about the Church and some of them are now members of the Church.

It was Brigham Young who said: "If the people will let us alone, we will convert the world; if they persecute us, we will do it the quicker."[9] (65–02)

Never apologize for our doctrines. As I grow in age and experience, I grow ever *less* concerned over whether others agree with us. I grow ever *more* concerned that they understand us. If they do understand, they have their agency and can accept or reject the gospel as they please.

It is not an easy thing for us to defend the position that bothers so many others.

Brethren and sisters, never be ashamed of the gospel of Jesus Christ. Never apologize for the sacred doctrines of the gospel.

Never feel inadequate and unsettled because you cannot explain them to the satisfaction of all who might inquire of you.

Do not be ill at ease or uncomfortable because you can give little more than your conviction.

Be assured that, if you will explain what you know and testify of what you feel, you may plant a seed that will one day grow and blossom into a testimony of the gospel of Jesus Christ. (85–13, p. 83)

Prerequisite courses are required to understand some principles. In the gospel there are some prerequisite courses without which the deeper meaning of some principles of the gospel may not be understood, in fact which may be completely misunderstood. For instance, the conditions under which personal revelation can be received could hardly be accepted or understood by one who has not completed the prerequisite courses of faith, repentance, baptism, and the reception of the Holy Ghost.

The bottom line is that we must never allow ourselves to be ashamed of the gospel because someone doesn't agree with us, even if that person is apparently alert, intelligent, and well-intentioned. Don't falter because you can't explain it in his terminology, in his context. (66–02, p. 103)

Bring all the truth you have. We do not claim that others have no truth. The Lord described them as having "a form of godliness." Converts to the Church may bring with them all the truth they possess and have it added upon.

We are not free to alter this fundamental doctrine of the gospel, not even in the face of the tribulation prophesied in that revelation.[10] Popularity and the approval of the world perhaps must remain ever beyond our reach. (85–13, p. 82)

Missionary work is work. Missionary work is work! It can be dull and repetitive and difficult, and at once exalting and marvelous, but it is work. It is patterning your habits, getting up early, and going about the work day after day. You will not be measured by the number of baptisms you have. You will be measured by the work you do.

When you stand on a doorstep and bear witness, that doorstep was sanctified for that time. You have done missionary work. You may go to many doorsteps without having the satisfaction of having someone who will listen to you, but you will have been a success judged by your determination to keep going. (02–07)

The importance of obedience. There is a word that young people do not like very much—obedience! That is something you may not yet know very much about. You will learn the importance of being obedient.

One day you are going to find out that the key to leadership is "followship." That comes from obedience. If you will learn to follow, the rules and counsel and policy are just like an armor. Wear it well, and it will protect you. (02–07)

Follow the rules. On very rare occasions we find a missionary who does not like to conform to rules. If you have such a companion and he tempts you to follow him in some activity contrary to what you know is right, do not follow him. If he asks, "If I do it, will you report it to the mission president?" You answer, "Of course I will!" We are servants of the Lord. We have an obligation to Him and to the Church. That is our first loyalty. . . .

By following the rules, you will never make a serious mistake. You can never make a serious mistake without being warned. You will never take the wrong road or go around the wrong bend or make the wrong decision without your having been warned. That pattern is the pattern of the Latter-day Saint. You were confirmed a member of the Church, and you had conferred upon you the gift of the Holy Ghost to be a guide and a companion to you, to be a comfort to you. (02–07)

Problems in the mission field come from the undisciplined. Our problems come from the undisciplined.

I want to define the word *disciplined* in this frame of reference. It is misused in the school classroom. That isn't what I am talking about. I'm not talking about coercion. I'm not talking about any false compulsions. I am talking about the discipline that comes from the root meaning of the word disciple or follower. This, of course, is self-discipline. And so to define again and say that the problems come from among those who are not really disciples, who are not really followers—the undisciplined in the mission field and in the Church. (64–08)

Missionaries are on stage all the time. You do not know that you are on stage all of the time. Every minute you are on stage. People are watching you. You stand out. You are different from the rank and file

In China while traveling with the BYU Young Ambassadors, May 1981

of the people that you will be working among. Just that! You have to be in character and on guard all of the time. Someone is always watching you. You are preaching the gospel all of the time. (03–03)

Missionaries can grow from a sense of duty to a sense of devotion. Some elders find themselves in the mission field and do not quite know how they got there, and wonder, are they really qualified or are they there in some measure under false pretenses? Was it only to please his parents? That is all right. For while they may go on a mission for a superficial reason, they stay on their mission for the right reason. They may go out of *duty*, but they stay out of *devotion*. For, on the mission, there comes an individual testimony of the gospel. (83–02, p. 59)

A little discouragement is normal. There is in the mission field the tendency to be discouraged. Sometimes a missionary will tell me, "I have had just a miserable day. Everything has gone wrong, and I am discouraged. It just isn't going to go right. I feel very depressed."

Should that be you, I would say, "Well, I am glad to hear that. At least I know you are normal! Did you know that it is not either normal or healthy to be on cloud nine all of the time?"

There is a little couplet:

> *Life is full of problems,*
> *It's full of ifs and buts,*
> *And the man that's grinning all the time*
> *Must be completely nuts!*[11]

Learn that there must be ups and downs in your life. You can find that explained to you in the doctrine: "For it must needs be, that there is an opposition in all things. If not so, my first-born [as the Prophet said], righteousness could not be brought to pass, neither wickedness, neither holiness nor misery, neither good nor bad."[12] That is part of life! You are learning that already. (02–07)

Avoid dwelling on physical problems. I was once in a university town with a friend. I learned that a doctor from my hometown was the university doctor. I wanted to see him and went over to the clinic.

We sat in the waiting room. There on a low table were stacks of pamphlets of all kinds. Each pamphlet described a disease. We sat there for a little while, and my companion said, "Look at those pamphlets! You look at them long enough and you will think that you have got it!"

You should learn as a young missionary the power of impression of that kind. It is something you need to understand and manage.

When you write your mother about a little indisposition of some kind, be careful not to say much about it. Did you not know that if you are in Australia and you write to Canada, a sniffle in Australia is double pneumonia by the time your mother reads that letter? We do not need to talk much about our aches and pains.

I knew that a missionary had something wrong with him. I knew it, but I never could figure it out. I interviewed him searchingly. He was performing well. He eventually became a zone leader. It was not until near the time he was released that one of the other missionaries told me he suffered from migraine headaches, terrible migraine headaches. I did not ever know it, because he would not tell me. He was on his mission, and the headaches were not going to be his preoccupation. I admired him greatly. A few years later I saw him. He was married, had a family, doing well, working, and the headaches were gone. (02–07)

A mission can be a great time of healing. You face the challenges in a world where being depressed and sad and having emotional difficulties is almost a popular thing to do. That is all right for somebody else, but it is not all right for you. Your mission is the great time of healing. That is the time that you leave behind those things that have been troubling and so distressing to you. You will find that work is a tremendous therapy. You will find that you can gain not just a knowledge of the gospel but a standard of emotional health that is beyond anything that you had thought possible.

It is true that you may have your limitations. Some of them you will have all of your life. That is the pattern of life. As you move into life, you will find that you always have your cross to bear of one kind or another. The great blessing is that, if you live properly, only those close to you will ever know. (02–07)

Inspired counsel to missionaries. You will find that the Lord will lead you. He can fix things up. He will prepare your converts. Keep the rules and cast off the depression and your feelings of inferiority and remember that you are sons and daughters of God. His power is with us and is available to us. If you will listen spiritually, you will be good enough for all you are called to do.

If another can memorize the scripture in one reading and it takes you ten readings and you still have not quite got it, so what? You will have earned it, and, in due course, it will last longer. You will be all right. You are as good as you ought to be, because you will have the power of the Almighty to answer your prayers and to be with you. (02–04)

Teach missionaries what they are to be. There is so much difference between teaching the missionaries what they are to do as compared to concentrating on what they are to be. The first will produce salesmen. The second will produce Saints. (00–04)

Teach missionaries with the tongue of angels. You could do much for [missionaries] if you teach them the patterns of discipline and organization and efficiency. That could not equal in a tiny percent what you would do for them if you cause them to gain a knowledge of the doctrines, a knowledge of the truths that are found in the scriptures and the revelations. And the way you teach it is the way you teach it. And if you teach it right, angels will attend you.[13] If you teach it properly you will speak with the tongues of angels.[14] If you teach it properly they will read and will know that they have heard His voice and have that revelation.[15] (93–03)

RETURNED MISSIONARIES

"Transferred" versus "Returned" missionaries. I wish we could phase out that title "the returned missionary."

The adjective "returned" connotes finished, over with, done, completed, accomplished, past.

If I could, I would replace it in your mind with the idea "transferred."

During your mission, you will have a number of transfers, none of which permits a reduction of commitment, only a change of environment. Your transfer home at the end of your mission should be the same.

You will have learned to obey the rules. The rules will change in some respects. Mission rules forbid you from any intimate association with one of the opposite gender. And there is a permanent injunction against any intimate physical association with one of the same gender. Some rules will change with your release, but not that one.

After your mission—reasonably soon after—you will be expected to develop an intimate association with one of the opposite gender. That relationship will lead to a consummation within the bonds of marriage.

Those experiences which result in your becoming a father or a mother are to be shared only with one to whom you are legally and lawfully married and sealed.

Those relationships, now forbidden, will then be more than a privilege to be enjoyed; but a commandment to be obeyed. The spirit you will have enjoyed in the mission field will be not less, but more important. You will have a closer companion and a fulness of life. You will need the Spirit of the Lord to lead you.

You are expected to go onward, ever onward, as constantly as you did on your mission, and use the knowledge you have shared, expand it, increase it, in a never-ending quest. You are expected to use it. That is the ideal way to firm up your possession of it.

If the idea, the title "returned missionary," seems to authorize you to let down, to lower your standard, to lessen your commitment, then your mission will be a chapter in, rather than the foundation of your life. (96–02)

Those who have filled a full-time mission should be determined to go "onward, ever onward." One problem we should not have in the Church is the falling away of missionaries after their release. Why, in heaven's name, should we need to worry about them?

You are prepared, you are trained, with years learning the gospel.

Teaching is the best way to learn. You will have lived away from home and matured in an ideal environment. No one is blessed with comparable opportunity.

Surely we don't need another Church program to tend missionaries after they return home.

Your life following your release should be a continuation of the interest, the commitment, and the dedication which typified your service in the field.

> *Onward, ever onward, as we glory in his name;*
> *Onward, ever onward, as we glory in his name;*
> *Forward, pressing forward, as a triumph song we sing.*
> *God our strength will be; press forward ever,*
> *Called to serve our King.*
> *Onward, ever onward, as we glory in His name.*[16]

You have, as the scriptures say, "Put your hand to the plow," never to look back. "Onward, ever onward." (96–02)

Counsel to those who have filled full-time missions. Too often a missionary returns to the dress standards of the world.

You loosen up, relax, let down your standards—first of grooming, then your behavior.

You may say, "I am home now so I can listen to the world's music. It may not be the best, but I won't pay attention to the words or the beat."

Some former missionaries become singles-ward hoppers. No bishop can shepherd these members. Few, if any, assignments are given to these missionaries who, prior to this time, have been totally immersed in Church service.[17]

"We will prove them herewith, to see if they will do all things whatsoever the Lord their God shall command them."[18]

To "do all things whatsoever the Lord . . . shall command" becomes the mission of every mortal, or missionary, who comes to earth. In this context, such terms as returned missionary or released missionary seem inappropriate since no one is ever returned or released from the mission or charge given in our pre-earthly existence.

Reference might be made to those who have filled full-time missions rather than referring to them as returned missionaries or even as those who have served missions. The connotation of the word fill implies "fulfilling the requirements of," "making full or complete," or "giving a full measure." (96–02)

Missionary experience should lead one to spiritual self-reliance. As one with missionary experience, you should be spiritually self-reliant. You should be the last one a bishop should need to be worried about.

When you get home, don't expect to be rewarded or served or tended. Don't be a ward-hopping single, bouncing around looking for someone good enough to fulfill your ideal. Rather work on yourself with the hope of fulfilling someone else's ideals. . . . If you are on course, His way will be your way. (96–02)

A sufficient cause for missionary service. If nothing else came from missionary work, if no converts came from it, the training and the installation in the hearts of our missionaries of the knowledge of the revelations would be sufficient cause for our missionary service. (93–03)

Missionaries who learn to teach by the Spirit will affect the Church forever. If you can see the power in one another and see the power in this pattern of teaching by the Spirit, then the end of it will never come. It will not come in your lives, because when you get to be old like I am and like these other Brethren are, you will be recalling scriptures that you learned as a missionary. And you will have as your compensation not just a testimony. That can come quickly and easily. But you will have the resources, and you will have treasured up in your mind scriptures that will be helpful not just to teach an investigator, but to teach a son or a daughter or to teach a Sunday School class. This is going to affect the Church forever. (04–10)

The benefits of a mission. The most important lasting evidence that you have served a mission will not be in your life. However important that may be, it will be in the lives of those you taught, by precept, by example, whose lives were changed and given a spiritual dignity and an imperishable value that they did not possess before you taught them.

There are many benefits in your own life. The missionary grows up and matures. He develops a confidence. He learns to speak up. He learns to organize his time. He learns about people. He learns about places. He learns to learn. He takes on a cleanliness, a neatness in appearance, a dignity that he did not possess. He learns to set goals. And there are many other things. He marries later than he might have and approaches marriage with the maturity that has come to him. These are benefits, lasting benefits, that come as something of a reward for his service.

But these things do not compare with the most important and most lasting of the rewards that come from serving on a mission. The choicest pearl, the one of greatest price that is to be found in this selfless service is to learn at an early age how one is guided by the Spirit of the Lord. We have had conferred upon us the gift of the Holy Ghost, a supernal gift, to be a guide, a shield and a protection to us if we employ it properly. (82–05)

MEMBER MISSIONARIES

We are to be conveyers of the gospel. There is a lesson that few members of the Church ever seem to learn. The lesson is this: We are not merely receptacles for the gospel; we are also conveyers of it. This idea is so important. (*TYD*, p. 185)

The Church is wherever you are. The Church is wherever you are, even when you're alone. And when you go looking for the Church when you may be in some isolated spot, just remember, brethren, there may be somebody else looking for the Church and when they have found you they have found it. (68–10)

We must provide nourishment to the spiritually underfed.
Undernourished children must be carefully fed; so it is with the spiritually underfed. Some are so weakened by mischief and sin that to begin with they reject the rich food we offer. They must be fed carefully and gently.

Some are so near spiritual death that they must be spoon-fed on the broth of fellowship, or nourished carefully on activities and programs. As the scriptures say, they must have milk before meat.[19] But we must take care lest the only nourishment they receive thereafter is that broth.

But feed them we must. We are commanded to preach the gospel to every nation, kindred, tongue, and people. That message . . . appears more than eighty times in the scriptures. (84–04, p. 42)

How can we warn our neighbors? Now the Lord has said that in His church and kingdom there is safety and that we will be protected. That is the only place on earth where this protection is. It behooves every man and every woman and every child who has been warned to warn his neighbors. We can do this in two ways. First, we can live the gospel completely, live it religiously. . . . Second, we can strive for perfection in being missionaries. And if we are not perfect in all things, at least we can seriously heed the warnings that are given. (76–09, pp. 82–83)

A mission for those with disabilities. If you have been handicapped by some accident of nature or by disease or disability, perhaps you may want to go on a mission. But you cannot serve a regular mission because of a wheelchair, or a brace, or a tongue or eyes or ears that will not respond properly. You can serve a different type of a mission, one which in your case is equally approved by the Lord. Perhaps a stake mission, perhaps not that—but the Lord loves you and will bless you for your desire and compensate you in other ways. You can at least be an example of *wanting to go.* You can inspire, or perhaps even shame, some indecisive youth who has the physical capacity to serve a mission but who does not want to go. (83–02, p. 59)

A mission for those who did not serve as missionaries. I am sure there are listening those who did not serve a mission. Perhaps you did not really understand. Perhaps your decision for one reason or another was that you could not go. Perhaps you were not in the Church at that age. Some missed their mission because of military service.

Whatever the reason, there is no time to brood over that now. Every member is a missionary. Devote attention to encouraging and financing and preparing your children and others to serve on missions. Many dreams are realized through our children. The time may come when you may go as a missionary couple.

Look forward, not backward. Magnify your priesthood. (83–02, pp. 59–60)

CHAPTER 25

The Gospel in Our Lives

"The standards of the world are constantly adjusted to what is. Our standards are fixed on what ought to be." (95–04)

CHARACTER

Be careful not to compare yourself with others. You ought to be glad you are here. Quit wishing you were somewhere else. Quit wishing you were somebody else. When you compare yourself with others you can be led astray. Compare yourself with what you used to be and you will progress. (79–02)

Be glad that you are you. Now be glad that you live in stormy, troubled times, and be glad that you are you. Never, never wish that you were someone else. You *are* you. You always will be you.

You may complain with your lot in life. Your social or economic inheritance may not be to your desire. You may think yourself limited mentally (we probably don't use 15 percent of our capacity). You may not like the body you are inhabiting—remember ultimately it may be perfected. You are you—a separate individual intelligence. You are a spirit inhabiting a body: "And the spirit and the body are the soul of man."[1] Sometimes we make an appraisal of ourselves in comparison with another and foolishly wish we were somebody else. Never do that. Thank the Lord for who you are and what you may become. "As man is, God once was; as God is, man may become."[2] (69–02, pp. 97–98)

What is success? Now I have lived long enough to see what success is and what it can be and what it isn't. If you just remain halfway decent Latter-day Saints and keep the commandments, then you will be somebody. It may well be that your name is never in the newspaper; you may never receive honors and awards and achievements that are recognition from the world, but you can, each of you, do that thing which is most worth doing. That is the thing that all of you want most to do—that is to find a companion, be married, raise a family and to struggle, going step by step, periodically to the edge of the light and into the darkness. (95–07)

The real valedictorians in mortality. There are members across the world that live out their lives in obscurity, and they end up the valedictorians in mortality. I know we look at those that are great and are well paid and highly acclaimed, but when you get across the veil (and we know a little about what is there) the real valedictorians in mortality will be just what the prophet said, a man and a woman living together in love and raising a family under ordinary circumstances, doing the best they can with what they have got, wondering why someone else had the prominence and the good fortune, and ending up finding out that they had it all. (98–02)

Heroism versus sainthood. Knowledge is depicted often as a lamp or as a torch, suggesting light. It has been said that a hero is one who walks the dark pathways of life setting torches along the way so that others may see; a saint is one who walks the dark pathways of life and is himself a light. On the matter of a heroism—and a sainthood—open to us all, an unidentified poet has written:

> *We cannot all be heroes*
> *And thrill a hemisphere*

With some great, daring venture,
Some deed that mocks at fear.
But we can fill a lifetime
With kindly acts, and true.
For there's always noble service
For noble souls to do.

May you each find your way to that kind of heroism, which is a mark of the educated soul. (83–03, p. 30)

Any virtue pressed to extreme may become a vice. A virtue when pressed to the extreme may turn into a vice. Unreasonable devotion to an ideal, without considering the practical application of it, can ruin the ideal itself. (90–09, p. 85)

Extending trust makes one happier. As I begin a new relationship with anyone—students, missionaries, or those with whom I associate or whom I supervise—it is on the basis of confidence and trust. I have been much happier since. Of course, there have been times when I have been disappointed, and a few times when I have been badly used. I do not care about that. Who am I not to be so misused or abused? Why should I be above that? If that is the price of extending trust to everyone, I am glad to pay it.

I have come to be much less afraid of that possibility than I was before. It is sometimes painful when one is misused or when trust or confidence is not honored. That kind of pain, however, is not unbearable, for it is only pain; it is not agony. The only agony I know is when I discover that inadvertently I have misused someone else. That is torture; that I will *avoid.* (TYD, pp. 95–96)

Our responsibility as Latter-day Saints. It is up to the Latter-day Saint to leaven the loaf. We are they who should be honest and responsible and moral people. We are they who should be devout and reverent. We are they who should be a church-going people and a church-building people. We are they who should pray, who should render service, who should preach the gospel to our fellowmen. We should give of ourselves and our means to sustain missionaries and to carry on the work of the Lord. We are they who should be honest in our dealings with our fellowmen; and look upon the basic principles of morality and integrity as worth holding.

In this way, perhaps, the Lord will guide our history, that metes and bounds will yet be set and that this invasion will be thwarted and conquered and that we might live freely from the domination of the adversary.

We are they who should look to our homes, each Monday night assembled as families. We should look upon our marriage covenants as sacred, even eternal. We should look upon our responsibilities as parents as being a sacred obligation to ourselves, to our Church, to our Father in Heaven. (71–07, pp. 217–18)

GOALS AND GOSPEL LIVING

Righteous goals give us a feeling of destiny. In a society which often drifts without direction, a personal, private set of goals is a great blessing. Goals give youth something to which they can aspire. Something which places in their heart a feeling of destiny not only regarding themselves, but regarding the Kingdom of God. (71–06)

Toward what goals can we strive? If neither wealth nor prominence are ideal objectives, how can we then be motivated to excellence? Toward what goals can we strive?

There are two that I would suggest. Excellence itself is a worthy goal—to be good, very good, at whatever you do; to develop your own talents to the fullest extent that you can; to develop a balanced, worthy, sensible individual.

The Lord said it. "Be ye therefore perfect, even as your Father which is in heaven is perfect."[3]

The other goal is service. "When ye are in the service of your fellow beings ye are only in the service of your God."[4] (80–08, p. 6)

The present not the future is our challenge. I meet so many people who are "en route," anxious to finish their present task so that they may begin to live, yet nervous about the uncertainty and the storm clouds ahead. Don't be that way; settle down. Here in school, look forward, but remember life is *today*. Settle into your studies, particularly into your ward assignments . . . your spiritual growth. Settle down permanently where you are. Relax, enjoy it, though you know, as students, you will not be here very long. The *future* is not your challenge, nor will it ever be. The *present* is your challenge; so remember, set your course "steady as she goes." (69–02, p. 97)

With the Lord change is possible. In this life we are constantly confronted with a spirit of competition. Teams contest one against another in an adversary relationship in order that one will be chosen a winner. We come to believe that wherever there is a winner there must also be a loser. To believe that is to be misled.

In the eyes of the Lord, everyone may be a winner. Now it is true that we must earn it; but if there is competition in His work, it is not with another soul—it's with our own former selves.

I do not say that it is easy. I am not talking about appearing to change. I am talking about *changing*. I do not say it is easy. I say it is possible and quickly possible. (75–03, pp. 105–6)

Now is the time to change. If there is something about yourself that you do not like, now is the time to change it. If there is something in your past that has been disabling, spiritually or otherwise, now is the time to rise above it. (*TYD,* p. 95)

We obey the command to do everything in His name. We obey the commandment "Whatsoever ye shall do, ye shall do it in my name."[5] Every prayer we offer is in His name. Every ordinance performed is in His name. Every baptism, confirmation, blessing, ordination, every sermon, every testimony is concluded with the invocation of His sacred name. It is in His name that we heal the sick and perform other miracles of which we do not, cannot, speak.

In the sacrament we take upon ourselves the name of Christ. We covenant to remember Him and keep His commandments. He is present in all that we believe. (98–01, p. 64)

INTEGRITY AND KEEPING CONFIDENCES

Importance of keeping confidences. Talents and abilities and training may set us far above people in general. However, if there is a flaw in our character and we cannot be trusted—if we do not keep confidences—all of these other qualifications may not be sufficient to make us of real service.

Some who are not blessed with much ability, perhaps are even handicapped, are of great service to this kingdom because of what they are—trustworthy!

If we cannot keep a confidence, despite our other attributes, we may be more of a disservice than a service to the Church and kingdom of God. (80–02)

We must demonstrate our trustworthiness. Many years ago, long before I was called to be one of the General Authorities, I came in contact with some of them through my employment. On occasions I would hear them make comments or tell experiences. I made this rule for myself; I've been grateful many times that I had the inspiration to do this:

If I should be in a small group, in a closed meeting, and one of the Brethren made an expression or told of an experience, I would never repeat it. I took that as an expression of confidence, as being a gesture of trust, and I was obliged not to betray it. If, however, on some occasion I heard those same things spoken by that General Authority in a public meeting, I felt, thereafter, free to make comment on them. . . .

I came to know later, that the Lord and His servants value very greatly the strength of character evidenced by the keeping of confidences. I came to know that the Lord will test us. He will find out just how trustworthy we will be. (80–02)

Bishops and stake presidents have a spiritual obligation to keep confidences. I could give a sermon about the obligation of a bishop or a stake president to keep confidences. They come to know many things that are very personal and important to individual members of the Church in the course of their interviews and their duties. Bishops, stake presidents, and other ecclesiastical officers are obliged, by spiritual commitment, not to reveal those things, but to keep them as sacred and confidential. (80–02)

Avoid the tendency to judge the gospel against the principles of your profession. A brother told me of an accident involving one of his children and asked counsel. It had been a serious injury. The driver of the automobile was insured. My counsel to him (and it would be to you) was—don't try to make a living off such things. I suggested that he would do well to keep the case open until sensible, kind, adequate compensation had been made by way of taking care of doctor bills, etc. But, that to insist on extra large amounts to cover things that never could be compensated by money would accomplish little, and would ultimately bring to himself and to his family the spirit of greed and the tendency to equate things that are sacred and priceless in terms of dollar value.

We live in a world of materialistic pressure. You don't have to find temptation of this kind; it runs into you at the intersection. The prevailing attitude is, as long as it is legal, why not get all you can? An alert attorney can build the issues in a case and make small things, ordinarily ignored, the basis for a handsome settlement. And you may have had encouragement from an attorney (who may be a member of the Church). "Why shouldn't you? After all, it's perfectly legal." Why shouldn't you?

It is the tendency of almost all men to judge the gospel of Jesus Christ against principles of his profession. . . . Whether you are going into the legal profession or any other profession or vocation, guard yourselves against the pitfall of substituting the accepted principles of that profession in preference to the principles of the gospel of Jesus Christ. (67–03)

Avoid lawsuits with little or no merit. When you seek financial gain, you may be tempted by others to miscalculate, even ignore, risks. When things go wrong—and they can go wrong even in carefully managed affairs—some look for others to blame. They want some "deep pocket" to make them whole. They want someone else to carry their responsibility like the scapegoat of Old Testament times, which was ceremonially burdened with the sins of others and left to wander in the wilderness.

They have little difficulty finding some attorney willing to act as high priest in transferring their responsibility to someone else. They file suit with little or no merit, intending to force others to settle in order to avoid the unconscionable cost of defending themselves in court.

There is no dishonor in appealing to a court of law for either justice or protection. I refer to those who do so to justify themselves and shift their own responsibility to someone else.

Such efforts are successful often enough to permit self-serving lawyers to convince yet another client that he need not honor his own commitments. The word *integrity* becomes tarnished by counsel and client alike. And there follows that long trail of acrimony with brother against brother over property or money. (87–07, p. 16)

Lawyers are needed to be defenders of the faith. I wonder if you who are now lawyers or you who are students of the law know how much you are needed as defenders of the faith. Be willing to give of your time and of your means and your expertise to the building up of the Church and the kingdom of God and the establishment of Zion, which we are under covenant to do—not just to the Church as an institution, but to members and ordinary people who need your professional protection. (04–02, p. 11)

I charge each of you lawyers and judges and put you on alert: These are days of great spiritual danger for this people. The world is spiraling downward at an ever-quickening pace. I am sorry to tell you that it will not get better.

I know of nothing in the history of the Church or in the history of the world to compare with our present circumstances. Nothing happened in Sodom and Gomorrah which exceeds the wickedness and depravity which surrounds us now.

Satan uses every intrigue to disrupt the family. The sacred relationship between man and woman, husband and wife, through which mortal bodies are conceived and life is passed from one generation to the next generation, is being showered with filth.

Profanity, vulgarity, blasphemy, and pornography are broadcast into the homes and minds of the innocent. Unspeakable wickedness, perversion, and abuse—not even exempting little children—once hidden in dark places, now seeks protection from courts and judges.

The Lord needs you who are trained in the law. You can do for this people what others cannot do. We should not need to go beyond the members of the Church to find superior legal counsel.

Now I caution you, as President John Taylor warned James Moyle and as Joseph Smith warned Stephen A. Douglas at the pinnacle of his political triumph, "If ever you turn your hand against . . . the Latter-day Saints, you will feel the weight of the hand of Almighty upon you."[6]

We must look to you for legal counsel. You have, or should have, the spirit of discernment. It was given you when you had conferred upon you the gift of the Holy Ghost.

You must locate where the snares are hidden and help guide our footsteps around them. (04–02, p. 9)

JOY AND HAPPINESS

Understand and follow the plan. If you understand the great plan of happiness and follow it, what goes on in the world will not determine your happiness. (94–01, p. 20)

Our happiness depends on living gospel standards. I have lived a long time and watched the standards upon which civilization must depend for survival swept aside one piece at a time. We live in a day when the age-old standards of morality, marriage, home, and family suffer defeat after defeat in courts and councils, in parliaments and classrooms. Our happiness depends upon living those very standards. (05–08, p. 70)

The laws of God are ordained to make us happy. (90–09, p. 84)

Joy is spiritual in nature. "Adam fell that men might be; and men are, that they might have joy."[7]

There is another revelation in which John said. "I have no greater joy than to hear that my children walk in truth."[8]

As you look through the revelations, you find that the word *joy* is used a lot, mostly in modern-day revelations. You young people can come to know that joy is a very deep, personal emotion, spiritual in nature, that is different from contentment, different from happiness. (08–03)

Happiness is inseparably connected with decent behavior. How many times have you heard someone say, after doing some generous or heroic deed or simply helping others, how *good* it made them feel? Like any natural feeling or emotion, that reaction is inborn in you. Surely you have experienced that yourself! Happiness is inseparably connected with decent, clean behavior. (97–02, p. 10)

A good sense of humor is pleasing. Someone has said that a sense of humor is oil for the machinery of life. A good sense of humor is a characteristic of a well-balanced person. It has always been apparent that the prophets were men with very alert and pleasing senses of humor. Despite the fact that they are dealing with the most serious and sometimes the most tragic and difficult things in life, the Brethren can always smile. (*TYD*, p. 249)

Happiness depends on what we do with what we are given. Happiness will depend on what each of us does with what each has, what we learn from what we do, and what we do thereafter. These are the things that will be reviewed in the days of judgment. (80–08, p. 6)

One cannot be happy and at once be wicked. We must come to understand that there are basic truths and basic principles, basic conformities necessary to achieve happiness. There are some things that are false, that are wrong. One cannot be happy and at once be wicked, regardless of how generally accepted that course may be. If it were printed in every book, run on every news press, set forth in every magazine, if it were broadcast on every frequency, televised from every station, declared from every pulpit, advocated in every classroom, and contended in every conversation, still it would be wrong. "Wickedness never was happiness,"[9] neither indeed can it be, neither indeed will it ever be. (65–05)

On getting "somewhere." College graduates embarking on a new phase of life often say to themselves, "I've got a degree. Now I am really going to get somewhere in life!" There is virtue in thinking that perhaps you really will get somewhere in life. Along the way you are sure to lament, as all of us have, "I'm just not getting anywhere in my life!"

Do you know where this somewhere is located, or this anywhere you think you may not reach? I know where somewhere is. I will try to tell you how to find it. . . .

Before telling you where it is, I must list three places you will probably look for it and, to your regret, not find it. Many have, and some of you surely will spend your lives chasing one of these "wheres," only to find it isn't the somewhere of your dreams. . . .

The first mirage I list is prosperity—money, wealth, riches. You can get them and still not be anywhere.

The second mirage is fame and acclaim. You may reach the pinnacle of popularity and find you are really nowhere.

The third mirage is intellectual achievement as an end in itself. You may end up "ever learning, and never able to come to the knowledge of the truth."[10] You still will not be somewhere.

The remarkable thing is, you can have any or all three of them together—prosperity, acclaim, and intellectual achievement—and also really be somewhere. . . .

Where is somewhere to be found? You have been told over and over and over and over and over and over and over again where to find it. It is within you. It is home. It is family.

The somewhere isn't a "where" at all! It is a condition! And if you find it, you will find it at home. You may be only one at home and wish you were two. You may be only two at home and wish there were more. Nevertheless, "Be it ever so humble, there's no place like home. . . ."

There is a map to somewhere in the books—those books written by the prophets. There is a key to somewhere in the temple. And there is an ever-present guide to somewhere reminding you of what is right and what is wrong.

Our family ties can be eternal. To know that our marriage will endure and that our children and their children are linked together by covenants and sacred ordinances is the source of supreme joy.

I finally came to understand that each of us has only two lines in our eternal pedigree: one line for us and one for our Heavenly Father. I came to know His Son as my Redeemer, my Savior, my Friend.

And now, I know that when I go home, I really am somewhere. (99–03)

GOSPEL STANDARDS VERSUS THE WORLD

Maintaining gospel standards will keep you safe. You will be safe if you look like and groom like and act like an ordinary Latter-day Saint: dress modestly, attend your meetings, pay tithes, take the sacrament, honor the priesthood, honor your parents, follow your leaders, read the scriptures, study the Book of Mormon, and pray, always pray. An unseen power will hold your hand as you hold to the iron rod.

Will this solve all your problems? Of course not! That would be contrary to the purpose of your coming into mortality. It will, however, give you a solid foundation on which to build your life.[11] (07–01, p. 261)

Righteousness and virtue will ultimately win. Every once in a while you'll do some obscure little ordinary thing and a light will turn on within you. You will experience a feeling of pure joy. You will come to know that good and righteousness and virtue always, inevitably, will win—conclusively!

Regardless of what the scoreboard says at the moment, regardless of how many examples of those living unworthily and yet seeming to accrue all of the things that seem to be so valuable, ultimately righteousness and virtue will be fully and completely rewarded. (79–02)

Our high standards are a magnet. Some suppose that our high standards will repel growth. It is just the opposite. High standards are a magnet. We are all children of God, drawn to the truth and to good. (06–07, p. 87)

We must live in the world, not like the world. We have to live in the world, but we don't have to live like the world. We can keep our standards, and they ought to be high standards. (98–02)

We must be careful not to fit too easily into the world. In the Church we are in the world, but we are not of the world. If you fit too easily and too quickly into the world, if your protective coloration against the background of the world leaves you too secure, you ought to worry just a little. If you look like, and dress like, and particularly if you act like the world, then you ought to wonder just who you care the most about—what the world says and thinks, what the world establishes as standards, or what the Lord thinks. (75–04)

We must be distinguishable from the world if we want the Spirit. If you want the Spirit of the Lord to operate through you, there is a price to pay, and the Lord will want you easily recognized for who you are and what you are.

That's not easy. Yet we can be in the world and yet not of the world, and staying in the world is part of our responsibility. We don't expect our young people to be hermits or nuts or oddballs, or to be so sanctimonious and sour and supposedly spiritual that they are so miserable that nobody can be around them. That isn't what it's all about. We can be happy, and we can be pleasant, but we need to be distinguishable from the world. (75–04)

Do not follow the image of the world. Young Latter-day Saints, young adults, the major decisions in your life are yet ahead of you and those things can be all that is wonderful. Yesterday alone, today a friend, tomorrow—happiness, happiness that need never end. But it will cost you, and it will not come from following the pattern and the image of the world. (75–04)

We are to warn the world. It isn't possible for us to come out of the world.

The Lord, when He taught His disciples, prayed for them. And He said, "I pray not that thou shouldest take them out of the world, but that thou shouldest keep them from evil."[12] We have as much obligation to stay in the world as we do to stay away from sin. Why? Because we are to warn the world. (76–06, p. 222)

CHRISTMAS

What Christmas is about. There have been many great men— wonderful, religious teachers who have taught men how to live—

There has been but *one Messiah.*

Jesus the Christ, the Son of God, the only begotten of the Father in the flesh. He is the Savior, the Messiah. He made atonement for our sins and opened the resurrection.

This is what Christmas is about.

Those of us who know the plan, know what Christmas really is all about! (79–14)

Christmas and becoming like a child. We lose our bearing if we leave the Christmas of childhood disillusioned. It is easy thereafter to feel that "Seeing is believing." If you are fixed on that, you do not have the hope of ever again finding Christmas as it once was and as it ought to be, because it works the other way around: "Believing is seeing." . . .

If you would see what you get in exchange for giving up the childish illusion of Christmas, you could look forward to the greatest of all discoveries. No matter what your age, you can find and can keep that "little-kid" feeling about Christmas.

The Christmas story in the second chapter of Luke takes, I suppose, a minute and a half to read. It might take a minute more to ponder on it. Yet how infrequently, how remarkably infrequently, does the reading of this sacred account find its way into the family festivities at Christmastime.

The Christmas story does not end there. It is only the beginning. When we, as adults, accept a new status as children of our God, our Father, we may humble ourselves and believe again and in so doing begin to see that in exchange for the fanciful poetry of *The Night Before Christmas* comes the miracle of the first Christmas that grows in every season.

The whole account—from Bethlehem to Calvary—is the Christmas story, and it takes simple, childlike faith to find that out.

It is sophistication that makes Christmas bells ring discordant notes to some, but it is humility that causes others to become as children. Believing is seeing! . . .

Of all times of the year, at Christmastime Latter-day Saints ought to be the most joyful, ought to have greater cause for festivity than anyone, ought to enjoy the Christmas tree and the holly wreath and the stockings and the mistletoe and gifts and toys and children and even reindeer that can fly! When you accept the true account of the birth of Christ, it will indeed "Bring thee the light of thy childhood again."[13] (97–05, pp. 3–8)

Christmas traditions can be positive. I have no quarrel with that well-fed gentleman with the red suit and the white whiskers. He was very generous to me when I was a boy. Now it is for our grandchildren and we still look forward with great anticipation to his visit to our home each year. The tree is always there, the holly wreath, the stockings hung along the fireplace mantle. When I was a boy we had no fireplace, so our stockings were hung on the back of the chairs. It worked wonderfully well for all ten of us. I know of few things on this earth quite so celestial as the face of a little youngster, happy, hopeful, and believing, with Christmas almost here. That is the gift that children give to parents at Christmastime. Those things about Christmas are good because they are for children—except, I suppose, the mistletoe. (97–05, p. 3)

The time we celebrate Christmas is not the important thing. You already know that Christmas commemorates the birthday of Jesus Christ. The date is not right, but the spirit is right, and it doesn't matter that we celebrate it now.

We commemorate His birthday with more preparation and celebration than any other holiday. Not just because He was a great man, or because He had so great an influence on human history.

Every time we write a date, every time we read a calendar, it somehow honors Him because time is measured from His birth. Every time you write the date you can be reminded of that.

Nor do we honor Him just because He showed us how to live. Other great teachers have told people to be honest and to be virtuous and to do good.

There is something about Him that is different from any other that ever lived. There is something He did which no one else could do. (79–14)

CHAPTER 26

Music and the Arts

"I [have] learned what power there can be in music.
When music is reverently presented, it can be akin to revelation.
At times, I think, it cannot be separated from the voice of the Lord,
the quiet, still voice of the Spirit." (07–04, p. 26)

Music is of enormous importance in our worship services. Music is of enormous importance in our worship services. I believe that those who choose, conduct, present, and accompany the music may influence the spirit of reverence in our meetings more than a speaker does. God bless them.

Music can set an atmosphere of worship which invites that spirit of revelation, of testimony. . . .

An organist who has the sensitivity to quietly play prelude music from the hymnbook tempers our feelings and causes us to go over in our minds the lyrics which teach the peaceable things of the kingdom. If we will listen, they are teaching the gospel, for the hymns of the Restoration are, in fact, a course in doctrine! (91–06, p. 22)

Care must be taken in the selection of music for worship services. For some reason it takes a constant vigilance on the part of priesthood leaders—both general and local—to ensure that music presented in our worship and devotional services is music that is appropriate for worship and devotional services. I have heard presidents of the Church declare after a general conference, or after a temple dedication, words to this effect (and I am quoting verbatim from one such experience):

"I suppose we did not give enough attention to the music. It seems that our musicians must take such liberties. Something spiritual was lost from our meetings because the music was not what it should have been. Next time we must remember to give them more careful instructions."

Why is it that the President of the Church, or the president of the stake, or the bishop of the ward must be so attentive in arranging music for worship services and conference meetings? Why should the anxiety persist that if the musicians are left to do what they want to do, the result will not invite the Spirit of the Lord? (76–01, p. 277)

So often our leaders in music feel the necessity, feel responsible, to "upgrade" and introduce "culture" into our worship services by performing music that is either secular or sectarian, chosen solely because it demonstrates their ability, but is not in keeping with the spirit of the gospel. Such music has an important place—but not in our worship services.

Someone will now say that I don't know much about music. To this I quickly confess. I do know, however, when the Spirit of the Lord is present; and that Spirit rarely yields itself to music that is merely well performed or dignified, any more than it is called forth by the speech of the world, however articulate it might be. (66–02, p. 97)

Prelude music, reverently played, invites inspiration. Prelude music, reverently played, is nourishment for the spirit. It invites inspiration. That is a time to, as the poet said, "go to your bosom . . . and ask your heart what it doth know."[1] Do not ever disturb prelude music for others, for reverence is essential to revelation. "Be still," He said, "and know that I am God."[2] (94–05, p. 61)

The power of inspired music. I have sometimes struggled without much success to teach sacred things which have been preceded by music that is secular or uninspired. Let me mention the other side of it.

I have been in places where I have felt insecure and unprepared. I have yearned inwardly in great agony for some power to pave the way or loosen my tongue, that an opportunity would not be lost because of my weakness and inadequacy. On more than a few occasions my prayers have been answered by the power of inspired music. I have been lifted above myself and beyond myself when the Spirit of the Lord has poured in upon the meeting, drawn there by beautiful, appropriate music. I stand indebted to the gifted among us who have that unusual sense of spiritual propriety. (76–01, p. 287)

Sacred music will prepare one to be instructed by the Spirit. Make wholesome music of all kinds a part of your life.

Then learn what *sacred* music has to do with revelation. The Lord said, "My soul delighteth in the song of the *heart;* yea, the song of the righteous is a prayer unto me, and it shall be answered with a blessing upon their heads."[3]

Secular music may be inspiring in a classical or popular sense, but it will not prepare your mind to be instructed by the Spirit as will sacred music.

The Apostle Paul counseled the Ephesians to "be filled with the Spirit; *speaking to yourselves* in psalms and hymns and spiritual songs, singing and making melody *in your heart* to the Lord."[4] (94–05, p. 61)

Our musicians should desire to truly inspire. Very frequently when our musicians, particularly the more highly trained among them, are left to do what they want to do, they perform in such a way as to call attention to themselves and their ability. They do this rather than give prayerful attention to what will inspire. I do not mean "inspire" as the music or art of the world can inspire. I mean *inspire!* (76–01, p. 279)

It is important that all sing. I have noticed that an increasing number of our leaders and members do not sing the congregational songs. Perhaps they do not know them or there are not enough hymnbooks. We should sing the songs of Zion—they are an essential part of our worship. We must not neglect the hymns nor the exalted anthems of the Restoration. (91–06, p. 22)

Do not let secular music replace the sacred. Do not let our sacred music slip away from us, nor allow secular music to replace it.

When music is presented which, however appropriate for other occasions, does not fit the Sabbath, much is lost.

A choir which favors secular music above sacred music on the Sabbath becomes a chorus. In that respect, they teach the ways of men and, in doing so, miss the opportunity to inspire, and deny the power that they might otherwise have. The Spirit does not ratify speech nor confirm music which lacks spiritual substance. (91–06, p. 22)

A caution about tying inappropriate music to a gospel theme. There have been a number of efforts to take sacred gospel themes and tie them to modern music in the hope of attracting our young people to the message. Few events in all of human history surpass the spiritual majesty of the First Vision. We would be ill advised to describe that event, the visit of Elohim and Jehovah, in company with rock music, even soft rock music, or to take equally sacred themes and set them to a modern beat. I do not know how that can be done and result in increased spirituality. I think it cannot be done.

When highly trained artists insist, as they occasionally do, that they receive spiritual experience in tying a sacred gospel theme to an inappropriate art form, I must conclude that they do not know, not really, the difference between when the Spirit of the Lord is present and when it is not. (76–01, p. 279)

We need more inspiring hymns and artwork. Our hymns speak the truth as far as they go. They could speak more of it if we had more of them, specifically teaching the principles of the restored gospel of Jesus Christ.

If I had my way there would be many new hymns with lyrics near scriptural in their power, bonded to music that would inspire people to worship. Think how much we could be helped by an inspired anthem or hymn of the Restoration! Think how we could be helped by an inspired painting on a scriptural theme or on one which depicts our heritage. How much we could be aided by a graceful and modest dance, by a persuasive narrative, or poem, or drama! We could have the Spirit of the Lord more frequently and in almost unlimited intensity if we would. (76–01, p. 281)

Inspirational compositions and art will come by dedication. It is a mistake to assume that one can follow the ways of the world and then somehow, in a moment of intruded inspiration, compose a great anthem of the Restoration, or in a moment of singular inspiration paint the great painting. When it is done, it will be done by one who has yearned and tried and longed fervently to do it, not by one who has condescended to do it. It will take quite as much preparation and work as any masterpiece, and a different kind of inspiration.

There is a test you might apply if you are among the gifted. Ask yourself this question: When I am free to do what I really want to do, what will it be? (76–01, p. 281)

Be careful that your ladder is not leaning against the wrong wall. The reason why we have not yet produced a greater heritage in art and literature and music and drama is not, I am very certain, because we have not had talented people. For over the years we have had not only good ones but great ones. Some have reached great heights in their chosen fields. But few have captured the spirit of the gospel of Jesus Christ and the restoration of it in music, in art, in literature. They have not, therefore, even though they were gifted, made a lasting contribution to the on rolling of the Church and kingdom of God in the dispensation of the fulness of times. They have therefore missed doing what they might have done, and they have missed being what they might have become. I am reminded of the statement: "There are many who struggle and climb and finally reach the top of the ladder only to find that it is leaning against the wrong wall." (76–01, p. 275)

Proper use of gifts. You who have such talents might well ask, "Whence comes this gift?" And gift it is. You may have cultivated it and developed it, but it was given to you. Most of us do not have it. You were not more deserving than we, but you are a good deal more responsible. If you use your gift properly, opportunities for service are opened that will be beneficial eternally for you and for others.

Has it ever occurred to you that you may leave this life without it? If the gift is yours because of the shape of your vocal cords, or the strength of your lungs, or because of the coordination of your hands, or because your eye registers form and color, you may leave the gift behind. You may have to be content with what you have become, because you possessed it while you were here. It has not been revealed just how this would be. I rather suspect that those gifts which we use properly will stay with us beyond the veil. And I repeat, you who are gifted may not be more deserving, but you are much more responsible than the rest of us. (76–01, p. 276)

Bless others with your gift. Go to, then, you who are gifted; cultivate your gift. Develop it in any of the arts and in every worthy example of them. If you have the ability and the desire, seek a career or employ your talent as an avocation or cultivate it as a hobby. But in all ways bless others with it. Set a standard of excellence. Employ it in the secular sense to every worthy advantage, but never use it profanely. Never express your gift unworthily. Increase our spiritual heritage in music, in art, in literature, in dance, in drama.

When we have done it, our activities will be a standard to the world. And our worship and devotion will remain as unique from the world as the Church is different from the world. Let the use of your gift be an expression of your devotion to Him who has given it to you. (76–01, pp. 287–88)

The greatest works will be produced by the most inspired. The greatest hymns and anthems have not been composed, nor have the greatest illustrations been set down, nor the poems written, nor the paintings finished. When they are produced, who will produce them? Will it be the most talented and the most highly trained among us? I rather think it will not. They will be produced by those who are the most inspired among us. Inspiration can come to those whose talents

*Elder and Sister Packer with BYU President Jeffrey R. Holland
and his wife, Patricia Holland, in China while traveling with the BYU
Young Ambassadors, May 1981*

are barely adequate, and their contribution will be felt for generations; and the Church and kingdom of God will move forward just a little more easily because they have been here.

Some of our most gifted people struggle to produce a work of art, hoping that it will be described by the world as masterpiece! monumental! epic! when in truth the simple, compelling theme of "I Am a Child of God" has moved and will move more souls to salvation than would such a work were they to succeed. (76–01, p. 285)

The right kind of music can prepare you to receive inspiration. I know that some young people resent it a little when we comment upon such things as the wild music that is served up nowadays.

Can you not see that you're not going to get much inspiration while your mind is filled with that?

The right kind of music, on the other hand, can prepare you to receive inspiration. (79–10, p. 20)

We ought to be surrounded by good music. There is so much wonderful, uplifting music available that we can experience to our advantage. Our people ought to be surrounded by good music of all kinds. (73–09, p. 27)

Satan seeks to cover the voice of the Spirit. The Church and individual members of it have always been, are now, and ever will be under siege from the adversary. He will cover, even erase the still, small voice through loud and dissonant music awash with lyrics that cannot be understood—or worse, by lyrics that can be understood. He will carefully lead us astray with every other temptation he could devise. (07–04, p. 28)

Music has been corrupted. In our day music itself has been corrupted. Music can, by its tempo, by its beat, by its intensity, dull the spiritual sensitivity of men.

Studies citing physiological effects from some of the extreme music of today neglect the most serious thing concerning it.

Our youth have been brought up on a diet of music that is loud and fast, more intended to agitate than to pacify, more intended to excite than to calm. Even so, there is a breadth of it, some soft enough to be innocent and appealing to our youth, and that which is hard, and that is where the problem is. (73–09, p. 25)

Some music is spiritually destructive. Now a warning! Some music is spiritually very destructive. You young people know what kind that is. The tempo, the sounds, and the lifestyle of those who perform it repel the Spirit. It is far more dangerous than you may suppose, for it can smother your spiritual senses. (94–05, p. 61)

I know some music is spiritually destructive; it's bad and dangerous! Young people, leave it alone! (99–07, p. 24)

Avoid the hard music of our day. Young people, you cannot afford to fill your mind with the unworthy hard music of our day. It is *not* harmless. It can welcome onto the stage of your mind unworthy thoughts and set the tempo to which they dance and to which you may act.

You degrade yourself when you identify with all of those things which seem now to surround such extremes in music: the shabbiness, the irreverence, the immorality, and the addictions. Such music as that is not worthy of you. You should have self-respect.

You are a son or a daughter of Almighty God. He has inspired a world full of wonderful things to learn and to do, uplifting music of many kinds that you may enjoy. (73–09, p. 28)

Avoid improper music. I learned something, and I have since lived that way. When some ugly thought from the nether kingdom tries to get into my mind, I move it out with good music, hymns.[5]

That is one of the reasons why you are very, very, very, very, very, very foolish when you like to participate in music that is dark and noisy. Worthy inspiration cannot get through to you where you are. No matter how popular it may be or how much you want to belong, just remember that there are those angels of the devil using you. (03–04, p. 172)

A recommendation to clean up your music collections. I would recommend that you go through your [music] and set aside [the music] that promote[s] the so-called new morality, the drug, or the hard-rock culture. Such music ought not to belong to young people concerned about spiritual development.

Why not go through your collection? Get rid of the worst of it. Keep just the best of it. Be selective in what you consume and what you produce. It becomes a part of you. (73–09, p. 27)

Parents should show interest in their children's music. We urge parents in the Church to show as much interest in the [music] their children purchase as they would the books and magazines they bring into the home. There are many parents who would not for one moment tolerate a pornographic magazine in their homes who unwittingly provide money for music, some of which in its influence can be quite as damaging. (73–09, p. 25)

Parents should foster good music. Parents ought to foster good music in the home and cultivate a desire to have their children learn the hymns of inspiration.

The time for music lessons seems to come along when there are so many other expenses for the family with little children. But we encourage parents to include musical training in the lives of their children. (73–09, p. 27)

CHAPTER 27

To the Youth of the Church

*"I have the conviction that against what was surely coming
and the prophecies that were given, the Lord has reserved special spirits to
bring forth at this time to see that His Church and kingdom are protected
and moved forward in the world." (07–01, p. 265)*

You, our wonderful youth, are an example to untold millions.
Society is on a course that has caused the destruction of civilizations and
is now ripening in iniquity. Civilization itself is at stake. You, our wonderful youth, are an example to untold millions of good people worldwide.

I think of the joy and happiness that await you in this life and the
work you are to do, and I cannot be discouraged. Peter, the Apostle who
stood next to the Lord, said of you, "Ye are a chosen generation, a royal
priesthood, an holy nation, a peculiar people; that ye should shew forth
the praises of him who hath called you out of darkness into his marvel-
lous light."[1]

Remember this great prophecy: "The Standard of Truth has been
erected; no unhallowed hand can stop the work from progressing; . . .
the truth of God will go forth boldly, nobly, and independent, till it has
penetrated every continent, visited every clime, swept every country,
and sounded in every ear, till the purposes of God shall be

accomplished, and the Great Jehovah shall say the work is done."[2] (03–09, pp. 26–27)

Youth: remember who you are. You remember who you are. Hold fast to your roots. You are a son or a daughter of Almighty God. Never forsake your spiritual heritage. I repeat, you are a son or a daughter of God. Go forth in your true identity. Help others to find what you have found. Do not ever travel in disguise and be wary of others who do. (77–09)

You are a child of God. You are a child of God. He is the father of your spirit. Spiritually you are of noble birth, the offspring of the King of Heaven. Fix that truth in your mind and hold to it. However many generations in your mortal ancestry, no matter what race or people you represent, the pedigree of your spirit can be written on a single line. You are a child of God!

You are a dual being, a spirit clothed in a mortal body. Your body is the instrument of your mind and the foundation of your character. Take nothing into your body which may harm it or disturb the functions of your mind and spirit. Anything that is addictive is dangerous.

Within your body is the power to beget life, to share in creation. The only legitimate expression of that power is within the covenant of marriage. The worthy use of it is the very key to your happiness. Do not use that power prematurely, not with anyone. The misuse of it cannot be made right by making it popular.

Your spirit operates through your mind, but cultivating your intellect is not enough. Reason alone will neither protect nor redeem you. Reason nourished by faith can do both. (89–01, p. 54)

Youth in the Church were reserved to come in this day. As I have looked at the youth of the Church today and at some of the things that are happening, I marvel. I am confident that never in the history of the human family have we had the choice, powerful spirits that the Lord has sent today. That to me is reasonable. If I were directing a large battle, I would be mighty careful to hold in abeyance, in reserve, some of the choice and the elite against the time when the enemy had lifted all his resources and sent them against us. (70–12)

We see a strength in youth beyond what we have seen before. Now another generation of youth comes forward. We see a strength in them beyond what we have seen before. Drinking and drugs and moral mischief are not a part of their lives. They band together in study of the gospel, in socials, and in service. They are not perfect. Not yet. They are doing the best they can, and they are stronger than the generations that came before. (04–09, p. 87)

Youth, your challenge is much greater than was ours. I wish we could promise you that the world will be safer and easier for you than for us. But we cannot make that promise, for just the opposite is true.

There are temptations beckoning to you that were not there when we were teenagers. AIDS was not known when we were young, and drugs were something a doctor prescribed. We knew about opium from reading mysteries, but steroids, pills, and crack and all the rest belonged to future imaginations.

Modesty was not mocked then. Morality and courtesy were fostered in books and films as much as their opposites are today. Perversion was not talked about, much less endorsed as a lifestyle. What was shunned then as pornographic, you see now on prime-time television.

Your challenge is *much* greater than was ours. Few of us would trade places with you. Frankly, we are quite relieved that we are not back where you are. Few of us would be equal to it.

But, oh, what a wonderful time to be young! You have knowledge of many more things than we needed to have. It is my conviction that your generation is better and stronger than was ours—better in many ways! I have faith that you young men and young women can meet the world on its own terms and conquer it! (89–01, p. 54)

Youth face decisions almost every day. You too live in a time of war, the spiritual war that will never end. War itself now dominates the affairs of mankind. Your world at war has lost its innocence. There is nothing, however crude or unworthy, that is not deemed acceptable for movies or plays or music or conversation. The world seems to be turned upside down.[3]

Formality, respect for authority, dignity, and nobility are mocked. Modesty and neatness yield to slouchiness and shabbiness in dress and grooming. The rules of honesty and integrity and basic morality are now ignored. Conversation is laced with profanity. You see that in art and literature, in drama and entertainment. Instead of being refined, they become coarse.[4]

You have decisions almost every day as to whether you will follow those trends. You have many tests ahead. (07–01, pp. 256–57)

Youth will be tried individually. As young Latter-day Saints, you are singled out among all of the people of the world, and, in due time, you will be tried individually as few people in the world will be tried. Live the gospel. (01–01)

The requirements of the Church are the highway to happiness. Young people sometimes get the mistaken notion that a religious attitude and spirituality interfere with youthful growth. They assume that the requirements of the Church are interferences and aggravations that thwart the full expression of young manhood and young womanhood.

How foolish is the youth who feels that the Church is a fence around love to keep him out! O youth, if you could know! The requirements of the Church are the highway to love and to happiness, with guardrails securely in place, with guideposts plainly marked, and with help along the way. How unfortunate to resent counsel and restraint. How fortunate are you who follow the standards of the Church, even if just from sheer obedience or habit. You will find a rapture and a joy fulfilled. (*TYD*, p. 295)

Your errand from the Lord. Jacob, a great Book of Mormon prophet, was teaching his people in the temple, and we find this descriptive verse: "Wherefore I, Jacob, gave unto them these words as I taught them in the temple, having first obtained mine errand from the Lord."[5] I repeat, "having first obtained mine errand from the Lord." It is about this errand, your errand, that I would speak. . . .

To achieve this spiritual preparation you must set out on a quest. The quest has all of the aspects of high adventure. It will require the gallantry of knighthood, all of the virtues of the storybook princess. It will take the resourcefulness of the pioneer, the courage of the astronaut, and the humility of a true saint. It will require some unteenage-like maturity. I say this because right now as teenagers you are trying to assert yourselves, trying to say to the world, mostly to yourselves, "I am *somebody*." But, this preparation will require some different attributes, some that perhaps have not matured in you as yet. It is almost out of keeping with your teenage personalities for you to be submissive and humble, isn't it? . . .

The errand, the quest, is the search for a testimony—an individual conviction, a certain knowledge that Jesus is the Christ, that God lives. Although much of religious expression is in group activity, this matter of testimony is not. It is individual—on your own, by yourself. . . .

Once you have a testimony of your own, some things won't seem to change a great deal. You will still have to work for what you get. You won't be immune to illness or death. You will still have problems to solve, but you will have great strength, and you will be prompted by the Spirit of the Lord in the solution of these problems. (62–06, pp. 924–26)

We invite all youth to come where a standard is kept. We make no apologies for holding to a standard that the Lord has set. In this ominous day when spiritual strength is so desperately needed, we invite all youth to come where a standard is kept, where the challenge is great, where much is required, where the gospel is lived. (63–01, p. 515)

Living water can come only when you consent. Youth suffer from a lingering thirst that has become a drive. Though it gnaws within them, it is not physical. They want to know what it all means—they are seeking the true meaning of life. There is something missing from their lives, some vital substance that they have not tasted.

Many of them unfortunately seek it in physical satisfaction. They smash down the boundaries of morality and wantonly indulge themselves in every manner conceivable to the limit of physical experience, seeking in physical gratification some taste of life. They come away less satisfied than before, the thirst and the craving more acute.

Then many of them turn elsewhere, seeking to escape the futility in life. They turn to drugs and find for a moment the escape they seek. At last their spirits soar. They reach beyond themselves, erase all limitations, and taste for a moment, as they suppose, that which they have been seeking. But it is a synthetic, a wicked counterfeit, for they return to a depression worse than the one they left.

Then they become players in the saddest of human tragedies. For, as they turn again to this release, they are not seeking what they sought before, but indulge to escape the consequences of each previous adventure with drugs. This is addiction! This is tragedy! This is slavery! When a remedy becomes worse than the disease, then we have found futility itself. . . .

When we mention that there is a spiritual answer to your need, I hope you don't dismiss it or ridicule the possibility. . . .

You may say you've been to church, that you've tried religion and not been satisfied. That is little wonder. It isn't in them all, you know, only a flavoring of it. The substance of it, the fulness of it can be found in only one place. Perhaps you have looked for it here, in that one place, and have not found it. And so I repeat, you might try fishing on the right side.

No one can compel you to taste of this living water. It can come only when you consent. There are no conscripts, only volunteers. (69–07, pp. 57–58)

Learn in your youth to follow the scriptures and our leaders. In your youth you can learn that the scriptures are powerful, that they're righteous, that in this Church we learn the scriptures, that we accept them, that we determine to live by them. Learn that there is a constituted authority—that our leaders are ordained by those who are in authority, and it is known throughout the Church. Nothing is done in the corner where there might be room for doubt or confusion or misunderstanding. We all have the right to go before the Lord to appeal in prayer and to receive inspiration and revelation for ourselves, so that each of us will know. (77–04, pp. 19–20)

Learn to follow the promptings of the Holy Ghost. You live in an interesting generation where trials will be constant in your life. Learn to follow the promptings of the Holy Ghost. It is to be a shield and a protection and a teacher for you. Never be ashamed or embarrassed about the doctrines of the gospel or about the standards that we teach in the Church. You always, if you are faithful in the Church, will be that much different from the world at large. (07–01, p. 263)

Youth need to understand what the gift of the Holy Ghost is. Every young Latter-day Saint in the Church has not only the right but the obligation to understand what the gift of the Holy Ghost is. When you do, the Spirit will be present with you often enough and in such power as will protect you in whatever you do. That will be particularly true in the choices—the choice of whom you should marry and what you should do by way of occupation. It will bless you in the times of struggle and difficulty that certainly will be part of your life. We hope it will be, because this is a life of testing. We use the gift so little and so infrequently, but it is ours, and if we prepare ourselves, that voice will speak to us. (00–01)

You have a built-in alarm system. You have an alarm system built into both body and spirit. In your body it is pain; in your spirit it is guilt—or spiritual pain. While neither pain nor guilt is pleasant, and an excess of either can be destructive, both are a protection, for they sound the alarm "Don't do that again!"

Be grateful for both. . . . If the nerve endings in your hands were altered so that you couldn't feel pain, you might put them in fire or machinery and destroy them. In your teenage heart of hearts, you know right from wrong.[6] Learn to pay attention to that spiritual voice of warning within you. (89–01, pp. 54–59)

Preparation for inspiration. Young people, carry a prayer in your heart always. Let sleep come every night with your mind centered in prayer.

Keep the Word of Wisdom.

Read the scriptures.

Listen to your parents and to the leaders of the Church.

Stay away from places and things that common sense tells you will interfere with inspiration.

Develop your spiritual capacities.

Learn to tune out the static and the interference.

Avoid the substitutes and the counterfeits!

Learn to be inspired and directed by the Holy Ghost. (79–10, p. 21)

Do not commit to positions that you may later regret. In your youth don't do things or commit yourselves to positions or involve yourselves in activities that might be spiritually embarrassing for you later in your lives that might limit you spiritually. (67–07)

Make every effort to overcome your weaknesses. When you look at yourself, why don't you make a list of your strengths and weaknesses. Do not try to hide them. You know them. You can look right through yourself. The Lord knows them and looks at you. I have learned from personal experience that His servants can do the same—look into you and see you.

After you have appraised your weaknesses, start acting like a Latter-day Saint. As you do this, avoid the circumstances that bring out your weaknesses. Stay away from them. When you look at yourself, if you find something unpleasant there (I have, a time or two—I guess all of you have or will), get rid of it.

If it is of severe intensity and ugly too and you do not quite know what to do, go see your bishop. He is a judge in Israel—an agent of the Lord. He has the formula. And there is no use your carrying this about. (62–01, pp. 204–5)

Be patient with your parents. Be patient with your parents. They love you so deeply. They are emotionally involved with you, and they may become too vigorous as they set their guidelines for you to follow. But be patient. Remember, they are involved in a big do-it-yourself child-raising project, and this is their first time through. They have never raised a child just like you before.

Give them the right to misunderstand and to make a mistake or two. They have accorded you that right. Recognize their authority. Be grateful for their discipline. Such discipline may set you on the path to greatness. (*TYD,* p. 295)

The love of parents is not divisible. One day each of you will know that some things are not divisible. The love of your parents is one of them. Parents do not love one child more than another—nor less. Each receives all of it. (80–10, p. 22)

You are never alone. If you, our youth, feel alone, remember there are millions of you in the Church now. Tens of thousands of you at this moment serve missions. You are a visible example, a testimony of the Restoration, even to those who will not listen to your message. Wherever you are—in school, at work or play, in the military—you are never alone. (03–09, p. 26)

Youth take hold of your lives. Young Latter-day Saints, shape up! Face up! Take hold of your lives! Take control of your mind, your thoughts! If you have friends that are not a good influence, make changes, even if you face loneliness, even rejection.

If you have already made bad mistakes, there are ways to fix things up, and eventually it will be as though they never happened.

Sometimes guilt controls our minds and takes us prisoner in our thoughts. How foolish to remain in prison when the door stands open. Now, don't tell yourself that sin really doesn't matter. That won't help; repentance will.

Take charge of yourself. How wonderful to be a young Latter-day Saint in this wonderful, challenging time.

Paul told young Timothy, "Let no man despise thy youth."[7]

And Louisa May Alcott was only fourteen when she wrote:

> *A little kingdom I possess,*
> *Where thoughts and feelings dwell,*
> *And very hard I find the task*
> *Of governing it well; . . .*
> *I do not ask for any crown*
> *But that which all may win,*
> *Nor seek to conquer any world*
> *Except the one within.*

You can do it—you must do it. Our future depends on you, our children and youth. (99–07, p. 24)

Learn to ask the right kind of questions. In your youth, as you prepare, learn to ask the right kind of questions. . . . There are no "have to's" in the gospel of Jesus Christ; they are all "get to's." (70–04)

Faith of youth is not dependent on money. Remember, the faith of our youth does not depend on how much money we can spend on them. (88–02)

A testimony and encouragement for children. Little ones, you will be tested, perhaps more than any generation that ever lived here. You will meet many people who do not believe in Christ. Some will be agents for the evil one and teach wickedness. Sometimes this will be very tempting. There will be times when you will make mistakes (and all of us make mistakes). There will be times when you will wonder if you can live the way He taught we should live. When you are tested, when you are disappointed, or ashamed, or when you are sad, remember Him and pray to your Heavenly Father in His name.

Some men will say that He did not come to earth. But He did. Some will say that He is not the Son of God. But He is. Some will say that He has no servants upon the face of the earth. But He has. For He lives. I know that He lives. In His church there are many thousands who can bear witness of Him, and I bear witness of Him, and tell you again the things you should remember, things you should learn when you are yet a little one.

Remember that each of you is a child of our Heavenly Father. That is why we call Him our Father.

You lived before you came to this earth. You came to receive a mortal body and to be tested.

When your life is over, your spirit and body will be separated. We call that death.

Our Heavenly Father sent His Son, Jesus Christ, to redeem us. Because of what He has done we will be resurrected.

There is another kind of death you should think of. That is the separation from the presence of our Heavenly Father. If we will be baptized and live His gospel, we may be redeemed from this second death.

Our Heavenly Father loves us, and we have a Lord and Savior.

I thank God for a church where you, our little children, are precious above all things. I thank God for our Savior who suffered the little children to come unto Him. (73–04, p. 54)

CHAPTER 28

I Have That Witness

*"I do not know now any more surely that Jesus is the Christ,
the Son of God, the Only Begotten of the Father, than I did then as a soldier
boy sitting on the cliff on that tiny speck of an island [in the Pacific Ocean].
There is one difference—now I know the Lord." (04–01, p. 6)*

A witness is not just a belief. I want to bear witness to you of
something that I know. The knowledge that I testify of is a personal witness. It is knowledge. It is not just belief.

I recall a friend of mine was on the stand in a court case. The attorney who was questioning him said, "You believe that such and such."

My friend said, "I did not say I believed it. I know it! If I didn't
know it, I wouldn't testify to it. It is past belief. I know it."

The Restoration has taken place. The Church is on the mission and
commission to bear witness to all the world, to redeem all the living,
and to redeem all the dead. (02–08)

I have that witness. Now, I wonder with you why one such as I
should be called to the holy apostleship. There are so many qualifications that I lack. There is so much in my effort to serve that is wanting.
As I have pondered on it, I have come to only one single thing, one

qualification in which there may be cause, and that is, I have *that* witness.

I declare to you that I know that Jesus is the Christ. I know that He lives. He was born in the meridian of time. He taught His gospel, was tried, was crucified. He rose on the third day. He was the first fruits of the resurrection. He has a body of flesh and bone. Of this I bear testimony. Of Him I am a witness. In the name of Jesus Christ, amen. (71–04, p. 88)

A personal witness that the gospel is true. I bear witness that Jesus is the Christ, the Son of God, that the gospel of Jesus Christ is true, that you as young members of the Church may look forward to a wonderful life of challenges and happiness and responsibility. It is a wonderful time to live and to be young. I envy you. As I said in the beginning, you are young and I am not. And yet in the eternal scheme of things, I am just as young as you are. Maybe a little closer to the final curtain on Act II, but I know, for I have seen a little behind the curtain into Act III and bear personal witness that the gospel is true, and bear witness of Jesus Christ. (95–06, p. 9)

No power can thwart this work. There is no power that can thwart this work. It is the Lord's work. He directs it. He is no stranger to His servants on this earth. He guides it and directs it. Of Him I bear witness, in the name of Jesus Christ, amen. (74–01, p. 133)

The only true and living church. I bear testimony that The Church of Jesus Christ of Latter-day Saints is, as the Lord declared, the only true and living church upon the face of the earth; that with it, He is well pleased, speaking of the Church collectively. And that, individually, if we are humble and faithful, we can stand approved of Him. (85–13, p. 83)

I feel a great obligation to the truth. I feel a great obligation to truth. Now, truth is independent of anyone's belief, regardless of what the pragmatist says. Truth is truth, and it is independent of whether it is believed or not, and I fully expect to be held accountable for anything I say that misleads or invents or enlarges or fabricates. But I have also come to the conclusion, just the last month or two, that I'll be likewise under condemnation for diluting or minimizing or watering down or apologizing or avoiding, and it is in the face of this that I have my greatest concern. There is an obligation to speak the truth, not just to know it. We should not exceed it, but we should not fall short of it. It is my greatest concern, my greatest obligation, and my greatest desire to do one simple thing—to bear witness that Jesus is the Christ, to bear witness that my Redeemer lives. (64–07)

I must know for sure. During my military service, my crew was sent to Seattle, Washington, where we boarded a ship headed into the Pacific by night. I remember lying on my bunk among the many men and reading my Book of Mormon. Many passages held special meaning for me.

In 1 Nephi 15:11, I read the promise: "If ye will not harden your hearts, and ask me in faith, believing that ye shall receive, with diligence in keeping my commandments, surely these things shall be made known unto you."

When I reached the final promise in Moroni 10:4–5, I blocked it in solid red: "And when ye shall receive these things, I would exhort you that ye would ask God, the Eternal Father, in the name of Christ, if these things are not true; and if ye shall ask with a sincere heart, with real intent, having faith in Christ, he will manifest the truth of it unto you, by the power of the Holy Ghost. And by the power of the Holy Ghost ye may know the truth of all things."

On a crowded ship taking a horde of men into battle, I explained to the Lord that I wanted to know whether the Book of Mormon was or was not true. "I must know for sure that it is," I fervently prayed, "for if it is not true, then I'm not sure that it is important whether or not I come back, because things in the world seem to be all undone anyway." And so I continued to plead for an answer—an answer which, in time and in the Lord's way, came to me. (02–06, p. 36)

A question often asked. Everywhere we go . . . we are often asked the question, "Have you seen the Lord? You are an Apostle. Have you seen the Lord?"

I always have the same answer. I say that when I was called to the Twelve, I answered that question in a general conference, and I will send you a copy of that talk. In substance it says this: I have not asked that question of anyone. I have never asked that question of my Brethren. I know the answer, but I have never asked it, supposing that would be so sacred and so personal that it would be among the things that the Lord had in mind when He said, "It is given unto many to know the mysteries of God; nevertheless they are laid under a strict command that they shall not impart only according to the portion of his word which he doth grant unto the children of men, according to the heed and diligence which they give unto him."[1] (90–08)

I wish there were authorization to say more. I bear witness that the Lord lives, that Jesus is the Christ. This I know. I know that He lives. I know that He directs this Church. Sometimes I wish that there were the authorization to say more, say it plainer, but that is the way we say it—the same as a Primary child would say it, that He lives, that we know. (88–05)

The gospel is true. The gospel is true, and it is exactly and precisely like you should hope it to be. The President of the Church is a prophet. The Twelve are Apostles, and they are witnesses of the Lord Jesus Christ. The Church and kingdom of God has been established, and the Lord does direct it. The kingdom will roll forth. It will fill the whole earth. The resurrection is a reality. There is a tremendous work of responsibility upon the Church and the kingdom of God. (*ABE*, p. 306)

Notes

PREFACE

1. See Jacob 1:17.
2. See Alma 42:8.
3. Lucile C. Tate, *Boyd K. Packer: A Watchman on the Tower,* (Salt Lake City: Bookcraft, 1995), 242.

CHAPTER 1: THE GREAT PLAN OF HAPPINESS

1. See Alma 42:8.
2. See *Teachings of the Prophet Joseph Smith* (Salt Lake City: Deseret Book, 1976), 157–58, 208; D&C 93:29–31.
3. See Numbers 16:22; Hebrews 12:9; D&C 76:24.
4. See D&C 77:2.
5. See D&C 132:63; Moses 6:9, 10; Abraham 4:27.
6. See *Teachings of the Prophet Joseph Smith,* 348–49.
7. See Alma 34:9.
8. See Abraham 3:24.
9. See Moses 6:8–10, 22, 59; Abraham 4:26–27.
10. See Abraham 3:25.
11. See Alma 13:3–5.
12. See *Teachings of the Prophet Joseph Smith,* 357.
13. See Moses 4:1–2; Abraham 3:22–27.

14. See Revelation 12:7–13; D&C 29:36; 76:28; Moses 4:3.
15. See Abraham 3:26.
16. See Acts 17:26; Deuteronomy 32:8.
17. See Alma 13:7–9; Abraham 3:23; *Teachings of the Prophet Joseph Smith*, 365.
18. See Abraham 5:4.
19. See Moses 1:34; 3:7; 4:26; 6:3–10, 22, 59.
20. See Moses 3:23–24.
21. See 2 Nephi 2:23.
22. See Moses 4:6, 19.
23. See Alma 12:22; Moses 2:28; 3:17; 4:13.
24. See 2 Nephi 2:20.
25. See Moses 5:4–9; 6:48–62.
26. See Alma 42:7–9; Helaman 14:16–18.
27. See Helaman 14:15.
28. See Articles of Faith 1:3; *Teachings of the Prophet Joseph Smith*, 48.
29. See *Teachings of the Prophet Joseph Smith*, 58–60, 308, 367.
30. See *Teachings of the Prophet Joseph Smith*, 158.
31. See D&C 27:12–13; 110; *Teachings of the Prophet Joseph Smith*, 157.
32. See *Teachings of the Prophet Joseph Smith*, 309–10.
33. See 2 Nephi 9:10–16; Alma 40:7–14.
34. See D&C 138:10–22.
35. *Teachings of the Prophet Joseph Smith*, 219.
36. See Mosiah 3:18.
37. See 1 Corinthians 15:21–22.
38. See 1 Corinthians 15:40–42.
39. See Romans 8:17; D&C 76:94–95; 84:34; 132:19–20; *Teachings of the Prophet Joseph Smith*, 374.
40. See Jude 1:6; Abraham 3:26, 28.
41. Alma 12:32; emphasis added.
42. See "Loyalty," address to religious educators, July 1966, 5.
43. Moses 1:39.
44. D&C 38:30.
45. Alma 42:8.
46. See D&C 84:19–22.
47. See D&C 93:29–33; Abraham 3:22.
48. See D&C 77:2.
49. See Ether 3:16.
50. See D&C 29:35; Moses 4:3.
51. D&C 93:29.
52. See Abraham 3:22.
53. See Alma 13:1–4.
54. Abraham 3:23; see also D&C 29:36; Moses 4:1–3.
55. *Teachings of the Prophet Joseph Smith*, 354.
56. D&C 93:38.
57. 2 Nephi 2:5.
58. 2 Nephi 9:28; Alma 12:4–5.
59. 3 Nephi 1:16; see also Helaman 2:8; D&C 10:12.
60. Joshua 24:15; see also Alma 30:8; D&C 127:2; Moses 6:33.
61. See D&C 76:24; see also Numbers 16:22; Hebrews 12:9.
62. See D&C 132:63; First Presidency, "Origin of Man" (Nov. 1909), in James R.

Clark, comp., *Messages of the First Presidency of The Church of Jesus Christ of Latter-day Saints*, 6 vols. (Salt Lake City: Bookcraft, 1965–75), 4:203; see also Spencer W. Kimball, *Ensign*, Mar. 1976, 71; Gordon B. Hinckley, *Ensign*, Nov. 1983, 83, "The Family: A Proclamation to the World," *Ensign*, Nov. 1995, 102.

63. See *Teachings of the Prophet Joseph Smith*, 348–49, 357, 365.
64. See Abraham 3:24–27.
65. See Jarom 1:2; Alma 24:14; 42:5; Moses 6:62.
66. See Jacob 6:8; Alma 12:25–36; 17:16; 18:39; 22:13–14; 39:18; 42:11, 13.
67. Alma 42:8.
68. See Alma 42:2–5.
69. See 2 Nephi 9:28; Alma 12:4–5; Helaman 2:8; 3 Nephi 1:16; D&C 10:12, 23; Moses 4:3.
70. See *Teachings of the Prophet Joseph Smith*, 181, 297.
71. See *Teachings of the Prophet Joseph Smith*, 181.
72. Titus 1:2.
73. Isaiah 14:12.
74. D&C 76:25–26.
75. Revelation 12:9.
76. See Abraham 4:1.
77. See Moses 2:25.
78. Moses 2:27.
79. See Moses 3:5.
80. Genesis 1:2.
81. See Genesis 1–2; Moses 2–3; Abraham 4–5.
82. See Abraham 4:1, 12, 15, 25, 30.
83. D&C 93:33.
84. Genesis 1:2; Moses 2:2.
85. D&C 93:29.
86. See D&C 101:33–34.
87. D&C 88:66.
88. See D&C 130:20.
89. Revelation 10:6; see also D&C 84:100.
90. Alma 40:8.
91. Moses 3:9.
92. Moses 3:17.
93. See Moses 4:10–12.
94. 2 Nephi 2:25.
95. D&C 29:41.
96. See D&C 29:42.
97. Alma 42:8.
98. D&C 29:42.
99. Moses 3:17.
100. 2 Nephi 2:25.
101. Leviticus 17:14; see also Deuteronomy 12:23; *Teachings of the Prophet Joseph Smith*, 199–200, 367.
102. Spencer W. Kimball, *Ensign*, Sept. 1978, 5.
103. See 2 Nephi 9:28.
104. See Alma 12:4–5.
105. See Helaman 2:8.
106. See 3 Nephi 1:16.

107. See 2 Nephi 2:18; 28:20.
108. See Alma 39:5; Moroni 9:9.
109. Moroni 7:12, 17.
110. See 1 Nephi 8:25, 28.
111. *Teachings of the Prophet Joseph Smith*, 181.
112. See Matthew 8:31.
113. 2 Nephi 2:27.
114. See D&C 132:28–31.
115. 2 Nephi 2:5.
116. 2 Nephi 2:5; see also Helaman 14:31.
117. See James 1:13–15.
118. See Alma 7:10–13; 15:8.
119. 2 Nephi 9:25.
120. Alma 42:17–18.
121. See 2 Nephi 2:22; D&C 77:2; Moses 3:9; Abraham 4:11–12, 24.
122. D&C 76:94.
123. See Galatians 5:22–23; Alma 7:23–24; D&C 4:5–6.
124. See D&C 131:2.
125. D&C 93:33.
126. D&C 88:15.
127. See 2 Nephi 9:11.
128. 2 Nephi 9:7–9.
129. 1 Nephi 10:21.
130. 2 Nephi 2:26.
131. 2 Nephi 9:13.
132. 2 Nephi 2:18.
133. D&C 4:3.
134. D&C 128:7.
135. Robert Keen, "How Firm a Foundation," *Hymns of The Church of Jesus Christ of Latter-day Saints* (Salt Lake City: The Church of Jesus Christ of Latter-day Saints, 1985), no. 85, v. 6.
136. See 2 Nephi 9:7–9.
137. 1 Corinthians 15:19.
138. Philippians 4:7.
139. See Alma 42:16–22.
140. Ezekiel 36:26.
141. D&C 19:16.
142. Alma 12:32.
143. John 19:10–11.
144. 1 Timothy 2:5.
145. 2 Nephi 2:7.
146. Alma 42:8.
147. D&C 101:36.
148. See D&C 137.
149. Philippians 4:7.
150. D&C 76:35, 37.
151. D&C 76:7, 8.
152. See D&C 84:38.

CHAPTER 2: OBEDIENCE AND FAITH

1. Mosiah 5:8.
2. See Moses 5:6–9.
3. Alma 29:4–5.
4. Matthew 5:48.
5. D&C 105:6.
6. John 8:32.
7. 2 Nephi 9:28; see also 2 Nephi 9:42; 28:15.

CHAPTER 3: REPENTANCE AND FORGIVENESS

1. Alma 36:19.
2. D&C 58:42; see also Hebrews 8:12; 10:17.
3. Isaiah 1:18.
4. D&C 18:11.
5. See 2 Nephi 1:13; 9:45; Jacob 3:11; Alma 26:13–14.
6. D&C 18:10.
7. D&C 46:15.
8. See Isaiah 43:25; Hebrews 8:12; 10:17; Alma 36:19; D&C 58:42.
9. Alma 42:16.
10. Alma 42:16.
11. See Matthew 12:31.
12. See D&C 132:38–39; see also Psalm 16:10; Acts 2:25–27; *Teachings of the Prophet Joseph Smith* (Salt Lake City: Deseret Book, 1976), 339.
13. 2 Nephi 2:7.
14. See Genesis 19:26.
15. See Hebrews 12:6–9; Helaman 15:3; D&C 95:1.
16. See D&C 101:78.
17. See *Teachings of the Prophet Joseph Smith,* 256–57.
18. See D&C 138.
19. D&C 58:42–43.
20. See D&C 42:25.
21. See Acts 5:31; Ephesians 1:7; Mosiah 4:2; 26:29; D&C 1:31–32; 58:42; 61:2.
22. See Isaiah 1:18.
23. Book of Mormon title page.
24. D&C 18:13.
25. D&C 1:31–32.
26. D&C 58:42.
27. D&C 58:42.
28. Isaiah 43:25.
29. Mormon 8:20.

CHAPTER 4: COVENANTS, BAPTISM, AND THE GIFT OF THE HOLY GHOST

1. *Doctrines of Salvation,* comp. Bruce R. McConkie, 3 vols. (Salt Lake City: Bookcraft, 1954–56), 1:152.
2. See D&C 22:1; 66:2.
3. See 2 Nephi 31:17; D&C 19:31.

4. Mosiah 3:21.
5. Moroni 8:12.
6. Moroni 8:20.
7. Moroni 8:14, 16.
8. See D&C 68:27.
9. Mosiah 18:10.
10. Articles of Faith 1:4.
11. See D&C 8:2–4.
12. Acts 2:2–4.
13. See Acts 2:7–11.
14. See Acts 2:38.
15. Acts 19:2.
16. Acts 19:5.
17. Acts 19:6.
18. See Moses 6:65–66.
19. Articles of Faith 1:4.
20. Articles of Faith 1:3.
21. Revelation 3:20.
22. 2 Nephi 9:39.
23. D&C 89:19.
24. D&C 9:7–8; emphasis added.
25. See 1 Nephi 14:28–30; 2 Nephi 32:7; Alma 12:9–11.
26. D&C 85:6.
27. 1 Nephi 17:45.
28. D&C 110:1.
29. D&C 8:2.
30. D&C 6:15.
31. D&C 100:5.
32. See D&C 8:2–3; 9:7–9.
33. D&C 121:46.
34. Moroni 10:5; see also 2 Nephi 32:5.
35. 2 Nephi 32:3.
36. 2 Nephi 31:13; 32:2.
37. 3 Nephi 9:20.
38. See 3 Nephi 9:20.
39. 3 Nephi 9:20; emphasis added.

CHAPTER 5: SPIRITUAL DEVELOPMENT

1. See Revelation 3:20.
2. See Mosiah 27:1–17.
3. See Mosiah 29:42–43; Alma 36:3–24.
4. D&C 98:12.
5. Moroni 7:38.
6. See 1 Corinthians 14:12.
7. See Mark 16:17–18.
8. Matthew 12:39; 16:4; see also Luke 11:29; D&C 63:7–10.
9. D&C 84:46; emphasis added.
10. D&C 88:13; see also John 1:4–9; D&C 84:45–47; 88:6; 93:9.
11. D&C 84:45.

12. 2 Corinthians 3:18; see also Mosiah 25:24.
13. D&C 93:26.
14. D&C 88:6.
15. D&C 46:17.
16. D&C 45:57.
17. "'Receiving' the Holy Ghost," *Improvement Era*, March 1916, 460.
18. John 1:9.
19. See D&C 93:23, 29–30.
20. See D&C 1:35.
21. 2 Nephi 2:11.
22. Moroni 7:17–18.
23. Moroni 7:19.
24. See Moroni 7:16.
25. See Moroni 7:17.
26. See 2 Nephi 2:11, 16.
27. See Galatians 6:7–9.
28. See Joseph Fielding Smith, *Doctrines of Salvation*, comp. Bruce R. McConkie, 3 vols. (Salt Lake City: Bookcraft, 1954–56), 1:54.
29. Article of Faith 1:3.
30. Article of Faith 1:4.
31. See Article of Faith 1:5.
32. See 1 Nephi 8:28.
33. *Teachings of the Prophet Joseph Smith* (Salt Lake City: Deseret Book, 1976), 151.
34. 1 Corinthians 2:13–14.
35. Jacob 4:14.
36. 1 Corinthians 2:14.
37. See 3 Nephi 9:20.
38. 3 Nephi 9:20.
39. Proverbs 20:27.
40. James 1:22.
41. John 7:17.

CHAPTER 6: REVELATION AND SPIRITUAL EXPERIENCES

1. See 1 Kings 19:1–12
2. D&C 88:15.
3. See Jeremiah 5:21; Ephesians 1:18; 2 Nephi 21:3; D&C 110:1; 138:11, 29.
4. Ether 4:15.
5. See Deuteronomy 28:28; Ephesians 4:18; D&C 58:15.
6. 1 Nephi 17:45.
7. See 1 Kings 19:12; 1 Nephi 17:45.
8. 1 Nephi 17:45; emphasis added.
9. See 1 Nephi 17:45.
10. 2 Nephi 32:3.
11. See 1 Nephi 17:45.
12. D&C 121:45.
13. 1 Corinthians 2:14.
14. 1 Samuel 3:10.
15. 2 Nephi 32:3.
16. See Exodus 18:14–18, 21–22.

17. Proverbs 29:18.
18. 2 Nephi 32:3.
19. See D&C 9:7–9.
20. D&C 88:124.
21. John 14:26.
22. See D&C 43:25.
23. D&C 1:38.
24. *Teachings of the Prophet Joseph Smith* (Salt Lake City: Deseret Book, 1976), 21.
25. Alma 12:9.
26. See Alma 12:9.
27. See D&C 42:11.
28. D&C 1:39.
29. Articles of Faith 1:9.
30. *The Teachings of Harold B. Lee,* ed. Clyde J. Williams (Salt Lake City: Bookcraft, 1996), 488–89.
31. Patriarchal blessing of Boyd K. Packer, 15 January 1944, 2.
32. Adam counseled and blessed his posterity (see D&C 107:42–56); Jacob blessed his sons and their descendants (see Genesis 49:1–28); Lehi blessed his posterity (see 2 Nephi 4:3–11).
33. The Savior ordained apostles, prophets, and evangelists (see Ephesians 4:11); the duty of the Twelve is to ordain evangelists (see D&C 107:39); Hyrum Smith was to take the office of patriarch (see D&C 124:91–92, 124; 135:1).
34. 2 Nephi 9:28.
35. D&C 4:7.
36. See Matthew 6:24; Luke 16:13; James 1:8.
37. See D&C 46:7.
38. See Matthew 24:24.
39. See Moroni 7:17.
40. D&C 50:2; see also D&C 50:3.
41. Moroni 7:17.
42. *Teachings of the Prophet Joseph Smith,* 205.
43. 2 Nephi 32:8–9.
44. Jacob 6:8; emphasis added.

CHAPTER 7: THE SCRIPTURES

1. 2 Timothy 3:2–4.
2. 2 Timothy 3:13.
3. 2 Timothy 3:15.
4. Matthew 13:46.
5. William Williams, "Guide Us, O Thou Great Jehovah," *Hymns of The Church of Jesus Christ of Latter-day Saints* (Salt Lake City: The Church of Jesus Christ of Latter-day Saints, 1985), no. 83.
6. D&C 1:20.
7. 2 Nephi 11:8; emphasis added; see also 1 Nephi 19:23–24; 2 Nephi 6:5; 11:2.
8. Jacob 1:4.
9. D&C 89:3.
10. See 2 Nephi 9:28–29.
11. Alma 42:8; see also Alma 42:5, 12, 30.
12. See 2 Nephi 31:2–21; 32:1–6; 3 Nephi 11:31–40; 27:13–21.

13. See 2 Nephi 9:4–6; Mosiah 16:8–9; Alma 12:25–27.
14. See Alma 40:11–14.
15. See 2 Nephi 2:27; Alma 28:13; 3 Nephi 2:2.
16. See Mosiah 29:42; Alma 4:20; 5:3, 44; 13:1–10.
17. See Moroni 4:3; 5:2.
18. See Moroni 7:16.
19. See Mosiah 4:26.
20. See D&C 20:9.
21. 1 Nephi 13:28.
22. See 1 Nephi 13:20–42; 14:23.
23. 1 Nephi 8:12.
24. 2 Nephi 4:15.
25. Amos 8:11.
26. Moroni 10:4–5.
27. See John 10:16.

CHAPTER 8: RIGHTEOUSNESS AND PERFECTION

1. Matthew 5:48.
2. 3 Nephi 9:20; emphasis added.
3. D&C 117:13.
4. D&C 117:13.
5. 3 Nephi 27:7.
6. D&C 121:45–46.
7. Proverbs 23:7.
8. Moses 3:17; emphasis added.
9. John 14:26.
10. Author unknown, "All the Water in the World," in *Best-Loved Poems of the LDS People,* ed. Jack M. Lyon, and others (Salt Lake City: Deseret Book, 1996), 302.
11. See Alma 12:14.
12. D&C 93:27–30.
13. D&C 101:78; emphasis added.
14. See 2 Nephi 2:5.
15. See D&C 101:78.
16. Moroni 8:14; compare D&C 18:42; 29:46–49; 68:25; 137:10.
17. See D&C 29:50.
18. John 8:31–32.
19. D&C 101:78; emphasis added.
20. D&C 101:97–98; emphasis added.
21. *Poor Richard's Almanac,* 1743.
22. 1 Corinthians 15:19.
23. See D&C 124:33–41.
24. Alma 62:39–41; emphasis added.
25. 2 Nephi 2:11.
26. Joseph Smith, *History of The Church of Jesus Christ of Latter-day Saints,* edited by B. H. Roberts, 7 vols., 2nd ed. rev. (Salt Lake City: The Church of Jesus Christ of Latter-day Saints, 1932–51), 4:570.
27. *History of the Church,* 4:570.
28. See John 9:1–3.
29. D&C 138:17.

CHAPTER 9: MEASURABLE PRINCIPLES

1. Mark 2:27–28.
2. See Exodus 12.
3. Hebrews 10:10, 12.
4. 1 Corinthians 3:16–17.
5. D&C 88:124.
6. D&C 89:2.
7. See D&C 89:3–9.
8. See D&C 89:18.
9. D&C 89:19.
10. D&C 89:3.
11. D&C 58:26.
12. D&C 89:3.
13. D&C 89:20.
14. D&C 89:19.
15. See D&C 89.
16. D&C 89:19.
17. D&C 89:1, 3.
18. D&C 89:18, 20–21.
19. D&C 89:19.
20. D&C 89:3; emphasis added.
21. See D&C 89:12.
22. D&C 49:18. The context for verse 18 is verse 19: "For, behold, the beasts of the field and the fowls of the air . . . [are] ordained for the use of man for food." Section 49 was specifically directed to members of the United Society of Believers in Christ's Second Appearing [the Shakers] to correct some of their erroneous doctrines. One of their beliefs was not to eat flesh—meat or fish.

CHAPTER 10: CHASTITY AND DATING

1. See Acts 17:29; D&C 93:33–35; Abraham 3:22–23; 5:7.
2. See Genesis 1:27; Matthew 19:4; Mark 10:6; D&C 20:17–18; 132:63; Moses 2:27; 6:9; Abraham 4:27.
3. See Alma 13:3.
4. Alma 38:12.
5. See Joseph F. Smith, *Gospel Doctrine* (Salt Lake City: Deseret Book, 1977), 309.
6. See *The Teachings of Harold B. Lee,* ed. Clyde J. Williams (Salt Lake City: Bookcraft, 1996), 220.
7. See "Your Greatest Challenge, Mother," *Ensign,* Nov. 2000, 97.
8. See 1 Corinthians 6:19–20.
9. See Jacob 3:12; D&C 42:24; 104:8–9.
10. 1 Corinthians 10:13.
11. See Joseph Smith–History 1:15–16.
12. See James 4:7.
13. See D&C 10:22; see also Luke 22:3; 2 Nephi 2:17–18, 27; 3 Nephi 18:18; D&C 50:3.
14. See Alma 41:10.
15. Alma 41:10.
16. See John 8:34; 2 Peter 2:12–14, 18–19.

17. See D&C 42:22.
18. See James 4:6–8; 2 Nephi 9:39; Mosiah 3:19.
19. 1 Corinthians 10:13; see also D&C 62:1.
20. Romans 1:24, 27.
21. Romans 1:26.
22. See 2 Nephi 2:26–27.
23. See 2 Nephi 2:25; 9:18; D&C 11:13; 42:61; 101:36.
24. Alma 41:10.
25. See Genesis 13:13 n. 13b; 18:20–22 n. 20b; 19:4–9; JST Genesis 19:9–15; Leviticus 18:22, 29; 20:13 n. 13a; Deuteronomy 23:17 n. 17b; Romans 1:24–27; 1 Corinthians 6:9 nn. 9e, 9f; 1 Timothy 1:9–10 n. 10b.
26. 1 Nephi 8:23; 12:17.
27. See 1 Nephi 8:23–32.
28. See 1 Corinthians 6:9; 1 Thessalonians 5:22; 2 Timothy 2:22; D&C 9:13.
29. See Genesis 1:26–27; Moses 2:26–27; 6:9; Abraham 4:26–27.
30. See 2 Nephi 2:1–6.
31. See Alma 7:11–12.
32. See D&C 101:78; Articles of Faith 1:2.
33. Alma 41:10.
34. D&C 59:6; emphasis added.
35. Ether 8:19.
36. Exodus 20:13; see also 2 Nephi 9:35.
37. D&C 59:6.

Chapter 11: Marriage

1. D&C 49:17.
2. Alma 42:8.
3. Psalm 127:3.
4. See D&C 130:2; 131:2; 1 Corinthians 11:11; Ephesians 5:31.
5. See Moses 6:8–9.
6. See Moses 3:8.
7. See Moses 6:67.
8. See Moses 3:18.
9. See Moses 3:23–24.
10. D&C 42:22; emphasis added.
11. See D&C 131:1–3.
12. *Mormon Doctrine,* 2nd ed. (Salt Lake City: Bookcraft, 1966), 118.
13. Moses 1:39.
14. 2 Nephi 2:25.
15. Genesis 2:18; Abraham 5:14.
16. See Genesis 1:28.
17. See *Teachings of the Prophet Joseph Smith* (Salt Lake City: Deseret Book, 1976), 308.
18. Alma 22:13.
19. Genesis 2:18; Abraham 5:14.
20. Moses 4:26.
21. David O. McKay, *Gospel Ideals* (Salt Lake City: The Improvement Era, 1953), 469.
22. *Gospel Ideals,* 466.
23. Alma 5:58.

24. Romans 1:26.
25. Matthew 20:7.
26. See D&C 137:7–9.
27. *Millennial Star* 61 (31 Aug. 1899): 547.
28. 1 Corinthians 15:19.

CHAPTER 12: FAMILY RELATIONSHIPS

1. See "The Family: A Proclamation to the World," *Ensign,* Nov. 1995, 102.
2. Revelation 12:12.
3. See Alma 42:8, 16.
4. Psalm 127:3.
5. See Alma 42:8.
6. See Matthew 6:33; Mark 1:14–15; D&C 65:2–6; 84:34; 88:78; 105:32; 138:44.
7. D&C 124:34.
8. See D&C 68:25–28.
9. *Church Handbook of Instructions, Book 2: Priesthood and Auxiliary Leaders* (Salt Lake City: The Church of Jesus Christ of Latter-day Saints, 1998), 178.
10. Ephesians 4:14.
11. In Conference Report, 6 Oct. 1961, 79.
12. See "Message From the First Presidency," *Family Home Evening Resource Book* (Salt Lake City: The Church of Jesus Christ of Latter-day Saints, 1983), iv.
13. *Ensign,* Nov. 1995, 102.
14. See Genesis 1:28; Moses 2:28.
15. D&C 137:9.
16. D&C 83:4.
17. Mosiah 4:14.
18. D&C 93:40.
19. Mosiah 4:15.
20. Matthew 18:6.
21. See D&C 68:25, 28.
22. D&C 93:36–37, 40; emphasis added.
23. Ether 8:24.
24. Helaman 12:1–3; emphasis added.
25. See D&C 20:41, 43; 33:15.
26. D&C 121:26.
27. 2 Nephi 32:3.
28. See D&C 6:36.
29. D&C 132:63.
30. Psalm 127:3.
31. See Harold B. Lee, *Ensign,* July 1973, 98.
32. Quoted by David O. McKay, *Improvement Era,* June 1964, 445.
33. Orson F. Whitney, in Conference Report, Apr. 1929, 110.
34. 3 John 1:4.
35. See D&C 131:1–3.
36. See D&C 131:1–4; 132:19–21.
37. D&C 58:3–4.
38. Proverbs 29:15.
39. D&C 68:25.
40. Conference Report, Oct. 1942, 12–13.

41. D&C 93:40; see D&C 93:36–40.
42. See D&C 83:2.
43. See D&C 93:40.
44. See D&C 121:41–43.
45. D&C 121:37.
46. D&C 84:39.
47. D&C 121:37.
48. See D&C 9:8–9.
49. See D&C 8:2–3.

Chapter 13: Teaching and Church Doctrine

1. Job 32:8.
2. Joseph Smith–Matthew 1:22.
3. D&C 121:26.
4. D&C 1:20.
5. Matthew 23:11.
6. 2 Timothy 3:1–7.
7. 2 Timothy 3:13–17.
8. D&C 42:14.
9. Jacob 1:17; emphasis added.
10. D&C 88:78; emphasis added.
11. D&C 88:79–80.
12. See Alma 29:8.
13. D&C 88:78.
14. D&C 84:85.
15. Matthew 10:39.
16. D&C 84:85; see also D&C 100:6; Matthew 10:19–20.
17. D&C 84:85.
18. 3 Nephi 27:27.

Chapter 14: Learning and Scholarship

1. 2 Timothy 3:7.
2. 2 Nephi 9:28–29; emphasis and comma added; see also 2 Nephi 9:42, 28:15; Alma 32:23; D&C 58:10.
3. D&C 93:2.
4. D&C 88:118; emphasis added.
5. D&C 88:79.
6. D&C 88:118.
7. Matthew 15:13.
8. D&C 90:15.
9. D&C 88:118.
10. D&C 82:3.
11. 1 Nephi 8:10, 12.
12. D&C 121:35.

Chaper 15: Economics and Welfare Principles

1. D&C 75:28; emphasis added.
2. 2 Nephi 2:11.

3. D&C 9:7–9.
4. See D&C 9:7–9.

CHAPTER 16: GOVERNMENT, LAWS, WAR, AND FREEDOM

1. Mosiah 29:26–27.
2. Conference Report, April 1955, p. 24.
3. Alma 60:13.
4. "Ancestral Home," by Boyd K. Packer, from Donna S. Packer, *On Footings from the Past* (Salt Lake City: Bookcraft, 1988), 401.
5. See Brigham Young, Journal History, 4 July 1854; *Church News,* 15 December 1948.
6. John 8:31–32.
7. Brigham Young in Journal History, 4 July 1854.
8. See, for example, 1 Nephi 2:20 and 2 Nephi 1:5.
9. See 2 Nephi 1:7.
10. D&C 101:80.
11. John 8:32.

CHAPTER 17: CHURCH HISTORY AND THE RESTORATION

1. Moroni 7:37.
2. See Joseph Smith–History 1:33.
3. D&C 121:16.
4. Joseph Smith–History 1:19; see also Matthew 15:9.
5. See D&C 27:12–13.
6. See 1 Nephi 10:17–19.
7. Joseph Smith–History 1:17.
8. See Joseph Smith–History 1:68–72.
9. See D&C 27:12.
10. Articles of Faith 1:5; see also Joseph Smith–History 1:1–75; D&C 20:1–84.
11. See D&C 110:11–16; 128:19–21.
12. D&C 13:1.
13. See D&C 20:41; 33:15.
14. See D&C 27:12–13; Joseph Smith–History 1:72.
15. D&C 107:3.
16. See D&C 110.
17. See D&C 18:9; 20:1–2; 107:22, 29.
18. See Articles of Faith 1:6; Ephesians 2:20.
19. Conference Report, April 1948, 11–17.

CHAPTER 18: PREPARING IN THE LAST DAYS

1. D&C 35:13; see also D&C 1:19–23; 1 Corinthians 1:27.
2. D&C 121:19–22.
3. D&C 65:2.
4. See Acts 26:26.
5. See D&C 42:11.
6. Acts 26:26.
7. D&C 42:11; emphasis added.

8. D&C 20:65.
9. Acts 2:38.
10. See D&C 49:7.
11. D&C 88:73.
12. See D&C 115:5–6; Isaiah 11:12; 2 Nephi 21:12.
13. 3 Nephi 21:28.
14. Moses 7:61.
15. 2 Timothy 3:1–7.
16. See Helaman 5:12.
17. See 3 Nephi 18:25; D&C 9:8.
18. Joshua 24:15.
19. Matthew 5:11–12.
20. See D&C 121:16–21.
21. D&C 105:14.
22. 3 Nephi 11:29.
23. 1 Nephi 8:28; emphasis added.
24. Nehemiah 4:2–3.
25. Nehemiah 4:6.
26. Nehemiah 6:2–3.
27. Nehemiah 4:9.

CHAPTER 19: MEETINGS AND AUXILIARIES

1. Numbers 21:7–9.
2. 1 Nephi 17:41.
3. D&C 1:38.
4. Articles of Faith 1:13.
5. *A Centenary of Relief Society, 1842–1942* (Salt Lake City: General Board of the Relief Society, 1942), 7.
6. See First Presidency letter, 19 Mar. 2003.

CHAPTER 20: PRIESTHOOD AND ITS EXERCISE

1. See JST, Genesis 14:28–31.
2. See D&C 84:33, 43–44.
3. D&C 84:38–40.
4. See 3 Nephi 27:1–10.
5. D&C 36:2; emphasis added.
6. See D&C 84:6, 14–16; 107:40–41; Abraham 1:3–4.
7. See Alma 29:8; D&C 133:37.
8. See D&C 20:38.
9. D&C 84:18.
10. D&C 107:13.
11. D&C 107:14.
12. D&C 107:1–3.
13. D&C 84:18–19.
14. D&C 124:123; see also D&C 76:57.
15. D&C 107:4.
16. See D&C 84:6–17; 107:40–57.
17. D&C 107:5.

18. Philip Doddridge, "How Gentle God's Commands," *Hymns of The Church of Jesus Christ of Latter-day Saints* (Salt Lake City: The Church of Jesus Christ of Latter-day Saints, 1985), no. 125.
19. Isaiah 55:9.
20. See D&C 27:13; 110:11–16; 112:30.
21. See D&C 132:7.
22. D&C 42:11.

Chapter 21: Leadership and Following the Brethren

1. Articles of Faith 1:5.
2. *Improvement Era,* June 1951, 412.
3. See Exodus 17:8–13.
4. D&C 124:45.
5. 3 Nephi 12:1.
6. D&C 124:46.
7. See John 6:60; 1 Nephi 16:2; 2 Nephi 9:40; Helaman 14:10.
8. Matthew 5:11–12; see also Luke 21:12; John 15:20; 3 Nephi 12:12.
9. Isaiah 29:21; see also 2 Nephi 27:32.
10. D&C 121:16–17, 19–21.
11. See D&C 58:43.
12. D&C 46:27.
13. Draft Declaration of the Twelve Apostles, reporting March 1844 meeting of Twelve, Brigham Young Papers, LDS Church Archives.
14. D&C 112:26.
15. D&C 1:38.
16. Psalm 119:105.
17. D&C 107:27, 29.
18. Isaiah 55:8–9.
19. Jacob 1:17; emphasis added.
20. In Conference Report, April 1951, 154.
21. Articles of Faith 1:5.
22. 1 Corinthians 2:14; emphasis added.
23. See D&C 41:9.
24. D&C 42:11.
25. See D&C 20:65.
26. See D&C 42:11.
27. D&C 36:2.
28. D&C 9:8.
29. D&C 58:18; emphasis added.
30. Articles of Faith 1:5.
31. D&C 115:3–4.

Chapter 22: The Kingdom Rolls Forth

1. D&C 65:2.
2. See Joseph Smith, *History of The Church of Jesus Christ of Latter-day Saints,* edited by B. H. Roberts, 7 vols., 2nd ed. rev. (Salt Lake City: The Church of Jesus Christ of Latter-day Saints, 1932–51), 4:540.
3. See Alma 34:15–16.

4. See D&C 76:3.
5. D&C 128:5.
6. *History of the Church,* 4:129.
7. D&C 97:21.
8. Conference Report, Apr. 1975, 4.
9. See 1 Nephi 14:12.

CHAPTER 23: TEMPLE WORK

1. 1 Corinthians 3:16–17; see also 1 Corinthians 6:19–20.
2. Bruce R. McConkie, *Mormon Doctrine* (Salt Lake City: Bookcraft, 1966), 227.
3. 2 Nephi 9:25.
4. See 1 Corinthians 15:29; D&C 124:29; 127:5–9; 138:33.
5. Articles of Faith 1:3.
6. 1 Nephi 10:19; Alma 7:20; 37:12.
7. *Discourses of Wilford Woodruff,* edited by G. Homer Durham (Salt Lake City: Bookcraft, 1946), 153.

CHAPTER 24: SPREADING THE GOSPEL

1. See 1 Kings 17:8–16.
2. See John 21:15–17.
3. D&C 50:21.
4. Book of Mormon title page.
5. Romans 2:21.
6. D&C 123:12.
7. D&C 1:30.
8. Nehemiah 6:2–3.
9. *History of The Church of Jesus Christ of Latter-day Saints,* edited by B. H. Roberts, 7 vols., 2nd ed. rev. (Salt Lake City: The Church of Jesus Christ of Latter-day Saints, 1932–51), 7:307–8.
10. See D&C 78.
11. Author unknown.
12. 2 Nephi 2:11.
13. See Moroni 7:31–33.
14. See 2 Nephi 32:3–4.
15. See D&C 18:33–36.
16. Grace Gordon, "Called to Serve," *Hymns of The Church of Jesus Christ of Latter-day Saints* (Salt Lake City: The Church of Jesus Christ of Latter-day Saints, 1985), no. 249.
17. See Marion G. Romney, Regional Representatives' Seminar, October 1984.
18. Abraham 3:25.
19. See 1 Corinthians 3:2; D&C 19:22.

CHAPTER 25: THE GOSPEL IN OUR LIVES

1. D&C 88:15.
2. *The Teachings of Lorenzo Snow,* edited by Clyde J. Williams (Salt Lake City: Bookcraft, 1984), 2.
3. Matthew 5:48.

4. Mosiah 2:17.

5. 3 Nephi 27:7.

6. Joseph Smith, *History of The Church of Jesus Christ of Latter-day Saints,* edited by B. H. Roberts, 7 vols., 2nd ed. rev. (Salt Lake City: The Church of Jesus Christ of Latter-day Saints, 1932–51), 5:394.

7. 2 Nephi 2:25.

8. 3 John 1:4.

9. Alma 41:10.

10. 2 Timothy 3:7.

11. See Helaman 5:12.

12. John 17:15.

13. Author unknown, "Answer to Rock Me to Sleep," in Martha Louise Rayne, *What Can a Woman Do* (Detroit: F. B. Dickerson and Co., 1884), 314.

CHAPTER 26: MUSIC AND THE ARTS

1. William Shakespeare, *Measure for Measure,* act 2, scene 2, lines 136–37.

2. Psalm 46:10.

3. D&C 25:12; emphasis added.

4. Ephesians 5:18–19; emphasis added.

5. See D&C 25:12.

CHAPTER 27: TO THE YOUTH OF THE CHURCH

1. 1 Peter 2:9.

2. Joseph Smith, *History of The Church of Jesus Christ of Latter-day Saints,* edited by B. H. Roberts, 7 vols., 2nd ed. rev. (Salt Lake City: The Church of Jesus Christ of Latter-day Saints, 1932–51), 4:540.

3. See 2 Peter 2:1–22.

4. See 1 Timothy 4:1–3; 2 Timothy 3:1–9.

5. Jacob 1:17.

6. See 2 Nephi 2:5.

7. 1 Timothy 4:12.

CHAPTER 28: I HAVE THAT WITNESS

1. Alma 12:9.

Sources

The following is a list of over four hundred sermons or writings from which the passages in this book were selected. References in the book correspond to the four-digit codes that precede each source listing below. The first two digits in the code indicate the year of delivery or publication, and the last two digits refer to the chronological order within that year. Thus, a reference to 85–04 would indicate the fourth item in 1985. In many cases these sermons were published in more than one source. These duplications have been listed together under the original delivery or publication date (for example, see 80–09 or 88–08). Sources indicated by a double "X" represent sermons or writings for which the delivery or publication date is unknown.

Four books containing collections of Boyd K. Packer's addresses have been published. The first was *That All May Be Edified* (Bookcraft, 1982), which is cited in the source list as *ABE*. The next book, *Let Not Your Heart Be Troubled* (Bookcraft, 1991), is cited as *HBT*. The third book, *The Things of the Soul* (Bookcraft, 1996), is cited as *TOS*. The fourth book, *The Shield of Faith* (Bookcraft, 1998), is cited as *SOF*. These four books are collections of complete talks by President Packer, whereas this volume is a compilation of topically arranged excerpts.

Additionally, President Packer has published three books from which excerpts have been taken. They are *Teach Ye Diligently*, rev. ed. (Deseret Book, 1991), cited in the book as *TYD; The Holy Temple* (Deseret Book, 1980), cited in the book as *THT;* and *Our Father's Plan* (Deseret Book, 1994), cited in the book as *OFP*.

Sermons and Articles

XX–01   "Home—Family Life." Unknown date.

XX–02   "Young Man Who Desires to Be Obedient." Unknown date.

55–01   "Talk on Patriotism."

58–01   "Teachers, the Treasurers of Time." *Improvement Era* 61 (February 1958): 102–3, 108.

58–02   "Problems in Teaching the Moral Standard." Address to seminary and institute faculty at Brigham Young University, 15 July 1958.

59–01   "On Teaching the Moral Standard." *Improvement Era* 62 (January 1959): 24–25, 59–62.

59–02   "Seminaries." *Improvement Era* 62 (September 1959): 656–59, 692–93.

59–03   "Joseph Smith—Prophet Teacher." Address at Logan Institute, 6 December 1959; *Millennial Star,* January 1967; *TOS,* ch. 5, pp. 34–44.

61–01   "Remember the Sabbath Day." *The Instructor,* August 1961, pp. 268–70.

62–01   "Your Articles of Faith." Address to Brigham Young University student body, 21 March 1962; *HBT,* ch. 21, pp. 199–209.

62–02   Conference Report, 8 April 1962, pp. 118–20; "A Challenge to Youth." *Improvement Era* 65 (June 1962): 460–62.

62–03   Address at MIA Conference, 17 June 1962.

62–04   "The Ideal Teacher." Address to seminary and institute teachers, 28 June 1962; *ABE,* ch. 10, pp. 97–108.

62–05   Address at Brigham Young University freshmen orientation, Provo, Utah, 19 September 1962.

62–06   Conference Report, 6 October 1962, pp. 47–50; "The Errand of Youth." *Improvement Era* 65 (December 1962): 924–27.

62–07   Address at Air Force Academy, 24 November 1962.

62–08   "Keeping Christmas." *Brigham Young University Speeches of the Year,* Provo, Utah, 19 December 1962.

63–01   Conference Report, 7 April 1963, pp. 106–9; "Principle with a Promise." *Improvement Era* 66 (June 1963): 514–15.

63–02   Ricks College baccalaureate. Ricks College Speeches to Remember, Rexburg, Idaho, 28 May 1963.

63–03   "Prove Up to the Blessings." Address at Brigham Young University Education Week devotional, 13 June 1963; *ABE,* ch. 24, pp. 225–35.

63–04   Address at Alaska conference—Juneau, Alaska, 19 August 1963; excerpts printed in *Indian Liahona,* 1963–64 Winter Issue.

63–05   Conference Report, 5 October 1963, pp. 62–65; "Where Is Your Power?" *Improvement Era* 66 (December 1963): 1084–86, *SOF,* ch. 2, pp. 9–14.

63–06   "Eternal Love." Address to students at Brigham Young University, 3 November 1963; *Eternal Love* (Salt Lake City: Deseret Book, 1973): 1–22.

63–07   Address at Family Life Conference, 8 November 1963.

64–01   *The Very Key,* Church Educational System filmstrip, 1964.

64–02   Address at Farmers' Union meeting, 7 February 1964.

64–03   Address at Junior Sunday School departmental meeting, 5 April 1964.

64–04   "Teaching Is an Art." Excerpts from an address at Sunday School General Conference, April 1964.

64–05   Conference Report, 5 April 1964, pp. 84–86; "Suffer the Little Children." *Improvement Era* 67 (June 1964): 491–92.

64–06   Mission presidents' seminar, 22 June 1964.

64–07   Address to seminary and institute personnel at Brigham Young University, 1 July 1964.

64–08   Brigham Young University devotional address, 30 July 1964.

64–09   "For the Blessing of the Lamanites." *Relief Society Magazine,* August 1964, pp. 564–66.

64–10   Mexico stake conference address, 30 August 1964.

64–11   "Children Are an Heritage of the Lord." Address given over the Columbia Broadcasting System's "Church of the Air" program, 1964.

64–12   Conference Report, 4 October 1964, pp. 126–29; "Can I Really Know?" *Improvement Era* 67 (December 1964): 1096–97; *HBT,* ch. 23, pp. 217–21.

64–13   Address at Rodo, Uruguay, 6 November 1964.

65–01   "Follow the Brethren." Address at Brigham Young University, 23 March 1965; *ABE,* ch. 25, pp. 236–45.

65–02   Seventy's Conference address, 3 April 1965.

65–03   Conference Report, 5 April 1965, pp. 69–71; "Youth's Obligation to Parents." *Improvement Era* 68 (June 1965): 517–18; *HBT,* ch. 15, pp. 137–42; *New Era,* June 2004, pp. 4–9.

65–04   Address at Weber College to Ogden Institute, 2 May 1965.

65–05   El Camino College baccalaureate, 13 June 1965.

66–01   Conference Report, 10 April 1966, pp. 145–48; "The Secret of Service." *Improvement Era* 69 (June 1966): 550–52.

66–02   "Shall the Youth of Zion Falter?" *Brigham Young University Speeches of the Year,* Provo, Utah, 12 April 1966; *TOS,* ch. 11, pp. 96–104; see also "The Spirit Speaks Eloquently." *The Instructor,* June 1970, pp. 210–12.

66–03   Address at Sunday School Convention, 30 September 1966.

66–04   Conference Report, 2 October 1966, pp. 131–33; "Children Are an Heritage of the Lord." *Improvement Era* 69 (December 1966): 1149–50.

66–05   "Let Not Your Heart Be Troubled." Address to Brigham Young University student body, 4 October 1966; *HBT,* ch. 26, pp. 243–53.

67–01   Excerpts from an address at Sunday School General Conference, 3 April 1967.

67–02   Address to Rotary Club of Boston, 15 March 1967.

67–03   "The Gospel and the College Student." Address at Utah State University as part of the "Religion in Life" Series, 7 April 1967.

67–04   Conference Report, 9 April 1967, pp. 129–33; "A Call to the Christian Clergy." *Improvement Era* 70 (June 1967): 107–9.

67–05   "Let Virtue Garnish Thy Thoughts." Address at Brigham Young University, 26 September 1967; *ABE,* ch. 4, pp. 31–40.

67–06   Conference Report, 1 October 1967, pp. 126–29; "The Disease of Profanity." *Improvement Era* 70 (December 1967): 96–97; reprinted as "The Clean Voice of Youth." *New Era,* January 1976, pp. 4–6.

67–07   Fireside address, 29 October 1967. Location of delivery unknown.

67–08   Address to combined wards in Boston Stake, Weston Ward, 24 December 1967.

68–01   "Testimony." Letter to missionaries in the New England Mission following zone conference, 1968.

68–02   "Teaching the Word of Wisdom." Letter to missionaries in the New England Mission, 1968.

68–03   Conference Report, 5 April 1968, pp. 33–36; "The Member and the Military." *Improvement Era* 71 (June 1968): 58–61.

68–04   "The Disease of Impenitence." Address at Boston Stake fireside, 5 May 1968; *TOS,* ch. 8, pp. 71–80.

68–05   "Keeper of the Faith." Address to Department of Seminaries and Institutes of Religion at Brigham Young University, 17 July 1968; *HBT,* ch. 16, pp. 145–57.

68–06   "Going 'Somewhere.'" Brigham Young University commencement, 23 August 1968.

68–07   Conference Report, 5 October 1968, pp. 73–76; "The Great Witness from These Conferences." *Improvement Era* 71 (December 1968): 79–80; *SOF,* ch. 6, pp. 39–44.

68–08   "Faith." *Improvement Era* 71 (November 1968): 60–63; see also "What Is Faith?" *Faith* (Salt Lake City: Deseret Book, 1983): 40–44.

68–09   Address at servicemen's seminar, Oakland, California, 6 December 1968.

68–10   Address at servicemen's seminar, Oakland, California, 7 December 1968.

68–11   Address at servicemen's seminar concluding testimony meeting, Oakland, California, 7 December 1968.

69–01   "Living Gospel Standards in Military Service." 1969. Published in pamphlet form, April 1970, pp. 1–11.

69–02   "Steady As She Goes." Address to Brigham Young University student body, 7 January 1969; *HBT,* ch. 11, pp. 93–100.

69–03   "In the Spirit of Testimony." Given at a priesthood board meeting, 19 February 1969; *HBT,* ch. 2, pp. 12–21.

69–04   Conference Report, 5 April 1969, pp. 104–7; "The Armor of God." *Improvement Era* 72 (June 1969): 93–95.

69–05   "A Dedication—to Faith." Address to Brigham Young University student body at dedication of Daniel H. Wells ROTC Building, 29 April 1969.

69–06   "The Pattern of Our Parentage." MIA Conference Sunday session, 29 June 1969.

69–07   Conference Report, 3 October 1969, pp. 36–38; "The Other Side of the Ship." *Improvement Era* 72 (December 1969): 57–59.

69–08   Address at Utah Farm Bureau convention, 21 November 1969.

69–09   Presentation at Murdock Travel Christmas party held at Lion House, 16 December 1969.

70–01   Address at Brighton High seminary dedication, 1970.

70–02   Opening remarks at Annual Meeting of Commanders of Military Bases in Utah and Representatives of Chambers of Commerce at Dugway Proving Grounds, 29 January 1970.

70–03 Address at Church College of Hawaii, 16 February 1970.

70–04 Address at University of Utah Latter-day Saints Student Association women's meeting in the Salt Lake Tabernacle, 4 March 1970.

70–05 "Children—Our Primary Responsibility." General session of Primary Conference, 2 April 1970.

70–06 Conference Report, 4 April 1970, pp. 40–43; "The Path to Manhood." *Improvement Era* 73 (June 1970): 51–54.

70–07 "Eternal Marriage." Address to Brigham Young University student body, 14 April 1970; *TOS*, ch. 23, pp. 219–28.

70–08 Address at Lamanite Youth Conference held at Brigham Young University, 8 May 1970.

70–09 "To Those Who Teach in Troubled Times." Address at Brigham Young University to seminary and institute personnel, June 1970; titled "Stand Steady" in *ABE*, ch. 27, pp. 262–73.

70–10 Address at Weber State College baccalaureate, 5 June 1970.

70–11 "The Family and Eternity." Address at a genealogical seminar, 6 August 1970; *Ensign,* February 1971, pp. 7–11; *ABE*, ch. 18, pp. 172–78.

70–12 "The Student Association." Address at convention of the Latter-day Saints Student Association, August 1970.

70–13 Address at Brigham Young University baccalaureate service, 20 August 1970.

70–14 Address at Laurelife Leadership Conference, 25 August 1970.

70–15 Address at Relief Society Conference, 1 October 1970.

70–16 Conference Report, 4 October 1970, pp. 118–22; "Families and Fences." *Improvement Era* 73 (December 1970): 106–9; *ABE*, ch. 14, pp. 137–43.

71–01 "Lectures in Theology: 'Last Message Series.'" Address at Salt Lake Institute of Religion, 12 February 1971.

71–02 "Cerritos Institute of Religion Dedicatory Address." Given at Cerritos Institute of Religion, Cerritos, California, 28 February 1971.

71–03 "Bulwark Against Evil (Family Home Evening.)" Article written for *Church News,* 6 March 1971.

71–04 Conference Report, 6 April 1971, pp. 122–25; "The Spirit Beareth Record." *Ensign,* June 1971, pp. 87–88; *ABE*, ch. 31, pp. 311–16.

71–05 Address at funeral of Gary Willis, 4 June 1971.

71–06 Address at morning session of the MIA Conference, 25 June 1971.

71–07 "God's Sacred Word among Us." Address at British Area Conference, 28 August 1971, pp. 55–59; *ABE*, ch. 22, pp. 213–18.

71–08 Address at British Area Conference, 28 August 1971, pp. 126–29.

71–09 "Begin Where You Are—At Home." Address at Relief Society Conference, 30 September 1971; *Ensign,* February 1972, pp. 69–74; "To Help a Miracle." *ABE*, ch. 7, pp. 70–78.

71–10 Conference Report, 1 October 1971, pp. 7–11; "The Only True and Living Church." *Ensign,* December 1971, pp. 40–42; *TOS*, ch. 13, pp. 121–26.

71–11 "Obedience." Address at Brigham Young University, 7 December 1971; *ABE*, ch. 26, pp. 253–61.

72–01 Conference Report, 9 April 1972, pp. 136–40; "Why Stay Morally Clean."

> *Ensign,* July 1972, pp. 111–13; *ABE,* ch. 19, pp. 179–86; address at Scandinavian Area Conference, 17 August 1974, pp. 81–85.

72–02   Address to Japan Central Mission, 18 April 1972.

72–03   Address to Ricks College faculty, 22 August 1972.

72–04   "A New Dimension to the Sunday School." Address at Sunday School Administrator's Breakfast, 7 October 1972.

72–05   Conference Report, 7 October 1972, pp. 100–104; "The Saints Securely Dwell." *Ensign,* January 1973, pp. 88–90; *HBT,* ch. 19, pp. 182–90.

72–06   Address at a meeting of military chaplains, 9 October 1972.

73–01   Address at Logan Institute of Religion, 23 January 1973.

73–02   Address at Young Adult Women's Fireside, 28 February 1973.

73–03   "Called of God by Prophecy." Address at Brigham Young University devotional, 27 March 1973; *Speeches of the Year 1972–1973,* pp. 119–30; *New Era,* September 1978, pp. 33–37; *TOS,* ch. 3, pp. 17–26.

73–04   Conference Report, 7 April 1973, pp. 78–82; "Behold Your Little Ones." *Ensign,* July 1973, pp. 51–54; *ABE,* ch. 2, pp. 16–22; reprinted in abbreviated form as "An Apostle Speaks to Children." *Friend,* July 1973, p. 32.

73–05   "What Every Freshman Should Know." Address at Utah State University baccalaureate service, 8 June 1973; *ABE,* ch. 17, pp. 162–71.

73–06   Address at Melchizedek Priesthood MIA Conference, 22 June 1973.

73–07   Address at Brigham Young University Faculty and Staff Pre-School Conference Dinner, 28 August 1973.

73–08   Address at Relief Society Conference, 3 October 1973.

73–09   Conference Report, 5 October 1973, pp. 21–25; "Inspiring Music—Worthy Thoughts." *Ensign,* January 1974, pp. 25–28.

74–01   "A Change in Command." *ABE,* ch. 12, pp. 121–33.

74–02   "President Spencer W. Kimball: No Ordinary Man." *Ensign,* March 1974, pp. 2–13.

74–03   Conference Report, 7 April 1974, pp. 135–39; "We Believe All That God Has Revealed." *Ensign,* May 1974, pp. 93–95; *TOS,* ch. 2, pp. 10–16.

74–04   "Seek Learning Even by Study and Also by Faith." Brigham Young University Religious Instruction, 10 April 1974; *ABE,* ch. 5, pp. 41–55.

74–05   Address at Box Elder High School graduation, 23 May 1974.

74–06   "Live by the Spirit." Address at Scandinavian Area Conference, 17 August 1974; *HBT,* ch. 25, pp. 229–39.

74–07   Address at open house of the Washington D.C. Temple, 11 September 1974.

74–08   Conference Report, 6 October 1974, pp. 125–29; "Where Much Is Given, Much Is Required." *Ensign,* November 1974, pp. 87–90; *HBT,* ch. 18, pp. 175–81; *Friend,* July 1987, inside front cover.

74–09   A tribute to Ronald Ira Packer, given in Brigham City, Utah, on 5 November 1974.

74–10   Address at a Veteran's Day concert, 13 November 1974.

75–01   "Self-Reliance." Fireside address at Brigham Young University, 2 March 1975; *Speeches of the Year 1975,* pp. 343–60; *Ensign,* August 1975, pp. 85–89.

75–02   "Equally Yoked Together." Address at Regional Representatives' Seminar, with stake presidents and Church Educational System personnel, 3 April 1975.

75–03   Conference Report, 6 April 1975, pp. 154–58; "An Appeal to Prospective Elders." *Ensign,* May 1975, pp. 104–6; *ABE,* ch. 8, pp. 79–87.

75–04   Address at Valleywide Young Adult Fireside, 13 April 1975.

75–05   Address at Brigham Young University graduation, 18 April 1975.

75–06   Conference Report, 5 October 1975, pp. 145–49; "The Redemption of the Dead." *Ensign,* November 1975, pp. 97–99; *ABE,* ch. 34, pp. 325–32; *HBT,* ch. 5, pp. 37–44.

75–07   Address at a meeting with Genealogical Department employees, 18 November 1975.

76–01   "The Arts and the Spirit of the Lord." Address at a Brigham Young University twelve-stake fireside, 1 February 1976; *Speeches of the Year 1976,* pp. 265–82; *ABE,* ch. 28, pp. 274–89.

76–02   Address at Ogden Division Mid-Year Convention, 6 February 1976.

76–03   Conference Report, 3 April 1976, pp. 44–48; "Spiritual Crocodiles." *Ensign,* May 1976, pp. 30–32; *New Era,* August 1976, pp. 4–7; *ABE,* ch. 21, pp. 207–12; *New Era,* October 2001, pp. 8–11.

76–04   Address at The Exchange Club of Salt Lake City, 5 May 1976.

76–05   "The Forces of Righteousness." Address at Scandinavian Area Conference (Copenhagen), 4 August 1976.

76–06   "A Voice of Warning." Address at Scandinavian Area Conference (Copenhagen), 4 August 1976; *ABE,* pp. 219–24.

76–07   "The Virtue of Hope." Address at mother-daughter session of the Dortmund Germany Area Conference, 7 August 1976.

76–08   "It Is the Position That Counts." Address at priesthood session of the Dortmund Germany Area Conference, 7 August 1976; *New Era,* June 1977, pp. 50–52.

76–09   "Language of the Spirit." Address at Dortmund Germany Area Conference, 7 August 1976; *New Era,* March 1977, pp. 4–7; *SOF,* ch. 11, pp. 79–83.

76–10   "Sustain Your Leaders." Address at Amsterdam Area Conference, 8 August 1976.

77–01   *Mothers,* booklet (Salt Lake City: Deseret Book, 1977, 1999.)

77–02   "Someone Up There Loves You." *Ensign,* January 1977, pp. 8–12; *ABE,* ch. 30, pp. 296–304; *THT,* pp. 230–38.

77–03   "The Equal Rights Amendment." Address at Pocatello public meeting, Pocatello, Idaho, 8 January 1977; *Ensign,* March 1977, pp. 6–9.

77–04   "Follow the Rule." Address at Brigham Young University–Hawaii devotional, 14 January 1977; *Speeches of the Year 1977,* pp. 17–24.

77–05   "That They May Be Redeemed." Address at Regional Representatives' Seminar, 1 April 1977.

77–06   Conference Report, 3 April 1977, pp. 77–81; "The Mediator." *Ensign,* May 1977, pp. 54–56; *The Mediator* (Salt Lake City: Deseret Book, 1978); *ABE,* ch. 32, pp. 316–22.

77–07   Address to experienced personnel of the Department of Seminaries and Institutes of Religion, 6 May 1977.

77–08   "Moral and Spiritual Values in Character Education." Address to Utah Association of Secondary School Principals, 14 June 1977; *HBT,* pp. 158–74.

77–09   Address at Brigham Young University graduation, 19 August 1977.

77–10   Conference Report, 2 October 1977, pp. 89–92; "The Balm of Gilead." *Ensign,* November 1977, pp. 59–61; *New Era,* August 1979, pp. 36–39; *ABE,* ch. 6, pp. 63–69.

77–11   "Teach the Scriptures." Address to Church Educational System full-time religious educators, 14 October 1977, pp. 1–9.

78–01   "To the One." Address at Brigham Young University fireside, 5 March 1978; *Speeches of the Year 1978,* pp. 33–40; *ABE,* ch. 20, pp. 186–99.

78–02   Conference Report, 2 April 1978, pp. 135–40; "Solving Emotional Problems in the Lord's Own Way." *Ensign,* May 1978, pp. 91–93; *ABE,* ch. 9, pp. 87–96.

78–03   Address at Dixie College commencement, 2 June 1978.

78–04   Notes of address for Brockbank funeral, 7 September 1978.

78–05   "To Help a Miracle." Address at Relief Society Conference, October 1978; *ABE,* ch. 7, pp. 70–78.

78–06   Conference Report, 30 September 1978, pp. 8–11; "The Relief Society." *Ensign,* November 1978, pp. 7–9; *HBT,* ch. 20, pp. 190–95.

78–07   Address at priesthood session of the South America Area Conference, October 1978.

78–08   Address at general session of the South America Area Conference, October 1978.

78–09   "We Are Going to Find Him." Address at dedication of the São Paulo Brazil Temple, 2 November 1978; *ABE,* ch. 13, pp. 134–36.

78–10   "A Voice We Feel." Address at Brazil Area Conference, 4 November 1978.

78–11   "A Priesthood of Preparation." Address at priesthood session of the Brazil Area Conference, 4 November 1978; *New Era,* May 1979, pp. 42–44.

79–01   Address at Brigham Young University Indian Week banquet, 15 February 1979.

79–02   Address at Ricks College fireside, 25 February 1979.

79–03   Conference Report, 1 April 1979, pp. 109–13; "Judge Not According to the Appearance." *Ensign,* May 1979, pp. 79–81; *ABE,* ch. 16, pp. 155–61.

79–04   Address at Mission Presidents' Seminar, 20 June 1979.

79–05   Pioneer Day address at Ogden, Utah, 22 July 1979.

79–06   Address at women's session of the Madison Wisconsin Area Conference, 4 August 1979.

79–07   Address at Sunday session of the Madison Wisconsin Area Conference, 5 August 1979.

79–08   "What Think Ye of Christ?" Address to Presbyterian Ministry at Westminster College, 21 August 1979.

79–09   "Which Way Do You Face?" Unpublished address, 3 October 1979.

79–10   Conference Report, 6 October 1979, pp. 27–31; "Prayers and Answers." *Ensign,* November 1979, pp. 19–21; *ABE,* ch. 1, pp. 9–15.

79–11   Address at Mexico City Mexico Temple groundbreaking, 30 October 1979.

79–12   Address at Mexico City Mission Presidents' Seminar, 30 October 1979.

79–13   "The Most Sacred Work." November 1979; *TOS,* ch. 22, pp. 204–18.

79–14	Address to Temple Square Mission, 5 December 1979; published in the booklet *The Light of Thy Childhood Again* (Salt Lake City: Deseret Book, 1997).
79–15	Address to Salt Lake Association of Insurance Underwriters, 7 December 1979.
80–01	Address to University of Utah Institute of Religion, 6 January 1980.
80–02	"Keeping Confidences." Address at Church Employees Lecture Series, 18 January 1980.
80–03	"Ordinances." Address at Brigham Young University fourteen-stake fireside, 3 February 1980; *Speeches of the Year 1980,* pp. 12–18; *TOS,* ch. 20, pp. 185–95.
80–04	Conference Report, 6 April 1980, pp. 82–86; "A Tribute to the Rank and File of the Church." *Ensign,* May 1980, pp. 62–65; *ABE,* ch. 15, pp. 144–50.
80–05	Address at priesthood session of Pago Pago Samoa Stake conference, 13 April 1980.
80–06	Address at general session of Pago Pago Samoa Stake conference, 13 April 1980.
80–07	Devotional address at Missionary Training Center, Provo, Utah, 22 April 1980.
80–08	"The Decision of Life." Address to Brigham Young University faculty and staff, 27 August 1980; *New Era,* August 1989, pp. 4–6.
80–09	"The Circle of Sisters." Address at general Relief Society meeting, 27 September 1980; *Ensign,* November 1980, pp. 109–11; *TOS,* ch. 15, pp. 140–46.
80–10	Conference Report, 4 October 1980, pp. 26–30; "The Choice." *Ensign,* November 1980, pp. 20–22; *SOF,* ch. 14, pp. 113–19.
80–11	Address at funeral service of Tom Clark, 5 November 1980.
81–01	Devotional address at Missionary Training Center, Provo, Utah, 27 January 1981.
81–02	"A Worm for a Wing Feather." Address to Brigham Young University–Hawaii student body, 20 February 1981.
81–03	"Member Activation." Unpublished address, 3 April 1981.
81–04	Conference Report, 4 April 1981, pp. 14–17; "Marriage." *Ensign,* May 1981, pp. 13–15; *ABE,* ch. 29, pp. 290–95.
81–05	Address at Ricks College baccalaureate, 23 April 1981.
81–06	"An Obligation and a Blessing." Address at Brigham Young University summer commencement, 21 August 1981.
81–07	"The Mantle Is Far, Far Greater Than the Intellect." Address at Fifth Annual Church Educational System Religious Educators' Symposium at Brigham Young University, 22 August 1981; *HBT,* ch. 12, pp. 101–22.
81–08	Conference Report, 3 October 1981, pp. 43–48; "The Aaronic Priesthood." *Ensign,* November 1981, pp. 30–33; *New Era,* May 1985, pp. 4–7; *ABE,* ch. 3, pp. 23–30.
81–09	"We Can Point to the Temples." Address at Jordan River Utah Temple dedication, 17 November 1981; *TOS,* ch. 19, pp. 179–84.
82–01	"A Worthy, Faithful Handmaiden of the Lord." Address at funeral service of Belle S. Spafford, 5 February 1982; *ABE,* ch. 11, pp. 115–20.
82–02	"Shepherds of the Flock." Unpublished address, 2 April 1982.
82–03	Conference Report, 3 April 1982, pp. 121–25; "The Gospel—The Foundation for Our Career." *Ensign,* May 1982, pp. 84–87; *SOF,* ch. 9, pp. 63–70.

82–04   "The Candle of the Lord." Address at seminar for new mission presidents, 25 June 1982; *Ensign,* January 1983, pp. 51–56; *ABE,* ch. 35, pp. 333–43; see "The Quest for Spiritual Knowledge." *New Era,* January 2007, pp. 2–7.

82–05   Addresses at mission presidents' seminars in Argentina, Chile, Peru, and Bolivia, 4–9 September 1982.

82–06   Conference Report, 3 October 1982, pp. 73–77; "Scriptures." *Ensign,* November 1982, pp. 51–53; *HBT,* ch. 1, pp. 5–11.

82–07   Address at Founder's Day devotional at Brigham Young University, 12 October 1982.

82–08   Address at funeral service of Monte L. Bean, 20 October 1982.

83–01   Conference Report, 3 April 1983, pp. 89–92; "Agency and Control." *Ensign,* May 1983, pp. 66–68; *SOF,* ch. 16, pp. 128–33.

83–02   "Come, All Ye Sons of God." Address at Churchwide fireside commemorating the restoration of the priesthood, 15 May 1983; *Ensign,* August 1983, pp. 68–71; *SOF,* ch. 8, pp. 53–60.

83–03   "The Essence of Education." Address at Weber College graduation, 10 June 1983; *HBT,* ch. 3, pp. 22–30.

83–04   Address at mission presidents' seminar, 23 June 1983.

83–05   Conference Report, 1 October 1983, pp. 19–23; "The Mystery of Life." *Ensign,* November 1983, pp. 16–18; *HBT,* ch. 24, pp. 222–28.

84–01   Address at funeral service of Elder Mark E. Petersen, 16 January 1984.

84–02   Address at dedication of the Museum of Church History and Art, 4 April 1984.

84–03   "Principles." *Ensign,* March 1985, pp. 6–10; *TOS,* ch. 7, pp. 63–70.

84–04   Conference Report, 7 April 1984, pp. 59–62; "Feed My Sheep." *Ensign,* May 1984, pp. 41–43; *New Era,* October 1987, pp. 4–7; *HBT,* ch. 4, pp. 31–36; *New Era,* January 2003, pp. 4–9.

84–05   "The Plan." Address at new mission presidents' seminar, 20 June 1984.

84–06   Address at Buenos Aires member meeting, 12 August 1984.

84–07   Conference Report, 7 October 1984, pp. 81–85; "The Pattern of Our Parentage." *Ensign,* November 1984, pp. 66–69; *HBT,* ch. 30, pp. 286–93.

84–08   Address to Brigham Young University administration, 18 October 1984.

85–01   "A Parable." 1985. Exact date and location of delivery unknown.

85–02   "The Plan of Salvation." 1985. Exact date and location of delivery unknown.

85–03   Address at funeral service of Elder G. Homer Durham, 14 January 1985.

85–04   Address at LDS Business College devotional, 27 February 1985.

85–05   "Using the New Scriptures." Address given in Churchwide satellite fireside, 10 March 1985; *Ensign,* December 1985, pp. 49–53.

85–06   "By the Spirit of Truth." Address at mission presidents' seminar, 3 April 1985.

85–07   "Called to Serve." Address at Regional Representatives' Seminar, April 1985; *TOS,* ch. 14, pp. 127–39.

85–08   Conference Report, 6 April 1985, pp. 41–45; "From Such Turn Away." *Ensign,* May 1985, pp. 33–35; *HBT,* ch. 14, pp. 129–36.

85–09   "Sentiment and Sober Thinking." Address at Brigham Young University graduation, 19 April 1985.

85–10   "Bruce R. McConkie, Apostle." Address at funeral service of Elder Bruce R. McConkie, 23 April 1985; *HBT,* ch. 28, pp. 259–67.

85–11   Address at funeral service of Vivian McConkie, 14 May 1985.

85–12   Address at funeral service of J. Willard Marriott, 17 August 1985.

85–13   Conference Report, 6 October 1985, pp. 103–7; "The Only True Church." *Ensign,* November 1985, pp. 80–83; *HBT,* ch. 10, pp. 82–89.

85–14   "Roland and Dora Mae." An address at dedication of the Crabtree Technology Building at Brigham Young University, 29 October 1985; *Brigham Young University Speeches 1985–86,* pp. 38–41.

85–15   Address at inauguration of Joe J. Christensen as president of Ricks College, 8 November 1985.

85–16   Address at funeral service of Leon Claron Packer, 29 November 1985.

86–01   "Keeping Covenants." Address at Buenos Aires Argentina Temple dedication, 19 January 1986; *HBT,* ch. 27, pp. 254–58.

86–02   Conference Report, 6 April 1986, pp. 73–77. "The Things of My Soul." *Ensign,* May 1986, pp. 59–61; *TOS,* ch. 1, pp. 3–9.

86–03   Address at Beneficial Life Insurance meeting in California, July 1986.

86–04   "The Book of Mormon." 11 September 1986, transcript for 1987 video presentation titled "The Things of My Soul"; *HBT,* ch. 29, pp. 268–85.

86–05   Conference Report, 4 October 1986, pp. 18–22; "Little Children." *Ensign,* November 1986, pp. 16–18; *SOF,* ch. 4. pp. 22–29.

86–06   "A Christmas Parable." Booklet (Salt Lake City: Bookcraft, 1986).

86–07   Address at funeral service of A. Theodore Tuttle, 2 December 1986.

87–01   "Gifts of the Spirit." Address at Brigham Young University sixteen-stake fireside, 4 January 1987; *SOF,* ch. 13, pp. 92–110.

87–02   "Covenants." Unpublished address, 3 April 1987.

87–03   Conference Report, 4 April 1987, pp. 24–28; "Covenants." *Ensign,* May 1987, pp. 22–25.

87–04   Address given in the video conference "Accomplishing the Mission of the Church." Broadcast 28 June 1987.

87–05   Address at Brigham Young University graduation, 14 August 1987.

87–06   Unpublished address, 8 September 1987.

87–07   Conference Report, 3 October 1987, pp. 17–21; "The Balm of Gilead." *Ensign,* November 1987, pp. 16–18; titled "Peace in Forgiving." *The Friend,* September 1994, inside front cover.

88–01   "There Is Cause to Rejoice!" Address to an unknown audience, 7 January 1988.

88–02   Unpublished address, 1 April 1988.

88–03   Conference Report, 3 April 1988, pp. 80–84; "Atonement, Agency, Accountability." *Ensign,* May 1988, pp. 69–72; *Ensign,* March 2008, pp. 13–19.

88–04   Address at Beneficial Life Insurance convention in California, 11 July 1988.

88–05   Address at Ricks College Faculty and Staff Dinner, 24 August 1988.

88–06   Address given to LDS booksellers (a review of Sister Donna Packer's book, *On Footings from the Past*), 26 August 1988.

88–07   Conference Report, 1 October 1988, pp. 22–26; "Funerals—A Time for Reverence." *Ensign,* November 1988, pp. 18–21.

88–08   "The Law and the Light." Address at Book of Mormon Symposium at Brigham Young University, 30 October 1988; *The Book of Mormon: Jacob Through Words of Mormon, To Learn with Joy* (Salt Lake City: Bookcraft, 1990), pp. 1–27.

88–09   Address at Missionary Training Center staff devotional, Provo, Utah, 9 November 1988.

88–10   Address at Employee Meeting to Commemorate the Fiftieth Anniversary of Microfilming, 16 November 1988.

89–01   Conference Report, 2 April 1989, pp. 70–73; "To Young Women and Men." *Ensign,* May 1989, pp. 53–59; titled "Your Test of Courage," *New Era,* March 1990, pp. 4–8; *HBT,* ch. 6, pp. 47–53; titled "A Few Simple Lessons," *New Era,* August 2002, pp. 4–9.

89–02   "A Tribute to Women." Address at Priesthood Commemoration Fireside, 7 May 1989; *TOS,* ch. 18, pp. 168–75.

89–03   "The Country with a Conscience." Address at American Freedom Festival, Provo, Utah, 25 June 1989; *HBT,* ch. 7, pp. 54–68.

89–04   Conference Report, 30 September 1989, pp. 16–19; "Revelation in a Changing World." *Ensign,* November 1989, pp. 14–16; *HBT,* ch. 22, pp. 210–16.

90–01   Address at dedication of Beehive Clothing Mills new facility, 26 January 1990.

90–02   "Father Ordaining Son." A letter written to Elder George I. Cannon, 7 February 1990.

90–03   "Teach Them Correct Principles." Address at Member Finances Fireside broadcast, 18 February 1990; *Ensign,* May 1990, pp. 89–91; *TOS,* ch. 17, pp. 161–67.

90–04   "The Edge of the Light." Address at Brigham Young University eighteen-stake fireside, 4 March 1990; *Brigham Young University Today,* March 1991, pp. 22–24, 38–43.

90–05   Unpublished address, 30 March 1990.

90–06   Conference Report, 31 March 1990, pp. 47–51; "The Library of the Lord." *Ensign,* May 1990, pp. 36–38; *TOS,* ch. 4, pp. 27–33.

90–07   Address at meetings of Beneficial Life Insurance Company, Vail, Colorado, 11 July 1990.

90–08   Devotional address at Missionary Training Center, Provo, Utah, 21 August 1990.

90–09   Conference Report, 7 October 1990, pp. 107–10; "Covenants." *Ensign,* November 1990, pp. 84–86; *TOS,* ch. 9, pp. 81–88.

91–01   "I Say Unto You, Be One." Brigham Young University devotional address, 12 February 1991; *Brigham Young University Speeches, 1990–91,* pp. 81–91.

91–02   Conference Report, 6 April 1991, pp. 6–9; "The Moving of the Water." *Ensign,* May 1991, pp. 7–9; *SOF,* ch. 5, pp. 30–36.

91–03   Address at University of Utah Institute fireside, 19 May 1991.

91–04   "The Language of the Spirit." Address at new mission presidents' seminar, 19 June 1991.

91–05   "Spirit Directed." Address at Seminary and Church Educational System broadcast, 22 June 1991.

91–06   Conference Report, 5 October 1991, pp. 26–30; "Reverence Invites Revelation." *Ensign,* November 1991, pp. 21–23; *TOS,* ch. 10, pp. 89–95.

91–07   Address at Ricks College four-stake fireside, 13 October 1991.

91–08   Address at Tuesday Night Missionary Training Center Devotional, 12 November 1991.

92–01   Address at funeral of Joseph Anderson, 17 March 1992.

92–02   "The Fountain of Life." Address at Brigham Young University eighteen-stake fireside, 29 March 1992; *TOS*, pp. 105–17.

92–03   Conference Report, 5 April 1992, pp. 91–95; "Our Moral Environment." *Ensign*, May 1992, pp. 66–68; *SOF*, ch. 15, pp. 120–27.

92–04   "What Every Elder Should Know—and Every Sister As Well: A Primer on Principles of Priesthood Government." 8 April 1992; *Ensign*, February 1993, pp. 6–13; *TOS*, ch. 16, pp. 147–60.

92–05   Conference Report, 4 October 1992, pp. 98–102; "To Be Learned Is Good If . . ." *Ensign*, November 1992, pp. 71–73; *SOF*, ch. 10, pp. 71–78.

93–01   Conference Report, 3 April 1993, pp. 21–25; "The Temple, the Priesthood." *Ensign*, May 1993, pp. 18–21; *TOS*, ch. 21, pp. 196–203.

93–02   Unpublished address, 18 May 1993.

93–03   Address at mission presidents' seminar, 23 June 1993.

93–04   "A Temple to Exalt." *Ensign*, August 1993, pp. 6–15; *SOF*, ch. 21, pp. 168–85.

93–05   "The Great Plan of Happiness." Address at 17th Annual Church Educational System Religious Educators Symposium, 10 August 1993.

93–06   Conference Report, 2 October 1993, pp. 27–32; "For Time and All Eternity." *Ensign*, November 1993, pp. 21–24; *TOS*, ch. 24, pp. 229–37; also published as a booklet (Salt Lake City: Deseret Book, 1994).

93–07   "The Great Plan of Happiness and Personal Revelation." Address at Young Adults Church Educational System broadcast, 7 November 1993; *TOS*, pp. 45–60.

94–01   Conference Report, 2 April 1994, pp. 23–27; "The Father and the Family." *Ensign*, May 1994, pp. 19–21; *SOF*, ch. 1, pp. 3–8.

94–02   Closing remarks at Brigham Young University commencement, 21 April 1994.

94–03   Address at funeral of President Ezra Taft Benson, 4 June 1994; "We Honor Now His Journey." *Ensign*, July 1994, pp. 32–34.

94–04   Address at new mission presidents' seminar, 24 June 1994.

94–05   Conference Report, 2 October 1994, pp. 76–80; "Personal Revelation: The Gift, the Test, and the Promise." *Ensign*, November 1994, pp. 59–62; *SOF*, ch. 12, pp. 84–91.

95–01   Address at Salt Lake Cottonwood Creek Stake women's conference, 28 January 1995.

95–02   "The Holy Temple." *Ensign*, February 1995, pp. 32–37; *SOF*, ch. 18, pp. 143–51.

95–03   "President Howard W. Hunter—He Endured to the End." Address at funeral of President Howard W. Hunter, 8 March 1995.

95–04   "The Shield of Faith." Address at BYU Management Society dinner, Washington, D.C., 18 March 1995.

95–05   Conference Report, 1 April 1995, pp. 5–9; "The Shield of Faith." *Ensign*, May 1995, pp. 7–9; *SOF*, ch. 3, pp. 15–21; adaptation in *Friend*, July 2003, p. 39.

95–06   "The Play and the Plan." Address at Church Educational System fireside, Kirkland Washington Stake center, 7 May 1995, pp. 1–9.

95–07   Address at LDS Business College graduation, 8 June 1995.

95–08   Address at new mission presidents' seminar, 21 June 1995.

95–09   Address at 90th anniversary of Beneficial Life Insurance Company, 11 July 1995.

95–10   "The Snow-White Birds." Address at 1995 annual Brigham Young University Conference, 29 August 1995; published in *Brigham Young Magazine,* November 1995, pp. 47–52.

95–11   Ricks College devotional address, 19 September 1995.

95–12   Conference Report, 30 September 1995, pp. 21–25; "The Brilliant Morning of Forgiveness." *Ensign,* October 1995, pp. 18–21; *SOF,* ch. 20, pp. 160–67; edited version printed in *New Era,* April 2005, pp. 4–8.

95–13   Address at Jordan River temple workers fireside, 26 November 1995.

96–01   Conference Report, 6 April 1996, pp. 21–25; "The Word of Wisdom: The Principle and the Promises." *Ensign,* May 1996, pp. 17–19; *SOF,* ch. 17, pp. 134–40.

96–02   "Onward, Ever Onward." Address at new mission presidents' seminar, 19 June 1996.

96–03   "Even As I Am." Transcript of video clip used for Church Educational System Symposium, August 1996.

96–04   "Jesus, the Master Teacher." Transcript of video clip used for Church Educational System Symposium, August 1996.

96–05   Conference Report, 5 October 1996, pp. 4–9; "The Twelve Apostles." *Ensign,* November 1996, pp. 6–8; *SOF,* ch. 7, pp. 45–52; reprinted in *Ensign,* September 2005, pp. 16–20.

96–06   Address at Brigham Young University David O. McKay Symposium, 9 October 1996.

96–07   Unpublished address, October 1996.

97–01   Prospective Missionary Fireside address, 26 February 1997.

97–02   Conference Report, 5 April 1997, pp. 8–11; "Washed Clean." *Ensign,* May 1997, pp. 9–11; *New Era,* April 1998, pp. 4–9; *SOF,* ch. 19, pp. 152–59; adapted version in *Friend,* April 1999, inside front cover.

97–03   Address at new mission presidents' seminar, 24 June 1997.

97–04   Conference Report, 4 October 1997, pp. 4–8; "Called to Serve." *Ensign,* November 1997, 6–8.

97–05   "The Light of Thy Childhood Again." Booklet (Salt Lake City: Deseret Book, 1997), October 1997.

98–01   "The Peaceable Followers of Christ." Address at eighteen-stake Church Educational System fireside satellite broadcast at Brigham Young University, 1 February 1998; *Ensign,* April 1998, pp. 62–67.

98–02   "The Artist and the Spirit." An Interview with President Boyd K. Packer and James C. Christensen for the Mormon Festival of the Arts, St. George, Utah, 2 March 1998.

98–03   Conference Report, 5 April 1998, pp. 94–98; "The Relief Society." *Ensign,* May 1998, pp. 72–74.

98–04   "Convert Retention." Address at new mission presidents' seminar, 23 June 1998.

98–05   Address at funeral of Sister June Oaks, 25 July 1998.

98–06   Address at announcement of the Brigham Young University School of Family Life, 10 September 1998.

98–07   Conference Report, 3 October 1998, pp. 27–30; "Parents in Zion." *Ensign,* November 1998, pp. 22–24.

98–08   Family History satellite broadcast, 8 November 1998.

99–01   Conference Report, 4 April 1999, pp. 77–80; "The Bishop and His Counselors." *Ensign,* May 1999, pp. 57–63.

99–02   Address at funeral service of Elder Carlos E. Asay, 13 April 1999.

99–03   "Somewhere." Address at Brigham Young University commencement exercises, 22 April 1999.

99–04   "Teaching the Gospel Video Presentations—Equally Yoked Together." Script used in a Church Educational System teacher training video segment, June 1999.

99–05   "Missionaries and Doctrine." Address at new mission presidents' seminar, 22 June 1999.

99–06   "Teach the Children." Brigham Young University Education Week devotional address, 17 August 1999; *Ensign,* February 2000, pp. 10–17.

99–07   Conference Report, 2 October 1999, pp. 27–30; "The Spirit of Revelation." *Ensign,* November 1999, pp. 23–25.

99–08   Address given for Family History broadcast, 18 November 1999.

99–09   Missionary Training Center Christmas Devotional address, Provo, Utah, 25 December 1999.

00–01   "And They Knew It Not." Church Educational System Fireside for Young Adults at Utah Valley State College, 5 March 2000.

00–02   Conference Report, 1 April 2000, pp. 6–9; "The Cloven Tongues of Fire." *Ensign,* May 2000, pp. 7–9.

00–03   *Special Witnesses of Christ.* Video transcript of video presentation of the testimonies of the First Presidency and Quorum of the Twelve, April 2000.

00–04   "Discipline—Principles to Consider." Address at Provo Missionary Training Center for the new mission presidents' seminar, 20 June 2000.

00–05   Provo Missionary Training Center devotional address, 22 August 2000.

00–06   Conference Report, 8 October 2000, pp. 93–96; "Ye Are the Temple of God." *Ensign,* May 2000, pp. 72–74.

00–07   Forest Bend Ward Christmas message, 24 December 2000.

01–01   University of Utah six-stake fireside address, 21 January 2001.

01–02   "The Parable of the Family." Unpublished address, 29 March 2001.

01–03   Conference Report, 31 March 2001, pp. 27–30; "The Touch of the Master's Hand." *Ensign,* May 2001, pp. 22–24.

01–04   Address at new mission presidents' seminar, 26 June 2001.

01–05   Conference Report, 7 October 2001, pp. 74–78; "The Book of Mormon: Another Testament of Jesus Christ." *Ensign,* November 2001, pp. 62–64.

01–06   Forest Bend Ward Christmas message, 23 December 2001.

02–01   "Special Witness: We Have a Savior." *Friend,* March 2002, p. 7; adapted from "An Apostle Speaks to the Children," *Friend,* July 1973, p. 32.

02–02   "The Twenty-Mark Note." Address at Brigham Young University–Idaho devotional, 12 March 2002.

02–03   Conference Report, 6 April 2002, pp. 6–9; "Children." *Ensign,* May 2002, pp. 7–10.

02–04   Devotional address at Missionary Training Center, Provo, Utah, 30 April 2002.

02–05   Address at South Jordan Utah Veterans' Memorial dedication, 4 May 2002.

02–06   "By the Power of the Spirit: In the Lord's Way." *New Era,* June 2002, p. 36.

02–07   "Some Things Every Missionary Should Know." Address at new mission presidents' seminar, 26 June 2002.

02–08   Address at a Family and Church History Department fireside, 13 September 2002.

02–09   Conference Report, 5 October 2002, pp. 45–49; "The Stake Patriarch." *Ensign,* November 2002, pp. 42–45.

03–01   "Restoration." Address at First Worldwide Leadership Training Meeting, 11 January 2003.

03–02   Address at an all-employee meeting at Missionary Training Center, Provo, Utah, 12 January 2003.

03–03   Devotional address at Missionary Training Center, Provo, Utah, 12 January 2003.

03–04   "The Instrument of Your Mind and the Foundation of Your Character." Fireside address at Brigham Young University, 2 February 2003; *Brigham Young University 2002–2003 Speeches,* pp. 167–75.

03–05   Conference Report, 6 April 2003, pp. 86–89; "The Golden Years." *Ensign,* May 2003, pp. 82–84.

03–06   Missionary training satellite broadcast, 25 April 2003.

03–07   "How to Confer the Priesthood: The Doctrine, the Principle, and the Practice." Address at Worldwide Leadership Training Broadcast, 21 June 2003, pp. 1–4.

03–08   "The Gift of the Holy Ghost: What Every Missionary Should Know—And Every Member As Well." Address at new mission presidents' seminar, 24 June 2003; *Ensign,* August 2006, pp. 46–52.

03–09   Conference Report, 4 October 2003, pp. 24–29; "The Standard of Truth Has Been Erected." *Ensign,* November 2003, pp. 24–27.

04–01   "The One Pure Defense." Address to Church Educational System Religious Educators, 6 February 2004; *Religious Educator* 5:2, pp. 1–11.

04–02   "On the Shoulders of Giants." Address at Brigham Young University J. Reuben Clark Law Society devotional, 28 February 2004; printed in *Clark Memorandum,* J. Reuben Clark Law School, Brigham Young University, Fall 2004, pp. 2–11.

04–03   Conference Report, 4 April 2004, pp. 78–82; "Do Not Fear." *Ensign,* May 2004, pp. 77–80.

04–04   "A Kingdom of Priests." Address at fireside for the 175th anniversary of the restoration of the priesthood, 16 May 2004.

04–05   "The Light of Christ: What Everyone Called to Preach the Gospel, Teach the Gospel, or Live the Gospel Should Know." Address at new mission presidents' seminar, Missionary Training Center, Provo, Utah, 22 June 2004; *Ensign,* April 2005, pp. 8–14.

04–06 Address at funeral for Neal A. Maxwell, 27 July 2004.

04–07 Address at funeral for David B. Haight, 5 August 2004.

04–08 Address at multistake and district conference, Osaka, Japan, 15 August 2004.

04–09 Conference Report, 3 October 2004, pp. 90–93; "The Least of These." *Ensign,* November 2004, pp. 86–88.

04–10 Remarks during the "Preach My Gospel" satellite broadcast to missionaries throughout the world, October 2004.

04–11 Address at Japan stake conference broadcast, 6 November 2004.

04–12 Devotional address to Temple Square Mission, 29 December 2004.

05–01 "The Office of Patriarch." Address at Worldwide Leadership Training Meeting, 8 January 2005.

05–02 Devotional address at Brigham Young University–Hawaii, 1 March 2005.

05–03 Conference Report, 5 April 2005, pp. 5–9; "The Book of Mormon: Another Testament of Jesus Christ: Plain and Precious Things." *Ensign,* May 2005, pp. 6–9.

05–04 Address at New England stake conference broadcast, 22 May 2005.

05–05 Remarks at new mission presidents' seminar, 21 June 2005.

05–06 "One in Thine Hand." Address at new mission presidents' seminar, 22 June 2005.

05–07 Introduction to a DVD for Latter-day Saint military servicemen titled "Let Not Your Heart Be Troubled." October 2005.

05–08 Conference Report, 2 October 2005, pp. 71–75; "On Zion's Hill." *Ensign,* November 2005, pp. 70–73.

05–09 Address at chaplain's seminar, 4 October 2005.

05–10 Address at northern Utah stake conference broadcast, 6 November 2005.

05–11 Address at eastern and southern Utah stake conference broadcast, 13 November 2005.

06–01 Address at Tonga, Fiji, and Kiribati stake conference broadcast, 11 March 2006.

06–02 Conference Report, 1 April 2006, pp. 25–28; "I Will Remember Your Sins No More." *Ensign,* May 2006, pp. 25–28.

06–03 "Children of God." Address at Brigham Young University Women's Conference, 5 May 2006.

06–04 "A Teacher of Teachers." Address to faculty of the David O. McKay School of Education, 24 May 2006; *McKay Today Magazine,* Fall 2006, pp. 2–5, 24.

06–05 Address at Handcart Pioneer Commemoration Fireside broadcast from Iowa State University, 11 June 2006.

06–06 "The Gathering." Address at new mission presidents' seminar, 29 June 2006.

06–07 Conference Report, 1 October 2006, pp. 91–94; "A Defense and a Refuge." *Ensign,* November 2006, pp. 85–88.

06–08 "Building Bridges of Understanding: The Church and the World of Islam." Introduction of Dr. Alwi Shihab at Brigham Young University Forum, 10 October 2006.

06–09   Missionary Training Center, Provo, Utah Sunday evening fireside address, 15 October 2006.

06–10   Address at Davis County stake conference broadcast, 5 November 2006.

06–11   Address at Christmas Eve sacrament meeting of the Forest Bend Ward, 24 December 2006.

07–01   "Lehi's Dream and You." Address at Brigham Young University devotional, 16 January 2007; *Brigham Young University 2006–2007 Speeches,* pp. 255–65.

07–02   Address at Central Mexico stake conference broadcast, 21 January 2007.

07–03   "Principles of Teaching and Learning." Address at Worldwide Leadership Training Meeting, 10 February 2007.

07–04   Conference Report, 31 March 2007, pp. 24–27; "The Spirit of the Tabernacle," *Ensign,* May 2007, pp. 26–29.

07–05   Address at eastern United States stake conference broadcast, 6 May 2007.

07–06   Address at Scandinavia stake conference broadcast, 17 June 2007.

07–07   "A Call to Faith." Address at new mission presidents' seminar, 27 June 2007.

07–08   Conference Report, 6 October 2007, pp. 3–7; "The Weak and Simple of the Church," *Ensign,* November 2007, pp. 6–9.

07–09   "Be Not Afraid." Address at Salt Lake City South Stake conference broadcast, 21 October 2007.

08–01   "The Proclamation on the Family." Address at Worldwide Leadership Training Meeting, 9 February 2008.

08–02   Unpublished document, February 2008.

08–03   Funeral services for Ruth Wright Faust, 13 February 2008.

08–04   Address at West Jordan Utah Cobble Creek Stake conference, 17 February 2008.

08–05   "Conversation with Teachers." Address at a Church Educational System Evening with a General Authority, 29 February 2008.

08–06   "Who Is Jesus Christ?" *Ensign,* March 2008, pp. 13–19. See 88–03.

08–07   Address at Bolivia stake conference broadcast, 16 March 2008.

08–08   Address at Salt Lake Hunter Copperhill Stake conference, 23 March 2008.

08–09   Conference Report, 6 April 2008, pp. 81–85; "The Twelve," *Ensign,* May 2008, pp. 83–87.

Index

617